Outline Contents

D0552929

Detailed Contents

Foreword

Media and entertainment law is probably the most immediate and entertaining branch of the law these days. By 'immediate', I don't just mean that claimants are constantly ringing up judges in the middle of the night to get urgent super-injunctions whose very existence is unreportable. The subject is immediate because it's racy, fast-moving and liable to change at a moment's notice. Just look at a couple of the cases that came up while I was reading a proof copy of this book. The European Court of Human Rights held that the *Daily Mirror*'s freedom of expression had been breached because it had been ordered to pay £365,000 in 'success fees' to Naomi Campbell's lawyers. This was a clear victory for free speech. But it came just a week after Max Mosley had asked the same court to protect his privacy by requiring newspapers to notify those whose private lives they were about to expose.

Thanks to personalities like these, privacy law is expanding at breakneck speed; it hardly existed less than a decade ago when I started work on my own book *Privacy and the Press*. At the same time, though, libel law is about to be reined back. The government has promised to publish a draft defamation bill this spring, redressing the imbalance that has made London the libel capital of the world. I'll be happy if I never see another libel tourist here again.

In describing the subject of this book as probably the most entertaining branch of the law, I had in mind the stars and the bands, the footballers and the politicians who give up both their private lives and their money to further its development. Without their stories, recounted here in lavish detail, this book would be a lot less interesting. And without their wealth and a certain willingness to see their names in the law reports, the common law would shrivel up and die.

But it's not just the law that's developing at an alarming pace. From Ursula Smartt's chapters on copyright I learned about new developments in technology, new methods of transmitting words, images and sounds that were never envisaged when legislation was drawn up. At first the law seems unable to help those in the vanguard: Gilbert and Sullivan were as powerless to prevent *Iolanthe* being ripped off in the United States as contemporary composers were in the face of illegal file-sharing. But then the law usually catches up with technology and those who understand its powers will find themselves in the ascendant. So far, I have been talking about those who use – or who are used by – the mass media. But things are changing there too. Until little more than a decade ago, we used to have a daily news cycle, with announcements being geared to the following day's newspapers and breakfast news shows. As recently as 2000, when I moved from broadcasting to newspapers, I was told to use the word 'yesterday' in my copy as often as possible – to show how up-to-date my reports were. When I suggested that this made them seem rather old, I was told this was the best a newspaper could do.

But the writing was already on the wall – or, I suppose, in the ether. BBC News had launched its website in 1997, ahead of the competition – for once – because those responsible for online coverage had simply gone ahead without worrying too much about what the bosses might think. To catch up, newspapers launched or re-launched their own websites – which soon began 'scooping' the print editions and securing headlines in rival news outlets.

The 24-hour news channels had to move from an hourly cycle to one that couldn't even wait for the reporter to come out of court and face the cameras. That was because judges decided at the end of 2010 that reporters would sometimes be allowed to send emails and tweets from court during a hearing. But trained reporters are not the only people who use Twitter. How do you make sure that cases are reported accurately by tweeters and that people who know nothing about media law do not break restrictions designed to ensure a fair trial? We have already seen the first injunction ordering the media not to report a particular tweet that the judge regarded as prejudicial. But a tweet can go halfway round the blogosphere before a judge has got his boots on.

Social networks are among the biggest challenges that media and entertainment law currently faces. We can now see that Twitter is more than just a series of fragmented conversations: it has become a means by which huge numbers of people can contribute to a discussion on a single topic. But there is little that can be done to stop people sending tweets that are defamatory or even incite violence. Moderating readers' posts on a newspaper website is a doddle in comparison.

Of course, it's not just tweeters who behave as if there were no restrictions on freedom of speech. Websites like WikiLeaks seem to regard themselves as above the law. In practice, they may be. And yet it is less than 25 years since a book such as *Spycatcher* could be published in the United States and injuncted in the United Kingdom.

The speed at which media and entertainment law is changing makes it all the more important to have an up-to-date account of it. News organisations generally abide by the law – except, perhaps, when they hack into people's mobile phone messages – but they need to know what's permitted and what's not. For as long as we have media and entertainment, we shall need media and entertainment law.

Joshua Rozenberg
January 2011

Preface

The principle of a free press has a long and proud history in the UK. But there are many who wish it was not quite as free as it is. Over centuries – since the collection and printing of information first began to be common practice – some people in authority have sought to keep knowledge to a limited few. After all, as the saying goes, knowledge is power.

There are good reasons why there are some secrets. Most people agree that national security is important – some would argue that it is one of the most important functions of government. And some element of individual privacy is vital in any civilized society.

So, is the right to say whatever you like to anyone about anything absolute? The nineteenth-century writer Evelyn Beatrice Hall famously quoted the French philosopher Voltaire as declaring, 'I disapprove of what you say, but I will defend to the death your right to say it.' Nowadays, many countries in the world declare that a 'right to free speech' is a cornerstone of a liberal democracy.

So does it exist anywhere? Can you express any view without fear of consequence? The answer is no – in most cases. There are legal constraints on what can be said in public, and sometimes in relative privacy, in countries throughout the globe. What differs widely, though, is just how free speech is from one nation to the next.

In some areas, the law allows views to be expressed on most subjects quite freely though, as the reader will discover, even in countries considered to be the most liberal, condoning or encouraging violence or discrimination, for instance, can invite prosecution. And one person cannot say damaging things about another without running the risk of having to prove what they say is true or justified. Elsewhere, however, merely expressing mild dissent to a particular belief – be it political, philosophical or religious – can easily threaten your life.

But, in the twenty-first century, the debate about restrictions on freedom of speech is intensifying as technology provides more and more people with a platform. The Internet in particular has changed the face of interpersonal communication, largely because it is global and difficult, or perhaps impossible, to control.

While, not so long ago, most views would be expressed to a handful of others at the most – at home to the family, in a pub or restaurant to friends, or to a small gathering in a town or village – today the Internet allows anyone to reach what can be a worldwide audience. And this is often done anonymously because hiding one's real identity online is relatively easy.

Of course, what is perfectly legal in one part of the world can be very much against the law elsewhere. So expressing a view – particularly a contentious or controversial one – can quickly become much more hazardous than it used to be.

But the media – as the world of art, entertainment and communication has come to be known – is not just about the written or spoken word. It now embraces all kinds of creativity and the question of who owns what – who initiated a work and who has the rights to exploit it – is now one of the most complicated branches of the law. Largely because of the speed with which new technology now develops, it is also one of the most changeable.

This book sets out to provide a solid grounding for those either working in media and entertainment or proposing to do so. It covers many legal milestones over the years – from Magna Carta to the *Digital Economy Act* 2010.

But today, as new ways of producing and distributing material of all sorts are being initiated – almost hourly it sometimes seems – the law is very often out of date even before it hits the statute book. So it is vitally important that those involved should have as much knowledge of the law as possible and, although what this book contains was up to the minute at the time of publication, constant vigilance of how things change in future is essential.

Ursula Smartt
October 2010

Acknowledgements

There have been a number of individuals who have shaped and influenced the writing and compiling of this book – above all, my wonderful husband and brilliant journalist, **Mike Smartt**.

As founder and editor-in-chief of BBC News online – Mike has been my guiding light to write (and complete) this book.

There were moments when I admired his patience – for example, when he explained peer-to-peer file-sharing or the differences between uploading and downloading – and he was instrumental in the more nerdy sections of the book concerning IT and the digital media future. Mike is also a brilliant photographer, as evidenced on the cover of this book.

My grateful thanks go to **A** and **B**, the two anonymous reviewers of this book. Though I have not met them, I hope that I will soon so that I can thank them in person for their meticulous and detailed notes over nine months that shaped the accuracy of this book.

There are others whose kind help and advice has been much appreciated. Many of them are either from the media and entertainment industries, or lawyers in the field whose time really does mean 'money'. All of them gave me their time freely as I was constantly aware of their pressurized professional lives and the cut-throat industries they work in.

I am indebted to **Joshua Rozenberg** for writing the foreword to this book. He is the best-known legal commentator. I particularly enjoyed listening to his presentations of the BBC's popular Radio 4 series, *Law in Action*, which I downloaded as podcasts and listened to while going to the gym early in the mornings, before I sat down for hours to write this book.

I first met him when he was the BBC's legal correspondent, before he moved to the *Daily Telegraph*, where I have enjoyed reading his legal coverage of some of the most famous cases. I get equal pleasure from reading his legal blogs in *The Guardian*. He makes law sound so simple and I admire Joshua for his independence and authoritative law reporting, particularly when writing about complicated legal issues. He writes with clarity and wit – even on freedom of information!

Cheryl Grant – Managing Director of Whitelabel Productions, Whitfield Street, London W1. Apart from being my best mate and training buddy in the gym, she is one of the most entrepreneurial people I have ever met. She is a specialist in artist imaging and design, video production and multilingual editorials of audio and audio-visual production, and remains inspirational in her very competitive field, the classical music industry, where record margins get ever tighter and the threat from music downloads and file-sharing is ever greater. Above all, she makes me laugh.

Media lawyer **Mark Stephens** – Partner and Head of International Law at Finers Stephens Innocent LLP, London. I met him very early on in the project and he was instrumental in shaping the ideas and layout of the book. He proved to be an inspirational mentor. I admire his sharp brain, as he alerted me to the 'hot' topics in privacy (superinjunctions) and child protection (IWF) and enthused me about 'obscenity and blasphemy' laws, with his keen interest in art censorship.

I have particularly enjoyed meeting with entertainment and music lawyers, such as **Lorna Aizlewood** – Vice President, Legal and Business Affairs Lawyer at EMI Classics, Kensington, London. Lorna is a brilliant lawyer and in a very short time managed to focus my attention on the basic copyright structure with applied relevance to the music industry. I also thank her for ploughing through the 'entertainment' chapter, which she said would have helped her tremendously at the start of her career following her LPC. Her passion to protect artists' copyright rubbed off on me. She is a tireless campaigner for the protection of performers' and artists' rights.

Then there are the Business Affairs Manager of EMI's 'Pop and Contemporary Music' labels, **Dina Mystris** and the Business Manager at EMI, **Dawn Burnett**, who patiently managed to talk me through the complex area of collecting agencies and royalties attribution in music publishing. It all made sense in the end!

Legal Counsel, **Florian Koempel**, who advises UK Music on copyright and EU legislation, also enthused about collecting societies in music publishing and performance rights; he was particularly helpful in explaining the passage of the Digital Economy Bill through Parliament and shone a light on the various EU copyright laws.

Master **Roger Venne** – Registrar of Criminal Appeals and Courts Martial Appeals, Master of the Crown Office, Queen's Coroner and Attorney at the Royal Courts of Justice – for his excellent advice on the latest court reporting restrictions – and for being a good friend. He has been a wonderful host to my law students when we visit the Royal Courts of Justice, allowing us to meet with him in his magnificent chambers, as well as arranging my visits to the Criminal Court of Appeal.

Lord Avebury – my friend Eric – who has arranged for countless visits to House of Lords debates for myself and my students; his knowledge has enhanced not only my teaching of Constitutional Law but also the practical understanding of how laws are made; a highlight for me was one of the final debates of the Digital Economy Bill during the 'wash-up' period in April 2010.

And finally the two people who commissioned and edited the book – **Fiona Kinnear** and **Lloyd Langman**. We shaped the content and layout of the book during the freezing cold spell in January 2010 when I arrived in an orange ski suit all the way from deepest snowbound Surrey, only to find that there was no snow at all on London's South Bank. Lloyd has been a hard taskmaster, constantly reminding me (and reviewers A and B) of the publishing deadlines and monthly submission of each chapter. Thank you both for making this book happen.

Guide to Using the Book

Media and Entertainment Law is rich with features designed to support and reinforce your learning. This Guided Tour shows you how to make the most of your textbook by illustrating each of the features used by the author.

4.1 Overview

This chapter looks at the common law d
which some foreign jurisdictions regard a
exists in common as well as statutory law i
There are three types of contempt under
statutory provision; these are:

1. interfering with 'pending or immi
   interfere with a trial which is under

Chapter Overviews
These overviews are a brief introduction to the core themes and issues you will encounter in each chapter.

◉ FOR THOUGHT

Why did Mr Mosley not simply file a cla
with injury his reputation? (You may
question.)

'For Thought'
'For Thought' boxes encourage discussion on topical issues and help you to critique current law and reflect on how and in which direction it may develop in the future.

❖ KEY CASE — *Kennedy v*

Facts:
The appellant, Dominic Kennedy (K) ap
Tribunal upholding a ruling of the firs
rejecting a complaint against the
Commission (C) to supply him with in
Appeal in 2003.

Key Cases
A variety of landmark cases are highlighted in text boxes for ease of reference. The facts and decisions are presented to help you reach an understanding of how and why the court reached the conclusion it did.

received money from the Iraqi regin
non-charitable purposes. The newspa
the MP had been given a percentage c
it calculated, would be worth about :
tions and commenced his l
Telegraph [2004].⁵³ Despite
Mr Kennedy, the three inq
withheld under s. 32 FOIA. This wa
Charity Commission's inquiry into t
public concern. But Mr Kennedy's ap¡

Cross-References
Related material is linked together by a
series of clearly marked cross-references.

4.10 Summary of key poir

- Strict liability contempt means that a p
  sub judice period) can be treated as a coı
  less of intent to do (s. 1 CCA);
- A 'publication' includes any speech,
  addressed to the public at large (s. 2 (
- A journalist, editor, publisher or broaɛ
  fair and accurate report of legal procee
  (s. 4 CCA 1981).

Chapter Summaries
The essential points and concepts covered
in each chapter are distilled into bulleted
summaries at the end of each chapter in
order to provide you with an at-a-glance
reference point for each topic.

6.7 Further reading

Goldberg, D. (2009) 'Freedom of informatio
    In Communications, 2009, 14(2), 50–6.
Johnson, H. (2008a) 'Freedom of informatic
    Disclosure'. In: Communications Law,
Klang, M. and Murray, A. (2004) Human Riç
Weber, R.H. (2010) Shaping Internet Goverı
    Mirina Grosz and Romana Weber). Zür

Further Reading
Selected further reading is included at the
end of each chapter to provide a pathway for
further study.

Glossary of acronyms ɑ

A

Actio injuriarum (or: iniuriarum) Scots priv
law 'injuries to honour'; action covers affron
based delicts such as defamation, wrongful
arrest, personal molestation and harassmer

Glossary
A useful Glossary provides clear definitions
of all the keywords and specialist terms
used in the text.

Glossary of acronyms and legal terms

A

Acte clair EU Law: the idea that there is no need to refer a point of law, which is reasonably clear and free from doubt, to the European Court of Justice (ECJ), e.g. this court found the matter acte clair and declined to refer the interpretation of Art.5 to the ECJ.

Actio injuriarum (or: iniuriarum) Scots private law 'injuries to honour'; action covers affront-based delicts such as defamation, wrongful arrest, personal molestation and harassment, breaches of confidentiality and privacy.

Adduce Introduce.

Admissible evidence Evidence allowed in proceedings.

ADSL Asymmetric Digital Subscriber Line – a broadband technology using the copper wire phone network.

Advocate General The European Court of Justice (ECJ or 'Court of Justice') is composed of 27 Judges and eight Advocates General. Advocates General are appointed by Governments of Member States for a term of six years (renewable) (see also: European Court of Justice).

Affidavit A written, sworn statement of evidence.

AG Attorney General (also: Authors Guild).

Alternative dispute resolution (ADR) Collective description of methods of resolving disputes otherwise than through the normal trial process.

A & R Artists and Repertoire. The division of a record label that is responsible for talent-scouting and the artistic development of a recording artist. A & R acts as liaison between artist and record label.

Arraign To put charges to the defendant in open court in the Crown Court.

Arraignment The formal process of putting charges to the defendant in the Crown Court which consists of three parts: (1) calling him to the bar by name, (2) putting the charges to him by reading from the indictment and (3) asking him whether he pleads guilty or not guilty.

ASA Advertising Standards Authority.

Assignment The transfer of property or rights from one party to another (copyright).

Authorities Judicial decisions or opinions of authors of repute used as grounds of statements of law.

AVMS Audio Visual Media Services Directive.

B

BBC British Broadcasting Corporation.

BBFC British Board of Film Classification.

Bill of indictment A written accusation of a crime against one or more persons – a criminal trial in the Crown Court cannot start without a valid indictment.

BitTorrent BitTorrent tracker is a server that assists in the communication between peers using the BitTorrent protocol for peer-to-peer (P2P) file-sharing. These sites are typically used to upload music files.

BPI British Phonographic Industry (originally 'The British Recorded Music Industry').

BSI British Standards Institution.

BTOP Broadband Technology Opportunities Programme – a US government project.

C

Case stated An appeal to the High Court against the decision of a magistrates court on the basis that the decision was wrong in law or in excess of the magistrates' jurisdiction.

CDPA Copyright, Designs and Patents Act 1988.

In chambers Proceedings which may be held in private.

Committal Sending someone to a court (usually from a magistrates' court to the Crown Court) or to prison.

Committal proceedings Preliminary hearing in a magistrates' court before a case is sent to be tried before a jury in the Crown Court.

Complainant A person who makes a formal complaint. In relation to an offence of rape or other sexual offences the complainant is the person against whom the offence is alleged to have been committed.

Contempt of court Disobedience or wilful disregard to the judicial process (Contempt of Court Act 1981).

Convention right A right under the European Convention on Human Rights (see: ECHR).

Counsel Barrister.

Counterclaim A claim brought by a defendant in response to the claimant's claim, which is included in the same proceedings as the claimant's claim.

CPD Criminal Practice Direction.

CPR Civil Procedure Rules or Criminal Procedure Rules.

Contra mundum An injunction (restraining order) 'against the world'.

Cross-examination Questioning of a witness by a party other than the party who called the witness.

D

DAB Digital Audio Broadcasting.

Damages A sum of money awarded by the court as compensation to the claimant.

Declaration of incompatibility A declaration by a court that a piece of UK legislation is incompatible with the provisions of the European Convention on Human Rights (see: ECHR).

De minimis 'De minimis non curat lex' ('about very little there is no attention to law') means the law has no interest in trivial matters; something which is unworthy of the law's attention.

Deposition Written record of a witness's written evidence.

Derivative work A work that is based on (derived from) another work (copyright), e.g. a painting of a photograph. As the adaption of copyright work is a restricted act, unless covered under fair dealing rules, the artist will normally require the permission of the copyright owner before making a derivative work.

Dictum (pl. dicta) 'Remark'; refers to a judge's comment in a ruling or decision which is not required to reach the decision, but may state the judge's interpretation of a related legal principle. A dictum does not have the full force of a precedent since it was not part of the legal basis for judgment, but may be cited in legal argument, e.g. in a counter argument, it is only dictum (or dicta).

Diplock courts Juryless courts in Northern Ireland from 1973 to 2007.

DMB-A Digital Multimedia Broadcasting – Audio.

DNS Domain Name System.

DOCSIS Data Over Cable Service Interface Specification – a technology for next generation broadband services over the cable network.

DPI Digital Phone Interphase Technology.

DRM Digital Rights Management.

DS Developers' System.

DSL See ADSL.

E

ECHR European Convention on Human Rights and Fundamental Freedoms (The Convention); also refers to the European Court of Human Rights in Strasbourg (ECtHR).

Estoppel Equitable doctrine that may be used to prevent a person from relying upon certain rights or facts, e.g. words said or actions performed, which is different from an earlier set of facts.

Estreatment (of recognizance) Forfeiture.

European Court of Justice (ECJ) or 'Court of Justice'. With the Treaty of Lisbon (1 December 2009), the EU now has legal personality; 'Community law' has become European Union law; the term 'Community law' is still used where case law of the ECJ relates to entry before the Lisbon Treaty. The ECJ can sit as a full court in a Grand Chamber of 13 Judges or in Chambers of three or five Judges (see also: The General Court).

Evidence in chief The evidence given by a witness for the party who called him.

Examining justice A magistrate carrying out his or her function of checking that a case appears on the face of the prosecution case papers to exist against an accused before the case is put forward for trial in the Crown Court (see committal).

Ex parte A hearing where only one party is allowed to attend and make submissions e.g. judicial review.

F

Fair dealing (or 'fair use') Acts which are allowable in relation to copyright works under statutory legislation. What constitutes 'fair use' may differ from country to country, but normally includes educational and private study and news reporting.

FOIA or FOI Freedom of Information Act 2000.

Footprints Deliberate mistakes or hidden elements that are only known to the author or creator of a work (copyright), e.g. the software designer who includes redundant subroutines that identify the author in some way.

Forfeiture by peaceable re-entry The repossession by a landlord of premises occupied by tenants.

Forum conveniens A discretionary power in common law where a foreign court will accept jurisdiction over matters where there is a more appropriate forum available to the parties.

Forum non conveniens This doctrine is employed when the court chosen by the plaintiff is inconvenient for witnesses or poses an undue hardship on the defendants, who must petition the court for an order transferring the case to a more convenient court, e.g. a lawsuit arising from an accident involving a foreign resident who files the complaint in his home country when the witnesses and doctors who treated the plaintiff are in the country where the accident occurred, which makes the latter country the most convenient location for trial.

FTT First Tier Tribunal (formerly: Information Tribunal').

G

General Court Formerly Court of First Instance as part of the European Court of Justice.

H

Hearsay evidence Oral or written statements made by someone who is not a witness in the case but which the court is asked to accept as proving what they say. This expression is defined further by the Criminal Procedure Rules rule 34.1 for the purposes of Part 34, and by rule 57.1 for the purposes of Parts 57–61.

HRA Human Rights Act 1998.

HSDPA High-Speed Downlink Packet Access – an enhanced 3G service for data transfer.

I

IAB Internet Advertising Bureau.

IC Information Commissioner (see also: FOIA).

ICT Information and Communication Technology.

IFPI International Federation of the Phonographic Industry represents the recording industry worldwide. IFPI safeguards the rights of record producers and expands the commercial uses of recorded music (see: BPI).

In camera Court proceedings in private where the public is not allowed access, though the media may be permitted access by special permission from the legal adviser or judge.

Indemnity A right of someone to recover from a third party the whole amount which he himself is liable to pay.

Informant Someone who lays information.

Infringement (copyright) The act of copying, distributing or adapting a work without permission.

Indictment The document containing the formal charges against a defendant; a trial in the Crown Court cannot start without this.

Injunction A court order prohibiting a person from doing something or requiring a person to do something.

Intellectual property A product of the intellect, including copyright works, trademarks and patents.

Inter partes A hearing where both parties attend and can make submissions (see: ex parte).

Interdict Scottish Court order similar to an injunction, which prohibits behaviour by the person named in the order from taking any action specified in the order.

Interested party A person or organization who is not the prosecutor or defendant, but who has some other legal interest in a case. This expression is defined further in the Criminal Procedure Rules, rule 66.1, for the purposes of Part 66 only.

IP Intellectual Property (or Internet Protocol).

IPTV Internet Protocol Television – television services delivered over the Internet.

ISB Independent Spectrum Broker.

ISDN Integrated Services Digital Network – a data transfer technology using the copper phone network.

ISP Internet Service Provider.

IWF Internet Watch Foundation.

J

Judge rapporteur EU law: the Judge Rapporteur draws up the preliminary report of the general meeting of the judges and the Advocates General before the Court of Justice known as 'measures of inquiry' (see also: European Court of Justice).

L

Laches A defence to an equitable action that bars recovery by the plaintiff because of the plaintiff's undue delay in seeking relief.

Leave to appeal Permission granted to appeal the decision of a court.

Licence An agreement in copyright that allows use of a work subject to conditions imposed by the copyright owner.

Limited right Right by virtue of the HRA (see HRA) – so that, within the scope of the limitation, the infringement of a guaranteed right may not contravene the Convention.

M

Mandatory order Order from the divisional Court of the Queen's Bench Division ordering a body (such as a magistrates' court) to do something (such as rehear a case).

MCPS The Mechanical Copyright Protection Society (now part of PRS). Collects royalties whenever a piece of music is reproduced for broadcast or online. (See: MCPS-PRS alliance.)

Moral rights Are concerned in copyright with the protection of the reputation of the author, in particular the right to be attributed for the creation of a work, and the right to object to defamatory treatment.

N

NDPB Non-departmental public body (see also: Quango).

Nobile officium The equitable power of the court (Scotland) which allows the court to provide a remedy when none other exists. The equitable jurisdiction in Scotland of the High Court of Justiciary or the Inner House of the Court of Session can provide a remedy where none other would be available, or to soften the effect of the law in a particular circumstance.

Nolle prosequi 'Will not prosecute'; formal entry in the records of the case in the court by the prosecutor in criminal case that they are not willing to go any further in the case. This means that the CPS withdraws the charge/s against the defendant/s.

Notice of transfer Procedure used in cases of serious and complex fraud, and in certain cases involving child witnesses, whereby the prosecution can, without seeking judicial approval, have the case sent direct to the Crown Court without the need to have the accused committed for trial.

O

OECD Organisation for Economic Cooperation and Development.

Ofcom The Office for Communications.

Offence triable either way An offence which may be tried either in the magistrates' court or in the Crown Court.

Offence triable only on indictment An offence which can be tried only in the Crown Court.

Offence triable only summarily An offence which can be tried only in a magistrates' court.

OFT Office of Fair Trading.

OGC Office of Government Commerce.

Ombudsman Or: Parliamentary Commissioner for Administration (Parliamentary Ombudsman); investigates complaints from members of the public about government departments; has wide powers to obtain evidence; makes recommendations about cases s/he hears.

In open court In a courtroom which is open to the public (see: open justice principle; in camera).

Open justice principle The public (and media) has the statutory right to attend most court proceedings – unless held in camera (see: in camera; see: in open court).

Order of committal An order sending someone to prison for contempt of court. (See: Criminal Procedure (Amendment No. 2) Rules 2010.)

P

PACT Producers Alliance of Cinema and Television.

Passing off Using the work or name of an organization or individual without consent to promote a competing product or service (copyright).

Patent A grant made by a government that confers upon the creator of an invention the sole right to make, use and sell that invention for a set period of time.

PCC Press Complaints Commission.

PLR Public Lending Right.

Phonogram copyright The 'P' in a circle is a distinct right applied to an individual sound recording, which will operate separately from rights existing in the underlying musical composition.

PPL Phonographic Performance Ltd licenses sound recordings and music videos for use in broadcast, public performance and new media.

Practice direction Direction relating to the practice and procedure of the courts.

Preliminary ruling EU Law: to ensure effective and uniform application of EU law, national courts can refer to the Court of Justice (or ECJ) and ask it to clarify a point in EU law; reference for a preliminary ruling can also seek the review of the validity of an act of EU law (Treaty provision).

Prima facie case A prosecution case which is strong enough to require the defendant to answer it.

Primary legislation Acts of Parliament.

Privilege The right of a party to refuse to disclose a document or produce a document or to refuse to answer questions on the ground of some special interest recognized by law.

PRS The Performing Rights Society. Body which represents music publishers (see also: MCPS).

PSB Public Service Broadcasting.

PSN Public Sector Network.

Q

Qualified right Right by virtue of the HRA (see HRA) so that in certain circumstances and under certain conditions, it can be interfered with.

Quango Quasi-autonomous non-governmental organization.

R

Recognizance Formal undertaking to pay the Crown a specified sum if an accused fails to surrender to custody.

Remand A criminal court sends a person away when a case is adjourned until another date; the person may be remanded on bail (when he can leave, subject to conditions) or in custody.

Representation order An order authorizing payment of legal aid for a defendant.

Respondent The other party (to the appellant) in a case which is the subject of an appeal.

Restraint order An order prohibiting a person from dealing with any realizable property held by him.

Requisition A document issued under s. 29 *Criminal Justice Act 2003*, requiring a person to appear before a magistrates' court to answer a written charge.

RIPA Regulation of Investigatory Powers Act 2000.

Royalties A share paid to an author or a composer out of the proceeds resulting from the sale or performance of his or her work (copyright).

S

Security Money deposited to ensure that the defendant attends court.

Sending For Trial Procedure whereby indictable offences are transferred to the Crown Court without the need for a committal hearing in the magistrates' court.

Set aside Cancelling a judgment or order or a step taken by a party in the proceedings.

SI Statutory Instrument.

Skeleton argument A document prepared by a party or their legal representative, setting out the basis of the party's argument, including any arguments based on law; the court may require such documents to be served on the court and on the other party prior to a trial.

Slander Spoken words which have a damaging effect on a person's reputation.

SOCA Serious Organised Crime Agency.

Solatium Scots law; action that deals with the delict of 'wounded' or 'injured feelings' (see also: *actio injuriarum*).

Special measures Measures which can be put in place to provide protection and/or anonymity to a witness (e.g. a screen separating witness from the accused; or hearing child witnesses on live link).

Stay A stay imposes a halt on proceedings, apart from taking any steps allowed by the Rules or the terms of the stay. Proceedings can be continued if a stay is lifted.

Strict liability Not all offences require proof of mens rea. By a crime of strict liability is meant an offence of which a person may be convicted without proof of intention (*mens rea*), recklessness or even negligence. The prosecution are only obliged to prove the commission of the actus reus and the absence of any recognized defence (see: *Adomako* (1994)).

Strike out Striking out means the court ordering written material to be deleted so that it may no longer be relied upon.

Subpoena A summons issued to a person directing their attendance in court to give evidence.

Summons A document signed by a magistrate after information is laid before him/her which sets out the basis of the accusation against the accused and the time and place when they must appear.

Surety A person who guarantees that a defendant will attend court.

T

Territorial Authority A national authority which has power to do certain things in connection with cooperation with other countries and international organizations in relation to the collection of the hearing of evidence.

Timeshifting A person is allowed to make a copy of a broadcast for private and domestic use to watch or listen to at a more convenient time; or for educational purposes, such as video recording or the BBC iPlayer©.

Trademark ™ or ® A name, symbol, or other device identifying a product or company. Trademarks are registered via national trademark or patent offices and legally restrict the use of the device to the owner; it is illegal to use the ® symbol or state that the trademark is registered until the trademark has in fact been registered.

TSI Trading Standards Institute.

U

UKCCIS UK Council for Child Internet Safety.

V

Venire de novo A QBD order requiring a new trial following a verdict given in an inferior court. In criminal matters the court of trial may, before verdict, discharge the jury and direct a fresh jury to be summoned, and even after verdict, if the findings are so imperfect as amount to no verdict at all.

VCS Video Standards Council – regulator of the video industry.

W

Warrant of distress Court order to arrest a person (also known as 'distress warrant').

Wasted costs order An order that a barrister or solicitor is not to be paid fees that they would normally be paid by the Legal Services Commission.

WIPO World Intellectual Property Organization.

Without prejudice Negotiations with a view to a settlement are usually conducted 'without prejudice', which means that the circumstances in which the content of those negotiations may be revealed to the court are very restricted.

Written charge A document, issued by a public prosecutor under s. 29 CJA 2003, which institutes criminal proceedings by charging a person with an offence.

Table of Cases

Table of Legislation

Legislation for England, Wales, Northern Ireland and Scotland
Unless otherwise stated, the following statutes cover the jurisdiction of Great Britain. Please note that certain enactments may not extend to Scotland, Northern Ireland and the Channel Islands where different legislation may apply.

Statutes

Table of International Instruments and Treaties

Decisions

Directives

Recommendations

Regulations

Resolutions

Chapter 1

Media Freedom

Chapter Contents

1.1 Overview

The historical overview in this chapter charts some of the limitations imposed on many writers and philosophers over the centuries to their freedom of speech. The theoretical foundations of 'free speech' will be examined in democratic as well as non-democratic societies. Freedom of expression will be compared with an individual's right to privacy.

This first chapter links the concepts of freedom of expression and a free press to the open justice principle, as there has been a long-standing rule that judicial proceedings are held in public and that all parties in a UK court of law are named. Freedom of expression and freedom of the press are of course not identical, though the press (or media) often equate them.[1] The fundamental principle of open justice and the right to freely report in the press will be examined; the latter basically means that everything that is heard in courts and tribunals can be reported by the media, as long as it adheres to contemporaneous and verbatim reporting rules. This text will also touch on proceedings in Scotland such as different libel proceedings or *actio injuriarum* ('injuries to honour'), or youth justice proceedings in the form of the Children's Hearing system.

1.2 Historical development of free speech

It was **Magna Carta** in 1215 – also known as the Great Charter of Freedoms – that first recognized free speech as the cornerstone of liberty in England, albeit in a very limited sense. In it, King John agreed to the right of barons to consult with and advise the King in a Great Council. For our purposes here, the final chapter of **Magna Carta** is the most important, because it confirmed the people's right to free speech which remains relevant to this day.

In Tudor and Jacobean England, press censorship existed as a means of royal repression and for the suppression of religious dissent, particularly under Elizabeth I, when it was the Crown which, to all intents and purposes, controlled all printing. The Church also issued edicts of what could and could not be printed and used the Court of High Commission and Court of Star Chamber to enforce its will. Clegg (2001: 4) refers to it simply as 'censorship' and curtailment of free speech. One of the key issues of the English Civil War (1642 to 1649) was freedom of speech and one of the first great proponents of free speech was Cromwell's secretary, the great poet John Milton (see his *Areopagitica* – see section 1.2.2 below).

The 1688 **Bill of Rights** granted the basic right of 'freedom of speech in Parliament', after James II was overthrown and William and Mary were installed as co-rulers.[2] Whereas **Magna Carta** can broadly be regarded as a declaration of the rights of the individual, the **Bill of Rights** is a statement of rights of the subject as represented by Parliament:

> ... that the Freedome of Speech and Debates or Proceedings in Parlyament ought not to be impeached or questioned in any Court or Place out of Parlyament (in the original).

---

1 See also the problems that arose in respect of 'the right of reply' in the US Supreme Court decision in *Miami Herald Publishing Co. v Tornillo* [1974]. The US Supreme Court overturned a Florida state law requiring newspapers to allow equal space in their newspapers to political candidates in the case of a political editorial or endorsement content, thereby reaffirming the constitutional principle of freedom of the press, detailed in the First Amendment, which prevented state governments from controlling the content of the press. The case demonstrates the most constitutional protection of the press, while *Red Lion Broadcasting Co. v Federal Communications Commission* [1969] represents the medium with the least protection in broadcast TV and radio.

2 On 4 November 1677 the Protestant Mary Stuart married the Dutch Protestant William of Orange, Charles I's grandson. This marriage strengthened William's claim to the English throne. The *Bill of Rights* was confirmed by an Act of Parliament on 16 December 1689.

The **Bill of Rights** dealt mostly with constitutional matters and 'parliamentary privilege', which guaranteed members of Parliament a certain amount of immunity including slander laws. Freedom of speech in Parliament significantly related to debates and proceedings in Parliament, and that these ought not to be questioned in any court. In essence, parliamentary privilege was developed as a means of stopping a monarch from interfering with the workings of Parliament. Parliamentary privilege means that – to this day – Parliamentarians have the right to say whatever they like in Parliament without fear of being sued for libel or slander. It also means the media have a right to report what is said in Parliament. As time has progressed, parliamentary privilege now also covers debates in Parliament, tabled questions and notes.

See Chapter
← 3

Other basic rights enshrined in the **Bill of Rights 1688** are trial by jury and the presumption of innocence:

> . . . that all Grants and Promises of Fines and Forfeitures of particular persons before Conviction are illegall and void.[3]

The **Bill of Rights 1688** was invoked as recently as 1 December 2010, when four members of Parliament tried to claim parliamentary privilege as a defence to charges of false accounting and misappropriation of public funds under the **Theft Act 1968**, resulting from the parliamentary expenses scandal in 2009. Sitting with nine Lords Justice, the Supreme Court unanimously dismissed the 3 appeals (Morley, Chaytor, Devine) whether the criminal courts are prevented from trying MPs.

1.2.1 International treaties

The First Amendment of the US **Bill of Rights** 1791 guaranteed freedoms of religion, speech, the press and the right to free assembly.[4] In Europe, after the twentieth century dictatorships of Adolf Hitler[5] in Germany, Benito Mussolini[6] in Italy and General Franco in Spain,[7] freedom of speech was formally identified as an absolute human right under Article 19 of the **Universal Declaration of Human Rights** of 1948.[8]

One thing these dictatorships had in common was the implementation of severe measures to curtail press freedom and the systematic suppression of dissident views through censorship and coercion. For example, under Goebbels during Germany's Nazi regime, a decree in 1935 banned any foreign press or radio broadcasts, punishing those who disobeyed the law with either imprisonment or the death penalty.[9] Other decrees banned national newspapers issued by the Catholic press (the *Generalanzeiger*) but permitted the *Frankfurter Zeitung*, the *Kölnische Zeitung* and the *Deutsche Allgemeine Zeitung* since the regime needed them to shape public opinion abroad. Further decrees paved the way for the National Socialist Press.[10]

In 1948, the **Universal Declaration of Human Rights** was adopted by the UN General Assembly. Its main aim was to promote human, civil, economic and social rights, including freedom of expression and religion, amongst all its subscribing nations. Additionally, the

---

3 Art 12 Bill of Rights 1688 (from the original).
4 The first ten amendments to the US Constitution are collectively known as the 'Bill of Rights'; there are five freedoms guaranteed by the First Amendment, the fifth being the right 'to petition the government for a redress of grievances'.
5 Chancellor of Nazi Germany 1933–45.
6 Italian Fascist dictator and founder of the Organizzazione per la Vigilanza e la Repressione dell'Antifascismo (OVRA) (Organization for Vigilance and Repression of Anti-Fascism), 1927–45, the Italian equivalent of the German Gestapo.
7 General Francisco Franco, the military head of Spain from 1936 to 1975.
8 The Universal Declaration of Human Rights (UDHR) is a milestone document in the history of human rights. Drafted by representatives with different legal and cultural backgrounds from all regions of the world, the Declaration was proclaimed by the United Nations General Assembly in Paris on 10 December 1948 (Resolution 217 A III).
9 Decree issued on 24 April 1935 by President Amann of the Reich Press Chamber.
10 Source: *New York Times* (2001) *Political Censorship*, pp. 119ff.

4 I MEDIA FREEDOM

International Covenant on Civil and Political Rights 1966 (ICCPR) recognizes the right to freedom of speech as 'the right to hold opinions without interference'.[11]

1.2.2 Fighters for freedom of speech

The list of those who have led either public or private crusades for the advancement of free speech is endless and only a few can be mentioned here. The Italian physicist and astronomer Galileo Galilei, having used his newly invented telescope, was brought before the Inquisition of the Roman Catholic Church in Rome in 1633 after claiming the sun did not revolve around the earth. The Roman Catholic Church condemned this theory – heliocentrism – as false and contrary to Scripture in 1616. Galileio's fight for the truth was picked up by Bertold Brecht in his drama *Leben des Galilei*[12] (Life of Galileo).

The play was written between 1937 and 1939 while Brecht was living in exile in Denmark, escaping the Nazi regime of the Third Reich in Germany. The astronomer Galileo's life was clearly seen as a metaphor for Brecht's own persecution and fight for free speech. *Galilei* was first performed during 1943 in Zürich, Switzerland, and was seen as a clear attack on the Hitler regime and Brecht's fight against censorship of literary works by the state.

John Milton, the English poet and author, vehemently opposed literary censorship and argued so eloquently in his *Areopagitica* (1644).[13] Parliament had issued the 'Licensing Order of 16 June 1643', designed to bring publishing under Crown control by creating a number of official censors to whom authors would submit their work for approval prior to publication. The Stationers' Company was the official legal protection agency that had been granted the official monopoly of printing books. This meant that the Stationers effectively assisted the Crown in its censorship role and Milton clearly saw this authority as a by-product of state control of both publishing and freedom of expression. In *Areopagitica* Milton appealed to Parliament to rescind the 'Licensing Order', arguing that pre-censorship of authors was little more than an excuse for state control of freedom of speech and thought. While Milton acknowledged that libel had to be kept under control and that authors had to be accountable for their works, he also felt that legal responsibility could be imposed on both printers and authors for the published content, when he wrote:

> . . . give me the liberty to know, to utter, and to argue freely according to conscience, above all liberties.[14]

Areopagitica contains Milton's objections to prior restraint to publication and is a manifestation of free speech. It remains the most influential and eloquent philosophical work defending the principle of the right to freedom of expression and embodies the cornerstone of press freedom. Pre-publication licensing was abolished in 1695.

One of the causes of the French Revolution of 1789 during the bourgeoisie's struggle for 'liberté, égalité, fraternité' was the egalitarian principles of freedom of speech which led to the *Déclaration des droits de l'homme et du citoyen* ('Declaration of the Rights of Man and Citizen') in 1793. Additionally, the European educated middle classes were inspired by philosophers such as Immanuel Kant, Voltaire, Jean-Jacques Rousseau and John Locke, who had spread the ideas and values of the Age of Enlightenment through the late seventeenth and early eighteenth centuries, when the concepts of equality and freedom of the individual had become paramount.

---

11 International Covenant on Civil and Political Rights (ICCPR), United Nations Treaty, New York, 16 December 1966. UN Treaty Series, vol. 999, p. 171 and vol. 1057, p. 407 (procès-verbal of rectification of the authentic Spanish text); depositary notification C.N.782.2001.
12 See: Brecht (2005) (New edition).
13 Milton (1644).
14 Ibid., p. 41.

When Edmund Burke, an intellectual Protestant and a Whig in Parliament, published his criticism of the French Revolution in his *Reflections* (1790),[15] he repudiated the belief in divinely-appointed monarchic authority and the idea that the people had no right to depose an oppressive government. Burke advocated as alternative central roles, private property, tradition and adherence as values regardless of their rational basis. These, he felt, would give citizens a stake in their nation's social order and constitutional reform rather than revolution. Above all, Burke advocated specific rights for the individual including freedom of speech, writing and printing as protection against governmental oppression.

In his essay *On Liberty* in 1859, John Stuart Mill, the English philosopher and Member of Parliament, argued in favour of tolerance, individuality and freedom of expression:

> . . . if any opinion is compelled to silence, that opinion may, for aught we can certainly know, be true. To deny this is to assume our own infallibility.[16]

John Stuart Mill also argued in favour of 'liberty of the press' as one of the most important securities against 'corrupt or tyrannical government'. He referred to other countries where governments had tried to control the expression of opinion:

> . . . though the law of England, on the subject of the press, is as servile to this day as it was in the time of the Tudors, there is little danger of its being actually put in force against political discussion, except during some temporary panic, when fear of insurrection drives ministers and judges from their propriety . . . The best government has no more title to it than the worst. It is as noxious, or more noxious, when exerted in accordance with public opinion, than when in opposition to it.

> . . . But the peculiar evil of silencing the expression of an opinion is, that it is robbing the human race; posterity as well as the existing generation; those who dissent from the opinion, still more than those who hold it.[17]

Postmodernist writers suffered exile and death threats because of their dissident publications against the totalitarian regime in which they lived. The Russian author Aleksandr Solzhenitsyn published a courageous and critical novel, *One Day in the Life of Ivan Denisovich* in 1962, describing a carpenter's life in a Siberian labour camp ('the Gulag') during the Stalinist era.[18] *One Day* is an autobiographical account of Solzhenitsyn's own experience of the Gulag where he was imprisoned for eight years after 1945 for writing, when a Red Army soldier during the Second World War, a derogatory comment about the Russian leader Joseph Stalin. Released from exile in 1954, Solzhenitsyn continued his secret writings against what he called the newly reformed Stalinist security apparatus of the Khrushchev regime. He was arrested on 12 February 1974, stripped of his Soviet citizenship and deported to Frankfurt (West Germany), after the KGB had found the secret manuscript of his *Gulag Archipelago*.

Expelled from the Soviet Union, Solzhenitsyn first resided in Cologne with the German author Heinrich Böll, who himself had been criticized, following the publication of his short novel *Die verlorene Ehre der Katharina Blum* (*The Lost Honour of Katharina Blum*) in 1974, by the German government for being a Baader-Meinhoff sympathizer. *Katharina Blum* became more popular abroad than in Germany, charting media intrusion by 'die Zeitung' (the newspaper), a clear criticism of the popular German

---

15 See: Burke (1790).
16 Mill (1859) Introduction, p. 26.
17 Ibid., Chapter II, 'Of the liberty of thought and discussion', pp. 30ff.
18 Solzhenitsyn (1962), first published in the Soviet literary magazine *Noviy Mir* ('New World') in November 1962.

tabloid *Bild Zeitung*' (or 'Bild'). Solzhenitsyn continued to live in exile in the US state of Vermont until he returned to Russia in 1994, where his Soviet citizenship was restored.[19]

Sir Salman Rushdie, the British–Indian writer, is another dissident who had to live in a different kind of exile – in secret, guarded round the clock – from 1989 until 1998 for publishing *The Satanic Verses*. The Iranian leader Ayatollah Khomeini issued a fatwa – taken by many to be a death threat – against the author (and publishers) for the 'blasphemous' content of his novel. The title of the novel refers to a group of Qur'anic verses that allowed for prayers of intercession to be made to three pagan goddesses in Mecca. Rushdie's novel caused great controversy in the Islamic world, with the book being banned in India and burnt during Muslim demonstrations in the UK when it was first published in 1988.

There are others whose lives have been threatened because of their dissident views against Islam. Nigerian journalist Isioma Daniel incensed Muslims in November 2002 by writing about the Prophet Muhammad in a newspaper article. In her fashion column for a Lagos newspaper she commented about the Miss World pageant which was about to be held in Nigeria:

> . . . the Muslims thought it was immoral to bring 92 women to Nigeria and ask them to revel in vanity. What would Mohammed think? In all honesty, he would probably have chosen a wife from one of them.[20]

The article incited major religious riots and a fatwa was issued on the journalist by the deputy governor of Zamfara State, who likened Daniel's article to the blasphemous publications of Salman Rushdie. The information minister of Zamfara, Umar Dangaladima, confirmed the state's policy:

> . . . it's a fact that Islam prescribes the death penalty on anybody, no matter his faith, who insults the Prophet.[21]

The Netherlands was shocked on 2 November 2004 by the murder of the film-maker Theo van Gogh. The killing crystallized fears about international terrorism and national identity in a country where 20 per cent of the population is of foreign descent. The motive for van Gogh's killing was his film *Submission*, released the summer before the murder. It told the fictional stories of four Muslim women who suffered physical and sexual abuse. Verses from the Qur'an were superimposed on the bodies of near-naked women, scenes which many Muslims found deeply offensive. Van Gogh believed that the film would encourage public discourse. Van Gogh's killer, 27-year-old Mohammed Bouyeri, an Amsterdam-born Muslim of Moroccan descent, pleaded guilty to murder and was given a life sentence on 27 July 2005.[22]

In February 2009, the far-right Dutch politician Geert Wilders, who leads his own Freedom party in the Netherlands, the anti-Islam PVV, was prevented from entering Britain by Labour Home Secretary Jacqui Smith, who argued that his presence was likely to incite racial hatred. Wilders is an outspoken critic of Islam, having called it 'the ideology of a retarded culture' and compared the Qur'an to Hitler's *Mein Kampf*. The UK government's attempt to ban Wilders, after lobbying from Lord Ahmed and some Muslim organizations, was provoked by a film he planned to screen at the House of Lords that showed the aftermath of Islamist terror atrocities, including 9/11 and the 7/7 bombings, intercut with selected verses from the Qur'an. The film, called *Fitna* (Arabic for strife), denounces Islam as a 'fascist' religion.

---

19 For further reading see Ericson and Mahoney (2009).
20 Source: *Thisday* press office release, Kaduna, 27 November 2002.
21 Source: 'Fatwa is issued against Nigerian journalist', by James Astill and Owen Bowcott, *The Guardian*, 27 November 2002.
22 Source: 'Unrepentant killer of Dutch film-maker jailed for life', by Ian Traynor, *The Guardian*, 27 July 2005.

Backed by his British host and then UK Independence Party (UKIP) leader Lord Pearson of Rannoch, Wilders won an appeal in October 2009. The Asylum and Immigration Tribunal upheld the appeal on the grounds of freedom of speech. Such cases increasingly raise issues of conflict between Article 9 and 10 ECHR (see also: *Otto-Preminger-Institut v Austria* (1994)[23]). In her annual speech on 21 September 2010, Queen Beatrix of the Netherlands referred to the need for unity and a 'harmonious society' which can only build on respect, acceptance and courtesy towards others. This, she said, requires 'give and take, tolerance and also adaptation. This is the responsibility of us all.'[24] Geert Wilders told Dutch newspaper the *Telegraaf* that the Queen's speech had been a direct attack on his party. Wilders described the speech, in which the Queen said that stable government was necessary for economic recovery, as a 'total nothing' – thereby also accusing the Prime Minister, Jan Peter Balkenende, who writes the speech for the monarch, of 'rabble rousing'.[25]

There have been many individuals and organizations around the world – such as UNICEF, as part of their educational activities – who have been dedicated to upholding freedom of speech, and many work in trying circumstances as we have seen above. Comedian Stephen Grant from Brighton spent two years fighting for his freedom of expression to tell jokes about his (former) wife Anneliese. As part of the divorce settlement she had insisted that he could not include any jokes as part of his stand-up routine that referred to their break-up. In September 2010 he won his High Court action – invoking Article 10 ECHR – and the right to discuss his former wife on stage. Solicitors acting for Ms Anneliese Holland had demanded he sign a 'gagging order' stopping him from discussing her negatively. At last Mr Grant was able to include some of the following jokes in his next performance:

> . . . this was a woman so two-faced it took ages to upload Facebook pictures of her because I had to tag her twice.

> When I finally got the house back, the only thing she left was a broomstick, which was odd, because I thought she might have needed it for transport.[26]

1.3 Theoretical foundations of media freedom

Press freedom can be defined as the ability and opportunity for journalists to say and write what they want without restriction or interference from the state and elsewhere. Absolute press freedom, though, is uncommon, even in the most democratic societies. Judith Lichtenberg (1995) argues that freedom of the press is not necessarily a substitute for freedom of speech because there can be too many legal constraints on the press which restrain freedom of speech. Philosopher Onora O'Neill, in the 2002 BBC Reith lectures, stated that:

> . . . a free press is not an unconditional good. It is good because and insofar as it helps the public to explore and test opinions and to judge for themselves whom and what to believe. If powerful institutions are allowed to publish, circulate and promote material without indicating what is known and what is rumour; what is derived from a reputable source and what is invented, what is standard analysis and what is speculation; which sources may be knowledge-able and which are probably not, they damage our public culture and all our lives. Good public debate must not only be accessible to but also assessable by its audiences. The press are

---

23 [1994] *ECHR* 26 (Case No 13470/87) 20 September 1994 (ECHR).
24 For a full Dutch text of the Queen's speech, see 'De volledige tekst van de troonrede', 21 September 2010: available (in Dutch) at <http://www.volkskrant.nl/binnenland/article1421683.ece/De_volledige_tekst_van_de_troonrede>, accessed 17 November 2010.
25 Source: 'Beatrix peilt meningen na val kabinet', *De Telegraaf*, 22 September 2010.
26 Source: 'Comedian wins legal battle to joke about divorce', by Caroline Gammell, *Daily Telegraph*, 1 October 2010.

skilled at making material accessible, but erratic about making it assessable. This may be why opinion polls and social surveys now show that the public in the UK claim that they trust newspaper journalists less than any other profession.[27]

Though the UK prides itself on having a free press, journalistic activities today are restricted by numerous pieces of legislation, the majority of which form the subject matter of this book. As common law has developed, particularly in the area of human rights, it will be demonstrated that the courts have attempted to strike a fine balance between the freedoms and responsibilities of the press, while safeguarding an individual's right to privacy. Some argue this amounts to a certain measure of censorship of the press by the courts.

1.3.1 Censorship and licensing

Every society determines its own position on freedom of expression according to its own history and constitutional make-up. This means that the laws governing such freedoms will change over time (see section 1.2.1). Many constitutions and international treaties now guarantee freedom of speech, such as the German Constitution (*Grundgesetz*), which was certainly not the case during the Third Reich or the Weimar Republic.[28]

The struggle for press freedom in England resulted in a royal proclamation in 1534, requiring pre-publication licensing, particularly in relation to religious matters (see section 1.2.2). The Tudor and Stuart monarchs introduced restrictive measures in the form of censorship, particularly aimed at political and religious criticism. Severe restrictions on the press also existed in seditious libel and blasphemy laws, which made it an offence to criticize government or members of Parliament in speech or writing or to challenge the orthodoxy of the Church of England. Not only writers but also printers could be arrested and imprisoned for publishing seditious material. Any criticism of the government was considered libellous and it was not until the mid-nineteenth century that 'truth' became an admissible defence in the tort of defamation.

The idea that citizens can receive free and objective information and engage in free debate and critical reflection was adopted in the twentieth century by the German philosopher Jürgen Habermas, who traced the rise of free speech back to the Age of Enlightenment, made possible by a free press (see section 1.2.2). Habermas believed that the emancipation of the informed citizen could only be brought about by 'critical communication and analysis of modern institutions'. The only way such informed criticism could take shape was through a free and uncensored press, which he included in his 'Three Normative Models of Democracy'.[29]

1.3.2 Press freedom in the twenty-first century

Today press freedom accepts certain restrictions on providing information, such as war-reporting,[30] contempt, blasphemy, the protection of minors, racial discrimination and national security. Frost (2007: 49) argues that it can be rather confusing that many people in Britain and other Western European countries appear to support freedom of speech and a free press on the one hand, while supporting censorship on specific matters on the other, such as the coverage of terrorism or sexually explicit material. Ultimately, there are ethical and moral issues that govern war-reporting, for instance, or newsgathering and broadcasting. These are usually left to broadcasting organizations' policy.

---

27 Source: 'A question of trust'. The 2002 BBC Reith Lectures. Lecture 5. Available at <http://www.bbc.co.uk/radio4/reith2002/lecture5.shtml>, accessed 17 November 2010.
28 For further discussion see: Stein (2000), pp. 347ff.
29 See: Habermas (1994).
30 For further discussion see: Burchill, White and Morris (2005).

FOR THOUGHT

You advise the editor of a public broadcasting TV channel on the aftermath coverage of a devastating earthquake. The editor wants to show close-ups of a pile of dead children in the street. What advice would you give?

1.3.3 Press coverage of terrorism

The coverage of terrorism is particularly difficult, as Karen Sanders points out in her book *Ethics and Journalism* (2003: 71). She comments on broadcast reporting during the Troubles in Northern Ireland in the 1990s, citing interviews with IRA (Irish Republican Army) and INLA (Irish National Liberation Army) members and referring to the broadcasting bans introduced by Douglas Hurd, Conservative Home Secretary in 1988, which affected 11 loyalist and republican organizations. Sinn Fein, the political wing of the IRA, had been the main target of this legislation and their spokesmen's voices were replaced by actors for many years during broadcasts until the beginning of the Northern Ireland peace talks in 1994. These were difficult times for press freedom.

In 1985, the British government banned a BBC documentary by Paul Hamann about Northern Ireland, featuring an extended interview with Martin McGuinness of Sinn Fein. This caused a huge row with the National Union of Journalists (NUJ) and led to a 24-hour walk-out by BBC staff. Media restrictions were eventually lifted in 1994 following the announcement by the IRA of a ceasefire and the documentary – *Real Lives: At The Edge Of The Union* – could finally be shown. But it was not until December 2005 that *The Guardian* obtained details of the extent of censorship, under the **Freedom of Information Act 2000**.

See Chapter 6

The Guardian traced the row back to June 1985, when Prime Minister Margaret Thatcher had already warned that broadcasters must 'starve' IRA terrorists of the 'oxygen of publicity'. At the time the Irish question was deeply entrenched and there had been a spate of kidnappings in the Irish Republic, attempted assassinations and the bomb at the seafront hotel in Brighton where many members of the government, including Mrs Thatcher, were staying during the Conservative Party conference. Paul Hamann's film was set against that background. He had secured an exclusive interview with Martin McGuinness and his wife, as well as his unionist counterpart, Gregory Campbell, leader of the Democratic Unionists.[31] Arguably, these broadcasting restrictions failed and controversy continues about the true nature of the relationship between Sinn Fein and the IRA.

FOR THOUGHT

Do you think that members of Sinn Fein should have been allowed to communicate their arguments freely to the media at the time of the Troubles in Northern Ireland?[32]

---

31 Source: 'The truth behind Real Lives', by Lisa O'Carroll, *Media Guardian*, 12 December 2005. http://www.guardian.co.uk/media/2005/dec/12/mondaymediasection.northernireland, accessed 1 February 2011.

32 'The Troubles' generally defines a period of communal violence in Northern Ireland, involving paramilitary organizations from both sides of the community as well as the locally recruited police force, the Royal Ulster Constabulary (RUC), the British Army and others, from the late 1960s until the late 1990s, ending with the 'Good Friday Agreement' (or 'Belfast Agreement') of 10 April 1998. Source: Smartt (2009), Chapter 3.4 on Northern Ireland, pp. 43ff.

1.3.4 Do the rich and famous have a right to privacy?

Though the 'Internet' concept had been in existence since 1962, as an 'Intranet' for the purpose of academic social networking in the United States (as discussed by J.C.R. Licklider in August 1962 in his 'Galactic Network'[33]), the global 'World Wide Web' as we know it today came about in 1995 when The Federal Networking Council (FNC) agreed on the definition of the term 'Internet', referring to the global information system that was logically linked together by a unique address space based on the Internet Protocol.[34] Today, personal information about people, particularly celebrities and royalty as well as those in political life, is shared freely on social networking sites such as Facebook or Twitter, or via a blog, encouraging people's obsession with the rich and famous and stimulating extensive uncensored expressions of personal opinion. Material that was once only the domain of the print press – and over which some editorial control had been exercised, however lightly – is now openly accessible via the Google or YouTube search engines.

There is, as yet, no apparent legal censorship on those websites that demand the stoning of gays or the subjugation of women. No censor authorized the taking-down of the 'Stop Rod Liddle' blog campaign in January 2010, when a petition gathered over 3,000 signatures protesting against the proposal that the polemical journalist would become the new editor of The Independent newspaper. There was no realistic legal avenue that Mr Liddle could have taken to sue the originators for libel other than action against the internet service provider (ISP) (see: Godfrey v Demon Internet (2001)).[35]

Public interest can be particularly heightened when celebrities go to extensive – and expensive – lengths to stop reporting of various activities. The England football captain John Terry asked the courts for what became known as a 'superinjunction' in January 2010 to cover up his alleged affair with a French lingerie model. This prevented not only reporting of the affair but even reporting of the existence of the injunction itself. After initially granting the injunction, Tugendhat J[36] overturned the decision a few days later after an outcry, particularly in the press, led by The Guardian newspaper, against media restrictions by the courts. This had the opposite effect to the one Terry was hoping for, resulting in blanket coverage in the tabloid press for days.

Formula One motor racing chief Max Mosley sought the right to privacy after the News of the World had exposed his alleged penchant for call girls dressed up in Nazi uniform (Mosley v Newsgroup Newspapers Ltd. (2008)). Then there was the German gossip magazine that tried to expose photographs of the stormy marriage between Princess Caroline of Monaco and Prince Ernst August von Hannover (see: von Hannover v Germany (2005)).

See Chapter 2 →

The public interest defence in coverage of celebrities and royalty is deemed to be legitimate from the point of view of transparency and democratic control. But can this principle be automatically applied to any public figure anywhere?

It can be argued that everyone, no matter how famous, has some right to privacy, particularly within the realms of their own home, when they are hospitalized or undergoing rehabilitative treatment (see: Campbell v Mirror Group Newspapers Ltd (2004)).[37] It is only when a fine balance has been struck between the competing rights of the personality and the right to free speech that the issue of whether a matter is in the public interest can be decided. Publication at all costs, merely designed to satisfy the public's curiosity and to increase newspaper sales, should be avoided.

---

33 See: Mitchell Waldrop (2002).
34 Source: Leiner et al. (2003).
35 [2001] QB 201.
36 Mr Justice Tugendhat (Sir Michael George) took over from Mr Justice Eady (now Sir David Eady) on 1 October 2010 as the most senior 'media' judge in charge of the Queen's Bench jury and non-jury lists. Source: Judicial Communications' Office, The Ministry of Justice, Press Release of 13 September 2010, news release bulletin 25/2010.
37 [2004] UKHL 22.

1.3.5 Unlimited freedom of speech via the Internet

There is no doubt that the Internet has considerably widened public interest in what goes on. Not only national but international newspapers can be read online, but we can also read any exposé on Facebook, Twitter or MySpace, or even view video footage on YouTube of material which was either in the private domain or had been restrained ('gagged') by the courts, such as the 'Trafigura' superinjunction. In December 2010, Lord Judge LCJ even gave the go-ahead to 'tweeting' in court, during the bail applications by Wikileaks' founder, Julian Assange.

Some would say that freedom of speech might have got out of hand in that there is, at present, very little (if any) legislation which allows control of what is published on the Internet. There now exists Internet-freedom of expression which carries enormous privileges but, with them, implied moral and ethical responsibilities not to write anything about people or organizations which may well harm them.

Freedom of speech means different things to different societies. When Google, for instance, launched its search engine service in China in 2005, the US company had to give an undertaking (known as 'the great firewall of China') to the Chinese government which allowed the People's Republic of China (PRC) to censor sensitive material, for example any references to the pro-democracy protests in Tiananmen Square in 1989.[38] On 13 January 2010, Google served notice on the PRC that it was no longer willing to permit this kind of censorship by Chinese government officials.

In its infancy, the movement in the developed world against censorship and repressive state forces was led by writers and philosophers, like John Stuart Mill and John Milton (see section 1.2.2). How difficult was it for D.H. Lawrence to get his *Lady Chatterley's Lover*, considered obscene by many at the time, published in 1960 or for Michael Bogdanov to have the *The Romans in Britain*, in which simulated homosexual rape was performed, staged at the National Theatre in 1980?

There is precious little that can be banned from the Internet today, though there are organizations like the UK Internet Watch Foundation that have the power to inform law enforcement agencies of paedophilic activity on individual's home computers, websites and servers, which has increasingly led to prosecutions.

Despite contempt of court legislation and strict anonymity orders, police suspects and people standing trial are sometimes featured on the US-based video-sharing site YouTube. This was the case with the identification of Baby P's mother, Tracey Connelly, 28, of Tottenham, who was fully identifiable via YouTube, in spite of strict anonymity orders which had been placed on her and her boyfriend. Anonymity given at trial to the child's mother and her boyfriend was granted under section 4(2) **Contempt of Court Act 1981**. The purpose of the anonymity orders was not to protect other children in this case but to ensure a fair hearing under Art 6 ECHR of the mother's boyfriend who, at the time of the trial for the killing of Baby P, was facing a further charge of raping another child. Baby P – later named as Peter Connelly – had been on Haringey Council's child protection register throughout eight months of abuse in which he suffered more than 50 injuries. His family had been seen 60 times by agencies including social workers from the council, which had previously found itself at the centre of a national outcry over the murder of Victoria Climbié by her great-aunt and her boyfriend. On 11 November 2008, Peter's stepfather, Steven Barker, and Barker's brother, Jason Owen, were convicted of causing or allowing Baby Peter's death. The baby's mother, Tracey Connelly, had already pleaded guilty to this charge. Connelly and Barker were named in August 2009 after the identification banning order had been lifted. In May 2009, Barker was convicted of raping a 2-year-old girl, who was also on Haringey's child protection register, though Connelly was cleared of cruelty towards the girl. Later that month

---

38 Source: 'US asks China to explain Google hacking claims', by Bobbie Johnson, *The Guardian*, 13 January 2010.

Barker was jailed for life, with a minimum term of 12 years; Connelly was jailed indefinitely, with a minimum term of five years. Lodger Jason Owen was originally given an indeterminate sentence for the protection of the public, with a minimum term of three years, for causing or allowing the death of 17-month-old Baby Peter. But in October 2009, three appeal court judges replaced it with a sentence of six years imprisonment after ruling he was not a significant enough risk to the public to warrant the open sentence. The purpose of court orders and protective child legislation will be further argued in Chapters 4 and 5.

So, just about anything can be said and shared via the World Wide Web. The Internet has become a worldwide collective of free speech, which some say has spiralled out of control. Others defend it strenuously, arguing that the Web is the one place where the essence of free speech lives unmolested.

FOR THOUGHT

Should there be sufficient safeguards to prevent the intrusion into someone's private life or personal safety on the Internet? And if so, who should be responsible?

1.4 The open justice principle

It is generally accepted that there are two systems of criminal trial, the inquisitorial and the accusatorial. The latter is practised in the Anglo-Saxon tradition and the former in continental European jurisdictions and elsewhere.

The English accusatorial tradition dates back to the twelfth and thirteenth centuries, which was also the beginning of the common law system. Trials were conducted in *judicium dei*; that is, judgment before God rather than the court. The inquisitorial system involves the judge or magistrate finding out for himself what happened in a case, by asking the parties in court questions. This is commonly practised in France, Germany, Spain and other Roman law-based jurisdictions.

The American legal theorist John Rawls (1921–2002) developed the concept of open justice and the 'difference principle', which asserts the notion of inequality and the (unfair) distribution of scarce goods in society, such as power, money and access to justice. In *A Theory of Justice* (1971), Rawls equates 'justice' with 'fairness'. This notion rests on three principles:

(1) the principle of equal liberty in that each person has an equal right to the most extensive system of equal basic liberties compatible with a similar system of liberty for all;
(2) the principle of equality of fair opportunity, open to all under conditions in which persons of similar abilities have equal access to office;
(3) the difference principle which requires social and economic institutions to be arranged in such a way that they equally benefit the worst-off.

The open justice principle has been recognized by the UK Parliament and all British courts for hundreds of years. This means that theoretically the public and the press cannot be excluded from court proceedings. The general principle behind open justice is that this discourages any abuse of the judicial process on the basis that, as expressed by Jeremy Bentham:

> . . . publicity is the very soul of justice. It is the keenest spur to exertion and the surest of all guards against improbity. It keeps the judge himself while trying under trial.[39]

---

39 Bentham (1843), p. 316.

1.4.1 'Justice should not only be done, but should manifestly and undoubtedly be seen to be done'

All lawyers will recognize the much-cited dictum of Lord Hewart from *Rex v Sussex Justices; Ex parte McCarthy* of 1924:

> . . . it is not merely of some importance but is of fundamental importance, that justice should not only be done, but should manifestly and undoubtedly be seen to be done.[40]

It is the duty of the press to report court proceedings 'in the public interest', necessary for those in society who cannot attend daily court proceedings, confirmed by Lord Atkin when he said, 'justice is not a cloistered virtue'.[41] In the nineteenth century many couples would doubtless have been only too pleased to agree to have their divorce heard in private. But the court sat in public and reports of the evidence, often recounting high-class intrigues, were published in the newspapers, as was the case in *Scott v Scott* (1913) (see below),[42] where, in the first instance, the judge was criticized for hearing the nullity proceedings in private. Adverse reports in the gossip columns of the late nineteenth century, particularly popular among servants, gave rise to some attempts to introduce legislative controls. But all attempts failed, partly because the unpleasant publicity was thought to act as a welcome deterrent against couples divorcing. In *Scott v Scott*, the House of Lords affirmed in the strongest possible terms the long-established dictum that all court hearings should be held in public, unless statute specifically provided for a private *in camera* hearing (where the journalists and public are either asked to leave the court or prevented from reporting proceedings). As Professor Richard Meredith Jackson so eloquently commented in his first edition of *The Machinery of Justice* (1903), the common law rule of open court eventually triumphed in *Scott v Scott*.

❖ KEY CASE   *Scott v Scott* (1913) AC 417 of 5 May 1913 (HL)

Facts:

Mrs Scott filed her petition for divorce against her husband to declare their marriage as null and void because of his impotence. She asked that the petition be heard in camera, which was granted by the judge. The decree of nullity was granted and made absolute on 15 January 1912. A public transcript of the shorthand proceedings was issued to Mr Scott and his mother. Mrs Scott and Mr Braby, her solicitor, subsequently objected to the court transcripts being made public, claiming that these had been in camera proceedings. Upon their objection, it was decided that the two appellants were guilty of contempt of court. They were ordered to pay costs. They appealed against the order.

There were a number of questions before their Lordships. Firstly whether divorce (nullity) proceedings ought to be heard in camera. Secondly, whether a judge had the power to make such an order, which not only excluded the public from the hearing, but restrained the parties from afterwards making public the details of what took place. Thirdly, did the communication of a transcript of the court proceedings constitute a contemptuous disobedience? And lastly, was that order itself properly and legitimately pronounced?

---

40 *R v Sussex Justices, Ex parte McCarthy* [1924] 1 KB 256 at 259 (Lord Hewart).
41 *Ambard v Attorney-General for Trinidad and Tobago* [1936] AC 322 at 335 (Lord Atkin).
42 [1913] AC 417.

Their Lordships looked at the practice of the Ecclesiastical Courts (Ecclesiastical Commissioners of 1832) and the **Matrimonial Causes Act 1857**, both of which stated that divorce petitions should be heard in open court.

Decision:
The House of Lords ruled that there was nothing in the 1857 Act which authorized in camera proceedings and that there was nothing that 'authorised the exclusion of bona fide representatives of a newspaper or news agency' (at para 485); that the original order of the nullity proceedings should never have been made by the first judge and that all transcriptions of the proceedings could be made public including the full names of the parties. Consequently the appeal was dismissed.

Lord Halsbury LC referred to press reporting of proceedings in court as going beyond 'merely enlarging the area of the court, and communicating to all, that which all had the right to know',[43] as a positive duty to report proceedings and to act as the 'eyes and ears' of society and to inform members of the public about issues of public interest in the civil, criminal and administrative courts of justice. It is for this reason that everyone involved in court proceedings can be identified, including the parties and the justices.[44] Lord Diplock explained in *AG v Leveller Magazine Ltd* (1979)[45] that proceedings being held in open court meant that not only the general public as well as the press were permitted to attend court proceedings, but also that nothing should be done to discourage the publication of fair and accurate reporting of proceedings.

Justices have the power under common law to order that a name or other matter be withheld from publication, which departs from the general rule of open justice. As Lord Diplock stated:

> . . . since the purpose of the general rule is to serve the ends of justice, it may be necessary to depart from it where the nature or circumstances of the particular proceeding are such that the application of the general rule in its entirety would frustrate or render impractical the administration of Justice . . . only to the extent and no more than the extent that the court reasonably believes it to be necessary in order to serve the ends of justice.[46]

There are occasions when statute automatically restricts reporting of court proceedings, most common in youth justice proceedings where strict reporting restrictions and anonymity orders apply to children under the age of 18 in England and Wales.[47] This differs in Scotland, where if a person under 17 years old is in custody or charged with a criminal offence or involved in the Children's Hearing system, there should be no reporting.[48] The occasions where the public is being excluded, or where anonymity orders are being issued, is widening, such as in terrorism cases, which are increasingly heard in camera (see: Re. *Guardian News and Media Ltd* (2010)).[49] These exceptions and restrictions will be further discussed in Chapter 5.

---

43 *MacDougall v Knight* [1889] AC at 200 (Lord Halsbury LC).
44 *R v Felixstowe Justices Ex parte Leigh and Another* [1987] 1 All ER 551.
45 [1979] AC 440.
46 Ibid. at 750 (Lord Diplock).
47 ss. 39 and 49 *Children and Young Persons Act* 1933.
48 s. 46 *Children and Young Persons (Scotland) Act* 1937.
49 *Guardian News and Media Ltd and others in Her Majesty's Treasury v Mohammed Jabar Ahmed and others* (FC); also cited as: *Her Majesty's Treasury v Mohammed al-Ghabra* (FC); *R (on the application of Hani El Sayed Sabaei Youssef) v Her Majesty's Treasury* [2010] UKSC 1 of 27 January 2010.

> 👁 **FOR THOUGHT**
>
> Do you agree with the open justice principle? When, in your opinion, should the public be excluded from court proceedings and in camera proceedings should be issued by the presiding magistrate or judge?

1.5 Scotland's privacy principle of *actio injuriarum* ('wounded feelings')

In the Roman law tradition, an attack on someone's honour (*injuria*) has historically been regarded as an invasion of privacy and a violation of personality. This concept has been used in Scottish courts of record since 1500.[50] For example, calling someone a liar or cheat amounted to a verbal injury and the private pursuer had to seek redress in the criminal courts by way of 'solatium' for pain and suffering or disfigurement. The doctrine of *solatium* in Scots law is an action that deals with the delict (tort) of 'wounded' or 'injured feelings' (*injuria* or *iniuria* = injury, insult or affront) and is part of property law.[51] *Solatium* generally arises from an infringement of a non-patrimonial right of personality by *injuria* and is regarded as a subjective wrong. *Injuria* can only be identified as an invasion of the right to peace of mind, human dignity and an invasion of privacy; it is not calculable as an objective loss and it has to be borne in mind that 'wounded feelings' are not the same as psychiatric injury.[52]

1.5.1 Rights of personality and the action for *solatium* for affront

The Roman law concept of a man's 'injuries to honour' was adopted in Scottish law and indeed the tort laws (*delicts*) of most Western European jurisdictions, such as the Netherlands,[53] Germany and France, where the rights to dignity and honour are still protected in their respective Civil Codes today.[54] The doctrine in its modern form comprises a right of personality, providing for a principled legal framework covering actions such as defamation, privacy and harassment. The right to dignity properly understood in Roman law is a non-patrimonial right of personality, and in Scots law such an infringed right is remedied by a claim for *solatium* for 'wounded feelings' by the *actio injuriarum*; this includes post-mortem cases, the main common law authority being *Pollok v Workman* (1900)[55]).

Today, Scottish delict and property law provides a sophisticated structure of real rights and (as is also the case in German law) of acquiring things – deriving from Roman Civil law through the *ius commune*.[56] The tort defamation is then regarded as 'delictual liability' in Scots law and amounts to an infringement of a personality right. In summary, *actio injuriarum* covers affront-based delicts in a wide jurisprudential field of Scots private law, such as defamation ('verbal injury'), the interference with liberty – such as a wrongful arrest – personal

See Chapter ◄ 3

---

50 Source: Zimmermann, (1996), Chapter 31.
51 See: Duncan, Gordon, Gamble and Reid (1996); also: Reid and Zimmermann (2000).
52 See: Whitty [2005].
53 See: Neethling, Potgieter and Visser (1996); also: Neethling, Potgieter and Scott (1995).
54 Source: Zweigert and Kötz (1998), Chapter 43.
55 [1900] 2 F 354 (Scottish Inner House). This case concerned the interest in a person's dead body on the part of the surviving spouse.
56 See: Carey Miller, D.L. and Irvine, D. (2005), paras 1.17–1.18.

molestation – such as harassment or stalking – and breaches of confidentiality and privacy.[57] It also covers medical law (see: *Stevens v Yorkhill NHS Trust*[58]).

> 👁 **FOR THOUGHT**
>
> What do you think are the possible reasons for retaining the doctrine of *actio injuriarum* in Scots law? Could it be an inherent dislike of English law and its common law tradition?

1.6 The boundaries of a free press: analysis and discussion

How impartial should the media be? What is the difference between comment, conjecture and fact? Traditionally, in Britain at least, a person's choice of newspaper is seen as a reflection of their views and values. If we buy *The Guardian*, for instance, we are seen as slightly left-wing, whereas the *Daily Telegraph* reader will be seen as more conservative, with the *Daily Mail* often being seen as appealing particularly to a female readership. Some newspaper proprietors pin their political allegiances to one party, though not necessarily the same one all the time. Rupert Murdoch's *Sun* newspaper, for example, changed its allegiance to the Conservative Party and its leader David Cameron prior to the May 2010 General Election.

Public broadcasting organizations, like the BBC, are required by law to be impartial, giving equal and adequate space in political coverage. All registered political parties, once they have reached a certain threshold, have their say in proportion to their significance. The controversial British National Party (BNP) and the anti-European Union UK Independence Party (UKIP) have no representation in the national Parliament, but their representatives have appeared on the BBC's *Question Time* panel, for instance.

We do not expect our newspapers to be impartial, but what we do expect is accuracy in news reporting. Newspapers, however, also generally contain opinion pieces and editorials, which usually reflect the views of that newspaper's editor and proprietor. These comment pieces are not required to be impartial – the Press Complaints Commission's *Code of Practice* reflects this, stating that:

> . . . the press, whilst free to be partisan, must distinguish clearly between comment, conjecture and fact.

One of the few certainties in the world of journalism and editorial policy is that the age-old tension between freedom of expression ('freedom of speech') and the right to robust and occasionally rude debate will, from time to time, come into conflict with the sensibilities of those who feel insulted or abused and minorities who can feel oppressed by the slights, real or imagined, of the majority.

There was a Christian outrage at the National Theatre's stage play *Jerry Springer: The Opera* and Catholic anger at the BBC's commissioning of the controversial animated sitcom *Popetown*. There was the escalating row over the publication of a series of cartoons, some depicting the Prophet Muhammad as a terrorist, published by the Danish newspaper *Jyllands-Posten* on 30 September 2005. The cartoons initially had little impact, but when they were reprinted by

---

57 Source: Reid (1993), vol 18 paras 4ff; 539ff.

58 [2006] SLT 889 Outer House, 13 September 2006. This was one of many cases covering the 'organ scandals' at Bristol and Alder Hey (Liverpool) hospitals. In this Scottish case the mother of a child born on 30 June 1995 with a congenital abnormality of the diaphragm, raised an action of damages in *actio injuriarum* against the health trust for psychiatric injury allegedly sustained following the defendant's disclosure that her daughter's brain had been removed in the course of a post-mortem.

Norwegian and French newspapers a storm erupted, with violent protests across the Middle East, resulting in hundreds of Iranians attacking the Danish embassy in Tehran. Saudi Arabia recalled its ambassador to Denmark, while Libya closed its embassy in Copenhagen and Lebanese demonstrators set the Danish embassy in Beirut on fire. Denmark's foreign ministry urged all Danes to leave Indonesia over intelligence fears that they might be targeted. One of the cartoons, which featured a caricature of a bearded man with a bomb in his turban, became the most talked-about of the cartoons; its creator, Kurt Westergarrd, suffered an attempted attack on his home. By 2009, 11 Danish newspapers had been contacted by the Saudi lawyer Faisal Yamani, representing eight Muslim organizations claiming to represent in turn 94,923 descendants of Muhammad, demanding that they remove the cartoons from their websites and print apologies. On 26 February 2010, Danish newspaper *Politiken* published an apology for reprinting the cartoons. Though this was welcomed by the Danish prime minister, he equally stressed the importance of press freedom. The editor of *Jyllands-Posten*, which originally printed the cartoons in 2005, said that its sister paper had failed in the fight for freedom of speech and called it a 'sad day' for the Danish press.[59]

So media outlets nowadays have to consider clear editorial justification for publication, supporting free speech on the one hand as well as demonstrating awareness of religious sensitivities and discrimination on the other.

When it comes to balancing the freedom of expression and the right to privacy in human rights law (Article 10 versus Article 8 ECHR), the Strasbourg court has repeatedly stressed the limitation on freedom of expression, but equally the limitations for an individual's right to privacy; that is, Article 8 should not extend to the protection of someone's reputation or commercial interest (*Karakó v Hungary* (2009)).[60]

❖ **KEY CASE** *Karakó v Hungary* (2009) European Court of Human Rights

Facts:
During the Hungarian parliamentary elections of 2002, Mr László Karakó, a delegate of the political party Fidesz (the Civic Union) was a candidate in one of the electoral districts of Szabolcs-Szatmár-Bereg County. On 19 April 2002, prior to the second ballot round, a flyer was distributed in the applicant's electoral district, signed by L.H., chairman of the Szabolcs-Szatmár-Bereg County Regional General Assembly. The flyer read:

> Dr. László Karakó, in his capacity as a member of the Fidesz . . . in the Regional General Assembly, regularly voted against the interests of the county. Moreover, in the debate concerning the route of the M3 highway, he did not support the version favourable to the county, with which – aside from the county – he probably harmed his own electoral district the most.

On 15 May 2002, Mr Karakó filed a criminal libel complaint against L.H. with the Nyíregyháza District Court, which was eventually declined by the Public Prosecutor's Office on 3 May 2004 for any further action.

Mr Karakó filed an application to the Strasbourg court in October 2005, alleging that the Hungarian authorities had failed to assist him to pursue his libel actions against his

---

59 Source: 'Danish newspaper apologises in Muhammad cartoons row', by Lars Eriksen, *The Guardian*, 26 February 2010.
60 [2009] (Application no. 39311/05) Strasbourg, 28 April 2009.

political opponent, claiming a breach of his Article 8 right to privacy. He claimed, inter alia, that this had violated his right to reputation.

Decision:
The Court commented that the right to privacy as protected by Article 8 did not imply a right to reputation; there is no positive state obligation to protect a person's reputation. There had been no violation of Article 8.

In *Karakó*, the Strasbourg court reaffirmed its jurisprudence that reputation may form part of a personality right under Article 8 ECHR, thereby elevating a qualification under Art 10(2) to an equal balancing interest under Article 8.[61]

In *Lindon v France* (2007)[62] the European Court of Human Rights (ECtHR) determined that the right to reputation should always have been considered to be safeguarded by Article 8 of the **European Convention**. The case arose from a novel published in France entitled 'Jean-Marie Le Pen on Trial' (*Le Procès de Jean-Marie Le Pen*)[63] in respect of which Monsieur Le Pen and his National Front party brought defamation proceedings in France against the writer and publisher of the book. The serious and murderous allegations against Le Pen and the National Front were found to be factually incorrect, defamatory and unproven. Upholding the defamation claims, the Paris Criminal Court noted that:

> . . . whilst Article 10 of the Convention . . . recognizes, in its first paragraph, that everyone has the right to freedom of expression, that provision states, in its second paragraph, that the exercise of this right, carrying with it duties and responsibilities, may be subject to such formalities, conditions, restrictions or penalties as are prescribed by law and are necessary in a democratic society for the protection and reputation of others.

After an appeal by the writer and publisher – Monsieur Lindon and Monsieur Otchakovsky-Laurens – failed, the matter went to the ECtHR, where all three defendants claimed that their Article 10 rights had been breached by the decision of the French court. The ECtHR noted the importance of Article 10 and that any exceptions to freedom of expression should be 'construed strictly'; equally that politicians must 'display a great degree of tolerance'. But the Strasbourg court concluded that the French appeal court had made a reasonable assessment of the facts in finding that to liken an individual, although he be a politician, to the 'chief of a gang of killers', to assert that a murder, even when committed by a fictional character, was 'advocated' by him, and to describe him as a 'vampire who thrives on the bitterness of his electorate, but sometimes also in their blood' overstepped the permissible limits of freedom of expression.

Judge Loucaides' opinion recognized that the ECtHR may, in the past, have gone too far in protecting the right of freedom of expression at the expense of the rights of reputation enshrined in Article 8; he observed:

> . . . the suppression of untrue defamatory statements, apart from protecting the dignity of individuals, discourages false speech and encourages the overall quality of public debate through a chilling effect on irresponsible journalism . . . The prohibition of defamatory speech also eliminates misinformation in the mass media and effectively protects the right of the public to

---

61 For further discussion see: Milo (2008, pp. 15–43(29)).
62 *Lindon, Otchakovsky-Laurens and July v France* (2007) (Applications nos. 21279/02 and 36448/02) judgment of 22 October 2007 (ECHR).
63 See: Lindon (1998).

truthful information. Furthermore, false accusations concerning public officials, including candidates for public office, may drive capable persons away from government service, thus frustrating rather than furthering the political process.

The right to reputation having the same legal status as freedom of speech as explained above is entitled to effective protection so that under any circumstances, any false defamatory state- ment, whether or not it is malicious and whether or not it may be inevitable for an uninhibited debate on public issues or the essential function of the press, should not be allowed to remain unchecked. . . . Furthermore, they [the media] should remain legally accountable to the persons concerned for any false defamatory allegations. Like any power, the mass media cannot be accountable only to themselves. A contrary position would lead to arbitrariness and impunity, which undermine democracy itself.

In a direct challenge to the *Reynolds* jurisprudence in the UK, Judge Loucaides placed striking emphasis both on the importance of truth and on the importance of powerful media organizations being accountable to those against whom they make false or defama- tory allegations. This point will also be discussed in the next chapter in the light of the *von Hannover* judgment[64].

See Chapter
◀ **3.2.6**

See Chapter
◀ **2.4.6**

This chapter has discussed freedom of speech as a fundamental human right, protected by a number of international conventions. This protection includes the necessity for freedom of expression, regardless of the medium used to convey the message. Some authoritarian regimes were highlighted where writers and authors were not able to freely exercise their power of free expression and have had to go into exile. The notion of censorship was highlighted, where governments have tried to suppress or restrict freedom of speech and the press.

What is and is not allowed on the Internet is one of biggest challenges currently facing many governments. Lord Mandelson's controversial Digital Economy Bill 2009, which became the **Digital Economy Act 2010** aims to punish illegal internet file-sharing and repeated unauthorized musical downloads and make ISPs responsible for all content posted on their server.[65] Governments issuing such legislation have to balance the interests and freedom of internet users and the protection of personal integrity with the requirement for commercial and personal security so that the Internet is not being misused.

⊙ FOR THOUGHT

Should cyber-warfare and cyber-espionage on the Internet be stopped by legislative means? Or does this amount to a threat to freedom of expression under Article 10 of the European Convention?

Some argue that the many challenges facing the use of new technologies reflect a need for more stringent compliance with international rules and conventions that protect freedom of expression. Just how this can be achieved is also the subject of much debate. Certainly, there needs to be clarification as to how human rights are to be protected if there is to be freedom of expression in electronic media.

---

64 *von Hannover v Germany* (2005) (Application no. 59320/00) 40 EHRR 1, 24 June 2004.
65 Section 3 *Digital Economy Act 2010* 'Obligation to notify subscribers of reported infringements' and section 4 'Obligation to provide infringement lists to copyright owners'.

Freedom of expression and freedom of the press do not always go hand in hand: there can be abuses by powerful media moguls which threaten media pluralism, such as the ever-growing Murdoch or Berlusconi media conglomerates. In its leader column on 20 September 2010, the *Financial Times* (FT) cited the growing dominance of Rupert Murdoch's News Corp's UK media assets – the *Sun, News of the World, The Times* and *Sunday Times*, which account for 37 per cent of national newspaper circulation, while BSkyB accounted (at that time) for 35 per cent of TV revenues – noting that 'in a few years time BSkyB may have almost half the British TV market [in terms of revenue]'. The FT argued that there was a 'clear risk' that News Corp could 'dominate the media scene, lock out challengers and stifle the diversity of debate'. Before Mr Murdoch seizes more territory by taking complete control of BSkyB, the FT urged the Business Secretary, Vince Cable, to call a halt and establish whether this deal really would serve the public interest. It further called on Mr Cable to examine the deal under British and EU competition rules that govern media diversity.[66]

1.7 Summary of key points

- **Magna Carta** 1215 recognizes free speech;
- **Bill of Rights 1688** grants basic right of freedom of speech in Parliament and 'Parliamentary privilege';
- In *Areopagitica* (1644) John Milton opposes literary censorship;
- US **Bill of Rights** 1791 (First Amendment) guarantees freedom of religion, speech, the press and the right to assembly;
- John Stuart Mill argues in favour of tolerance, individuality and freedom of expression in *On Liberty* (1859);
- Article 19 of the UN **Universal Declaration of Human Rights 1948** guarantees freedom of speech as absolute human right;
- *One Day in the Life of Ivan Denisovich* (1962) by Aleksandr Solzhenitsyn, critical novel about the Russian Gulag and Stalin regime;
- The UN **International Covenant on Civil and Political Rights 1966** (ICCPR) recognizes the right to freedom of speech as 'the right to hold opinions without interference';
- Conservative government bans BBC documentary by Paul Hamann about Northern Ireland in 1985;
- Conservative government orders broadcasting ban on Sinn Fein in Northern Ireland in 1988; Gerry Adams' voice synchronized by an actor until 1994;
- Fatwa issue, in 1989 by Ayatollah Khomeini against Salman Rushdie for writing *The Satanic Verses*;
- Fatwa issue, against Nigerian journalist Isioma Daniel in November 2002, for writing about Prophet Muhammad and 'Miss World' in Lagos newspaper *ThisDay*;
- Dutch film-maker Theo van Gogh is killed on 2 November 2004 after his film *Submission* is released; his killer, 27-year-old Mohammed Bouyeri, is sentenced to 'life' on 27 July 2005;
- Open justice principle means that the public and press cannot be excluded from (adult) court proceedings;
- Doctrine of *solatium*, an action in Scots law, dealing with the delict (tort) of 'wounded' or 'injured' feelings (*injuria* or *iniuria* = injury, insult or affront);
- *Actio injuriarum*, cause of action in Scots law, for affront-based delicts, e.g. defamation, wrongful arrest or imprisonment.

---

66 Source: 'Cable should call Murdoch to heel', *The Financial Times*, 19 September 2010.

1.8 Further reading

Carey Miller, D. L. and Irvine, D. (2005) *Corporeal Moveables in Scots Law*. 2nd Revised Edition. Edinburgh: W. Green Publishers.

Frost, C. (2007) *Journalism, Ethics and Regulation*. 2nd Edition. Harlow: Pearson Longman.

Lichtenberg, J. (1995) 'Foundations and limits of freedom of the press.' In: Lichtenberg, J. (ed.) *Democracy and the Mass Media*. Cambridge: Cambridge University Press.

Rawls, J. (orig. 1971; 1999) *A Theory of Justice*. Reprinted and updated edition. Oxford: Oxford University Press.

Reid, K.G.C. and Zimmermann, R. (2000) *A History of Private Law in Scotland*. Oxford: Oxford University Press.

Sanders, K. (2003) *Ethics and Journalism*. London: Sage.

Spencer, J.R. (1989) *Jackson's Machinery of Justice*. 8th Edition (on the original publication by Professor R.M. Jackson in 1903). Cambridge: Cambridge University Press.

Zimmermann, R. (1996) *The Law of Obligations, Roman Foundations of the Civilian Tradition*. Oxford: Clarendon Press.

Zweigert, K. and Kötz, H. (1998) *An Introduction to Comparative Law*, 3rd Edition. Oxford: Clarendon Press.

Chapter 2

Privacy and Confidentiality

Chapter Contents

2.1 Overview

The cover of the magazine *Paris Match* in April 2010 said a great deal about a new wave of French press freedom: 'Zahia: celle par qui le scandale arrive' (showing a picture of 17-year-old Zahia Dehar on the cover with the headline 'Zahia: for whom the scandal arrived').[1] This was a daring move by one of the oldest names in the French press, in a country where press freedom has been notoriously limited and where 'red tops' and tabloid journalism simply do not exist. If one wants to read about the private lives of footballers, one usually has to turn to the British press. The magazine had revealed the secret of footballer Franck Ribéry, a winger for Bayern Munich at the time, who had bought himself the 'escort' girl Zahia for his birthday. Nobody understood why this famous soccer player, a married man who had converted to Islam for the love of his wife, had to pay for sex. This open revelation was something new for French journalism, where no editor would dare to publish anything too salacious because judges habitually forbade journalists from writing about private matters of the rich and famous. The revelations about Franck Ribéry's affair were an audacious move by Arnaud Lagardère, owner of *Paris Match*. There had been rumours about other soccer heroes but no journalist had reported on them. Why now? Maybe because many other European papers had been writing about the Ribéry story but maybe because things in relation to privacy laws were changing?[2]

It is our human craving for stories and gossip that helps keep the newspaper and magazine industries alive. This chapter looks at the development of popular journalism, with the main focus on the way courts have made use of orders, particularly injunctions, to restrain publication of material that some people would rather was not published for a whole variety of reasons. The aim of the chapter is to clarify the terms 'confidentiality' and 'privacy' in English common law and European Court of Human Rights (ECtHR) jurisprudence, particularly in the shape of Articles 8 'the right to privacy' and 10 'freedom of expression' of the **European Convention on Human Rights** (ECHR) and the various subcategories of 'private life' and 'confidentiality' that have been identified by UK common law and Strasbourg jurisprudence (see: *Karakó v Hungary* (2009)[3]) (see section 1.6 above).

See Chapter ◄ 1.6

Following on from Chapter 1, privacy as non-existent in English legislation remains a thorny issue. Some newspaper editors, like Paul Dacre of the *Daily Mail*, have argued that common law development in the area of privacy and confidentiality has undermined press freedom. Mr Dacre referred to Mr Justice Eady's ruling in the Max Mosley case as privacy legislation via the back door (see below 2.4.5). This notion will be examined by looking at a number of cases, including this one, which concerned a person's right to privacy and the freedom of expression, both before and after the ECHR came into UK law in the form of the **Human Rights Act 1998** (HRA) (see below 2.4). Whenever there is an application by either an individual or an organization to the courts to make an injunction, Article 12 of the **Human Rights Act 1998** is applied to derogate from the basic principle of freedom of expression under Article 10 of the ECHR (see below 2.4.1).

The term 'superinjunction' made the headlines a number of times in 2009 and 2010, particularly when Mr Justice Tugendhat lifted a pre-publication restraining order on the then England football captain, John Terry, on material concerning his extramarital infidelities.[4] Such orders were previously used mainly in family court proceedings to protect the anonymity of children and vulnerable persons. But they began to appear more frequently, used by the rich and famous to try to silence the press. Whether superinjunctions have become a form of press censorship by the courts will be discussed in the light of the John Terry and other cases, where it appears that celebrity

---

1 Source: *Paris Match*, 28 April 2010.
2 See also: 'Franck Ribéry football scandal prostitute breaks her silence', by Peter Allan, *Daily Telegraph*, 21 April 2010.
3 (2009) (Application no. 39311/05) Strasbourg, 28 April 2009.
4 *John Terry (previously referred to as LNS) v Persons Unknown* [2010] EWHC 119 (QB) (sub nom 'John Terry Superinjunction').

claimants' law firms may have given the impression that extensive derogations from open justice should be routine in claims for misuse of private information under the umbrella of the protection of confidentiality (see below 2.7.2).

Increasing coverage of popular culture for its prime-time audience does not finish at tabloid journalism but extends to the Internet, with online chat rooms, social networking sites, tweets and video sharing on YouTube. The chapter closes with a discussion about whether the courts or legislation, such as the **Digital Economy Act 2010**, can regulate privacy on the World Wide Web or whether it is simply too late. The blogosphere now cites personal information and gossip about celebrities, sports personalities and politicians' indiscretions, even if there are superinjunctions in place. The World Wide Web now renders territorial demarcation lines of national jurisdictions almost ineffective. As the line between public and private blurs on the Internet, can the courts truly protect what they regard as 'private' and 'confidential' in an attempt to protect a person's reputation, including personal image and photographs (see below 2.8)?

2.2 Historical developments: protection of private and confidential information

2.2.1 The emergence of public opinion and the print press

The modern concept of public opinion emerged with the production of relatively cheap newspapers in the seventeenth century. Following on from Jürgen Habermas' concept of the public sphere, already discussed in Chapter 1, where the German philosopher called the public sphere an area in social life where people could get together and freely discuss and identify societal problems, Habermas pointed out that it is as a result of public discussion and debate that public opinion can develop and then influence political action in a democratic society. He further argues that the emergence of newspapers and the mass media brought freedom of expression into the public domain.[5] Arguably, Twitter is now a modern version of Habermas' public sphere.

The Daily Universal Register, launched in January 1785 by John Walter (1793–1812), could be regarded as the beginning of mass publication. Former coal merchant and Lloyd's underwriter Walter turned his hand to printing and developed and patented the revolutionary logographic printing press, greatly speeding up typesetting. The Daily Universal Register was renamed The Times in 1788. As editor-in-chief, Walter used contributions from significant political and intellectual writers. He also pioneered 'news from the continent', concentrating in the main on news about the French Revolution with coverage of the fall of the Bastille on 14 July 1789 and extensive reports of the Battle of Waterloo in June 1815. The Times correspondent in France brought extensive coverage of the trial and execution of Queen Marie Antoinette, with detailed descriptions of her being guillotined at Place de la Révolution at 1pm on 16 October 1793.[6]

A couple of spats with the law, when he was convicted of libelling the Duke of York and the Prince of Wales in 1789, prevented Walter from running his press. He ran his business from Newgate Prison for a short while. Ten years later, Walter was again convicted of technical libel on Lord Cowper by republication. Because of the accessible reporting style, Times readers rapidly shaped public opinion, followed by those of other newspapers.

---

5 See: Raymond (1998), pp. 109–36.
6 Source: Aubrey (1895), Vol 3, p. 311.

2.2.2 Common law development in privacy and confidentiality

As newspapers became more widespread and readership interest in gossip and tittle-tattle increased, intrusion into people's private and personal lives grew. To this day, there is no UK statute which covers expressly an individual's right to privacy, as the court in *Kaye v Robertson* (1991)[7] famously and uncompromisingly pointed out: there is no tort of privacy known to English law.

The protection of someone's privacy is frequently seen as a way of drawing the line at how far society can intrude into an individual's private affairs. To define 'privacy' is perhaps the most difficult, as the notion of privacy differs from country to country and from culture to culture. Individual states have defined their constitutional laws and substantive case law as the notion of privacy has developed.[8]

In English law, the terms 'privacy' and 'confidentiality' have remained flexible and have frequently been tested in common law. Definitions of the terms vary widely according to context and environment and it is important not to confuse privacy law with the modern notion of data protection, which deals with the management of personal information. A privacy right serves to protect a personal and private state of affairs, preventing information that the individual has chosen not to convey from being disclosed. This justification was first coined by John Stuart Mill in his writings 'on liberty' where he argued that privacy allows people to engage in 'experiments in living'.[9]

See Chapter 6.4

See Chapter 1.2.2

Privacy prevents others from learning everything about our activities.[10] If we look at the Tiger Woods affair[11] – where a superinjunction was sought in the UK courts, but was subsequently not granted – we can see that where celebrities are concerned it is often not so much about the protection of their privacy but about the safeguarding of their image, carefully constructed for the purposes of exploiting image rights and sponsorship contracts. The Americans call this the 'publicity right'.

Before we look at the wealth of common law, it might be an idea to consider some definitions of the meaning and coverage of 'privacy'. For this purpose, the following categories may assist, which have been devised by American political sociologist Barrington Moore (1984):

- **Information Privacy** involves the establishment of rules governing the collection and handling of personal data such as credit information and medical records;
- **Bodily privacy** concerns the protection of people's physical selves against invasive procedures such as drug testing;
- **Privacy of communications** covers the security and privacy of mail, telephones, email and other forms of communication; and
- **Territorial privacy** concerns the setting of limits on intrusion into the domestic environment such as the workplace or public sphere; to control the channels through which one's image is distributed.[12]

---

7 (1991) FSR 62.
8 See: Hixson (1987).
9 Mill (1859).
10 See: Barber (2003), pp. 602–10.
11 On 27 November 2009 the famous golfer, Tiger Woods, was injured in a car accident, hitting a fire hydrant and a tree in his driveway in Orlando, Florida. US gossip websites speculated that the incident might have been connected to reports in the *National Enquirer*, alleging Woods had an affair with a New York nightclub hostess, Rachel Uchitel. On 2 December, *US Weekly* magazine published an interview with a cocktail waitress, Jaimee Grubbs, who claimed to have had a 31-month affair with Woods. Several other women then claimed to have had flings with the golf star, including a porn actress, a pancake house waitress and a Las Vegas club promoter. On 23 August 2010 Judge Judy Pittman Biebel finalized Tiger Woods' and his wife Elin Nordegren's divorce in a hearing lasting less than 10 minutes.
12 Source: Moore (1984), p. 5ff.

As privacy law developed by way of common law jurisdiction in the English courts, the notion of 'confidence' developed alongside. Neither concept ever made it into the torts (*delicts*) of privacy in continental European jurisdictions, such as France or Germany, where strict privacy laws prevail (see below 2.2.3). Rachels (1975) argues that privacy is valuable in that it allows us to limit the information that others know about us: that there are different sorts of social relationships that bring different levels of intimacy. Some information remains confidential to us.[13]

To date, no government has attempted to introduce privacy legislation into Parliament. The Younger Committee, for instance, advised in 1973 against enactment of any general tort of invasion of privacy. This meant the courts continued to iron out deficiencies in existing law with piecemeal common law jurisdiction.[14] 'Younger' recommended that the then Press Council should deal with the continued regulation of the print press and any breaches of privacy and confidentiality on a case by case basis. In 1990, the Calcutt Committee[15] recommended that a tort of infringement of privacy should not be introduced.[16]

See Chapter 10.3.2 →

2.2.3 Privacy in other jurisdictions

The *delict* of privacy in French law was first identified in Article 2 of the 'Déclaration des droits de l'homme et du citoyen 1789' ('Declaration of the Rights of Man and of the Citizen'), first applied in the 'The Rachel affaire' (1858), which made sensational headlines in both London and Paris at the time (see below). The 1789 Declaration, proclaimed by the French National Assembly and comprising 17 articles, stated that the 'imprescriptible rights of man' were 'liberty, property, security and resistance to oppression'.

The 'Rachel affaire' extended the privacy concept in French law to the protection of the private life of the dead. The (in)famous French actress and courtesan Mademoiselle Rachel (1821–58), daughter of Jewish peasants from the Alsace, had risen to pan-European stardom through determined self-education. Among her many lovers were Napoleon I's illegitimate son, Alexandre Joseph Count Colonna-Walewski, with whom she had a son. While touring in London, Rachel had a brief affair with Louis Napoleon Bonaparte (later Napoleon III). There was considerable public and press interest in 'la Rachel', and when she died the Parisian tabloid press even wanted to show an image of her on her deathbed. The 'Tribunal de la Seine' of 1858 ruled that the protection of private life in death was absolute, which included respect for the grieving family.[17] The private life of dead persons has been part of the theoretical framework of French personality rights ever since, a right which cannot be 'seized, given up, transmitted or acquired'.[18]

The Anglo-American Philosopher Jeremy Bentham (1748–1832) relentlessly criticized the 1789 French Declaration when he wrote:

> . . . it is in England, rather than in France that the discovery of the rights of man ought naturally to have taken its rise: it is we English, that have the better *right* to it . . . Our right to this precious discovery, such as it is, of the rights of man, must, I repeat it, have been prior to that of the French. It has been seen how peculiarly rich we are in materials for making it. *Right*, the substantive *right*, is the child of law: from *real* laws come *real* rights; but from *imaginary* laws, from laws of nature, fancied and invented by poets, rhetoricians, and dealers in moral and intellectual poisons, come *imaginary* rights.[19]

---

13 See: Rachels (1975), pp. 323ff.
14 Source: House of Commons (1973) Privacy: Younger Committee's Report. HC Debate 6 June 1973.
15 House of Commons (1990) Calcutt Report. HC Debate 21 June 1990.
16 For further discussion see: Robertson and Nicol (2007), Chapter 14, 'Media Self Regulation', pp. 759–95.
17 Tribunal civil de la Seine, 16 juin 1858, D. P. 1858. 3. 62.
18 For further discussion see: Deringer (2003), p. 191.
19 Bentham (1843, reprinted 2001), L2 at 10.

Lord Hoffmann (2009) re-examined the universal claim by the French 'Declaration' on human rights and agreed with Bentham's disdain, stating that the French claim rested purely on philosophical foundations rather than actual humanitarian principles.[20]

Freedom of expression in French law derives from the Act of 29 July 1881 (amended by 'Ordonnance' of August 1944), which included the general principle of freedom of the press. This marked the end of censorship and pre-licence authorization, though the statute limited the freedom of speech concerning political opinion. Though the privacy right was not explicitly included in the French Constitution of 1958, the Cour de Cassation (French Constitutional Court) ruled in 1994 that the right of privacy was implicit in the Constitution because it had been added to the French Civil Code in 1970.

Article 9 of the Code Civil of 17 July 1970 provides for the 'protection of private life', which inherently includes protection from the media.[21] Article 22 of the Code Civil additionally restricts the scope of private life to 'intimate private life' (intimité de la vie privée). This permits the courts to order urgent measures in the form of restraint of publication or even seizure of articles and photographs. One such case concerned the unauthorized publication of Marlene Dietrich's personal memoirs in a weekly magazine. She was granted compensation for the breach of confidentiality and invasion of her privacy.[22]

Dupré (2000) notes that there is hardly any French case law which covers breaches of privacy by the media because the French courts have 'always sought to protect private life in an efficient and appropriate manner'.[23] The Cour de Cassation frequently refers to the 'right to privacy' under Article 8 and judges make interim injunctions in form of a référé, if a media organization is in breach of Art 9 Code Civil 1970.

After the totalitarian Nazi regime of the Third Reich it was important for Germany to adopt the principle of free speech in its constitution. The German Constitution – the Basic Law (Grundgesetz – GG) of 1949[24] – guarantees freedom of speech under Article 5 GG. The Grundgesetz additionally grants protection to all aspects of human personality, whether they concern an individual's privacy or commercial concerns, known as the 'general personality right' (allgemeines Persönlichkeitsrecht). General personality rights are fundamental human rights and include the 'right to human dignity' the 'right of free development' under Articles 1(1) and 2(1) GG. Additionally Article 10 GG enshrines the protection of privacy in 'letters, post and telecommunications', which 'shall be inviolable'.

After the Human Rights Court ruling in von Hannover,[25] the German courts had to review their legislation when the ECtHR upheld several claims submitted by Princess Caroline of Monaco, stating that the German courts had failed to recognize her and her family's right to private life under Art 8 ECHR (see below 2.4.6). The Swedish Constitution provides very similar protection of an individual's right to privacy. Press freedom is specifically guaranteed under Article 2 of the **Instrument of Government Act 1974**[26] and the **Freedom of the Press Act 1949**.[27]

The US 'Declaration of Independence' drafted by Thomas Jefferson in 1776 stated:

> ... we hold these truths to be self-evident, that all men are created equal, that they are endowed by their Creator with certain unalienable rights, that among these are life, liberty and the pursuit of happiness.

---

20 Hoffmann, Lord (2009) 'The universality of human rights', LQR at 421–23.
21 Article 9 of the Civil Code, Statute No. 70–643 of 17 July 1970; Décision 94–352 du Conseil Constitutionnel du 18 Janvier 1995.
22 Cour d'appel Paris, 17 mars 1966.
23 See: Dupré (2000), pp. 627–49.
24 Grundgesetz (GG) of 23 May 1949; last updated 29.7.2009 I 2248 GG.
25 von Hannover v Germany (2005) (Application no. 59320/00) 40 EHRR 1, 24 June 2004.
26 Regeringsformen, SFS 1974: 152.
27 Tryckfrihetsförordningen, SFS 1949: 105.

As common law developed in England in the area of privacy and confidentiality, American privacy law borrowed heavily from English court rulings. The result were the First, Fourth and Fifth Amendments of the US **Bill of Rights 1791**, increasingly protecting the freedom of individuals to choose whether or not to perform certain acts or subject themselves to certain experiences.[28] The 'liberty' clause was added later with the bill's Fourteenth Amendment, granting individuals anonymity rights in terms of 'intimacy' and 'solitude'. 'Liberty' was narrowly defined, generally only protecting privacy of family, marriage, motherhood, procreation and child-rearing to this very day. This means a general right to personal autonomy has never been granted.[29]

Towards the end of the nineteenth century, two partners in a Boston law firm, one of them being US Supreme Court Justice Louis Brandeis, articulated the English 'revolutionary concept of privacy' in an article in the *Harvard Law Review*, stating that an individual's right to be left alone should also be recognized in US legislation and remain untouched. Warren and Brandeis (1890) argued that privacy was the most cherished of freedoms in a democracy and should be reflected in the Constitution.[30] They further argued:

> . . . the press is overstepping in every direction the obvious bounds of propriety and decency. Gossip is no longer the resource of the idle and of the vicious, but has become a trade, which is pursued with industry as well as effrontery. To satisfy a prurient taste the details of sexual relations are spread broadcast in the columns of the daily papers.[31]

This also gave rise to a positive right to control the use of image for commercial purposes, known as the 'publicity right' (see: *Midler (Bette) v Ford Motor Co and Young & Rubicam* (1988)[32]).

2.2.4 The public interest and the public domain

Whenever journalists or publishers defend a publication which has been or is about to be restrained by the courts, they try to stop the injunction by fiercely contending that publication will be 'in the public interest'. Public interest is the most common justification for publishing information which is either confidential or which has been challenged in the tort of defamation. Before the **Human Rights Act 1998** came into force in 2000 (1998 in Scotland), English common law recognized that the public interest could justify the publication of information that was known to have been disclosed in breach of confidence. This was initially limited under the 'iniquity rule', whereby confidentiality could not be relied upon to conceal wrongdoing, upheld in *Lion Laboratories v Evans* (1985).[33]

See Chapter 3 →

How can the 'public domain' be defined? The term generally applies where there has been sufficient prior publication so that there is nothing left which an injunction can, or should, protect (see: *AG v Guardian Newspapers Ltd*. Nr. 2 (1990) '*Spycatcher Nr 2*').[34] However, the courts have ruled that the public interest test does not always amount to a justification for publication of confidential information. In some cases repetition of a publication already made may amount to a threat to public security and could be prevented by an (interim) injunction.

---

28 For further comparative analysis see: Schilling (1991), pp. 169–76.
29 For further discussion see: Strachan and Singh (2002), pp. 129–61.
30 Warren and Brandeis (1890), pp. 193–220.
31 Ibid., at p. 196.
32 *Midler (Bette) v Ford Motor Company and Young & Rubicam* [1988] 849 F 2d 460 Case N°: 87–6168) United States Court of Appeals (for the Ninth Circuit) on 22 June 1988. This case centred on the protectability of the voice of a celebrated chanteuse from commercial exploitation without her consent.
33 [1985] QB 526.
34 [1990] 1 AC 109.

2.2.5 What is a breach of confidence?

The common law or, more precisely, the courts of equity, have long afforded protection to the wrongful use of private information by means of the cause of action which became known as breach of confidence. A breach of confidence was restrained as a form of unconscionable conduct, akin to a breach of trust. Today this term can be misleading. A breach of confidence goes back to the time when the cause of action was based on improper use of information disclosed by one person to another in confidence. To attract protection the information had to be of a confidential nature. But the gist of the cause of action was that information of this character had been disclosed by one person to another in circumstances 'importing an obligation of confidence' (*Coco v A. N. Clark (Engineers) Ltd.* (1969)[35]).

In other words, a duty of confidence arises when information comes to the knowledge of a person in circumstances where he has notice, or is held to have agreed, that the information is confidential. A breach of confidence occurs where there has been an unauthorized use or disclosure.

When breach of confidence exists a remedy is possible, but the orthodox definition of a 'breach' needs to be made up of three essential elements:

1. the information itself must have the 'necessary quality of confidence' about it;
2. the information 'must have been imparted in circumstances importing an obligation of confidence'; and
3. there must have been an 'unauthorized use of that information to the detriment of the party communicating it'.[36]

As regards the damages recoverable for breach of confidence, Sir Robert Megarry VC commented on the unsatisfactory state in the law of equity in that:

> . . . the right of confidentiality is an equitable right which is still in the course of development, and is usually protected by the grant of an injunction to prevent disclosure of the confidence. Under Lord Cairns' Act 1858 damages may be granted in substitution for an injunction; yet if there is no case for the grant of an injunction, as when the disclosure has already been made, the unsatisfactory result seems to be that no damages can be awarded under this head . . . In such a case, where there is no breach of contract or other orthodox foundation for damages at common law, it seems doubtful whether there is any right to damages, as distinct from an account of profits.[37]

We then see two branches of confidentiality developing, one in relation to trade and business secrets – as per *Coco v A. N. Clark (Engineers) Ltd.* – and the misuse of private information. It is important not to confuse these two branches of law.

In 1984 the Court of Appeal granted an injunction, based on breach of confidence, restraining the *Daily Mirror*, its editor and two journalists from publishing information which had been received from unidentified persons, including one who had obtained the information by tapping the plaintiffs' telephones (see: *Francome v Mirror Group Newspapers Ltd.* (1984)[38]). The court stressed that in such cases, proper authorities and sources are required before the public interest could be raised, which was later developed in the *Reynolds* defence.

See Chapter ◄ 3.2.6

---

35 [1969] RPC 41 at 47 (Megarry J).
36 Ibid., at 47.
37 *Malone v Metropolitan Police Commissioner* [1979] 1 Ch 344 (Sir Robert Megarry VC).
38 [1984] 1 WLR 892.

As common law developed, a breach of confidence was no longer constrained by notions of unconscionable conduct or a breach of trust as established in the *Coco Engineering* case. Additionally, there was no longer the need to prove an initial confidential relationship. This development was clearly recognized by the House of Lords in their judgment as pronounced by Lord Goff of Chieveley in the *Spycatcher Nr 2*[39] action, outlining the general principles as regards confidential information, and the corresponding duty *not* to disclose such information, when he stated:

> . . . a duty of confidence arises when confidential information comes to the knowledge of a person (the confidant) in circumstances where he has notice, or is held to have agreed, that the information is confidential, with the effect that it would be just in all the circumstances that he should be precluded from disclosing the information to others.

> I have used the word 'notice' advisedly, in order to avoid the (here unnecessary) question of the extent to which actual knowledge is necessary; though I of course understand knowledge to include circumstances where the confidant has deliberately closed his eyes to the obvious. The existence of this broad principle reflects the fact that there is such a public interest in the maintenance of confidences, that the law will provide remedies for their protection.[40]

Since *Spycatcher Nr 2* the law imposes a 'duty of confidence' whenever a person receives information which he knows or ought to know is fairly and reasonably to be regarded as confidential. Nevertheless, the law remains awkward and bewildering, caused partly by confusing case law relating to trade secrets with misuse of private personal information, which may require different parameters and treatment. This has given rise to ever greater legal actions. Arguably, the use of 'duty of confidence' and definition of information being 'confidential' still has not been adequately defined in common law and the courts have been skirting around the issue since the early 1990s. Would it not be simpler to say that the information is 'private'?

For example, Naomi Campbell's common law claim was presented to the courts exclusively on the basis of breach of confidence, that is, the wrongful *publication* by the 'Mirror' of private information[41] (see below 2.4.4). In *Jameel (Mohammed) v Wall Street Journal* (2007),[42] Lord Bingham made the following observations in the context of qualified privilege in the law of defamation, within the context of confidentiality:

> . . . the necessary precondition of reliance on qualified privilege in this context is that the matter published should be one of public interest. In the present case the subject matter of the article complained of was of undoubted public interest. But that is not always, perhaps not usually, so. It has been repeatedly and rightly said that what engages the interest of the public may not be material which engages the public interest.[43]

See Chapter 3 →

See Chapter 1.5.1 →

Showing an individual in a false or unfavourable light is largely remedied in English tort law, through defamation or 'malicious falsehood'; all other remedies rest in common law. In Scotland there is a general right to privacy through the principle of *actio injuriarum*, providing a remedy for 'injuries to honour'.[44]

---

39 *AG v Guardian Newspapers Ltd. (Nr. 2)* ('*Spycatcher Nr 2*') [1990] 1 AC 109.
40 Ibid., at 281 (Lord Goff of Chieveley).
41 *Campbell v Mirror Group Newspapers Ltd* [2004] 2 AC 457.
42 [2007] 1 AC 359.
43 Ibid., at 31–3 (Lord Bingham).
44 Kilbrandon (1971), p. 128.

At a trial for a claim for misuse of private and confidential information, a claimant must now first establish that he has a reasonable expectation of privacy in relation to the confidential information of which disclosure is threatened, as established in *Murray v Express Newspapers* (2008):[45]

> ... whether a reasonable person of ordinary sensibilities would feel if he or she was placed in the same position as the claimant and faced the same publicity.[46]

That case concerned photographs of a young child in a public place taken covertly and published without the parents' permission (see below in 2.6).

2.2.6 Restraining unauthorized publications: what do Prince Albert and Prince Charles have in common?

Both Prince Albert and Prince Charles have asked the courts to restrain 'mass' publication of their private thoughts. Prince Albert's was in the form of some drawings which he and his wife Queen Victoria had made to amuse themselves about goings-on at the court in Windsor and Osborne House on the Isle of Wight. Some 157 year later, the Prince of Wales, Prince Charles, found that his private travel journals had fallen into the wrong hands and were about to be published in the press. Both princes tried to stop publication by way of court injunctions, on the grounds of breach of confidentiality and their right to privacy.

In *(Prince) Albert v Strange and Others* (1849)[47] His Royal Highness, the Prince Consort, Prince Albert, asked the courts to restrain the printer William Strange and the publishers Jasper Tomsett Judge and his son from reproducing private royal household and family drawings in the form of etchings and to exhibit these 'sketches'. Both Prince Charles' travel journals and Prince Albert's etchings had fallen into the hands of 'trusted' servants, who had gone to the press in order to divulge royal secrets and make a little bit of money.

Jasper Judge had 'appropriated' copies of the etchings from Mr Strange and had published naughty little books for public titillation, with titles such as *A Handbook to the New Royal Stables and Riding House at Windsor Castle*. The 'Royal accomplishments' were frequently discussed in the papers, since people liked to know what their Queen and her German husband were up to. Were they really clever enough to produce such etchings?

Much to Prince Albert's chagrin, Jasper Judge had reproduced the drawings without their Majesties' permission, though Strange and Judge always added admiring notes to the etchings in the *Morning Herald*, *The Weekly Dispatch*, *Britannia* and other popular tabloids of the time. The final affront to Prince Albert's integrity came when Strange published *The Royal Etchings*, a booklet which provided interesting little secrets about the royal household, including servants' salaries. Strange also published an announcement in *The Times* on 7 September 1848 and some provincial newspapers about a 'perfectly unique collection' of some hundred royal etchings which would 'enable the whole nation to form an opinion of Her Majesty's and the Prince Consort's great merits in a branch of the fine arts in which it is so difficult to excel'. An exhibition catalogue was to be sold separately: 'A Descriptive Catalogue of the Royal Victoria and Albert Gallery of Etchings – Price Sixpence.'

Prince Albert filed his law suit ('the bill') against the culprits on 20 October 1848, demanding that these 'types of men' be summarily imprisoned so that they could be prevented from publishing his private drawings. The Prince's main concern was that the sketches should not be mass reproduced in a catalogue which the defendants intended to sell for vast profit to the world at large. The

---

45 [2008] EWCA Civ 446.
46 Ibid., at 24.
47 (1849) 41 ER 1171.

Prince also asserted his copyright in the etchings. The bill cited the defendants William Strange, Jasper Tomsett Judge and J.A.F. Judge (his son), the publishers in London. The Attorney General was made a co-defendant on the bill representing the interest of Her Majesty, Queen Victoria, in the subject matter of the suit.

A court injunction was granted on 6 November 1848, followed by the defendants' counter-claim opposing the restraining order and explaining to the Vice Chancellor, Knight Bruce, that the injunction was preventing them from going about their business and thereby robbing them of their income. The application was refused on 16 January 1849. At appeal, the case was considered before the Lord Chancellor, Lord Cottenham, who stated that the drawings had been made 'in private' by Queen Victoria and her husband Prince Albert for 'their own amusement'. The etchings had been kept under lock and key at Her Majesty's private apartments at Windsor, yet had fallen into the hands of Strange and Mr Judge and Son, who had surreptitiously taken impressions from the plates.

The *Prince Albert* case set the precedent for any subsequent similar actions in privacy and confidentiality, taking into account any copyright actions where the Lord Chancellor ruled that the right and property of an author or composer in his work (published or unpublished), kept under lock and key for his private use or pleasure, entitled the owner to withhold the material completely from the public knowledge of others. This has caused a certain degree of subsequent jurisprudential confusion about the basis of a confidence action, that is, whether confidential information is 'property', which stems from the rather sweeping nature of the judgment in this case. The court held that it will interfere by injunction with *any* party who avails themselves of unauthorized material in violation of any right or breach of confidence or contractual nature.

See Chapter
8.2 →

What happened to the defendants Mr Strange, Mr Judge and his son? In her fascinating national archival account *The Married Life of Queen Victoria*, Clare Jerrold (1913) chronicles that Mr Judge (Senior) was ordered to 'deliver up' the pictures and etching plates but refused to do so, claiming that he had bought them fairly (it is believed from a footman to Prince Albert). Strange and the Judges gave an undertaking that they would no longer publish the drawings. Strange Senior was ordered to pay £700 in court costs with an additional 'execution' on his premises for £200 for resisting the first injunction. Following non-payment, Strange lost his business and went abroad for fear of further prosecution. After persistent nagging from Mrs Judge, Mr Judge finally wrote a letter to Prince Albert asking for mercy, pleading *in forma pauperis*. His court costs and fine were eventually settled by Queen Victoria.[48]

The *Prince Albert* case extensively influenced American jurisdiction and laid the foundation for the tort of invasion of privacy.[49] The case of *Carsons* concluded:

> . . . we do not need a First Amendment to preserve the freedom of the press, but the abuse of that freedom can be ensured only by the enforcement of a right to privacy. This right has so long been disregarded here that it can be recognized now only by the legislature. Especially since there is available in the United States a wealth of experience of the enforcement of this right both at common law and also under statute, it is to be hoped that the making good of this signal shortcoming in our law will not be long delayed.[50]

Some 157 years later, the *Prince Charles* case[51] (see below) provides us with a *déjà vu* court challenge very similar to the *Prince Albert* action, where Blackburne J cited *Albert v Strange* in his final ruling on grounds for breach of confidence and copyright. In the Prince Charles case, the *Mail on Sunday*

---

48 Source: Jerrold (1913), pp. 250ff.
49 Restatement (Second) of Torts § 652B–652E (1976).
50 *Carson v Here's Johnny Portable Toilets Inc.* [1983] 698 F 2 d 838 at 835.
51 *HRH Prince of Wales v Associated Newspapers* [2006] EWHC 522 (Ch)

(Associated Newspapers) had published extracts from the first of the Prince of Wales' travel journals. Prince Charles asked the courts to restrain any further publications of the other seven journals, citing breach of confidence and copyright as well has his right to privacy under Art 8 ECHR.

The defendants' counterclaim was that the public had a right to know about the future King's political views, in this case his derisive and mocking remarks on the Chinese hierarchy at the time that Hong Kong was to pass back to China. They also argued that the diaries and journals were in the public domain since Prince Charles had been on official Crown business. Associated Newspapers argued that the journals were subject to Crown copyright under s. 163 of the **Copyright, Designs and Patents Act 1988**, as the Prince had been engaged in the service of the executive branch of government and the journals were made 'in the course of his duties' (see also: *Ashdown v Telegraph Group Ltd.* (2001)[52]).

❖ KEY CASE — *HRH Prince of Wales v Associated Newspapers* (2006)

Facts:

In March 2006, the *Mail on Sunday* published extracts from the first of seven 3,000-word travel journals by Prince Charles. At the time of his official tour of Hong Kong, which was about to be handed over to China, in 1997, the Prince of Wales referred to the Chinese leadership as 'appalling old waxworks' in the journal 'The Handover of Hong Kong or "The Great Chinese Takeaway" June 27 – July 3 1997'. The *Mail* diary editor had received the journals via an 'intermediary' of the royal household in May 2005.

The Prince sought a restraining order to stop the newspaper from disclosing the contents of the other seven journals, citing *inter alia* breach of copyright and asked for delivery up. He argued that: (1) the journals set out his private and personal thoughts, which were not matters for the public domain and constituted confidential information; (2) he had kept the handwritten travel journals under lock and key at Highgrove with photocopies at St James's Palace; (3) the journals were original literary works under the **Copyright, Designs and Patents Act 1988**.

Decision:

The application was granted in that the Prince of Wales' journals were his private and confidential thoughts; that the journals received by the newspaper were not legitimately obtained. The public interest factor was therefore irrelevant. Since the entries were of a highly personal or private nature, the Prince could reasonably expect privacy in the matters within the journals which were not intended for public scrutiny. Balancing Articles 8 and 10 ECHR, the court ruled that Prince Charles' entitlement to confidentiality in respect of the journals should prevail. The issue of copyright was partly allowed, though it could not prevent the journals being officially published in future as an official record.

Understandably, the *Prince Charles* ruling was not very popular with the press, with some dissenting opinions expressed in media blogs, such as the one by journalist and author Max Hastings:

> . . . I would have had enormous sympathy if this case had involved the Queen, because she has always gone to great pains to ensure that her private opinions remain so. But Prince Charles

---

52 [2001] Ch 685 (Ch D).

decided a long time ago to exploit publicity when it suited his interests. His views have been widely broadcast and he has chosen to selectively leak information to the press. He's tried to be this semi-public, semi-private figure, dancing between the two as it suits him, and I don't think it washes.[53]

2.2.7 There is no right to privacy in English law

The case which established that there is no tort of privacy in English law is *Kaye v Robertson* (1991),[54] where the editor and publishers of the *Sunday Sport* newspaper, with its 'lurid and sensational style' (as per Potter J), appealed against the grant of an interlocutory injunction restraining them from publishing an interview and photograph of the well-known actor, Gorden Kaye (René in *'Allo 'Allo*). Mr Kaye was recovering in hospital after he sustained severe head injuries on 25 January 1990 when, as he was driving in London during a gale, a piece of wood from an advertisement hoarding smashed through his windscreen and struck him on the head. Mr Kaye was on life support until 2 February.

On 13 February, as Mr Kaye was recovering in a private room, a newspaper journalist and photographer gained access without permission and interviewed Mr Kaye, who was incapable of giving consent. A day later the defendants showed the plaintiff a draft of the proposed article in two parts with a photo for the front-page story. At trial they claimed that Mr Kaye had given consent.

Gorden Kaye argued that he had no recollection of the 'interview', arguing partly in the tort of defamation, partly in malicious falsehood, that he had been libelled. The court could not grant an interlocutory injunction after the jury could not find libel – though he partly succeeded in malicious falsehood later. Glidewell LJ gave the famous *obiter* judgment:

> ... it is well known that in English law there is no right to privacy, and accordingly there is no right of action for breach of a person's privacy. The facts of the present case are a graphic illustration of the desirability of Parliament considering whether and in what circumstances statutory provision can be made to protect the privacy of individuals.[55]

Clearly, Gorden Kaye's story was likely to be valuable to him and that value would be decreased if published in the *Sunday Sport*. The theory behind the 'confidentiality' factor in this case meant that a celebrity's identity could be valuable to that person, for example in the promotion of products or the course of a business, a principle which had been developed as the 'right of publicity' protecting commercial interests of celebrities in their identities (see: *Barber v Time Inc.* (1942)[56]). The interest of a celebrity may be protected from the unauthorized commercial exploitation of their identity. Famous personalities 'have an exclusive legal right during life to control and profit from the commercial use of their name and personality'.[57]

The *Kaye* case has been cited by Markesinis and Unberath (2002), acutely highlighting the failure of both English common law and statute to protect in an effective way the personal privacy of individual citizens. They wrote that English law compares rather unfavourably with German or French law in that some aspects of human personality and privacy are protected by a multitude of existing torts. In English common law, this means fitting the facts of each case into the pigeon-hole of an existing tort, a process involving legal constraints often leaving the deserving plaintiff without

---

53 Source: 'Charles claims victory in Hong Kong diary case', *Media Guardian* online comments 18 March 2006, at <http://www.guardian.co.uk/media/2006/mar/18/mailonsunday.associatednewspapers>, accessed 18 November 2010.
54 (1991) FSR 62.
55 Ibid. at 66 (Glidewell LJ).
56 (1942) 159 SW 2.
57 Ibid., at 291.

a remedy.[58] One could further argue that the House of Lords in *Campbell v Mirror Group* (2004)[59] were *de facto* granting a privacy action under the guise of expanded confidence law.

> ⊙ **FOR THOUGHT**
>
> Some argue that the Gordon Kaye case demonstrated the acute need for a law of privacy to protect individuals from the invasions of the press. Do you agree?

2.3 Media practices and human rights

The Second World War and the Nuremberg war trials left Europe in a state of shock. As a result, the Council of Europe was founded in 1949 to guard against the rise of new dictatorships and any further European wars. The Council recognized that dictatorships did not arrive overnight but arose gradually; the first steps usually being the suppression of individual rights, for example restricting the freedom of speech or censorship of the press.[60] It was for this reason that the **European Convention on Human Rights** was drafted in 1950 and ratified in 1953 (see below 2.3.1).

> ⊙ **FOR THOUGHT**
>
> What do you think was the Council of Europe's main aim when drafting the **European Convention on Human Rights and Fundamental Freedoms**, first signed by Robert Schumann on 4 November 1950?

Article 8(1) of the European Convention makes it clear that the concept of privacy is not limited to isolated individuals, but includes the general 'zone' of the family, the home, correspondence with others, telephone conversations and a person's well-being. In the absence of a right to privacy in English law, there exists a general concern as to the limited availability of legal remedies in English law for the invasion of someone's privacy.

In the domestic action of *Malone* (1979),[61] Megarry VC held that a telephone conversation could not be said to be 'confidential information' because:

> . . . it seems to me that a person who utters confidential information must accept the risk of any unknown overhearing, that is inherent in the circumstances of communication . . . when this is applied to telephone conversation, it appears to me that the speaker is taking such risks of being overheard as are inherent in the system.[62]

---

58 See: Markesinis and Unberath (2002).
59 [2004] 2 AC 457.
60 See: Lester, Panick and Herberg (eds) (2009), Chapter 1.
61 *Malone v Metropolitan Police Commissioner* [1979] 1 Ch 344.
62 Ibid., at 405.

In the Human Rights Court action *Malone v UK* (1984),[63] Malone alleged that the Metropolitan Police had infringed his right to privacy under Article 8 ECHR by tapping his telephone. The ECtHR held that the UK had breached Art 8(1) of the Convention because the police had not sought the specific court's permission to intercept the applicant's telephone communications, including the unauthorized release of metering records and telephone numbers dialled. The clandestine recording by the Metropolitan Police amounted to a breach of the applicant's right to privacy and an unauthorized interference by the state. But the ECtHR also found that the power to tap telephones in the UK was not subject to any clearly defined legal restraints and that there were no remedies available to Mr Malone for such a breach. As a result of the *Malone* judgment, the UK Parliament passed the **Interception and Communications Act 1985**, where section 1 established a statutory offence of the interception of telephone communications[64] (see also: **The Regulation of Investigatory Powers Act 2000** (RIPA), which regulates the powers of public bodies to carry out surveillance and investigation and covers the interception of communications, including the Internet).

There are numerous examples of invasion of privacy in the British press, often revealing the most private and embarrassing facts about famous TV, film or football stars. Above all, the British 'red tops' take great pleasure in delving into the private lives of those who are meant to be moral pillars of society, such as politicians. In 1992 a Scottish paper revealed that the then Leader of the Liberal Party, Paddy Ashdown, was having an extramarital affair. The information had been stolen from the office of the politician's solicitor. Mr Ashdown sought an *interdict* from the Scottish High Court in Edinburgh to stop the press from revealing his infidelities, but he was unsuccessful because the story was already in the public domain and the Scottish courts ruled in favour of the public interest.

A year later, another political scandal hit the headline when another politician, David Mellor, became the centre of media attention where it was revealed that the then Conservative Secretary of State for National Heritage was having an extramarital affair with an actress, Antonia de Sancha. The press had obtained the information by recording the Minister's phone conversations. Seeking an injunction and criminal charges against the newspapers, the Minister had to learn that the courts could not find a contravention of s. 1 **Interception and Communications Act 1985** as the recordings were made on another phone extension from the subscriber's telephone. The Minister was forced to resign.

Inquiries into journalistic practices regarding illegal phone-tapping, clandestine recording devices and subterfuge have not ceased, and have been pursued by *The Guardian* since 2007, resulting in the publication of the (new) Press Complaints Commission (PCC) *Code for Editors* covering, specifically, the area of phone-tapping. On 9 July 2009, *The Guardian* reported that phone-tapping and subterfuge in certain journalistic quarters, such as the *News of the World*, was still going on, despite the PCC's investigations in 2007 and the new Clause 10 of the PCC Code. Criminal convictions followed, and the action against now was still pursued in 2011.

See Chapter
10.3.3 →

In *Hector v Attorney-General of Antigua and Barbuda* (1990)[65], Lord Bridge of Harwich said:

> . . . in a free democratic society it is almost too obvious to need stating that those who hold office in government and who are responsible for public administration must always be open to criticism. Any attempt to stifle or fetter such criticism amounts to political censorship of the

---

63 (1984) 7 EHRR 14.
64 In order for a civil action to be brought, the party to the intercepted conversation must identify himself, and such identification may also be inevitable in any criminal proceedings. Section 2 of the Act established the exception, essentially giving legislative approval to the old system of ministerial warrants for interception of telecommunications or postal communications, with a quasi-judicial system of review in the form of a tribunal added via s. 7. This gives the state the right to intercept telephone conversations in the interests of national security and the purpose of detecting or preventing serious crime under ss. 2(2) (a) and (b).
65 [1990] 2 AC 312.

most insidious and objectionable kind. At the same time it is no less obvious that the very purpose of criticism levelled at those who have the conduct of public affairs by their political opponents is to undermine public confidence in their stewardship and to persuade the electorate that the opponents would make a better job of it than those presently holding office.[66]

In this case, the Judicial Committee of the Privy Council held that a statutory provision which made the printing or distribution of any false statement likely to undermine public confidence in the conduct of public affairs a criminal offence contravened the provisions of the constitution protecting freedom of speech.

There is no doubt that the **European Convention on Human Rights** and Strasbourg jurisprudence have had a significant influence in this area of the common law. The provisions of Article 8 ECHR, concerning respect for private and family life, and Article 10 ECHR, concerning freedom of expression – and the interaction of the two – have prompted the UK courts to identify more clearly the different factors involved in cases where one or other of these two interests is present. Where both are present, the courts are increasingly explicit in evaluating the competing considerations involved and the courts have identified and evaluated the factors encapsulated in these two articles.

But judicial commentary by European judges suggests that a development of a breach of confidence action could fill the gap in English law. Convention rights were tested in the 'Earl Spencer' case[67] immediately before the **Human Rights Act 1998** came into force in the UK (see below in 2.3.7).

2.3.1 The European Convention for the Protection of Human Rights and Fundamental Freedoms 1950

There is no doubt that the **European Convention on Human Rights and Fundamental Freedoms** of 1950 ('the Convention') has influenced the respect for private life in English common law. Furthermore, the horizontal effect of the Convention, based on Strasbourg jurisprudence, has provided the impetus for the development of the breach of confidence in tort law. Convention rights which particularly influenced and affect the freedom of the press and freedom of speech are:

- Article 8: the right to respect for private and family life, home and correspondence; and
- Article 10: the freedom of expression.

Moreham (2008) specifies several privacy rights under the Art 8 jurisprudence: the right to be free from interference with physical and psychological integrity, the right from unwanted access to and collection of information; the right to be free to develop one's identity; and the right to live one's life in the manner of one's choosing, developed from the Strasbourg court's own observations about the scope of Art 8 ECHR.[68]

The Human Rights Court has acknowledged the various meanings of 'privacy' in a number of ways, such as the right to live privately and protected from publicity (*X v Iceland* (1976)[69]). The term was extended to 'private life', which was to include the physical and psychological integrity of a person as in *Peck*[70] and *Pretty*.[71] The right to establish details of an individual's identity as an individual human being was established in *Goodwin*[72] and *von Hannover*.[73]

See Chapter
◀ 7.4.2

---

66 Ibid., at 318 (Lord Bridge of Harwich).
67 *Earl Spencer and Countess Spencer v United Kingdom* (1998) 25 EHRR CD105 App. Nos 28851/95, 28852/95) of 16 January 1998.
68 Moreham (2008), pp. 44–79.
69 (1976) 5 D. & R. 86.
70 *Peck v the United Kingdom* (2003) 36 EHRR 41.
71 *Pretty v United Kingdom* (2002) 35 EHRR 1.
72 *Goodwin v United Kingdom* (2002) 35 EHRR 18.
73 *von Hannover v Germany* (2005) 40 EHRR 1.

Once there is a challenge before the Human Rights Court in respect of Article 8, the court usually asks two questions:

1.   Has there been an interference with a person's rights as specified in Art 8(1); and if so,
2.   Was the interference justified under Art 8(2)?

This principle is known as the Court's 'negative obligation' and any interference must have been made in accordance with domestic law (*Malone v UK* (1984)[74]); the court must also find that the state should have provided a measure of legal protection against arbitrary interference by public authorities (*Segerstedt-Wiberg v Sweden* (2007)[75]). The measure must then be shown to have served one of the legitimate aims specified in Art 8(2); that is the interests of national security, public safety, economic well-being, the prevention of disorder or crime or the protection of health, morals, or the rights and freedoms of others.[76] The measure must be 'necessary in a democratic society'[77] and there must be a 'pressing social need for the interference.[78]

Strasbourg case law provides us with plenty of examples of situations where the public interest in the receipt of information protected by Article 10 has prevailed over restraints on publication that were lawful under domestic law. Generally, the ECtHR views with disfavour any attempts to suppress publication of information which is of genuine public interest. Article 10 is then to be regarded as protecting journalists' (including photojournalists') rights to divulge information of general public interest, provided the publication acted in good faith, was factually accurate and was in accordance with the ethics of journalism.

In *Jersild v Denmark* (1994)[79] the ECtHR commented that it was not for national courts to substitute their own views for those of the press as to what technique of reporting should be adopted by journalists, for this would amount to censorship of the press by the courts.

See Chapter
7.4.2 →

Furthermore, the ECtHR stressed that Article 10 not only protects the substance of ideas and information expressed but also the form in which these are conveyed, such as photographs and broadcast and other media. The Human Rights Court has essentially left it up to each state's media editorial policy and ethical practice as to the revelation of someone's identity, in line with the message an article or broadcast intend to convey (see: *Re. S (A Child) (Identification: Restriction on Publication)* (2004)[80]). As Lord Hoffmann opined in *Campbell v MGN Ltd.* (2004), judges are not newspaper editors; neither are they broadcasting editors.[81] The issue as to where the balance is to be struck between the competing rights of Articles 8 and 10 must be approached on this basis.

This means there are numerous ECHR decisions which contain as a common theme the importance of the role of the press in a democratic society, which is to be interpreted broadly as the support for the freedom of expression, as formulated in *Fressoz and Roire v France* (1999):[82]

> . . . (i) Freedom of expression constitutes one of the essential foundations of a democratic society. Subject to paragraph 2 of article 10, it is applicable not only to 'information' or 'ideas' that are favourably received or regarded as inoffensive or as a matter of indifference, but also to those that offend, shock or disturb. Such are the demands of pluralism, tolerance and broadmindedness without which there is no 'democratic society'.

---

74 (1984) 7 EHRR 14.
75 (2007) 44 EHRR 2.
76 For further reference see: Harris et al. (2009), pp. 290ff.
77 See: Clayton and Tomlinson (2009), para 6ff.
78 See: Fenwick and Phillipson (2006), pp. 104–6.
79 (1994) 19 EHRR 1.
80 [2004] UKHL 47.
81 [2004] 2 AC 457 at 59 (Lord Hoffmann).
82 (1999) 31 EHRR 28.

(ii) The press plays an essential role in a democratic society. Although it must not overstep certain bounds, in particular in respect of the reputation and rights of others and the need to prevent the disclosure of confidential information, its duty is nevertheless to impart – in a manner consistent with its obligations and responsibilities – information and ideas on all matters of public interest. In addition, the court is mindful of the fact that journalistic freedom also covers possible recourse to a degree of exaggeration, or even provocation.[83]

The time has come to recognize in UK domestic law that the values enshrined in Articles 8 and 10 of the Convention have become part of the cause of action for breach of confidence and equally in the right to privacy, as Lord Woolf CJ stressed in *A v B plc* (2003).[84]

2.3.2 Official secrets and national security: from the Crossman Diaries to David Shayler

The British secret services, particularly MI5, have always been the object of conspiracy theories, in the words of Cambridge professor Christopher Andrew, author of the first official history of MI5.[85] For a long time, what MI5, the domestic part of the service, was up to was generally defined as 'defence of the realm' and they were left to get on with it. Their activities were partly exposed by the 'Profumo' affair in 1963. John Dennis Profumo, Tory Secretary of State for War, had a brief and passionate affair with a call girl, Christine Keeler, at the same time as there were reports that she was consorting with a naval attaché at the Soviet Embassy in London. Profumo made a fundamental error: he lied to the House of Commons. In March 1963 he told the chamber that there was 'no impropriety whatever' in his relationship with Miss Keeler. Ten weeks later he appeared before MPs again to say 'with deep remorse' that he had misled the House, and would resign.

The secret service continued to be protected by layers of official secrecy, until the publication *Spycatcher* came onto the (Australian) market, in which former MI5 officer Peter Wright described how 'we bugged and burgled our way across London at the State's behest, while pompous, bowler-hatted civil servants in Whitehall pretended to look the other way'.[86]

Secrecy may be essential in the case of a respondent who, if tipped off, is likely to defeat the purposes of an application by publishing the material before he can be shown to have had notice of the injunction, or before it can be granted. There may be compelling reasons why the Crown or the Attorney General apply for an injunction on the grounds of public security and state secrecy.

There have been three famous cases in UK legal history which have tested the notion of state secrecy and confidentiality; two were decided prior to the **Human Rights Act 1998**, namely the *Crossman Diaries*[87] and *Spycatcher*, with the *David Shayler* case decided post the European Convention's incorporation into UK law involving criminal action. In *Crossman Diaries* and *Spycatcher*, prior restraint orders to stop publication were applied for by the Attorney General on behalf of the respective government at the time citing breach of confidence.

The 'Crossman Diaries' case (*Attorney General v Jonathan Cape Ltd.* (1976))[88] presented the first court action that tested the paradigm of restraint of a government minister's publication of cabinet 'secrets'. The government had applied via the Attorney General to injunct the publication of cabinet minister Richard Crossman's posthumous diaries. The courts, in turn, had to balance the competing interests, namely the public's right to know about government secrets and indiscretions ('the public

---

83 Ibid., at 45.
84 [2003] QB 195 at 202 (Lord Woolf CJ).
85 See: Andrew (2009).
86 See: Wright (1987), pp. 104–6.
87 See: Crossman (1976–7).
88 [1976] QB 752.

interest test') and cabinet confidentiality and government secrecy. Lord Widgery CJ's judgment makes this abundantly clear when he lifted the injunction and the publication of the three volumes of diaries could go ahead:

> . . . it is unacceptable in our democratic society that there should be a restraint on the publication of information relating to government when the only vice of that information is that it enables the public to discuss, review and criticise government action. Accordingly, the court will determine the government's claim to confidentiality by reference to the public interest. Unless disclosure is likely to injure the public interest, it will not be protected.[89]

The *Spycatcher* action followed, arguably best known for its numerous injunctions (see: *AG v Guardian Newspapers Ltd.* (Nr 1) (1987)[90] and 'Nr 2' (1990)[91]). Former MI5 spy Peter Wright had entered into a publishing contract with an Australian company in 1985 after he had retired to Tasmania, where he had written his memoirs: *Spycatcher: the candid autobiography of a senior intelligence officer*. The first court action ('Spycatcher Nr 1') concerned the application by the Attorney General to restrain prior publication of the book in order to preserve the confidentiality of the Wright material, subject to him signing the contract of employment which inherently included the **Official Secrets Act 1911**.[92] Once the British government learnt that *Spycatcher* was going to be published on a large scale in the Antipodes and North America, it was said the British secret services of MI5 and its international counterpart MI6 would never be truly secret and confidential again. The question arose in the UK High Court whether the Crown could injunct a publication outside the United Kingdom.[93]

❖ **KEY CASE**   *'Spycatcher' (Nr 1): AG v Guardian Newspapers Ltd. (Nr 1) (1987)*

Facts:
Former MI5 member of the British secret service, Peter Wright (W), had written his memoirs of 20 years in the secret service, during his retirement in Tasmania, under the title *Spycatcher*. The book alleged unlawful activities carried out by MI5 during W's period of service, such as allegations of activities by certain MI5 officers with the intention of destabilizing the Harold Wilson administration and of surveillance of Mr Wilson in 1977.

The Crown took steps in the form of an injunction to stop the book being published in New South Wales and the United States, because it disclosed information that constituted a breach of confidentiality owed to the Crown and on the grounds that if publication took place, the conduct of MI5 investigations and operations might be compromised and put at risk. *The Independent, The Guardian* and *Observer* newspapers reported on the intended press 'gagging' orders, stating that this amounted to an interference with the freedom of the press.

On 11 July 1986 Millett J granted injunctions against the newspapers, restraining them from disclosing or publishing any information about W. The newspapers appealed and their appeal was dismissed on 25 July 1986 by the Court of Appeal. On 27 April 1987, *The*

---

89 (1976) QB 752 at 735 (Lord Widgery).
90 [1987] 1 WLR 1248.
91 [1990] 1 AC 109.
92 For further discussion see: Barendt (1989), pp. 204ff; also: Bindman (1989), pp. 94ff.
93 See also: Lee (1987), pp. 506ff; see also: Leigh (1992), pp. 200ff.

Independent published a summary of allegations contained in *Spycatcher*. The AG commenced contempt of court proceedings against *The Independent. The Guardian* and *Observer* applied for the discharge of their injunctions on the grounds that there had been a significant change of circumstances since July 1986.

On 2 June 1987, Sir Nicolas Browne-Wilkinson VC held that the publication in *The Independent* and two London evening newspapers could not amount to 'contempt' because there was no injunction restraining publication by *The Independent* or any newspaper, apart from *The Guardian* and the *Observer*.

On 12 July 1987, the *Sunday Times* published extracts from the book, having bought the serialization rights to *Spycatcher* from the Australian publisher, timed to coincide with the book's publication in the USA. On 13 July 1987 the Attorney General commenced 'contempt' proceedings against the *Sunday Times* for publishing the article while a restraining order was still in place. On 17 July the Court of Appeal held that the publication by *The Independent* amounted to a contempt of court.

On 22 July the Vice Chancellor discharged all injunctions, allowing a cross-appeal from the Attorney General at the Court of Appeal on 24 July, modifying the injunctions by allowing the newspapers to publish a summary of Peter Wright's book with its allegations.

Decision:
The CA upheld all interim injunctions against the newspapers and agreed with the AG that they were necessary to maintain the efficiency of the security services upon which the safety of the realm was dependent.

The basic argument by defendant newspapers in *Spycatcher* Nr 2[94] was that the information contained in Peter Wright's book was public property and already public knowledge in that the book had already been published in Australia and the United States. Therefore, the plaintiff (the Attorney General) had to show not only that the information was confidential in quality and that it was imparted so as to import an obligation of confidence, but also that there would be 'an unauthorised use of that information to the detriment of the party communicating', as per *Coco v A. N. Clark (Engineers) Ltd.* (1969).[95]

In the second *Spycatcher* action, the House of Lords was sympathetic to the Attorney General's fear that newspapers might publish the contents of such a book without careful consideration of the public interest in non-disclosure and without giving him the opportunity, if he challenged the editors' judgment, to have the issue determined by the court. It was for this reason that the first judge, Scott J, had granted the injunction in *Spycatcher* Nr 1.

Lord Griffiths in *Spycatcher* Nr 2 referred to the provision of freedom of expression under Article 10 ECHR, commenting that he saw no reason why English law should take a different approach in relation to confidentiality.[96] Lord Goff of Chieveley, in his judgment, identified the following limiting principles where the law would protect the notion of 'confidence':

94 *AG v Guardian Newspapers Ltd.* (Nr. 2) ('Spycatcher Nr 2)' [1990] 1 AC 109.
95 [1969] RPC 41.
96 Ibid., at 273 (Lord Griffiths).

> . . . although the basis of the law's protection of confidence is that there is a public interest that confidences should be preserved and protected by the law, nevertheless that public interest may be outweighed by some other countervailing public interest which favours disclosure. This limitation may apply . . . to all types of confidential information. It is this limiting principle which may require a court to carry out a balancing operation, weighing the public interest in maintaining confidence against a countervailing public interest favouring disclosure.[97]

While the courts condemned Peter Wright's conduct, it was still unavoidable that British citizens had either read reports or reviews of the book, or comments on it in the newspapers, or they had bought a copy of *Spycatcher* in foreign bookshops. In its judgment in *Spycatcher* Nr 2, the House of Lords held that the book contained material prejudicial to national security and was in serious breach of confidence. In the end their Lordships had no choice but to lift the injunction because a restraining order could not be applied against Peter Wright and the publishers because they were resident outside the UK, which provided them with a jurisdictional shield. This meant that a UK court order could not bind the High Court of Australia, the New Zealand Court of Appeal or indeed any other foreign jurisdiction. Since the book had already been published in New South Wales, New Zealand and the United States, *Spycatcher* was already in the public domain and an injunction would effectively be worthless.

It is worth mentioning that the *Sunday Times* publishers and its editor Andrew Neil were severely criticized in *Spycatcher* Nr 2: they were held liable to account to the Crown for profits because they had ignored the existing court injunction and the newspaper had still gone ahead and published extracts from the book in July 1987. The publishers and editor were found guilty of contempt of court and Lord Keith of Kinkel specifically referred to Mr Neil's blatantly ignoring the interim injunction as employing 'peculiarly sneaky methods'.[98]

The *Spycatcher* litigation was viewed by some foreign jurisdictions as an authoritarian attempt by the British government over its former Commonwealth to quash freedom of speech, freedom of access to information and freedom to publish. Unsurprisingly, English judges took a different view.

The *David Shayler* case (R v *Shayler* (2003)[99]) was different. The case concerned a 'whistleblower', former MI5 agent David Shayler, who took it upon himself to disclose British secret service information by publishing articles in the press during August 1997. On 24 August, the *Mail on Sunday* ran a front-page story headlined 'MI5 Bugged Mandelson', with the claim that Tony Blair's favourite minister had his phone tapped for three years during the late 1970s. Not only did Shayler not succeed in publishing his memoirs but he was also convicted for unlawfully disclosing official documents to the press, while at the same time breaching the **Official Secrets Act** 1989 as part of his employment.[100] When a prosecution against Mr Shayler ensued for seriously breaching the Act, he used the right to freedom of expression under Art 10 ECHR as a defence.[101]

❖ **KEY CASE**   *R v Shayler* (2003) 1 AC 247 (House of Lords)

Facts:
MI5 agent David Shayler was a member of the security service from November 1991 to October 1996. As part of his contract, he had signed the **Official Secrets Act 1989**, acknowledging the confidential nature of documents and other information relating to security or intelligence that might come into his possession. On leaving the service he

---

97 ibid., at 282 (Lord Goff of Chieveley).
98 *AG v Guardian Newspapers* (No.2) [1990] 1 A.C. 109 at 261 (Lord Keith of Kinkel).
99 [2003] 1 AC 247.
100 For further discussion see: Hollingsworth and Fielding (1999).
101 HRA 1998, Sch. 1, Pt I.

signed a declaration acknowledging that the provisions of the Act continued to apply. In 1997 Mr Shayler disclosed documents relating to security and intelligence matters to a national newspaper, claiming that MI5 held files on more than 500,000 subjects, including two cabinet ministers. He also alleged that Britain had tried to assassinate the Libyan leader, Colonel Gaddafi. Shayler escaped to France to avoid prosecution for breaching secrecy laws. In 1999, government lawyers applied for an injunction to block the publication of his memoirs. In August 2000 he returned to the UK and was arrested and charged with disclosing documents without lawful authority, contrary to ss. 1 and 4 of the 1989 Act.

At trial at the Old Bailey, Moses J ruled that the defence of duress or necessity of circumstances was not available to the defendant, implied in the 1989 Act. Shayler was also not permitted to invoke Article 10 ECHR, claiming that the disclosures were necessary in the public interest to avert damage to life or limb or serious damage to property. The CA dismissed Shayler's appeal, ruling that, having regard to national security, the restrictions placed on past and present members of the security service were not a contravention of their right to freedom of expression, and that the judge had been entitled to make the ruling he did.

Decision:
Their Lordships dismissed the appeal on the grounds that ss. 1(1)(a), 3(a) and 4(1) of the 1989 Act, when given their plain and natural meaning and read in the context of the Act as a whole, made it clear that Parliament did not intend that a defendant prosecuted under those sections should be acquitted if he showed that it was, or that he believed that it was, in the public or national interest to make the disclosure in question, or if the jury concluded that it might have been, or that the defendant might have believed it to be, in the public or national interest to make the disclosure. The prosecution did not have to prove that the disclosure was damaging or was not in the public interest. For that reason, the defendant was not entitled to argue as a defence that the unauthorized disclosures he had made were made in the public interest. David Shayler was sentenced to six months in prison.

Their Lordships stated *obiter*, that in order to 'whistleblow' on irregularities or unlawful practices within the security services Mr Shayler should have sought judicial review as the right course of effective action. Instead, Mr Shayler chose to impart highly confidential information to a national newspaper for financial and professional gain.

Spycatcher had clearly smoothed the path to future publications of memoirs or biographies from or about the British secret services, such as by the first female heads of MI5, Stella Rimington[102] or Eliza Manningham-Buller.[103]

2.3.3 Kiss and tell and domestic intimacy
When people kiss and later one of them tells, the second person is almost certainly breaking a confidential arrangement. Though it is necessary for the press to report on all proceedings in open court, as was held in the divorce proceedings in *Scott v Scott* (1913),[104] the courts have never given a carte blanche approach to the disclosure of private communication between couples and free distribution to the press of private correspondence. This point was further

See Chapter
◀ 1.4.1

---

102 See: Rimington (2002).
103 See: Hewitt (2010).
104 [1913] AC 417.

developed in the 'Duchess and Duke of Argyll' case relating to confidentiality (see below: 2.3.4; see also: *Stephens v Avery* (1988)[105]).

The European Human Rights court has consistently applied its jurisdiction on the subject of Article 8 ECHR when determining what is necessary in a particular state's society where an action is being brought. This is widely acknowledged where the Court has held that it will apply narrower measures with reference to an aspect of a person's private life, such as one's sexuality.[106] A variety of different interferences fall within the category of 'private life style' and interest, including unwanted observation and intrusion into one's home and the workplace as well as the unwanted dissemination of images (*Peck v UK* (2003)[107]).

Recognition of the need to protect against such interferences is unsurprising. Although English courts have not yet recognized physical intrusion as part of the tort of privacy, there are a number of Strasbourg rulings which could be regarded as persuasive, such as the right to be free from physical assault or bodily searches, surveillance and the dissemination of images (*YF v Turkey* (2004)[108]); or where the Court expressly held that an individual's mental and physical health is part of a person's 'physical or moral integrity' (*Bensaid v UK* (2001)[109]). The next challenge to privacy will be aerial kite photography, used already for military reconnaissance.

2.3.4 The scandal that rocked the nation: *The Duchess of Argyll v The Duke of Argyll*

The eleventh Duke of Argyll had been unlucky in love. Twice divorced, he then met Margaret Whigham, a millionaire's daughter, and divorcee, on a blind date in London. They were married in 1951 and the Duke took her north to his ancestral seat at Inveraray Castle. But the Duchess of Argyll was soon bored. By early 1954, the Duke had accused Margaret of a string of affairs, filing for divorce in 1959.

The Duke's main evidence was his wife's diaries and explosive photographs which had been taken with a Polaroid camera; the so-called 'headless' photos. All items of personal property had been seized by gaining unauthorized entry to the Duchess' house at 48 Upper Grosvenor Street, which her father had left Margaret as personal property. This raid was key to the Duke's divorce case. The Polaroids, dated on the back 1957, showed the Duchess wearing nothing but a string of pearls performing fellatio on her lover, while revealing a shot of another man in a gilt mirror, performing a sex act on the first naked man. The men's heads had been cropped out of the photograph. The photos were commonly referred to as the 'headless men' Polaroids.

Allegation followed allegation in an incredible war of words, injunctions and two-way adultery claims – which may well have been the basis for today's superinjunctions. The lawyers were kept fully employed. As the Duke pursued his adultery claims, the Duchess cross-petitioned and alleged that he was having an affair with her own stepmother; she later withdrew the preposterous claim and paid out £25,000 when she was sued. After three years of legal wrangling, the case was finally heard at an 11-day hearing at the Edinburgh High Court in 1962, whereby the Duke finally obtained his divorce on the grounds of her adultery. The court heard details of her salacious behaviour inside the Georgian house in London's Mayfair, and Margaret was pilloried as a high-class harlot.

The Duke had originally listed 88 possible lovers, but the judge found Margaret had committed adultery with three, namely John Cohane, an American businessman, Harvey Combe, a former press officer for the Savoy Hotel who lived in Ross-shire, and Sigismund von Braun, a German

---

105 [1988] 1 Ch 449.
106 *Norris v Ireland* (1989) 13 EHRR 186.
107 (2003) 36 EHRR 41.
108 (2004) 39 EHRR 34.
109 (2001) 33 EHRR 10.

diplomat, whose letters were regarded as sufficient evidence to prove adultery. The sexually explicit photos were central to the Argyll divorce proceedings and formed part of the 'confidentiality' action in *Argyll v Argyll* (1967).[110] The photos even became part of a government investigation led by Lord Denning, who had been given the task of establishing the identities of the Duchess' 'headless' lovers to establish the infidelity action. However, the identities of the two headless men in the photos were not revealed in court.

Following the decree of divorce, the Edinburgh court granted an injunction that the subject matter of the action should never be made public despite the fact that the Duchess had allowed certain articles relating to her infidelities to appear in the *People* newspaper. It followed that it was unlawful to publish or make public any offensive material (including the headless photographs) or name any party cited during the infidelity proceedings.[111] The judgment was not pronounced until 8 May 1963, when Lord Wheatley read the four-and-a-half-hour judgment, including: 'She is a highly sexed woman who has ceased to be satisfied with normal sexual activities and has started to indulge in disgusting sexual activities to gratify a debased sexual appetite.' While the judgment was being read out, the Duchess was in Paris for a dress fitting. The Argyll judgment was heard in the same month when John Profumo lied to the Commons about his relationship Christine Keeler. *Argyll v Argyll* became the longest and most sensational divorce to occur in Britain. Below is the summarized judgment by Lord Wheatley, which was later applied in similar relationship cases, such as *Barrymore* (see below: 2.3.5):

1. A breach of confidence or trust or faith can arise independently of any right in property or contract and that the court in the exercise of its equitable jurisdiction will restrain a breach of confidence independently of any right at law;
2. that the principle applies even *after* divorce or *after* adultery or previous disclosures;
3. the confidential nature of the marital relationship is of its very essence and so obviously and necessarily implicit in it that there is no need for it to be expressed. This would apply not merely to private affairs but business matters and things discovered by one party to the marriage about the other which but for the close relationship they would not have discovered. It also encompasses things done as well as things talked about.[112]

The *Argyll* ruling states that confidential communication between husband and wife – in the form of letters, diary entries or photographs – is within the scope of the court's protection against breach of confidence. In the Duchess of Argyll's case, her immorality did not nullify her right to protection against breach of confidence relating to past events, prior to the breakdown of the marriage.

The identity of the 'headless men' in the Duchess of Argyll's Polaroid snaps was eventually revealed some 41 years after the event on 10 August 2000, when a Channel 4 documentary alleged that there had been two different 'headless men' in the photographs. The programme named the actor Douglas Fairbanks Jr (after his death) and cabinet minister Duncan Sandys (who had died in 1987).[113]

In 1978, John Lennon of The Beatles was not able to restrain breaches of marital confidences and disclosures by his first wife, published in the *News of the World*, on the grounds that:

(1) He himself had publicized the most intimate details of their marriage; and
(2) There was nothing left which was confidential; all the information was already in the public domain.[114]

---

110 [1967] Ch 301.
111 Section 1 *Judicial Proceedings (Regulation of Reports) Act 1926*.
112 (1967) Ch 301 at 632 (Lord Wheatley).
113 Source: 'Headless men' in sex scandal finally named', by Sarah Hall, *The Guardian*, 10 August 2000.
114 *Lennon v News Group Newspapers* [1978] FSR 573.

2.3.5 Domestic partnerships: the Michael Barrymore case

On 17 March 1997, the *Sun* released extracts from confidential handwritten letters between TV personality Michael Barrymore and his lover Paul Wilcott. Though Mr Barrymore had made it known in August 1995 to his wife and close family members that he was homosexual, the matter was not of general public knowledge at the time.

On the day the *Sun* outed Michael Barrymore as gay, he sought an *ex parte* injunction from the High Court, claiming breach of confidence at common law and in equity and in relation to 'A Trust and Confidence Agreement' made between the second plaintiff, the company owned jointly by Barrymore and his wife, and Paul Wincott (*Barrymore v News Group Newspapers Limited and Another* (1997)[115]). The agreement – made by deed – included the obligation not to disclose or make use of any confidential business or personal information. The High Court granted the injunction to restrain any further publications, citing Lord Wheatley's judgment in *Argyll*, extending the principle of confidentiality in correspondence between married couples to that of 'close relationships'.

It is then only common sense if people enter into a personal relationship and exchange letters, photographs or other means of correspondence that this is not done for the purpose of publication in the press or any other medium. It would be highly unlikely in personal relationships that the parties draw up a contract to keep their relationship confidential and if there is a breach of confidentiality, and one party 'kisses and tells', only common law may provide a remedy to stop the papers from printing such information as outlined in *Scott v Scott*, the *Duke and Duchess of Argyll case* and *Barrymore*.

2.3.6 Breach of confidence and court remedies

The press, being fed information by a jilted partner about letters or emails exchanged between the couple when they were still in love, will always try to publish a juicy story. BBC TV and Radio 1 presenter Jamie Theakston attempted to block certain photographs and a story about visits to a Mayfair brothel, where he had engaged in sexual activity with three prostitutes, appearing in the *Sunday People* and the *News of the World*. But the judge rejected, in part, his application for an injunction on the grounds of privacy and confidentiality.

In *Theakston v MGN* (2002),[116] the court granted the injunction in part under s. 12(3) HRA 1998, restraining the publication of the photographs, stating that there was no public interest in their publication, no consent had been given to their being taken and there was no similar material that had been placed in the public domain. But the court was not prepared to grant the celebrity a restraining order on the article and ruled in favour of freedom of expression, because Theakston's 'one-night stand' with the prostitutes could hardly be described as a 'close relationship', and a brothel did not constitute a private place for the purposes of Article 8 ECHR. The relationship between a prostitute in a brothel and the customer was not confidential in nature and the fact that sexual activity had taken place did not, of itself, create a relationship of confidentiality; though, no doubt, they shared a few secrets and experiences. The prostitute wanted to share these experiences with the public and the press; clearly Theakston did not. It was because Mr Theakston was a presenter of programmes aimed at young viewers, like *Top of the Pops* and *Live and Kicking*, that it was considered there was an element of public interest in some of the material being published and Article 10 was given greater weight. After the injunction was refused and the article was published in the *Sunday People*, Theakston was forced to excuse his behaviour in a public broadcast, stating that he was 'totally drunk' and 'I thought, why not? It's Christmas'.[117]

---

115 [1997] ESR 600.
116 [2002] EWHC 137 (QB).
117 Source: 'Theakston "sorry" over sex stories', BBC *news online*, 27 January 2002, available at <http://news.bbc.co.uk/1/hi/entertainment/1785264.stm>, accessed 18 November 2010.

Remedy for breach of confidence exists, but to qualify three essential elements must be present:

1. The information itself must have 'the necessary quality of confidence about it';
2. The information 'must have been imparted in circumstances importing an obligation of confidence'; and
3. There must have been an 'unauthorised use of that information to the detriment of the party communicating it'.[118]

The civil remedies available include:

1. injunction;
2. compensatory damages;
3. exemplary damages;
4. account of profits;
5. delivery-up;
6. costs.

But it is not quite that straightforward, as damages for breach of confidence are not always recoverable, as Sir Robert Megarry, VC, stated in *Malone v Metropolitan Police Commissioner* (1979):[119]

> . . . the right of confidentiality is an equitable right which is still in the course of development, and is usually protected by the grant of an injunction to prevent disclosure of the confidence. Under Lord Cairns' Act 1858 damages may be granted in substitution for an injunction; yet if there is no case for the grant of an injunction, as when the disclosure has already been made, the unsatisfactory result seems to be that no damages can be awarded under this head . . . In such a case, where there is no breach of contract or other orthodox foundation for damages at common law, it seems doubtful whether there is any right to damages, as distinct from an account of profits.[120]

As mentioned above in section 2.3.2, an order of an account of profits was made against the *Sunday Times* in '*Spycatcher Nr 2*'.[121] The remedy of 'account of profits' was ordered as an alternative to damages for breach of confidence despite the equitable nature of the wrong, through a beneficent interpretation of the **Chancery Amendment Act 1858** (Lord Cairns' Act). Because of the difficulties often arising out of confidence action, the taking of account of profit is therefore regarded as a more satisfactory remedy, at least in cases where the confidential information is of a commercial nature and quantifiable damage may therefore have been suffered.

In *Barrymore*, the High Court granted an injunction to restrain further publication in the newspaper of information released by Paul Wincott. But the question of compensation was a tricky one, as Jacobs J stated:

> . . . the financial consequences will no doubt be a matter for the court to decide in due course. I say no more at this stage other than that newspapers which think that they can pay their way out of breach of confidence may find it more expensive than it is worth to print the material.[122]

---

118 *Coco v A. N. Clarke* (Engineers) Ltd. [1969] RPC 41 at 47.
119 [1979] 1 Ch 344.
120 Ibid., at 468 (Sir Robert Megarry VC).
121 [1990] 1 AC 109 at 286 (Lord Goff).
122 *Barrymore v News Group Newspapers* [1997] ESR at 602 (Jacobs J).

This leaves the concept of breach of confidentiality rather too open and flexible and will, no doubt, be decided by the courts on a case-by-case basis. As common law on privacy and confidentiality has advanced and has gradually merged the two concepts, they tend to have a rather uneasy relationship with the right to freedom of expression under Article 10 of the Convention, as demonstrated in the *Earl Spencer* case (below). This tension is particularly acute where people in a relationship share confidential information and one partner discloses it, usually for financial gain, after the relationship has gone sour.

2.3.7 Privacy and the Human Rights Court: the Earl Spencer case

In his privacy action before the Strasbourg court, the ninth Earl Spencer, brother of the deceased Princess Diana, submitted that the United Kingdom had failed to comply with its obligations under the Convention to protect his right to respect for his private life under Article 8 ECHR. He claimed that the state had failed to prohibit the publication and dissemination of information relating to his wife's private affairs and to provide a legal remedy; that is, the UK ought to have prevented the release of private and confidential information concerning the Spencers' private affairs in the form of restraining newspaper publications and should have provided damages thereafter for the distress caused.

In the 'Earl Spencer' case,[123] the second applicant, Countess Spencer, referred to long-lens photography taken of her in the grounds of a private rehabilitation clinic without her knowledge or consent. Both applicants invoked Articles 8 and 13 ('right to an effective remedy') of the Convention. The first publication concerned an article in the *News of the World* on 2 April 1995, headlined 'Di's sister-in-law in booze and bulimia clinic'. It went into considerable detail about the Countess' personal and family problems. The article was accompanied by a photograph taken with a telephoto lens while she walked in the grounds of the private clinic, captioned 'SO THIN: Victoria walks in the clinic grounds this week'. The second publication was an article in the *People* on the same day, referring to the Countess' admission to a private clinic for an eating disorder. The third article was published in the *Sunday Mirror*, also on the same day, alleging that the Countess had a drink problem. Later, on 2 April 1995, Earl Spencer condemned the intrusion into his wife's personal affairs, arguing that she needed privacy and freedom from harassment since she was suffering from a psychological disorder.

The editor of the *News of the World* issued a statement on 14 Mary 1995 that the Countess was a public figure by birth and the public had a right to know about the Spencer family affairs, given that they were related to Princess Diana, the Princess of Wales; in any case the Countess had herself publically confirmed at a charity event of the Eating Disorders Association on 5 August 1993 that she suffered from an eating disorder; so the information was in the public domain.

On 3 April 1995, Earl Spencer complained to the Press Complaints Commission (PCC) about the articles, claiming breaches under the PCC Code of Practice relating to privacy (Clause 4), intrusion by journalists in hospitals (Clause 6) and harassment (Clause 8). The PCC concluded that the *News of the World* and other newspapers had breached the Code of Practice, but excused the *Daily Mirror* because its editor had published an apology prior to the PCC's adjudication. On 17 May the Earl and his wife issued a High Court writ against two former friends, threatening breach of confidence for releasing personal information in the form of a letter written by the Countess which had resulted in the *News of the World* article. The writ sought a permanent injunction to restrain the defendants from disclosing, publishing or revealing to any party whomsoever *any* information concerning the Spencers' private lives including their children, relatives, guests and visitors, including members of the Royal Family and their staff. This was not granted and the Earl and Countess Spencer sought

---

123 *Earl Spencer and Countess Spencer v United Kingdom* (1998) 25 EHRR CD 105.

redress before the Human Rights Court, which sadly occurred at the time that Princess Diana died in Paris in the tragic car accident.

Apart from arguing the breach of confidence action, the Spencers complained that the UK had no effective remedy in common law for the invasion of their privacy by the media. Citing the *Barrymore* judgment, they submitted that it must be shown that the relevant newspapers had been put on notice *prior* to publication and that the disclosure of confidential information amounted to a breach of a duty of confidence owed by the source to the subject of the information. In practice this would have meant that the couple would have had to prove that the newspapers had the requisite notice both of the friends' duty of confidence *and* of their breach of that duty; in conclusion, that such a duty would and could not exist in the majority of cases of media intrusion and, if it did exist, was near impossible to establish. As to the remedies available for a breach of confidence, Earl Spencer and his wife referred to the impossibility of obtaining an injunction *prior* to publication in the absence of prior warning. In short, the court would not make a restraining order if the material information has already been published.

The European Human Rights Commission rejected the Spencers' complaints under Article 8 on the basis that the couple had not completely exhausted the domestic remedies available to them for breach of confidence as outlined in *Spycatcher* Nr 2 and *Barrymore*. The Commission also found their complaint under Article 13 ill-founded within the meaning of Article 27(2) of the Convention. Accordingly, the remedy of an action in breach of confidence against the relevant newspapers had been accessible to the applicants and was capable of providing redress for their complaints. The court commented that the UK's common law provisions offered reasonable prospects of success and that there were effective remedies which the Spencers chose not to avail themselves of before taking their action to the Human Rights Court.

2.4 The impact of the Human Rights Act 1998 on UK common law

The **Human Rights Act 1998** (HRA) came into effect in October 2000, importing the European Convention on Human Rights into UK law. Since this chapter deals mainly with challenges under Articles 8 and 10 of the Convention – the right to privacy and freedom of expression – it is fair to say that not all cases have been reported and many of them have been settled out of court. Most actions have claimed injunctions under Article 8, which have been filed against the most popular 'red tops' and their senior editors.

For example, famous children's author J.K. Rowling obtained a successful injunction in June 2005 prior to the publication of *Harry Potter and the Half-Blood Prince* in order to keep the contents of the book confidential. Attempts had been made by two men to sell stolen copies of the book to the media. Rowling's lawyer, David Hooper, had obtained a 'John Doe' injunction citing Article 8 as one of the main reasons.[124] This meant that no newspaper or other media outlet could publish anything on the book and if they did, they would be in contempt of court.

In November 2008, movie actress Sienna Miller reached a settlement with an agency of paparazzi photographers, 'Big Pictures', after claiming an invasion of her privacy and harassment over her alleged relationship with Balthazar Getty, soon after she broke off a relationship with the Welsh actor Rhys Ifans. Ms Miller reportedly reached an out-of-court settlement against Big Pictures

---

124 A 'John Doe' injunction binds any unnamed and presently unknown persons who wrongfully come into possession of any original material not to disclose the original work.

for £16,000 in damages and succeeded in a similar privacy claim against the *Sun* and *News of the World* newspapers amounting to £35,000 in damages.[125]

> ### 👁 FOR THOUGHT
>
> 'The original purpose of the Council of Europe Convention on Human Rights was to enable public attention to be drawn to any revival of totalitarian methods of government and to provide a forum in which the appropriate action could be discussed and decided' (Simpson 2004: 777). In the light of Professor Simpson's quotation, do you not think it remarkable that the European Convention has one fundamental flaw in the basic concept of having an international court of human rights that deals with the concrete application of those rights in different countries?

As stated before, the main conflict rests on the courts' striking the right balance between Articles 8 and 10 ECHR as well as paying attention to the rights protected by both articles, which are subject to limitations prescribed by law necessary in a democratic society and in the public interest. A survey by legal publishers Sweet & Maxwell found that in the 12 months to October 2009, there were 51 cases, or 15 per cent, that involved human rights issues before the House of Lords, an increase of more than a third on the 38 reported the year before. The figures also showed that more cases were making use of the **Human Rights Act** than in the previous seven years. Researchers found a rise of 90 per cent in disputes with government agencies brought by businesses, corporations or firms making use of the 1998 Act, which meant that businesses were using the HRA as much as prisoners.[126]

Unsuccessful court actions, particularly involving high-profile celebrities, are often reported. But those settled out of court are rarely reported, because that will be part of the settlement and 'compromise agreement'). Moreover, we can glean some idea of human rights challenges when reading some of the PCC adjudications (online) which mostly concern the intrusion into a person's privacy (Clause 3 of the PCC Code).

One such complaint was by Prince Harry in 2004, who was pursued by paparazzi when sunning himself with his girlfriend Chelsy Davy on a public beach in Mozambique. He instructed the PR officer at Clarence House in London to contact the PCC so that they could instruct the paparazzi to stop harassing him and his lady friend. The PCC's Director, Tim Toulmin and the then chairman, Sir Christopher Meyer, explained to the Royal Press Office that privacy on a public beach could not generally be guaranteed, even to members of the Royal Family.[127]

2.4.1 Article 12 HRA: restraining publication and the freedom of expression

A claimant who applies for an interim order restraining a defendant from publishing allegedly private or confidential information has to give advance notice of the application under Article 12 of the **Human Rights Act 1998** (HRA) and of the injunctive relief sought to any non-party on whom

---

125 Source: 'Sienna Miller gets £53k for press intrusion', by Mark Sweney, *The Guardian*, 22 November 2008.
126 Poole and Shah (2009), pp. 347–71. The research paper outlines the background and methodology adopted and the main findings on whether the House showed a greater willingness after the Act's commencement to grant leave to appeal in cases raising human rights issues.
127 Source: 'Photos of Prince Harry prompt privacy row: PCC may get complaint over snaps taken at holiday resort', by Owen Gibson, Media Correspondent, *The Guardian*, 21 December 2004.

the claimant intends to serve the order, so as to bind that party by application of the '*Spycatcher*' principle (see above 2.3.2), *unless*:

(1)   The claimant has no reason to believe that the non-party has or may have an existing specific interest in the outcome of the application; or

(2)   The claimant is unable to notify the non-party having taken all practicable steps to do so; or

(3)   There are compelling reasons why the non-party should not be notified.

Article 12 HRA will only apply at any trial or at the application of a superinjunction or possible life-long anonymity order when the freedom of expression is challenged; s. 12 HRA reads:

(1) This section applies if a court is considering whether to grant any relief which, if granted, might affect the exercise of the Convention right to freedom of expression.

(2) If the person against whom the application for relief is made ('the respondent') is neither present nor represented, no such relief is to be granted unless the court is satisfied:

(a)   that the applicant has taken all practicable steps to notify the respondent; or

(b)   that there are compelling reasons why the respondent should not be notified.

(3) No such relief is to be granted so as to restrain publication before trial unless the court is satisfied that the applicant is likely to establish that publication should not be allowed.

(4) The court must have particular regard to the importance of the Convention right to freedom of expression and, where the proceedings relate to material which the respondent claims, or which appears to the court, to be journalistic, literary or artistic material (or to conduct connected with such material), to:

(a)   the extent to which (i) the material has, or is about to, become available to the public; or (ii) it is, or would be, in the public interest for the material to be published;

(b)   any relevant privacy code[128].

The problem in the John Terry superinjunction[129] was that the applicant claimed not to know the name of the media organization that had a specific interest in his story (see below 2.7.7). Tugendhat J, hearing the application, could not accept that explanation. It was evident that the *News of the World* intended to publish the story about footballer John Terry's affair on Sunday 24 January 2010, but the applicant did not know what the story would be about. This meant that the newspaper group should have been given notice by Mr Terry's lawyers under s. 12 HRA confirming the application to have the story injuncted. According to Mr Justice Tugendhat's judgment this did not happen, or rather, it happened too late, pending the handing-down of the judgment of 29 January 2010.

In the application to curtail freedom of expression under s. 12 HRA there lies an inherent dilemma for the applicant: if he or she gives notice to the media to have the impending story or publication injuncted, the very information upon which an attempt is being made to keep secret is revealed. It is possible that, up until then, the newspaper to which notice is being given knows only part of the story and the attempt to injunct may confirm as fact what is at that stage only rumour.

When the *Guardian* requested sight of the evidence in opposing the John Terry injunction, the newspaper's lawyer, Gillian Phillips, made the following four points:

---

128 For example the PCC Code Clause 3 'Privacy'.
129 See: *LNS v Persons Unknown* [2010] EWHC 119 (QB).

. . . it appears to me that this latest order is symptomatic of a trend whereby this sort of order is (1) sought against persons unknown, by which I deduce that no one was heard in opposition to the injunction request. No advance notice was given to the media; (2) immediately served on the legal departments of the national media, who are not defendants to the action; (3) dispenses with any obligation to serve evidence in support; (4) protects an anonymous claimant.[130]

In response to *The Guardian*'s request for sight of the evidence, the solicitors for the applicant footballer asked for an undertaking that the information be kept secure and not disclosed. Because of the limited reporting of such cases, frequently known only by acronyms and randomly selected letters of the alphabet, it is difficult to come to a single and rigid standard conclusion governing all applications for superinjunctions (see: *G and G v Wikimedia Foundation Inc* (2009)).[131]

The effect of section 12(3) HRA is that a court is not to make an interim restraint order unless satisfied that the applicant's prospects of success at trial are sufficiently favourable to justify such an order being made in the particular circumstances of the case and taking into account the relevant jurisprudence under Article 10 ECHR. Looking at the judgment by Tugendhat J in *LNS*, it appears that the general approach by the courts in the granting of superinjunctions tends to be 'exceedingly slow' by making an interim restraint order where the applicant has not satisfied the court that he would probably succeed at the trial.[132] However, where the potential adverse consequences of disclosure are particularly grave – say, in family cases, or where a short-lived injunction is needed to enable the court to hear and give proper consideration to an application for interim relief pending trial or any relevant appeal – the courts have granted such restraining orders under s. 12 HRA with great expediency (see: *X (a woman formerly known as Mary Bell) and another v O'Brien and others* (2003)[133] – see below: 2.6.2).

On 29 September 2008, Max Mosley filed an application before the European Court of Human Rights in Strasbourg. On 11 January 2011, Mr Mosley asked the ECtHR to rule in favour of 'prior notification', which would compel the UK press to notify the subject of a story before publication. It had already been established in the High Court that Mr Mosley was the subject of an illegal and devastating invasion of his private life by the *News of the World* (see 2.4.5 below). The current position in the UK is that, although we all have a right to privacy, it is entirely up to the editor of a newspaper whether or not we are able to exercise that right in any effective or meaningful way. The editor of a newspaper (or online edition), acting alone, can take a decision to publish material which may ruin a life or destroy a family, safe in the knowledge that even if publication is later held to be unlawful, there will be no significant consequences for him or his employers. As Eady J observed in his judgment, the UK media is well aware that most people would not have taken legal action had they been in Mr Mosley's shoes.

Bringing a privacy claim for damages in the High Court is extremely costly and puts the very information the claimant wishes to keep private back in the public domain. Because of the greater chance of an injunction, a newspaper editor will be even less likely to notify an individual with a very strong privacy claim (perhaps concerning particularly intrusive material) because this individual will almost certainly not sue once the material has been published. By placing this claim before the Strasbourg Human Rights Court, Mr Mosley is not seeking any further damages. If the application is successful, and effective measures are implemented as a result, everyone in the UK will equally share in the right to have an editor's decision to publish reviewed by a judge (if the individual so wishes) before irreparable damage can be done. This does not mean that the editor is

---

130 Quote by Gillian Phillips, Director of Editorial Legal Services to Guardian News Media Ltd. as cited in *LNS v Persons Unknown* [2010] EWHC 119 (QB) at 116.
131 [2009] EWHC 3148 (QB).
132 *LNS v Persons Unknown* [2010] EWHC 119 (QB) at 120 (Tugendhat J).
133 [2003] EWHC 1101 (QB).

sacrificing freedom of expression, jeopardizing the freedom of the press, by notifying an individual *before* publishing private material: he is merely affording that individual an opportunity to protect his right to privacy by seeking an injunction. In any case, a (super) injunction will always be refused if there is a strong and legitimate public interest in publication, in which case the editor can continue to publish and recover the newspaper's legal costs from the applicant. Max Mosley's ruling sought in Strasbourg will thus have no 'chilling effect' on investigative journalism where the exposure of private material has a legitimate purpose or is genuinely in the public interest.

 FOR THOUGHT

With a click of the web one can now discover hundreds of websites and blogs that offer gossip and 'Wikileaks' on celebrities. Once the information about a famous personality's private life is in the public domain, is there much point to superinjunctions in the future?

2.4.2 Entertainment or reality? Balancing the freedom of expression and the right to privacy

It has already been discussed that the press fulfils the function of forming public opinion (see above 2.2.1); this does not exclude entertainment, which also plays a role in the formation of opinions. Arguably, entertainment literature, such as glossy magazines, can, at times, stimulate or influence public opinion more than purely factual information and it can be observed that there is a growing tendency in the media to replace news-type information in favour of 'infotainment'. Consequently, many readers obtain information they consider to be important or interesting from entertainment coverage and the Internet.

Entertainment provides amusement, relaxation and escapism. But entertainment can also convey images of reality and thereby spark a process of discussion and debate linked to lifestyle and philosophies, moral values and behaviour patterns. In that respect it fulfils important social functions and should therefore be equally protected under 'press freedom' and the scope of the fundamental human right of freedom of expression enshrined in Article 10 of the Convention.

Every journalist will confirm that personalization is an important journalistic tool for attracting a reader's attention. This can be an interest in a particular event or situation or a personality. To some of the general public, celebrities embody certain moral values and lifestyles which people seek to emulate; be it a famous model like Naomi Campbell or a member of a European Royal Family like Princess Caroline of Monaco. Glossy magazines like *Hello!* or *OK!*, appeal to some members of society, because they can base their choice of lifestyle on their role model. It is this which explains the public interest in entertainment magazines or online versions of gossip magazines.

The lives and lifestyles of politicians have always been matters of public interest; and always deemed to be legitimate from the point of view of transparency and democratic control. It is then a duty and function of the press to show people in situations that are not limited to specific functions or events, and this also falls within the sphere of protection of press freedom. It is only when a balancing exercise is struck between competing personality rights that an issue arises as to whether matters of essential interest for the public are at issue and treated seriously and objectively or whether private matters, designed merely to satisfy the public's curiosity, are being disseminated.

See Chapter 6.3.2

Since the **Human Rights Act 1998** came into force there have been a number of challenges concerning breach of confidence and the right to an individual's privacy. Central to the argument in each case has been the interaction of the rights and the qualifications of those rights set out in

Articles 8 and 10 of the Convention as set out in the **Human Rights Act 1998**.[134] This has been criticized by senior media editors such as the *Daily Mail*'s Paul Dacre. In his address to the Society of Editors in November 2008, Dacre – also Chairman of the PCC's Editor's Code Committee at the time – openly attacked the courts for their judgment in the Max Mosley case, where Mosley was granted the right to privacy.

Apart from attacking the UK libel laws, Mr Dacre concentrated most of his speech on what he said was an erosion of free speech and press freedom by the courts. He argued in the strongest terms that courts were imposing a privacy law 'by the back door' rather than such a law coming from Parliament. He referred to 'arrogant and amoral judgments' that were being passed down by the courts, particularly criticizing Mr Justice Eady in the *Max Mosley* case which, Mr Dacre argued, had completely corrupted the right to freedom of expression and was introducing a privacy law through the back door:

> . . . Justice Eady effectively ruled that it's perfectly acceptable for the multi-millionaire head of a multibillion-pound sport that is followed by countless young people to pay five women £2,500 to take part in acts of unimaginable sexual depravity with him. The judge found for Max Mosley because he had not engaged in a 'sick Nazi orgy' as the *News of the World* contested, though some of the participants were dressed in military-style uniform. Mosley was issuing commands in German while one prostitute pretended to pick lice from his hair, a second fellated him and a third caned his backside until blood was drawn. Now most people would consider such activities to be perverted, depraved, the very abrogation of civilised behaviour of which the law is supposed to be the safeguard. Not Justice Eady. To him such behaviour was merely 'unconventional' . . .

> But what is most worrying about Justice Eady's decision is that he is ruling that – when it comes to morality – the law in Britain is now effectively neutral, which is why I accuse him, in his judgments, of being 'amoral' . . . In the Mosley case, the judge is ruling that there is no public interest in revealing a public figure's involvement in acts of depravity. . . . What the judge loftily calls the 'new rights-based jurisprudence' of the Human Rights Act seems to be ruling out any such thing as public standards of morality and decency, and the right of newspapers to report on digressions from those standards. But most worrying is that when it comes to suppressing media freedom, the good Justice Eady is seemingly ubiquitous.[135]

2.4.3 Exclusivity and privacy of wedding photos: the Douglas and *Hello!* case

The background to *Douglas v Hello! Ltd.* (2001)[136] is well known and therefore only a brief summary is given here. Prior to their wedding on 18 November 2000 at the Plaza Hotel in New York, Michael Douglas and Catherine Zeta-Jones contracted with *OK!* magazine the exclusive right to publish photographs of the event at which all other photography would be forbidden. For this, they would receive £1 million. In order to protect this 'trade secret', all wedding guests had to sign exclusivity clauses not to take any photographs at the wedding. Only this way could the picture release to *OK!* be controlled.

The rival magazine *Hello!* published photographs in its now famous issue No. 639, which it knew to have been surreptitiously taken by an unauthorized photographer, Rupert Thorpe, pretending to

---

134 *Human Rights Act* 1998, Schedule 1, Part 1.
135 Source: Paul Dacre's speech in full to the Society of Editors: *Press Gazette*, 9 November 2008, available at <www.pressgazette. co.uk/story.asp?sectioncode=1&storycode=42394&c=1>, accessed 18 November 2010.
136 [2001] QB 967.

be a waiter at the Plaza Hotel.[137] OK! obtained an *ex parte* injunction restraining publication of *Hello!*'s issue 639 on 20 November 2000, which was granted – perhaps a little too hastily. Counsel for the Douglases had argued that the illicit photos breached their right to privacy under Art 8(1) of the **European Convention on Human Rights**, which had only just become effective in English law.

On 23 November the injunction was discharged by the Court of Appeal and the photographs were published on the following day by *Hello!* A few hours earlier on the same day, *OK!* published its own photographs, having brought forward its date of publication on account of what it knew to be the imminent publication by *Hello!* Also on the same day, some of the unauthorized pictures were, without objection by *Hello!*, published in national daily newspapers.

Reasons for the Court of Appeal's discharging the injunction were partly because the Douglases had sold most of their privacy rights to *OK!* and partly because, had the restraining order been wrongly granted, it would have been very difficult to quantify the damage suffered. The claimants had entered into a contract with *OK!* for profit and all exclusive rights had been granted to *OK!*, who were able to exploit the commercialization of the wedding in its entirety and attract large amounts of advertising revenue given the special wedding feature. Additionally, the Douglas wedding did not remain private for long as they were happy for it to be widely publicized by *OK!*'s special wedding issue.

Lord Justice Sedley's observations in this case in respect of balancing the Douglases' right to privacy and the media's freedom of expression are highly relevant when he said:

> . . . the Convention right, when one turns to it, is qualified in favour of the reputation and rights of others and the protection of information received in confidence. In other words you cannot have particular regard to Article 10 without having equally particular regard at the very least to Article 8.[138]

The Douglases did not succeed in the first 2001 action claiming a right to privacy under Article 8, though Lindsay J held *Hello!* liable for breach of confidence, applying the well-known criteria summarized by Megarry J in *Coco v AN Clark (Engineers) Ltd* (1969):

> . . . first, the information itself . . . must 'have the necessary quality of confidence about it. Secondly, that information must have been imparted in circumstances importing an obligation of confidence. Thirdly, there must be an unauthorised use of that information to the detriment of the party communicating it.[139]

For this purpose the judge identified the information as being photographic images of the wedding. Not information about the wedding generally; anyone was free to communicate the information that the Douglases had been married, describe what the bride wore and so forth. The claim was only that there had been a breach of an obligation of confidence in respect of photographic images.

This was challenged in the follow-up seven-year action in the Chancery Division, where *OK!* and the Douglases sued *Hello!* for breach of confidence and for the tort of causing loss by unlawful means.[140] This case should not be confused with the first action in 2001, which challenged the fundamental principles of Articles 8 and 10 ECHR. The 2003 to 2007 Chancery Division action concerned a commercial breach of confidence and privacy was only used by the claimants to bolster their position. The obligation of confidence was therefore binding upon *Hello!* and the third

---

137 For further discussion see: Moreham (2001), pp. 767ff.
138 [2001] QB 967 at 134 (Sedley LJ).
139 [1969] RPC 41 at 47 (Megarry J).
140 *OBG Ltd. and others v Allan and others; Douglas and another and others v Hello! Ltd and others; Mainstream Properties Ltd. v Young and others and another* [2007] UKHL 21 (sub nom 'Douglas v Hello! No. 7')

Coco requirement of use to the detriment of *OK!* was plainly satisfied. In the No. 7 action Lindsay J therefore decided that *Hello!* was liable to *OK!* for the loss caused by the publication, which he later assessed at £1,033,156.[141]

The Court of Appeal (Lord Phillips of Worth Matravers MR, Clarke and Neuberger LJJ) reversed the judge's decision on the ground that the obligation of confidence for the benefit of *OK!* attached only to the photographs which the Douglases authorized them to publish.[142] They did not have the benefit of an obligation of confidence in respect of any other photographs. Their publication may have invaded a residual right of privacy retained by the Douglases but did not infringe any right of *OK!* Lord Hoffmann, when reading the final judgment in the Douglases' No. 7 case to the House of Lords on 2 May 2007, made it abundantly clear that the final appeal was not concerned with the protection of privacy under Article 8 nor the freedom of expression under Article 10 of the Convention:

> . . . so your Lordships need not be concerned with Convention rights. *OK!* has no claim to privacy under article 8 nor can it make a claim which is parasitic upon the Douglases' right to privacy.[143]

The fact that the information happened to have been about the personal life of the Douglases was irrelevant. It could have been information about anything that a newspaper was willing to pay for. What mattered was that the Douglases, by the way they arranged their wedding, were in a position to impose an obligation of confidence – that is the control of information of photographic images. If *OK!* was willing to pay for the right to be the only source of that particular form of information and did not mind that others were free to communicate other forms of information about the wedding, then the Douglases should have been able to impose a suitably limited obligation of confidence. As the Court of Appeal put it when stating *OK!*'s argument:

> . . . the photographs published by *Hello!* fell within a generic class of commercially confidential information . . . which *OK!* were entitled to protect.[144]

For this reason *OK!*'s final appeal was allowed.

👁 FOR THOUGHT

Would you agree that – since *Douglas v Hello!* (2001) – English courts have found the right balance between an individual's application to his right to privacy conferred by Article 8 ECHR and the media's right to freedom of expression conferred by Article 10? Discuss the remedies available for breach of confidence for an unauthorized disclosure of personal information with reference to common law that followed.

In the David and Victoria Beckham case (*Beckham v MGN* (2001)),[145] Mr Justice Eady upheld an interim injunction in favour of the famous footballer and his pop star wife, preventing the *Sunday People* from publishing photographs of their matrimonial home and protecting the claimants from

---

141 *Douglas v Hello! No.7* [2007] UKHL 21 at 115.
142 *Douglas v Hello! Ltd.* (No. 6); [2003] EWHC 786.
143 [2007] UKHL 21 at 118 (Lord Hoffmann).
144 [2006] QB at para 138.
145 *Beckham v MGN Ltd.* (June 28, 2001; unreported).

unwarranted intrusions into their privacy under Article 8, 'with regard to material which the law recognises as being confidential'.[146]

Increasingly, however, the courts have been faced with the protection of an individual's identity where the single most important element of the information sought by way of photographs was the detection of the future identity of individuals who had committed famous crimes, such as the Bulger killers – Thompson and Venables – or Maxine Carr, who had lied on behalf of her boyfriend Ian Huntley in the Soham killings. In these cases the courts had to decide what type of information ought to be protected under the right to privacy and why the media had sought such information. This will be further discussed in later chapters (see: *V v UK; T v UK* (1999))[147]; also see below 2.6.2).

2.4.4 Privacy in rehabilitation and treatment: the Naomi Campbell case

Photographs are a record of a frozen moment in time and therefore have a permanence and presentational power which the human eye and words alone cannot capture. We have seen in the *Douglas v Hello!* (2001) case that the mere taking of photographs is not of itself actionable except where the photographing itself represents a misuse of confidential information when protected by contract. Photographs can have a special intrusive effect, as was held in the *Beckham* case, (above) conveying visual information which words alone cannot achieve. In determining whether photographs taken in a public place are capable of protection the courts have taken account of the context in which the photographs were taken and published, and whether the person photographed had a reasonable expectation of privacy in relation to their subject matter, and whether the photographs were taken surreptitiously (see: *von Hannover v Germany* (2005)[148]; also see below 2.4.6).

Additionally, the information conveyed by photographs has to be judged by reference to the captions and surrounding text. A cause of action arose upon the publication of surreptitiously taken photos when the *Daily Mirror* published an image and extensive articles on the famous supermodel Naomi Campbell receiving drug rehabilitation treatment at a Narcotics Anonymous clinic in 2001. Naomi Campbell sued the newspaper for damages for breach of confidentiality (*Campbell v Mirror Group Newspapers Ltd* (2002)[149]).

On 1 February 2001 the *Mirror* had carried the first of a number of subsequent stories on the supermodel, headed: 'Naomi: I am a drug addict'. The article was supported by a slightly indistinct picture of a smiling, relaxed Miss Campbell, dressed in baseball cap and jeans, over a caption stating that she was leaving the therapy clinic. On the same day, Miss Campbell commenced proceedings against Mirror Group. The *Mirror*'s response was to continue publishing further articles, such as on 5 February an article headlined: 'Pathetic – No hiding Naomi.'

During the first proceedings Miss Campbell claimed damages for breach of confidence and compensation under the **Data Protection Act 1998**. Morland J upheld Miss Campbell's claim in parts, though not granting her right to privacy under Article 8. She was awarded £2,500 plus £1,000 aggravated damages.[150] The newspaper appealed and the Court of Appeal allowed the appeal and discharged the injunction. Miss Campbell appealed to the House of Lords on 23 February 2003. Their Lordships Lord Nicholls of Birkenhead, Lord Hoffmann, Lord Hope of Craighead, Baroness Hale of Richmond and Lord Carswell commented that the law of confidence does not protect the trivial and that the courts have a duty to strike a fair balance between the competing rights of the claimant to respect for her private life under Article 8 and of the defendant newspaper

---

146 Ibid., at 9, line C (Eady J).
147 (1999) 30 EHRR 121.
148 (2005) 40 EHRR 1.
149 [2002] EWHC 499 (QB).
150 Ibid. at 502 (Morland J).

to freedom of expression under Article 10 of the Convention (*Campbell v Mirror Group Newspapers Ltd* (2004)).[151] Neither article has pre-eminence over the other and – as has been held in all the previous cases in common law and Strasbourg jurisdiction – each court has to consider the proportionality of the proposed interference with each right in turn, weighing those features which enhance the importance of each right in the particular case. There is no public interest in publishing information merely because its subject is a well-known person.

The articles in question in the *Mirror* contained the information that Campbell was a drug addict, that she was receiving treatment, and that she was attending Narcotics Anonymous, together with the details of that treatment and photographs of her leaving Narcotics Anonymous with other patients after having had treatment. The House of Lords stated that Miss Campbell could not complain of the exposure of her drug-taking, especially since she had previously denied that she was a drug addict, but it felt that the Court of Appeal had erred in holding that the details of the claimant's treatment and attendance at the clinic plus the photographs were not private and confidential and that the article could not credibly have been written without the inclusion of that material.

Allowing the appeal (Lord Nicholls of Birkenhead and Lord Hoffmann dissenting), the House of Lords set the threshold test as to whether information was private: whether a reasonable person of ordinary sensibilities, placed in the same situation as the subject of the disclosure (rather than its recipient) would find the disclosure offensive. Miss Campbell's details of her drug therapy should have been afforded privacy related to her physical and mental health. The treatment she was receiving amounted to confidential information contained in her medical records and the publication clearly breached that confidentiality and her right to privacy. Their Lordships found the disclosure of the photographs highly offensive, stating that this had caused the claimant a setback in her recovery. The publication of that information went beyond disclosure which was necessary to add credibility to the legitimate story that the claimant had deceived the public and went beyond the journalistic margin of appreciation allowed to a free press. Though the photographs of Miss Campbell were taken in a public place, the context in which they were used and linked to the articles added to the overall intrusion into the claimant's private life. On 18 January 2011, the European Court of Human Rights ruled that the recovery of 'success fees' by lawyers in privacy and defamation actions significantly violates freedom of expression. The case was brought by the publishers of the *Daily Mirror*. The ECtHR said the requirement to pay these fees was 'disproportionate'.[152]

In summary, looking at the publication as a whole and taking account of all the circumstances, the claimant's right under Article 8 outweighed the newspaper's right to freedom of expression. Accordingly, the publication of the articles and the accompanying photos in the *Mirror* constituted an unjustified infringement of Naomi Campbell's right to privacy for which she was entitled to damages.

2.4.5 Social utility and the protection of private information: the Max Mosley case

When a public figure chooses to make untrue statements about their private life, as was the case with Naomi Campbell, isn't the press entitled to set the record straight? Should disclosure not be justified when it serves to prevent members of the public from being misled? The *Daily Mirror* would argue that the photos and details about the Naomi Campbell's drug treatment exposed her lies, demonstrating that the newspaper had done an excellent piece of investigative journalism. But the House of Lords' ruling in *Campbell* demonstrated that there is a margin of latitude in what journalists are entitled to publish. It depends how the information is obtained and by what means, such as by covert or surreptitious means, though in law a complainant would have no ground for complaining

---

151 [2004] 2 AC 457.
152 Ibid., at 51–3 (Lord Hoffmann).

that she was photographed without her consent in a public place (see: *Wainwright v Home Office* (2004)[153]; *Fressoz and Roire v France* (1999)[154]; *Jersild v Denmark* (1994)[155]; *Peck v UK* (2003)[156]).

The law of confidence does not protect useless information or trivia. It only bites on information which is significant or of substantial concern to the claimant. The test of what is 'highly offensive' is objective for the 'sober and reasonable man' and a public figure like Max Mosley must accept that his actions will be closely scrutinized by the court (see: *Mosley v News Group Newspapers Ltd* (2008)[157]). In the Max Mosley case, Eady J extended the privacy and confidentiality notion to what amounts to personal conduct and what would be regarded as 'socially harmful'. He then applied the term 'social utility', first coined in *Francome v Mirror Group Newspapers Ltd.* (1984)[158] by Sir John Donaldson MR, where he explained that:

> . . . the 'media', to use a term which comprises not only the newspapers, but also television and radio, are an essential foundation of any democracy. In exposing crime, anti-social behaviour and hypocrisy and in campaigning for reform and propagating the view of minorities, they perform an invaluable function.[159]

Max Mosley sued the *News of the World* (News Group Newspapers Ltd), complaining of a number of articles. One was by Neville Thurlbeck in a 30 March 2008 'exclusive' issue, headlined: 'F1 Boss Has Sick Nazi Orgy With 5 Hookers', accompanied by the subheading: 'Son of Hitler-loving fascist in sex shame'. It concerned an event which took place on 28 March, described by the paper as 'an orgy'. There were explicit photographs of the event and the same information and images were on the newspaper's website, which also contained video footage.

As soon as the *News of the World* published their article and video footage, Mr Mosley's right to respect for his privacy was lost. Mr Mosley knew nothing of the article before publication: the first he knew of it was on the same Sunday that millions of people were reading the article and watching the footage on the website. Following the publication that Sunday, the only legal remedy available to Mr Mosley in the UK was to bring a claim for damages, that is financial compensation. He succeeded in this claim and was awarded £60,000 plus his costs. Although this is the highest sum ever achieved in a claim for an invasion of privacy, it is not an effective remedy. The only effective remedy would have been to prevent the publication in the first place by means of an injunction; but because he did not know about the article beforehand, the opportunity of an injunction was not open to him. Colin Myler – then editor of the *News of the World* – admitted in court that the main reason why he did not notify Mr Mosley before deciding to publish this private material was that he knew Mr Mosley would seek an injunction. Mr Myler was quite safe making this admission in Court because in the UK there is no legal or regulatory obligation upon newspaper editors to notify those whose private lives they intend to expose.

Mr Mosley further complained about a follow-up article on 6 April headed: 'Exclusive: Mosley Hooker Tells All: My Nazi Orgy with F1 Boss.' This consisted of an interview with 'Woman E', who had been present at the event and had filmed what took place clandestinely with a camera concealed in her clothing, supplied and paid for by the *News of the World*. The cause of action was breach of confidence and the unauthorized disclosure of personal information, said to infringe Max Mosley's right of privacy under Article 8 ECHR. Clearly, it was not alleged that the Formula 1 boss[160] had

---

153 [2004] 2 AC 406.
154 (1999) 31 EHRR 28.
155 (1994) 19 EHRR 1.
156 (2003) 36 EHRR 719.
157 [2008] EWHC 1777 (QB).
158 [1984] 1 WLR 892.
159 Ibid., at 989 (Sir John Donaldson MR).
160 Mr Mosley had been President of the Fédération Internationale de l'Automobile (motor racing's ruling body) since 1993.

engaged in unlawful activity, since the matter at trial concerned sexual activities between consenting adults in private. But Mr Justice Eady referred to the principle of 'social utility', where revealing someone's identity in court and therefore in the media was useful to society and 'of social utility', for the purpose of revealing criminal misconduct and antisocial behaviour (see: *X v Persons Unknown* (2006)[161]).

Eady J stressed that not all conduct that is socially harmful is unlawful and that the law is rather inconsistent in this area. He drew the analogy between the law on consumption of alcohol with that on other intoxicating substances: was such conduct in private and by consenting adults in the public interest and of social utility? He stated that in our plural society there will be some who would suggest that what Mr Mosley did ought to be discouraged, supported by the 'red top' press, some of which will make this editorial policy. In conclusion, Eady J decided that the photographs and articles of Mr Mosley's sado-masochistic (S and M) activities with hired call girls were of no social utility and amounted to 'old-fashioned breach of confidence by way of conduct inconsistent with a pre-existing relationship, rather than simply of the purloining of private information'.[162] Eady J argued not only that the content of the published material was inherently private in nature, consisting of S and M and some sexual activities, but that there had also been a pre-existing relationship of confidentiality between the participants, who had all known each other for some time and took part in such activities on the understanding that they would be private and that none of them would reveal what had taken place. Clearly 'Woman E' breached that trust by recording her fellow participants.

Although the law of 'old-fashioned breach of confidence' has been well established for many years, and derives historically from equitable principles (see above 2.2.2), these were extended with the introduction of the **Human Rights Act 1998** and the content of the European Convention. Since the rulings in *Campbell* and *Max Mosley*, the law now affords protection to information in respect of which there is a reasonable expectation of privacy, even in circumstances where there is no pre-existing relationship giving rise of itself to an enforceable duty of confidence. The law now seems to be concerned with the prevention of the violation of a person's autonomy, dignity and self-esteem and since Parliament enacted the **1998 Human Rights Act**, the courts now require these values to be acknowledged. The issue of pre-notification to the subject prior to publication was still subject to the ECHR's adjudication in the Max Mosley application at the time of going to print.

FOR THOUGHT

Why did Mr Mosley not simply file a claim in the tort of defamation? Was he not concerned with injury his reputation? (You may wish to read Chapter 3 in conjunction with this question.)

2.4.6 Celebrities in the public eye and the special status of photographs: the *von Hannover* case

Since the **Human Rights Act 1998** came into existence, we live in a rights-based environment which was largely unfamiliar to the English common law tradition. Other European countries and signatories to the Council of Europe have been signatories to the European Convention since 1950

---

161 [2006] EWHC 2783 (QB).
162 [2008] EWHC 1777 QB at 2–6 (Eady J).

and 1953. Strasbourg case law has identified infringements of a person's Article 8 rights particularly where personal identification in the form of photography is at issue. The only permitted exception for publication appears to have been where there is a countervailing public interest which – given particular circumstances – is strong enough to outweigh the right to privacy. The domestic courts should then ask:

1. Was it necessary and proportionate for the intrusion to take place, for example, in order to expose illegal activity or to prevent the public from being significantly misled by public claims hitherto made by the individual concerned, such as Naomi Campbell's public denials of drug-taking?; or

2. Was it necessary because the information would make a contribution to a debate of general interest?

The German weekly 'gossip' magazines have always been particularly interested in the private lives of European royalty, focusing in this particular case on Princess Caroline of Monaco during her various marriages.[163] The case was particularly poignant following the untimely death of Princess Diana on 31 August 1997 when she was being chased by paparazzi during a car chase in Paris. It is possible that the ECHR ruling in *von Hannover* may have been influenced by this kind of personal harassment of a celebrity.

Because he is in the line of succession to the British Crown, the German press has been keenly interested in the personal life of Prince Ernst August von Hannover, especially when he married Princess Caroline in 1999. The *von Hannover* action concerned Princess Caroline (von Hannover)'s complaint to the Strasbourg Human Rights Court about repeated intrusion into her private life.[164] Princess Caroline had on several occasions unsuccessfully applied to the German courts for injunctions to prevent the publication of photographs of her in German magazines, namely *Bunte*, *Freizeit Revue* (published by Burda) and *Neue Post* (published by Heinrich Bauer Verlag). On 13 August 1993, for instance, Princess Caroline had sought an injunction in the Hamburg Regional Court against any further publication by the Burda publishing company of a series of photos on the ground that they infringed her right to protection of her personality rights guaranteed by Articles 1(1) and 2(1) of the German Constitution (*Grundgesetz*) as well as her right to protection of her private life under Article 8 ECHR. The Princess also complained that the magazine had used her image without consent arguing the provisions under Articles 22 and 23 of the *Kunsturhebergesetz* (KUG – 'the German Arts Domain Copyright Act') on which the civil courts based their decisions. This states that publications of images need the consent of the person whose image has been either painted or photographed. Consent is implied where the person has received a fee.

Under Article 2(1) of the *Grundgesetz*, general personality rights are guaranteed only within the framework of the constitutional order. The provisions concerning the publication of photographical representations of persons listed in Arts 22 and 23 KUG are part of that constitutional order. They derive from an incident which at the time caused a scandal – namely photos of Bismarck on his deathbed – and from the ensuing politico-legal debate sparked by this incident; these provisions aim to strike a fair balance between respect for personality rights and the community's interest in being informed. This means that under Art 22 KUG, pictures can only be disseminated or exposed to the public eye with the express approval of the person represented. Pictures relating to contemporary society are excluded from that rule under Art 23(1) KUG. This means that if a celebrity or politician is photographed in public performing a public office or duty, the publication of these images is

---

163 Her official title is: Princess Caroline Louise Marguerite, Prinzessin von Hannover, Herzogin zu Braunschweig und Lüneburg. She married Ernst August Prinz von Hannover on 23 January 1999, her second marriage, after Caroline of Monaco had married Philippe Junot on 28 June 1978; their marriage was annulled on 9 October 1980.

164 *von Hannover v Germany* (2005) 40 EHRR 1.

allowed. However, that exception does not apply where the dissemination interferes with a legitimate private interest of that person (Art 23(2) KUG). This makes the German 'Arts Domain Copyright Act' a rather complex piece of legislation granting protection to (famous) individuals only by degrees and favours, in general, society's desire to be informed, which the press can usually supply and satisfy.

Ever since Prince Rainier and his glamorous American actress wife, Grace Kelly, sold photographs of the newborn Princess Caroline to a French newspaper in 1957, Monaco's royal family has had an uneasy relationship with the press. The paparazzi soon discovered Princess Caroline's aversion to intrusions into her private life. The three-times-married Princess not only exploited the strict French privacy laws but also took Germany to task, where she initially did not find the support of the courts. Among the many photographic incidents complained about by Princess Caroline, there was issue No. 30 of the *Freizeit Revue* of 22 July 1993, which showed her in the company of the actor Vincent Lindon after the tragic death of her second husband, Stefano Casiraghi. Lindon and the Princess were photographed at the far end of a restaurant courtyard in Saint-Rémy-de-Provence, captioned: 'These photos are evidence of the tenderest romance of our time' – following the dating gossip about the Princess' numerous suitors.

Another photo sequence in issue No. 37 of the *Neue Post* (1997) showed Caroline dating Prince von Hannover while he was still married to his first wife, headlined: 'Prince Ernst August played fisticuffs and Princess Caroline fell flat on her face.' Later articles and photographs alleged domestic violence incidents between Prince von Hannover and Princess Caroline after their marriage in 1999, linking his well-documented violent temper to alleged domestic violence incidents. The German tabloid *Bild* had referred to him as the 'Prügel Prinz' (battery prince) after he had been convicted of assault on a TV cameraman in 1998 and breaking his nose.

Article 23 of the *Kunsturhebergesetz* (KUG) affords individuals only limited protection when photographed in public and does not guarantee a right to privacy or right of control if the image is 'incidental' within the surroundings; this could conceivably include photos of politicians exercising official functions or a princess dining in a public restaurant. It is for this reason that Princess Caroline did not succeed in her German court actions; she applied for leave to appeal to the Strasbourg Human Rights Court. Not surprisingly, the ECtHR found that the German 'copyright' statute was ambiguous and misleading in respect of the meaning of 'private individual'. The German press had argued that there undoubtedly was a legitimate public interest in publishing photos of Princess Caroline as a 'public figure par excellence', in that she was a member of a royal family (Monaco) and had married into another prominent European royal family, namely the House of Hannover; but they had to admit that she was not in herself exercising any official functions. The German courts had interpreted its 'Arts Domain Copyright Act' narrowly in order to ensure that the state complies with its positive obligation to protect private life.

The Strasbourg court criticized the German courts' decision for making a distinction between figures of contemporary society 'par excellence' and merely 'relative' public figures. For this reason the Strasbourg court granted Princess Caroline her right to privacy under Art 8. Concurring with the opinion of Judge Cabral Barreto, Judge Zupani stated that the distinctions between the different levels of permitted exposure in German copyright and constitutional jurisprudence were far too complex (*Begriffsjurisprudenz*). But Judge Zupani also observed that the 'balancing test between the public's right to know on the one hand and the affected person's right to privacy on the other hand must be adequately performed', commenting:

> . . . he who willingly steps upon the public stage cannot claim to be a private person entitled to anonymity. Royalty, actors, academics, politicians etc. perform whatever they perform publicly. They may not seek publicity, yet, by definition, their image is to some extent public property.[165]

---

165 *von Hannover* (2005) 40 EHRR 1 at 32 (Judge Zupani).

The complex and multifaceted German legislation had established criteria of interpretation that had not sufficiently ensured protection to Princess Caroline. It also meant a complex balancing exercise for journalists and photographers: they would first have to establish whether the (famous) individual was in a 'protected sphere', or whether the 'sphere' was 'public', in which case they could interfere with that person's privacy.[166] In the light of the ECtHR ruling, the German Federal Supreme Court (Bundesgerichtshof) had to depart from its media-friendly principle in order to give a new interpretation to the well-established principle of 'graduated concept of protection' (*abgestuftes Schutzkonzept*). By doing so, the traditional differentiation between 'absolute' and 'relative persons' of contemporary history had to be amended.[167]

The ruling in *von Hannover* is significant and impacts on media practices throughout Europe. Whenever a photograph becomes a complaint issue in privacy and confidentiality, the domestic courts now have to weigh up whether the photo was taken in public, whether it was taken secretly or by clandestine means, whether by long-lens paparazzi or close-up, whether the image shows the individual undertaking an official duty or whether the 'public figure' is in a 'private sphere' or setting. If it is found that the picture was of public interest it can be published, irrespective of consent. Applying the ruling in *von Hannover*, the Bundesgerichtshof dismissed a further privacy claim by Princess Caroline on 1 July 2008, permitting the publication of holiday snaps in a street in France in a magazine to which the von Hannovers had not consented.[168]

2.5 Photojournalism in public places

On Sunday morning, 29 November 2009, BBC stills photographer Jeff Overs told Andrew Marr's BBC TV Sunday breakfast programme that he had been stopped by two Police Community Support Officers (PCSOs) on the previous Wednesday for taking photos at sunset of St Paul's Cathedral in London. Reasons given by an over-zealous PCSO included her newly acquired 'extended stop and search powers', which she cited as pursuant under section 44 of the **Terrorism Act 2000**. She informed Mr Overs that he might be doing a 'keen amateur recce' aimed at future terrorism attacks on London's landmarks.[169] The *London Evening Standard* also featured Mr Overs' story, headlined: 'BBC Man in Terror Quiz for photographing St Paul's sunset', as they quoted Mr Overs:

> . . . I was outraged at such an infringement of my liberty. I pointed out that nearly every other person walking along the South Bank was taking pictures of the view using their mobile phones and we had drawn her attention because we were using cameras.[170]

When looking closely at section 44 of the **Terrorism Act 2000** ('power to stop and search'), it does not specifically refer to 'illegal photography' when it states under 'authorisations':

> (1) An authorisation under this subsection authorises any constable in uniform to stop a vehicle in an area or at a place specified in the authorisation and to search–
>
> > (a) the vehicle;
> > (b) the driver of the vehicle;

166 s. 23(2) KUG.
167 For further discussion see: Clark (2009), pp. 107–11.
168 Urlaubsfoto von Caroline (Holiday picture of Caroline) Bundesgerichtshof. BGH, VI ZR 67/08, 1 July 2008.
169 Source: 'BBC photographer on being stopped by police', The Andrew Marr Show, BBC TV, 29 November 2009, available at <http://news.bbc.co.uk/1/hi/8384972.stm>, accessed 18 November 2010.
170 Source: the *London Evening Standard*, 27 November 2009.

(c) a passenger in the vehicle;

(d) anything in or on the vehicle or carried by the driver or a passenger.

(2) An authorisation under this subsection authorises any constable in uniform to stop a pedestrian in an area or at a place specified in the authorisation and to search–

(a) the pedestrian;

(b) anything carried by him.

Section 43 ('search of persons') of the same Act still does not say anything specifically about the
prevention of taking photographs; it says:

(1) A constable may stop and search a person whom he reasonably suspects to be a terrorist to
discover whether he has in his possession anything which may constitute evidence that he is a
terrorist.

This means neither section 43 nor 44 of the 2000 Act specifically prohibits the taking of photographs, digital images or film in public or of public buildings. In other words, press and indeed
amateur photographers should not be prevented from taking photographs in public or of public
buildings.

The provision was further amended by s. 76 of the **Counter-Terrorism Act 2008** ('Offences
relating to information about members of armed forces'), which makes it an offence – punishable
by 10 years' imprisonment – 'to publish or communicate any such information'.[171] This means that
an offence could now be committed whether or not the photographer has any intention that the
information or record on his camera could or would be used for terrorist activity. All that is required
is that the material is of a kind 'likely to be useful'. This broad definition has led police officers to
stop, search and confiscate cameras, photo or mobile phone memory cards. On 16 February 2009,
the NUJ led a demonstration of photographers against s. 76 of the **Counter-Terrorism Act 2008**,
the day it came into force.

In a speech to the House of Commons on 8 July 2010, the new Conservative Home Secretary
Theresa May put an end to one of Britain's most controversial pieces of legislation – section 44
of the **Terrorism Act 2000** – which had been increasingly used by police officers to restrict
photographers working in public places. In an oral statement, Mrs May stated that police officers
would not be able to use section 44 'stop-and-search powers' on individuals, but that sections 43
and 44 would remain available to police officers wishing to search vehicles. Instead, they will
have to rely on section 43 powers – which require officers to reasonably suspect the person to
be a terrorist, and officers will only be able to use section 44 in relation to the searches of
vehicles.

These interim measures brought police stop and search powers fully into line with the
European Court's judgment in *Gillan and Quinton v UK* (2010).[172] In this case, Kevin Gillan and Pennie
Quinton were both stopped during a London-based arms trade show on 9 September 2003
('Defence Systems and Equipment International Exhibition' at the Excel Centre in Docklands) by
London 'Met' police officers under sections 44–47 of the 2000 Act. Gillan and Quinton were on
their way to a demonstration close to the arms fair. Nothing incriminating was found on either of
them and they went to court questioning the legality of stop and search powers. The High Court

---

171 After s. 58 Terrorism Act 2000 the following insert provision is to be made: section 58A 'Eliciting, publishing or
   communicating information about members of armed forces etc'.
172 *Gillan and Quinton v United Kingdom* [2010] ECHR 28 of 12 January 2010 (Application no. 4158/05) (ECHR). The Strasbourg
   Court's judgment became final on 28 June 2010.

and the Court of Appeal said the powers were legitimate given the risk of terrorism in London. But the Human Rights Court disagreed.

The Grand Chamber of the ECtHR found on 12 June 2010 that the two protesters' rights had been violated under Article 8 ECHR:

> ... the Court observes that although the length of time during which each applicant was stopped and search did not in either case exceed 30 minutes, during this period the applicants were entirely deprived of any freedom of movement. They were obliged to remain where they were and submit to the search and if they had refused they would have been liable to arrest, detention at a police station and criminal charges.[173]

The court stated that the use of section 44 to stop and search people is illegal, that the powers lack proper 'safeguards against abuse', and that 'the public nature of the search, with the discomfort of having personal information exposed to public view, might even in certain cases compound the seriousness of the interference because of an element of humiliation and embarrassment'.[174] The court added that it was 'struck by the statistical and other evidence showing the extent to which police officers resorted to the powers of stop and search under section 44 of the Act' and found that there was 'a clear risk of arbitrariness in granting such broad discretion to the police officer.'[175] Mr Gillan and Miss Quinton were awarded more than £30,000 compensation between them.

Moreover, the Strasbourg Court noted that there was an increased risk that such a widely framed powers could be misused against demonstrators and protestors in breach of Article 10 and/or 11 of the Convention. In this connection the Court was struck by the statistical evidence, provided by the UK Ministry of Justice (MOJ), showing the extent to which police had resorted to section 44 powers. In 2004/5, the MOJ had recorded a total of 33,177 stops and searches, in 2005/6 there were 44,545 and in 2007/8 there were 117,278.[176] (see also: *Foka v Turkey* (2008)[177]).

The *Gillan and Quinton* judgment was welcomed by photojournalists in particular since they had long felt that the stop and search powers granted under section 44 of the **Terrorism Act 2000** amount to the violation of their right to a private life. The ECtHR found that the powers were drawn too broadly at the time of their initial authorization and that the powers contained insufficient safeguards to protect civil liberties.

2.5.1 Police treatment of photographers under terrorism legislation

In view of the *Gillan and Quinton* judgment, a police officer can only stop and search a person if he *reasonably* suspects him to be a terrorist – and this now largely extends to the search of motor vehicles only. Since 2003, police have increasingly used sections 43 and 44 of the **Terrorism Act 2000** with regard to demonstrators and journalists, which, as the National Union of Journalists (NUJ) argues, is symptomatic of a 'creeping crackdown on freedom of expression'.[178] There have been numerous reports in the NUJ journal where digital images have been viewed and camera equipment has been seized by police. In spite of the *Gillan and Quinton* judgment, the Home Office

---

173 Ibid. at para 57.
174 2010 judgment, ECHR 28 at para 83.
175 Ibid.
176 Ibid. at paras 44–6.
177 (2008) (Application No. 28940/09) of 24 June 2008 (ECHR).
178 Source: 'The force is with them', *The Journalist*, May/June 2009, pp. 14–15.

issued additional guidance to officers and the public, citing it as perfectly legitimate that officers may conduct a stop and search of anyone taking photos in public and that cameras, film or mobile phone memory cards may be seized if the officer 'reasonably suspects' that these may constitute evidence that the person is a terrorist.[179]

Freelance stills photographer Justin Leighton, who shoots behind-the-scenes for the BBC's *Top Gear* programme and magazine, said that taking photos in London increasingly raises suspicion with the police. Leighton told *Amateur Photographer*: 'Met Police and PCSOs are a nightmare. They haven't got a clue what they are doing', citing a recent incident when a PCSO quizzed him when he was photographing three supercars early one morning on Westminster Bridge, even though clearance had already been provided by the authorities.[180]

With mobile phone cameras becoming ever more discreet, why would any would-be terrorist need to use an obvious camera? In any case, most 'target' buildings are freely available on the Internet via Google maps and 'street view'. It appears that the legislation on police powers to stop and search is either being misinterpreted or misdirected in order to prevent terrorism.

◉ FOR THOUGHT

How appropriate is recent terrorism legislation? Will it stop aspiring terrorists from targeting important public buildings?

2.5.2 Publication of personal identity and photographs

Photographs attract special protection because they can be much more intrusive and informative than words. This was evident in the Douglas and the Naomi Campbell cases. As the Court of Appeal stated in *Douglas v Hello! Ltd (No 3)* (2006):

> . . . Special considerations attach to photographs in the field of privacy. They are not merely a method of conveying information that is an alternative to verbal description. They enable the person viewing the photograph to act as a spectator, in some circumstances voyeur would be the more appropriate noun, of whatever it is that the photograph depicts. As a means of invading privacy, a photograph is particularly intrusive. This is quite apart from the fact that the camera, and the telephoto lens, can give access to the viewer of the photograph to scenes where those photographed could reasonably expect that their appearances or actions would not be brought to the notice of the public.[181]

The question before the courts if a challenge arises to 'injunct' photographs revealing a person's identity is: is there a reasonable expectation and justification under Article 10 ECHR to publish the images in the public interest? It was acknowledged by Lord Hoffmann in *Campbell*[182] that there could be a genuine public interest in the disclosure of the existence of a sexual relationship. But he went on to warn that the addition of salacious details or intimate photographs would be disproportionate and unacceptable.

---

179 Source: 'Photography and Counter-Terrorism legislation', Home Office Circular 012/2009 of 18 August 2009.
180 Source: 'BBC Top Gear photographer: Met Police are a "nightmare"', by Chris Cheesman, *Amateur Photographer Magazine*, 2 December 2009.
181 [2006] QB 125 at 84.
182 [2004] 2 AC 457 at 60 (Lord Hoffmann).

At the Court of Appeal stage of *Campbell* (2003), Lord Phillips stated that, provided the publication of particular confidential information is justifiable in the public interest, the journalist must be given reasonable latitude as to the manner in which the information is conveyed to the public[183] (see also: *Fressoz v France* (1999)[184]).

There is an abundance of case law that has emerged from the Strasbourg Human Rights court, regarding the concept of private life and elements of Article 8 of the Convention which relate to personal identity, such as one's name or image,[185] or the publication of a person's photograph, particularly when this falls within the scope of the private life of a public figure.[186] It is yet to be determined how far the *von Hannover* doctrine will go when being tested in the UK courts in relation to photography in public places, as the ECtHR differentiated between 'ordinary' and 'public' persons and their 'sphere of interaction', which has broadened the scope of interpretation, recognizing that certain 'public persons' have a definite right to privacy and prevention from identification and others have not. If *von Hannover* is to be taken literally, it would mean a very significant change in what is permitted. It could have a profound effect on the tabloid and celebrity culture to which we have become accustomed.

2.6 A child's right to privacy

Children occupy a very special place in society and a number of treaties[187] as well as statute[188] and common law recognize that a child's interests and welfare are paramount, as Lord Oliver emphasized in his judgment in *Re KD* (1988):[189]

> . . . Parenthood, in most civilised societies, is generally conceived of as conferring upon parents the exclusive privilege of ordering, within the family, the upbringing of children of tender age, with all that entails.[190]

In *Re. Z* (1996),[191] the Court of Appeal granted an injunction preventing Channel 4 TV from broadcasting the identity of a child with special educational needs, in spite of the fact that its mother had given permission to film and identify her child, who attended a special school. The broadcast of *Boys and Girls Alone* did not go ahead after complaints had been received from Cornwall County Council that the programme-makers had 'emotionally abused' the young participants, seeking an injunction. Channel 4 producers had argued the programme was in the public interest by showing the children's learning difficulties.

There is a general presumption that a child's anonymity is protected under superinjunctions, when they and their parents are participating in court proceedings, as Lord Steyn said in *Re. S (A Child) (Identification on Publication)* (2004)[192]:

---

183 [2003] QB 633 at 64 (Lord Phillips).
184 (1999) 31 EHRR 28.
185 *Nikolaishvili v Georgia*, 13 January 2009 (Case No 37048/04) (ECHR). See also: *Schüssel v Austria*, Decision of 21 February 2002 (Case No. 42409/98) regarding the former Prime Minister of Austria who complained about an electoral poster reproducing his face half-mixed with that of right-wing extremist Jörg Haider.
186 See: *Toma v Roumania* [2009] ECHR; *Khuzin and others v Russia* [2008]; *Pfeifer v Austria* [2007]; *White v Sweden* [2006]; *Sciacca v Italy* [2005] ECHR – where the applicant complained about the disclosure of her photograph during a press conference organized by the Italian Prosecutor and the Financial Squad; *PG and JH v UK* [2001].
187 Such as the UN Convention on the Rights of the Child 1989 or the EU Charter of Fundamental Rights 2000 where Art 24(2) states: 'In all actions relating to children, whether taken by public authorities or private institutions, the child's best interests must be a primary consideration.'
188 For example the Children and Young Persons Act 1933 (for further discussion see Chapter 5).
189 *KD (A Minor) (Ward: Termination of Access)* [1988] FCR 657 (HL).
190 Ibid. at pp. 672–3 (Lord Oliver).
191 *Re. Z. (A Minor) (Identification: Restrictions on Publication)* [1996] 2 FCR 164.
192 [2004] UKHL 47; that case concerned the reporting of a trial of a parent charged with murder of a son.

... it is important to bear in mind that from a newspaper's point of view a report of a sensational trial without revealing the identity of the defendant would be a very much disembodied
trial. If the newspapers choose not to contest such an injunction, they are less likely to give
prominence to reports of the trial. Certainly, readers will be less interested and editors will act
accordingly. Informed debate about criminal justice will suffer.[193]

2.6.1 Children of famous parents: the J.K. Rowling photo case

There have been times when the courts have interfered in parental responsibility on behalf of children and in the child's interest, for example when parents refuse to consent to a blood transfusion
on religious grounds or when it is in the child's interest not to appear on TV in spite of a mother's
consent, as in Re. Z.

The Court of Appeal ruled in the J.K. Rowling 'Big Pictures' photo case (*Murray v Express Newspapers
and others* (2008)[194]) that a child's right of privacy is distinct from that of each of its parents
owing to its vulnerability and youth.[195] This case concerned the publication of a photograph of
J.K. Rowling's son, David Murray, in the *Sunday Express* magazine in April 2005, accompanied by an
article on the famous children's author's attitude to motherhood. The child, aged 19 months at
the time, was photographed in a buggy as the author was strolling in a public street in Edinburgh.
The photo had been taken covertly in November 2004 with a long lens by a photographer from
Big Pictures, a celebrity photo agency which licenses its photos in the UK and internationally.
David's parents began injunction proceedings against Big Pictures and the *Express* in June 2005,
citing a breach of confidence of the photograph and Article 8 on behalf of the child. A further
claim was made under the **Data Protection Act 1998**. The injunction against the picture agency
was not granted and the case against the *Express* was settled out of court. David Murray's parents
appealed.

The Court of Appeal *Murray* case reversed Patten J's decision at first instance on the basis that he
focused too much on the parents and not enough on the child. Lord Hope stated that Art 8 is more
likely to be engaged if the information in question concerns a child because the circumstances in
which a child has a legitimate expectation of privacy are wider than those in which an adult has
such expectations: adults can expect a greater degree of intrusion as part of their daily lives. Citing
the 'legitimate expectation' test in *Campbell v MGN Ltd*, Lord Hope questioned:

... what a reasonable person of ordinary sensibilities would feel if she was placed in the same
position as the claimant and faced with the same publicity?[196]

Unlike adults, children are very unlikely to derive any benefit from publication of information. This
does not mean that children should never be photographed in public, as long as it is not detrimental to the child at the time of publication or in the future. In any case this should be in line with
normal parental responsibility and the statutory duty to protect the child's well-being. As has already
been discussed above, there is a trend to include children of famous personalities in lifestyle magazines or reality programmes which enhance celebrities' status as a 'yummy mummy' or 'super dad'.
The *Murray* case was concerned with the issue of whether parents can validly waive their child's
right to privacy. The court ruling stated that they cannot: a child's right to privacy is distinct from
that of its parents.

193 Ibid., at 34 (Lord Steyn).
194 [2008] EWCA Civ 446 (also cited as: 'Murray v Big Pictures (UK) Ltd').
195 For further discussion see: Carter-Silk and Cartwright-Hignett (2009), pp. 212–17.
196 *Campbell v MGN Ltd* [2004] 2 AC 457 (HL).

The PCC has also considered cases in its adjudications of intrusion into celebrity children's lives with long-lens photography (see: *Elle Macpherson v Hello!* PCC Report 74). The Code provides particular protection to children under 16. PCC Code 6 (ii) 'Children' states:

> . . . a child under 16 must not be interviewed or photographed on issues involving their own or another child's welfare unless a custodial parent or similarly responsible adult consents;

and Code 6 (v) states:

> . . . editors must not use the fame, notoriety or position of a parent or guardian as sole justification for publishing details of a child's private life.

When J.K.Rowling complained to the PCC, asking the regulator to stop publication of images of her daughter in a swimsuit while on a family holiday, taken by a photographer using a long lens, the PCC adjudicated that there needs to be a substantial reason for publishing photographs featuring children, other than the fame of a parent.[197] The author had gone to considerable lengths to keep her daughter, young Miss Rowling Arantes, out of the public eye and the publication was clearly not in the interests of the child.[198]

2.6.2 Lifelong anonymity for child killers

The issue of lifelong injunctions in respect of child murderers was first raised in the case of Mary Bell when, in 1968, 10-year-old Mary was convicted at Newcastle Crown Court of the murder of two little boys, aged three and four, by strangulation. After conviction Mary Bell spent 12 years at Red Bank Approved School near Newton-le-Willows in Lancashire and was released on licence in 1980 with a new identity. There followed a number of applications to the courts for the anonymity order to continue beyond her coming of age. The first application on 25 May 1984 concerned an injunction to conceal the identity of her baby daughter (Y) and the baby's father after the *News of the World* had tracked down Mary Bell and her child (*Re X* (1985)[199]). Mr Justice Balcombe granted a restraining order on Y's eighteenth birthday, preventing identification of Mary's daughter as well as the child's father, and continuing the order on Mary (X) indefinitely. A further injunction was granted in 1988 when the identities of X and Y (then aged four) had been revealed to the press by villagers where the mother and daughter lived at the time.

The third period was in 1998 after the publication of Gita Sereny's book on the 'story of Mary Bell', whereby Sereny had paid Mary a 'substantial sum of money' to co-author the book.[200] Home Secretary Jack Straw did not succeed in injuncting the publication of the book and condemned the payment to Bell in an open letter to the *Sun*, stating that by collaboration on the book, Mary Bell should forfeit her right to anonymity. Prime Minister Tony Blair equally criticized the payments to the former child killer as 'inherently repugnant'.

The fourth period began in December 2002 when Mary's acquitted co-accused 'Norma' demanded in the *Sunday Sun* on 15 December that it was 'time to unmask Mary Bell'. The Newcastle *Evening Chronicle* published a lead article on 11 April 2003, 'Still haunted', in which family members of the two killed boys demanded that Mary Bell's identity be disclosed. The following court action ensued.

---

197 *Rowling v Daily Mirror* PCC Report 72.
198 For further discussion see: Carter-Silk, A. and Cartwright-Hignett (2009), pp. 212–17.
199 *Re. X (a woman formerly known as Mary Bell) and CC v A* [1985] 1 All ER 53.
200 See: Sereny (1998).

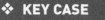
❖ KEY CASE   *Re. X (a woman formerly known as Mary Bell)* (2003)[201]

Facts:
Over the years there were consistent press reports of Mary Bell sightings, such as the Newcastle *Evening Chronicle* displaying the headline on 11 April 2003: 'Time to unmask Mary Bell', with the intention to name and shame her. Y (Mary's daughter) argued that her situation was so inextricably linked up with that of X (Mary Bell) that it was not possible to treat them separately. Section 12 HRA 1998 required the court to balance the possible interference with the claimant's Art 8 rights against the right to freedom of expression found in Art 10.

Decision:
Dame Elizabeth Butler-Sloss, President of the High Court Family Division, granted a life-long anonymity order (*injunction contra mundum*) after carefully balancing Arts 8 and 10 ECHR. She stated that the situation could only be resolved by recognizing the confidenti-ality of some information to protect the claimants, in particular claimant Y. The grounds were based on the risk, both for X and for Y, of breaches of the law of confidence (Schedule 1 HRA 1998).

The waiver of a child's privacy may not be permanent. The court can reimpose privacy even if it has previously been waved. This was demonstrated by probably the most extreme case in British crim-inal legal history, involving child murderers Jon Venables and Robert Thompson, who were convicted in November 1993 at Preston Crown Court for abducting and torturing to death 18-month-old James Bulger. After their conviction at the adult crown court, the judge had lifted the child anonymity order imposed under s. 39 **Children and Young Persons Act 1933**, because he felt the public had a right to know about their crime. This resulted in a media frenzy in which the families and friends of the two convicted boys went into police protection programmes for fear of vigilante reprisals.

In *Venables and Thompson v News Group Newspapers* (2001),[202] Dame Elizabeth Butler-Sloss, P granted an injunction for life *contra mundum* with an anonymity order on Venables and Thompson at the point in their lives when the young killers turned 18 and faced imminent release from juvenile secure detention. This was after Lord Chief Justice Woolf had issued the unprecedented step for the convicted killers not to enter adult custody. The teenagers were released from their secure unit on licence into the community with new identities. Part of the order was not to associate with each other.

The President of the Family Court Division ordered lifelong anonymity on the Bulger killers citing Article 2 ECHR, 'right to life', as she feared that if their identity was revealed by the media the young men's lives would be in serious danger. Butler-Sloss P referred to 20 newspaper articles as testimony, among them:

'Society must be protected from this pair of monsters', Denise Bulger said: '. . . I will do every-thing in my power to keep them caged and I hope that Jack Straw will back me up. If they ever do get out I have sworn to go looking for them. When I find them they will wish they were dead.

---

201 *Re. X (a woman formerly known as Mary Bell) and another v O'Brien and others* [2003] EWHC 1101 (QB).
202 [2001] Fam 430 (also cited as 'Thompson and Venables v NGN').

I will make sure they know what it is to really suffer . . . wherever they go mothers like me will be after their blood.' (the *Sunday Mirror*, 31 October 1999)

Throw away the key . . . if Venables and Thompson returned to Liverpool they would be lynched – and nobody would shed a tear. The pair of them should stay inside for the rest of their natural lives. They took a baby's life. So why should they be allowed a life of their own? (the *Sunday Mirror*, 27 August 2000)

. . . like Mary Bell . . . they are likely to be constantly looking over their shoulders in fear they have been tracked down by vigilantes. (the *Daily Mail*, 27 October 2000)[203]

Mr Pike, solicitor for the defendant newspapers, made a statement in support of lifting all injunctions for the newspapers, arguing that the rehabilitation process and education of the released Venables and Thompson were matters of genuine public interest and for that reason their identities should be revealed, citing freedom of expression. He said that the circumstances surrounding the death of James Bulger were extraordinary largely as a result of the young age of the claimants at the time they committed the brutal and horrific crime. He did not accept that the level of media interest was other than proper and legitimate. But Dame Elizabeth remained steadfast, reasoning that the immediate and future well-being of the claimants and that of their families was at risk from vigilante groups; and for that reason the courts had a duty of care to grant lifelong anonymity orders on the teenagers (see also: *Davies v Taylor* (1974)[204]; *Re. H (Minors) (Sexual Abuse: Standard of Proof)* (1996)[205]). Summing up, Butler-Sloss P relied on Lord Goff of Chieveley's statement in '*Spycatcher Nr 2*' (1990) that an equitable duty of confidence arose from an obligation of conscience whether a reasonable person would recognize public disclosure as not being 'just in all the circumstances' and that there need not be a 'formal relationship' between the parties.[206]

A controversial decision by Eady J concerned his ruling in the Maxine Carr judgment of February 2005, when he ordered that the 27-year-old's identity needed to be kept secret 'for her own safety' under Art 2 ECHR, following her release on probation after serving half of a 42-month sentence for perverting the course of justice. In the 'Soham murder' trial in 2003, Maxine Carr had been convicted of conspiring with Ian Huntley, who killed the schoolgirls Holly Wells and Jessica Chapman in August 2002. Following sentencing, Carr had complained to the courts that the press had hounded her and that she was suffering stress-related psychiatric disorders including anorexia and panic attacks. Apart from the request for a new identity, she had asked the High Court for a complete anonymity order.

At a two-day hearing, Eady J ruled that Carr's identity needed to be kept a secret for her own safety, citing the case of child killer Mary Bell (see above). He said the injunction was 'necessary and proportionate' as there was clear evidence of danger to her life and physical well-being.[207] At the hearing, the *Sun*, the *News of the World* and the Mirror Group argued that the injunction was contravening their freedom of expression and that the public had a right to know about Carr's new identity and whereabouts: after all, she had been an adult accomplice when she provided the alibi for Ian Huntley at the time of the Soham murders.[208] Eady J granted an indefinite injunction, banning

---

203 [2001] Fam 430 at 457 (Dame Elizabeth Butler-Sloss P).
204 [1974] AC 207.
205 [1996] AC 563 (Lord Nicholls of Birkenhead at 585).
206 [1990] 1 AC 109 at 281 (Lord Goff of Chieveley).
207 Source: *The Times*, 24 February 2005.
208 Source: 'Lawyers seek lifelong anonymity for Maxine Carr', by Clare Cozens, *The Guardian*, 25 February 2005.

any publication of any details on Maxine Carr for life so that her new identity could never be revealed.

2.6.3 Identification of child killers: the Jon Venables case

On 8 March 2010, the news broke that Jon Venables was back in prison on suspicion of a 'serious sexual offence'. The Mirror had first got hold of the 'scoop', reporting that the reason for his recall to prison – being on life licence – was an offence of child pornography and related internet offences. The Ministry of Justice released a press statement which confirmed the identity of the Bulger-killer in preventive custody, though it stated that Venables, now 27, had not been charged. Minister of Justice, Jack Straw, did not confirm the nature of the alleged offence. This angered the press and the blogosphere was wild with speculation about Venables' identity. The Mirror and Sun demanded that the lifelong anonymity order on Venables and his accomplice Thompson be lifted.

Agreeing with Justice Secretary Jack Straw that the anonymity order must never be lifted, Baroness Butler-Sloss addressed the House of Lords on 9 March 2010, giving reasons why the Bulger killers should remain anonymous. The former President of the Family Court Division reiterated her original ruling that there had been enough evidence before the court at the time of making the order in 2001 that the boys' future lives would be in substantial danger and that it was the court's duty to protect individuals' lives under Art 2 ECHR. She opined that the risk of harm to Venables would be too great and the court had a duty of care to protect even the most dangerous offenders (see: Osman v UK (1998)[209]).

On 13 March 2010, the newly appointed Children's Commissioner for England, Dr Maggie Atkinson, told The Times that most criminals under 12 did not fully understand their actions and that the Bulger killers should never have been tried in an adult court. Instead, she believed that Venables and Thompson should have been helped to change their lives. The Children's Commissioner stated that a civilized society should recognize that children who commit offences needed to be treated differently from adult criminals. Dr Atkinson said:

> . . . what they did was exceptionally unpleasant and the fact that a little boy ended up dead is not something the nation can easily forget, but they shouldn't have been tried in an adult court because they were still children.[210]

The Children's Commissioner called for the age of criminal responsibility to be raised, in line with other European countries, where the ranges are between 14 and 16. Currently, the age of criminal responsibility in England, Wales and Northern Ireland is 10.[211] Scotland raised the age from 8 to 12 in March 2009.

Following Dr Atkins' comments, the Sun reported that Denise Fergus, James Bulger's mother, had called for the Children's Commissioner 'to be sacked'.[212] Justice Minister Jack Straw responded that the government had no intention of raising the age of criminal responsibility in England and Wales and that custody for under-18-year-olds was always a last resort, used for the most serious, persistent and violent offenders.[213]

---

209 (1998) 29 EHRR 245.
210 Source: 'Even Bulger killers were just children, says Maggie Atkinson, Children's Commissioner', by Alice Thomson and Rachel Sylvester, The Times, 13 March 2010.
211 The age of criminal responsibility in England was reduced from 13 to 10 by Jack Straw in 1998, when he, as the first New Labour Home Secretary, ended the presumption that children under 14 did not know the difference between right and wrong, thereby abolishing the doctrine of doli incapax.
212 Source: the Sun, 14 March 2010.
213 Source: 'Ministry of Justice dismisses adviser's claim', by Robin Henry, The Times, 13 March 2010.

On 23 July 2010, Venables pleaded guilty to three offences under the **Protection of Children Act 1978**. The first involved downloading 57 indecent pictures of children between February 2009 and February 2010. The second involved distributing three indecent photographs of children in February 2010, while a third involved distributing 42 images in February 2008. Mr Justice Bean, sitting at the Old Bailey, said Venables had 'colluded in the harm of children'. However, the judge said it would be 'wrong' for Venables' sentence to be increased because of his previous crime. Jon Venables, 27, was sentenced to two years' imprisonment. The judge had refused to lift reporting restrictions, and Venables appeared at the Old Bailey via video link from prison to admit downloading and distributing scores of indecent images of children.[214]

In January 2010, the 'red tops' had demanded that the identity of the 'Edlington killers' be released. Mr Justice Keith had passed an indeterminate life sentence for public protection on the two 'Edlington boys', two brothers, aged 10 and 11, for 'unimaginable' violence executed against an 11-year-old and 9-year-old boy in Edlington, near Doncaster, South Yorkshire in April 2009. The boys had admitted the torturous killing on 4 September 2009.[215]

On 18 January 2010, following the sentencing of the Edlington boys, BBC's Newsnight revealed part of a report by the Doncaster Children's Safety Board which described the brutal attacks by the young killers on the children in their neighbourhood. The popular press demanded the full release of the Doncaster children's and social services' report 'in the public interest', stating that the public had a right to know the 'multiple failings by nine different agencies over fourteen years in this case'. The court heard during the boys' guilty plea in September 2009 that the boys' mother – who like her sons was never identified – had begged social workers for support for more than two years before their brutal attack on the two children on 4 April 2009.[216] The Ministry of Justice denied the media access to the Social Services Reports and ordered that the Edlington boys' identities be protected for life.

The British media has always been fascinated by child-killer stories or the maltreatment of children, ever since 10-year-old Mary Bell killed two little boys by strangulation in 1968. That said, the press provides a valuable public service. The media has uncovered a number of horrendous stories involving children, such as the tragic death of Victoria Climbié in 2000 or that of 17-month-old baby Peter in 2007 – both in Haringey. Superinjunctions are meant to be for the protection of children and the vulnerable in family courts and it should remain the courts' duty to ensure the lifelong protection of some youngsters who were convicted, not only for their own but also for their families' protection.

See Chapter
◄ 5.4

Was it just that Eady J granted a lifelong injunction on Maxine Carr restraining any future publication? Why should her anonymity be protected? After all, she was not a child when committing her offence as a lying accomplice to Ian Huntley in the Soham murders. It might therefore be understandable that in Carr's case the press was rightly angered and could not understand why they were 'gagged' by the court's injunction contra mundum. On the other hand, it could be argued that the lifelong injunction granted Maxine Carr some form of closure.

2.7 Superinjunctions: protection of privacy or reputation?

There have been a number of high-profile cases where celebrities have sought privacy injunctions and – in turn – were granted so-called 'super-injunctions' (or 'superinjunctions') by the courts.

214 Source: 'Sordid secret life of Bulger killer exposed as he is jailed for two years over shocking child pornography', by Nicola Boden, Daily Mail, 30 July 2010.
215 Source: 'Reign of terror that took them to the brink of murder: The descent of two brothers into depravity', by Arthur Martin, Fay Schlesinger and Paul Harris, Daily Mail, 4 September 2009.
216 Source: BBC Newsnight, 18 January 2010.

These can restrain the disclosure of the fact that a privacy injunction has been obtained. Superinjunctions (also known as 'double gagging orders' by the media) have attracted a great deal of criticism in that justice is being done behind closed doors.

The use of such injunctions to stop reporting of potentially embarrassing revelations is a growing trend among sports stars, who have the financial means to use expensive lawyers to exercise legal rights denied to ordinary members of the public. Superinjunctions sought but subsequently lifted (or not granted) involved Chelsea football captain John Terry, England striker Wayne Rooney and golfer Tiger Woods. Though the golfer's British lawyers, Schillings, denied in December 2009 that any nude photos of Woods and his mistresses exist, the images were in circulation via American websites. Woods was not able to avail himself of superinjunctions in the US courts, because privacy law is weaker in America than in the UK. It is not articulated as a constitutional right in the US and is subject to much stronger rights to publish. Some argue that, with material now readily available on the World Wide Web, there is no point maintaining an injunction that is completely pointless.

A number of superinjunctions were exposed on social networking sites, such as Twitter and Facebook or online blogs during 2009 and 2010, making the double gagging orders effectively worthless. None of these were linked to children but involved either famous celebrities or company misdemeanours. The public learnt about The Guardian's successful fight against the 'Trafigura' superinjunction and interim orders on Portsmouth football manager Avram Grant[217], footballer Ashley Cole[218] and TV presenter Vernon Kay.[219]

See Chapter
6.3.6 →

Superinjunctions are interim court orders which prevent news organizations from revealing the identities of those involved in legal disputes, or even reporting the existence of the injunction at all. They were originally used exclusively in the family courts as a result of privacy and in camera proceedings, mostly concerning the protection of juveniles and children in care and adoption proceedings. In their simplest form, superinjunctions prevent the media from reporting what happens in court, usually on the basis that doing so could prejudice a trial or someone's right to privacy. Superinjunctions in their strictest form mean a derogation from the open justice principle in that they seek:

1. a private hearing (in camera);
2. anonymity for the applicant (and other persons involved in the 'relationship');
3. that the entire court file should be sealed;[220]
4. that the court order should prohibit publication of the existence of the proceedings, and usually, until after the conclusion of any trial.

What must be borne in mind is that if an individual is properly entitled to a privacy injunction, the whole purpose of that injunction may in some situations be undermined by disclosure of the fact that an injunction has been obtained by that individual. In such circumstances the alternative to justice being done behind closed doors is that justice will not be done at all.

When are superinjunctions granted? In the first instance, it is up to the courts to assess whether there is a 'pressing social need' for any restriction by making an injunction after applying the public interest test and a certain margin of appreciation of an individual's right to privacy and the confidentiality of the subject matter. Arguably, it should be in the public interest of our democratic society to ensure that the freedom of the press is maintained. Similarly, courts should weigh up, if they place any reporting restriction or superinjunctions on a publication, whether this measure is

---

217 Source: 'Get any Rompy Pompey Avram?' by Tom Wells, Jamie Pyatt and Alex Peake, the Sun, 5 February 2010.
218 Source: 'Chelsea's Cole is a love cheat' by Richard White and Philip Chase, the Sun, 25 January 2010.
219 Source: 'Vernon Kay admits sending racy text and Twitter messages to Page 3 girl behind wife Tess Daly's back', Daily Mail, 9 February 2010.
220 Criminal Procedure Rule (CPR) 5. 4C(7)

proportionate to the legitimate aim pursued. Where the published information invades an individual's right of privacy, as protected by Article 8 ECHR, the court ought to give careful consideration as to whether the information is truly of public interest rather than merely of interest to the
public. This is a fundamental distinction. As the Strasbourg Court observed in *von Hannover*:

> . . . the court considers that a fundamental distinction needs to be made between reporting
> facts – even controversial ones – capable of contributing to a debate in a democratic society
> relating to politicians in the exercise of their functions, for example, and reporting details of the
> private life of an individual who, moreover, as in this case, does not exercise official functions.
> While in the former case the press exercises its vital role of 'watchdog' in a democracy by
> contributing to 'impart[ing] information and ideas on matters of public interest' it does not do
> so in the latter case.[221]

In the case where a litigant intends to serve a prohibitory injunction upon a publication, the courts
rely on the *Spycatcher* principle, in that the individual author, journalist or publisher should be given
a realistic opportunity to be heard on the appropriateness of granting the injunction and the scope
of its terms, mirrored closely by the provisions contained in section 12 HRA 1998.

2.7.1 Double gagging orders: the John Terry superinjunction

The 'John Terry Superinjunction' (*LNS v Persons Unknown* (2010)[222]) had been sought by Mr Richard
Spearman QC, instructed by the applicant's lawyers Schillings on 22 January 2010. He asked for a
prohibition in the form of an interim superinjunction on publishing details of a 'specific personal
relationship' between their client and another person. The injunction sought complete privacy,
stating that *any* publication of *any* information including photographs evidencing the extramarital
relationship could lead to harming the private family life of the applicant. Footballer John Terry's
lawyers argued that the intended publication in the *News of the World* would amount to a breach of
confidence and misuse of private information in that £1 million had been promised to an informant
to keep the story quiet. The newspaper was about to publish their scoop on the then England football captain's adulterous affair with a French underwear model who happened to be the former
girlfriend of Terry's friend and team-mate, Wayne Bridge. The story was to be the front-page headline on Sunday 24 January 2010.

Opposing the injunction at the hearing on 29 January 2010, the *News of the World* (News Group
Newspapers) made a strong submission before Mr Justice Tugendhat, supporting freedom of
expression under Article 10 and the public's 'right to know' in this case. Tugendhat J considered
Articles 6, 8 and 10 of the Convention in turn, giving additional consideration to the open justice
principle. Balancing one right against the other, he considered the right to speak freely, the right to
private life and reputation and the right to a fair hearing. Tugendhat J applied the 'confidentiality
test' as cited in the 'Prince Charles' Diaries' case'[223] (see above 2.2.6):

> . . . not simply whether the information is a matter of public interest but whether, in all the
> circumstances, it is in the public interest that the duty of confidence should be breached.[224]

Tugendhat J noted that there was no evidence before the court and no personal representation from
the applicant of proof to convince him to apply the right to privacy under Article 8, nor was there

---

221 *von Hannover v Germany* [2005] 40 EHRR 1 at 63.
222 [2010] EWHC 119 (sub nom 'John Terry Superinjunction').
223 *Associated Newspapers Ltd v HRH Prince of Wales* [2006] EWCA Civ 1776; [2008] Ch 57 (sub nom 'The Prince Charles' Diaries' case).
224 Ibid., at 68 (Tugendhat J).

proof that any confidentiality had been breached: no photographs were produced nor was there any confidential or private information disclosed (see: X v Persons Unknown (2006)[225]). For this reason Tugendhat J lifted a superinjunction granted initially a few days earlier, stating that privacy law was not there to protect someone's reputation; which in his case meant the footballer's commercial interests.

John Terry did indeed have some very lucrative contracts and sponsorship deals at the time. For example, in 2009 the footballer had been named 'Dad of the Year', landing a sponsorship deal with Daddies Sauce. Other commercial deals included Umbro, Samsung and Nationwide. Most of Terry's lucrative advertising deals were aimed at either children or young family men. After Terry's failed appeal regarding the superinjunction, he may well have gone down badly in the estimation of the public after his sex scandal revelations. Summing up, Mr Justice Tugendhat said:

> . . . that is why sponsors may be sensitive to the public image of those sportspersons whom they pay to promote their products. Freedom to live as one chooses is one of the most valuable freedoms. But so is the freedom to criticise (within the limits of the law) the conduct of other members of society as being socially harmful, or wrong.[226]

The lifting of the 'John Terry superinjunction' sent screams of delight through the tabloid press, who naturally became more aggressive in their revelations about the infidelities and indiscretions of celebrities where superinjunctions may well have been in place. But no one really knows – by the very nature of these double gagging orders – how many are in place at any one time. Some media lawyers have guessed at around two hundred per year. Tom Crone, the News of the World's legal manager, called the Tugendhat ruling a 'long overdue breath of fresh air and common sense'.[227]

As we have seen from the Strasbourg Human Rights Court jurisdiction, there is now a basic framework within Articles 8 and 10 that provides for a social equilibrium between individuals, the media and society. It is argued that superinjunctions have curtailed the extent to which a newspaper or media organization can report on individuals in the public interest. The Tugendhat ruling in the John Terry case has given hope to the media where the conflict between an individual's right to privacy – extending to his reputation and commercial interests – has been overridden by the freedom of expression and press freedom in the interest of the public.

In April 2010, Lord Neuberger, the Master of the Rolls, set up a committee to examine the use by the courts of media injunctions. The remit for the committee includes the question of superinjunctions which prevent not only the reporting of a story but the existence of the injunction. Members of the committee include Lord Justice Moore-Bick and Mr Justice Tugendhat alongside libel silk and former chairman of the Bar Council Desmond Browne QC. They were joined by Alasdair Pepper, partner at Carter Ruck, and Rod Christie-Miller, partner at Schillings. Guardian News and Media were also represented by director of editorial legal services Gill Phillips and Trinity Mirror by group legal director Marcus Partington.[228]

As common law and Human Rights Courts rulings have developed, the courts have stressed that the 'necessity' for any restriction on freedom of expression must be convincingly established as a matter of general principle (see: Fressoz and Roire v France (1999)[229]).

225 [2006] EWHC 2783 (QB) at 290.
226 LNS v Persons Unknown [2010] EWHC 119 (QB) at 104 (Tugendhat J).
227 Source: 'Privacy on the back foot', by Stephen Brook and Steve Busfield in Media Guardian, 22 February 2010.
228 Source: 'Lord Neuberger sets up "super injunctions" committee', Solicitors Journal, 6 April 2010.
229 [1999] 31 EHRR 28.

2.8 Internet privacy

We live in an era where people routinely share extremely personal information online via a whole host of sites including Facebook, Twitter, YouTube and mobile phone messaging. Can the World Wide Web be controlled by privacy and censorship legislation? The rise of social networking has blurred the boundaries of what can be considered private online, making it less of a defence in law.

Dr Kieron O'Hara, senior research fellow in Electronics and Computer Science at the University of Southampton, has called for more public awareness of publications online. Addressing a conference in January 2010 at the London School of Economics, he said:

> . . . if you look at privacy in law, one important concept is a reasonable expectation of privacy. As more private lives are exposed online, reasonable expectations are diminishing.[230]

Talking at the 'Crunchie' awards in San Francisco, the 25-year-old chief executive and founder of the world's most popular social network, Facebook, Dr Mark Zuckerberg, stated that privacy was no longer a 'social norm'. With 350 million users in 2009, Facebook became the most successful social networking site. Dr Zuckerberg stated:

> . . . people have really gotten comfortable not only sharing more information and different kinds, but more openly and with more people. That social norm is just something that has evolved over time.

How – if at all – can legislation manage the privacy of online users? If people voluntarily post their most intimate details and thoughts, what protection is there for them? And if information which a site visitor thinks is secure can be harvested by illegal – and sometimes legal – means, what can be done about it, especially if the information-thief or snooper is in a country many thousands of miles away?

2.8.1 A right to privacy on Facebook?

In July 2009 Facebook's users were given the chance to alter security settings on items they upload to the site, such as photographs and videos. This meant that their status updates could automatically be made public unless they specified otherwise. Privacy groups, including the American Civil Liberties Union and the Electronic Frontier Foundation, were outraged, calling the developments 'flawed' and 'worrisome'.[231] As a result of this pressure group action, Facebook changed the privacy settings.

Much of this chapter has dealt with how professional writers and publishers are dealt with by the courts when it comes to privacy. But there are now literally millions of amateurs who blog online and who will be less knowledgeable about the restraints that do and do not exist in law on reportage, comment, rumour and abuse. The coming years are going to present many challenges for the legislators and the courts in dealing with online content.

And what about material that is intended to be shared privately by individuals or groups online that up until now could be locked away as it travelled across the Internet? The technology that allows that privacy can be denied to online users as per sections 3 and 4 of the **Digital Economy**

230 Source: Conference paper (unpublished) by Dr Kieron O'Hara, University of Southampton, at the 'Media, Communications and Cultural Studies Association' (MeCCSA) conference, held on 6–8 January 2010 at the London School of Economics (LSE).
231 Source: 'Facebook's new privacy changes: the good, the bad and the ugly', online blog by Kevin Bankston, 9 December 2009, available at <http://www.eff.org/deeplinks/2009/12/facebooks-new-privacy-changes-good-bad-and-ugly>, accessed 18 November 2010.

Act 2010, which allow courts to order all of Britain's ISPs to shut off 'web lockers' (also known as 'cyberlockers') if they are found to be involved with copyright or privacy infringement. In its initial draft, the Digital Economy Bill only dealt with certain types of copyright infringement, namely peer-to-peer (P2P) file-sharing, because about 35 per cent of all online copyright infringement took place on P2P sites and services at the time the research was conducted between 2007 and 2009. Particular threats concern 'cyberlockers' which are hosted abroad. There are websites which consistently infringe copyright, many of them based outside the UK in countries such as Russia and beyond the jurisdiction of the UK courts. Many of these websites refuse to stop supplying access to illegal content.

Activist, science fiction author and co-editor of the blog 'Boing Boing', Cory Doctorow, was outraged about this proposal and voiced his opinion in *Media Guardian*, stressing the absolute necessity of web lockers:

> . . . as our routine media files have increased in size – multi-megapixel images, home videos, audio recordings of meetings and so on – it's become increasingly difficult to use email to share data privately with family, friends and colleagues, because most email servers croak over really big files.[232]

Doctorow pointed out that the sound editor for his podcasts uses a web locker to send mastered audiofiles to him for reviews and that his parents, living in Canada, regularly availed themselves of the web locker device for videos sent online of their granddaughter, which made their home movies available on the public Internet but not for public consumption. What was being asked was: did the peers understand web lockers are used to support both piracy and privacy? A statute to end web lockers – Doctorow argues – is a 'call to eliminate the public's ability to exchange personal information out of sight of the wide world'.[233]

2.9 Summary of key points

- There is no right of privacy in English common law and legislation (*Kaye v Robertson* (1991));
- 'Confidence' arises when information comes to the knowledge of a person, in circumstances where he has notice, or is held to have agreed, that the information is confidential; or objectively is deemed as a reasonable person to know it is confidential;
- 'Breach of confidence' is where there has been an unauthorized use or disclosure;
- 'Duty of confidence' arises when a person receives information he knows is reasonably regarded as confidential; or obtains confidential trade secrets (*Coco v A. N. Clarke (Engineers) Ltd.* (1969) – anchored to Megarry's J formula);
- confidence will protect the disclosure of:

  i) Private communications whether orally or in writing, such as letters, telephone calls, emails in marital or close relationships (*Argyll v Argyll* (1967); *Barrymore* (1997));

  ii) Private thoughts or expressions committed to writing or recorded in some way, such as diaries, tape recordings, etchings (*Albert v Strange* (1849); *Prince of Wales v Associated Newspapers* (2006));

  iii) Private conduct particularly sexual (*Mosley v Newsgroup Newspapers* (2008));

---

232 Source: 'My Lords, you can't please the entertainment industry and sustain privacy', by Cory Doctorow, *Media Guardian*, 4 March 2010.
233 Ibid.

- Articles 8 'right to privacy' and 10 ECHR 'freedom of expression' are part of a cause of action for breach of confidence;
- 'Freedom of expression' will prevail where:

i) disclosure of information is in the public interest;

ii) the person has consented to disclosure, expressly, or impliedly by reason of his conduct;

iii) the information is already in the public domain, such as book publication; news item on the Internet; newspaper;

iv) the person is not otherwise subject to a duty of good faith in respect of the information;

- The law is developing a very fluid manner in the area of 'confidentiality' and boundaries and conditions of its application are uncertain; the above conditions are applied in a very expansive manner on different occasions by a number of different judges.

2.10 Further reading

Barber, N.W. (2003) 'A right to privacy?' *Public Law*, 2003, Win, 602–10.

Barendt, E. (1989) 'Spycatcher and freedom of speech'. *Public Law*, 204.

Bingham, T. (1996) 'Should there be a law to protect rights of personal privacy?' In: *European Human Rights Law Review 1996*, 5: 455–62.

Carter-Silk, A. and Cartwright-Hignett, C. (2009) 'A child's right to privacy: "out of a parent's hands" '. *Entertainment Law Review* 2009, 20(6), 212–17.

Clayton, R. and Tomlinson, H. (2009) *The Law of Human Rights*. 2nd Edition. Oxford: Oxford University Press.

Deringer, K.F. (2003) 'Privacy and the press: the convergence of British and French law in accordance with the European Convention of Human Rights.' Summer, 2003. Penn State *International Law Review*, 22. Carlisle, PA: Dickinson School of Law.

Fenwick, H. and Phillipson, G. (2006) *Media Freedom under the Human Rights Act*. Oxford: Oxford University Press.

Harris, D., O'Boyle, M., Warbrick, C., Bates, E. and Buckley, C. (2009) *Law of the European Convention on Human Rights*. 2nd Edition. Oxford: Oxford University Press.

Hixson, R. (1987) *Privacy in a Public Society: Human Rights in Conflict*. Oxford: Oxford University Press.

Hoffmann, Lord (2009) 'The universality of human rights'. *Law Quarterly Review*. 125 (Jul), 416–32.

Lord Lester of Herne Hill, Lord David Panick and Javan Herberg (eds) (2009) *Human Rights Law and Practice*. 3rd revised edition. London: LexisNexis.

Moore, B. (1984) *Privacy: Studies in Social and Cultural History*. Armonk/New York: M.E. Sharpe Publishing.

Moreham, N A. (2008) 'The right to respect for private life in the European Convention on Human Rights: a re-examination'. *European Human Rights Law Review*, 1: 44–79.

Schilling, K. (1991) 'Privacy and the press: breach of confidence – the nemesis of the tabloids?' *Entertainment Law Review*, 2(6): 169–76.

Strachan, J. (2002) 'The right to privacy in English law'. *European Human Rights Law Review*, 2, 129–61.

Zimmermann, R. (1996) *The Law of Obligations, Roman Foundations of the Civilian Tradition*. Oxford: Clarendon Press.

Chapter 3

Defamation

Chapter Contents

3.1 Overview

On 1 April 2010, science writer Dr Simon Singh (*BCA v Singh*) won an action in the Court of Appeal, relying on the defence of fair comment in a long-drawn-out legal battle in which he had been accused of libel by the British Chiropractic Association (BCA).[1] In an article in *The Guardian* in April 2008, Singh had criticized claims by some chiropractors that they could successfully treat children and babies for conditions such as asthma, colic and ear infections. Dr Singh had suggested there was a lack of evidence.[2]

The BCA had taken immediate exception to Dr Singh's description of these treatments as 'bogus' and to his view that there was not a 'jot of evidence' to support them, and being denied a right of reply. Instead, the BCA alleged that the reputation of chiropractors was damaged and sued him personally rather than bringing an action against *The Guardian* newspaper group. Singh's primary defence to libel was that his were expressions of opinion and fair comment in the public interest (see also: *Galloway v Telegraph Group Ltd.* (2004)[3]).

In a preliminary ruling in the High Court in May 2009, Eady J ruled that Mr Singh's comments were factual assertions rather than expressions of opinion; this meant that he could not use the defence of fair comment. But on 1 April 2010 the Court of Appeal disagreed with Eady J's judgment. Allowing Dr Singh's appeal, the Court of Appeal in a unanimous judgment by the most senior law lords – Lord Chief Justice Lord Judge, Master of the Rolls Lord Neuberger and Lord Justice Sedley – Lord Justice Judge pronounced that the original judge had 'erred in his approach', stating that:

> . . . it is now nearly two years since the publication of the offending article. It seems unlikely that anyone would dare repeat the opinions expressed by Dr Singh for fear of a writ. Accordingly, this litigation has almost certainly had a chilling effect on public debate which might otherwise have assisted potential patients to make informed choices about the possible use of chiropractic.[4]

Lord Judge quoted US Chief Judge Easterbrook of the seventh circuit who said in the 1994 libel action of *Underwager v Salter*:

> . . . [claimants] cannot, by simply filing suit and crying 'character assassination!', silence those who hold divergent views, no matter how adverse those views may be to claimants' interests. Scientific controversies must be settled by the methods of science rather than by the methods of litigation [. . .] More papers, more discussion, better data, and more satisfactory models – not larger awards of damages – mark the path towards superior understanding of the world around us.[5]

On 15 April 2010 the British Chiropractic Association dropped its continuing libel action against Dr Singh by filing a notice of discontinuation in the High Court.[6] Following his successful appeal, Simon Singh commented in *The Guardian* that defending his libel action had taken up most of his time since the spring of 2008 and had cost him nearly £200,000. But apart from achieving justice

---

1 Source: 'Science writer wins libel appeal,' *BBC News online*, 1 April 2010, available at <http://news.bbc.co.uk/1/hi/8598472.stm>, accessed 19 November 2010.
2 See also: Singh and Ernst (2009).
3 [2004] EWHC 2786 (QB).
4 Source: 'Simon Singh libel case dropped' by Sarah Boseley, *The Guardian*, 15 April 2010.
5 *Ralph Underwager and Hollida Wakefield (Claimants-appellants) v. Anna Salter, et al., (Defendants-appellees)*. United States Court of Appeals, Seventh Circuit. 22 F.3d 730 Argued December 10, 1993. Decided April 25, 1994, quoted at para 34.
6 Source: *The Guardian*, 15 April 2010.

for free scientific and academic speech, Dr Singh thought it 'good news' that the BCA no longer promoted the 'bizarre belief that spinal manipulation could help children with colic, ear infections and asthma' on its website; further that his original article had been reinstated on *The Guardian* website. He urged readers to support his petition for libel reform and hoped that a new government (following the then forthcoming general election) would address new legislation on libel to protect the right of defendants to speak freely.

The Simon Singh case is a good example of the law of libel in action today, which has stressed the demand for reform particularly with the predicament of claimants who might be in danger of jeopardizing their career and reputation in the name of 'freedom of expression'. Mullins and Scott (2009) express concern as libel laws are being reviewed that the present libel regime is too broad and the reforms proposed by Lord Lester's 'Libel Bill' (Defamation Bill 2010) are too sweeping and indiscriminate. They argue that the public commentary on the law of defamation has been remarkably one-sided, and in some respects dangerously oversimplified, stating in their libel law critique:

> . . . we are nervous that the important societal functions performed by libel law have been underplayed. Libel reform should be coherent, not piecemeal and un(der)-principled.[7]

Everyone has a reputation, as outlined by Clement Gatley during the 1930s in his famous textbook on libel and slander.[8] People have been fascinated by high-profile cases for more than three hundred years. The civil law on defamation has developed through the common law over hundreds of years, periodically being supplemented by statute, most 'recently' by the **Defamation Acts of 1952 and 1996**. The 'offer of amends' was introduced in 1996 as well as the High Court's encouragement to settle matters out of court by way of an apology and damages (see below 3.5.2).[9]

Obscene libel was one of four forms of criminal libel originally covered only in common law and later in statute (**Criminal Libel Act 1819**).[10] Obscene and seditious libel were superseded by the **Obscene Publications Act 1959**, whereby the common law offence of 'obscene libel' was rendered nugatory by section 2(4) of the 1959 Act.[11] Criminal libel was eventually abolished in 2009.[12]

See Chapter 7.3 →

This chapter is primarily concerned with the common law development of the tort of defamation and the protection of an individual's reputation. Not all cases can be covered, but some in-depth examination of substantive common law will indicate some of the priorities set by individuals and organizations which they have attached to their reputation through the centuries. As John Disley said when he and Chris Brasher won their libel action in 1995, 'Take away my good name and you take away my life.'[13]

Brasher and Disley, original founders and organizers of the London Marathon, accepted more than £380,000 in libel damages in an out-of-court settlement on 23 May 1995 over magazine and TV allegations that they used the London Marathon to enrich themselves. George Carman QC, for Brasher and Disley, told Mr Justice Waller at the first hearing in the High Court that the allegations had caused both men serious distress and damage through the magazine publication in July 1990 and the Channel 4 *Dispatches* broadcast in March 1991. The allegations that they had been consistently guilty of fraud, deception and dishonesty were 'entirely untrue'. Brasher said afterwards:

---

7 See: Mullins and Scott (2009), pp. 173–83.
8 Now edited by Rogers and Parkes (2010) in its 11th edition.
9 See also: Gibbons (1996).
10 For further discussion see: Spencer (1977), pp. 383ff.
11 See also: Kearns, P. (2007).
12 s. 73 Coroners and Justice Act 2009 abolished the common law offences of 'sedition', 'seditious libel', 'defamatory libel' and 'obscene libel' in England, Wales and Northern Ireland.
13 Source: *The Reunion: The first London Marathon*, BBC Radio 4, 4 April 2010.

'Now our reputations have been completely cleared. I am only sorry that it has taken four years – four years of hell for us and our families – for the *New Statesman* and Channel 4 to admit that the allegations made were completely unfounded.'[14]

The idea that loss of reputation has such a high perceived monetary effect on the accused is regarded as a difficult notion to accept in the modern age. After all, reputations are formed and reformed by the near-constant barrage of information available to us every day. But the basic principle remains: the tort of defamation exists to protect against blatantly untrue damaging statements. This chapter then discusses the closely related tort of malicious falsehood, an alternative complaints procedure to the civil action, open to a defamed person (see below 3.4.1).

The law of defamation is at times concerned with conflicting issues of great sensitivity, involving both the protection of good reputation and the maintenance of the principles of free expression. In defending a libel action the difference between a statement of verifiable fact and one of opinion can be crucial. A defendant who has to justify a statement of fact, as in the case of *Singh*, has to prove that the statement was true. This can involve calling vast amounts of evidence at huge cost. Defending a statement of opinion, as long as it is honestly held, is much less onerous and far cheaper. Extortionate costs and the lack of legal aid will be discussed later in relation to a few well-known cases (see below 3.5.1).

Gatley's standard textbook on 'Libel and Slander' states that the defence of 'fair comment' is still 'dogged by misleading terminology'.[15] Other common law countries, like New Zealand, Australia and the Republic of Ireland, now describe the defence of fair comment as 'honest opinion'. The right to privacy and freedom of speech have already been discussed in the previous two chapters and will be followed up here in relation to the defence of qualified privilege and the *Reynolds* defence. The House of Lords in *Jameel v Wall Street Journal* (2007)[16] affirmed the importance of freedom of expression as a matter of public concern paving the way to responsible journalism (see 3.7.3).

The unique problems in relation to defamation conducted on the Internet will be explored in detail and lead to the discussion and analysis of the concept of self-governance in cyberspace as opposed to governmental territorial legislation (see below 3.8.2).

3.2 History

3.2.1 Libel tourism

The *Daily Telegraph* reported in September 2010 that libel challenges by actors and celebrities in the London courts had trebled over the past year, adding to fears over press freedom.[17] Pop stars Lily Allen, Sir Elton John and Peter Andre, the actress Kate Winslet and the former England football captain David Beckham all sued during 2009 and 2010. They were among 30 celebrities who began defamation claims (compared with 11 in 2008–9), according to the figures from the legal information provider Sweet & Maxwell. The researchers revealed that the surge in reported cases was due to closer ties between the managing agents of celebrities and law firms that specialize in defamation claims against the media. Celebrities are increasingly taking advantage of 'no win, no fee' agreements to start lawsuits that might not be affordable otherwise and their representatives are making more use of digital media monitoring services to identify potentially damaging material.

The rise in defamation cases linked to the Internet has been inevitable, where bloggers or tweets have failed to put in place the same kind of pre-publication controls that traditional media

---

14 Source: 'Brasher and Disley win libel case', *The Independent*, 24 May 1995.
15 See: Milmo et al. (2010).
16 [2007] 1 AC 359.
17 Source: 'Celebrities have driven a 46 per cent increase in the number of defamation actions from 57 in 2007–08 to 83 in 2009–10', *Daily Telegraph*, 3 September 2010.

use. As a result, there exists an ongoing battle between individuals trying to protect their privacy and the media trying to publish ostensibly private material. Critics of Britain's libel laws have warned that they let powerful foreign figures use the London courts to restrict the freedoms of international media. In August 2010, President Obama signed into law an act protecting American citizens from British libel judgments, which means that UK judgments cannot be enforced in the United States.

Why has London often been described as 'the libel capital of the world'? Why has the High Court in London attracted some famous celebrities and foreign citizens to conduct lawsuits against other foreign individuals rather than in their own jurisdictions? A 2008 Oxford University study found the average defamation costs in England and Wales to be 140 times the average for the rest of Europe. Even the Law Lords have talked about the 'blackmailing effect' of solicitors using costs as a weapon to force silence, and numerous reports have mentioned the 'chilling effect' of British defamation laws on free speech.

English libel law is generally regarded as claimant-friendly. As the present law stands, a libel defendant is guilty until proven innocent, resulting in a disproportionate number of libel cases, both from British citizens and 'libel tourists', who sue in UK courts (including Scotland; see below 3.3.4). Libel tourists know that forcing defendants to prove their innocence may lead to a retraction of the alleged libel and discourage other writers from publishing similar statements, also known as the 'chilling effect' of free speech. The chances of covering up whatever it was that a celebrity wanted to keep quiet are quite high. Should a newspaper decide to settle – a decision that may well be taken by the publishers' insurers rather than the editor, as *Guardian* editor Alan Rusbridger has argued in the *Spectator* – it could well end up paying its solicitor anything between £400 and £800 an hour for the duration of the battle.[18] The longer the editor holds out, the higher the chances he will end up writing a cheque for six or seven figures. Not for damages: they rarely exceed £15,000 to £25,000 for most run-of-the-mill libels these days. The money all goes in costs.

An example is that of a Russian businessman, Boris Berezovsky, who sued the UK edition of *Forbes* magazine in the London courts. At the time of the defamation action in 2000, the UK readership of *Forbes* was 6,000 compared with a circulation of 785,000 in the United States. *Forbes* is a bi-weekly magazine, with a total circulation of over 900,000, published by a private equity firm, Forbes Inc. Together with its online provision, Forbes reaches about 40 million business leaders each month. It is probably one of the most trusted resources for senior business executives, providing them with real-time reporting, uncompromising commentary and concise analysis, to assist the business community to succeed at work and to profit from their investment. Forbes journalism covers business, technology, personal finance and entrepreneurship and is regarded as some of the best in the world. One of its major attractions is the 'Forbes Rich List' of the world's top billionaires, topped by software king, Bill Gates, at $54bn and Facebook founder, Mark Zuckerberg's fortune at $6.9bn in 2010.[19]

In *Berezovsky v Michaels* (2000),[20] the Russian tycoon's libel action against Forbes took six years before being resolved in the magazine's favour. Though the case would have been more suited to an action in either the United States or Russia, the House of Lords gave leave to Mr Berezovsky to sue in England, based on his connection to and reputation in England, applying the Duke of Brunswick principle (see below 3.2.4). English common law on defamation has been copied and implemented in many (but not all) Commonwealth nations, and the ruling in *Berezovsky* was followed in *Dow Jones v Gutnick* (2002)[21] by the High Court of Australia.

18 Source: 'How to stifle the press', by Alan Rusbridger, *The Spectator*, 18 September 2010 at p. 17.
19 Source: 'The World's Billionaires', edited by Luisa Kroll and Matthew Miller, Forbes.com, 3 October 2010.
20 [2000] UKHL 25.
21 [2002] CLR 575.

British libel laws are seen as more favourable to pursuing a defamation action than those in the United States, where libel laws are not only less generous to claimants but there is also the single publication rule. It is for these reasons that claimants choose to seek redress in the London courts (see: *Lewis v King* (2004)[22]; *Richardson v Schwarzenegger* (2004)[23]; *New York Times v Sullivan*[24]).

In February 2010, *The Guardian*'s director of editorial legal services, Gill Phillips, chaired a panel discussion between media lawyers: Dominic Crossley from the law firm Collyer Bristow; Sarah Webb from Russell Jones & Walker; Jonathan Coad from Swan Turton, a barrister who represents the press; Gavin Millar QC from Doughty Street Chambers; and John Kampfner, chief executive of Index on Censorship. The topic of debate was 'libel tourism' and the assertion that English law is being abused by claimants from overseas. Mr Kampfner asked at the start:

> . . . why is it that so many of the world's rich and powerful use English jurisdiction to sue for libel? Why are they not using the French or German courts?[25]

John Kampfner argued that the ease with which claimants with little connection to the UK could sue in the English courts allowed wealthy people from abroad to bring cases without difficulty. This point of view was strongly contested by some of the famous claimants' lawyers. Mr Crossley argued that the UK was not an attractive place to sue a claimant who has no links here, stating:

> . . . it's very expensive and it takes a long time. Any lawyer would soon send that kind of claimant packing.[26]

Panellists found more common ground on the problem of spiralling costs in libel cases.

Milo (2008) argues that the law of defamation is outdated and conflicts with human rights legislation such as Article 10 'freedom of expression' and possibly a person's right to a fair trial under Article 6 ECHR[27].

Prior to the General Election in May 2010, the government had been consulting about introducing interim measures to deal with disproportionate costs in libel cases while it considered wider proposals that could see radical reductions in conditional fee agreements (CFAs) or 'no win, no fee' deals. The potential cost of defending claims (even with a strong defence) is inhibiting the media from publishing stories in the public interest. This is sometimes known as the 'chilling effect' that excessive costs have on freedom of expression. This problem was highlighted by Eady J in *Peacock v MGN Limited* (2009)[28] where he stated:

> . . . as is obvious, the considerations that arise in defamation are rather special – not least because of the rights to freedom of expression protected under Article 10 of the ECHR. There is no doubt that the costs of libel litigation generally, and the implications of CFAs in particular,

---

22 [2004] EWCA Civ 1329. The case concerned Don King, the US boxing promoter, who was suing Judd Burstein for remarks he made about him on a couple of boxing websites. The High Court and Court of Appeal held that England was an appropriate forum for the case.

23 [2004] EWHC 2422. The claimant was a British TV host who accused Arnold Schwarzenegger of touching her breast during the course of his election campaign. Mr Schwarzenegger's publicist alleged that it was Ms Richardson who had behaved provocatively and that Ms Richardson had concocted her story. This allegation was reported in the *Los Angeles Times*. Hard copies of this paper were published in England and the article was also posted on the Internet. The High Court refused to set aside the Master's order giving permission to serve the second defendant outside the jurisdiction.

24 376 US 254.

25 Source: 'Libel law: who's rooting for reform?' *Media Guardian*, 15 February 2010, available at <http://www.guardian.co.uk/media/2010/feb/15/libel-law-reform>, accessed 19 November 2010.

26 Ibid.

27 See: Milo (2008), pp. 5ff.

28 [2009] EWHC 769 (QB).

are capable of exerting a significant chilling effect on freedom of expression. As has been pointed out, on more than one occasion, there is a huge incentive in some cases to settle for purely commercial reasons without reference to the merits of any defences that may be available.

Under a CFA, the solicitor can charge a success fee to reward their risk-taking in the event of a win. This can be as much as double their fees. Of course, they receive nothing if they lose. The client can take out after-the-event (ATE) insurance to cover their costs if the case fails. A hundred per cent success fee means some claimant lawyers have been charging an outrageous £700 an hour – double their normal £350 hourly rate – and because the cost of ATE insurance is beyond the means of most claimants, defendants are exposed on costs, win or lose. On the other hand, claimants – especially in malicious libel actions – are not means tested, as the Naomi Campbell action showed.[29]

The 'chilling effect' of CFAs in defamation actions has been a hot topic ever since the ruling of Eady J in the case of *Adam Musa King v Telegraph* (2004).[30] It was the first case in which a court considered the use of a CFA[31] in a defamation action which was later appealed.[32] Mr King had been represented by Mr Justin Rushbrooke of Peter Carter-Ruck & Partners on a CFA. The newspaper defendants maintained that the claimant's 'Mathaba' website contained and provided direct access to websites which contained Islamic extremist propaganda. The claimant complained about the allegations made in two articles in the *Sunday Telegraph* in October and December 2001, entitled 'Two white suspects in bin Laden probe' and 'British Muslim targeted by FBI for terror links'. The *Sunday Telegraph* applied to have the case struck out and one argument was that the means of funding amounted to 'an abuse of process'.

Lord Justice Brooke was extremely critical of the way in which Mr King's legal representatives had gone about certain aspects of the claim. Nonetheless the court affirmed the costs order in the court below and ordered the defendants – the Telegraph Group Ltd – to pay 70 per cent of Adam Musa King's costs of the appeal. Lord Justice Brooke said:

> . . . what is at issue in this case, however, is the appropriateness of arrangements whereby a defendant publisher will be required to pay up to twice the reasonable and proportionate costs of the claimant if he loses or concedes liability, and will almost certainly have to bear his own costs [estimated in this case to be about £400,000] if he wins. The obvious unfairness of such a system is bound to have the chilling effect on a newspaper exercising its right to freedom of expression . . . and to lead to the danger of self-imposed restraints on publication which he [Mr Beabey for the *Telegraph*] so much feared.[33]

In January 2010, Lord Justice Jackson condemned the system of recoverable success fees, which could force a losing party to pay fees that could be double the winning side's initial costs. Presently, cases are being settled, and stories retracted, when there is no editorial reason to do so. These problems are exacerbated in cases where the claimant is represented under a Conditional Fee Agreement (CFA) with a success fee. The outcome is that claimants worthy of censure are succeeding with claims simply because the media cannot afford to defend them.

---

29 See: *Campbell v Mirror Group Newspapers Ltd* [2002] EWHC 499 (QB).
30 *King (Adam Musa) v Telegraph Group Ltd.* [2004] EWCA Civ 613 of May 18, 2004 (CA Civ Div).
31 The CFA included a 100 per cent success fee, although in respect of the solicitors the amount claimed between the parties was 96.5 per cent to take account of the irrecoverable element based on the fact that the solicitors would not be paid until the end of the case.
32 In the High Court of Justice, Queen's Bench Division before Costs Judge Hirst (Claim No: HQ02X03462) on 2 December 2005.
33 *King v Telegraph Group Ltd* [2004] op cit. at para. 99 (Lord Justice Brooke).

The Government's draft Defamation Bill announced by Justice Secretary Kenneth Clarke in March 2011 seeks to ensure that anyone who makes a statement of fact or expresses an honest opinion can do so with confidence. The draft bill includes provision for:

- A new 'public interest' defence;
- A requirement for claimants to demonstrate substantial harm before they can sue;
- Reducing so-called 'libel tourism' by making it tougher to bring overseas claims which have little connection to the UK in the English courts;
- A 'single publication' rule, meaning repeat claims for libel cannot be made every time a publication is accessed on the Internet.

◉ FOR THOUGHT

Is it wrong that rich people should be advised on a CFA? Why should the likes of Naomi Campbell, Sara Cox[34] or Keith Bennett[35] not benefit from the 'no win, no fee' agreements? Do you agree with the ECtHR judgment in *MGN Ltd v UK* (2011)?

3.2.2 Libel or slander?

Defamation is the collective term for libel and slander, and occurs when a person communicates material to a third party, in words or any other form, containing an untrue imputation against the reputation of a claimant. Material is libellous where it is communicated in a permanent form or broadcast, or forms part of a theatrical performance. If the material is spoken or takes some other transient form, then it is classed as slander. Whether material is defamatory is a matter for the courts to determine.

A defamatory publication is usually in words, but pictures, gestures, and other acts can also be defamatory. Defamation is a publication of an untrue statement about a person that tends to lower his reputation in the opinion of 'right-thinking members of the community' (*Sim v Stretch* (1936)[36]) or to make them shun or avoid him. The main tests established by the courts in deciding whether material is defamatory are whether the words used 'tend to lower the claimant in the estimation of right-thinking members of society generally',[37] 'without justification or lawful excuse [are] calculated to injure the reputation of another, by exposing him to hatred, contempt, or ridicule',[38] or tend to make the claimant 'be shunned and avoided and that without any moral discredit on [the claimant's] part'.[39]

The basis of the tort is injury to reputation, so it must be proved that the statement was communicated to someone other than the person defamed – a third party – because it can reasonably be assumed that a third party may well communicate the information independently of the author of it. If the statement is not obviously defamatory, the claimant must show that it would be

---

34 BBC Radio 1 breakfast presenter Sara Cox and her husband, DJ Jon Carter, were photographed naked on their honeymoon on a private island in the Seychelles in October 2001. They won a privacy action against the *People*, who agreed to pay Cox £30,000 and her husband Jon Carter £20,000 in an out of court settlement. The couple split up in 2005.
35 In July 2003, Keith Bennett, Labour party election agent to the former Foreign Office minister Keith Vaz, accepted substantial undisclosed damages in his action against the *Sunday Telegraph*. This concerned an article wrongly alleging that he misused his privileged status as a passholder at the Palace of Westminster and breached House of Commons rules.
36 [1936] 2 All ER 1237 (Lord Atkin).
37 Ibid.
38 *Parmiter v Coupland* (1840) 6 M & W 105 at 108 (Lord Wensleydale; then Parke B)
39 *Youssoupoff v MGM Pictures Ltd.* (1934) 50 TLR 581 at 587 (Slesser LJ).

understood in a defamatory sense, such as by some innuendo. It is not necessary to prove that the defendant intended to refer to the claimant. The test is whether reasonable people would think the statement referred to him, but the defendant may escape liability for *unintentional defamation* by making an out of court settlement by way of an apology and damages ('an offer of amends'). Other defences are justification, fair comment, and absolute and qualified privilege (see below 3.2.5 and 3.2.7).

3.2.3 On whom is the burden of proof?

Usually, a claimant in civil law has to prove his case to succeed at trial. Not so in a defamation action: here the claimant claims that a publication is false and the defendant has to prove the statement at the heart of the case is true. It seems ironic that the defendant's burden of proof was established to protect a person's honour and that this ancient common law principle has now resulted in London being the libel capital of the western world. Old libel laws were initially designed to protect the integrity of the Crown and members of Parliament through the courts. Now the charge is that it is increasingly being used by the rich and famous, from home and abroad, to silence free speech and the freedom of the press in the UK (see below 3.3.1).

So, the burden of proving material is defamatory lies with the claimant. However, the claimant is not required to show that the material is false; there is a rebuttable presumption that this is the case and it is for the defendant to prove otherwise. For an action to be successful, not only does the meaning of the material complained of have to be defamatory, the statement must refer to the claimant and have been communicated to a third party. This rule was introduced by the Victorians, who thought it inconceivable that a gentleman should have to prove that something said about him was a lie. This effectively means the claimant does not have to do anything except make an application to the court; the onus is then on the party defending the claim (unlike in 'ordinary' civil or criminal matters where 'he who alleges must prove').

This issue has been particularly controversial, since there is a presumption of falsity when publication takes place of material which could be defamatory. This means that a defendant being sued over, say, a scientific issue – as in the *Simon Singh* case[40] – has the burden of trying to prove that something is good science over bad science. The Ministry of Justice (MOJ) consultation document of 2009 proposed a shifting in the burden of proof, so that claimants have to prove their case.[41]

3.2.4 The multiple publication rule and secondary publication: the Duke of Brunswick case

There exists a long-standing principle in the tort of defamation that each publication of a defamatory statement, publication or broadcast gives rise to a separate cause of action which is subject to its own limitation period. It is known as the 'multiple publication rule'. The Law Commission considered the multiple publication rule in its 2002 scoping study 'Defamation and the Internet'[42] and concluded that 'there is a need to review the way in which the multiple publication rule interacts with the limitation period applying to archived material' (see below 3.7.2).

---

40 *British Chiropractic Association v Simon Singh* [2010] EWCA Civ 350.
41 Ministry of Justice (2009b) 'Defamation and the Internet: the multiple publication rule'. Consultation Paper, CP20/09, 16 September 2009, available at <http://www.justice.gov.uk/consultations/defamation-internet-consultation-paper.htm>, accessed 19 November 2010.
42 Source: Law Commission, Defamation and the Internet: A Preliminary Investigation, Scoping Study No 2, December 2002.

The multiple publication rule stems from the early nineteenth-century case of *Duke of Brunswick v Harmer* (1849).[43] The central character in this case was an exiled German ruler, Karl II.[44] In 1848, the Duke sent a servant to procure a copy of an article which had been published in 1830, containing an alleged defamatory statement about the Duke. The statement had been known to him since its original publication. Clearly, the then six-year limitation period for bringing an action for defamation had expired, but still, the Duke sent his servant to procure copies of the offending article and brought defamation proceedings for injury to his reputation. After obtaining a fresh copy of the said article from the London publishers, the Duke promptly sued on the basis that he had the original copy and a fresh copy of the article, thereby suing for republication.

The Queen's Bench held that the act of procuring the 'fresh' article by the Duke amounted to a new publication of a libel, giving rise to a fresh cause of action in respect of each article; and that was in spite of the fact that there was a statute in place which limited the bringing of such a civil action to six years. The court held that publisher Harmer's back-issue of the offending publication in 1848 constituted a separate act of publication and was therefore within the statutory time limit. The new action commenced at the point in time when the publication was received, rather than the date of its original printing and distribution 17 years previously.

Astonishingly, the *Brunswick* ruling on republication still governs the law of defamation today. The effect of the ruling is that each individual access to an alleged libellous publication can give rise to a separate cause of action, with a separate limitation period attached to it (see below 3.7.2). What has changed since the Duke of Brunswick case is the limitation period when an action in defamation can be brought. This is now *one* year under section 4A of the **Limitation Act 1980**, which also covers an action in malicious falsehood. Each separate publication is subject to the one-year limitation period and runs from the time at which the material is accessed. A defendant will also be liable if he is a 'secondary publisher' and cannot use the defence contained in section 1 of the **Defamation Act 1996** (see below 3.5.2).

There are several arguments that arise over whether the multiple publication rule should have a place in the modern law of defamation and it is necessary to examine how the courts have addressed the balance between freedom of expression and an individual's claim in defamation. In principle, it is valid that an individual ought to be able to take action in respect of defamatory publications which damage his reputation. One argument for maintaining the multiple publication rule is that there is a limited likelihood of actions being brought in respect of archive material only; and that where a cause of action does arise, it seems unfair to deny a claimant the right to redress if they were to become aware of the publication of defamatory material through accessing archive material rather than the initial publication. The counter-argument could be that such a rule creates potentially open-ended liability and therefore defeats the purpose of having a limitation period to protect defendants from extended liability. It could also be argued that in many cases archives are 'stale news' and that therefore any injury to reputation will be minimal and damages awarded as a result will be small. It could equally be argued by a claimant that material published by online media and news providers is not 'stale' because the immediacy of access across the world makes the impression more permanent, as the World Wide Web allows material to be instantly displayed, distributed and downloaded for many years after first publication. If an action does arise, a defendant may have problems mounting a defence if a long period of time has elapsed and memories have faded or evidence has been destroyed.

---

43 [1849] 14 QB 185.
44 Official title: Herzog zu Braunschweig–Lüneburg–Wolfenbüttel.

> ⊙ **FOR THOUGHT**
>
> Do you think it is fair to adopt a new and proper procedure in law, where the claimant in a defamation action has to prove the presumption of falsity? Do you think the present system is outdated?

3.2.5 Substantive defences

A defendant will be liable if material meets the criteria that the defendant is the primary publisher of the material and does not succeed in establishing any of the defences in the **Defamation Act 1952**, namely:

1. **justification** that the material is true;
2. **fair comment**, which protects statements of opinion or comment on matters of public interest (with no malice);
3. **absolute privilege**, which guarantees immunity from liability in certain situations such as in Parliamentary and court proceedings;
4. **qualified privilege**, which grants limited protection on public policy grounds to statements in the media provided that certain requirements are met (see also below 3.8.1).

A defendant is not a 'secondary publisher' and will not be liable where he:

1. is not the author, editor or publisher of the statement complained of;
2. took reasonable care in relation to its publication; and
3. did not know, and had no reason to believe, that what he did caused or contributed to the publication of a defamatory statement.

In addition, section 2 of the 1996 Act provides a procedure by which a defendant can make an offer of amends to enable valid claims to be settled without the need for court proceedings. Section 2(4) provides that an offer to make amends is an offer to:

1. make a suitable correction of the statement complained of and a sufficient apology to the aggrieved party;
2. publish the correction and apology in a manner that is reasonable and practicable in the circumstances; and
3. pay to the aggrieved party such compensation (if any), and such costs, as may be agreed or determined to be payable.

An offer of amends (out of court settlement under s.3 **Defamation Act 1996**) is not regarded as an admission of liability and is, in fact, a form of defence (unless it was published with malice and clearly referring to the claimant). The offer may be withdrawn before it is accepted. A full and rapid apology can earn up to 50 per cent discount on damages. If an offer is accepted, the party accepting the offer may not bring or continue defamation proceedings in respect of the publication concerned against the person making the offer. If a case does go to court and the claimant succeeds, the court may award a range of remedies including damages and injunctions.

3.2.6 Historic doctrine of absolute privilege

Absolute privilege gives the author of a 'defamatory' statement utter freedom in the communication of views and information. This privilege of free speech, dating back to Article 9 of the **Bill of**

Rights 1689, is extended to all members of Parliament and to statements made during judicial or tribunal proceedings. However, absolute privilege does not protect ministers or peers outside the Houses of Parliament (such as on College Green) or outside the courthouse (see: *Church of Scientology of California v Johnson-Smith* (1972)[45]).

The doctrine of absolute privilege covers:

See Chapter
◄ 1.2

- Any statement made in Parliament (Bill of Rights 1689); but a member of Parliament can waive the privilege if he so wishes (s. 13 **Defamation Act 1996**).
- Any report published by the Houses of Parliament such as Hansard (s. 1 **Parliamentary Papers Act 1840**);
- Any statement by officer of state to another such as a Secretary of State or Minister in the course of his duty;
- Statements made in judicial proceedings and tribunals;
- Fair and accurate reporting of public judicial proceedings (s. 14 **Defamation Act 1996**) (contemporaneous reports of court proceedings are absolutely privileged);
- Any statement made by one spouse to another;
- Any statements by officials of the European Union; European Court of Justice, the European Court of Human Rights and the United Nations in exercising their functions (s. 14 **Defamation Act 1996**).

In *Westcott v Westcott* (2009),[46] Richard Westcott sought damages for slander and libel as well as an injunction to restrain further publication against his daughter-in-law, the defendant Sarah Westcott, over allegations which she had made about him during an interview with the police. After a heated family argument, Mrs Westcott had telephoned the police and claimed in an oral and written statement that Mr Westcott, her father-in-law, had assaulted her and her baby. But the police decided to take no further action. Mr Westcott then sued Sarah Westcott for defamation. It was held that the police investigation and proceedings were protected by absolute privilege. The Court of Appeal in *Westcott* relied on *Taylor*,[47] establishing that immunity for out-of-court statements was not confined to persons who were subsequently called as witnesses. The policy of 'absolute privilege' was therefore applied and extended to police investigations, enabling people to speak freely, without inhibition and without fear of being sued.

Society expects that if criminal activity is reported, the police will investigate and, where appropriate, prosecute. If there is insufficient evidence, they and the Crown Prosecution Service will drop the case. Making an oral complaint is therefore the first step in the criminal justice process and in order to have confidence that protection will be afforded to an informer or complainant, the police have to give the assurance that immunity will be granted from any attack; that includes immunity from a defamatory action.

Any inhibition on the freedom to complain would seriously erode the rigours of the criminal justice system and be contrary to the public interest. Witness immunity has to be guaranteed from the onset. It is for this reason that criminal investigations are subject to absolute privilege in respect of statements made. This principle is applied to informants, investigators and prosecutors (see also: *D v NSPCC* (1978)[48]; *Evans v London Hospital Medial College* (1981)[49]).

---

45 [1972] 1 QB 522.
46 [2009] QB 407; [2009] 2 WLR 838.
47 *Taylor v Director of the Serious Fraud Office* [1999] 2 AC 177 (HL).
48 [1978] AC 171 (HL).
49 [1981] 1 WLR 184 (QBD).

3.2.7 The *Reynolds* qualified privilege and public interest defence

Newspapers exist to supply information to the public and journalists, and editors and publishers may regard themselves as under a 'social and moral duty' to publish the information contained in their articles. Qualified privilege arises where media freedom warrants some additional protection from the threat of litigation, particularly relevant to newspaper reports of public meetings or court proceedings. 'Qualified' means it is not 'absolute' and there will be certain conditions put on the author of the statement. A statement made in the performance of a duty may attract the defence of qualified privilege under common law,[50] provided that the person making the statement has a legal, moral or social duty to make the statement and the person receiving it has an interest in doing so in that it allows such person to make a quality decision.

Section 15 **Defamation Act 1996** regrettably does not define 'qualified privilege'; it just states that the publication must not be made with malice. Otherwise 'there is no defence'. There are a number of situations defined in Schedule 1 of the 1996 Act which detail 'qualified privilege' scenarios. The prima facie defence of qualified privilege is lost if the claimant can prove that the defendant was motivated by 'actual' or 'express malice', though there is no sufficient definition in common law as to the meaning of 'malice' (see below 3.4). A defendant establishes a prima facie defence of qualified privilege to an action in defamation if he can show that the publication was made by him in pursuance of a duty or in protection of an interest to a person who had a duty or interest in hearing the matter published.[51] Though the privilege existed, it was extended by section 4 **Law of Libel (Amendment) Act 1888**[52] which read:

> . . . a fair and accurate report published in any newspaper of the proceedings of a public meeting, or (except where neither the public nor any newspaper reporter is admitted) of any meeting of a vestry, town council, school board, board of guardians, board of local authority formed or constituted under the provisions of any Act of Parliament, or of any committee appointed by any of the above-mentioned bodies, or of any meeting of any commissioners authorised to act by letters patent, Act of Parliament, warrant under the Royal Sign Manual, or other lawful warrant or authority, select committees of either House of Parliament, justices of the peace in quarter sessions assembled for administrative or deliberative purposes, and the publication at the request of any Government office or department, officer of state, commissioner of police, or chief constable of any notice or report issued by them for the information of the public shall be privileged, unless it shall be proved that such report or publication was published or made maliciously: Provided that nothing in this section shall authorise the publication of any blasphemous or indecent matter . . .

Lord Diplock defined the meaning 'public interest' in the passage below established in *Horrocks v Lowe* (1975):[53]

> . . . the public interest that the law should provide an effective means whereby a man can vindicate his reputation against calumny has nevertheless to be accommodated to the competing public interest in permitting men to communicate frankly and freely with one another about matters in respect of which the law recognises that they have a duty to perform or an interest to protect in doing so. What is published in good faith on matters of these kinds is published on a privileged occasion. It is not actionable even though it be defamatory and turns out to be

---

50 Common law is recognized by s. 15(4) Defamation Act 1996.
51 *Hebditch v MacIlwaine* [1894] 2 QB 54.
52 Section 4 is now repealed.
53 [1975] AC 135.

untrue. With some exceptions which are irrelevant to the instant appeal, the privilege is not absolute but qualified. It is lost if the occasion which gives rise to it is misused.[54]

The qualified privilege common law defence was extended by way of the 'circumstantial' test established by the Court of Appeal in the 'Albert Reynolds' case, 'where the nature, status and source of the material, and the circumstances of the publication, such that the publication should in the public interest be protected in the absence of proof of express malice'[55] (though this was rejected in the House of Lords). In his 'libel' action against The Times, the former Irish Taoiseach (Prime Minister), Albert Reynolds, found himself embroiled in a political crisis in 1994. The Irish section of The Times had alleged that Mr Reynolds had misled the Irish Parliament with the UK version of the paper omitting the Taoiseach's 'right to reply'. After a number of cross appeals, the House of Lords[56] set the precedent for the now famous 'Reynolds defence of qualified privilege', which set the tone for future media cases in defamation. However, a series of allegations emerged about Reynolds' appointing a new President of the High Court, Harry Whelehan, whom Reynolds had elevated to that post from Attorney General in the midst of the affair. The charges implicated Whelehan, then serving as Attorney General, in delaying the extradition of a couple of Irish priests who were wanted in the Belfast court for alleged child sex abuse. Both Reynolds and AG Whelehan procrastinated in signing the extradition warrants for the priests for Northern Ireland, which caused enormous political embarrassment for Reynolds, and his government fell shortly thereafter, resulting in the piece in The Times.

Lord Nicholls, giving the leading judgment in Reynolds, then provided a 10-point list of factors to take into account when deciding whether the defence should be available.

The House of Lords 10-point-Reynolds test

(1) **The seriousness of the allegation**. The more serious the charge, the more the public is misinformed and the individual harmed, if the allegation is not true.
(2) **The nature of the information**, and the extent to which the subject matter is a matter of public concern.
(3) **The source of the information**. Some informants have no direct knowledge of the events. Some have their own axes to grind, or are being paid for their stories.
(4) **The steps taken to verify the information**.
(5) **The status of the information**. The allegation may have already been the subject of an investigation which commands respect.
(6) **The urgency of the matter**. News is often a perishable commodity.
(7) **Whether comment was sought from the claimant**. He may have information others do not possess or have not disclosed. An approach to the claimant will not always be necessary.
(8) Whether the article contained the **gist of the claimant's side of the story**.
(9) **The tone of the article**. A newspaper can raise queries or call for an investigation. It need not adopt allegations as statements of fact.
(10) **The circumstances of the publication**, including the timing.[57]

---

54 Ibid. at 149 (Lord Diplock).
55 *Reynolds v Times Newspapers Ltd* [1998] 3 All ER 961 at 995a (CA).
56 The UK Supreme Court was established by Part 3 of the Constitutional Reform Act 2005 and came into being on 1 October 2009. It replaced the House of Lords in its judicial capacity and has assumed the jurisdiction of the House of Lords under the Appellate Jurisdiction Acts 1876 and 1888. The Supreme Court also has jurisdiction in relation to devolution matters under the Scotland Act 1998, the Northern Ireland Act 1988 and the Government of Wales Act 2006; this was transferred to the Supreme Court from the Judicial Committee of the Privy Council.
57 [2001] 2 AC at para. 205 (Lord Nicholls of Birkenhead).

The House of Lords ruling in Reynolds provided what is now known as the 'Reynolds defence'. This can be raised where it is clear that a journalist, accused of defamation, has a duty to meet the '10-point' test in order to claim qualified privilege. The subsequent case of *Jameel v Wall Street Journal* (2007)[58] affirmed this defence (see below 3.8.2).

This means that newspapers, broadcasters and online editors should take steps – wherever practicable – when publishing 'in the public interest' statements to which the defence of justification cannot be applied, to verify the truth of what is being reported. Fairness to those whose names appear in newspapers may require an opportunity to comment by being given a 'right to reply' published by the newspaper. Publications in the public interest are now protected by qualified privilege after the House of Lords established the 10-point criteria for 'responsible journalism' in *Reynolds*[59]. If these criteria are met, they act as a complete defence in a libel action.

The 'Reynolds defence' has been regarded as a divisive and controversial issue. Clayton and Tomlinson (2009) argued that *Reynolds* qualified privilege left the law of defamation in a state of uncertainty in relation to media discussion of matters of public interest, stating:

> . . . in the absence of a developed body of case law, a responsible media organisation publishing material relating to matters of 'public interest' will be unable to determine whether a defence is available. It seems that the full background to the publication will have to be investigated in each case in order to satisfy the court that there is a 'right to know'. It is arguable that this uncertainty, of itself, constitutes an unacceptable restriction on freedom of expression.[60]

Clayton and Tomlinson further criticized the *Reynolds* ten-point criteria in that they did not support journalistic practice and free speech under Article 10 ECHR as a defence of qualified privilege in 'matters of legitimate public concern'[61] (see also: *Bergens Tidende v Norway* (2000)[62]).

How useful are the *Reynolds* 10-point-test criteria and to whom? Those who read or hear defamatory imputations and allegations about a person are unlikely to have any means of knowing whether such statements are true or not. If a newspaper is understandably unwilling to disclose its sources, a claimant can be deprived access to material necessary to prove, or even allege, that the newspaper acted recklessly in publishing as it did without further verification. In the absence of any additional safeguard for reputation, a newspaper, anxious to be first with a 'scoop', would, in practice, be free to publish seriously defamatory misstatements of fact based on the slenderest of materials. Unless the paper chose later to withdraw the allegations, a defamed individual would have no means of clearing his name and the public would have no means of knowing where the truth lay. That said, the *Reynolds* criteria are said to have achieved further protection for reputation without a disproportionate incursion into freedom of expression.

The *Reynolds* 10-point test was applied in the 'George Galloway' case (*Galloway v Telegraph* (2004)),[63] where the former Glasgow MP sued the *Daily Telegraph* for publishing libellous articles during April 2003, claiming that Mr Galloway had 'received money from the Iraqi ruler Saddam Hussein's regime, taking a slice of oil earnings worth £375,000 a year', and that the Scottish MP had asked for 'a greater cut of Iraq's exports and 'was profiting from food contracts'. A further article

had stated that, according to the claimant's Iraqi intelligence profile, the claimant 'had a family history of loyalty to Saddam Hussein's Ba'ath Party', and referred to him as a 'sympathiser with Iraq' (see also: *Kennedy v Information Commissioner* (2010)[64]). The defendant

---

58 [2007] 1 AC 359.
59 *Reynolds v Times Newspapers Ltd.* [2001] 2 AC 127 (HL).
60 Clayton and Tomlinson (2009) at para.15.249.
61 Ibid.
62 App. No.26132/95 (ECHR).
63 [2004] EWHC 2786 (QB).
64 [2010] EWHC 475 (Admin) of 19 January 2010 (QBD).

newspaper did not seek to plead justification but raised the defences under the *Reynolds* criteria of qualified privilege; in respect of two leader articles and the two respective headlines, the *Telegraph* also raised the defence of 'fair comment'.

The High Court ruled that the defendants could not rely on the *Reynolds* test, because not all of the 10-point criteria were satisfied (affirmed by the Court of Appeal). Though the court said that the subject matter was 'undoubtedly of public concern', the sources of information could not be regarded as 'inherently reliable', and the *Telegraph* publishers and editor had not taken sufficient steps to verify the information. The court, presiding without a jury, ruled in favour of Mr Galloway, who was awarded £150,000 in damages.

What can be concluded from *Galloway* is that a newspaper which obtains critical material from an anonymous or slightly dubious source will not be able to rely on the qualified privilege defence unless the source material passes the *Reynolds* – qualified privilege – test. George Galloway's success against the *Telegraph* effectively meant that breaking *any one* of the 10-point *Reynolds* criteria means the defence may be lost.

The New Zealand Court of Appeal argued in the case of *Lange v Atkinson* (2000)[65] that the *Reynolds* test had created excessive uncertainty. This case concerned an article by a political scientist accusing the former Prime Minister, David Lange, of hypocrisy. The defendant pleaded qualified privilege and was successful before the High Court. The Court of Appeal dismissed the appeal but the Privy Council, on appeal, sent the case back to the New Zealand Court of Appeal to take into account the House of Lords decision in *Reynolds* and the 'generic' qualified privilege defence criteria.[66]

The decision of the House of Lords in *Reynolds* built on the traditional foundations of qualified privilege but carried the law forward in a way which gave much greater weight than earlier law had done to the value of informed public debate of significant public issues. Lord Nicholls listed certain matters – the 10-point test – which might be taken into account in deciding whether the test of responsible journalism was satisfied. He intended these as pointers which might be more or less indicative, depending on the circumstances of a particular case. However, many media and publishing defendants have since seen this test as too great a hurdle and argue that they can no longer successfully rely on qualified privilege.

In *Seaga v Harper* (2008),[67] the Privy Council dismissed an appeal by the defendant, Mr Edward Seaga, from the dismissal by the Court of Appeal of Jamaica of his appeal from Brooks J, who on 11 December 2003 had awarded the claimant, Mr Leslie Harper, damages of $3,500,000 for slander in respect of statements made on 2 October 1996 at the Wyndham Hotel, Kingston, Jamaica. The Court of Appeal reduced the damages to $1,500,000. In this high-profile Caribbean case, the politician and opposition leader Mr Seaga had made defamatory statements about Mr Harper, a deputy police commissioner, at a public meeting, which were widely reported throughout Jamaica. Mr Harper issued proceedings for slander. Mr Seaga said he had received information from senior members of his party, and also that many people had telephoned him to warn him about Mr Harper. Mr Seaga said he accepted their word and did not seek to question the information. The problem was that Mr Seaga did not name his informants, which made matters difficult when the court wanted to apply the *Reynolds* criteria. The Privy Council held that the words complained of were defamatory. The sole defence was that the words spoken had been justified by a plea of fair comment claiming, inter alia, qualified privilege. There was no plea of malice.

The Privy Council stated that the *Reynolds* privilege was based on liberalizing the media and there was no reason why the privilege should not be extended to publications – other than newspapers or broadcasts – made by any person who published material of public interest in any

65 [2000] 3 NZLR 385.
66 See: Atkin (2001) at p. 237, where he argues that the later decision of the New Zealand Court of Appeal bears more similarities to the judgment in Reynolds than to their original judgment.
67 [2008] 1 All ER 965 (Privy Council).

medium, so long as the requirements of the statement were of public interest and the test of responsible journalism was met. Their Lordships accepted the trial judge's analysis of the *Reynolds* factors, but Lord Carswell pointed out that this case was more about an election campaign and therefore amounted to an aggressive political attack on a holder of a public office rather than being of genuine public interest as stipulated by *Reynolds*.[68] There was therefore no valid reason why the *Reynolds* defence should be available in this case either to the defendant politician or to the media in general. The Privy Council warned that it was inadequate to rely merely on the conclusions of others without demonstrating the validity of those conclusions; and if qualified privilege was to be successfully claimed, it had to satisfy the *Reynolds* principles in relation to 'responsible journalism'.

Generally speaking, the *Reynolds* 10-point test has had a 'chilling effect' on journalistic practice with the defence of qualified privilege being a very tall order to meet. Once any one of the 10-point criteria are not met, the whole defence is effectively lost, as *Galloway* proved.[69]

However, as the later case of *Jameel* demonstrates, the House of Lords provided a fresh impetus to 'responsible journalism' which depreciated the importance of the Reynolds 10-point test to a certain extent (see also: *Hughes v Rusbridger* (2010)[70]) (see below 3.8.2).

👁 FOR THOUGHT

Do you think that the public interest test in libel actions should be expanded? Do you think the *Reynolds* defence is too great a hurdle for the media to take in respect of the 10-point criteria test? Should the reason of the public interest defence not be enough in allowing news to be published without fear that a particular error of fact will restrict the willingness of the press to work in a certain fashion?

3.3 General framework for defamation law

The disappearance of four-year-old Madeleine McCann grasped Europe's attention and led to some of the most aggressive tabloid journalism of recent times. Madeleine, from Rothley, Leicestershire, went missing on 3 May 2007 from the Algarve apartment in Praia da Luz where she was on holiday with her parents Kate and Gerry McCann and their two-year-old twins, Sean and Amelie. Few could have anticipated the enormity of the story and the distressing facts were often blurred by rumour and counter rumour in the media, including misunderstandings about the Portuguese criminal justice system and widespread unsupported allegations in the 'red top' tabloid press in 'trial by media'-style reporting, either accusing the McCanns themselves or vehemently supporting the couple, apparently ignoring the most basic principles of defamation law and ethical journalism.[71]

One of the most notable defeats of the press concerned substantial payouts to the parents of Madeleine McCann and to Robert Murat, who lived near to where Madeleine disappeared. The McCanns won £550,000 in damages in March 2008 from Express Newspapers following 'grotesque and grossly defamatory' allegations contained in more than a hundred articles following their daughter's disappearance.[72] From January 2010 onwards, Kate and Gerry McCann also faced legal

---

68 Ibid., at para 14 (Lord Carswell).
69 For further discussion, see: Barendt, Lustgarten, Norrie and Stephenson, (1997) at p.1032, referred to in *Reynolds* [2001] 2 AC 127.
70 [2010] EWHC 491 of 11 March 2010 (QB).
71 For further discussion see: Johnson (2008b).
72 See: 'Murat's £800,000 – a minor marketing expense', by Peter Wilby, *The Guardian*, 21 July 2008; see also: 'Free rein for m'learned friends', by Peter Preston, the *Observer*, 20 July 2008.

action in Portugal, suing former detective, Gonçalo Amaral, in a libel action at the Lisbon High Court. Mr Amaral had accused Mrs McCann of faking her daughter Madeleine's abduction to cover up her death. He published his book, *a Verdade da Mentira* ('the truth of the lie') in July 2008, claiming that Madeleine died accidentally in the apartment, and that her parents fabricated the abduction story. The McCanns successfully applied for an injunction, which was granted by the Portuguese court in September 2009, banning any further sales of the book. On 18 February 2010, Mr Amaral lost his appeal to lift the injunction.[73]

The main problem in the McCann and Murat cases was that the press ignored the most basic principles of defamation law. The principle of sound journalism, including story and source verification and ethics, was ignored. Robert Murat, a British expat and property developer, had assisted the police and the McCanns with translation in the first few days after little Madeleine's disappearance. The Portuguese police then made him an *arguido* (suspect), but Mr Murat strongly protested his innocence. Mr Murat won £600,000 in libel damages in proceedings which he had brought against Associated Newspapers, Express Newspapers, Mirror Group Newspapers (MGN) Ltd. and News Group Newspapers. Stephen Glover commented in *The Independent*:

> . . . to differing degrees, the newspapers, which include pretty well every tabloid in the country behaved abominably . . . I don't for a moment imagine that having collectively forked out a relatively modest £600,000 plus costs, the tabloids will behave much better in the future. Nor do I suppose that next time the qualities will act differently. They will go on pretending they inhabit a separate moral universe while committing many of the same faults as the tabloids.[74]

Robert Murat had taken advantage of the CFA – the conditional fee agreement, targeted for abolition by the then Justice Minister Jack Straw in his Libel Reform Bill in March 2010. Mr Straw announced to Parliament that he intended to bring an end to 'libel tourism', citing the 'shocking example' of the British doctor Peter Wilmshurst, who was, at that time, being sued by a US company after he questioned the effectiveness of a heart implant.[75] Though rejected by Parliament just as the General Election was called in April 2010, Lord Lester introduced the Defamation Bill 2010 at the start of the new Parliament in the House of Lords on 9 July 2010 (second reading).

The bill has much to offer the media defendant, such as the introduction of a single publication rule and the widening of the categories of information to which statutory privilege applies. If the bill becomes law, reports of academic conferences will be protected and claimants will no longer be able to rely on a case decided more than 150 years ago (see: *Duke of Brunswick v Harmer* (1849)). However, the bill does not propose to reverse the burden of proof – a present bugbear for defendants. Instead, the 'Lord Lester Libel Bill' establishes some new hurdles for the claimant, such as the need to establish serious damage to reputation. Lester also proposes the presumption of the right to a jury trial – after all, privacy cases are already heard by a judge alone.

The bill clarifies existing law to make it more user-friendly and consolidates common law with existing statute in defamation. The proposed legislation makes the defences of 'fair comment' and 'Reynolds privilege' more accessible, in line with the *Jameel* ruling of 'responsible journalism' and 'honest opinion'. The bill includes Lord Nicholls' 10-point factors in Reynolds, which must be taken into account by the court when deciding whether a defendant has acted responsibly. But the bill makes no reference to the need for the courts to give weight to judgments made by editorial staff at the time of publication, which was so helpfully included in the House of Lords'

---

73 Source: 'Madeleine McCann detective loses attempt to overturn book ban', by Esther Addley, *The Guardian*, 18 February 2010.
74 Source: 'Murat's victory should serve as warning to the entire British press', by Stephen Glover, *The Independent*, Media Section, 21 July, 2008 at p. 7.
75 Source: 'Reform of libel laws will protect freedom of expression', Ministry of Justice News release, 23 March 2010, at <http://www.justice.gov.uk/news/newsrelease230310b.htm>, accessed 19 November 2010.

Jameel judgment. The bill also includes in its 'responsible publication' test that the media must be seen to have complied with codes of conduct, such as the Press Complaints Commission's Editors' Code of Practice (latest version: January 2011). This leads to the question whether the Defamation Bill is for everybody or just for traditional media which have codes of conduct (for example bloggers do not).

See Chapter 10.3.4 →

To date, the defamation laws of England and Wales are stacked heavily against the defendant and can often involve monumental costs with no possibility of legal aid. It is argued that they amount, in effect, to censorship by private interests: as George Monbiot commented in *The Guardian*, 'a sedition law for the exclusive use of millionaires'.[76]

3.3.1 Exposure to hatred and ridicule: common law development

Professor Winfield gave the widely accepted definition of a defamatory statement:

> . . . [one which] tends to lower a person in the estimation of right thinking members of society generally; or which tends to make them shun or avoid that person.[77]

One such example was the case of *Gillick*,[78] where the claimant, Mrs Victoria Gillick, a mother of ten, appeared on a live BBC TV chat show. During the programme it was implied that she was morally responsible for the deaths of pregnant girls, following her campaign through the 1980s to prevent doctors from giving contraceptive advice to under-16-year-old girls without their parents' consent.[79] There is an abundance of case law where a claimant has been the subject of a comical or satirical portrayal subjecting him or her to ridicule or contempt (see: *Dunlop Rubber Co. Ltd v Dunlop* (1921)[80]; *Hulton v Jones* (1910)[81]).

3.3.2 *Scandalum magnatum*: criminal libel and the Star Chamber

The early history of the law of 'defamation' is somewhat obscure, though civil actions for damages seem to have been reasonably frequent as far back as the reign of Edward I (1272–1307). There was no distinction drawn between words written and spoken and 'libel' was the most commonly used generic term. When no pecuniary penalty was involved, cases fell within the old jurisdiction of the ecclesiastical courts.[82] The crime of *scandalum magnatum*, spreading false reports about the magnates of the realm – such as 'Great Officers of the State' or peers – was formally established by the **Statute of Westminster 1275**, which provided that:

> . . . from henceforth none be so hardy to tell or publish any false News or Tales, whereby discord, or occasion of discord or slander may grow between the King and his People, or the Great Men of the Realm.[83]

Scandalum magnatum was both a tort and a criminal offence and is based on Roman law, which treated libel as a breach of the peace. The law aimed to give sufficient scope for the discussion of a man's character, while it protected him from needless insult and pain.

---

76 Source: 'Censored by money', by George Monbiot, *The Guardian*, 15 July 2008.
77 Winfield (1937).
78 *Gillick v British Broadcasting Corporation* [1996] EMLR 267 (CA).
79 *Gillick v Department of Health and Social Security* [1986] AC 112 (HL).
80 [1921] 1 AC 367 (HL).
81 *Hulton (E) & Co. v Jones* [1910] AC 20 (HL).
82 See: Pike (1894), pp. 215–17.
83 3 Edw. 1, Stat. Westm. prim. at 34.

According to Roman jurist Ulpian (Gnaeus Domitius Annius Ulpianus, circa 170–223 AD),[84] a defamatory and injurous statement made in a public manner (*convicium adversus bonos mores*) became subject to monetary penalties. The *Praetorian Edict* codified remedies for verbal and more serious libels in 130 AD, where anonymous accusations were regarded as particularly dangerous and punished severely where they contained untrue or false statements. The later notion of 'maliciousness' is based on this principle (see: 3.4.1).

The ancient high court of England, the Star Chamber, created by King Henry VII in 1487, was a monarchical instrument and consisted of royal councillors and two royal judges. The Star Chamber in the Palace of Westminster was so called because of stars painted on the ceiling. The court of the Star Chamber developed from the judicial proceedings traditionally carried out by the king and his council, and was entirely separate from the common law courts of the day. The Star Chamber originally assisted the king in purely administrative matters, but soon relieved the sovereign of the burden of hearing cases personally. The purpose of the Star Chamber was to protect the sovereign from criticism, insurrection and breaches of the peace by trying libel, treason and sedition cases against nobles who were too powerful to be tried in the lower courts. Under Chancellor Wolsey's leadership (1515–29), the court of Star Chamber became a political weapon, bringing actions against opponents of the decrees and edicts of Henry VIII.

In 1530 the Star Chamber became a 'proper' court of equity, granting remedies unavailable in the common law courts. The court, which sat without a jury and in secret, was often used as a political weapon and a device of royal tyranny. During the mid-sixteenth century, the Star Chamber also acquired criminal jurisdiction, hearing cases on issues concerning the security of the realm, such as sedition and criminal libel, conspiracy and forgery.[85] Though the common-law courts originally presided over defamation cases, the Star Chamber soon took over the laws governing (seditious) libel and contempt of court and it was here that the common law of criminal libel was first recorded.

As printing was introduced in England during the fifteenth and sixteenth centuries, increasing the importance of newspapers, the monarchy tried to control and influence public opinion by regulating the press through the Stationers' Company,[86] which effectively had the monopoly over printing and publishing in England from 1556 onwards. The right to regulate the press stemmed from the royal prerogative.[87]

See Chapter 2.2.1

A decree issued by the Star Chamber in 1586, and an ordinance in 1637, imposed stringent regulations for licensing. They were seen as necessary to maintain complete control of the press in the face of increasing political and religious discord. The regulation was covered by laws relating to treason, and by other criminal offences such as sedition, heresy or blasphemy, some of which were, from time to time, equated with treason. Punishments included cutting off hands or ears or cutting out tongues.[88] The Star Chamber was abolished in 1641 by Parliament for abuses of power and the prohibition of *scandalum magnatum* was finally repealed by the **Statute Law Revision Act 1887**.

See Chapter 7.2.1

3.3.3 Seditious libel

While 'libel' or 'slander' may be different legal concepts today, most early legal systems relate back to verbal injuries, largely treated as a criminal or quasi-criminal offence. The essence of the injury

---

84 Source: Ulpianus libro 56 ad edictum, 47.10.1., Domini nostri sacratissimi principis iustiniani iuris enucleati ex omni vetere iure collecti. Digestorum seu pandectarum. Liber quadragensimus septimus. Based on the Latin text of Mommsen's edition, 'History of Rome', 1954.
85 Source: Van Vechten (1903 and 1904), p. 33 and p. 546.
86 The Stationers' Company was an amalgamation of associations of writers, printers, illuminators, binders and other similar crafts.
87 For further discussion see: Oats and Sadler (2002).
88 See: Holdsworth (1920), pp. 841ff.

lay not in pecuniary loss but in personal insult which had to be atoned for by a vindictive penalty which replaced personal revenge.[89] During the seventeenth century, the crime of 'seditious libel' encompassed conduct or language directed unlawfully against a state authority, public commotion and any political criticism that threatened to diminish respect for the government, its laws or public officials. Commonly this would include political cartoons directed against the monarch or prominent politicians.[90]

On 17 January 1712, Queen Anne called on Parliament to consider curbing the perceived menace of the unregulated press:

> . . . Her Majesty finds it necessary to observe, how great licence is taken in publishing false and scandalous libels such as are a reproach to any government. This evil seems to be grown too strong for the laws now in force; it is therefore recommended to you to find a remedy equal to the mischief.[91]

The Commons' reply the following day was as follows:

> . . . we are very sensible how much the Liberty of the Press is abused, by turning it into such a licentiousness as is a just reproach to the nation; since not only false and scandalous libels are printed and published against your Majesty's government, but the most horrid blasphemies against God and religion; and we beg leave humbly to assure your majesty, that we will do utmost to find out a remedy equal to this mischief, and that may effectually cure it.[92]

James Fitzjames Stephen commented on the definition of seditious libel as an offence 'to excite Her Majesty's subjects to attempt otherwise than by lawful means the alteration of any matter in Church or State by law established'.[93] Stephen argued that by keeping seditious libel as a criminal offence, Queen Anne created discontent and disaffection among the general population because it curtailed freedom of speech. The doctrine of libel was wholly inconsistent with any serious public discussion of political affairs and arguably amounted to a censorship of the press by the state.[94]

'Fox's Libel Act' of 1792[95] provided for significant changes in English libel laws in that the Act codified 'seditious libel' by making it a crime punishable by fine or imprisonment. Criminal libel then meant to speak disparagingly of the national government or government officials in a manner intending to hold them up to public ridicule and erode their authority. **The Libel Act 1792** restored the right of juries (which had been abolished by the Star Chamber) to decide whether an allegedly libellous article had been published, what constituted libel and whether or not a defendant was guilty of libel. The Act was seen as a liberalization of English libel laws in so far as it allowed evidence of the truth of a charge against the government to be entered into the defence at a trial and allowed the jury to be the judge not only of the fact of publication, but also of the allegedly seditious character of the published matter.[96]

By the end of the nineteenth century, the meaning of seditious libel had narrowed, as Stephen commented, to 'nothing short of direct incitement to disorder and violence is a seditious libel'.[97] He said further:

---

89 For further discussion see: Spencer (1977), pp. 383ff.
90 See: Pike (1894) pp. 218–227.
91 10 Anne, c.19, CXV.
92 Source: Cobbett (1806), Vol. 6, col. 1063.
93 See: Stephen (1883), p. 298 on the subject of seditious libel.
94 Ibid., p. 348.
95 Charles James Fox (1749–1806) was a prominent Whig whose Parliamentary career spanned 38 years. He was the arch-rival of William Pitt the Younger.
96 See: Holdsworth (1942), Vol. III.
97 Op. cit. (1883) p. 375.

. . . there can be no such offence as sedition. There may indeed be breaches of the peace which may destroy or endanger life, limb, or property, and there may be incitements to such offences, but no imaginable censure of the government, short of a censure which has an immediate tendency to produce such a breach of the peace, ought to be regarded as criminal.[98]

Barnum (2006), in a discussion of seditious libel, links its historical legal roots to the **Terrorism Act 2006**, arguing that the offence of 'indirect encouragement' to acts of terrorism, following the attacks on London in 2005, relates back to the ancient concept of seditious libel, which punished freedom of speech during riotous public congregations.[99] The origins of the offence of blasphemy also lie in seditious libel and were extended to 'obscene' libel by the Star Chamber in 1641. Historically guarded and overseen by the ecclesiastical courts in medieval times, 'obscenity' laws covered an attack on the Church or its doctrine and publications which were said to be blasphemous, containing any 'contemptuous, reviling, scurrilous or ludicrous matter relating to God, Jesus Christ, or the Bible, or the formularies of the Church of England as by law established'.[100] Part 2, section 73 of the **Coroners and Justice Act 2009** abolished criminal libel and linked offences such as seditious libel, defamatory libel and obscene libel.

See Chapter 7

3.3.4 Defamation in Scotland

It might be thought that when police constable Leslie Fraser was awarded £5,000 damages in the Court of Session in 1990, after being defamed by a man who claimed he had been arrested because he was coloured and a Justice of the Peace, the sum involved was large. However, compared to the libel damages awarded by an English jury of £1.5 million to Lord Aldington or the £60,000 to the Yorkshire Ripper's wife Sonia Sutcliffe in her libel suit against *Private Eye* – where the High Court jury had initially awarded her £600,000 – awards in the Scottish courts are a mere fraction of what the English courts have awarded in the past.[101]

Until PC Fraser's case, there had only been four reported cases of defamation since 1950 in Scotland, the highest award being that to Sam McCluskie of the National Union of Seamen (NUS) of £7,500 in 1988 in a case involving defamatory letters sent to Michael Foot MP. Lord Murray, who sat in judgment, thought that this was a serious case of defamation and would have assessed damages at £10,000 had it not been for mitigating factors, such as the limited circulation of the letters and the fact that Mr McCluskie had been elected as general secretary of the NUS in the interim.

Another exceptionally high award of £302,000 was awarded in 1978, a case involving Capital Life Assurance Society Ltd and the publishers of the Scottish *Sunday Mail*. The loss of profit calculations by the company suffered due to the defamatory publication made up the high award of damages.

What are the reasons for the discrepancy in libel damages between the Scottish and the English courts? Are Scots more robust in their feelings and less affronted by libellous publications or slanderous comments? The two main reasons the Scots law towards damages in general and the almost total absence of a jury in defamation cases.

While some areas of Scottish jurisprudence clearly derived from the civil Roman law tradition (or Canon law), the tort (or *delict*) of defamation cannot be readily attributed to the differences in the sources of the two systems.[102] As far as the delict of defamation is concerned,

98 Ibid., pp. 299–300.
99 See: Barnum (2006).
100 See: Nokes (1928), p. 103.
101 See: *Sutcliffe v Pressdram Ltd.* [1991] 1 QB 153.
102 For a historical overview, see: Normand (1938), pp. 327–338.

Scots law is not substantially different from English (and Welsh) law. Nor can it be said that the seventeenth-century institutional writer Viscount Stair contributed much information in this area of Scots law.[103]

In a short passage in his *Institutions of the Law of Scotland* (1681) on 'defamation', Stair simply notes that English law is identical to the law of Scotland in so far as claims for damages for defamation are concerned with some minor procedural differences. He writes that such actions:

> . . . upon injurious words, as they relate to damage in means, are frequent and curious among the English, but with us there is little of it accustomed to be pursued, though we own the same grounds, and would proceed to the same effects with them, if questioned.[104]

There are, however, some distinctive features which differ between the two jurisdictions. In English law, a distinction is made between defamation in permanent form (libel) and not in permanent form (slander). This distinction is not made in Scotland. In Scots law, 'defamation' is a separate delict amounting to 'verbal injury' or '*convicium*'. The pursuer's claim is largely of the nature of *solatium* for hurt feelings or an award of damages for the loss proved or presumed from a reputation unjustly attacked. Scottish judges find it difficult to put a precise figure on an injured reputation or hurt feelings and they have little in the way of precedent to guide them – circumstances which might be taken into account in order to assess the seriousness of the defamation both of itself and in relation to the defender. Allegations of drunkenness made about a minister or of dishonesty made about a solicitor would be treated more seriously than if the same statement was made about an ordinary member of the public.

See Chapter 1.5 → There is also a separate delict of 'invasion of privacy' linked to Article 8 of the **European Convention**, in which the making of a statement may give rise to liability. Neither of these delicts comes under the general heading of 'defamation'.

Jury trials in Scottish defamation cases are extremely rare, brought about by changes made by the **Evidence (Scotland) Act of 1866** (still in force today), which makes judge-alone trials possible if 'special cause' can be shown.[105] Though 'special cause' is not defined in either common law or statute, it is generally assumed that it means 'special circumstances' depending on each individual case (see below 3.6).

Once a Scottish court holds the words to be capable of bearing a defamatory meaning, the following are presumed:

1.   that the words are false;
2.   that the words are spoken with intent to injure; and
3.   that the pursuer has suffered some form of material injury which must result in financial compensation being due from the defender.

Most importantly, there is a reverse onus (the same as in England): that is, it is up to the defender to prove his case if the defence is based on *veritas* (justification). The pursuer in a Scottish defamation action enjoys the same advantage as his English counterpart. Although Scottish judges have largely followed English precedent in the law of defamation, there are certain procedural differences. The main one is that there is no jury, which many Scottish lawyers regard as an advantage compared with 'libel' juries south of the border, who have repeatedly allowed substantial punitive awards of

---

103 See: Smartt (2006) pp. 231–71.
104 See: Stair, Viscount – The Stair Society (1981), Chapter I, ix, p. 4.
105 Non-jury trials in defamation actions equally take place in England and Wales, determined by the amount of damages claimed. The venue will then be the county court for claims less than £10,000. See also proposals in Lord Lester's Defamation Bill to abolish 'libel juries'.

damages as in the 'Elton John'[106] or 'Esther Rantzen'[107] cases. Contrary to English and Welsh jurisdiction, conditional fee arrangements (CFA – 'no win, no fee') are not available in Scotland. Neither is summary disposal. The remedies which can be sought usually amount to damages and injunction (see below 3.5.1).

In cases where publication has been with malice, aggravated damages will be awarded if the case is proved. Even if the statement is truthful but designed to injure the claimant out of malice, an action can be brought when a statement is communicated; but only to the person defamed. This action includes injury to the feelings of the person defamed as well as injury to reputation. The pursuer of such a 'personal injury' claim cannot take advantage of the Court of Session procedure afforded to accident cases, for example.[108] The Scottish courts regard money damages as the remedy for a wrong done. Damages are always to compensate, never to punish. As Lord Neaves remarked in 1874:

> . . . money is the universal solvent; everything can be turned into money that is either a gain or a loss.

In 1908, Lord President Dunedin reviewed the question of punitive or exemplary damages and could find no authority for them in the law of Scotland. In fact, he felt that the heading of 'reparation' under which the matter is treated in the textbooks excluded the very idea of exemplary damages. When the argument was again raised in a defamation case sixty years later, Lord Justice Clerk Grant held that the fact that a libel was actuated by malice was not enough to entitle the pursuer to greater damages.

In *Baigent v BBC* (1999),[109] temporary Judge Coutts QC awarded exceptionally high damages. The case concerned a television programme which alleged that the owners of a nursing home were operating 'a callous and uncaring regime'. Mrs Baigent was awarded £60,000, Mr Baigent £50,000 and each of the three Baigent children £20,000 (upheld on appeal). The Baigent case probably marked the turning point when the Scottish courts began to award similarly high damages to the English courts. Coutts J stressed, that damages in Scottish libel actions are compensatory rather than punitive. Similarly high awards, each of £60,000, were made in *Clinton v News Group Newspapers Ltd* (1999)[110] and *Wray v Associated Newspapers Ltd* (2000).[111]

Another major difference is the limitation period afforded to a pursuer in Scots law, which makes litigation in the Scottish courts more attractive to litigants. Section 17 of the **Prescription and Limitation Act (Scotland) 1973** grants a litigant three years in which to raise proceedings (compared to the one-year time limit in England and Wales). While Art 6 ECHR permits access to a court, that right is not absolute and the granting of an award of caution is a permissible limitation to that right (see: *Monarch Energy Ltd v Powergen Retail Ltd* (2006)[112]).

So-called 'serial litigant' Terence Patrick Ewing took advantage of Scottish legislation when he sued in both the delict of 'personal injury' and 'injury to privacy'. However, judging that Mr Ewing was a 'vexatious litigant', the Edinburgh High Court of Sessions took the unprecedented step of merely granting the pursuer a motion for caution in the sum of £15,000. In *Ewing v Times Newspapers Ltd* (2008),[113] Lord Brodie additionally refused leave to reclaim any damages at a later hearing (though it is understood that Mr Ewing marked an appeal). The pursuer, Mr Ewing, co-founder of

---

106 *John v Mirror Group Newspapers Ltd.* [1997] QB 586.
107 *Rantzen v Mirror Group Newspapers (1986) Ltd.* [1994] QB 670.
108 Practice Note No 2 of 2003 explaining rule 43.1 of the Rules of the Court of Session 1994.
109 [1999] SCLR 787.
110 [1999] SC 367.
111 [2000] SLT 869.
112 [2006] SLT 743.
113 [2008] CSOH 169. Outer House, Court of Session, Edinburgh.

the Euston Trust, whose members travel around the UK to make objections to planning applications, filed a 'defamation' claim against the Scottish edition of the *Sunday Times* in respect of an online article of 11 February 2007, entitled 'Heritage Fakers Hold Builders to Ransom', in which investigative journalists Daniel Foggo and Robert Booth had claimed to have exposed Mr Ewing as a fraudster; and also of having considerable debts from statutory demands for payment of fines. The publication in question had been downloaded by Mr Ewing's companion at the Edinburgh City Library.[114]

Mr Ewing sued for defamation, claiming, *inter alia*, breach of data protection, invasion of his privacy and harassment as well as breach of confidence. The court held that there was a 'stateable case' on his pleadings, confined the pursuer's damages to a claim that that would not be 'substantial' because his case did not have 'serious merits' and was an 'artificial litigation,'[115] based on Lord Donaldson's ruling in *Henry J Garratt & Co v Ewing* (1991).[116] One crucial factor for the court's decision was that the pursuer had made 'at least 25 vexatious claims . . . none of this bodes well for the manner in which he is likely to conduct this action in a jurisdiction'[117] (see also: *Rush v Fife Regional Council* (1985)[118]).

Henderson (2009) argues that it would be wrong to presume that the finding in the *Ewing* claim (including privacy) was not stateable, as disclosing any emerging principle of the approach that the Scots courts will take to such actions.[119] Firstly there was an absence of any expectation of privacy on the part of the pursuer and secondly the context of the libel complaint had to be taken into account in that Mr Ewing had simply supplied a photocopy of the cases cited, where the court held that the pursuer 'did not set out in any comprehensive way in his pleadings the basis upon which he avers that delictual liability has been incurred'.[120]

The 'Frances Curran'[121] case (below) was seen as a major victory for press freedom and equally a resounding result for the *Reynolds* qualified privilege defence, ensuring that all Scottish newspapers could continue to report fearlessly. Mrs Justice Wise QC held that the focus of the 'eye-catching' article and photograph was on the leadership of a political party and the ability or inability of some of its members to work with each other. Accordingly she did not consider that this was an attack on the private character of the pursuer, Frances Curran, but rather on her political decisions and political loyalties (see also: *McLeod v News Quest (Sunday Herald) Ltd.* (2007)[122]).

❖ **KEY CASE**　　　*Frances Curran v Scottish Daily Record* (2010)

Facts:

The pursuer, Frances Curran,[123] was a member of the Scottish Socialist Party (SSP) and Member of the Scottish Parliament (MSP); the defenders the publishers of the *Daily Record*. On 7 August 2006 the defenders published a four-page article based on an interview with Tommy Sheridan,[124] in which certain remarks were made about the pursuer and three other MSPs, Colin Fox, Rosie Kane and Carolyn Leckie, accompanied by

---

114　Ibid., at paras 3 and 21.
115　Ibid., at para 25.
116　[1991] 1 WLR 1356 at 1357E (Lord Donaldson MR).
117　[2008] CSOH at para. 29 (Lord Brodie).
118　[1985] SLT 451 (Lord Wheatley).
119　Source: Henderson (2009).
120　[2008] CSOH 169 at para 28 (Lord Brodie).
121　*Curran (Frances) v Scottish Daily Record, Sunday Mail Ltd.* [2010] (A 952/08) CSOH 44 (2010 WL 902938) Outer House, Court of Session of 26 March 2010.
122　[2007] SCLR 555.
123　Frances Curran (born 21 May 1961 in Glasgow) is joint national spokesperson of the Scottish Socialist Party. She was MSP for West Scotland in 2003–7 and lost in the July 2008 Glasgow East by-election.
124　Tommy Sheridan MSP, also a member of the SSP, won a libel action against the *News of the World* on 4 August 2006 when the jury returned their verdict, finding in favour of Mr Sheridan, awarding him damages of £200,000.

photographs. The headline on the front page of the *Daily Record* read: 'I'LL DESTROY THE SCABS WHO TRIED TO RUIN ME: Tommy vows to win back leadership of Scottish Socialists.' The defenders sought dismissal of the action on the basis that no relevant case of defamation was made out in the pursuer's pleadings and an *esto* position that, were the action to proceed to proof before answer, deletions would require to be made.

It was submitted on behalf of the defenders that criticism by an MSP of another MSP did not amount to defamation because of the permitted latitude in criticizing those who hold public office. Further, it was submitted that the comments made in the article were protected by the *Reynolds* qualified privilege and that the pursuer would require to aver malice, which she had not done.

Counsel for the defenders submitted that the article be looked at as a whole, representing an attack on the public as well as the political activities of the pursuer and her colleagues and that the term 'scab' in the article referred to her being a 'political scab'.

Counsel for Ms Curran submitted that the case should be sent to proof and submitted that the tenor of the article was that she was guilty of dishonest conduct with base motives and went beyond fair criticism of a holder of a public office.

Opinion:

Temporary Judge Mrs Morag Wise QC dismissed the action. She considered whether the article, taken as a whole, would tend to lower the pursuer in the estimation of right-thinking members of society generally, or be likely to affect her adversely in the estimation of reasonable people generally. She ruled:

> . . . I do not consider that it would have that effect. Right thinking members of society are well able to read an article of this sort and see it as no more than a robust criticism of the pursuer as a former colleague and ally of Mr Sheridan. The reference to the pursuer as a 'scab' simply has no context without the detail given of the political plot alleged by Mr Sheridan and the references to collaboration with 'the enemy' namely Newsgroup Newspapers Limited.[125]

In relation to the photograph this should not be seen in isolation but as part of the whole article, as demonstrated in *Charleston v News Group Newspapers Ltd.* (1995).[126]

In October 2010, Mr Sheridan and his wife, Gail, were on trial at the Scottish High Court, in Glasgow accused of perjury. The couple were accused of lying in court to help Mr Sheridan successfully sue the *News of the World* in 2006. The couple denied lying in court. The former Scottish Socialist Party (SSP) leader Tommy Sheridan had won £200,000 in damages after the newspaper printed allegations about his private life, claiming that he was an adulterer who had visited a swingers' club. Gail Sheridan, a star witness in the defamation case, famously told the jury that her husband would have ended up 'in the Clyde with a piece of concrete tied round him' if she thought the allegations were true. However, within weeks the Crown Office instructed Lothian and Borders Police to investigate whether any witnesses had lied and Mr and Mrs Sheridan were arrested and charged with

125 [2010] CSOH 44 at para 29 (Judge Morag Wise, QC).
126 [1995] 2 AC 65 (HL).

perjury in February 2009. The perjury trial at Glasgow's High Court proved to be one of Scotland's most high-profile courtroom sensations of the twenty-first century so far. On 23 December 2010, Tommy Sheridan was convicted of perjury. He was sentenced to three years imprisonment. His wife Gail was acquitted. Live updates on Twitter were allowed by trial judge Lord Bracadale.

Similar to its English counterpart, Scots common law development in defamation, coupled with 'privacy' challenges, is in a state of flux in that even relatively recent decisions can soon become out of date and is best illustrated with reference to cases involving photographs. This is exemplified by the fact that Scottish courts have frequently referred to the *von Hannover*[127] decision in relation to the invasion of someone's privacy when defamatory actions are being considered.

See Chapter 2.4.6 →

When the court considered privacy in the *Ewing* action it referred, inter alia, to *Reklos v Greece* (2009).[128] In this action, Greek nationals Dimitrios Reklos and Vassiliki Davourli complained initially to the Athens Court of First Instance that the actual taking of the photograph of their newborn child, Anastasios Reklos, on 31 March 1997 in a private clinic, violated Article 8 ECHR. As part of the service at the clinic, a professional photographer had taken two photographs of Anastasios shortly after his birth. The parents objected to this intrusion, especially since the photos were taken in the sterile environment of the birthing unit and without their prior consent. But the Athens court dismissed their action as unfounded; the Court of Cassation upheld the decision at first instance and the couple proceeded to the Human Rights Court.

In a Chamber judgment of the European Court of Human Rights, President Nina Vajić held that the taking of clandestine photographs and the keeping of negatives of a newborn child, without parental consent, was an infringement of Article 8 – with the special provision in this case that the photos were taken in a sterile unit to which only medical staff and patients had access (see also: *Egeland and Hanseid v Norway* (2009)[129]).

In the 'Frances Curran' case, the Edinburgh court felt that the photo shot of the Scottish MPs neither amounted to defamation nor an infringement of their privacy under Article 8 ECHR, citing the *Reklos* judgment.

3.3.5 'Artemus Jones' and unintentional libel

What happens if a journalist unintentionally refers to a fictitious name which he has made up, and there is such a person 'out there'? The question should be: did the journalist or author intend to refer to an actual individual? Or was the individual unintentionally defamed? And what if the defendant uses a fictional name and a real person of that same name claims to have been defamed?

In *Hulton v Jones* (1910),[130] the *Sunday Chronicle* had published a light-hearted sketch in 1909 about a certain 'Artemus Jones' and the tendency of 'sober' Englishmen, once abroad, to lead a 'gay' life. The sketch had the subheading:

> . . . Whist! There's Artemus Jones with a woman who is not his wife, who must be, you know –
> the other thing . . . Whist!

The fictional character was described as a Churchwarden from Peckham but unfortunately, the article was read by an actual Artemus Jones, a barrister practising on the Welsh circuit. He sued the editor of the newspaper in libel, claiming that some of his friends thought that the article referred

---

127 *von Hannover v Germany* (2005) 40 EHRR 1 (ECHR).
128 (2009) (Application No. 1234/05) ECHR of 15 January 2009.
129 (2009) (Application no. 34438/04) Strasbourg, 16 April 2009 (ECHR).
130 (1910) AC 20 (HL).

to him. After a lengthy appeal, the House of Lords awarded the claimant substantial damages, ruling that though the defendants had seemingly not intended to 'name and shame', intention was immaterial; what mattered was whether the reasonable reader thought the words within the meaning of the article referred to the claimant.

Though the classic Artemus Jones case now appears rather dated, it still sets the precedent for strict liability in defamation law, placing the burden on the publisher to ensure – as a matter of principle – that no individual suffers as a result of that publication, even if the person concerned suffers damage wholly independently of any fault on the part of the publisher. *Hulton v Jones* thus established the strict liability principle for unintentional defamation.

What about the 'lookalike situation'? Shortly after the **European Convention** had entered UK law, Morland J endeavoured to strike a balance between freedom of expression and an individual's right for the protection of his privacy when considering strict liability libel in *O'Shea v MGN* (2001).[131] In this case the claimant bore a striking resemblance to a 'Miss E', who appeared in an advertisement for a pornographic Internet Service Provider (the second defendant), who in turn had advertised in the *Sunday Mirror*. The photograph in question did not name or identify the claimant, other than by virtue of the strong resemblance between her and Miss E.

Morland J had to decide whether a photograph (of Miss E) would be recognized by those who knew the claimant and would identify her – albeit wrongly – as being the person in the photograph, which would give her the cause of action in libel; as he observed, referring inter alia to *Hulton v Jones*:

> . . . The test in law is objective. Would the ordinary reader of the advertisement, having regard to the words complained of and the photograph in the context of the advertisement as a whole and clothed with the special knowledge of the publishers, that is that the photograph was the 'spit and image' of the claimant, have reasonably concluded that the woman speaking into the telephone [in the photograph] was the claimant?[132]

Morland J concluded, after considering Article 10 ECHR, that the strict liability principle should not cover the 'lookalike' situation. To allow it to do so would be an unjustifiable interference with the vital right of freedom of expression and the democratic principle of a free press. Consequently, young Miss O'Shea may well have suffered considerable embarrassment, but the court held that she was not protected under Article 8 ECHR, nor did she win her libel action.

To be successful in a libel action, the words complained of must be interpreted in their context and the claimant is not allowed to select passages which are prima facie libellous if the passage taken as a whole is not defamatory, for example just a newspaper headline (see: *Charleston v News Group Newspapers Ltd.* (1995)[133]).

3.4 The role of malice

The case of *Joyce v Sengupta* (1993)[134] raised the question of whether a claimant who may well lose in a defamatory action can instead bring an action in the tort of malicious falsehood. A most important factor is that the historically founded criminal action of 'maliciousness' is legally aided, whereas ordinary defamation actions are not. *Joyce v Sengupta* attracted considerable public attention at the time since it involved the Princess Royal's maid, Linda Joyce, and intimate love letters written by the Queen's daughter, Princess Anne. The disclosure that Princess Anne had received personal letters

---

131 [2001] EMLR 40 (QBD).
132 Ibid., at 84 (Morland J).
133 [1995] 2 AC 65 (HL).
134 [1993] 1 WLR 337.

from Royal Navy Commander Timothy Lawrence had sparked rumours about the Princess Royal's troubled 15-year-marriage to Captain Mark Phillips.

Kim Sengupta, Chief Crime Correspondent for the *Today* newspaper, had published an article on 25 April 1989 headlined, 'Royal Maid Stole Letters', clearly referring to the claimant, Ms Joyce, and that she allegedly stole the love letters from her employer, Princess Anne. Though the article appeared grossly defamatory, Ms Joyce did not have the money 'up front' to sue in libel and legal aid was clearly not available in 'ordinary' libel actions.[135] The claimant's legal counsel, Mr Geoffrey Robertson QC and Andrew Nicol QC, advised her to make a claim in malicious falsehood for which legal aid was duly granted. But the judge at first instance struck out her claim, stating that the [initial] action had been one of libel. Counsel argued before the Court of Appeal that there was a fundamental difference. The remedy provided by law for the damage to a person's reputation was granted by common law in defamation. But Ms Joyce's case concerned 'injurious falsehood' (also referred to as 'trade libel'), in that it had caused her financial loss; furthermore, that she had not only lost her reputation, but also her employment. She had clearly suffered economic loss and was most likely not going to get another job due to lack of references.

What is the difference between ordinary libel (defamation) and malicious (injurious) falsehood? An essential feature of both torts is injury to reputation, of one kind or another. The ordinary tort of defamation is the publication of words or matter to a third person injurious to the reputation of another.[136] It is not necessary for the claimant to prove 'special damage', that is, that he has suffered real damage to his reputation as a result of the statement.

The importance of *Joyce v Sengupta* lies in the fact that it established the precedent of actions in malicious falsehood which attract legal aid – though this is somewhat restrictive. Nowadays, Ms Joyce would probably have had to go via a CFA agreement. Malicious falsehood is 'an action which involves special damage sustained by reason of speaking or publication of the slander of the claimant's title'.[137] In *Joyce v Sengupta* the 'title' concerned Linda Joyce's position of employment as a royal maid and she claimed that the article had damaged her future employment prospects. Harm must be shown to have been caused which essentially involves damage to title: 'the damage actually done is the very gist of the action.'[138]

The burden of proving or disproving malice will vary, however, from case to case, and claimant to claimant, according to the nature of the action and the nature of the malice as well as the notion of express and implied malice, which therefore leaves the matter totally open to the courts.

3.4.1 Malicious falsehood and criminal libel

The issue of malice is complex: the 'mere absence of just cause or excuse' is not of itself malice. Malice in its proper and accurate sense is a question of motive, intention, or state of mind'.[139] In *Shapiro v La Morta* (1923), Scrutton LJ observed that the terms 'malice' and 'malicious' 'have caused more confusion in English law than any judge can hope to dispel'.[140]

Malice was aptly defined by Maugham J in *Balden v Shorter* (1933) when he said:

. . . it is now apparently settled that malice in the law of slander of title and other forms of injurious falsehood means some dishonest or otherwise improper motive. A bona fide

135 Legal Aid Act 1988, Schedule 2, Part 2, para 1.
136 See: Milmo et al. (2010), p. 4.
137 *Malachy v Soper* (1836) 3 Bing NC 371 (Lord Tindall LCJ).
138 *Ratcliffe v Evans* [1892] 2 QB 531 at 532.
139 British R.T. Co. v C.R.C. [1922] 2 KB at 269 (McCardie J).
140 (1923) 40 TLR 201 at 203 (Scrutton LJ).

assertion of title, however mistaken, if made for the protection of one's own interest or some other purpose, is not malicious.[141]

Part of the difficulty lies in the fact that the law distinguishes between actual (or express) malice and presumed malice. Actual malice is referred to as 'malice in fact', as opposed to presumed malice which is 'malice in law'. Actual malice amounts to maliciousness including ill-feeling and a desire to cause harm. Presumed malice can simply be a publication without lawful excuse, inferred malice either from the words used or from evidence of the circumstances which prompted the words. The courts have attempted to define actions of 'malice' though 'express malice' is still difficult to define in certain circumstances. What is important is that damages need to be quantified and the claimant has to prove economic (financial) loss, as was proved in the 'Stephane Grappelli' case.

In *Grappelli v Derek Block*,[142] the claimants were Stephane Grappelli, an internationally famous jazz violinist, and William Charles Disley ('Diz' Dizley), a professional guitarist and leader of the Grappelli Jazz Trio. The defendants Derek Block (Holdings) Ltd were concert promoters who had purported to arrange concerts for the claimants around June 1976 at, inter alia, Tameside, near Manchester, on 26 November 1976 and Milton Keynes on 4 December 1976. On 21 September 1976, the defendants told Tameside and Milton Keynes concert hall managers that the claimants' concerts had been cancelled because Mr Grappelli was 'very seriously ill in Paris' and it would be surprising 'if he ever toured again'. The claimants said that the defendants acted without their authority and Mr Grappelli stated that the statement about him was false, claiming damages for libel and slander, alleging that the facts gave rise to an innuendo that the claimants had given a reason for cancelling the concerts which they knew to be false. Though this statement was not in itself defamatory – as it was not damaging to Mr Grappelli's reputation to say that he was ill – this particular announcement was clearly damaging to Mr Grappelli's future career and success (see also: *Tolley v JS Fry & Sons Ltd* (1931)[143]). The court dismissed the defamation action when Lord Denning MR stated that the paragraphs alleging libel and slander could not stand, advising the claimants to file a new action relying on injurious falsehood and maliciousness. The claimants were eventually successful in their malicious falsehood action after they had provided the court with evidence of financial loss by way of a statement of quantum of damages and evidence of express malice.[144]

The controversy in the meaning of express or implied malice led Professor Loveland (1998) to observe that malice 'has become an horrendously imprecise facet of English defamation law'.[145] Loveland (2000) went on to criticize the application of the test for malice in English political libel cases because it failed to emphasize the electorate's entitlement to know the truth about its elected representatives, and he contrasted English law unfavourably with the US position.[146]

In summary, an action in malicious falsehood for a publication or statement in fact must be injurious to the character of another and must require proof of economic loss. It is only then that the law will consider the publication 'malicious' and the courts will interpret the meaning of 'malice' narrowly.[147] This should not be confused with a 'fair comment' defence where the courts have held that the presence of an ulterior motive – such as settling an old score or dislike – will not necessarily amount to malice if the opinion was honestly held. This defence can work where the allegedly libellous comments are statements of opinion rather than statements of fact.

---

141 [1933] Ch 427 at 430 (Maugham J).
142 *Grappelli v Derek Block* (Holdings) Ltd. [1981] 1 WLR 822.
143 [1931] AC 333 (HL).
144 Referring inter alia to *Wright v Woodgate* (1835) 2 CR M & R 573 at 577.
145 Loveland (1998), p. 637.
146 See: Loveland (2000).
147 For further discussion see: Mitchell (1999).

In *Branson v Bower* (2001),[148] the court provided an interesting perspective on one such defence, that of 'fair comment on a matter of public interest'. The case concerned Sir Richard Branson's allegation that he had been libelled by an article carried in the *Evening Standard* in December 1999. The article had suggested, among other things, that Sir Richard's bid to run the National Lottery was motivated by financial self-interest and the chance of free publicity for the Virgin brand. Sir Richard sued in defamation and the article's author, Tom Bower, claimed the defence of 'fair comment'. The critical issue before the court was the meaning of 'fair comment'. Sir Richard's lawyers argued that, in order for opinion to be 'fair comment', those views must satisfy a 'fairness' test: could a 'fair-minded man' honestly hold those views? If not, it was claimed, the defence should fail. Mr Bower argued on the other hand that the test was simply whether the stated opinions were honestly held.

The court decided that there was no case to answer for a 'fairness test' since the 'fair comment' defence already existed in common law to protect expressions of *genuine* opinion on matters of public interest. Most importantly, the defence existed to protect freedom to comment on public events. However, the court stressed that the 'fair comment' defence (in the public interest) will not succeed if the commentator's opinions are based on an inaccurate or distorted picture. Furthermore, the opinions must be honestly held. The test is an objective test and does not mean that the views must be fair. It simply means that 'fair comment' will not protect entirely unjustifiable or bizarre opinions, which anyone knowing the facts could not honestly hold. In the 'Richard Branson' case the court found that the opinions were clearly capable of being honestly held. Sir Richard could still succeed if he could establish that Mr Bower did not in fact honestly hold the views which he had expressed.

3.5 Remedies and damages

On 16 December 2009, Barry George accepted an undisclosed six-figure sum in libel damages and an apology from the *Sun* and the *News of the World* newspapers over a series of articles suggesting that he was responsible for the murder of TV presenter Jill Dando and was a stalker.[149] Following his acquittal at a retrial on 1 August 2008, the *Sun* published an article on 2 August about his retrial, describing a number of matters that had been kept from the jury. The *Sun* and *News of the World* also made various allegations between 1 August and 20 November 2008 that Mr George had become obsessed with the Sky News presenter Kay Burley and had also pestered Pam Wright, the fiancée of convicted 'Ipswich strangler' Steve Wright. Counsel for Mr George, Gordon Bishop QC, argued before Eady J that the tabloids alleged that there were grounds to suspect Barry George of the murder of Jill Dando despite his acquittal.

In addition to an action in defamation, there exists the 'cheaper' route via the Press Complaints Commission (PCC) and its Code of Practice for the print press (and online editions) and in terms of broadcast media under s. 319 of the **Communications Act 2003**, where there exists the obligation to correct inaccurate and misleading material. The PCC has no power to award monetary compensation.

See Chapter
10.3.3 →

---

148 [2001] EWCA Civ 791.
149 Barry George was first convicted in 2001 at the Old Bailey of shooting 37-year-old BBC *Crimewatch* and news presenter Miss Jill Dando on her doorstep on 26 April 1999. After two appeals, a retrial was ordered based on the unreliable evidence of the gunshot residue said to have been found on Mr George's clothing.

3.5.1 Extortionate libel damages

The 'Esther Rantzen' case[150] can be regarded as an illustration where a libel jury awarded exorbitant damages;[151] the judge took the unprecedented step of reducing the damages, stating that damages in defamatory actions should be interpreted in a manner consistent with the fundamental freedom of expression within the **European Convention**, though Article 10 at that time was not yet incorporated into UK law.

Popular TV presenter Esther Rantzen, who fronted the BBC consumer programme *That's Life* from 1973 to 1994,[152] sued the Mirror group for a defamatory article in the *People* newspaper that alleged that she had protected a child abuser by keeping secret the fact that he was an abuser. The 'red top' alleged that Ms Rantzen had put children at risk and had been insincere and hypocritical. The newspaper publishers pleaded justification as a defence, but were found guilty of libel. The jury made an award of £250,000 and the Mirror Group appealed, seeking a reduction in the level of damages. Under the provisions of section 8 of the **Courts and Legal Services Act 1990**, the Court of Appeal allowed the appeal and reduced the award to £110,000.

Section 8 of the **Courts and Legal Services Act 1990** permits jury awards to be quashed and the Ester Rantzen case was such an example. The Court of Appeal commented that the award bore no relation to the damage suffered by Ms Rantzen and was grossly excessive compared with awards in personal injury cases. Although it would not be right for juries to be referred to awards made in other cases, they should be told to consider the purchasing power of any award they might be minded to make.

More or less at the same time as Esther Rantzen's action, pop star Sir Elton John was initially awarded £350,000 by a libel jury against the *Sunday Mirror*.[153] The pop star's claims were over false allegations that he suffered from a bizarre eating disorder, headlined on 27 December 1992: 'Elton's Diet of Death'. Lord Williams QC, counsel for Mirror Group Newspapers, argued that the article, though inaccurate, was not libellous and that people would think none the worse of the pop star after reading it. When Sir Elton won his action in the High Court, Drake J asked the jury to 'keep a sense of proportion' in assessing damages and to resist the temptation to put 'a nought or two on the end' of the award. When the jury awarded £350,000 in damages, Mr Justice Drake reasoned that a personal injury award to a person who had lost an eye would only amount to around £20,000 compensation. The Court of Appeal reduced the amount of damages to £75,000.

Sir Elton John's initial jury award was the eighth largest libel settlement in the British 'libel top ten', with the highest award of £1.5m at that time given to Lord Aldington over false allegations made by Count Nikolai Tolstoy over the deaths of Cossacks in 1945. The essence of the libel in *Tolstoy-Miloslavsky v Aldington* (1995)[154] was that Lord Aldington was a major war criminal responsible for the massacre of 70,000 people in May 1945. After a two-month trial, Lord Aldington's reputation was vindicated, but in financial terms it was a Pyrrhic victory: of the two defendants, Nigel Watts had to pay £10,000 and Count Tolstoy, who had declared himself bankrupt, paid nothing. Count Tolstoy had sought to set aside the libel judgment on grounds of fraud and perjury.

Sir Elton John subsequently lost a libel action in December 2008 and the singer was refused leave to appeal by Mr Justice Tugendhat. This time Sir Elton had brought the action against the *Guardian*, following the publication in its *Weekend* magazine in July 2008 of a spoof diary written by Marina Hyde, entitled 'A peek at the diary of Sir Elton John'. This recorded his fictional thoughts

---

150 *Rantzen v Mirror Group Newspapers Ltd.* [1994] QB 670.
151 Section 8 of the Courts and Legal Services Act 1990.
152 Following the inclusion of some child protection items on the programme, Rantzen founded Britain's telephone helpline for children, ChildLine.
153 *John v Mirror Group Newspapers Ltd.* [1997] QB 586.
154 *Tolstoy-Miloslavsky v Aldington* [1996] Court of Appeal (Lord Justice Rose, Lord Justice Roch and Lord Justice Ward) 13 December 1995 (unreported).

about his annual 'White Tie and Tiara Ball', which raised millions of pounds for the Elton John Aids Foundation. The singer, represented by solicitors Carter-Ruck, claimed that the article suggested that Sir Elton's commitment to the charity is so insincere that he hosts the ball knowing that only a small proportion of the money raised will go to the charity, and that he uses the event 'as an occasion for meeting celebrities and self-promotion'. Sir Elton suggested that Hyde had acted maliciously in the 'diary'. The Guardian argued that no reasonable reader would have believed that the words were meant to be taken at face value. The judge agreed and ruled that the singer's sense of humour failure over a satirical piece by a Guardian columnist was 'a tantrum too far' and that 'irony' and 'teasing' did not amount to defamation.

This ruling was important for cartoonists and satirical sketch writers and, in the words of Mr Justice Tugendhat in his 17-page judgment, the opinion that irony is a figure of speech in which the intended meaning is the opposite of that expressed by the words used and that no reasonable reader could be misled by it. Media lawyer Mark Stephens called the ruling 'significant', stating that 'what Tugendhat has done is move us closer to the US system where you can't get damages for satire and humour, except in the most exceptional cases'.[155]

Libel cases are notoriously expensive and − in spite of the Human Rights Court ruling in 'McLibel' in 2005[156] that certain defendants in defamation cases ought to qualify for legal aid − the law in this respect has not changed. Some claimants have thought they warrant higher libel damages than anticipated. In 1998, Coronation Street star William Roache − who plays Ken Barlow − sued his law firm Peter Carter-Ruck & Partners for negligence over its handling of his libel action against the Sun in 1992.[157] Mr Roache won his action over a claim in November 1990 that he was as boring as his screen character and hated by his television colleagues. The defendants (News Group Newspapers Ltd, editor Kelvin Mackenzie and freelance journalist Ken Irwin) pleaded fair comment and, to a limited extent, justification. They paid first £25,000 and then a further £25,000 into court, but the claimant did not accept it because − he argued − the £50,000 would not cover his six-figure court costs. He had expected at least £100,000. The appeal judge looked closely at the facts of the 'Bill Roache' case and asked: 'Who, as a matter of substance and reality, has won? Has the plaintiff won anything of value which he could not have won without fighting the action through to the finish? Has the defendant substantially denied the plaintiff the prize which the plaintiff fought the action to win?'

Sir Thomas Bingham MR said two important principles were relevant here. The first was that costs normally followed the event, the winner recovering his costs from the loser. The second was that where a plaintiff claimed a financial remedy and the defendant paid into a court a sum, not accepted by the plaintiff, equal to or greater than the plaintiff recovered in the action, the plaintiff should pay the defendant's costs from the date of payment in. Consequently, the Court of Appeal allowed the defendant newspaper's appeal and Mr Roache had subsequently to declare himself bankrupt in 1999 with debts of around £300,000 after suing the Sun for libel and later suing his lawyers Peter Carter-Ruck.

Another libel action which practically bankrupted a claimant concerned the self-professed Third Reich specialist David Irving, who has consistently denied the Holocaust. In Irving v Penguin Books Ltd and Deborah Lipstadt (1996),[158] David Irving lost his lengthy libel action against American academic Deborah Lipstadt and her publishers Penguin. Lipstadt said in her 1994 book that Irving had misinterpreted historical evidence to minimize Hitler's culpability in the Holocaust.[159]

---

155 Source: 'A victory for irony as Elton John loses Guardian libel case', The Guardian, 13 December 2008.
156 Steel and Morris v United Kingdom [2005] ECHR (Application no. 68416/01); judgment of 15 February 2005.
157 See: Roache v Newsgroup Newspapers Ltd [1998] EMLR 161.
158 (1996) judgment of 11 April 2000 (QBD) (unreported).
159 See: Lipstadt (1994).

Gray J – sitting without a jury – ruled that Mr Irving was 'an active Holocaust denier, anti-Semitic and racist' who had 'distorted historical data to suit his own ideological agenda'.[160]

3.5.2 The offer of amends: has the Defamation Act 1996 limited the amount of damages?

When Parliament passed the **Defamation Act 1996**, its principal aim was to speed up the civil justice system in this area of law and to enable parties in defamation proceedings to achieve a relatively speedy and inexpensive disposal of a complaint of injury of reputation. The 'offer of amends' regime was part of this philosophy, usually accompanied by an apology and a withdrawal of the defamatory publication or statement. Thereafter, should a claimant still proceed with his action to a full trial, he must demonstrate that he has engaged fully with the regime as laid down by statute.

The sole defence of an 'offer of amends' was introduced by way of sections 2–4 of the **Defamation Act 1996** (DA). This offers a flexible defence to a defendant who has no other effective justification. It involves an admission of liability, an apology and usually the payment of damages. Sections 2–4 DA provide a defendant with an offer of amends and, if this is accepted and duly performed, then precludes the claimant bringing any further proceedings for defamation and terminates the proceedings. Actual as opposed to constructive knowledge is required as defined by Lord Diplock in *Horrocks v Lowe* (1975)[161] (see also: *Milne v Express Newspapers* (2005)[162]). Section 2 DA ('offer to make amends') reads:

(1)   A person who has published a statement alleged to be defamatory of another may offer to make amends under this section.

(2)   The offer may be in relation to the statement generally or in relation to a specific defamatory meaning which the person making the offer accepts that the statement conveys ('a qualified offer').

(3)   An offer to make amends –

    (a)   must be in writing,

    (b)   must be expressed to be an offer to make amends under section 2 of the Defamation Act 1996, and

    (c)   must state whether it is a qualified offer and, if so, set out the defamatory meaning in relation to which it is made.

There are three key elements outlined in section 2(4) DA:

(a)   to make a suitable correction of the statement complained of and a sufficient apology to the aggrieved party;

(b)   to publish the correction and apology in a manner that is reasonable and practicable in the circumstances; and

(c)   to pay to the aggrieved party such compensation (if any), and such costs, as may be agreed or determined to be payable.

---

160 Lipstadt (2006), quoting Gray J at p. 214.
161 [1975] AC 135 (Lord Diplock).
162 [2005] 1 All ER 1021.

The **Defamation Act 1996** also introduced a summary procedure for claims of less than £10,000 to be heard by a judge alone.[163] For actions involving claims in excess of £10,000, defamation hearings can still take place with a jury which decides the award of damages.[164]

Complexities can arise where there are joint defendants and where one makes an offer and the other does not (see: *Veliu v Mazrekaj* (2007)[165]). The 1996 Act also provided a defence in that, under s. 1 DA, a mere distributor of a book, newspaper, magazine, etc., may have a defence of *innocent dissemination* if he was not the author, editor or commercial publisher; took reasonable care in relation to the publication; and did not know and had no reason to know of its defamatory contents.

In 2004, *Auf Wiedersehen Pet* star Jimmy Nail won £37,500 libel damages over allegations about his sexual behaviour, greed and 'prima donna tendencies'.[166] Mr Nail had sued over an article in the *News Of The World* in May 2002, and a 1998 biography of him by Geraint Jones, entitled *Nailed*, published by Harper Collins. In both cases, unqualified offers of amends had been made and accepted, involving apologies which acceded that the material complained of was defamatory and untrue. Mr Justice Eady, sitting without a jury, observed at first instance:

> . . . the very adoption of the [offer of amends] procedure has therefore a major deflationary effect upon the appropriate level of compensation. This is for two reasons. From the defendant's perspective he is behaving reasonably. He puts his hands up, and accepts that he has to make amends for his wrongdoing. As to the claimant, the stress of litigation has from that moment at least been significantly reduced. On the whole, however, once the defendant has decided to go down this route, it would make sense to adopt a conciliatory approach and work towards genuine compromise over matters such as the terms of the apology or the level of compensation.'[167]

Similar to Bill Roache (above), the actor and singer-songwriter Jimmy Nail, facing estimated court costs of around £200,000, appealed against the libel award made by the court on 20 December 2004. Nail also lost his appeal. Moreover, the court reduced the damages award to £30,000, leaving him with an enormous bill.

It is important to note that the court now awards significant discounts to defendants – of up to 50 per cent in damages – if they make a full and rapid apology and offer of amends (see: *Campbell-James v Guardian Media Group* (2005)[168]).

Tom Crone, legal manager at the *News of the World*, said after Nail's appeal hearing:

> . . . this ruling sends a robust and significant signal. The *News of the World* will not be intimidated by either greedy litigants or their legal advisers. The *News of the World* offered Mr Jimmy Nail a full apology and a substantial sum of money in compensation, which he rejected. His response was to demand a sum five times greater than the court deemed appropriate. The court has shown its distaste for avaricious claimants who might be tempted to follow in Mr Nail's footsteps. Libel damages are designed to correct a wrong. They are not a guarantee to a one-way road to riches as the courts have increasingly recognized in recent years.[169]

---

163 ss. 8–10 DA 1996.
164 Unless the parties waive their right under s. 69 Senior Courts Act 1981 (Supreme Court Act 1981).
165 [2007] 1 WLR 495.
166 *Nail v News Group Newspapers Ltd. and others* [2005] EMLR 12.
167 Ibid., at para 35 (Eady J).
168 [2005] EMLR 24, where Eady J gave a discount of 40 per cent in spite of the fact there was no evidence of conciliation.
169 Quoted by Jenny Booth in: 'Jimmy Nail faces huge legal bill after losing his appeal over libel damages', *The Times*, 20 December 2004.

But what happens if the defendant has made an offer of amends under the **Defamation Act 1996** – which is accepted – and the defendant later wishes to change the offer? In *Warren v Random House* (2009)[170], boxing promoter Frank Warren claimed damages for libel in respect of three passages in a book published by Random House. The book was the autobiographical account by the boxer Ricky Hatton. One of the passages claimed that Warren had dishonestly conned the boxer Vince Phillips into accepting a pitiful fee for putting his life at risk by fighting Ricky Hatton, by lying to him that this was all that could be paid because American TV did not want to televise the fight ('the Phillips allegation').

Random House marketed and sold the book containing the 'Phillips allegation' over a period of several months, including the Christmas period in 2006. Thirty seven thousand copies of the book were sold – most of them *after* the complaint had been made by Mr Warren. On 7 March 2007, the publishers (Random) made an offer of amends (read out in open court) under ss. 2–4 DA which was duly accepted by the claimant. But before the court determined the level of compensation, Random House tried to withdraw the offer, trying to seek a plea of justification instead. The judge refused on the following grounds:

(i)   that, although the court had a residual discretion to allow a defendant to withdraw an offer of amends made, there were no exceptional circumstances in the present case and Random had made its offer of amends voluntarily;

ii)   that the claimant had duly accepted the offer;

iii)   the parties had ample time of freedom of expression under Article 10 ECHR.

In any case, there was nothing that would stop Random publishers choosing to plead justification in any subsequent action.

In *Tesco Stores Ltd v Guardian News & Media Ltd* (2009),[171] Eady J held that it was not possible for a claimant to elect neither to accept nor to reject an offer of amends indefinitely; to do so would undermine the statutory provision under the **Defamation Act 1996**, thereby making a nonsense of Parliament's intention to introduce the offer of amends. Following *The Guardian's* publication of defamatory statements, alleging that the Tesco supermarket chain had engaged in a scheme designed to avoid corporation tax, Tesco instigated a libel action against the *Guardian* newspaper group for a claim in malicious falsehood. *The Guardian* admitted the falsehood of its principal allegation, namely that the particular scheme in question did not involve the avoidance of corporation tax; the newspaper also admitted that the meanings pleaded by the supermarket corporation were defamatory. *The Guardian* published a retraction statement stating that Tesco had not been involved in the avoidance of corporation tax but rather an avoidance of stamp duty land tax. This statement was served 21 minutes after making an offer of amends pursuant to s. 2 DA. But Tesco neither accepted nor rejected that offer, arguing that, even if it accepted the offer of amends and obtained an apology and damages under the statutory scheme, it could go on and obtain a decision on the malicious falsehood issue so as to have the court's finding in relation to malice. Eady J stated that it would make a nonsense of the underlying policy of the DA; in any case, the claimant could still file a separate action in 'malice'. Therefore, the supermarket chain had to accept the offer of amends or else take on the risk of overcoming the statutory defence by proving malice at trial. Accordingly, the malicious falsehood claim was stayed.

In the high-profile 'Trafigura' case,[172] the BBC made a settlement on 17 December 2009 before Mr Justice Eady in a libel action which had been brought by the oil trading company

---

170 [2009] QB 600; [2008] EWCA Civ 834 (CA Civ Div).
171 [2009] EMLR 5 (Eady J) (QBD).
172 *Trafigura Limited v British Broadcasting Corporation* (2009) QBD 15 May 2009. Claim No: HQ09X02050. Unreported.

Trafigura. Trafigura, it was alleged, made thousands of people ill in Ivory Coast when it arranged to dump toxic oil waste there. The company sued BBC *Newsnight* for libel after it was criticized on the programme. It was one of a series of legal threats and actions brought by 'libel' solicitors, Carter-Ruck on behalf of Trafigura against the media in several countries. Carter-Ruck tried to suppress media reports by obtaining a superinjunction against *The Guardian* on 11 September 2009. Though the 'gagging order' was directed at *The Guardian*, this injunction 'against the world' meant that anyone aware of the order would be in breach of it if any reporting went ahead.

The subject of the superinjunction was published via Twitter and Wikileaks on 12 October 2009, reflecting outrage that Trafigura's lawyers had tried to suppress a question in the House of Commons by Paul Farrelly MP on the subject. Mr Farrelly's question concerned the effectiveness of legislation in relation to allegations of the illegal dumping of toxic waste by Trafigura. But the superinjunction prevented *The Guardian* and all other media from identifying the MP, what the question in Parliament was, which minister might answer it and where the question was to be found. All that could be reported was that the case involved the London libel lawyers Peter Carter-Ruck.[173] This had a potential constitutional impact since it is crucial to the public interest to know what is being said and done in Parliament. On 13 October 2009, Carter-Ruck conceded and dropped the injunction, allowing publication of a scientific report obtained by *The Guardian* about the potential health dangers of the waste.[174]

As far as BBC *Newsnight* was concerned, its edition of 13 May 2009 had focused on the discharging of gasoline waste by Trafigura in Abidjan in Ivory Coast in August 2006 which was subsequently dumped by a local company. This was also published on the BBC news website. The report stated that Trafigura's actions had caused deaths, miscarriages, serious injuries and sickness with long-term chronic effects. In September 2009, Trafigura's lawyers, at the time Leigh Day, commenced libel proceedings against the BBC, claiming that the oil traders had been wrongly accused of causing deaths and not just sickness. After lengthy negotiations with Trafigura's Director, Eric de Turckheim, in December 2009, the BBC agreed to apologize for the *Newsnight* programme, pay £25,000 to a charity and withdraw any allegation that Trafigura's toxic waste dumped in West Africa had caused deaths. The apology statement as part of the 'offer of amends', endorsed by Mister Justice MacDuff – the judge who had been due to hear the trial – recorded that the experts instructed in that case had been unable to identify any link between exposure to the dumped material and the deaths, miscarriages and chronic and long-term injuries alleged. But, at the same time, the BBC issued a combative statement, pointing out that the dumping of Trafigura's hazardous waste had led to the British-based oil trader being forced to pay out £30m in compensation to victims. It read:

> . . . the BBC has played a leading role in bringing to the public's attention the actions of Trafigura in the illegal dumping of 500 tons of hazardous waste. The dumping caused a public health emergency with tens of thousands of people seeking treatment. Experts in the [compensation] case were not able to establish a link between the waste and serious long-term consequences, including deaths.

The BBC's decision to settle caused dismay in journalism circles because the public broadcaster was penalized for trying to report what had been factually raised in Parliament and by the United Nations 'Minton Report' (2009). But the BBC was concerned that costs of as much as £3m could be run up if the issue came to a full trial.

See Chapter 6.3.3 →

---

173 Source: 'Guardian gagged from reporting Parliament', *The Guardian*, 12 October 2009.
174 The United Nations 'Minton Report' (September 2009) had exposed a toxic waste dumping incident in August 2006 in Ivory Coast, involving the multinational Dutch oil company Trafigura.

3.6 Libel juries

Jury trial in defamation cases is a constitutional right, whose importance was well expressed by Nourse LJ in the Sonia Sutcliffe[175] case:

> . . . whether someone's reputation has or has not been falsely discredited ought to be tried by other ordinary men and women and, as Lord Camden said, it is the jury who are the people of England.[176]

The presence of a jury in libel actions can be a significant factor and it was claimed by pop star Michael Jackson's former bodyguard, Matthew (Matt) Fiddes, in his action against Channel 4 TV that it was his fundamental constitutional right to have a trial by (libel) jury to be judged by his fellow men and women because his honour was in jeopardy (see: *Fiddes v Channel 4 TV* (2010)[177]). Martial arts expert Matt Fiddes had commenced proceedings in December 2008 against the Channel 4 corporation, claiming he had been libelled in the programme entitled *The Jacksons are Coming*, part of the *Cutting Edge* series, transmitted on 27 November 2008. It described a visit to Britain by Jackson's older brother Tito, who was said to be planning a British equivalent of the Neverland ranch. The programme, watched by 1.88 million people, had Mr Fiddes as a 'manipulative and dishonest individual' who had betrayed the Jackson family by selling stories about them for his own benefit. Channel 4 had raised the defences of justification and fair comment.

The main issue in this case was that Tugendhat J had directed on 7 October 2009 that the action would be heard by judge alone and the question before the Court of Appeal was whether the judge had been entitled to make a section 69 order.[178] Dismissing the appeal, and handing down the judgment of the Court of Appeal in June 2010, Lord Neuberger of Abbotsbury MR stated in *Fiddes* that the original judge's decision of a judge-alone trial was correct and appropriate and that the trial could go ahead by judge alone.[179]

This had already been made clear by Bingham LCJ in the 'Jonathan Aitken' case,[180] where the court rejected the defendants' – *The Guardian* and *Granada TV* – submission that the public would perceive a jury trial as the appropriate way of deciding a dispute between a senior public figure, elected by and accountable to the public, and the media. Given the overall complexity of the case resulting from the proliferation of issues, the amount of detail and the large body of documentation, as well as the number of witnesses, the interests of justice were best served by a painstaking, dispassionate, impartial, orderly approach to deciding where the truth lay; that is, by a single judge. Former Conservative MP and government minister Jonathan Aitken had applied for his libel action to be heard by a jury.[181]

In both *Fiddes* and *Aitken* the Court of Appeal followed the principle enshrined in section 69 (1) **Senior Courts Act 1981**, which allows for a libel action to be heard by a judge alone. Both cases illustrate that defendants who 'sail under the flag of truth' – as Millett LJ put it in the course of the *Aitken* argument – are likely, in complex defamation cases, to find themselves doing so without a jury.

---

175 See: *Sutcliffe v Pressdram Ltd* [1991] 1 QB 153.
176 Ibid., at 182 (Nourse LJ).
177 [2010] EWCA Civ 730 of 10 June 2010.
178 ss. 69 (1) Senior Courts Act 1981 (as amended): '. . . the action shall be tried with a jury, unless the court is of opinion that the trial requires any prolonged examination of documents or accounts or any scientific or local investigation which cannot conveniently be made with a jury'.
179 *Re. Fiddes* [2010] EWCA Civ 730 at para 44 (Lord Neuberger MR).
180 See: *Aitken (Jonathan) v Preston* [1997] EMLR 415 (CA Civ Div).
181 In *Beta Construction Ltd. v Channel Four TV Co. Ltd.* [1990] 2 All ER 1012, the defendants had admitted liability and the only issue that remained to be tried was that relating to quantum of damages.

Consequently, Matt Fiddes dropped his libel action against Channel 4 in June 2010, and it is said that the legal bills for Mr Fiddes ran up to £1.3m for the trial on a no win, no fee basis. Mr Fiddes' counsel, Ron Thwaites QC, told Mr Justice Tugendhat that his client now 'publicly acknowledges that the programme was not "faked" as he had previously claimed'. He withdrew his allegations of malice. Channel 4 commented that they would not chase Mr Fiddes for the costs awarded against him.[182]

See Chapter 4.8.4 →

Unless the case requires a lengthy examination of documents or a complex scientific investigation, a jury will – at least up until now – decide whether the words complained of are defamatory. Libel juries are popular because they tend to make higher awards than judges and a claimant will usually exercise his right to a trial by jury.

As already stated, jury trials in defamation cases in Scotland are exceptionally rare in a country where civil juries virtually died out at the end of the fifteenth century (only momentarily reappearing in the early twentieth century).[183] Civil jury trials in Scotland were the subject of a number of investigations by at least two Royal Commissions. The Strachan Committee Report into civil jury trials of 1959 undertook a comprehensive review and decided to retain civil juries. One of the arguments advanced by the committee was that they award more realistic awards of damages than judges.[184] As civil jury trials declined, the Scottish Courts Administration issued a consultation paper in 1988, inviting views as to whether the right to a civil jury trial should be abolished. On Lord Advocate Lord Fraser of Carmyllie's suggestion, the matter was dropped and civil jury trials were retained.[185]

The Fiddes case illustrated the 'chilling effect' that exorbitant legal costs in conditional fee agreements in defamation actions can have on broadcasters' freedom of expression.

3.6.1 Jury or no jury?

On 23 July 2009 Express newspaper proprietor Richard Desmond lost a libel battle against the author and journalist Tom Bower. A jury at the high court in London returned a majority verdict rejecting Desmond's claim that he was defamed by Bower in a biography of the former Daily Telegraph boss Conrad Black. The trial centred on a passing reference to Mr Desmond in Bower's 2006 book, Conrad and Lady Black: Dancing on the Edge.[186] Richard Desmond had objected to a claim that he had told Sunday Express journalists to run a string of stories that were critical of Black, with whom he was then locked in a dispute over a joint business venture, and then authorized the paper to apologize for the stories. Mr Desmond alleged defamation, claiming that the book's reference had damaged his business reputation. The total legal bill for the trial amounted to nearly £1.25m.[187]

The collapse of the 'Jubilee Line' (2005)[188] trial on 22 March 2005 at the Old Bailey, which had run for 21 months, was widely regarded as the most disastrous jury trial in recent history. The case involved charges of corruption and conspiracy to defraud in relation to contracts for major construction work extending London Underground's Jubilee Line in the 1990s. The judge discharged the jury after the prosecution conceded that that the trial was no longer viable.[189] Following the trial's collapse, media attention focused on the question of the suitability of juries in

---

182 Source: 'Jackson bodyguard drops libel action against Channel 4', by Steve Doughty, Daily Mail, 22 June 2010.
183 See: Smith (1964), pp. 1076ff.
184 See: Strachan (1959).
185 Source: 'Lord Advocate plans review of civil juries', Glasgow Herald, 12 May 1989.
186 See: Bower (2006).
187 Source: 'Richard Desmond loses libel case against Tom Bower,' by Helen Pidd and Chris Tryhorn, The Guardian, 23 July 2009.
188 Rayment and others [2005] (unreported).
189 For further discussion on related jury research see Lloyd-Bostock (2007). Her article draws on the HMCPSI report by Stephen Wooler and also reports on a retrospective case study of the experience of juries published by Matthews, Hancock and Briggs (2004).

complex fraud trials. Juror Helen Boyask, 62, gave an interview in *The Guardian*, expressing her 'disgust' about the collapse of the trial. She said that she was 'bewildered' and 'upset' and insisted that the fraud trial proceedings had been relatively easy to understand, but that it was intolerable to make a jury serve for such an inordinate time.[190]

Following the collapse of the Jubilee Line trial, the Attorney General asked HM Chief Inspector of the Crown Prosecution Service, Stephen Wooler, to conduct a review of the case with special consideration of the jury's perspective.[191] Wooler's report found that the jury had taken their role seriously but were extremely frustrated not to complete the trial. The report stated that the burden on jurors was 'quite intolerable', involving sackloads of complex technical evidence. The report concluded that the complexity of fraud trials far exceeded the limits of comprehension of ordinary members of the public on jury service.[192]

In March 2010 the first criminal trial without a jury was held, when John Twomey, Peter Blake, Glenn Cameron and Barry Hibberd were found guilty by a single judge at the Central Criminal Court, The Old Bailey, after he was satisfied that they carefully planned and coordinated the armed robbery of the Menzies World Cargo depot at Heathrow Airport, where more than £1,750,000 of various currencies was taken on 6 February 2004. The basis of the CPS application to the Court of Appeal to hold a juryless trial was that any future trial was likely to involve jury tampering and any protective measures for the jury could not sufficiently address the problem of potential interference. It was also felt that these measures, if they had to be implemented during the course of a trial, would have been too burdensome on the lives of potential jurors. It was six years since the offences were committed.

Many human rights lawyers saw this as the thin edge of the wedge, arguing that the British jury trial system would slowly be undermined by this first criminal judge-alone trial, arguing that it denied a defendant a fair trial under Article 6 of the **European Convention**. The CPS argued that witness intimidation and jury tampering was on the increase in serious criminal trials and that they would always apply the new legislation under sections 44–49 **Criminal Justice Act 2003**[193] provision if they felt that justice would not be served otherwise.[194]

Another problem in civil as well as criminal trials using juries is the Internet. Instances of jurors using internet search engines at home during a trial, or even during jury deliberations, and using their mobile phones to 'tweet' their friends is compromising the strict rule that the only information available to a jury be carefully vetted by lawyers so as not to prejudice the trial verdict. In July 2010, 19-year-old juror Danielle Robinson was found guilty of contempt of court for sending text messages to another woman sitting in a second trial at Hull Crown Court. She had passed on 'gossip' from the jury room, such as: 'Hi, it's Danielle from court. Are you doing the kid's case?' and 'He's been in prison before and is a paedo, and when he broke into the pub he took all the kids underwear xx.' Though both women were subsequently dismissed from sitting on the juries, it was touch and go whether the cases would be allowed to continue. Judge Roger Thorn QC called Robinson's texts a blatant attempt to influence a jury and said that her ignorance was no excuse for such contemptuous behaviour. She received an eight-months suspended sentence.[195]

The high-profile trial in August 2009 of Steven Barker, Jason Owen and Tracey Connelly, the defendants ultimately convicted of causing the death of Peter Connelly ('Baby P'), was almost

190 Source: 'Juror tells of outrage after collapsed trial,' by David Leigh, *The Guardian*, 24 March 2005.
191 See: Wooler (2006).
192 Ibid., at pages ii–v.
193 ss. 44 to 49 Criminal Justice Act 2003 came into force on 24 July 2006. Part 7 makes provision for non-jury trial in cases where there is danger of jury tampering or where jury tampering has taken place. Prosecutors must obtain CCP/Head of HQ Casework Division clearance (or the consent of a lawyer of Level E or above to whom the power to consent has been delegated) before applications or representations are made under Part 7 CJA 2003.
194 Source: Press release by the Crown Prosecution Service (CPS) 'Four armed robbers found guilty in first trial without jury', by Portia Ragnauth, Chief Crown Prosecutor for the Surrey Crown Prosecution Service, 31 March 2010.
195 Source: Teenager who jeopardised trials with texts to juror escapes jail', by Jo Adetunji, *The Guardian*, 14 July 2010.

jeopardized by internet sites like YouTube which revealed their identities and campaigned for justice in the case. The Attorney General, at the time Baroness Scotland, took unprecedented steps to restrict details being available online and to alert ISPs to ensure prejudicial information was removed from the Internet.[196]

The introduction of extraneous material into jury deliberations via online material is probably inevitable, though each judge will nowadays direct a jury not to look at the Internet in connection with the trial. If the Internet is used for 'research purposes' during a trial, it can just as easily influence the juror's mind as a discussion with a friend or neighbour which, of course, no juror is permitted to do during a trial. Juries accessing the Internet is becoming a big problem, particularly in cases involving disputed expert evidence or when there has been sensational and prejudicial reporting of a case or celebrity prior to the case coming to court, with some newspapers ignoring the 'contempt of court' legislation. Naturally, as stated above, the material will usually remain on online media archives. The US Supreme Court is now issuing explicit instructions to jurors (in criminal cases), banning them from using the Internet in conjunction with a case. The rules include that a juror must not use electronic devices or computers, must not communicate about the case, including tweeting, texting, blogging, emailing or posting information on a website or chatroom.

See Chapter 4.8.3 →

If and when Parliament considers a reform of the law of defamation, Lord Lester may well recommend judge-alone trials in defamation actions, as is already common practice in Scotland. On the other hand, human rights lawyers may well argue that the presence of a jury in libel cases is a very significant factor and has long been a principle of English law that when a man's life, liberty or honour is in jeopardy, he should have the right to be judged by his fellow men. As has been established in criminal trials, juries are one of the most democratic aspects of constitutional Britain, an institution which is open to the public, where ordinary people participate in decisions of such immediate importance and wield real power. There are jurors settling the fates of their fellow citizens in Crown Courts up and down the country every day of the week, determining by their verdicts whether or not defendants are guilty of the most serious crimes of violence and dishonesty such as murder, rape, robbery and fraud. And there are libel juries which determine the damages a claimant may receive (see the 'Elton John' case[197]).

Unless the case requires a lengthy examination of documents or a complex scientific investigation or language – as was the case in the David Irving trial – a jury decides whether the words complained of are defamatory. The jury, too, decides on the level of damages. Since juries are generally thought to make higher awards than judges, a claimant in England will usually exercise his right to a trial by jury. By bringing ordinary citizens into the system and placing them at the very heart of the decision-making process, trial by jury – whether criminal or in defamation cases – exposes the justice system to public scrutiny while ensuring citizens gain first-hand experience of how that system works. Trial by jury helps the justice system reflect the values and standards of the general public.

There is no absolute right to trial by jury in libel cases. Section 69 of the **Supreme Court Act 1981** says a libel action 'shall be tried with a jury unless the court is of the opinion that the trial requires any prolonged examination of documents', which could not be conveniently be made with a jury. When Tugendhat J ordered a judge-alone trial in the Matthew Fiddes libel action, he said that he was swayed by the cost implications of a jury trial. The Court of Appeal agreed with Tugendhat J in the *Fiddes* appeal, but the case throws the spotlight on whether trial by jury in defamation cases should be preserved.[198]

---

196 Source: 'Baby P killers unmasked', by Vanessa Allen, Colin Fernandez and Lucy Ballinger, *Daily Mail*, 11 August 2009.
197 *John (Elton) v Mirror Group Newspapers Ltd.* [1997] QB 586.
198 Source: 'Channel 4 libel case: court of appeal upholds decision to drop jury', *The Guardian*, 10 June 2010.

3.7 Cyberspace libel

Each year there are about 220 defamation cases issued in the High Court at the Royal Courts of Justice.[199] At the time of going to print, the Ministry of Justice (MOJ) could not provide any information on how many of these legal actions related to online publications or involved the application of the multiple publication rule. There was also no information available as to how many cases had been settled out of court each year, how many actions related to internet libel or how many actions were filed regarding archived news material.

Since the judgment in *Loutchansky*[200] was delivered in 2001 (see below 3.7.2), the use of the Internet, and in particular of internet search engines, has increased considerably, and so has the amount of material and information on the Internet. In 2001 there were relatively few years of back issues of newspapers or online news archives available. This has changed dramatically and has arguably increased litigation in defamation in that a person's reputation might be damaged 'for ever'. While print media may eventually fade in people's memories, online publications and news archives will potentially remain in cyberspace indefinitely. As Mister Justice Tugendhat remarked in *Clarke (t/a Elumina Iberica UK) v Bain & Anor* (2008): 'what is to be found on the Internet may become like a tattoo.'[201] The old *Duke of Brunswick* principle of republication was upheld in a range of different internet cases, as the House of Lords did in *Berezovsky v Michaels* (2000),[202] and the Court of Appeal in relation to archived material in *Loutchansky v Times Newspapers Ltd.* (2002),[203] although the latter was a controversial judgment (see below 3.7.2). The republication rule in the *Duke of Brunswick* case is therefore applicable to online publications and has established London as the most popular location for launching internet libel actions which know no geographical boundaries.

In *Flood v Times Newspapers Ltd.* (2009),[204] West Sussex Detective Sergeant Gary Flood argued that a story headlined, 'Detective Accused of Taking Bribes from Russian Exiles' was defamatory and that *The Times* publishers had shown utter disregard for his feelings and reputation. Flood suggested a compensation award in the region of £100,000. In a paper and online publication of June 2006, *The Times* had alleged that Mr Flood had abused his position as a police officer with the Metropolitan Police's extradition unit by corruptly accepting £20,000 in bribes from Russian criminals. The story claimed the bribes were for selling highly confidential Home Office and police intelligence about extradition attempts, and alleged Mr Flood had committed both an appalling breach of duty and betrayal of trust. *The Times* refused to apologize and continued to publish the story on its website.

Mr Justice Tugendhat ruled in *Flood* that the *Reynolds* defence of qualified privilege would succeed in respect of the print publication and website publications made up to 5 September 2007, but failed in respect of the website publication made after 5 September 2007, that is after the complainant had asked the newspaper to remove the offending article from its website. Tugendhat J referred to the ruling by the Court of Appeal in *Loutchansky* and said that the failure to remove the article from the *Times Online* website amounted to irresponsible journalism. It was not in the public interest nor in the interest of the claimant that there should be a permanent record questioning the claimant's honesty on the Internet, an issue which had been raised in 2006 and had long been forgotten.[205]

Republication on the Internet and online archives remain a problem where some actual and prospective employers, teachers or lecturers, for example, may well make checks on a person's name and background via the Internet and an old defamatory publication may blight that person's

---

199 Source: Ministry of Justice (2009b), Appendix 'Evidence Base', para. 1.5.
200 *Loutchansky v Times Newspapers Ltd* [2002] 1 All ER 652.
201 [2008] EWHC 2636 para 55 (Tugendhat J) (QB).
202 [2000] 1 WLR 1004.
203 [2002] 1 All ER 652.
204 [2009] EWHC 2375 (QB).
205 Ibid., at 249.

prospects and reputation 'for life'. Even if an allegation has been authoritatively refuted, it may still be on the Internet unless a court order has specifically been made to remove the offending material.[206]

3.7.1 There are no geographical borders in cyberspace

Cyberspace has no territorially based boundaries and messages or information can be instantaneously transmitted from one physical location to another. There are no physical barriers to prevent access of information from geographically remote places and in many cases we do not know the physical location of either an Internet Service Provider (ISP) or the server. For example, a server that hosts a '.uk' domain name may or may not be located in the United Kingdom; a server with a '.com' domain name could well be anywhere.

This makes defamation on the Internet a problematic issue. Cases with similar facts might have different outcomes in the United States compared with the UK, such as the different rulings in *Godfrey v Demon Internet Limited* (2001)[207] and *Lunney v Prodigy* (1999).[208] In *Godfrey*, the respondent ISP had received and stored on its news server an article defamatory of the respondent. The English High Court held that whenever an ISP transmitted a defamatory posting, this amounted to a new publication of that posting to any subscriber who accessed the material containing that posting on that server consistent with the old law established in the *Duke of Brunswick* case some 152 years earlier when the 'Galactic Network' was not even a twinkle in J.C.R. Licklider's imagination.

See Chapter 1.3.4 →

Furthermore, the court held in *Godfrey* that a defence to the defamation claim was not available to Demon Internet as s. 1 **Defamation Act 1996** was not satisfied, which states that the defendant only has a valid defence if he can show that:

(1) he was not the author, editor or publisher of the relevant statement;
(2) he took reasonable care in relation to the publication; and
(3) he did not know, and had no reason to believe, that what he did caused or contributed to the publication of a defamatory statement.

This also meant that every time one of Demon's customers accessed soc.culture.thai (in the present case) and saw the posting defaming the university lecturer, there was a publication to that customer. And because of Demon's refusal to remove the offending material from its bulletin board, the court held that the second and third requirements (above) had not been satisfied. As an argument in court, Demon referred to US case law on electronic commerce in relation to defamation and pointed out that US law clearly states that an ISP is only 'hosting' information on its server. But the English court rejected this argument.

In contrast, the US court in *Prodigy* ruled that an ISP cannot be held liable for any material posted on its server since it was merely a host. Regarding the defamatory message in question, the court accepted Prodigy's argument that the ISP had not 'participated in preparing the message, exercised any discretion or control over its communication, or in any way assumed responsibility'. In this case an unknown imposter had opened a number of accounts with the ISP, Prodigy Services Company, by assuming and usurping the (real) name of Alexander Lunney, a teenage Boy Scout and infant claimant in this appeal. The imposter posted two vulgar messages in Lunney's name on a Prodigy bulletin board and sent a threatening, profane email message in Lunney's name to a third person, with the subject line: 'HOW I'M GONNA'KILL U'. Lunney sued Prodigy (through his

---

206 For further discussion see: Macmillan (2009).
207 [2001] QB 201.
208 *Lunney (Alexander G.) & c. v Prodigy Services Company et al* (1999) 99 NY Int 0165.

father), asserting that he had been stigmatized by being falsely cast as the author of these messages. The principal issues before the New York Appeal Court were whether the ISP could be held liable for defamation or negligence. The court dismissed the complaint against Prodigy for the following reasons:

(1)   qualified privilege is based upon the fact that a party plays a passive role in publication;
(2)   the possible distinction between liability for defamatory emails as opposed to bulletin board messages, as sufficient control in the latter could amount to publishing; and
(3)   Lunney's claim that Prodigy had been negligent in allowing defamatory remarks to be attributed to the claimant, rejected in this case, may be a possible cause of action on different facts.

Even if Prodigy were a publisher (which the court held it was not), it was entitled to qualified privilege in the same way that telephone companies are protected from claims for defamation under the US law. Section 230(c)(1) **Telecommunications Act 1996** provides ISPs with a relatively early defence in that:

> . . . no provider or user of an interactive computer service shall be treated as the publisher or speaker of any information provided by another information provider.

Since the concept of the Internet originated in the United States, it stands to reason that US digital law is more developed than that in the rest of the world, though many governments are now responding to electronic communications crossing their territorial borders by trying to stop or regulate the flow of information as it crosses their borders by way of legislation. Article 15(1) of the **European e-Commerce Directive** obliges electronic service providers to police or monitor the content of archives for defamatory material.[209] All 27 EU member states are generally obliged under this legislation to monitor content on 'information society service providers'. Still, it is difficult to see how the multiple publication rule could effectively impose a monitoring obligation on intermediary service providers by virtue of Regulations 17 to 19 of the E-Commerce Regulations.[210] For example, German authorities sought to prevent violations of the country's laws against distribution of pornographic material by ordering CompuServe to disable access by German residents to certain available global Usenet newsgroups.[211]

Most protective schemes and attempts to restrict the flow of information based on geographical locations have proved futile so far. The French courts ruled, for example, that Yahoo! Inc. must block French users from its sites auctioning Nazi artefacts. Yahoo argued that it could not possibly limit access to certain geographical regions; alternatively, it could comply with French legislation and block everyone from bidding for the artefacts. The other difficulty is that policing any such legislation across cyber borders is very difficult to impossible. Time will tell how the new **Digital Economy Act 2010** will fare when the UK government makes its own efforts to regulate its affairs by informing its local residents that their accessing harmful information or illegal downloads may result in the user being cut off from his server. Arguably, the sheer volume of electronic communications crossing territorial boundaries is beyond the resources of any government authority for it to exercise meaningful control.

See Chapter 9

---

209   EU Directive 2000/31/EC on 'Liability of Intermediary Service Providers' on electronic commerce of 8 June 2000.
210   EU Regulations 2002/2013 EC on Electronic Commerce.
211   See: 'Germany Forces Online Service to Censor Internet', by Karen Kaplan, *L.A. Times*, 29 December 1995, p. A1; see also: 'Cyberporn Debate Goes International; Germany Pulls the Shade On CompuServe', by Karen Kaplan, *Washington Post*, 1 January 1996, p. F13, where she describes efforts by a local Bavarian police force requiring CompuServe to temporarily cut off the availability of news groups to its entire audience.

3.7.2 Internet archives and republication: the *Loutchansky* case

As already mentioned above, issues in relation to the multiple publication rule and online publications and archives are becoming increasingly disconcerting to news websites and online editors (see the 'Duke of Brunswick' case[212]). It is now common for media organizations to make previously published material available to everyone through online archives, such as those maintained by newspapers or the BBC. Blogs, online diaries and other discussion forums also fall within this category.

Taking the law on defamation literally and transposing it into the digital age, each view of a web page creates a new publication and therefore falls within the multiple publication rule, potentially giving rise to a separate cause of action should it contain defamatory material. Each cause of action has its own limitation period of one year, running from the time at which the material was accessed. One of the early concerns of the Internet was the possibility of defamation published via the World Wide Web. Case law has done very little to diminish those fears and there have been some high-profile cases highlighting the dangers of the Internet in this context.

The landmark ruling in Loutchansky[213] centred on the findings that The Times had libelled Tashkent-born international businessman Dr Grigori Loutchansky in articles accusing him of being the boss of a major Russian criminal organization involved in money-laundering. This case raised a number of issues relating to republication on the Internet. The Russian businessman brought two actions against the newspaper. The first related to articles published in October 1999, which were subsequently placed on The Times online archive and were available for the public to access. In his second action in December 2000, the claimant brought an action more than one year after the original publication in relation to the online archive. The Court of Appeal was asked to consider two issues in respect of the second action: the limitation period applicable to archives; and the nature of any privilege that should attach to them. On the issue of limitation, the Court held that 'it is a well-established principle of English law that each individual publication of a libel gives rise to a separate cause of action, subject to its own limitation period', referring to the Duke of Brunswick case.

The Times argued that the English courts should follow the approach taken by the US court in the Prodigy case, recognizing that there can only be one single act of publication, that being the date at which the act of publication occurred (see above 3.7.1). But the English courts thought differently, which makes the Loutchansky ruling very controversial, outraging not only British but also American journalists and publishers; the Scottish courts have also since applied the Loutchansky principle (see: Ewing v Times (2008)[214]). In Loutchansky, the Court of Appeal acknowledged that online archives were of 'social utility' but they also commented, *obiter*, that it was a 'comparatively insignificant aspect of freedom of expression'.[215] In relation to republication, the court accepted that the notion of permitting actions based on fresh disseminations was 'at odds with some of the reasons for the introduction of a twelve months limitation period' and stated that any resulting damages were 'likely to be modest'.[216]

The second issue in Loutchansky concerned the defence of 'privilege' and whether this could be attached to an online edition of a publication. The court dismissed The Times' defence of 'archive privilege'. The Court of Appeal held that as soon as The Times had become aware of the criticisms of the articles, and had not made any attempt to justify them, it should have drawn readers' attention to the fact that their truth was disputed. Its failure to do so meant that it was not entitled to rely on

---

212 Brunswick v Harmer (1849) 14 QB 185; see also Chapter 3.2.3.
213 Loutchansky v Times Newspapers Ltd (Nr 2) [2002] QB 783.
214 [2008] CSOH 169.
215 [2002] QB 783 at 676.
216 Ibid.

any protection by way of privilege attaching to the original articles. However, the appeal was allowed as the Court decided that the initial High Court ruling misapplied the test in relation to qualified privilege for determining whether *The Times* was under a duty to publish the articles. The case was remitted back to the High Court, which held that *The Times* had not made out the defence of qualified privilege and found in the claimant's favour.

❖ KEY CASE   *Loutchansky v Times Newspapers Ltd* (2002)

Facts:

International businessman Dr Grigori Loutchansky (of Russian and Israeli dual nationality) had been a regular visitor to the UK until he was excluded from entry in December 1994 by the Home Secretary on the ground that his presence in the UK was not conducive to the public good. *The Times* ran articles on 8 September 1999 and 14 October 1999 alleging that Dr Loutchansky was involved in Russian organized crime and money-laundering. The same articles were on *The Times'* website and online archive. The claimant complained in a letter on 17 November 1999 but *The Times* continued publication online, though a qualification was added to the website on 23 December 2000 in relation to the first article.

During the first action in 2001, the newspaper relied on the defence of qualified privilege. The judge at first instance struck out this defence because the appellants (*The Times*) had no reasonable grounds to contend after the date of publication that they remained under a duty to publish these articles on the Internet, nor could they sustain a separate argument for a special privilege on archived material. The judge at first instance, Mr Justice Grey, refused leave to amend because he thought that the appellants' argument was unsustainable and would require the creation of a new law. He said:

> . . . to succeed in a defence of qualified privilege the defendants had to show that they had been under a duty to publish the articles on the Internet. Only in exceptional circumstances can such a duty arise if the publisher has no honest belief in the truth of the matter published. No such special circumstances attended the publication on the Internet. Mr Brett [lawyer for *The Times*] had conceded that the defendants had no honest belief in the truth of what they had published. This was fatal to a defence of qualified privilege.[217]

The second action in 2002 related to the continued publication of *Times* online archived material without any qualification. *The Times* pleaded qualified privilege again and that the online archived material was an important international public service. The appellants argued that the limitation period began to run as soon as the allegedly defamatory article was first posted on the website and that subsequent occasions upon which the website was accessed did not give rise to separate causes of action; they also invoked Article 10 ECHR, arguing that if defamation actions were permitted more than a year after the initial publication, this amounted to a restriction on a writer's freedom of expression.

---

217 Ibid., at para 51 (Grey J).

Decision:

The Court of Appeal observed that the two libel actions related to the same articles and both had been commenced within 15 months of the initial publication of the articles. *The Times'* ability to defend itself effectively was not therefore hindered by the passage of time and the problems linked to ceaseless liability did not arise. The CA emphasized that while individuals who are defamed must have a real opportunity to defend their reputation, libel proceedings brought against a media publication after too long a period might well give rise to a disproportionate interference with Article 10.[218]

On 30 April 2002 the House of Lords refused leave to appeal, the main reason being that *The Times* had repeatedly republished defamatory material regarding the claimant on their Internet website and had kept the publications in their online archives without qualifying the allegations or seeking a response from the claimant, which had been prescribed under the 10-point *Reynolds* criteria. After *The Times* failed in the House of Lords, the newspaper publishers took their case to the Human Rights Court in March 2009, where they subsequently also lost.[219] The Strasbourg court – before President Garlicki and judges Sir Nicolas Bratza, Bonello, Mijovic, Hirvelä, Bianku and Vucinic – unanimously held that *The Times* had libelled Dr Loutchansky by its continued publication on the Internet and by keeping the two defamatory articles on its online archives, ruling also that there had not been a breach of Article 10 in that there had not been a disproportionate restriction on the newspaper's freedom of expression. The ECtHR noted that, while internet archives were an important source for education and historical research, the press had a duty to act in accordance with the principles of responsible journalism, which included accuracy and reliable sources of information. The Strasbourg court further noted that limitation periods in defamation proceedings were there to ensure that those who had to defend their actions were able to defend themselves effectively. In any case, it was for all contracting states to the Convention to set their appropriate limitation periods in domestic law. The ECtHR commented *obiter* that should a 'Duke of Brunswick' type action arise, it might well be contrary to Article 10 even in a fresh publication.

The Court of Appeal ruling in *Loutchansky* was considered in relation to a US website publication in *Firth v State of New York* (2002).[220] That case concerned a report published at a press conference which was then placed on the Internet the same day, but the claim was not filed for over a year. It was held that the limitation period ran from the time that the article was placed on the website, and that each 'hit' on the website did not amount to a new publication. It was also held that unrelated modifications made to other parts of the site were irrelevant and did not create a new publication.

The Court of Appeal judgment in *Loutchansky* meant that publishers and online editors could be potentially liable for *any* defamatory material published by them, no matter how old, stored in online archives of a news and media organization or broadcaster. Each 'view' on an internet search engine would effectively mean a new or republication of a libellous statement.[221]

---

218 Ibid., at para 76.
219 See: *Times Newspapers Ltd (Nos 1 and 2) v UK* (2009) (Applications 3002/03 and 23676/03, 10 March 2009, ECHR. Source: *Times Online* 11 March 2009, available at <http://business.timesonline.co.uk/tol/business/law/reports/article5883783.ece>, accessed 19 November 2010.
220 [2002] NY int 88.
221 For further discussion see: Dunlop (2006).

FOR THOUGHT

The *Loutchansky* case illustrates the dangers for those who host websites. It is common for newspapers and other publications to store archives of their publications. What if the original text was defamatory? Where does the 'duty' to publish end and the duty not to defame someone begin? What is the effect of the traditional rule of English law – under the *Duke of Brunswick* principle –that a publication takes place every time the statement is issued to a third party, including the author, editor, publisher – even the vendor of a newspaper on the high street?

3.7.3 Article 10 protection and online search engines: *Budu v BBC*

The Internet and the arrival of the Google search engine changed things for journalists and editors on newspapers and websites when it came to defamation. Mike Smartt, former editor-in-chief of BBC News Interactive, explains:

> . . . before the Internet, people were often unaware of material written about them. Unless they read an article themselves or a friend of relative pointed it out, they could easily be ignorant of what a publication had said about them. And because newspapers were all tomorrow's fish and chip wrapping, inaccuracies frequently went uncorrected.[222]

In the past, before the development of the Internet, even if someone was made aware of a reference to him and a possible defamatory statement in print, it would have required a trip to a newspaper's offices to search archives to confirm what had been written – just as the servant to the Duke of Brunswick had done over a hundred years ago. And then a relevant piece might be missing from the record anyway – local newspaper archives, in particular, were sometimes incomplete. However, as Mike Smartt comments, from day one everything on the BBC's news website was archived and, with a few exceptions, has remained there ever since. So articles are available at the click of a mouse, though very few visitors to the BBC news website searched its online archives during the early days.

Everything changed with the emergence of the Google search engine. People began to type in their own names and up came everything written about them. This meant that for the first time material that was incorrect – or in some cases possibly defamatory – was easy to find. Those unhappy about what had been written contemporaneously, on the day itself or the previous week or so, were relatively easy to deal with. Most media publishers make mistakes from time to time, the majority of which are not particularly serious. One big advantage of the Internet is that inaccuracies can be changed almost instantly and an apology provided if necessary. But there were a handful of cases where people read something in the online archive which dated back some years previously and they then might challenge the publications. Mike Smartt concludes:

> . . . the problem was that the journalist who had written the piece may have left, be unavailable or could not remember how the report was compiled. He or she would almost certainly have discarded their notes or wiped the recording device; therefore there was no record of what was said at the time or details of sources and investigating whether a complaint was indeed justified was very difficult.

---

222 Source: interview with and personal comment by Mike Smartt on 22 April 2010.

> In my nine years as responsible editorially for BBC News online, only once was an article the subject of possible legal action and that was settled out of court which, considering there were several million easily accessed reports by the end of that period, was not a bad record. It very soon dawned on writers and editors, though, that this new way of accessing archives online meant that accuracy and impartiality were even more important than they had been before.

The *Wall Street Journal* in *Jameel* (see below 3.8.2) relied on Article 10 of the Convention, but it proved that 'freedom of expression' is not a guaranteed and absolute right in that it may be restricted by prescribed law such as the tort of defamation, as confirmed in *Derbyshire*, that:

> ... the state therefore enjoys a margin of appreciation as to the means it provides under domestic law to enable a company to challenge the truth, and limit the damage, of allegations which risk harming its reputation.[223]

In a groundbreaking judgment by Mrs Justice Sharp, in *Budu v BBC* (2010),[224] she ruled that publishers cannot be held liable for slanderous material republished out of context on internet search engines. Revolving around the dispute between the BBC and Sam Budu, the High Court deemed that neither a search engine nor publisher should face libel claims, even if articles contain clearly libellous material, and that such contentious articles should only be read in context when filing a libel action.

The case concerned three online articles which Ghanaian-born Mr Budu found via the Google search engine when he entered his own name. The first article, which did not refer to the claimant by name, reported that Cambridgeshire police had been compelled to withdraw a job offer from 'an applicant' when it transpired that he was an illegal immigrant. The second and third article, giving Mr Budu's name, reported in June 2004 that Sam Budu, Ipswich and Suffolk Council's racial equality director, was later rejected as diversity manager after security vetting. Although the two later articles put the claimant's side of the story, Mr Budu alleged that they conveyed the defamatory meaning that he had failed a vetting process and posed a security risk.[225]

Following the *Loutchansky* judgment, in response to Mr Budu's complaint in July 2008, the BBC posted updating notices on the articles complained of, which stated that in 2004 the claimant had been granted indefinite leave to remain in the UK. It was for this reason alone that judge Sharp ruled that the BBC was not liable for the Google snippet (particularly of the second article) and that the 'snippet' was not capable of bearing the meaning advanced that the claimant alleged meant that he was a security risk. It then followed that there was no 'republication' for which the BBC could be liable.[226] Google could not be held liable for the snippet, following Eady J's decision in *Metropolitan International Schools v Designtechnica Corporation* (2009),[227] because e-commerce Regulations protect ISPs from liability for the information they pass on unless they have been told that it breaks the law. The articles had been archived on the BBC website and Mr Budu sued the BBC in respect of Google 'snippets' which could be found on the Internet – that is an extract from the second article which appeared above the hyperlink when conducting an online search for the claimant's name. Mr Budu alleged that this amounted to republication. Mr Budu commenced proceedings in May 2009, confining his claim to publications since May 2008 so that the one-year time limit was adhered to. Mrs Justice Sharp considered the practical issues of online archived material, applying the court's decisions in *Jameel*. She ruled in relation to the first article:

---

223 *Derbyshire County Council v Times Newspapers Ltd* [1993] AC 534 at para 94.
224 [2010] EWHC 616 (Sharp J) (QB).
225 Ibid., at paras 18, 23 and 25.
226 Ibid., at para 70.
227 [2009] EWHC 1765 (QB) (Eady J).

1. The claimant alleged that the imputation was that he was an illegal immigrant, pitched at his guilt. The judge ruled that this was not a meaning which the article was capable of bearing;
2. The issue on the meaning of the first article involved jigsaw identification which affected the way others would read it and how third parties would interpret it; the claimant's case was based on inference; the judge ruled that this was a hypothetical assumption, since he had not been identified by the publishers in the article; it would have required a hypothetical reader to have carried out a Google search.

In relation to the second and third article, Sharp J ruled:

3. A Google search did yield the claimant's name which could have linked back to the first article and related BBC online story (via hyperlinks); Sharp J held that the case on publication of the first article must be limited to persons who had also seen the later article, because it was only by searching and finding those that it was reasonable for a reader to have found the first article and understood it to refer to the claimant;[228]
4. Any reader who saw the first article would have also read the authoritative rejection of the allegation that the claimant was an illegal immigrant; Sharp J held that the claim was unsustainable.
5. As the articles were manifestly about the claimant's immigration status, Sharp J also ruled that the second and third articles were not capable of bearing the meaning pleaded that the claimant posed a security risk.[229]

Referring to the judgment in *Metropolitan Schools*, Sharp J noted that a search engine provider may be liable if publication of the 'snippet' continued after it had been notified of the specific URL. Mrs Justice Sharp noted that 'liability for publication cannot accrue by default' and that readers of Google search results are sufficiently web-literate to understand that such a snippet is merely part of a larger publication.[230]

> . . . if the real complaint is in respect of the original article or webpage from which the snippet is, or is said to be extracted, then a claimant genuinely interested in compensation or vindication can pursue a claim, including for injunctive relief, against the original publisher of that webpage. It would not be appropriate or just in my view to make the publisher of the original webpage responsible in law for a snippet which makes a defamatory allegation not made in the original webpage itself.[231]

In relation to press freedom and the journalist's freedom of expression under Article 10 ECHR, Sharp J focused on *Jameel*, stating that – irrespective of whether the claimant had a potential case or not – she would have struck out Mr Budu's claim because the articles were old and only available via the BBC online archive. Because of the passage of time it would have been difficult for the BBC to advance a *Reynolds* defence since the journalist concerned had already disposed of her notes in the normal course of events.[232] She concluded:

---

228 [2010] EWHC 616 (Sharp J) (QB) at para 44.
229 Ibid., at paras 55–56.
230 Ibid., at para 73 (Sharp J).
231 Ibid., at para 74.
232 Ibid., at para 128.

. . . generally it is a disproportionate interference with a party's Article 10 rights to bring a claim for libel after a significant period of time has elapsed.[233]

In those circumstances, permitting Mr Budu's action to continue would have constituted a disproportionate interference with the BBC's rights and would be an abuse of process.

FOR THOUGHT

If a defendant newspaper has archived materials that are or may be defamatory, would an appropriate notice warning against treating it as the truth remove the sting of the libel from the material or will the courts regard this publication as equally important to the dissemination of contemporary material?

3.8 Are UK libel laws in need of reform? Analysis and discussion

As has been demonstrated, the law of defamation is an accumulation of the common law over hundreds of years. It is phenomenally complex and technical. Some lawyers have suggested codifying the law in order to simplify libel actions by providing a procedural code and creating a rational way of resolving reputational disputes.

Following the judgment in *Singh*, can the media take comfort from the general trend of recent legal rulings where the influence of Article 10 ECHR and Strasbourg jurisprudence have led to a generally liberal interpretation of the defences available to the media in libel actions? The Ministry of Justice and the media have genuine concerns about the financial structure involved in bringing civil actions, particularly conditional and contingency fee agreements, compounded by a legalistic approach to the offer of amends defence introduced by the **Defamation Act 1996**. On 15 February 2010, the Department for Culture, Media and Sport issued its long-awaited report on libel and privacy. The report describes a law which has a 'worldwide chilling effect' that has put England at the heart of a clampdown of freedom of speech around the globe.

Another possible approach could be to amend the **Defamation Act 1996** to prevent actions in relation to publications online outside the one-year limitation period for the initial publication, unless the publisher refuses or neglects to update the electronic version, on request, with a reasonable letter or statement by the claimant by way of explanation or contradiction. This would reflect the Strasbourg ruling in *Times Newspapers v UK* (2009), which recognized the important role played by online archives in preserving and making available news and information as a public service and important educational research tool in our information society.

3.8.1 The sting of defamation is not as great as it once was

Ian Hislop, editor of *Private Eye*, suggested in a BBC interview for *Law in Action* in 2009 that the sting of defamation is not as great as it once was due to the more generous interpretation of qualified privilege following *Reynolds* and the de facto upper limit on damages under the offer of amends scheme. Hislop prides himself of being the most sued man in English legal

---

233 Ibid., at para 118.

history. When he took over the editorship of the weekly satirical magazine from Richard Ingrams aged only 26, the 'Eye' immediately faced a number of high-profile libel actions, including the Maxwell brothers and the wife of the 'Yorkshire Ripper', Sonia Sutcliffe. She won her libel action against *Private Eye* with damages awarded amounting to £600,000 (reduced to £60,000 on appeal – *Sutcliffe v Pressdram Ltd.* (1991);[234] see also: *AG v BBC and Hat Trick Productions Ltd.* (1997)[235]).

In 2001, a libel case was brought against the 'Eye' and its editor by Cornish accountant Stuart Condliffe, but the 'Eye' succeeded in having the case dismissed. Yet the magazine's publishers still had to pay costs after Mr Condliffe declared himself bankrupt. An old adversary of Hislop, former *Daily Mirror* editor Piers Morgan (2005) retaliated over the 'Eye's coverage of the *Mirror* share-dealing scandal by placing a full-page advert on page three of the red-top in 2002, offering a financial reward for information that would lead to the downfall of 'the gnome' (meaning Ian Hislop).[236]

Mr Hislop claims that the libel climate has changed over the past decade, thanks to changes in the law, partly – he claims – brought about by the Sonia Sutcliffe case. He also argues that the effective use of the offer of amends procedure and the one-year limitation period have eased the legal defamation challenges for the media.[237]

See Chapter ◄ 4.3.1

Johnson (2008b) argues that the substantive defences in a defamatory action, such as absolute and qualified privilege, are going 'quite strongly in favour of the publisher of the material'[238] and that the courts and human rights court rulings have been in favour of freedom of expression. But if the basic elements of responsible journalism such as accuracy and reliable sources are ignored, the courts will take a dim view of journalists if they put basic economics to sell newspapers or promote their web sites before truthful reporting.

3.8.2 Proposals for libel law reform: the responsible journalism test under *Jameel*

There has been much publicity on the harmful effects of UK libel tourism following the medical and science cases of Simon Singh, Peter Wilmshurst and the Danish radiologist Henrik Thomson, who all faced actions from overseas commercial interests. The fears of the medical and science community are well founded, particularly in the internet age, and the report on 'Press standards, privacy and libel' (2010) by the House of Commons Culture, Media and Sport Committee expressed strong concerns about the country's present libel laws, in particular the issue of fair comment in academic peer-reviewed publications.[239]

The modern history of failed attempts to reform UK libel laws goes back to 1938, when the government of the day managed to neuter a bill moved by A.P. Herbert with the support of E.M. Forster. The Second World War interrupted and then weakened the debate on libel reform, resulting in the **Defamation Act of 1952**. Things are about to change, following a private member's defamation bill from the Liberal Democrat peer Lord Lester, which proposes putting a defence of 'responsible publication on matters of public interest' on a statutory footing. This would also put an end to the 'Duke of Brunswick' rule of republication, where he sent his servant to the British Museum in 1849 in order to find a 17-year-old copy of the *Weekly Dispatch*, which he believed had libelled him. Lord Lester's Defamation Bill deals with the ludicrous state of affairs by which the repetition of information on the Internet is treated as serious republication.

---

234 [1991] 1 QB 153.
235 [1997] EMLR 76 ('*Have I Got News For You* case').
236 See: Morgan (2005).
237 Source: 'Ian Hislop: My 20 years at the Eye', *The Independent*, 23 October 2006.
238 See: Johnson (2008b), pp. 126–31.
239 See: House of Commons (2010a) at para. 142.

What may have changed the parliamentary mood is the case of scientist Dr Simon Singh, who wrote accurately on matters of the highest public interest in a journal, yet faced the most time-consuming and expensive battle against the British Chiropractic Association to defend his work. Then there was the lawsuit by oil traders Trafigura, who paid their lawyers Carter-Ruck to muzzle a question in Parliament and to stifle reporting of the dumping of toxic waste in Ivory Coast. The bill proposes to:

- introduce a statutory defence of responsible publication on a matter of public interest;
- clarify the defences of 'justification' and 'fair comment', renamed as 'truth' and 'honest opinion';
- respond to the problems of the internet age, including multiple publications and the responsibility of Internet Service Providers as 'hosts';
- protect those reporting on proceedings in Parliament and other issues of public concern;
- require claimants to show substantial harm, and corporate bodies to show financial loss;
- encourage the speedy settlement of disputes without recourse to costly litigation and CFAs.

At its second reading in July 2010, Parliament debated the adoption of a single publication rule which would impact on material published offline as well as online; though this leaves the contentious issue of online archives and a claimant's right to have any defamatory material removed from an ISP.

It is important to take note of the *Jameel* case (see below), the background to which was the destruction of the World Trade Center in New York on 11 September 2001 by terrorists, 15 of whom had been financed by Saudi Arabia. On 28 September 2001 the UN Security Council had passed Resolution 1373, which required all states to prevent and suppress the financing of terrorist acts with the United States making diplomatic efforts to secure the cooperation of the Saudi Arabian Monetary Authority (SAMA).

❖ **KEY CASE** — *Jameel (Mohammed) v Wall Street Journal* (2007) (HL)

Facts:
On 6 February 2002 the *Wall Street Journal* (W) published an article headlined 'Saudi Officials Monitor Certain Bank Accounts', claiming that SAMA, at the request of the US Treasury, was monitoring the accounts of certain named Saudi companies, including those of Mr Jameel (J),[240] principal director of the holding company named in the article, to trace whether any payments were finding their way to terrorist organizations. The article was written by James Dorsey, the W's special correspondent in Riyadh, and checked by financial journalist Glenn R Simpson. The claimants brought their proceedings in the UK against the publishers of the European edition of the *Wall Street Journal* (Europe), where the article also appeared.

The judge rejected the newspaper's claim to *Reynolds* privilege and the jury found that the article was defamatory of both claimants, J and the Jameel Group, culminating in awards of £30,000 and £10,000 respectively.

---

240 The Abdul Latif Jameel Company Ltd, the second claimant, was known as a substantial Saudi Arabian trading company with interests in a number of businesses, including the distribution of Toyota vehicles, part of an international group owned by the Jameel family, including Hartwell plc, a company which distributes vehicles in the United Kingdom. Mr Mohammed Abdul Latif Jameel, the first claimant, was general manager and president at the time.

The Court of Appeal refused W leave to raise a new ground of misdirection, and thought that the jury had 'almost certainly' based their answers on the impression made by witnesses in court.[241] The principal question before the House of Lords was whether the journal was entitled to the *Reynolds* defence of publication in the public interest.

Decision:
Lord Scott of Foscote summarized the HL judgment, stating that the original judge was wrong to withdraw from the jury the possibility that the author could reasonably have been intending to convey some lesser defamatory meaning than that of 'reasonable grounds to suspect' the conduct alleged. The original judge should not have withdrawn from the jury the possibility of finding at least that W could reasonably have been intending to convey some lesser defamatory meaning than reasonable grounds for suspicion. Hearsay evidence should have been admissible with regard to evaluating the plea of qualified privilege. Their Lordships ruled that the story was of international interest, not because of the identity of the names on the list, but that there *was* such a list, evidencing the highly important and significant cooperation between the US and the Saudi authorities in the fight against terror. The citation of the names gave credibility to the story.

The public had a right to the disclosure of the information and the journalists had a professional duty to disclose it, which amounted to the 'criterion of responsible journalism'.[242]

In the light of the House of Lords' judgment in *Jameel*, the following criteria emerged in addition to the *Reynolds* qualified privilege defence when the courts consider what amounts to 'responsible journalism' in similar cases:

1. Is the publication in the public interest in the context of the work as a whole?
2. Will the work or article pass the 'fairness' test'?
3. How much weight is attached to the professional judgment of the journalist and his reliable sources?

Since *Jameel*, there has been a shift towards accepting that responsible investigative journalism is embraced by Article 10 (1) ECHR, especially where there exists a genuine public interest.

Investigative journalism was given a major boost in *Charman v Orion* (2007),[243] after BBC reporter Graeme McLagan won his appeal together with his publishers Orion on 11 October 2007. The Court of Appeal found in favour of McLagan, whose book *Bent Coppers* was previously judged to have defamed a former Flying Squad officer, Michael Charman.[244] Applying the *Jameel* test and *Reynolds* privilege, Ward LJ allowed the appeal against the ruling of Gray J about allegedly defamatory passages in the book. Mr McLagan, who had worked as the BBC's expert on police corruption for more than twenty years, told reporters on the steps of the High Court:

---

241 [2003] EWHC 2322 (Eady J).
242 [2007] 1 AC at 113ff (Lord Scott of Foscote).
243 [2007] EWCA Civ 972 (CA Civ Div).
244 See: McLagan (2004).

> . . . this is a victory for solid, responsible investigative journalism. Exposing police corruption is obviously in the public interest, as was recognized by the trial judge, the appeal court and even by Michael Charman's own defence team.[245]

Running a *Reynolds* defence today means that – due to enormous costs – many cases do not actually reach court. The House of Lords judgment in *Jameel* was particularly welcome in that it tested the scope and application of the *Reynolds* privilege, emphasizing the need for flexibility of the defence so that it appropriately protects the media's freedom of expression. What remains of concern is that the defence remains costly and therefore inaccessible to many publishers and media outlets with poor financial resources.

English PEN[246] and Index on Censorship[247], two of the UK's leading freedom of expression organizations, have been campaigning to change libel laws. In November 2009 they conducted an opinion poll into defamation legislation, reflecting their increasing concern about the extent to which the British courts were stifling investigative journalism and free expression. PEN claimed that 'the cost of libel law puts free speech up for sale' and that defending a libel action in English law was on average 140 times more expensive than elsewhere in Europe, while the bizarre definition of 'publication' in English law has turned London into an international libel tribunal. Moreover, this was the only area of English law where the defendant is guilty until proven innocent. PEN have suggested a £10,000 cap on damages and a requirement that claimants prove that alleged defamatory statements are both false and damaging.[248]

In March 2010, Justice Secretary Jack Straw announced reforms of the defamation law. The proposals for a bill included:

- **The single publication rule** to ensure that claimants cannot bring a case against every publication or download of a story repeating the same claims;
- **The statutory 'public interest' defence** to support investigative journalism;
- **Amendments to the Civil Procedure Rules** to prevent 'libel tourism and inappropriate claims at an early stage before reaching court'.[249]

These have now been formalized in Lord Lester's Defamation Bill, currently before Parliament for debate at the time of going to print.

One of the main reasons why foreign nationals prefer the English courts in defamation actions is that the present law is loaded against the defendant. The simple fact remains that claimants from anywhere in the world can come to the London courts to defend their reputation by way of a defamation action by making use of the UK's archaic laws (see: *GKR Karate (UK) Ltd v Yorkshire Post Newspapers Ltd* (2000)[250]).

Dr Peter Wilmshurst, a consultant cardiologist at the Royal Shrewsbury Hospital, for example, was sued in London's High Court for comments made in America to a Canadian. Dr Wilmshurt's case began with his involvement in a study of a medical device made by NMT Medical called 'Starflex', designed to close a type of hole in the heart known as a patent foramen ovale (PFO). The study investigated Starflex as a potential treatment for migraine, which is significantly more common among people with a PFO, but failed to find benefits. At a cardiology conference in Washington in

---

245 Source: 'McLagan wins Reynolds appeal', by Chris Tryhorn, *The Guardian*, 11 October 2007.
246 English PEN is an organization that seeks to promote literature as a means of greater understanding between the world's people. PEN also defends the rights of persecuted writers.
247 Index on Censorship is a global organization that promotes freedom of expression.
248 Source: PEN/Index Libel Inquiry and Libel Reform campaign, Free Word Centre, 10 November 2009, available at <www.englishpen.org/aboutenglishpen/campaigns/reformingthelibellaws>, accessed 19 November 2010.
249 Source: 'Reform of libel laws will protect freedom of expression', Ministry of Justice, 23 March 2010, op cit fn. 75.
250 [2000] (Nr 1) 1 WLR 2571.

2007, Dr Wilmshurst criticized NMT in relation to the research. His comments were reported by *Heartwire*, a website, prompting NMT to sue him in libel in February 2009. NMT claimed that by talking about his concerns, Dr Wilmshurst had breached a confidentiality agreement. The company demanded that he apologize and pay damages.[251] For Dr Wilmshurst, this was not just a question of freedom of speech, but public access to information. He expressed his anger that he and his colleague at the Royal Shrewsbury Hospital were not allowed to see the detailed 'line data' (as opposed to summaries) to work out why the trials failed to alleviate migraine. NMT Medical is suing in England arguing that Dr Wilmshurst accused the US company of research fraud – a malicious libel.[252] Just as the British Chiropractic Association dropped its case against Simon Singh, it was hoped that NMT would do likewise in respect of Dr Wilmshurst.

It is relatively rare for individuals to defend a libel case successfully against a big corporation as the 'McLibel Two', gardener Helen Steel and postman David Morris, found during their seven-year action against McDonald's. Steel and Morris were found guilty in 1997 of libelling the world's largest hamburger corporation in a leaflet campaign issued by London Greenpeace. The 'McLibel Two' spent 314 days in the High Court defending themselves because defamation actions do not warrant legal aid. McDonald's were awarded £60,000 in damages (later reduced to £40,000 on appeal). The Human Rights Court ruled in February 2005 that Steel and Morris did not have a fair trial under Article 6 ECHR, because of the lack of legal aid available to libel defendants in the UK and that their freedom of expression had been violated by the 1997 judgment.[253] UK legislation has not changed in this respect, although there is the proviso for the Legal Services Commission to grant financial aid where it is felt that the case is in the public interest.

To date, we do not know how many internet bloggers have been asked to take down articles from the web after receiving a threatening letter from a lawyer. How many people, such as Dr Wilmshurst or Dr Singh, who expressed medical and scientific opinion, have either been bullied by libel lawyers or have been forced to settle out of court, admitting wrongdoing and forced to apologize, even when they may have been completely right?

There are indications that a 'libel law reform' may take place. There already exists a proposal by the Ministry of Justice in the form of the consultation paper 'Defamation and the Internet: the multiple publication rule' (2009).[254] The paper proposes a single publication rule which would permit only one action to be brought against particular defamatory material.

⊙ FOR THOUGHT

Do you think that the defamatory principle of a multiple publication rule should be retained or that a single publication rule be introduced? If your answer is 'yes' to the latter, can you think of ways in which a single publication rule might work in practice?

3.9 Summary of key points

- Defamation is the collective term for libel and slander;
- A person must communicate material to a third party, in words or any other form, containing an untrue imputation against the reputation of the claimant;

---

251 Source: 'Anger at bid to silence heart op whistleblower', by Jerome Burne, *Daily Mail*, 26 February 2009.
252 Source: British Medical Journal: Response by Dr Peter Wilmshurst', *British Medical Journal* 340, 2 March 2010.
253 *Steel and Morris v UK* (2005) (Application no. 68416/01) 15 February 2005 (ECHR).
254 Ministry of Justice (2009b); see also: Ministry of Justice (2009a).

- Libel is material communicated in permanent form, or broadcast, or theatrical performance, and is actionable without specific proof of damage; it is actionable per se;
- Slander is material in spoken form and generally only actionable if damage can be proved; it is not actionable per se;
- The judge determines whether the material is capable of being defamatory as a matter of law;
- The (libel) jury decides as a question of fact whether the material is defamatory in the particular context of the case;
- The meaning of the material complained of must be defamatory and the claimant must show that it refers to him, and that it has been communicated to a third party;
- The burden of proof that the material is prima facie defamatory lies with the claimant, who is presumed to be possessed of a good reputation; BUT he is not required to show that the material is false; it is for the defendant to prove otherwise;
- The burden of proving the words are true, or the defence of justification is on the defendant;
- 'Maliciousness' (or 'injurious falsehood') is an action that can be brought without the need for proof of loss of reputation but needs proof of economic loss;
- 'Malice' means to act without just cause or excuse and with some indirect, dishonest or improper motive; there needs to be the presence of an ulterior motive, otherwise the 'fair comment' defence will suffice (see: *Branson v Bower* (2001));
- The claimant must prove economic loss if he sues in 'malice';
- 'Absolute privilege' covers a range of situations but most importantly any statement made in Parliament or a court of law (**Bill of Rights 1689**);
- 'Qualified privilege' covers a range of situations but most importantly is not an absolute defence; it must meet the *Reynolds* criteria in the public interest (see also the provisions of s.15 **Defamation Act 1996**);
- 'Fair comment' means the words must be based on true facts, must be of genuine public interest (the judge decides) and honestly held opinion by the author of the comment;
- The time limit to bring an action in England and Wales is *one* year;
- The time limit in Scotland is *three* years;
- s. 73 **Coroners and Justice Act of 2009** abolished criminal libel;
- 'Repetition' and 'republication' means that *every* repetition of a defamatory statement or words spoken amounts to a fresh publication and creates a fresh cause of action;
- A libel which is reprinted brings new liability to the author, editor or publisher of that statement.;
- The 'offer of amends' potentially enables cases to be resolved in a fast track out of court action (ss. 2–4 **Defamation Act 1996** 'offer to make amends');
- In clear-cut cases where there is obviously no defence and less than £10,000 is being claimed, the summary procedure can be used by the defendant in the County Court, where there is clearly no cause of action by the claimant; the case will be dealt with in a judge-alone trial without jury (ss. 8–10 **Defamation Act 1996** 'summary disposal of claim');
- 'Summary relief' usually comprises a declaration that the statement was false and defamatory of the plaintiff; a published apology by the defendant; damages not exceeding £10,000; an order restraining the defendant from publishing any further matter complained of (s. 9(1) **Defamation Act 1996**).

📖 3.10 Further Reading

Barendt, E. (2007) *Freedom of Speech*. 2nd Edition. Oxford: Oxford University Press.

Carter-Ruck, P.F. (1990) *Memoirs of a Libel Lawyer*. London: Weidenfeld & Nicolson.

Crossan, S.J. and Wylie, A.B. (2010) *Introduction to Scots Law: Theory and Practice*. 2nd Edition. London: Hodder Gibson.

Dunlop, R. (2006) 'Article 10, the Reynolds test and the rule in the Duke of Brunswick's case – the decision in Times Newspapers Ltd v United Kingdom'. *European Human Rights Law Review*, 2006, 3, 327–39.

Johnson, H. (2008) 'Defamation: the media on the defensive?' *Communications Law*, 2008, 13(4), 126–31.

Loveland, I. (2000) *Political Libels: A Comparative Study*. Oxford: Hart Publishing.

Macmillan, K. (2009) 'Internet publication rule survives'. *Communications Law*, 14(3), 80–2.

Milmo, P., Rogers, W.V.H., Parkes, R., Walker, C. and Busuttil, G. (eds) (2010) *Gatley on Libel and Slander*. 11th edition: 1st supplement. London: Sweet & Maxwell.

Milo, D. (2008) *Defamation and Freedom of Speech*. Oxford: Oxford University Press.

Mitchell, P. (2005) *The Making of the Modern Law of Defamation*. Oxford/Oregon: Hart Publishing.

Mullins, A. and Scott, A (2009) 'Something rotten in the state of English Libel Law? A rejoinder to the clamour for reform of defamation'. *Communications Law*, 2009, 14(6): 173–83.

Rogers, W.V.H. and Parkes, R. (eds) (2010) *Gatley on Libel and Slander*. 11th Edition. London: Sweet & Maxwell.

Chapter 4

Contempt of Court

Chapter Contents

4.1 Overview

This chapter looks at the common law development of contempt of court, a criminal offence, which some foreign jurisdictions regard as a rather peculiar piece of UK law. 'Contempt' today exists in common as well as statutory law in the form of the **Contempt of Court Act 1981** (CCA). There are three types of contempt under common law which continue to exist alongside the statutory provision; these are:

1. interfering with 'pending or imminent' court proceedings; that is, conduct tending to interfere with a trial which is under way or just about to begin;[1]
2. contempt in the face of the court; and
3. scandalizing the courts.

Contempt covers both civil and criminal jurisdiction, meaning that anything which generally interferes with the course of justice may potentially amount to a contempt of court. Forms of contempt then include:

- the strict liability rule;
- common law contempt (see above);
- breach of publication bans (i.e. court injunctions).

Part 62 of the Criminal Procedure (Amendment No. 2) Rules 2010 deals with contempt by obstructive, disruptive, insulting or intimidating conduct in or near the courtroom (from 4 April 2011).

The practical function of the law of contempt, has the purpose of preserving the integrity of the legal process in order to provide a fair trial to all parties in court. It is particularly relevant in criminal proceedings, where 'the court is under a duty to ensure the accused a fair trial', also covered by Article 6 ECHR.[2] A judge may stay a trial if he feels the outcome would be deemed unfair or impossible for a jury to decide, the main one being unfair publicity shortly before or during the trial, known as 'active' proceedings.

The meaning of 'active' court proceedings will be discussed along with what is meant by *sub judice* proceedings (see below 4.3.3). Practical examples in common law will be given: when newspapers fall foul of the law of contempt, editors and publishers are punished via the Attorney General (see below 4.5.4). Since the law of contempt covers the whole of the United Kingdom, Scottish jurisprudence and authorities will be referred to, alerting the reader to the fact that Scottish courts take contempt very seriously (see below 4.7).

One major contempt risk involves reporting on matters involving forthcoming or ongoing criminal trial proceedings. Photographs can be a big problem when newspapers or broadcasters reveal a police suspect and identification at trial is an evidential issue. As the Court of Appeal indicated in R v Bieber (2006),[3] the publication of a photo can have an enormous prejudicial effect on a jury trial where visual identification is an issue and relied on. The closer the publication to a trial, the greater the risk of jury prejudice (see below 4.8.1).

There are two instances in English law where speech is 'criminalized' the areas of blasphemy and obscenity, which are thus a contempt of court. This makes the general

See Chapter 7

---

1 See: *Balogh v St Albans Crown Court* [1975] QB 73; also: *Rooney v Snaresbrook Crown Court* (1978) 68 Cr App R 78.
2 See also: *R v Sang* [1980] AC 402.
3 [2006] EWCA Crim 2776.

availability of defences and human rights legislation in this area of law a matter of great importance. How effective these defences are will be discussed (see below 4.7.1).[4]

Section 8 of the **Contempt of Court Act 1981** deals with the confidentiality of jury deliberations and will be linked to jury research and jury behaviour in the digital age (see below 4.8). There follows a look at courtroom TV coverage in the United States with a reflection on the O.J. Simpson trial and whether a more open approach to courtroom TV will shortly arrive in the UK (see below 4.8.4 and 4.8.6). This chapter will also briefly deal with the use of Diplock courts in Northern Ireland, which have been phased out and are being replaced by juries in 'schedule' offences involving terrorist trials in Belfast (see below 4.5.3).

The chapter concludes with the question: 'who still observes the law of contempt?' and looks at recent media coverage where the Attorney General did not take any action against publishers or editors who openly published during *sub judice* periods.

4.2 The common law development of contempt of court

The first published opinion on contempt was that of Wilmot J in *Rex v Almon* (1765). He said:[5]

> . . . it is a necessary incident to every court of justice to fine and imprison for a contempt to the court, acted in the face of it.[6]

The case concerned bookseller John Almon, who was tried on a charge of criminal libel (*scandalum magnatum*) for selling Junius's 'Letter to the King' in 1770, itself a breach of a court order. In this case, Lord Mansfield instructed the jury that there were two grounds for their consideration. First, of publication, and second, the construction put upon the publication by the prosecution, by inserting words where there were dashes and not words. Almon was found guilty of contempt and criminal libel because he had refused to obey a court injunction to stop selling the letter.

See Chapter 3.3.2 →

Blackstone wrote in his *Commentaries* (1825) about this type of contempt 'in the face of the court':

> . . . If the contempt be committed in the face of the court, the offender may be instantly apprehended and imprisoned, at the discretion of the judges.[7]

Contempt in the face of the court remains a summary offence today, whereby magistrates have the power to send the offender with immediate effect 'to the cells' in the courthouse until the end of the day's sitting.[8]

4.2.1 Contempt: an eccentricity of the British legal system

Contempt of court ('contempt') may be defined as the improper interference with the administration of justice. Common law and statutory provision ensures that a court – be it civil or criminal jurisdiction – is free to decide on the matters before it, without undue influence from the media. Contempt is closely linked to the Anglo-Saxon concept of trial by jury examined by the late Senior

---

4 For further discussion see: Jaconelli (2007).
5 (1765) Wilm. 243.
6 Ibid., at 254 (Wilmot J).
7 See: Commentaries (1825) 16th Edition, Book IV, p. 286.
8 s. 108 Magistrates' Courts Act 1980 applies by virtue of subsection s.12 Contempt of Court Act 1981.

Master of the Supreme Court Chancery Division, Sir John C. Fox,[9] who described contempt of court (*contemptus curiae*) as an 'eccentricity' of the English legal system and as a necessary regulatory evil to preserve the discipline of the courts and the defendant's right to a fair trial.[10] Penalties for breach can be by way of a fine or imprisonment. Proceedings for serious breaches are commenced by the Attorney General (AG) (see below 4.6.2).

4.2.2 'Thalidomide' and the permanent injunction 'against the world'

Before 'contempt' existed under statute, one of the leading authorities could be found in Lord Diplock's characterization of the term in the 'thalidomide' case,[11] when he said:

> . . . [contempt covers] particular conduct in court proceedings which tends to undermine that system or to inhibit citizens from availing themselves of it for the settlement of their disputes.[12]

In this case, involving decades of lengthy action by victims of the drug thalidomide, five Law Lords overruled the Court of Appeal and directed the Divisional Court to grant an injunction to the Attorney General against the *The Times* newspapers 'contra mundum', restraining the *Sunday Times* (and therefore all other media outlets) from publishing *any* matter which might prejudice present and future court proceedings involving Distillers Co. (Biochemicals) Ltd in respect of the manufacture, distribution and use of thalidomide. On 23 December 2009, some fifty years after one of the worst disasters in medical history, hundreds of survivors of the thalidomide scandal finally received an apology from the government with a new £20 million compensation package.[13]

There are 466 'Thalidomiders' − as they call themselves − all of them in middle age, born between 1958 and 1961 to mothers who unwittingly took the drug 'Distaval' for morning sickness in the early months of pregnancy. The babies suffered a variety of deformities, mostly to both arms, both legs or all four limbs. Some also suffered damage to their internal organs. Thalidomiders already receive support from a fund set up by the drugs company Distillers in 1971 during the first lengthy court battles, which began in 1961. But the payments were not sufficient and not flexible enough to meet people's changing needs. The Thalidomiders have been campaigning for government support for many years, backed by former *Sunday Times* editor Sir Harold Evans, whose paper championed the cause in the 1970s. The government should bear its share of responsibility for what happened, they said. Evans published an editorial article on 24 September 1972, in which he criticized Distillers for not offering parents of thalidomide-affected children more generous compensation. Evans had planned six further editorials on this subject, but was 'gagged' by the courts.

On 12 October 1972, Distillers asked the Attorney General (AG) to injunct any further publications, claiming 'contempt of court' since the (civil) court proceedings were still 'active'. An interim injunction was granted by the High Court. Harold Evans appealed to the Queen's Bench Division on 20 October, and the injunction was subsequently lifted. Evans had argued that he believed all the facts to be true and that the matter was in the public interest. There followed a cross-appeal by the AG on 17 November 1972 and a further injunction was granted. A heated parliamentary debate concerning press freedom followed.[14] The second injunction was discharged on 16 February 1973

---

9 See: Fox (1927), pp. 394ff.
10 See also: Goodhart (1935).
11 *AG v Times Newspapers* [1974] AC 273.
12 Ibid., at 298 (Lord Diplock).
13 Source: '50 years on, an apology to thalidomide scandal survivors', by Sarah Boseley, *The Guardian*, 15 January 2010.
14 See: Hansard, 29 November 1972.

by the Court of Appeal. The House of Lords heard the final appeal and – allowing the Attorney General's appeal – granted a permanent injunction *contra mundum* on 1 March 1973 for the duration all future thalidomide actions. This meant that nothing relating to Distillers or the thalidomide actions could be published until all actions had been settled.[15] The case set the precedent for contempt of court, with Lord Reid summing up:

> . . . there has long been and there still is in this country a strong and generally held feeling that trial by newspaper is wrong and should be prevented . . . What I think is regarded as most objectionable is that a newspaper or television programme should seek to persuade the public, by discussing the issues and evidence in a case before the court, where civil or criminal, that one side is right and the other wrong.

In response to the settlement agreed by Parliament, thalidomide victim Elizabeth Buckle, from the Isle of Lismore, Argyll, wrote in *The Guardian*:

> . . . it is a 'grant' of money to pay for healthcare and the adaptations that we need, and which the government and local authorities have singularly failed to provide for us until now. You would not believe the level of difficulty and struggle that we have had to endure – which practical help and payments could have made easier. Many of us have damaged our bodies further because we have never been given the help and the adaptations we should have had. Our government was complicit in allowing the drug to be used inappropriately, they stopped our parents' drive for proper legal justice (and compensation) and are still denying us compensation, which in terms of payments would be of an entirely different magnitude from that offered.[16]

The publisher, editor and a group of journalists of the *Sunday Times* filed an application with the European Commission of Human Rights in 1978, claiming that the injunction infringed their right to freedom of expression guaranteed by Article 10 of the European Convention. The ECtHR held – by 11 votes to nine – that the interference with the applicants' freedom of expression was *not* justified under Article 10(2) as a 'pressing social need' and could not therefore be regarded as 'necessary'.[17]

4.3 The Contempt of Court Act 1981

Reform of the law of contempt had been in the air since Lord Hailsham set up the Contempt of Court Committee in 1974. Lord Justice Phillimore had presented his report on the law of contempt of court to Parliament in December 1974 and the topic had been briefly discussed in Parliament at that time. The conclusions of the Phillimore Report revealed certain difficulties and deficiencies in the operation of the law of contempt, particularly in criminal contempt matters and that the freedom of the press, while paramount, involved a measure of restraint.[18] The Attorney General at the time of the Phillimore 'contempt' debate, Mr S.C. Silkin, raised the difficulties in drafting contempt legislation, to strike the right balance between media freedom in the public interest and the fair administration of justice. He referred to seriously prejudicial press reporting in the

15 For further comment on the court action, see the foreword by Sir Harold Evans in Smartt (2006) at pp. ix–xi.
16 Source: Letter to *The Guardian*, 16 January 2010.
17 See: *Sunday Times v UK* (1980) 2 EHRR 245 (ECHR).
18 See: Hansard, The Phillimore Report on 'Contempt', HC Deb 25 April 1978 vol 948 cc1340–50.

Poulson[19] and *Kray*[20] cases, where there had been widespread reports of proceedings against persons who were likely to be tried on other charges in the near future.[21]

Legislation was eventually hastened following the House of Lords' (1974) and the Human Rights Court (1979) judgments in the thalidomide case and the Green Paper followed by the Contempt of Court Bill proposed to deal specifically with criminal contempt.[22] The **Contempt of Court Act 1981** ('CCA') introduced the strict liability offence of interfering with active court proceedings. Section 1 CCA creates the strict liability rule, meaning that a journalist's conduct may be treated as a contempt of court by interfering with the course of justice in particular legal proceedings regardless of intent to do so.[23] This can be particularly pertinent in criminal proceedings during the *sub judice* ('active') period (see below 4.3.3).

The act was intended to liberalize the law and make it more certain than the vagueness of common law that had been evident in common law.[24]

4.3.1 The Yorkshire Ripper trial

Contempt risk starts before a suspect has been charged with a criminal offence, if he is the key suspect. There are proposals not to name a suspect until he has been charged, following the murder inquiry of Joanna Yates in Bristol and the wrongful arrest of her landlord in December 2010. As the **Contempt of Court Act** became law in the UK in 1981, the 'Yorkshire Ripper' – Peter Sutcliffe – was arrested on 2 January 1981 by West Yorkshire police. This marked the *sub judice* period and no reporting other than his name, address and charge was allowed.[25] On 5 January, 35-year-old Sutcliffe of 6 Garden Lane, Bradford, was charged at Dewsbury Magistrates' Court with the murder of 20-year-old Leeds university student Jacqueline Hill, who had been killed in December 1980.[26] Later, in total, Sutcliffe was charged with the murder of 13 women over a five-year period, most of them prostitutes.

---

19 See: *R v Poulson & Pottinger* [1974] Crim LR 141 where the trial judge said that he did not see how the press could report the evidence in the case without running the risk of being in contempt of other criminal proceedings which had already begun against Poulson and other defendants in respect of similar offences. The John Poulson trials through the 1970s were the most high-profile tax evasion cases brought by the Inland Revenue at that time, resulting, *inter alia*, in the resignation of the Conservative Home Secretary Reginald Maudling, who had formerly been chairman of two of Poulson's companies. Poulson had taken advantage of the post-war depression, using his political contacts to obtain large-scale civic building work. He used bribes as his main weapon. In the Sixties he built a series of public hospitals and grandiose new shopping centres, including the Arndale Centre in Leeds. By 1966 his turnover was £1.16m, with a net profit of £112,500. The Poulson case of 1972–1976 was the largest case of public corruption brought in Britain in the twentieth century, but was played down politically because both major parties were involved; as the Salmon Committee on 'Standards in Public Life' put it: 'We doubt if Mr Poulson would ever have been prosecuted but for his bankruptcy and his habit of meticulously preserving copies of everything he wrote or that was written to him.' Poulson's first conviction, for which he was sentenced to five years' imprisonment in February 1974, related to the development of a winter sports centre at Aviemore – the papers reported on the background during the case. The following month Poulson received a further sentence of seven years, to run concurrently, on further charges of conspiracy. The papers reported his previous conviction during the trial. Poulson was released from prison in 1977 and died in February 1993. A book on the subject (Tomkinson and Gillard, 1980) suggests that the bankruptcy proceedings instituted in 1972 were much hindered by unusual pressure put on Muir Hunter QC and the rest of the legal team representing the trustee in bankruptcy, and all involved in the case found themselves both lamed and discriminated against in their careers.

20 *R v Kray* (1969) 53 Cr App R 412.

21 Ibid at para 1348.

22 See: Young (1981).

23 The 'strict liability rule' is contained within s. 1 CCA 1981m and provides that 'conduct may be treated as a contempt of court, as tending to interfere with the course of justice in particular legal proceedings, regardless of intent to do so'.

24 ss. 7 and 8(3) CCA 1981 relate to proceedings for contempt under the strict liability rule. Section 8(3) relates to proceedings for contempt regarding breaches of confidentiality of jury deliberations. In both cases a court having jurisdiction may of its own motion bring proceedings.

25 ss. 8 Magistrates' Court Act 1980 ('Restrictions on reports of committal proceedings').

26 In connection with this allegation see: *Hill v Chief Constable of West Yorkshire Police* [1989] AC 53 where the plaintiff, Mrs Hill, mother of the deceased Jacqueline Hill, the last of the 'Yorkshire Ripper' victims, sued the police in negligence alleging that the police conduct and investigations relating to the earlier 'Ripper' murders in West Yorkshire could have prevented her daughter's killing. Mrs Hill claimed that the West Yorkshire Police had failed to apprehend Sutcliffe on a number of occasions. But the trial judge struck out Mrs Hill's claim, a decision upheld by the Court of Appeal and affirmed by the House of Lords on the grounds that there was no proximity between the parties. The police were granted the 'immunity' effect in respect of crime investigations and prevention.

There followed extensive 'red top' newspaper coverage, alleging that the Ripper's last murder victim could have been saved and implying total police incompetence during the five-year 'Ripper' investigation. The papers that said around 300,000 persons had been questioned in the hunt for the 'Yorkshire Ripper', one of them being Peter Sutcliffe in 1977. Following Sutcliffe's arrest, West Yorkshire Assistant Chief Constable George Oldfield gave every indication 'off the record' to the press that the 'Yorkshire Ripper' and prime suspect, long-distance lorry driver Peter Sutcliffe, were one and the same person, stating that the police were 'scaling down' their search for the 'Ripper'.

The government's Solicitor General, Sir Ian Percival, had issued a press warning, intimating that the media would be liable to prosecution if their stories impeded a fair trial for Sutcliffe. Nevertheless, long before any trial, there was sensational news coverage that the 'Yorkshire Ripper' had finally been arrested, including full background coverage of the accused. The tabloid press relied heavily on police-supported leaks. Journalists held their breath to discover whether the Attorney General, Sir Michael Havers QC, would act. But, despite recent legislation for contempt being in place, he did nothing.[27] After a two-week trial at the Old Bailey, Peter Sutcliffe was found guilty of 13 counts of murder and sentenced on Friday 22 May 1981 to 30 years behind bars.

Following Sutcliffe's arrest, *Private Eye* magazine accused his wife, Mrs Sonia Sutcliffe, of doing a deal with the *Daily Mail* worth £250,000, for telling the story of 'my life with the Yorkshire Ripper'. They said there had been a squalid race to buy her story and claimed she had negotiated with the press to profit from her fame as the wife of a serial killer. On 24 May 1989, Mrs Sutcliffe won a libel action against the 'Eye' and editor Ian Hislop. A jury at the High Court in London awarded £600,000 damages to Sonia Sutcliffe (the award being £100,000 more than any previous libel sum in the UK at the time). Mr Hislop commented afterwards: 'If this is justice, I'm a banana.' The sum was reduced to £60,000 on appeal. To date, about a quarter of the magazine's turnover is still set aside

See Chapter 3.8.1 →

each year for possible libel settlements. Mrs Sutcliffe's defence lawyer, Peter Carter-Ruck, had argued throughout the trial that she had not done a deal with the press, nor did she ever want to capitalize on what her husband had done.[28]

The Byford Report of 1981, released under the **Freedom of Information Act 2000** on 1 June 2006, exposed details of 'systematic failure' by the West Yorkshire Police in the 'Ripper' inquiry and the handling of the press. The report included a letter from Hillsborough MP, Martin Flannery, to the Home Secretary William Whitelaw, warning that police 'off the record' comments to the media about the prime suspect amounted to a 'presumption of guilt' and contempt of court, and that Peter Sutcliffe would never stand a chance of a fair trial.[29] The Report also included a copy of a letter by Lord Chancellor, Lord Hailsham, to then Attorney General, Sir Michael Havers, stating:

> . . . how can I be expected to get the Contempt Bill through Parliament in an acceptable form, or how can you be expected to operate the law at all, when the police, including a chief constable, behave like this?

Sir Lawrence Byford summarized:

> . . . since the Sutcliffe press conference, the Contempt of Court Act 1981 has become law. Neither the police nor the media can escape blame for the limitations clearly exposed in the Ripper case and both agencies should recognise their duty to act in furtherance of the public weal.[30]

---

27 Source: Press Council Report, House of Lords Debate; HL Deb 20 July 1983 vol 443 cc 1159–70.
28 See: *Sutcliffe v Pressdram Ltd.* [1991] 1 QB 153.
29 Source: Home Office (1987), paras 466–82.
30 Ibid., at paras 518–19; 667–8.

. . . not only in tracking down the killer Peter Sutcliffe and his continuing reign of terror, possibly committing more crimes than the 13 murders he was eventually convicted of, but also referring to inappropriate comments to the press made by Assistant Chief Constable George Oldfield shortly after Sutcliffe's arrest in January 1981.[31]

In 1983, the Press Council also conducted an inquiry, inviting views from the Attorney General, the police and the editors involved in the 'Ripper' investigation and trial proceedings.[32] The Report stated that there was a considerable degree of cooperation, but:

. . . regrettably the same cannot be said of the reaction of all the editors. While some editors were forthcoming, it required a prolonged and detailed correspondence to obtain from others information, often given unwillingly, about their own newspaper's attempts to buy the stories of people connected with the case.[33]

The Press Council had already expressed strong views about 'cheque book journalism' 17 years earlier after the trial judge in the 'Moors Murder' case (involving Myra Hindley and Ian Brady), Mr Justice Fenton Atkinson, had made his anxieties known to the then Attorney General (Lord Elwyn-Jones). The Press Council had issued a statement that no payment or offer of payment should be made by a newspaper to any person known or reasonably expected to be a witness in criminal proceedings already begun, in exchange for any story or information in connection with the proceedings, until they have been concluded.

This rule was deliberately breached by the *Sunday Telegraph* in 1979 when it entered into a contract with a prosecution witness in the Jeremy Thorpe trial and the Norman Scott affair. Scott had claimed to be the former homosexual lover of Liberal Party politician Jeremy Thorpe. Thorpe was charged with the attempted murder of Scott and stood trial at the Old Bailey on 8 May 1979. Chief prosecution witness, former Liberal MP Peter Bessell, claimed to have been present while the murder plot was discussed within the Liberal Party. His credibility was damaged because he sold his story to the *Sunday Telegraph* for a reported fee for £50,000. George Carman QC, counsel for Mr Thorpe, claimed that Scott had sought to blackmail Thorpe and that there was a serious contempt of court in the key witness being paid by the newspaper. The jury reached a verdict of not guilty, acquitting all four defendants on 22 June 1979.

The Press Council's 'cheque book journalism' code was equally breached by a number of newspapers in the Peter Sutcliffe case, including the *Sun*, the *Sunday People*, the *Daily Mail* and the *Daily Star*. Three days after Sutcliffe's arrest, the *Daily Express* reportedly made an offer of £80,000 to Sonia Sutcliffe. The Press Council stated in its report that, as she was a potential witness in the trial, this amounted to a possible statutory offence under the new **Contempt of Court Act 1981**.

Tabloid newspapers had repeatedly contacted Mrs Sutcliffe for over three months, deliberately allowing her to imagine that they intended to agree to a lucrative contract when they had no intention of signing any such contract. The Council said in its findings that a group of senior editorial executives not only set out to deceive Mrs Sutcliffe, but their conduct had the effect of artificially creating and sustaining a cheque book journalism market in her story, stating that the conduct of the *Daily Mail* editor amounted to 'gross misconduct'.[34] At least two newspapers published prominent close-up photographs of Mr Sutcliffe during the *sub judice* period when he was being questioned by police, before he had been charged, which amounted to serious danger of prejudicing any issue of identification at the eventual trial. The explanation given to the Council by the

31 Ibid., 'The police and the media' paras 664–8.
32 See: Press Council (1983).
33 Ibid., at para 2.12.
34 Ibid., at para 11.62.

editor of the *London Evening Standard* for this clear breach of strict liability contempt was that the police gave guidance to the newspapers that Mr Sutcliffe had confessed and that identification would not be in dispute. Yet Sutcliffe's features would later form part of the prosecution case.[35]

The House of Lords concluded in its review of the Press Council's enquiry into the 'Ripper' trial that:

> . . . it is a blunt reality that some sections of the press regard the Press Council with scarcely-veiled contempt. While some newspapers undoubtedly take the views of the council seriously . . . there is now a minority who care little for the council's views and are, as we have seen in the Sutcliffe case, prepared to say so in the most unambiguous language.[36]

Whether lessons were learnt from the 'Ripper' inquiry by the Press Council or the recommendations in the Byford report is unclear but will be further explored below in the 'Suffolk Ripper' story (see below 4.9). It will never be known whether the published material in the 'Ripper' trial ultimately prejudiced the considerations by the Old Bailey jury, but arguably it was potentially highly prejudicial and did not grant Mr Sutcliffe a fair trial. The Attorney General could have issued contempt proceedings under the new 1981 Act against a number of newspapers and their editors after the verdict, but he did not.[37]

4.3.2 Contempt by publication

Contempt covers media reporting by 'publication' which asserts or assumes, expressly or implicitly, the guilt of the defendant or possible negligence on behalf of the respondent in civil cases. In newspaper reporting terms, this can be just a single headline or in broadcasting terms it can be a biased commentary or news item before or during a trial. In criminal proceedings, extraneous information – such as background material on a defendant – might sway a juror's mind and prejudice a final verdict. In the case of an offending publication or broadcast, defence lawyers may well ask a trial judge to stay trial proceedings if they feel that their client has been adversely treated by the media.

In *R v Knight* (1995),[38] the accused, Ronnie Knight, the former husband of *EastEnders* star Barbara Windsor, was to stand trial at the Old Bailey in January 1994 for alleged involvement in the £7 million Security Express robbery in Shoreditch, East London, in 1983. Knight was the subject of extensive pre-trial reporting mentioning previous convictions and that he had been acquitted in 1980 of killing club-owner Alfredo Zomparelli. The 'red tops' alleged that he had spent 10 years in the 'Costa del Crime' in Spain after the arrest of his brother, John, who subsequently received a 22-year sentence for his part in the armed heist. The trial judge described the tabloid frenzy as 'scandalous' contempt and stayed the proceedings on the ground that a fair trial would be impossible, even if the trial were adjourned. The contempt proceedings were unsuccessful and Ronnie Knight eventually pleaded guilty at the Old Bailey in 1995 to receiving and handling stolen goods worth more than £300,000. He received a seven-year prison sentence.

The standard of proof of whether a publication amounts to strict liability contempt is the criminal 'heightened' standard – beyond reasonable doubt – that the publication may cause a substantial risk that the course of justice in the proceedings in question may be seriously impeded or prejudiced. If a trial is stayed – due to adverse media reporting for contempt of court – the accused will – in certain cases – never stand trial. This effectively means that justice will not be seen

---

35 Ibid., at para 10.16.
36 Source: House of Lords (1983) at p. 1164.
37 Press Council (1983) at paras 10.16 and 10.24.
38 (1995) Harrow Crown Court, 4 October 1995 (unreported).

to be done in the public interest. Paradoxically, the more publicity there is in a high-profile case the less likely it is that any *one* individual publication will have had a substantial affect on the reader. It may well be that the law of (criminal) contempt is in need of reform.

4.3.3 Active proceedings: *sub judice*

The **Contempt of Court Act 1981** provides for strict liability from the point a case becomes 'active'. This is known as the period of *sub judice*, as set out in section 1 CCA:

> ... the strict liability rule means the rule of law whereby conduct may be treated as a contempt of court as tending to interfere with the course of justice in particular legal proceedings regard-less of intent to do so.

The 'active' period in criminal proceedings begins when a person has been charged with a criminal offence; some would argue that active proceedings start when a person becomes a police suspect.[39] Contempt warnings by the Attorney General, Dominic Grieve QC, were ignored during the murder investigation of Joanna Yates when the course of justice was impeded by newspapers and commentary on Twitter implicated her landlord suspect Chris Jefferies. 'Active' proceedings are further defined by Schedule 1(4) CCA as:

1. An arrest without a warrant (in Scotland: 'the grant of a warrant of arrest');
2. A summons to appear before a court (in Scotland: 'that grant of a warrant to cite');
3. The serving of an indictment on a specific charge.[40]

Criminal appellate proceedings are active from the time when arraignments for the hearing are made.[41] Once the 'active' *sub judice* period has started, a journalist, broadcaster or publisher must adhere to the contempt legislation.[42] The publication or broadcast can mention the following when reporting on criminal proceedings:

● The name of the accused;
● His or her address;
● The offence he or she is charged with.

The law does not allow for any identification of children or young persons under 18 (England, Wales, Northern Ireland).[43] In Scotland the anonymity can be lifted as soon as the young person has reached the age of 16.[44] This can cause discrepancies, particularly when writing for an online (news) publication or a newspaper which is published north *and* south of the border, as was the case when Home Secretary Jack Straw's 17-year-old son was caught in a 'honey trap'.

See Chapter
◀ 5.3

On 13 December 1997, some tabloid newspapers discovered that Jack Straw's teenage son William had agreed to supply a young 'estate agent', whom he had met in a pub, with a small amount of cannabis. She was, in fact, Dawn Alford, a *Daily Mirror* reporter. As a result, she had a story

---

39 See: Schedule 1 Contempt of Court Act 1981 ('Times when proceedings are active').
40 Where as a result of an order under s. 54 Criminal Procedure and Investigations Act 1996 (acquittal tainted by an administration of justice offence) proceedings are brought against a person for an offence of which he has previously been acquitted, the initial step of the proceedings is a certification under subsection (2) of that section.
41 Schedule 1(12) CCA 1981.
42 Remand proceedings in the magistrates' court prior to committal are covered by s. 8 Magistrates' Court Act 1980; during the trial proceedings reporting is covered by s. 4 CCA 1981 ('contemporary reports of proceedings'). See also Chapter 4.4.
43 Automatic reporting restrictions and anonymity orders under ss. 39 and 49 Children and Young Persons Act 1933.
44 s. 47 Criminal Procedure (Scotland) Act 1995.

about the son of the first New Labour Home Secretary. William's father, Jack Straw, was the minister responsible for attempting to cut youth crime at that time, when he had vowed to be 'tough on crime – tough on the causes of crime' in his White Paper 'No more excuses' (1997), the basis for the **Crime and Disorder Act 1998**.[45] The *Mirror* had set up an in-depth investigation, alongside a campaign by *The Independent on Sunday*, to legalize cannabis. Jack Straw sought an immediate injunction and anonymity order from the High Court in London which was to cover him as Home Secretary, rather than the boy, who was covered by youth legislation and anonymity as he was under the age of 18. The order was granted.

Meanwhile, *Mirror* reporter Dawn Alford had been arrested on suspicion of possession of marijuana but had been freed on bail. *The Independent* headline read: 'Journalist Arrested Over Drugs Bought in "Sting" ' – and also reported that the police had taken no further action.[46] In the absence of an *interdict* by the Scottish High Court (which the Home Secretary had not obtained separately), three Scottish newspapers published, named and 'shamed' the Home Secretary's son William Straw, since reporting in Scotland on persons over the age of 16 is permitted. *The Scotsman* wrote, 'Straw's Son Cautioned in Drugs Case'.[47] Furthermore, Google news and discussion groups, such as alt.politics.british, had already revealed the identity of the Minister's son. There was also extensive news coverage in France which was available via online sources. Following the publications in Scotland, France and online, the *Sun* appealed against the (English) injunction and on 2 January 1998, the Attorney General ordered for the restraining order to be lifted, stating that the restriction was no longer realistic since the full information was now in the public domain.

The limitation of the scope of strict liability in relation to a publication is defined by s. 2 CCA:

Section 2 'Limitation of scope of strict liability'

(1) The strict liability rule applies only in relation to publications, and for this purpose 'publication' includes any speech, writing, programme included in a cable programme service, or other communication in whatever form, which is addressed to the public at large or any section of the public;[48]

(2) The strict liability rule applies only to a publication which creates a substantial risk that the course of justice in the proceedings in question will be seriously impeded or prejudiced;

(3) The strict liability rule applies to a publication only if the proceedings in question are active within the meaning of this section at the time of the publication.

Criminal proceedings are concluded by:

a) an acquittal or by sentence;
b) any other verdict, finding, order or decision which puts an end to the proceedings;
c) discontinuance of the charge.[49]

Civil and appellate proceedings are active from the time when arraignments for the hearing are made or – if no such arraignments are previously made – from the time the hearing begins, until the proceedings are disposed of or discontinued or withdrawn.[50]

45 See: Home Office (1997).
46 Source: John Penman, *The Independent*, 30 December 1997.
47 Source: John Penman, *The Scotsman*, 13 January 1998.
48 In this section 'programme service' has the same meaning as in the Broadcasting Act 1990: s. 2(5) inserted by Broadcasting Act 1990 (c. 42, SIF 96), s. 203(1), Sch. 20, para. 31(1)(b).
49 Schedule 1 (6) CCA; s.1 Powers of Criminal Courts (Sentencing) Act 2000; s. 219 or 432 Criminal Procedure (Scotland) Act 1975; Article 14 Treatment of Offenders (Northern Ireland) Order 1976.
50 Schedule 1(11) and 1(15) CCA 1981.

4.3.4 Strict liability and substantial risk

Section 1 CCA creates the strict liability rule, whereby conduct may be treated as a 'contempt of court' if it tends to interfere with the course of justice in particular legal proceedings, regardless of intent to do so. This means even the most experienced journalist can fall foul of the law of contempt, even if he just wants to write a background piece to a forthcoming trial – it may well be that the publication is deemed to interfere with the course of justice. It is for this reason that every journalist, editor and publisher ought to be familiar with current contempt legislation.

4.4 Reporting on court proceedings

If covering active court proceedings, a court reporter is allowed to report verbatim and contemporaneously what was said in court. This is covered by section 4(1) CCA which states that:

> . . . a person is not guilty of contempt of court under the strict liability rule in respect of a fair and accurate report of legal proceedings held in public, published contemporaneously and in good faith.

So a reporter or publisher is not guilty of strict liability contempt if the publication amounts to fair and accurate reporting of legal proceedings held in public and published 'in good faith'.

See Chapter
◄ 5

4.4.1 Contemporaneous court reporting

A court may postpone reporting until the completion of the trial or may make a complete anonymity order, banning any reporting until the proceedings are concluded.[51] This can happen in terrorism cases where the court deems it necessary for public security reasons and the protection of jury members.[52]

In Re. B (2006),[53] the BBC and other media organizations appealed against a High Court ruling that had ordered a complete reporting ban under s. 4(2) CCA until the conclusion of the proceedings. In this case, B and his co-defendant D had been arrested as part of an extensive police anti-terrorism operation which had been widely reported by the media. B and D were indicted for 23 offences, including conspiracy to commit murder and acts of terrorism. B had already pleaded guilty to some offences. B and D contended that the extraneous comments made by the media on B's previous sentencing hearing were potentially disastrous to a fair hearing in the present case and D's trial. The defendants argued that the media coverage might prejudice a (yet unselected) jury, arguing, inter alia, Article 6 ECHR and their right to a fair trial.

Allowing the appeal, Sir Igor Judge ruled that media editors ought to be trusted to fulfil their responsibilities and exercise sensible judgment in the publication of such information – after all, they were familiar with contempt legislation. Balancing the principles enshrined in human rights legislation, the Court of Appeal ruled in favour of 'freedom of expression' and that the media should act as the 'eyes and ears of the public' but should observe the contemporaneous reporting rules as ordered in statute. It was also held that the judge in any trial would give directions to the jury to act fairly and only decide on the facts of the case rather than be influenced by extraneous media coverage which may have preceded the trial.

---

51 s. 4(2) CCA.
52 Covered by s. 11 CCA 1981 ('Publication of matters exempted from disclosure in court'), i.e. permanent anonymity from reporting; some judges may postpone reporting until post-conviction and/or sentence; see the Baby P case.
53 R v B [2006] EWCA Crim 2692 ('re. B').

> ### ⊙ FOR THOUGHT
>
> Are contempt proceedings instigated by the Attorney General an unjustifiable interference with the right of freedom of expression guaranteed by Article 10 of the **European Convention on Human Rights**?

4.5 Problems of identification

The Attorney General's office issues frequent media warnings in high-profile cases that editors should not be complacent and rely on the fade factor (see below 4.5.2). There have been cases – such as the 'Yorkshire Ripper' case – where the Attorney General has not issued contempt proceedings even though contempt looked to have been committed, but this should not be seen as a precedent or give an automatic 'green light' to publish prejudicial material (see above 4.3.1). It is agreed, however, that common law development in this respect has not been very helpful. What's more, the Attorney General has not issued any hard and fast rules as to when he may commence contempt proceedings in relation to publication and active trial proceedings.

When former *Blue Peter* TV presenter, 38-year-old John Leslie, was arrested on 5 December 2002 in connection with allegations of rape and indecent assault on a woman dating back to 25 May and 28 May 1997, the Attorney General issued the following media warning via the Crown Prosecution Service, reminding the press of strict liability contempt in this high-profile case:

1. The **Sexual Offences (Amendment) Act 1992** gives anonymity during their lifetime to complainants.[54]
2. Anonymity for complainants of sexual offences is covered by the **Sexual Offences Acts 1976**[55] and **(Amendment Act) 1992**.[56] The anonymity for a complainant of a sexual offence covered by these Acts applies from the time an allegation is made and remains in force throughout their lifetime no matter what the outcome of the allegation. Under no circumstances must anything be published which identifies or could lead to the identification of a complainant.
3. All media are strongly reminded that proceedings are active in this case and are subject to the provisions of the **Contempt of Court Act 1981**. Media representatives are reminded of their responsibility not to publish any material that may prejudice proceedings.
4. The media are further reminded of the Attorney General's Note to Editors issued on 8 November 2002 and his request to the media 'to exercise appropriate and proportionate restraint in their reporting and their other conduct in connection with these matters' so as 'to seek to ensure that should any person be arrested or charged with any offence in connection with these allegations at any future date, a fair trial is not compromised by prejudicial prior publicity'.[57]

Former 'weather girl' and TV show host Ulrika Jonsson had alleged that she was 'date raped' in a hotel room as a 19-year-old by another well-known TV presenter. She made the allegations on a

---

54 The legislation in 1976 and 1988 dealt with rape, attempted rape, incitement to rape and accomplices to such offences. It did not deal with conspiracy to rape or burglary with intent to rape. Further it did not deal with other sexual offences where the victim might have been subjected to a whole range of forcible sexual acts which the law did not define as rape. The Sexual Offences (Amendment) Act 1992 extended the statutory anonymity of rape victims to other sexual offences.

55 s. 4 'Anonymity of complainants in rape etc cases'; see also: words substituted by Broadcasting Act 1990 (c. 42, SIF 96), s. 203(1), Sch. 20 para. 26(1)(a).

56 As amended by the Sexual Offences Act 2003.

57 Source: Archived CPS press release re. John Leslie, 8 November 2002.

Channel 4 TV programme, *Ulrika Jonsson: The Trouble With Men* on 17 October 2002. She made the same allegations in her autobiography *Honest*, published in May 2002. Though Jonsson did not specifically name John Leslie as the perpetrator, he was inadvertently identified by Matthew Wright on his live morning chat show *The Wright Stuff* when he blurted out Leslie's name after discussion about Ms Jonsson's book and her 'rape' claims on 'Five Live' on 23 October 2002.[58] Leslie was preparing to present his own TV show, *This Morning*, on Granada; following the allegations the TV company announced that Mr Leslie would not be presenting the show for the foreseeable future and was taking time off 'for personal reasons'. Clearly the adverse media coverage and identification of John Leslie was already destroying the career of one of Britain's leading television presenters.

On 18 June 2003, John Leslie was formally charged at Forest Gate police station with two counts of indecent assault and was bailed to appear at Bow Street Magistrates' Court on 2 July 2003. In spite of the Attorney General's press warnings being in place (see above), photographers from a number of tabloid newspapers captured Leslie's visits to the police station and the 'red tops' published police intelligence and identification photos in spite of *sub judice* proceedings. After all charges against John Leslie were dropped on 24 July 2003 (the prosecution failed to offer any evidence), the Attorney General did not issue any contempt proceedings against any of the offending newspapers or broadcasters. He decided that the media had not actually breached the strict liability contempt rule but merely the 'spirit' of the 1981 Act. In a statement, Ms Jonsson's lawyer, Keith Schilling, said that his client had never named her assailant nor had she ever had any intention of doing so.[59]

4.5.1 Photographs

Photographs are a major source of contempt by publication, particularly in criminal cases where a police suspect has not been positively identified by a witness, for example in an ID parade. At first hearing at the magistrates' court, the defendant may argue that he was not at the scene of the crime and plead not guilty. It is then not particularly helpful when a newspaper publishes a photo of the suspect.

As the Press Council argued in a 1983 report following the 'Yorkshire Ripper' investigation, the publication of a photograph of an accused man before his trial is potentially seriously prejudicial. The risk of prejudice in the Peter Sutcliffe case was greatly increased by the holding of police press conferences and photo-calls (attributed to Mr George Oldfield, West Yorkshire's assistant chief constable) following Sutcliffe's arrest on 2 January 1981 and questioning at Dewsbury police station. So photographs of police suspects in newspapers or on TV can be problematical, particularly where there are identification issues during primary disclosure. If the complainant has not managed to identify an aggressor – say, in an ID parade – but suddenly sees an image of the individual in a newspaper or on TV, how can a court be sure that the complainant did not identify the accused from the publication rather than from memory?

❖ **KEY CASE**   *Attorney General v Express Newspapers* (2004)[60]

Facts:
In October 2003, a 17-year-old schoolgirl had contacted publicist Max Clifford, claiming that she had been gang-raped by at least 10 Premiership footballers. The attack was

58 Source: 'Live TV slip links presenter to Ulrika Jonsson rape claim', by Adam Sherwin, *The Times*, 24 October 2002; see also: 'Leslie arrested by rape cops', by Mike Sullivan and Thomas Whitaker, the *Sun*, 6 December 2002.
59 Source: 'I blame myself: Ulrika Jonsson speaks about her date rape' by Keri Sutherland, *Daily Mail*, 21 March 2009, available at <http://www.dailymail.co.uk/tvshowbiz/article-1163642/I-blame-Ulrika-Jonsson-speaks-date-rape.html>, accessed 22 November 2010.
60 [2004] All ER (D) 394 (sub nom 'footballer rape case').

supposed to have taken place at the Grosvenor House Hotel, Park Lane, London. At the same time, the allegation was being investigated by the Metropolitan Police specialist sexual violence unit, 'Operation Sapphire'. Identification became an issue: the complainant had consented to sexual intercourse with one of the footballers but told the police that she had not consented to nine other players. She had not been able to identify or name any of the men and an ID parade had not yet been arranged.

The Attorney General had issued strict anonymity and contempt warnings to the media and in spite of overwhelming media curiosity, even the boldest 'red tops' had not published anything during the investigation period. Even the online gossip site *Popbitch* wrote: 'If you want to discuss the footballer rape story – don't do it here, go somewhere else.'

On 23 October 2003, the *Daily Star* named two footballers, accompanied by two photographs. The article alleged that the then Newcastle United defender Titus Bramble and then Chelsea forward Carlton Cole were possible suspects. The Attorney General, Lord Goldsmith, commenced immediate contempt proceedings against the Express Newspapers Group and applied for an injunction to halt the proceedings.

Decision:
Lord Justice Rose and Mr Justice Pitchman found the publishers and the newspaper's editor guilty of strict liability contempt in that the offending article had created 'a real, substantial, more than remote risk' that the course of justice would be 'seriously impeded or prejudiced'. Philip Havers QC, appearing for the AG, stated that the newspaper group had 'blatantly ignored the contempt laws' in order to gain sensational publicity and boost their sales. Express Newspapers were fined £60,000. None of the four footballers questioned by police were ever charged and the CPS dropped the case.

The naming by the *Daily Star* of Premiership footballers Titus Bramble and Carlton Cole, after they had been arrested in connection with the alleged gang rape of a 17-year-old girl, was a 'bad mistake'. The two were named, despite warnings from the Attorney General and the police, in the 'red top' piece including a pixilated photograph of Bramble headed 'Bramble is bailed'. Judges found this fulfilled the strict liability contempt criteria. Lord Justice Rose and Mr Justice Pitchford imposed the fine under the 'strict liability' contempt rules in respect of the naming, which came during investigations in which identity was said to be an issue. Clearly justice was not seen to be done in the 'footballer rape case' (*AG v Express Newspapers*) since no one was ever charged and the victim never received due justice. At the same time the alleged suspects were never able to clear their names.

There are of course exceptions where different considerations arise. For instance, the police and CPS may release a photograph of a criminal or suspect who is at large and whom the police want to apprehend.[61]

4.5.2 The fade factor

If strict liability contempt is alleged, there are two ways of dealing with criminal contempt: by the exercise of summary jurisdiction or by an application to a Divisional Court. Either the Divisional Court or the Attorney General will then assess the 'fade factor' in the light of a particular

---

61 See: *Atkins v London Weekend Television* [1978] JC 48.

publication. That is, whether the offending publication appeared shortly before an impending trial and whether this may have influenced the decision-making of that trial. If the publication was a long time previously – common law stipulates that this usually amounts to six to nine months prior to the trial – the court will say that the jurors' recollection of adverse publication in the media may well have faded (see: *AG v ITN* (1995)[62]). Simulated jury research has also proved this (see below 4.8.1). If the court then decides on the 'fade factor', this would make otherwise prejudicial reporting no longer contemptuous, especially when combined with appropriate jury direction by the presiding judge at the trial.

The risk of prejudice will depend on the nature and weight of the publication, the identity of the accused and the facts of the case. Sensational reporting of high-profile cases is likely to stay in the mind of potential jurors for much longer than more mundane events. Equally, local newspaper reporting or broadcasts are likely to impact more on a local jury than on a randomly selected jury at the Old Bailey.

4.5.3 Diplock courts and juries in Northern Ireland

From the 1920s until the 1970s, the legal system in Northern Ireland developed alongside the English legal system, with the final appeal from the Belfast courts to the House of Lords in London. Following increased sectarian and paramilitary terrorist violence after 1969, the British government responded with a series of anti-terrorism measures which included changes to the criminal court system in the province. In 1973, Lord Diplock introduced the idea of trials without juries for those accused of terrorism in Northern Ireland. 'Diplock courts' (juryless courts) were introduced for 'schedule offences' under Schedule 9 of the **Northern Ireland (Emergency Provisions) Act 1973**, covering terrorist offences, including serious sectarian violence.

Schedule crimes include terrorist bombing and other serious criminal offences linked to terrorist activities. Anyone charged with a schedule offence was automatically tried before a Diplock Court unless the Attorney General for Northern Ireland directed that the case be tried before a jury, known as 'descheduling', in which case the AG would apply a non-statutory test, usually connected with the emergency status in the province. Schedule offences could even be tried summarily before a resident magistrate, in which case the DPP had to issue a certificate of suitability for summary trial. Over the years, judges and to a lesser extent magistrates operating the Diplock system, were targeted by the IRA. Lord Justice Maurice Gibson, aged 74, and his wife, Lady Cecily, aged 67, were killed by a remote-controlled car bomb as they drove over the Irish border back into Northern Ireland on 27 April 1987.[63]

The Diplock Courts were proposed in response to the possibility that jurors could be intimidated by paramilitary groups and the belief that jurors might return verdicts that were favourable to their particular community. About 350 cases were prosecuted each year in juryless courts. One of the most contentious trials involved the 120-day 'supergrass' trial (December 1982 to August 1983) before Kelly J, where IRA member Christopher Black gave evidence against 38 defendants. The judge sentenced 22 of the accused to a total of 4,000 years' imprisonment.[64]

Among many killings during what became known as 'the Troubles' in Northern Ireland was that of a Belfast solicitor, Pat Finucane. A loyalist paramilitary, Ken Barrett, linked to Finucane's murder, was eventually tried before a single 'Diplock' judge at Belfast Crown Court in September 2004.

---

62 [1995] 2 All ER 370.
63 Source: The Cory Collusion Inquiry Report into the killing of Lord Justice Gibson and Lady Gibson 7 October 2003. The *Irish Times*, Special Report, 2003.
64 For further discussion see: Craig (2009).

❖ **KEY CASE**   The murder of Patrick Finucane[65]

Patrick 'Pat' Finucane was murdered in front of his wife and three children in his home on Sunday 12 February 1989. He was 39 years old and worked as a solicitor in Belfast. Mr Finucane was shot fourteen times by two masked gunmen who entered his house in the early evening. The gunmen escaped in a red Ford Sierra motor vehicle driven by an accomplice. The following day the Ulster Freedom Fighters (UFF) claimed responsibility for the murder. A number of suspects were identified and arrested by the RUC but by November 1989 the murder remained unsolved. The investigation ceased.

Finucane had won some famous IRA defence cases, such as 23 men allegedly involved in the murder of two British soldiers during an IRA funeral in 1988. One of his most famous clients was Bobby Sands, republican hunger striker in the Maze Prison.

In 1990 journalist Neil Mulholland provided new information about the Finucane murder. The intelligence came from William Stobie, claiming to be both a quartermaster for the Ulster Defence Association (UDA) and an agent of the RUC Special Branch. He admitted to Mulholland that he had supplied the murder weapon that had killed another man, Brian Adam Lambert, on 9 November 1987. Stobie was arrested and charged with the murder of Finucane and Lambert. The judge-alone trial was held at Belfast Crown Court in November 2001 when the key prosecution witness, Neil Mulholland, failed to give evidence on account of his mental state. Two weeks into the trial, Stobie was shot dead. His murder was claimed by the loyalist terrorist group the 'Red Hand Defenders'.

The Stevens Inquiry discovered a wealth of forensic material recovered from the loyalist paramilitary groups, resulting in the identification of 81 people who had left their fingerprints on classified documents that they had no lawful reason to possess, linked, *inter alia*, to Finucane's murder. Twenty-seven were arrested and interviewed; six persons were convicted in relation to possession of documents likely to be of use to terrorists. The remaining 21 cases failed to satisfy the prosecution test. Virtually all aspects of the investigations by Sir John Stevens' team concerned the widespread collusion between the loyalist paramilitaries, the RUC and the Army, including the allegation that the RUC had incited the death of Pat Finucane.

In May 2003 loyalist paramilitary Ken Barrett was charged with Finucane's murder. Though initially denying the charges, Barrett confessed during his trial at Belfast Crown Court in September 2004 before a single 'Diplock' judge. Barrett was sentenced to 22 years in prison, but was released early in May 2006 under the terms of the Good Friday Agreement.

The Stevens Inquiry concluded that the murders of Patrick Finucane and Brian Adam Lambert could have been prevented and that the RUC investigations into the murders should have resulted in the early arrest and detection of his killers. Sir John Stevens concluded that there had been wilful failure

---

65 Source: Stevens Inquiry (2003) Sir John Stevens QPM DL, Commissioner of the Metropolitan Police Service, 17 April 2003. The report focuses on three inquiries covering the years 1987 to 2002, regarding allegations of collusion between the security forces and loyalist paramilitaries in Northern Ireland and the murder of Pat Finucane. During the course of these three inquiries, 9,256 statements were taken, 10,391 documents recorded (totalling over 1 million pages) and 16,194 exhibits seized. This led to 144 arrests and by the time the report was published.

to keep police records and that intelligence and evidence had been withheld.[66] Michael Finucane, Patrick's son, now a Solicitor in his diseased father's practice, continues to fight for a full and independent public inquiry.

Northern Ireland (NI) now has its own judicial system, headed by the Lord Chief Justice of Northern Ireland. The Lord Chancellor is responsible for court administration through the NI Court Service and has general responsibility for legal aid, advice and assistance. Policy and legislation concerning criminal law, the police, prisons and probation are the responsibility of the Northern Ireland Office. Decisions to prosecute offences are made by the Public Prosecution Service (PPS) and are based on evidence gathered by the police. Statutes passed by the Northern Ireland Assembly must also be compatible with the **Human Rights Act 1998** and the **European Convention**.

On 1 August 2005 Secretary of State for Northern Ireland, Peter Hain, announced that the armed campaign and sectarian violence had ended. There followed the abolition of all counter-terrorist legislation, including the planned abolition of Diplock Courts, following Lord Carlile's 'Report on the Government's Independent Review of Terrorism Legislation'. From 2005 onwards, the number of scheduled cases at Diplock Court hearings decreased to about 60 a year compared with 300 cases in 2004.[67] From 2006 'normal' jury courts were gradually implemented at the Belfast Crown Court. When selecting a jury, criminal record checks are routinely carried out by the Northern Ireland Court Service.[68] Reasons for such stringent checks lie in the polarized nature of Northern Ireland society, in as much as some jurors may be unduly influenced by their political and religious backgrounds and beliefs in reaching a verdict.[69] In this context, jury checks limit the defendant's ability to 'pack a jury', thereby reducing the risk of perverse verdicts. A range of jury protection measures have been put in place since the (re)introduction of juries in criminal cases in order to reduce jury intimidation ('jury nobbling') (see below 4.6.1).

Diplock courts were formally brought to an end on 31 July 2007. But the provision of judge-alone trials and inquiries involving schedule offences remains a possibility under s.1(2) of the **Justice and Security (Northern Ireland) Act 2007** ('trials on indictment without a jury'), which states that the Director of Public Prosecutions of Northern Ireland may issue a certificate that a trial on indictment of a defendant can be conducted without a jury involving 'religious or political hostility', if it is felt that either the defendant or witnesses (or both) are associated with a proscribed terrorist organization or past members. Where a jury is constituted in schedule criminal cases, special measures will be put into place for jury protection, such as giving evidence behind a screen. Jurors are routinely balloted by number only and some jurors receive special police protection during or even after a trial (see: *Re. Officer L* (2007)[70], a case concerning the Robert Hamill Inquiry where former RUC officers requested totally anonymity in court). The juryless system which operated for more than twenty years has been vehemently criticized by human rights groups, invoking Article 6 ECHR and also asking the question why the Diplock courts were still operating 10 years after the Good Friday Agreement.[71]

FOR THOUGHT

Can impartial jury trials ever be achieved in Northern Ireland?

---

66 Stevens Inquiry (2003) ibid. at paras 4.6 and 4.7.
67 For further discussion see: Smartt (2009), pp. 48–53.
68 Article 3 and Schedule 1 of the Juries (Northern Ireland) Order 1996 set out the criteria for those persons who must be disqualified for jury service by virtue of their criminal record.
69 For further discussion see: McKittrick and McVea (2001).
70 [2007] UKHL 36.
71 Also known as the 'Belfast Agreement' of 10 April 1998.

4.6 Administration of justice

The worst outcome for trial proceedings and interference with fair justice takes place when a trial judge stays the entire court proceedings. Defence lawyers will frequently apply for proceedings to be stayed if there has been undue and adverse media coverage in a prominent case, arguing that the accused will not be granted a fair trial before the jury which, *inter alia*, will also be argued under the Article 6 ECHR provision (see: *AG v Express Newspapers* (2004)[72]).

4.6.1 The role of the Attorney General

The Attorney General (AG) is the government's chief legal adviser on domestic and international law and the Solicitor General is his or her deputy.[73] They also have public interest roles, for example in relation to criminal cases and contempt of court proceedings. The AG's main responsibilities are:

● Chief legal adviser to the government and Parliament;
● Guardian of the rule of law and the public interest;
● Superintendent of the prosecuting departments.

The AG has certain public interest functions: for example, in taking action to appeal unduly lenient sentences; giving consents for prosecutions; issuing a *nolle prosequi* ('will not prosecute'); referring to the Court of Appeal on a point of law; protecting charities; and bringing proceedings under the **Contempt of Court Act 1981**.

On 12 April 2010, devolution of power to the Northern Ireland Assembly was finally completed; this included the devolution of justice and policing matters and the appointment of the Advocate General for Northern Ireland (replacing the Attorney General for Northern Ireland) (see above: 4.5.3).

Contempt proceedings are public law proceedings brought by the Attorney General for England and Wales in the public interest. Section 14 CCA states that mode of trial in contempt proceedings does not apply and that the maximum punishment for strict liability contempt is two years' imprisonment, taking into account any relevant mitigating factors. Recent case law decisions generally fall into the following 'contempt' categories:

● Media publication of material which is prejudicial to trial proceedings;
● Abusing a judge, magistrate or other officer of court;
● Attempting to influence witnesses or jurors;
● Witnesses refusing to give evidence;
● Giving false statements (affidavit) before the court.

If the Attorney General believes that the strict liability contempt has been an issue, he (or she) will commence separate criminal proceedings against an offending publication or broadcaster, publisher and/or editor, usually after the (original) trial has concluded.[74]

4.6.2 Stayed court proceedings

During the (first) *sub judice* period in R v *Bowyer and Woodgate* (2000), the BBC TV's *Match of the Day* coverage on 26 November 2000 broadcast a cup match between Leeds United and Arsenal with the

---

72 [2004] EWHC 2859 (Ch).
73 The AG has a statutory duty to superintend the discharge of the duties of the Director of Public Prosecutions (DPP), the Director of the Serious Fraud Office (SFO) and the Director of the Revenue and Customs Prosecution Office (RCPO).
74 Rules of the Supreme Court Order 52 (RSC Ord 52); see: *Regina v M* [2008] EWCA Crim 1901.

Leeds United footballers, Jonathan Woodgate and Lee Bowyer, as pixelated (headless) players for fear of contravening the **Contempt of Court Act 1981**. Woodgate and Bowyer had been remanded on bail at the time, having been charged with serious wounding offences for an alleged serious assault on a young Asian student, Sarfraz Najeib, in a Leeds city centre nightclub in January 2000. The Leeds footballers' trial (Nr 1) took place at Hull Crown Court. At the start of the trial proceedings Poole J had emphasized to the jury that the accused were not charged with racism offences and that the jury should ignore such thoughts.

During the jury's deliberation in April 2001, the *Sunday Mirror* published an interview with the victim's father, Muhammed Najeib, alleging a racist attack. On application by the defence, Mr Justice Poole stayed the proceedings citing contempt of court and ordered a retrial. He made it clear that the newspaper had seriously prejudiced the jury verdict by its publication, stating that the editor should have known better, and ordering costs against the Trinity Mirror Group newspaper organization.[75] At their retrial a year later in 2002, Woodgate and Bowyer were acquitted of section 18 and 20 wounding charges (**Offences Against the Person Act 1861**). Woodgate pleaded guilty to affray and was sentenced to 100 hours' 'community service' and ordered to pay eight weeks' wages as a fine. Bowyer also pleaded guilty to affray and was fined four weeks' wages. After the conclusion of the second trial, the Attorney General issued contempt proceedings against the Trinity Mirror Group and the *Sunday Mirror's* editor, Colin Myler. They were found guilty of contempt and subsequently fined a total of £175,000. Colin Myler resigned. Kennedy LJ and Rafferty J contended that the offending article had seriously impeded justice during a lengthy, expensive, high-profile case at a crucially difficult time[76] (See also: R v West (Rosemary) (1996) 2 Cr App 374).

❖ KEY CASE   *Attorney General v ITV Central Ltd* [2008][77]

Facts:

A regional broadcaster, Central TV (B), had broadcast a 23-second news report referring to the trial of five men later that day. The reporter said that one of the accused was already serving a prison sentence for murder; that report was repeated on two late-morning news bulletins. Defence counsel brought B's broadcast to the attention of the trial judge and the trial was stayed. B offered an immediate and unreserved apology to the court, agreeing to pay all third-party costs to cover the postponement of the trial. Subsequently, all five defendants were convicted with court costs amounting to £37,014, which B paid.

After the trial, the Attorney General (AG) applied for an order for committal for contempt of court against B, contending that the news broadcast was a clear breach of liability contempt.

Decision:

The AG's application was granted for reasons that the 'publication' (the broadcast) had amounted to a 'serious and basic error' that created a real risk that the broadcast might be heard by members of the jury due to hear the trial. A charge of murder was serious, as was a conviction for murder and the 'simplicity' of the error could not detract from the seriousness of the publication. B should have known that where a person was

---

75 A 'wasted costs' order can be made against third parties here: the media – by the magistrates or presiding judge under the *Courts Act* 2003, for wasting the court's time in a 'cracked' trial (where a trial had to be abandoned).
76 See also: 'Exclusive: Bowyer's £170,000 to beaten student' by Graham Brough, *Daily Mirror*, 29 November 2005.
77 [2008] EWHC 1984 (Admin).

convicted of murder and was due to be tried on another charge of murder, his previous conviction should not be disclosed. The contempt had resulted in the disturbance of the court, delays and distress to third parties. B was fined £25,000 for contempt.

4.6.3 Criminal contempt: false statements in court

Contempt proceedings can also be brought against a person who makes a false disclosure statement (affidavit) for use in court without an honest belief that the statement was true, covered by the Civil Procedure Rules[78]:

> . . . rule 32.14 'False statements':
>
> (1)   Proceedings for contempt of court may be brought against a person if he makes, or causes to be made, a false statement in a document verified by a statement of truth without an honest belief in its truth.
>   (Part 22 makes provision for a statement of truth)
> (2)   Proceedings under this rule may be brought only –
>
>   (a)   by the Attorney General; or
>   (b)   with the permission of the court.

It was held in the 'Honda Superbikes' case (2008)[79] that prima facie contempt proceedings can follow immediately after the conclusion of the trial against a dishonest party who was found to give false evidence during the trial proceedings. In this civil case, key witness Anthony Hinton, general manager of Honda Motorcycles Australia, had admitted during cross-examination before the court that his 'truthful' affidavit statement had not been 'completely accurate'. Mr. Hinton was held in contempt of court in that he had lied by providing a false witness statement.

4.6.4 Impertinent courtroom behaviour

'Contempt' also covers courtroom behaviour, such as being disrespectful to a magistrates' bench, wearing inappropriate clothing in the public gallery or the use of mobile phones. On 11 May 2003, Judge Huw Daniel, sitting at Mold Crown Court, dismissed a potential juror for 'contempt in the face of the court'. The male juror was wearing a top with a 'mis-spelt Anglo Saxon word' (a French Connection 'FCUK' T-shirt). The judge said that this was not only a distraction but was disrespectful of court proceedings. The juror had to stand down and was asked to leave the court.[80]

The issue of taking photos in a courtroom was addressed in R v D (Vincent) (2004).[81] The law in this area is very old, covered by s. 41 **Criminal Justice Act 1925** ('Prohibition on taking photographs, &c., in court') and reads:

> (1) No person shall—

---

78 CPR 2010.
79 KJM Superbikes Ltd v Hinton [2008] EWCA Civ Div 1280 ('Practice Notice').
80 Source: 'Judge bars four-letter word T-shirt', BBC News Online, 11 May 2003.
81 [2004] EWCA Crim 1271.

(a)   take or attempt to take in any court any photograph, or with a view to publication make or attempt to make in any court any portrait or sketch, of any person, being a judge of the court or a juror or a witness in or a party to any proceedings before the court, whether civil or criminal; or

(b)   publish any photograph, portrait or sketch taken or made in contravention of the fore-going provisions of this section or any reproduction thereof;

and if any person acts in contravention of this section he shall, on summary conviction, be liable in respect of each offence to a fine.

R v D addressed the illegal use of mobile phone cameras in court. The juvenile appellant had taken three photographs with his mobile phone camera at Liverpool Crown Court: one in the court canteen; one from the public gallery towards the witness box; and the third of his brother in the secure dock. The last picture also revealed one of the security officers. The trial judge seized the appellant's mobile phone and charged him with the summary offence of criminal contempt.[82] The accused 'photographer' was convicted and sentenced to 12 months' imprisonment, whereupon he appealed against that sentence. The Court of Appeal had to decide whether the contemnor's sentence for contempt of court by using a mobile phone camera in the court room was manifestly excessive. Their Lordships expressed concern about the ease with which photos could now be passed on to third parties by electronic means and could easily fall into the wrong hands. Lord Aikens noted:

> . . . intimidation of juries and witnesses is a growing problem generally in criminal cases. Recently there have even been physical attacks on prosecuting counsel in a case. A person could use photographs of members of the jury or a witness or advocates or even a Judge in order to try to intimidate them or to take other reprisals. Witnesses who are only seen on a screen or who are meant to be known only by an initial could possibly be identified. The anonymity of dock officers or policemen who are involved in a case could be compromised if a photograph is taken and is used to identify them.[83]

Though the young appellant in R v D had argued that he had taken the photos in a 'spirit of fun', explaining that the photos of his brother in the dock were meant as a text message for his niece on her eighteenth birthday, the Court of Appeal upheld his sentence on the grounds that taking photos in a courthouse was illegal and gravely prejudiced the administration of justice because taking photos of witnesses or jury members could lead to their intimidation. The principle of fair justice and the right to a fair trial could be severely impeded.

4.7 Procedure and punishment

The courts' jurisdiction to deal with contempt is divided into two broad categories: criminal contempt and civil contempt. In essence, a criminal contempt, such as contempt in the face of the court, is an act which threatens the administration of justice. Courts are empowered to protect the administration of justice by acting on their own initiative, punishing those guilty of such contempt with detention in custody or a fine.

Civil contempt involves disobedience of a court order or undertaking by a party who is bound by it. The court's sanction in civil contempt has been seen primarily as coercive or remedial. Civil contempt has largely arisen in respect of an order or undertaking made in civil litigation. However,

---

82 s.41(1) Criminal Justice Act 1925 ('Prohibition on taking photographs, &c., in court').
83 (2004) EWCA Crim 1271 para 15 (Lord Aikens).

as some civil orders now are made in criminal cases, for example a restraint order considered in R v M,[84] a civil contempt may occur in the course of proceedings in a criminal court.

4.7.1 General defences and exceptions

Following the Human Rights Court ruling in *Sunday Times v UK* (1980),[85] the Strasbourg Court opined that the overriding importance of a free press had to be maintained in order to keep the public informed, thereby upholding Article 10.[86] This case followed on from the domestic court action in the thalidomide case and concerned a long-drawn-out action in damages and compensation (see also 4.2.2). The **Contempt of Court Act 1981** was enacted, following the *Sunday Times* case,[87] though the creation of such legislation had already been discussed much earlier by a House of Commons Committee on 'Contempt of Court' (1974).[88] At that time, the Committee could not agree on a general definition for a possible defence, and Chairman Phillimore LJ rejected the idea of a general defence for 'public benefit', which he said was difficult to define in statute for specific situations.[89]

General defences can be found under Schedule 1, section 3 CCA 1981:

(1)   A person is not guilty of contempt of court under the strict liability rule as the publisher of any matter to which that rule applies if at the time of publication (having taken all reasonable care) he does not know and has no reason to suspect that relevant proceedings are active;

(2)   A person is not guilty of contempt of court under the strict liability rule as the distributor of a publication containing any such matter if at the time of distribution (having taken all reasonable care) he does not know that it contains such matter and has no reason to suspect that it is likely to do so;

(3)   The burden of proof of any fact tending to establish a defence afforded by this section to any person lies upon that person.

If faced with contempt allegations by the Attorney General (or a Sheriff Court in Scotland), the burden of proof lies on the journalist, editor, publisher or contemnor to convince the court that they were not in contempt when publishing offending material. This will be advanced under s. 5 CCA (see below). A strong argument would be that the publication was made as part of a discussion, in good faith, of public affairs or as a matter of general public interest. It is up to the Attorney General to decide whether the strict liability contempt rules apply and whether there was a risk of impediment or prejudice to particular legal proceedings or whether the publication amounted to a mere incidental discussion.

Section 5 of the **Contempt of Court Act 1981** (CCA) provides a statutory defence concerning 'discussion of public affairs':

. . . a publication made as or as part of a discussion in good faith of public affairs or other matters of general public interest is not to be treated as a contempt of court under the strict liability rule if the risk of impediment or prejudice to particular legal proceedings is merely incidental to the discussion.

---

84   [2008] EWCA Crim 1901.
85   (1980) 2 EHRR 245 (ECHR).
86   Ibid., at para 66.
87   Source: House of Commons (1980).
88   Source: House of Commons (1974).
89   Ibid., at paras 143–5.

Section 5 CCA can save a publication that would otherwise fall foul of the strict liability rule (as defined in s.1 of the 1981 Act) if it is made a 'discussion of public affairs' and generally passes the public interest test (which is not defined by statute). This means that the section 5 defence is not altogether satisfactory, particularly where the restraint imposed would interfere with the journalist or publisher's freedom of expression as being 'necessary in a democratic society.' How do we know whether a publication or online report is crucial to the public interest aspect in a particular case?

As already stated, the principal aim of the 1981 'contempt' statute was to introduce the 'strict liability rule' under s.2(2) CCA, which only applies if a publication creates a 'substantial risk' of prejudicing forthcoming court proceedings or seriously impeding the course of justice (see above 4.3.2). The test whether the section 5 defence can be successfully applied is left to the Attorney General or the Divisional Court and usually comprises:

1. the size of the risk (of serious prejudice), and
2. the severity of impact of the publication.

Neither a remote risk of serious impediment nor a substantial risk of minor impediment will suffice.

Section 5 puts the public interest element secondary to the objectivity principle of assuring the unprejudiced administration of justice. But it is ultimately up to the Attorney General to decide whether a publication could have the potential of creating such a 'substantial risk' of serious prejudice to a trial. Since jury research is not permitted under section 8 CCA, there is no evidence whether a publication did create the liability for contempt or whether it was merely incidental to a particular trial (see below 4.8.1).

In *AG v English* (1982),[90] the House of Lords ruled that the section 5 CCA did amount to a defence to the *Daily Mail* columnist Malcolm Muggeridge, because his comment piece had been written in 'good faith' and the piece was in the public interest. For this reason Lord Diplock opined that this section provided the exception to the strict liability rule.[91] Mr Muggeridge had written an opinion piece in the *Mail* on mercy killing (euthanasia), commenting on the Sheffield paediatrician, Dr Arthur, who was standing trial at the time for murdering a prematurely born, severely disabled baby boy, by not operating on the child or giving life-sustaining treatment. Dr Arthur was acquitted by the jury.

A case where the 'public interest defence' under section 5 CCA did not succeed involved the popular BBC TV news quiz *Have I Got News For You*.[92]

❖ **KEY CASE**   *Attorney General v BBC and Hat Trick Productions Ltd* (1997)

Facts

Have I Got News For You was screened on BBC2 on Friday 29 April 1994 between 22.00 and 22.30 hours. One main topic of the news quiz was the forthcoming fraud trial of the Maxwell brothers, Kevin and Ian, sons of the deceased *Mirror* newspaper tycoon Robert Maxwell. The trial was scheduled for 31 October 1994. At the time of the broadcast the Maxwell brothers were charged with two counts of conspiracy to defraud the trustees

---

90 [1982] 2 All ER 903 (HL).
91 Ibid., at para 918f–g.
92 *AG v BBC and Hat Trick Productions* [1997] EMLR 76.

and beneficiaries of the Mirror Group Pension Fund. The news quiz was chaired by Angus Deayton.

When team leaders Ian Hislop, editor of *Private Eye*, and actor-comedian Paul Merton played the 'odd one out' round, the fourth photo showed some *Mirror* pensioners. The team members' repeated banter centred on the pensioners 'allegedly' defrauded by Robert Maxwell, implying 'guilt' of the Maxwell brothers. The programme was repeated the following night unedited.

At the start of the Maxwell sons' trial, their lawyers applied for proceedings to be stayed, arguing that the BBC news quiz had contravened contempt legislation and that Kevin and Ian Maxwell would not stand a fair trial due to adverse media coverage. Though the trial went ahead, and the Maxwell brothers were acquitted, the AG commenced contempt proceedings against the programme makers Hat Trick Productions and the BBC immediately after the conclusion of the fraud trial.

Decision:
The court found both parties guilty of strict liability contempt for reasons that the programme makers and the BBC should not have broadcast any material in connection with the forthcoming Maxwell trial during the *sub judice* period. The court further held that the public broadcaster had made no attempt to edit out the 'irrelevant' and 'rude' comments, particularly in its repeat programme. Hat Trick and the BBC were each fined £10,000.

Arguably the terms used in section 5 CCA may well form part of the *actus reus* of contempt. But the terms are separately defined in s. 2(2) CCA ('limitation of scope of strict liability') in the interests, presumably, of clarity and emphasis (see above 4.3.4). This then is the confusing part of the 1981 Act: to judge whether an element forms part of the *actus reus* of the strict liability crime or is a defence as strictly defined has of course a bearing on who carries the burden of proof. It might be for this very reason that the Attorney General increasingly does not prosecute for strict liability contempt because the statute is unclear on the matter of whether section 5 implies an exception to the 'strict liability' rule outlined in section 2 (see: R v Hunt (1987);[93] R v Lambert (2001)[94]).

Who then has to prove strict liability contempt? Clearly, the Attorney General will avail him or herself of the conditions set out in s. 2(2) CCA, in which case the onus must lie with the defendant to prove that it met the conditions set out under s. 5 CCA. Or should the burden of proof lie on the Attorney General to prove that section 5 will not apply in certain circumstances? This ultimately means that it is a question of law rather than fact.

More recently the courts have made exceptions and have allowed for a section 5 defence in the discussion of public affairs relating to permitting publication and even photographs during *sub judice* proceedings in terrorism related cases. Following the atrocities of the London bombings of 7 July 2005 and the attempted terrorism attacks of 21 July of the same year, the CPS issued new practice guidelines allowing the media to make more extensive use of publishing police intelligence during active proceedings (following pre-trial proceedings), such as photos and previous convictions of the suspects. This new practice guideline was issued in relation to the

---

93 [1987] AC 352 (HL).
94 [2001] UKHL 37 (HL).

suspected London bombers who had been arrested on 22 September 2005, namely Hussain Osman (27), Ibrahim Muktar Said (27), Yassin Hussan Omar (26) and Ramzi Mohamed (23). Their trial took two years to come to Woolwich Crown Court in 2007; yet the media was urged to release the following details and the BBC's *Crimewatch* encouraged members of the public to come forward with more information in 2005:

- Maps and diagrams of the scene of the crime;
- Photographs of the suspects, including custody photos of the accused;
- Police videos showing scenes of crime;
- Pictures of property seized such as weapons, clothing, drug hauls, stolen goods, etc.;
- Police reconstruction videos;
- CCTV footage of the accused and/or the scene of crime;
- Police interview tapes and transcripts.

Human rights lawyers have argued that media reporting of terrorist suspects amounts to strict liability contempt and does not grant the accused a fair trial because of the unduly sensational and inflammatory press coverage, with a slur on particular faiths and an imbalance of reporting previous convictions.

4.7.2 Sentencing contemnors

The penalties for contempt offences can be substantial, ranging from a fine not exceeding £2,500 to imprisonment to a maximum of one month in summary proceedings, to proceedings in the County or Crown Courts with an unlimited fine or a maximum two-year prison sentence[95] (see: R v Bolam, ex parte Haigh (1949)[96]).

In R v Montgomery (1995)[97], the contemnor-witness had given evidence in court relating to a confession made by the defendant who was charged with conspiracy to defraud. Similar to the Honda Superbikes case (see above), the contemnor's statement turned out to be false and he was subsequently charged with contempt of court. On his appeal, the Court of Appeal held that the question of sentencing the contemnor should best be left until the end of the original trial (i.e. the outcome of the *Montgomery* hearing). Following this trial, the CA made the following sentencing recommendations to be taken into account when sentencing contemnors:

- The gravity of the offence being tried;
- The effect upon the trial;
- The contemnor's reasons for failing to give evidence;
- Whether the contempt is aggravated by impertinent defiance to the judge;
- The scale of sentences in similar cases, albeit each case must turn on its own facts;
- The antecedents, personal circumstances and characteristics of the contemnor (for example, whether for the contemnor this would be his first time in prison or being institutionalized).[98]

The Court of Appeal in *Montgomery* then issued the following sentencing guidelines:

---

95 s. 14 CCA 1981; or proceedings brought by the AG for Northern Ireland under s. 18 CCA 1981; section 35 Criminal Justice Act (Northern Ireland) 1945 applies to fines imposed for contempt of court by any superior court other than the Crown Court as it applies to fines imposed by the Crown Court.
96 (1949) 93 SJ 220.
97 (1995) 16 Cr App R (S) 274.
98 See also: Part 62 Criminal Procedure Rules 2005 of 5 October 2009.

1. An immediate custodial sentence is the only appropriate sentence to impose upon a person who interferes with the administration of justice, unless the circumstances are wholly exceptional;

2. While review of the authorities suggests that interference with, or threats made to, jurors are usually visited with higher sentences than the case of a witness who refuses to give evidence, there is no rule or established practice to that effect; the circumstances of each case are all-important;

3. Although the maximum sentence for failing to comply with a witness order is three months, that should not inhibit a substantially longer sentence for a blatant contempt in the face of the court by a witness who has refused to testify;

4. The principal matters affecting sentence are the gravity of the offence being tried; the effect upon the trial; the contemnor's reasons for failing to give evidence; whether the contempt is aggravated by impertinence defiance rather than a simple and stubborn refusal to answer; the scale of sentences in similar cases; the antecedents, personal circumstances and characteristics of the contemnor; whether a special deterrent is needed.

As stated above, contempt proceedings are left until after the (original) trial or at least until the end of the prosecution case.[99]

4.7.3 Contempt proceedings in Scotland

Scottish contempt proceedings are dealt with either by the Sheriff or the District Court and are known as a breach of interdict.[100] Depending on the severity of the contempt, the penalty can range from a maximum Level 4 fine to two years' imprisonment (or both) (See: *Johnson v Grant* (1923)[101]; *Johnston v Johnston* (1996)[102]). Active civil proceedings in the Scottish courts are covered by Schedule 1(14) **Contempt of Court Act 1981**; active appellate criminal proceedings are covered by Schedule 1(16) CCA.

Scottish courts have traditionally punished contempt more harshly than English courts. This changed when Peter Cox, a former *Sun* newspaper executive 'south of the border', became editor of the Glasgow-based *Daily Record* in 1998. In this landmark case, commonly known as 'Cox and Griffiths' (see below), Peter Cox challenged the Scottish courts in contempt proceedings, arguing that the **1981 Contempt of Court Act** contravened human rights legislation and press freedom under Art 10 ECHR.

❖ **KEY CASE** | 'Cox and Griffiths' and Glasgow's *Daily Record* (1998)[103]

Facts:
On 10 April 1998, reporter Stuart Griffiths wrote a story for the tabloid *Daily Record*, head-lined 'Armed Convoy', with the subheading: 'Gun cops on guard as prisoners switch jails.' The story was about a dozen 'high-risk' prisoners who were transported 'under massive armed police guard' from Glasgow's Barlinnie Jail along the M8 Motorway to Saughton Prison near Edinburgh. The prisoners were to stand trial on serious drugs and fraud charges

---

99 See: *R v Richardson* [2004] EWCA Crim 758.
100 s. 15 CCA 1981 (incorporated by Criminal Procedure (Scotland) Act 1995).
101 [1923] SC 789.
102 [1996] SLT 499.
103 *Cox (Petitioner) and another* [1998] SCCR 561.

at the Edinburgh High Court on 14 April 1998. Griffiths quoted police fears that 'someone might try to bust them', and said that the police were 'taking no chances on this lot.'

At the start of the trial counsel for one of the defendants asked for proceedings to be stayed due to adverse media coverage, stating that Griffiths' article amounted to 'substantial risk of prejudice', and that the prisoners would not have a right to a fair trial under Art 6 ECHR in that the offending article had seriously impeded the forthcoming trial proceedings and would adversely influence the jury.

Immediately after the conclusion of the trial, editor Peter Cox and reporter Stuart Griffiths were both charged and found guilty of strict liability contempt at the Glasgow Sheriff Court and fined £1,500 each. They appealed against conviction and sentence (*nobile officium*) citing *inter alia* Art 10 ECHR. Counsel for the petitioners argued – citing AG v ITN[104] – that 'the odds against the potential juror reading any of the publications is multiplied by the long odds against a reader remembering it; the risk of prejudice is remote.'

Decision:
Lord Prosser allowed the petition by stating that 'juries are healthy bodies' and that they do not need a 'germ-free' media atmosphere. The finding of contempt was quashed.

The ruling by the Scottish Court of Appeal in 'Cox and Griffiths' was seen as rather liberal at the time, demonstrating a more tolerant attitude towards contempt and *sub judice* in the Scottish press. Some Scottish editors have interpreted Lord Prosser's approach in the case as too liberal, worried that 'Cox and Griffiths' may be misinterpreted, leading to greater liberties when reporting during a *sub judice* period. McInnes (2009b) undertook a research study whereby she examined court reporting and possible contempt situations. She concluded that there is a discrepancy between the Scottish and the English courts' contempt proceedings, arguing that contempt proceedings by the Attorney General 'south of the border' have become increasingly rare.[105]

In *Daily Record and Sunday Mail Ltd v Thomson* (2009),[106] Sheriff Allan found the *Scottish Sun*, the *Daily Record* and STV guilty of contempt. In this case the 'red tops' had reported on footballer Derek Riordan's dock identification and had simultaneously published a photograph of him. Mr Riordan and his cousin, Kevin Burrell, were being tried for assaulting two members of staff at Biddy Mulligan's pub in Edinburgh's Grassmarket and breach of the peace. Following the acquittal of both Riordan and Burrell, the Sheriff Court issued contempt proceedings against the publishers and editors of the said newspapers. The main issue was the Riordan photo because the two civilian complainants in the case had not yet identified the footballer, and Riordan had not yet been cross-examined. The complainants had also been expressly warned not to discuss their evidence with each other. Fining each media outlet £1,750 for contempt, Sheriff Allan concluded:

> . . . the fact that the name of Derek Riordan and his photograph might be well known to many persons who follow football is nothing to the point . . . If, as turned out to be the case here, neither of the two civilian witnesses knew or were ever aware of having previously seen or heard of Derek Riordan, the risk of prejudice or impediment to the course of justice was substantial . . . That is why such great care and attention requires to be given to the question of

---

104 [1995] 2 All ER 370.
105 See: McInnes (2009b).
106 [2009] SLT 363.

the publication of a photograph of an accused person in the course of a trial if identification is an issue.[107]

The *Daily Record*'s proprietors petitioned under *nobile officium* against the contempt finding, arguing that a celebrity footballer's photograph presented a slightly different position, particularly if he was well known. The petitioners accepted that normally the publication of a photo during *sub judice* proceedings would amount to contempt. On 12 March 2009, the Scottish Court of Appeal refused the petition, quoting Lord Justice General Hope in *HM Advocate v Caledonian Newspapers Ltd* (1995)[108], where the *Evening Times* was found in contempt for carrying photographs of the accused in an active case:

> . . . the publication of the photograph, linking the name of the accused to the offence with which he is charged, may assist witnesses in their identification of them as the perpetrator of it. The closer in time and place this is to the publication of the photograph, the greater the risk that this will occur. Similarly, the publication of a photograph . . . may affect the jury's determination of the issue of identification at the trial. The closer the trial is to the date of publication the greater will be the risk.[109]

Both the English and Scottish jurisdictions remain very strict where photographs and identifications are an issue; in this case contempt proceedings will usually ensue.[110]

4.8 Juries and contempt of court

See Chapter 3.6.1. ➔ For all that has already been said about juries, the jury system remains the 'the jewel in the Crown' and 'cornerstone' of the British justice system. Blackstone described the jury system as 'the palladium' and 'grand bulwark' of the Englishman's liberties,[111] and Sir Patrick Devlin spoke of it as 'a little Parliament' and the 'lamp that shows that freedom lives'.[112] But does the jury system still command public confidence as that hallowed institution which, because of its ancient origin and involvement of 12 randomly selected laypeople, serves the justice system best of all? Or are there certain areas of jurisprudence which would be best served without a jury, such as defamation?

The rules of evidence, developed over hundreds of years of jurisprudence, are there to ensure that the facts that go before a jury have been subjected to scrutiny and can be challenged from both sides. Jurors are not supposed to seek information outside of the courtroom. They are required to reach a verdict based only on the facts in the case and they are not supposed to see evidence that has been excluded as prejudicial.[113] In his address to law students at the University of Hertfordshire in November 2008, the Lord Chief Justice, Lord Judge, highlighted the problem the Internet and social networking sites are posing to jury trials. Jurors are increasingly using Twitter or are writing a blog about their court experiences. They might even take mobile phone or video footage of crime

---

107 Ibid., at para 567.
108 [1995] SLT 926.
109 Ibid., at para 931.
110 See: *Haney v HM Advocate* [2003] Appeal Court, High Court of Justiciary; also: *HM Advocate v McGee* [2005] High Court of Justiciary of 12 October 2005 (Lord Abernethy) (unreported); also: *HM Advocate v Cowan* [2007], 27 February 2007 (Sheriff Sinclair) (unreported).
111 Source: Blackstone (1776), vol. IV at page 347.
112 See: Devlin (1956, reprinted 1966), p. 164, quoting, at p. 165, Blackstone's *Commentaries*, at IV, pp 349–50.
113 For further discussion see: Barsby and Ashworth (2004).

scenes when they undertake a reconnaissance visit as part of the evidential stage which, in his experience, some jurors even uploaded on to YouTube.[114]

Can jurors be trusted to obey the judge's instructions to abandon their normal habit during trial proceedings? It would be unrealistic to expect judges or lawyers to police jurors' accessing the World Wide Web and there will be jurors who will seek information on Google about the people they have heard about in court. The use of BlackBerrys, iPhones, Twitter, Facebook and YouTube by jurors gathering and sending out information about cases is wreaking havoc on trials around the USA, upending deliberations and infuriating judges. Professor Gary Slapper (2009) argues that the decision of the Divisional Court by Lord Justice Pill and Mr Justice Sweeney on 20 May 2009 to fine the Times Newspapers £15,000 for a report about a jury's verdict in a manslaughter case strengthens the campaign for reform of the 'indefensible law of contempt of court'.[115]

There are rare occasions where a court orders in *camera* proceedings and a complete reporting ban until the completion of trial proceedings[116] (see: *R v Reigate Justices, ex parte Argus Newspapers and Larcombe* (1983)[117]). The section 11 CCA 1981 provision was invoked during the preliminary hearing of courts-martial proceedings[118] in *re Times Newspapers Ltd* (2008),[119] where Judge Advocate General Blackett, during the preliminary hearing on 4 February 2008, made an order that forthcoming proceedings were to be held in *camera*. The reasons were that there would be substantial risk to national security and a danger of prejudicing administration of justice. In this case, six soldiers – A, B, C, D, E and F – were charged on indictment with conspiracy to defraud.[120] *The Times*, Guardian Media Ltd and Solider B all appealed against the direction, relying on the open justice principle established in *Scott v Scott*[121] that all court proceedings be held in public. The Court of Appeal in *re Times Newspapers Ltd* applied the balancing test between, on the one hand, Article 10's 'freedom of expression' – that the press was entitled to report (supported by the 'contemporaneous' legislation enshrined in the **Contempt of Court Act 1981**), together with the protection and matters of safety concerning British soldiers involved in the war on terror in Afghanistan and Iraq – and, on the other hand, that such matters should be reported as part of the 'discussion on public affairs' as enshrined in s. 5 CCA.[122] The appeal (by the media to report and publish) was allowed.

4.8.1 Jury research

Approximately 800,000 jurors sit each year and yet this practice is still shrouded in secrecy because contempt legislation forbids *any* jury research. There have been numerous debates in Parliament on whether jury trials should be abolished. The 'Morris Committee on Jury Service' (1965) observed that 'in general [there is] an acceptance of the desirability of maintaining the jury system in criminal cases.'[123] The Runciman Royal Commission (1993) urged research into the workings and deliberations of juries, principally with a view to improving the system of jury trials; the report summarized:

> . . . we are conscious that the jury system is widely and firmly believed to be one of the corner-stones of our system of justice. We have received no evidence which would lead us to argue that

---

114 Source: Judge (2008).
115 Source: Commentary in *The Times* by Professor Gary Slapper, 23 May 2009.
116 s. 11 CCA 1981.
117 (1983) 5 Cr App R (S) 181.
118 Under s. 103(2) (mn) Army Act 1955, as inserted by s. 378 of and para. 21 of Schedule 16 Armed Forces Act 2006, and rule 90(I) (2) of the Courts-Martial (Army) Rules 2007 (SI 2007/3442).
119 [2008] EWCA Crim 2396. Courts-Martial Appeal Court.
120 s. 94(2) *Army Act* 1955.
121 [1913] AC 417 (Viscount Haldane).
122 Re. *Times Newspaper* [2008] at para 11.
123 Report of the Departmental Committee on Jury Service, (The Morris Report) (1965), paras 3 and 6.

an alternative method of arriving at a verdict in criminal trials would make the risk of a mistake significantly less.[124]

In his report of the 'Review of the Criminal Courts of England and Wales' (2001), Lord Justice Auld recommended a substantial, if not complete, departure from the present law on jury research as provided by section 8 CCA.[125] When section 8 of the Contempt Bill was first debated in Parliament during the 1980–81 session, it was initially aimed at prohibiting the publication and identification of a juror at trial.[126] Only a House of Lords amendment led to the section 8 regarding juries as it stands now. The then Lord Advocate, Lord Mackay, argued in vain that 'the jury system, great institution that it is, surely can stand up to properly conducted research'. Lord Chancellor Hailsham added that he would not vote for 'a new criminal offence which is to my mind thoroughly bad because it is too draconian'.[127]

Section 8 CCA was enacted after the *New Statesman* magazine was acquitted of 'contempt' by Lord Chief Justice Widgery in 1980,[128] against the background of publishing an interview with one of the witnesses in the sensational 1979 Old Bailey trial in which Jeremy Thorpe, the Liberal politician (and other defendants) were acquitted of conspiracy to murder. In relation to the contempt charge, the Attorney General (AG) had applied for an order at common law following the publication in the magazine of a juror's account of significant parts of the jury deliberations in the course of arriving at their verdict in the trial of Thorpe. The AG's application failed on the ground that the contents of the article did not justify the title of contempt in relation to jury verdicts. The court held that there were 'no special circumstances', other than publication of some of the secrets of the jury room that called for condemnation. Section 8 **Contempt of Court Act 1981** (CCA) creates an offence:

> . . . to obtain, disclose or solicit any particulars of statements made, opinions expressed, arguments advanced or votes cast by members of a jury in the course of their deliberations in any legal proceedings.

Since jury research is not permitted, we do not know what influences jurors or what could be the comparative impact of different forms of reporting, such as national versus local newspapers, broadcast versus print or the reading of an online report. We do not know how far jurors are able to put out of their minds reports which they have seen or heard or how far a true balance can be struck in the jury room between objectivity and the risk of real prejudice. The Society of Editors has called for the contempt of court legislation to be updated to address the restrictions on reporting of 'active' court proceedings and to look at possible jury research and a review of section 8 CCA 1981.

It would be unrealistic to assume that jurors always adhere to a judge's warning: material is easily accessible by jurors online during a trial. Lord Goldsmith, the former Attorney General, had begun to review contempt legislation in 2006 but Attorney General Baroness Scotland had not continued any reform of contempt legislation by the time the General Election was called on 6 May 2010.

Increasingly, jurors have been known to talk to the press 'off the record' after the completion of a trial. In April 2009, the Attorney General instigated legal proceedings against *The Times* and a jury foreman, Michael Seckerson, for breaching s. 8 CCA 1981. The criminal trial in question took place at Reading Crown Court in November 2007 and concerned childminder Mrs Keran

124 Report of the Royal Commission on Criminal Justice (1993), Chapter 1, para 8.
125 Ministry of Justice (2001), Chapter 5, para 98.
126 See: House of Commons (1980); see also: House of Commons (1981).
127 Source: Lord Advocate, Lord Mackay of Clashfern and Lord Hailsham LC, 416 House of Lords Debates, Hansard, col. 385, 20 January 1981.
128 *AG v New Statesman and Nation Publishing Co Ltd* [1981] QB 1.

Henderson, who was charged with manslaughter by shaking 11-month-old Maeve Sheppard from Slough to death. Mrs Henderson was convicted and given a three-year prison sentence; she served half her sentence and was released in May 2009. Following the trial, jury foreman Mr Seckerson published an article in *The Times* on 29 January 2008, expressing his strong disagreement with the majority jury verdict of 10:2. He believed the defendant had been wrongly convicted. He wrote:

> . . . I begin to hope that the accused is innocent, as I despise what seem like cheap tricks of interrogation . . . It remains for us to hear the summing up then retire to consider our verdict . . . Now we, the jury, culled from the streets and with scarcely a PhD among us, must judge this case.[129]

Criminal contempt charges against *The Times* and Mr Seckerson were subsequently brought by Baroness Scotland of Asthal, QC, the Attorney General, under section 8 CCA of the **Contempt of Court Act**, which bans disclosure of 'votes cast, statements made, opinions expressed or arguments advanced' by jurors in their deliberations. At the contempt hearing, lawyers for the *Times* newspaper group argued that 'freedom of expression' under Art 10 ECHR gave the press the right to reveal what went on in judicial proceedings, as long as it did not prejudice or jeopardize the authority and impartiality of the judiciary. Philip Havers QC, for the AG, accepted that the offending juror's article was in the public interest but argued that the case could have a serious effect on the willingness of jurors to raise concerns about verdicts in future. On 13 May 2009, jury foreman Michael Seckerson and *The Times* were found guilty of contempt. In his judgment, Lord Justice Pill said:

> . . . the disclosure of the 10:2 vote was a clear breach of section 8(1) CCA 1981. It was a breach as it disclosed a vote. Moreover, it revealed the opinions expressed by ten members of the jury, at an early stage of a long deliberation.[130]

The newspaper was fined £15,000 and Michael Seckerson was fined £500 on the same criminal contempt charge. The AG was awarded £27,426 costs, which had to be paid by *The Times* because Mr Seckerson was legally aided.

The Divisional Court concluded that the *Times* article breached section 8 CCA for two reasons. First, because the newspaper disclosed that the jury's verdict was split 10:2 immediately after the jurors began their deliberations and that there was 'no going back'. This meant that the jury had formed their views early, before closing speeches and the judge's direction, and they were clearly not going to change their minds. The second basis for contempt was that the article reported the foreman's concern that 'the case was decided by laymen and laywomen using that despicable enemy of correct and logical thinking, that wonderfully persuasive device, common sense', when there should have been careful consideration and analysis of expert evidence on behalf of each jury member. The Divisional Court held that this was to 'reveal the approach of the jury to the evidence in this case'.

Section 8 CCA does not permit the public interest defence. Otherwise *The Times* might have had a strong basis for arguing that alleged child cruelty is in the public interest in relation to how juries assess expert medical evidence, or whether they actually understand what was being said in court. At the time of publication, *The Times* and Mr Seckerson were seeking permission to appeal to the House of Lords against the High Court's findings.

---

129 Source: 'Juror speaks out' by Mike Seckerson, *The Times*, 29 January 2008.
130 Source: 'Times is accused of revealing jury room secrets' by Chris Smyth, *The Times*, 9 April 2009.

Section 8 CCA does not sit comfortably with section 5 defence (argued above) which states that a person is not guilty of the strict liability contempt if they can show that publication is part of a discussion in good faith and is a matter of public interest; and that the risk of impediment or prejudice is merely incidental to that discussion (see above 4.7.1)

Following the contempt findings in the *Times* case in May 2009, Lord (David) Pannick QC commented that section 8 CCA, as applied by the Divisional Court in the case, was 'an embarrassment to the legal system'. He argued further that there was no conceivable damage to the administration of justice as there was no naming of any individual juror. Only a volunteer, Michael Seckerson, had been identified (by himself); all other jurors had remained anonymous and had not been exposed. The court had punished *The Times* for publishing material which actually contributed to a debate on an important matter of public interest, namely child abuse. Lord Pannick concludes:

> . . . any sensible jury would unanimously conclude that Section 8 is guilty as charged and is badly in need of amendment.[131]

See Chapter 6 → There is increased openness regarding public information under the **Freedom of Information Act 2000**. Should there not be similar increased openness in the justice system? Does the public not have a right to know how a jury decides its verdict or how it reaches an award for damages in defamation actions? In 1957, Sir Patrick, later Lord, Devlin observed that abolishing juries was one of the first things a dictator taking over Britain would do, because 'no tyrant could afford to leave a subject's freedom in the hands of 12 of his countrymen'.[132] With anything this important, many would argue for the need to know how it works. In so far as Section 8 of the **Contempt of Court Act 1981** prevents research on how juries work, many feel it is an anachronistic law and should be reformed urgently.[133]

A groundbreaking piece of jury research was published in 2010, commissioned by the Ministry of Justice.[134] The research, and case simulation with real juries from Crown Courts at Winchester, Nottingham and Blackfriars (London), was conducted by Professor Cheryl Thomas, involving 797 jurors on 68 juries.[135] The study found little evidence that juries are not fair. However, it identified several areas where the criminal justice system could better assist jurors in performing this vital role. Professor Thomas' study observed an efficient and effective English jury system where a verdict was reached by deliberation on 89 per cent of all charges within the control groups. And once juries deliberated, they reached verdicts on virtually all charges (only 0.6 per cent of all verdicts are hung juries). Juries convict on almost two-thirds (64 per cent) of all charges presented to them.[136]

A total of 660 jurors were assessed in relation to media influence and their decision-making. Jurors serving on high-profile cases were almost seven times more likely to recall media coverage (70 per cent) than jurors serving on standard cases (11 per cent). In relation to 'the fade factor', Thomas' research established that most jurors only recalled media reports of their case during the time their trial was going on (see above 4.5.2). The further away media reports were from a trial the more likely they were to fade from jurors' memories. However, a third of jurors (35 per cent) on high-profile cases remembered pre-trial coverage. Those jurors who admitted they had 'researched' the case via the Internet were aged 30 and over (68 per cent). In high-profile cases

---

131 Source: Comment in *The Times* by Lord Pannick QC, 28 May 2009.
132 Devlin (1956 reprinted 1966), pp. 159–60.
133 See also: Home Office (2002).
134 Source: Ministry of Justice (2010a).
135 The case simulations were conducted with 41 all-white juries at Winchester and Nottingham Crown Courts (478 jurors). It replicated an earlier study of racially mixed juries at Blackfriars Crown Court in London (27 juries with 319 jurors); see also: Ministry of Justice (2007).
136 Source: Ministry of Justice (2010a), pp. 6–8.

some 81 per cent admitted searching the Internet for background information.[137] Most importantly, the study demonstrated that section 8 of the **Contempt of Court Act 1981** does not prevent comprehensive research about how juries reach their verdicts and that research from other jurisdictions should not be relied upon to understand juries in this country.

⊙ **FOR THOUGHT**

Is there a compelling argument to change or even repeal the law relating to contempt of court?

4.8.2 Juries and the digital age

We do not know how many jurors in today's digital society are obeying the judge's orders at a criminal trial. By using mobile phones or hand-held devices they can look up the name of a defendant on the Web or examine a crime's location by using Google Maps, thereby violating the legal system's complex rules of evidence. They can also tell their friends what is happening in the jury room via Twitter once they have left the courtroom, in spite of the fact that they will have been warned by the judge to keep their opinions and deliberations secret. However, a present-day jury direction at the start of a trial will normally include a warning not to consult the Internet or any other form of communication (including social networking sites) until the full conclusion of the trial. It is therefore generally assumed that the judge's directions are accepted and obeyed. The Wooler Report (2006)[138] on 'jury fitness' commented on increased problems with long and complex trials involving accusations of money-laundering or fraud. Often juries did not understand the proceedings or what was evidenced in court and would consult 'background' information to assist them during the trial.

In March 2009, the *New York Times* reported that a juror in a big federal drug trial in Florida had admitted to the judge that he had been doing 'research' on the background of the case on the Internet. Federal Judge William J. Zloch responded by telling the juror that he had directly violated the judge's instructions; at the same time the judge questioned the rest of the jury and learnt that eight other jurors had been doing the same thing. Judge Zloch declared a mistrial citing contempt of court.[139] There are signs that not only American jurors are using the Internet for background research during a trial. In R v *Thakrar* (2008),[140] six weeks into a complex money-laundering trial, the following note was sent from the jury foreman to the trial judge:

> . . . around the third week into this trial a fellow juror announced to us all that he had been looking on the Internet and found on www.bbc.co.uk information that related to one of the defendants, Mr Ketan Thakrar, who is alleged to have been arrested, tried and found guilty of money laundering in 2001. The juror said to us all that he felt it was fair that we knew all this.[141]

This resulted in a successful appeal by the defence citing contempt of court by way of section 8 CCA. Bearing in mind that only about one per cent of criminal trials are heard by a jury, it would be fair to assume that, from time to time, an individual juror will disregard the judge's directions and will make his own private enquiries into the background of a court hearing.

---

137 Ibid.
138 See: Wooler (2006).
139 Source: 'As jurors turn to web, mistrials are popping up', by John Schwartz, *The New York Times*, 17 March 2009.
140 [2008] EWCA Crim 2359.
141 Ibid., at para 2374.

👁 FOR THOUGHT

In our global world of regular internet use, blogs and social networking sites, do you think that jurors really are prejudiced by what they have seen or heard in the media? Can courts still rely on the 'fade factor', assuming that the risk of prejudice is greater, the nearer the reporting is to the trial, and fades over time?

4.8.3 Courtroom TV: the O.J. Simpson trial and the UK *Speechley* appeal

Contempt laws historically exist in the United States but are reportedly not often adhered to. However, Federal Judge Susan Webber Wright raised issues of 'contempt' in her well-publicized decision on 14 April 1999, concerning President Bill Clinton's lying on factual grounds in a deposition about his relationship with Monica Lewinsky. Judge Webber Wright held that the US President was in (civil) contempt of court by making Mr Clinton subject to a fine. Criminal contempt could have raised the question of whether the President had committed a crime for which he could have been subject to impeachment.

One of the most publicized criminal cases in US legal history was that of O.J. Simpson in 1995. It was also the first fully live broadcast criminal trial. The former American football hero and well-known actor stood trial for the murders of his former wife Nicole Brown Simpson and her gym friend Ronald Goldman, who had both been found stabbed to death at Nicole's house in Brentwood, Los Angeles on 12 June 1994. Every day for nine months, the public was glued to 'O.J. TV', with live coverage from the Superior Court of California in Los Angeles. Everyone knew there were 11 lawyers representing O.J., and that there were 150 witnesses giving evidence before a predominantly black jury from January until October 1995. The jury was never shown. But on 3 October 1995, 'Madam Foreperson' handed the jury verdict of 'not guilty' on both counts of murder to the court clerk, Mrs Robertson, who read out the verdict on the jury's behalf. Millions of people around the world then witnessed the visible grief and shock on the faces of the family victims caught on courtroom cameras.[142]

Following Simpson's not-guilty verdict, the Goldman family pursued O.J. Simpson in the civil courts. This trial was heard in 1997. Under California law, before the jury could award punitive damages they had to consider the reprehensibility of the alleged crime. The jury of six men and six women found O.J. Simpson liable for the deaths and ordered him to pay damages to the Goldman family of $38 million and to the Simpson family of $24 million.

As it is a fundamental right for jurors to speak out after a trial under the Seventh Amendment to the US Constitution, some jurors in the O.J. Simpson civil case gave interviews to the media after the conclusion of the trial (see: *Bridges v California* (1941)[143]). Juror No. 266, a woman in her 40s, told the press that her decision was based on everything she heard in court, especially the evidence that by now had become part of the nation's legal lore: the bloody-soled shoes, the incidents of wife-beating, the bloody gloves, the sweat-suited figure in the dark, Mr Simpson's taking the stand, the statement that 'he was not credible'.[144] The public also learnt from dissenting juror No. 294, a

---

142 BBC World Tonight OJ Simpson verdict 3 October 1995 (streamed audio broadcast) 'OJ Simpson is found not guilty of the murders of his ex-wife Nicole and her friend Ronald Goldman'; Bill Turnbull World Tonight report on the verdict available at <http://news.bbc.co.uk/player/nol/newsid_6560000/newsid_6568600/6568623.stm?bw=bb&mp=wm&news=1&bbcws=1>, accessed 30 November 2010.
143 [1941] 62 S. Ct. 190.
144 Source: 'Jury Decides Simpson Must Pay $25 Million in Punitive Award' By B. Drummond Ayres Jr., *The New York Times*, 11 February 1997, p. A1.

lady in her 20s, that there was a 10:2 verdict and that in her opinion the punitive damages should have been 'millions less' because she did not believe Mr Simpson had $25 million. A photo of nine jurors accompanied the *New York Times* article.

On 18 December 2009, Chief Judge Alex Kozinski of the United States Court of Appeals for the Ninth Circuit announced that video cameras would be allowed in civil trials. This meant that TV cameras and video recordings were installed in courtrooms in Alaska, Arizona, California, Hawaii, Idaho, Montana, Nevada, Oregon and Washington.[145] One of the first cases to be televised was the hearing concerning California's ban on same-sex marriages in January 2010.

In Britain, history was made in the Criminal Division of the Court of Appeal on 16 November 2004, when TV cameras were allowed to film and record the 'Speechley Appeal'.[146] Though the case was never broadcast, the pilot project was the first step towards the introduction of courtroom TV in England and Wales, approved by the Lord Chancellor, the Lord Chief Justice and the Master of the Rolls.

As part of a wider consultation project, the (then) Department of Constitutional Affairs (DCA) wanted to investigate the wider issues surrounding courtroom behaviour. The then Lord Chancellor, Lord Falconer, ordered the consultation project to seek wider views on the introduction of courtroom TV from the public, ministers, lawyers, judges and broadcasters. The O.J. experience from the United States was also taken into account. The overarching question was whether courtroom broadcasts would boost public confidence in the British legal system?

The 'Speechley Appeal' concerned former Lincolnshire County Council Leader Jim Speechley after he had been convicted at Sheffield Crown Court in April 2003 of 'misconduct in public office' and sentenced to 18 months imprisonment.[147] The councillor, who was released pending his appeal, was found to have tried to influence the route of the Crowland bypass to increase the value of a pocket of land he owned. The cameras were focused on the lawyers in the case and on the appeal judges, Lord Justice Kennedy (presiding), Mr Justice Bell and Mr Justice Hughes. William Harbage QC and Catarina Sjolin appeared for the appellant.[148] The recording took place at the Royal Courts of Justice from 16 to 18 November 2004, when robotic cameras focused mainly on the judges and barristers, but not on the dock or the witness box. Both the conviction and sentence were upheld, though Lord Justice Kennedy reduced £25,000 court costs to £10,000.

The case was taped and edited as if for broadcast by Roy Scotton of 'Bow Tie Television' (the company in charge of parliamentary and Supreme Court broadcasts) and the result was shown to a panel of government ministers and senior judges before a decision was made whether to take the idea of courtroom TV any further. The 'Speechley Appeal' was regarded as a resounding success and the panel commented that there should be no reason why such appeals should not be shown on public TV as part of bringing the 'open justice principle' to people who had otherwise no time or inclination to attend court. 'Speechley' and routine parliamentary and Supreme Court (Sky TV and BBC) public broadcasts have demonstrated that the technology is good enough and they make for interesting educational viewing – as long as there are proper safeguards in the provision of camera-free areas in court, such as the dock, the witness stand and the jury.

---

145 Source: 'Rule invites cameras into federal civil cases', by John Schwartz, *The New York Times*, 18 December 2009, p. A12.
146 *R v Speechley* [2004] (unreported) (CA).
147 Source: 'Cameras record High Court appeal', *BBC News Online*, 16 November 2004, available at <http://news.bbc.co.uk/1/hi/england/lincolnshire/4015977.stm>, accessed 22 November 2010.
148 Source: 'William Harbage QC filmed live in the court of appeal', 36 Bedford Row: the Chambers of Frances Oldham QC, 15 December 2004, available at <http://www.36bedfordrow.co.uk/new_news.php?news_id=42&news_type=-1>, accessed 22 November 2010.

4.8.4 The Lockerbie trial

On 22 December 1988, at 19.03 hours, Pan Am Flight 103 fell out of the sky over the Scottish town of Lockerbie. All 259 passengers and crew members and 11 residents of Lockerbie were killed. As a result, two men – Abdelbaset Ali Mohmed Al Megrahi and Al Amin Khalifa Fhimah – were arrested and their trial began on 2 February 2000 at the Scottish Court, but in the Netherlands (see below).[149] The Crown's case was that the cause of the disaster was that an explosive device had been introduced into the hold of the aircraft by the two accused. This device exploded when the aircraft was in Scottish airspace, thus causing the aircraft to disintegrate. Both accused were found guilty of murder.

The BBC had petitioned to the *nobile officium* of the Lord Advocate at the High Court of Justiciary in Edinburgh to seek permission to broadcast the proceedings which – for security reasons – were being held at Camp Zeist in the Netherlands.[150] Scottish Television Ltd and seven other TV broadcasting companies also sought the Scottish High Court's consent to broadcast the trial proceedings. The BBC's petition for consent read:

> . . . to televise the proceedings of the trial (a) for the purpose of broadcasting simultaneously the entire proceedings of the trial, (b) for the purpose of broadcasting edited portions of the proceedings of the trial in news broadcasts and other broadcasts of topical or other interest, and (c) for the compiling and broadcasting after the ending of the proceedings of the trial one or more documentary programmes on the circumstances surrounding the subject of the trial and including parts of the proceedings of the trial, and that subject to such conditions as to [the court] shall seem proper.[151]

Mr Martin QC for the first petitioners emphasized the unique nature of the application and the trial proceedings before a bench of three Lords Commissioners of Justiciary, sitting without a jury.[152] He stressed that the petitioners did not seek to establish any precedent, either in domestic Scots law or by reference to Article 10 ECHR, to the effect that broadcasters have a right to broadcast the proceedings in criminal trials generally. The Lockerbie trial proceedings in 2000 and appeal hearings in 2002 were broadcast live (in both English and Arabic) over the Internet by the BBC and streamed across the world.[153]

4.8.6 Pros and cons of courtroom broadcasts

One danger of courtroom TV is that it might be sensationalist and have a potential effect in high-profile trials, as already witnessed by the media circus which surrounded the 'Soham trial' of Ian

---

149 The judges were Lord Sutherland (presiding), Lord Coulsfield and Lord MacLean; an additional judge, Lord Abernethy, was also appointed to participate in deliberations and to act as a substitute if necessary.
150 *HM Advocate v Abdelbaset Ali Mohmed Al Megrahi and Al Amin Khalifa Fhimah (Prisoners in the Prison of Camp Zeist [Kamp van Zeist] v the Netherlands* [2000] Case No: 1475/99, in the High Court of Justiciary at Camp Zeist (sub nom 'The Lockerbie Trial').
151 British Broadcasting Corporation and others to the *nobile officium* of the High Court of Justiciary, Edinburgh, 7 March 2000, at para. 2.
152 The arrangements were regulated by an intergovernmental agreement between Her Majesty's Government and the Government of the Kingdom of the Netherlands. The legislative basis for the proceedings was: Order in Council made under s.1 United Nations Act 1946, namely the High Court of Justiciary (Proceedings in the Netherlands) (United Nations) Order 1998 (S.I. 1998 No. 2251) ('the Order'). Article 3 of the Order (1) enabled the High Court of Justiciary to sit in the Netherlands for the purpose of conducting the specified criminal proceedings on indictment against the first and second accused, and (2) provided that the proceedings before the court sitting in the Netherlands were to be conducted 'in accordance with the law relating to proceedings on indictment before the High Court of Justiciary in Scotland'. Article 5(1) provided for the appointment of three Lords Commissioners of Justiciary to constitute the court for the purposes of the trial to be conducted by virtue of the Order, and Article 5(3) provided that the trial be conducted without a jury.
153 See: *BBC News Online* live video coverage throughout the appeal of convicted Lockerbie bomber Abdelbaset Ali Mohmed Al Megrahi, 24 June 2002, available at <http://news.bbc.co.uk/1/hi/world/1766508.stm>, accessed 22 November 2010.

Huntley in December 2003. Huntley was the school caretaker accused of killing 10-year-old schoolgirls Holly Wells and Jessica Chapman in August 2002. The argument against courtroom TV rests on the belief that the camera's presence might intimidate witnesses and affect their testimony, thereby creating an O.J. Simpson-style media circus.

As the law stands, broadcasting images of the witness box would not comply with victim protection legislation such as the **Crime and Disorder Act 1998**, the **Protection from Harassment Act 1997** or the **Vulnerable Witness (Scotland) Act 2004**.[154] However, there could be a public interest in allowing filming of a prosecution or defence opening to a jury and of mitigation and sentence; judicial discretion should then allow or disallow filming built into contempt of court legislation.[155] But equally, as the Lockerbie trial and Speechley Appeal have shown, there is a strong case for courtroom broadcasting, not just for public interest concerns but also for educational reasons, such as law school training and introducing the open justice principle to schools and colleges.

The argument in favour of courtroom broadcasts is that television has long been the principal source of information for the majority of people. Just as parliamentary broadcasts are freely accessible, public broadcasting should now cover all aspects of public life, including the justice system. With the advancement of technology and the inclusion of internet video transmission on most public media websites, the administration of justice ought to be publically accessible.

On 1 October 2009, British legal history was made with the new Supreme Court taking over from the House of Lords as the highest court in the land and final appeal court in criminal matters. Now cases and judgments are broadcast live (by Sky News), in a move some legal experts believe could pave the way for more widespread televising of legal proceedings. The Supreme Court is the result of the **Constitutional Reform Act** of 2005, aimed at separating the highest appeal court from the upper house of Parliament – the House of Lords – and physically removing the Law Lords from the legislature.

But courtroom TV in ordinary courts, particularly family and criminal courts, as well as the Court of Appeal, needs a change in the law to allow cameras and live streaming in courtrooms, currently prevented by section 41 **Criminal Justice Act 1925** ('Prohibition on taking photographs in court') and general contempt legislation (see above 4.6.4).

It remains to be seen whether British courtroom TV will catch on and, if so, whether it will change public opinion towards the justice system by granting greater access to the open court system. However, it may be that courtroom TV could become primarily entertainment like the *Jeremy Kyle Show* or *Judge Judy*. In spite of the apparent success of the 'Speechley' courtroom TV trials, it is not envisaged that this practice will be adopted by the Royal Courts of Justice in the near future, according to Master Venne, Registrar of Criminal Appeals due to human rights issues, such as Article 6 ECHR, and the safe protection of vulnerable witnesses.[156] Generally, one would not anticipate a vast audience for routine court cases broadcast on the 'courtroom TV' channel, as is already the case with broadcasts on the BBC's Parliament channel.

4.9 The 'Suffolk Ripper': who still observes the law of contempt? Analysis and discussion

One story dominated the British 'red tops' from the beginning of December 2006, culminating in a *Sunday Mirror* 'scoop' on 17 December about someone dubbed the 'Suffolk Ripper', who had killed

---

154 The Vulnerable Witness (Scotland) Act 2004 is aimed at making it easier for child and adult vulnerable witnesses to give their best evidence by formalizing existing special measures for giving evidence and introducing new measures, such as locations outside the court house known as 'remote sites'.
155 ss. 4(2) and 11 CCA 1981 would still be available to the court should it be felt necessary.
156 Author's interview with Master Roger Venne on 21 September 2010 at the Royal Courts of Justice.

five prostitutes near Ipswich, Suffolk. The story featured Tom Stephens, a former Special Constable and supermarket worker. At that time, Stephens was merely a police suspect. Relentlessly, the story ran for days – including the full *sub judice* period – well into the middle of December 2006.

Identification was clearly an issue and police were still appealing for call girl witnesses to come forward. The story was likened to the Yorkshire Ripper story (see above 4.3.1). Tom Stephens was linked to the prostitutes by the *Sunday Mirror* because he had said on his social networking MySpace page that he knew and had befriended the girls. The *Mirror* used Stephens' own online blog title with its sensational headline: ' "Call Me The Bishop": Ripper Exclusive' on 19 December 2006.

It was problematic for the Attorney General's office and media editors, because, in the news-papers' defence, prime suspect Stephens had 'outed' himself via his own blog and further on local radio that he knew the murdered women intimately. BBC Radio Suffolk broadcast a live 36-minute interview conducted by Trudi Barber with Tom Stephens on 12 December – at which point he had been formally arrested by the Suffolk police. The interview included full comment and personal conjecture about the vice girls' brutal murders, where Stephens said: 'I had been a client of a number of the girls, including Gemma . . . I was probably the closest thing Tania had to a boyfriend . . . we had an arrangement that suited us both.'[157] Mr Stephens' request was that the broadcast was for background purposes only and was not originally intended for public use.

Was this not clearly contempt of court? Adrian Van-Klaveren, Deputy Director of BBC News at the time, thought not and defended the BBC's decision to broadcast the Stephens interview during the *sub judice* period via his editor's blog on 21 December 2006, where he wrote:

> . . . following Tom Stephens' arrest on Monday, we took the decision to transmit the interview on the basis that there had been an exceptional change in circumstances. The anonymity, which Mr Stephens had sought to preserve by making the interview for background only, no longer applied. His name and many other details about him were very much in the public domain. We felt there was a compelling public interest in letting the public hear what he had to say. He knew all five of the murdered women, two of them well. He had much to say about the world of drug dealers and financial pressures in which they lived. On balance it seemed to us to be wrong to deny people the opportunity to hear his thoughts on the events of the past few weeks. Of course, we reflected long and hard about the legal and ethical issues this interview raised. We are confident that nothing we have broadcast could prejudice any future trial. We also reached the conclusion that nothing we broadcast could reasonably be expected to impede the ongoing police investigation.[158]

Why did the Attorney General not intervene in the 'Suffolk Ripper' story? Why did contempt laws not defend a subsequently innocent Tom Stephens? One answer is that the initial prime suspect, Stephens, had openly disclosed himself via a social networking site and his BBC radio interview. In the end, a second man – Stephen Wright – was charged and found guilty of the murder of the five women. But had Tom Stephens been tried for their murder instead, it would have been open to the Attorney General to commence contempt proceedings against the media.

But the media coverage, even after Stephen Wright had become a (second) suspect in the pros-titute killings, continued to be relentless about Wright with full background coverage in the 'red tops'. Arguably, he did not stand a chance of a fair trial, particularly since it was held locally at the Crown Court in Ipswich with a local jury who would almost certainly have remembered the

157 Source: 'The Tom Stephens interview', BBC Radio Suffolk, 12 December 2006, available at <http://news.bbc.co.uk/player/nol/newsid_6190000/newsid_6190000/6190031.stm?bw=bb&mp=wm&news=1&ms3=6&ms_javascript=true&nol_storyid=6190031&bbcws=2>, accessed 1 February 2011.

158 Source: BBC editors' blog by Adrian van-Klaveren, Tuesday, 19 December 2006, available at <http://www.bbc.co.uk/blogs/theeditors/2006/12/the_tom_stephens_interview.html>, accessed 1 February 2011.

extensive media coverage at the time. Did Wright have a fair trial under contempt and human rights legislation (Article 6 ECHR)?[159] Forklift truck driver Stephen Wright, who had been arrested shortly after Tom Stephens on 19 December 2006, was found guilty of murder by a majority verdict by an Ipswich jury of nine men and three women on 21 February 2008.[160]

4.9.1 Does contempt law interfere with human rights?

By its nature, the law of contempt places restrictions on the freedom of expression and press freedom in general. Given a number of Strasbourg decisions, the UK courts must now give weight to Article 10 ECHR in relation to freedom of speech. In *Gregory v United Kingdom* (1997),[161] the Human Rights Court drew attention to its decision in *Remli v France* (1996),[162] commenting that Art 6(1) ECHR imposes an obligation on *every* national court to check whether it is 'an impartial tribunal' within the meaning of that provision, which was considered in relation to admissible (hearsay) evidence before a jury and whether such evidence adduced would jeopardize a fair trial. What if jurors 'research' the background to the trial via the Internet? Would that amount to jury bias? In *Remli* the trial judges had failed to react to an allegation that an identifiable juror had been overheard to say that he was a racist. In the circumstances, the court established within the meaning of Article 6(1) ECHR that sufficient guarantees were put in place to dispel any doubts.

In *Sander v United Kingdom* (2000),[163] an Asian accused was on trial with two others for conspiracy to defraud. The judge had almost completed his summing up when a juror handed a letter to the court usher in which he alleged that at least two of the jurors had been making openly racist remarks during the jury's deliberation; the said juror had expressed his concern that the defendants would not receive a fair trial verdict. The judge, having discussed the complaint with counsel in chambers, decided not to discharge the jury immediately or to conduct an inquiry. He told the jury to search their consciences overnight and to let the court know if they felt that they were not able to try the case solely on the evidence. Having received their assurances by letter the next morning that the jury would reach its verdict without racial bias, the judge allowed the trial to proceed and the accused were duly convicted.

In *Sander*, the ECtHR held that there had been a violation of Art 6(1) ECHR on the ground that the trial judge should have acted in a more robust manner; that he had failed to provide sufficient guarantees to exclude any objectively justified or legitimate doubts about the impartiality of the court. *Sander* is important because the Strasbourg Court took the opportunity to review its decision in *Gregory* (1997),[164] regarding the fundamental importance of public confidence in the courts and the rule governing the secrecy of jury deliberations.

The same question was addressed by the House of Lords in the two parallel appeals in *Mirza* and *Connor* (2004):[165] whether evidence about jury deliberations that revealed a lack of impartiality was always inadmissible under the common law secrecy rule. The issue in *Mirza* concerned a juror who had revealed after the verdict that, during jury deliberations, that some jury members were associated with a neo-Nazi group, and that they strongly influenced the conviction of the accused because he was a black immigrant. In *Connor*, a juror had revealed after the verdict that a majority of the jury refused to deliberate at all and had made up its mind virtually at the start of the trial; that jury ultimately arrived at a guilty verdict by spinning a coin.

---

159 For further discussion see: Smartt (2007).
160 Source: 'Steve Wright guilty of Ipswich prostitutes' murders', by Bonnie Malkin, *The Daily Telegraph*, 21 February 2008.
161 (1997) 25 EHRR 577.
162 (1996) 22 EHRR 253, 271–272, paras 47 and 48.
163 (2000) 31 EHRR 1003.
164 (1997) 25 EHRR 577.
165 *R v Connor and another; R v Mirza* [2004] (conjoined appeals) UKHL 2 (HL).

Dismissing appeals in both *Mirza* and *Connor*, the House of Lords stated that common and statutory provision of contempt of court was well established in the area of jury deliberations. However, their Lordships commented *obiter* that this law may not be altogether well suited towards the 'modern' jury member today and that the courts may have attached undue weight to the confidentiality of jury deliberations in the past. It was for these reasons that their Lordships did not admit the evidence and allegations in the letters by the jurors in both *Mirza* and *Connor*, stating that this was not a sound basis on which one could base an unsafe jury verdict. The appeals were dismissed. Their Lordships commented *inter alia* that the Court of Appeal could not be held in contempt of itself when exercising the jurisdiction to hear evidence about what happened in the jury room. For this reason section 8 CCA would not impinge on the jurisdiction of the Court of Appeal to receive evidence which it regards as relevant to the disposal of an appeal.

4.10 Summary of key points

- Strict liability contempt means that a publication or broadcast during 'active' proceedings (the *sub judice* period) can be treated as a contempt by interfering with the course of justice regardless of intent to do (s. 1 CCA 1981);
- A 'publication' includes any speech, writing, broadcast, online or other communication addressed to the public at large (s. 2(1) CCA);
- A journalist, editor, publisher or broadcaster is not guilty of contempt if the publication is a fair and accurate report of legal proceedings held in public and published contemporaneously (s. 4 CCA);
- The Attorney General (AG) brings contempt proceedings as part of the administrative court procedure (Rules of the Supreme Court Order 52);
- General defences can be found under Schedule 1, section 3 CCA;
- Section 5 CCA provides a statutory defence concerning 'discussion of public affairs';
- Jury research is not permitted under section 8 CCA;
- It is a contempt of court to obtain, disclose or solicit any particulars of jury statements made, opinions expressed, arguments advanced or votes cast by members of a jury in the course of their deliberations in any legal proceedings (s. 8 CCA);
- Proceedings for a contempt of court at common law are generally commenced with the consent of the Attorney General (in Scotland: Advocate General).

4.11 Further reading

Barendt, E. (2009) *Media Freedom and Contempt of Court: Library of Essays in Media Law*. London: Ashgate.

Barsby, C. and Ashworth, A. J. (2004) 'Juries: Contempt of Court Act 1981, s. 8. Case Comment.' *Criminal Law Review*. Crim. L.R. 2004, Dec, 1041–44.

Blackstone, Sir William (1825) *Commentaries on the Laws of England*. 16th Edition, Book IV. London: University of Cambridge.

Craig, R. (2009) 'Non-jury courts in Northern Ireland'. *Criminal Law and Justice Weekly*, 6 June, 2009, available at ←http://www.criminallawandjustice.co.uk/index.php?/Analysis/non-jury-courts-in-northern-ireland.html→, accessed 22 November 2010.

Fox, Sir John C. (1927) *The History of Contempt of Court. The Form of Trial and the Mode of Punishment*. Oxford: The Clarendon Press.

Jaconelli, J. (2007) 'Defences to speech crimes'. *European Human Rights Law Review*. 1, 27–46.

MacQueen, H. (2006) *Studying Scots Law*. 3rd Edition. Edinburgh: Tottel Publishing.

McInnes, R. (2009a) 'Footballers' faces: photographs, identification and publication contempt'. Scots Law Times, 21, 123–6.

Matthews, R., Hancock, L. and Briggs, D. (2004) 'Jurors' Perceptions, Understanding, Confidence and Satisfaction in the Jury System: a Study in Six Courts'. Research Development and Statistics Directorate. Home Office Report No. 05/04/2004.

Ministry of Justice (2010a) 'Are juries fair?' Research conducted by Professor Cheryl Thomas of the Centre for Empirical Legal Studies, University College. London Ministry of Justice Bulletin Number 39, March 2010.

Oswald, J.F. (2009) *Contempt of Court, Committal, and Attachment and Arrest Upon Civil Process*. London: BiblioBazaar.

Smartt, U. (2007) 'Who still observes the law of contempt?' Justice of the Peace, 3 February 2007, Vol. 171: 76–83

Young, J. (1981) 'The Contempt of Court Act 1981'. *British Journal of Law & Society*, Vol. 8, No 2, Winter 1981, pp. 243ff.

Chapter 5

Reporting Legal Proceedings

Chapter Contents

5.1 Overview

The open justice principle, as clearly recognized by Parliament and the courts, grants the public and media statutory and common law rights to attend all court proceedings in UK courts and tribunals.[1] There will be circumstances when the court may justify hearing a case *in camera* (in secret), for instance where the nature of the evidence, if made public, would cause harm to national security or identifying a person whose identity should be protected for strong public interest reasons. The test is one of necessity and an application to proceed *in camera* should be supported by relevant evidence.[2]

See Chapter
1.4

It is a particularly essential prerequisite that the criminal justice system be administered in public. However, there are a number of statutory exceptions. To date, there has been no formal guidance in relation to the issue of reporting restrictions in proceedings in the UK criminal courts, with the consequence that on occasion matters have been wrongly reported. The common law attaches a very high degree of importance to hearing cases in open court, also supported by Article 6 ECHR – the right to a public hearing and to public pronouncement of judgment – which are protected as part of the right to a fair trial.

To restrain the freedom of the press there should be a pressing social need for the restriction, convincingly established by proper, concrete evidence and the restrictions must be proportionate to the legitimate aim pursued. The need for any reporting restriction must be convincingly established and the terms of any order ought to be proportionate, going no further than is necessary to meet the relevant objective, as was held in *A-G v Leveller Magazine Ltd* (1979).[3] One example could be if one report refers to an unnamed defendant having been convicted of rape of his daughter and another report names the defendant but does not identify the relationship between the defendant and the witness. This is referred to as 'jigsaw identification'.

It is important where any automatic restriction applies or a discretionary order is made that it is made clear in the judgment of the court so that journalists understand the issue of such a discretionary order. This chapter looks at such proceedings and orders. Since reports may already have appeared before the case reaches the court, the court should be very slow to interfere with this agreed practice, even where interference is possible, since it may result in the sort of identification that the codes are intended to prevent (see: R v Southwark Crown Court Ex parte Godwin and Others (1992)[4] – below).

It is of course important to distinguish between reporting the facts and contents of a case and applying names to the participants – increasingly questions are being asked, particularly where children are involved, if it is sufficient if the content of the case is published without the need to provide specific identities – is the latter merely feeding a prurient public or meeting any justified wider public interest? It is also important that much of what we read about unjustified secrecy is being published by the very group who have a vested interest in minimal or no secrecy – it is not always easy to distinguish between bona fide arguments about open justice and a genuine public interest in knowledge as opposed to self-serving arguments to help boost circulation to a public avid for gory detail.

When the government announced plans to reform the coroner system by way of the Coroners Bill in June 2006, the draft Bill proposed a provision for coroners to impose reporting restrictions in inquests where there was no public interest, such as child deaths and some apparent suicides where the matters being aired at the inquest were of an entirely private nature. However, following extensive consultation, the Bill eventually recognized the fine balance between families' need to grieve privately and the public interest in inquests being transparent and open to scrutiny. The **Coroners and Justice Act 2009** no longer contained the original widely drafted clause allowing the

---

1 See also: *MacDougall v Knight* [1889] AC at 200 (Lord Halsbury LC).
2 See: *Scott v Scott* [1913] AC 417.
3 [1979] AC 440 at 450.
4 [1992] QB 190.

imposition of reporting restrictions and the holding of 'secret inquests', now covered by standard and justified reporting restrictions to protect matters of, say, national security (see below 5.2.4).

There will be occasions when the open justice principle and the right of the media to report are restricted in order to ensure fair trials for, and the protection of, those who are vulnerable such as children and victims of sexual offences. The media's recognition of this is reflected in their own codes of practice, such as the PCC's Code of Practice and Ofcom's broadcasting regulations.

See Chapters
10.3.4 →
and 10.4.2

There is extensive and sensible youth justice legislation which supports and encourages responsible reporting, to the extent of urging restraint even when the law increasingly allows publication. The Court of Appeal held in *Murray v Big Pictures (UK) Ltd*,[5] for instance, that a child has a civil right to privacy distinctly separate from that of each of its parents (see below 5.3).

See Chapter
2.6.1 →

5.2 Hearings from which the public are excluded

The democratic principles of a free and open society contain a number of essential features: the rule of law, accountable political institutions, an independent and impartial judiciary upholding the law and a free press whose journalistic investigations and ability to publish the results provide an essential part of a free and open society. Free media reporting includes court reporting of a fair and open justice system, thereby ensuring that those in authority are held to account and that the rule of law does not become something to which those in power simply pay lip service. As the nineteenth-century philosopher and jurist, Jeremy Bentham, put it:

> . . . publicity is the very soul of justice. It is the keenest spur to exertion, and the surest of all guards against improbity. It keeps the judge himself, while trying, under trial.[6]

Section 12 **Administration of Justice Act 1960** defines a number of specific situations where publication of information about proceedings in private (whether *in camera* or in chambers) constitutes a contempt of court. Those relevant are:

- Where the court sits in private for reasons of national security; and
- Where the court, having power to do so, expressly prohibits the publication of all or any information relating to the proceedings.

Like 'without notice' (formerly *ex parte*) hearings, hearings *in camera* raise concerns about fairness, particularly in light of the principle that justice should not only be done but appear to be done.[7] Generally, court proceedings attract reporting restrictions or anonymity orders where publicity would defeat the object of the hearing; for example, a trial concerned with protecting commercial secrets or where privacy is needed to protect the interests of a mental patient.

5.2.1 Automatic reporting restrictions

There are a number of automatic reporting restrictions, which are statutory exceptions to the open justice principle; these apply to:

---

5 See: *Murray v Express Newspapers and others* [2008] EWCA Civ 446.
6 Bentham cited in *Home Office v Harman* [1983] 1 AC at 303 (Lord Diplock).
7 See: *Hobbs v Tinling and Company Limited* [1929] 2 KB 1 at 33 per Lord Sankey LC; see also: *R v Sussex Justices; Ex parte McCarthy* [1924] 1 KB 256 at 259 per Lord Hewart CJ: 'it is not merely of some importance but is of fundamental importance, that justice should not only be done, but should manifestly and undoubtedly be seen to be done.'

- sexual offence victims;[8]
- appeals and preparatory appeal hearings;[9]
- prosecution appeals.[10]

The existence of an automatic restriction may render some discretionary restrictions unnecessary, such as in respect of child or young offender proceedings. In such cases the judge or magistrate will usually remind the media of any automatic restriction under section 39 of the **Children and Young Persons Act 1933** (see below 5.3.1). The court has power to restrict reporting about certain adult witnesses (other than the accused) in criminal proceedings on the application of any party to those proceedings for a 'reporting direction' under section 46 **Youth Justice and Criminal Evidence Act 1999**.

If a defendant in a criminal action requests an order for anonymity, the court has to be satisfied either that the administration of justice would be seriously affected or that there is a real and *immediate* risk to the life of a defendant if anonymity were not granted (e.g. a police informer). However, even a significant interference with the rights of the accused under Article 8 ECHR might be proportionate when account is taken of the weight that must be given to the competing right to freedom of expression under Article 10.[11] When a party makes such an application, the court must be satisfied that the quality of evidence or level of cooperation by the witness is likely to be diminished by reason of fear or distress in being identified by the public.[12] On appeal, automatic reporting restrictions apply from the moment the prosecution indicates its intention to appeal to prevent the publication of anything other than certain specified factual information.[13]

Freedom of expression – whether by individuals or by the media – and the ability to exercise it, is an essential feature of any open, liberal and democratic society, as Lord Bingham described it:

> . . . free communication of information, opinions and argument about the laws which a state should enact and the policies its Government at all levels should pursue is an essential condition of truly democratic Government.[14]

There is also a notable conflict between the open justice principle, injunctions and restraining ('gagging') orders. In essence, a court commentator cannot refer to such court orders or fully report on a case. Tugendhat J stressed in the 'John Terry' case, where an issue of reporting restrictions in the form of superinjunctions arose, that making such orders (superinjunctions) would require intense scrutiny by the court so that the open justice system and public confidence in the proper administration of justice are maintained.[15] Where justice is carried out in secret, away from public scrutiny, bad habits can develop; and if they do not develop, the impression may arise that they have done so. Neither reality nor suspicion is an acceptable feature of any open society.

Consistent with the requirement to protect the open justice principle and freedom of expression, an order under section 11 **Contempt of Court Act 1981** should only be made where the nature or circumstances of the proceedings are such that a hearing in open court would frustrate or render impracticable the administration of justice (see: *A-G v Leveller Magazine* (1979)[16]). The court may order the postponement of publication of a fair, accurate and contemporaneous report of its

---

8 s. 2 Sexual Offences (Amendment) Act 1992; a complainant may waive this entitlement.
9 Under s. 35 Criminal Procedure and Investigations Act 1996; s. 9(11) Criminal Justice Act 1987.
10 s. 58 Criminal Justice Act 2003.
11 see: AG's Ref (No.3 of 1999): BBC's application to set aside or vary reporting restrictions order [2009] UKHL 34 at para. 28.
12 Part 16 Criminal Procedure Rules.
13 s. 71 Criminal Justice Act 2003.
14 See: *R (Animal Defenders International) v Secretary of State for Culture, Media and Sport* [2008] 1 AC at 27 (Lord Bingham).
15 See: *John Terry (previously referred to as LNS) v Persons Unknown* [2010] EWHC 119 (QB) (Tugendhat J).
16 [1979] AC 440.

proceedings where that is necessary to avoid a substantial risk of prejudice to the administration of justice in those or other proceedings.[17] The court should only exercise its discretion to make an order after weighing the competing interests of open justice and fair trial. The courts have suggested that where possible the question of any imposition of reporting restrictions is best dealt with in advance of trial. The Crown Court has discretion to invite representations from the media or their legal representatives as to whether an order should be made, varied or lifted, or whether 'tweets' should be allowed. It may make a temporary order to restrict publication pending its hearing to determine whether an order should be made. Under section 159 **Criminal Justice Act 1988** the media has the formal right to apply for judicial review.

There will be cases where the court will be assisted before making an order by receiving either written or oral representations from the media. Factors known to the media may not be apparent from the case papers and neither the prosecution nor the defence may be aware of them or have any particular interest in advancing them. The court will usually invite representations from the media and this practice was encouraged by the Divisional Court in R v *Teesdale and Wear Valley Justices ex parte* M (2000)[18].

When a discretionary restriction order is made, it is clearly desirable that the media are given every assistance to comply with it. The judge usually makes a helpful direction, stating if there are any particular problems arising from the making of the order which the media wish to raise in a written note, further guidance will be given in open court. Usually, every court will ensure, given human rights challenges in line with Article 10 ECHR, that adequate steps are taken to draw any discretionary restriction order to the attention of media representatives who may not have been in court when the order was made, and a judge should ensure that the procedure has been followed.

As more and more soldiers face courts martial in the face of desertion from the armed forces after the war in Iraq and ongoing actions in Afghanistan, here follow some brief notes on court-martial proceedings. The principle of open justice as expressed in *Scott v Scott* also applies to courts martial. There is a statutory requirement that courts martial sit in open court unless there is a compelling reason for the judge to direct otherwise. For instance, cases involving matters which could lead to the disclosure of security classified information may be held in *camera*.[19]

5.2.2 Sexual offences

It is a principle of law in criminal proceedings that defendants are normally named. It is only in the most exceptional circumstances that courts are empowered by statute to make an order to the contrary. Section 1 of the **Sexual Offices (Amendment) Act 1992** imposes a lifetime ban on reporting the identity of the alleged victim once an allegation that an offence has been committed is made; this continues after someone has been charged. Section 1 ('anonymity of victims in certain offences') reads:

> (1) Where an allegation has been made that an offence to which this Act applies has been committed against a person, neither the name nor address, and no still or moving picture, of that person shall during that person's lifetime
>
> > (a)   be published in England and Wales in a written publication available to the public; or,
> > (b)   be included in a relevant programme for reception in England and Wales,

---

17 s. 4(2) Contempt of Court Act 1981.
18 (2000) of 7 February 2000 (unreported).
19 s. 158 Armed Forces Act 2006; rules 152 and 153 Armed Forces (Court-Martial) Rules 2009.

if it is likely to lead members of the public to identify that person as the person against whom the offence is alleged to have been committed.

Offences include rape,[20] indecent assault, gross indecency,[21] indecency with children, buggery[22] and the vast majority of other sexual offences.[23] A person charged with a sexual offence covered by these restrictions may apply to the court to direct that the restrictions shall not apply if such a direction is required to induce potential witnesses to come forward and the conduct of the defence is likely to be substantially prejudiced if no such direction is given. The trial judge has the discretion to lift or relax reporting restrictions if their effect is to impose a substantial and unreasonable restriction on reporting the proceedings at trial and it would be in the public interest to do so. The victim or alleged victim (aged 16 and over) may, in writing, agree to the restriction being lifted; there must be no coercion.[24]

In the case of C v D (2006),[25] Field J made an order at the end of the private prosecution that reporting restrictions be lifted both on the victim, 'Christopher', and Master Leslie, the abusing headmaster of the Roman Catholic Ealing Abbey school. In this case the first defendant was the claimant's headmaster when C attended the junior part of this boys' public school; the second defendants were the trustees of the school. C brought proceedings to recover damages for distress and psychiatric injury caused as a result of serious sexual assault when he was at the prep school. C was now 24. The accused head teacher had filmed his class in the showers, had exposed his genitals and sexually touched the penis of the boy on several occasions. On the evidence before the court, these incidents amounted to gross invasion of the boy's personal integrity at a time when he was especially vulnerable. The first defendant had been reckless as to whether he caused the claimant psychiatric injury and was found liable for that conduct. C had been through a long period of painful mental abnormality, and was awarded £20,000 in respect of damages.

The opinions of Christopher were sought and, with his permission, publication of the horrendous child sex abuse case was subsequently permitted, exposing an immense scandal surrounding that boys' public school, which was run by a religious order. Field J gave reasons, in the public interest, for lifting the anonymity order and allowing publication:

> . . . in my judgment, now that C's allegations have been fully tried out and proven to be true, the public interest requires that all parties to these proceedings should be identified. The public should know not only that C was sexually abused by his headmaster but also the identity of his abuser and the school where it happened. And if the defendants are to lose their anonymity, I can see no reason why the claimant should not lose his too. Accordingly, I discharge Master Leslie's order of the 13th June 2005.[26]

Arguably, an order protecting the identity of persons accused of child sex offences sets a dangerous precedent. For this reason restraining orders are rarely made by the courts because the public has

---

20 Definition of rape s. 1 Sexual Offences Act 1956; see also: Archbold 2004, 20–5. The offence applies to the rape of a woman or the rape of another man. The offence of rape was restated in s. 142 Criminal Justice & Public Order Act 1994, to include anal sexual intercourse with another man without consent. Following R v R [1992] AC 599 and the removal of the word 'unlawful' from the definition of rape, it is clear that a husband may be prosecuted for raping his wife. A boy under 14 is now capable in law of sexual intercourse – Sexual Offences Act 1993, sections 1 and 2 Archbold 2004, 20–3. A woman may be convicted as an aider and abettor.

21 s. 13 Sexual Offences Act 1956; see also: Archbold, 20–133.

22 The Sexual Offences (Amendment) Act 2000 amended the Sexual Offences Act 1956 and 1967 to reduce the minimum age of consent at which a person may lawfully consent to buggery and to certain homosexual acts from 18 to 16 in England and Wales.

23 see: Archbold 2000: 20–267.

24 see: Archbold 2000: 20–266 to 20–270.

25 [2006] EWHC 166 of 23 February 2006 (QB) ('the Ealing Abbey case').

26 Ibid., at para 116.

to be served by open and frank reporting in such cases, though different procedures may be relevant if a criminal as opposed to civil action is brought.

Under section 37 of the **Children and Young Persons Act 1933**, the court has the power to clear the courtroom if a child or young person (under 18) is appearing in adult court proceedings or is giving evidence in certain cases. This is particularly the case in relation to sexual offences or concerning conduct contrary to decency or morality. The court has no power to clear the court of media representatives but the public can be excluded. In the case of an adult involved in child sex offences, a section 39 order under the 1933 Act will be made by the courts in order to protect the identity of the child or young person. Usually, the media will respect the clear effect of such an order, which states that nothing can be reported on the case that would lead to the identification of that young person. Wherever a defendant has the same name as a child victim – therefore running the risk of jigsaw identification – a section 39 direction will usually be made (see below 5.3.1).

The argument for not naming a child and the linked adult defendant is usually because of the close nature of the community in which all these persons live. Thus naming the defendant is highly likely to have the effect of thereby identifying the child or other siblings. If it is apparent to a judge before a prosecution starts that the effect of naming defendants is almost inevitably going to be to identify the children concerned in the particular case, then it is only right that he should say so and, using his express power, make a section 39 order to avoid jigsaw identification. Once a section 39 order has been made and details are spelt out, the effect of the order is that the media must not reveal any names or addresses of the defendants.

5.2.3 Vulnerable witnesses and special measures

For some people the process of giving evidence in court can be particularly difficult, such as children, victims of sexual offences and people with communication or learning difficulties. They are described by the court services as 'vulnerable' or intimidated witnesses and are allowed to use 'special measures' to help them give their evidence in the best possible way.

In criminal proceedings particularly, witnesses can experience stress and fear during the police investigation of a crime and the process of attending and giving evidence to a court. Stress affects the quantity and quality of communication with witnesses of all ages. Also, certain witnesses have particular difficulties attending court and giving evidence due to their age or personal circumstances, or because of their particular needs or their fear of intimidation.

In October 2009, 19-year-old aspiring model Kara Hoyte suffered a horrendous attack, which resulted in permanent brain injuries, at the hands of her ex-partner, professional footballer Mario Celaire. Her tremendous courage in giving evidence contributed to the conviction of her ex-partner in a landmark case as Celaire had been acquitted six years earlier of the murder of Cassandra McDermott. Kara gave video evidence, played to the jury via a video screen, so that she was not in court and could not be 'eyeballed' by the accused while giving evidence. Kara's evidence resulted in the conviction of Celaire at the Central Criminal Court when he admitted to the manslaughter of Casandra McDermott and the attempted murder of Kara Hoyte.[27] Celaire had been cleared at the Old Bailey of murdering Ms McDermott in 2002. The double jeopardy rule that prevented anyone from being tried twice for the same crime was changed with the **Criminal Justice Act 2003**, which came into force on 1 April 2005 for cases where new and compelling evidence could be produced. After Ms Hoyte's evidence was heard, prosecution lawyers applied to reopen the inquiry into Ms McDermott's killing and successfully had the acquittal quashed in the Court of Appeal. Celaire received two life sentences with a minimum of 23 years' custody.[28]

---

27 See: Vulnerable witness transcript released by the CPS on Kara Hoyte, available at <http://www.cps.gov.uk/victims_witnesses/going_to_court/kara_transcript.html>, accessed 22 November 2010.

28 Source: 'How model found words to bring killer to justice', *The Times*, 4 July 2009.

The **Youth Justice and Criminal Evidence Act 1999** (YJCEA) introduced a range of measures to facilitate the gathering and giving of evidence by vulnerable and intimidated witnesses. They are collectively known as 'special measures'. They are subject to the discretion of the court and have to be applied for at least 14 days in advance of proceedings. Different presumptions apply to different categories of witness. Special measures that may be available are:

- **'Live link'**: giving evidence through a TV link where the victim or witness can sit in a room outside the courtroom and give evidence via a live television link to the courtroom. The witness will be able to see the courtroom and those in the courtroom can see the witness on a television screen (s. 24 YJCEA);
- **Video-recorded evidence**: The victim's or witness's evidence is videotaped and played to the court. The provision is available for all vulnerable witnesses in the Crown Court, but only for complainants in serious sexual offences (s. 27 YJCEA);
- **Video-recorded cross examination:** video-recorded cross-examination is also considered admissible if the witness has already been permitted to give their evidence-in-chief on video prior to the court case. As with evidence-in-chief, the recording can be excluded if CPR-rules have not been complied with (s. 28 YJCEA);
- **Screens** around the witness box (or sometimes the dock) to prevent the witness from having to see the defendant (known as 'eyeballing the victim') (s. 23 YJCEA);
- **Removal of wigs and gowns**: the judge and lawyers in the Crown Court do not wear gowns and wigs so that the court feels less formal; this is usual in child proceedings or where there are young accused or child witnesses (s. 26 YJCEA);
- **Evidence given in camera (private):** exclusion from the court of members of the public except for one named person to represent the press – will be considered in cases involving sexual offences or intimidation. Available for all vulnerable and intimidated witnesses (s. 25 YJCEA);
- **Communication aids**: communication will be permitted to enable the witness to give best evidence whether through a communicator or interpreter, or through a communication aid or technique, provided that the communication can be independently verified and understood by the court. This measure is only available to vulnerable witnesses (s. 30 YJCEA);
- **Examination through an intermediary**: an intermediary is someone who can help a witness understand questions that they are being asked, and can make his or her answers understood by the court (s. 29 YJCEA).

In addition to special measures, the YJCEA 1999 also contains the following provisions intended to enable vulnerable or intimidated witnesses[29] to give their best evidence:

- Mandatory protection of witness from cross-examination by the accused in person: an exception has been created which prohibits the unrepresented defendant from cross-examining vulnerable child and adult victims in certain classes of cases involving sexual offences (ss. 34 and 35 YJCEA);
- Discretionary protection of witness from cross-examination by the accused in person: in other types of offence, the court has a discretion to prohibit an unrepresented defendant from cross-examining the victim in person (s. 36 YJCEA);

---

29 ss. 16 and 17 YJCEA 1999 define the witnesses who are eligible for special measures such as vulnerable witnesses. Children are defined as vulnerable by reason of their age, s. 16(1)(a) YJCEA.

- Restrictions on evidence and questions about complainant's sexual behaviour: the 1999 Act restricts the circumstances in which the defence can bring evidence about the sexual behaviour of a complainant in cases of rape and other sexual offences (s. 41 YJCEA);
- Reporting restrictions: the Act provides for restrictions on the reporting by the media of information likely to lead to the identification of children under 18 and certain adult witnesses in criminal proceedings (ss. 44 to 46 YJCEA – see below 5.3).

Special measures for most vulnerable or intimidated witnesses[30] can be authorized only if they are likely to improve the quality of a witness's evidence. The single exception to this general rule is that this requirement is not applicable to children 'in need of special protection' (see below 5.3).

A complete reporting ban was ordered on all parties involved the tragic death of 'Baby P'.[31] The 17-month-old toddler had died on 3 August 2007 after enduring months of abuse in Haringey, North London. Initially it was not clear why his mother, for instance, could not be named, though anyone with an internet connection could have circumvented the court anonymity orders to find out that her name was Tracey Connelly and her boyfriend was Steven Barker. By simply typing 'Baby P Mother' into Google or YouTube all names and pictures connected to Baby P could be revealed in seconds, while the media continued to adhere to contempt of court rules for the best part of two years. Connelly's 'Friends Reunited' profile had been widely distributed and blogs and unofficial websites had openly published her details, with the result that Facebook was forced to shut down pages that revealed Connelly's and Barker's identities alongside comments promising violent retribution. All of this raised the question whether there was any point in reporting restriction laws in the digital age.

See Chapter 4.3.3 →

The complete reporting ban surrounding the Baby P case only became clear in the spring of 2009 once the section 4(2) CCA order was lifted, following the conviction and sentencing of Baby P's 'stepfather', Jason Owen, 37, who was found guilty of raping a two-year-old girl. The anal rape allegation came to light after Baby P's mother and Owen had been arrested over P's death. Both Tracey Connelly and Jason Owen were tried at the Old Bailey in relation to the girl under false names amid fears that an internet hate campaign would try to influence jurors, and to assure a fair trial. The jury of eight men and four women had no idea of the defendants' true identities. Connelly's charges were cruelty to the little girl and Owen's was rape.[32] Tracey Connelly and her boyfriend Steven Barker, 33, had already been found guilty of causing (allowing) baby Peter's death in early May 2009. Their lodger, Owen, later found to be Stephen Barker's brother, was given an indefinite sentence with a minimum term of three years for failing to take steps to save the child. With the additional sentence for rape of the little girl and for allowing baby Peter's death, Jason Owen received a life sentence with an additional order for 'public protection' as a real and future danger to the public.[33]

The Head of CPS London's Homicide Team, Judith Reed, said that her landmark decision to allow a four-year-old rape victim to give evidence in the Jason Owen case was the toughest of her career. She said, 'It was quite clear that she was raped by this man and I felt it was important for her that we went to trial. In the years to come she will know that the prosecution took her account seriously and worked hard to ensure that a jury were able to consider her evidence.'[34] The girl, who was two years old when she was raped, was interviewed by police some twelve months after her ordeal. Judith Reed continued: 'Having viewed the video of her interview I have to say she

---

30 Intimidated witnesses are defined by s. 17(1) YJCEA 1999, as those suffering from fear or distress in relation to testifying in the case.
31 The order was made under s. 4(2) Contempt of Court Act 1981.
32 Source: 'Baby P killers unmasked', by Vanessa Allen, Colin Fernandez and Lucy Ballinger, *Daily Mail*, 11 August 2009.
33 Source: 'Baby P "stepfather" guilty of raping two-year-old', The Press Association, 1 May 2009.
34 Source: 'Why I let four-year-old rape victim give evidence in court – prosecutor', CPS, press release, 1 May 2009.

was really quite remarkable. I'd never seen a child so young give as clear and consistent an account. . . The problem was we had very little corroborative evidence to draw on. . . I have never made a decision around a case of a child so young. Having said that, she was one of the best child witnesses of any age I've seen give evidence on video.'

During the lead-up to Owen's rape trial, the prosecution team faced relentless challenges relating to disclosure issues – many linked to the previous trial relating to Baby P's death. Despite complete reporting restrictions and a complete news blackout imposed by the court, the identities of the stepfather and Baby Peter's mother were revealed by websites. This encouraged the defence to argue that the defendants could not be guaranteed a fair hearing. But Jason Owen's rape trial (and Tracey Connelly's cruelty charge) at the Old Bailey was allowed to proceed. Three days before the trial, the CPS took the unusual step of allowing the little girl to watch the videotape of her interview to assure them that she would not say in court that she could not remember making it. During the trial the girl, the youngest rape victim in legal history to give evidence, was cross-examined for 45 minutes. She gave evidence by video-link from a room at the Old Bailey. Neither defendant gave evidence. Their counsel argued that the girl's evidence was not reliable and the allegation could have been suggested to her by another child or adult, or that someone else was responsible. Tracey Connelly (Baby Peter's mother) was acquitted of child cruelty in relation to the little girl; and given an indefinite sentence with a minimum term of five years for causing, or allowing, Baby Peter's death in August 2007.

'Quality' usually encompasses coherence, completeness and accuracy in the case of vulnerable witnesses. 'Coherence' in this sense means that the witness is able to address the questions put and give answers that can be understood, but as separate answers and when taken together as a complete statement of the witness's evidence. Other vulnerable witnesses include:

- those who have a mental disorder as defined under the **Mental Health Act 1983**;[35]
- those who are significantly impaired in relation to intelligence and social functioning, such as learning impaired or disabled witnesses;[36]
- physically disabled witnesses.[37]

Intimidated witnesses – defined by s. 17(4) YJCEA 1999 – include complainants in sexual assault or domestic violence cases, victims of racially motivated crime or those subject to repeat victimization; but also witnesses in honour-based crimes and the elderly and frail. Section 17(4) ('witnesses eligible for assistance on grounds of fear or distress about testifying') reads:

> . . . where the complainant in respect of a sexual offence is a witness in proceedings relating to that offence (or to that offence and any other offences), the witness is eligible for assistance in relation to those proceedings by virtue of this subsection unless the witness has informed the court of the witness' wish not to be so eligible by virtue of this subsection.

While the legislation distinguishes between vulnerable and intimidated witnesses in respect of the criteria for their eligibility for special measures, it must be recognized that:

- some witnesses may be vulnerable as well as intimidated;
- others may be vulnerable but not subject to intimidation;
- others may not be vulnerable but may be subject to possible intimidation.

---

35 s. 16(2)(a)(i)]; mental disorder is defined in s. 1(2) Mental Health Act 1983.
36 s. 16(2)(a)(ii) Youth Justice and Criminal Evidence Act 1999.
37 s. 16(2)(b) Youth Justice and Criminal Evidence Act 1999.

And it is important for the courts not to attempt to categorize witnesses too rigidly and to recognize that special measures are not automatically available at the trial. A prosecutor must make an application to the court for special measures within the given set timescales (see below),[38] usually agreed with the police officer in the case in conjunction with the considered needs of the victim or witnesses in the case.[39] The timescales are:

Youth Court
Within 28 days of the date on which the defendant first appears or is brought before the court in connection with the offence.

Magistrates' Court
Within 14 days of the defendant indicating his intention to plead not guilty to any charge brought against him and in relation to which a special measures direction may be sought.

Crown Court
Within 28 days of:

(i)   the committal of the defendant; or
(ii) the consent to the preferment of a bill of indictment in relation to the case; or
(iii) the service of a notice of transfer;[40] or
(iv) where a person is sent for trial;[41] or
(v)   the service of a Notice of Appeal from a decision of a youth court or a magistrates' court.

Judges and magistrates have to strike a balance under Article 6 ECHR between protecting the defendant's rights to a fair trial and Article 10 ensuring that trials and court hearings are openly reported to the public. While the YJCEA 1999 created an expectation that the court ought to be concerned that witnesses are enabled to give their best evidence, it also imposed an obligation on judges and magistrates to raise of their own volition the question of whether special measures should be used if the party has not applied for them; this is an example of the increasing inquisitorial nature of the justice system.[42]

Section 19 YJCEA deals with special measures directions relating to vulnerable and potentially intimidated witnesses. Information relating to intimidation may be potentially prejudicial to a defendant, but must be made known to a court if it is relevant to the making of a special measures direction, even if – as is likely – it is inadmissible as proof of the offence to be tried. The court must also take into account all the circumstances of the case and whether or not special measures – such as screens or evidence given via live link – are likely to inhibit the evidence being effectively tested by any party to the proceedings.[43]

5.2.4 Inquests

An inquest is a formal public inquiry into sudden or unexplained deaths for the public record. Very often deaths requiring investigation by a coroner[44] are, by their very nature, matters of the highest public concern. Section 5 of the **Coroners and Justice Act 2009** states:

---

38 Rules 29–31 Criminal Procedure Rules concern special measures and directions; Rule 30 concerns live links; Rule 31 concerns cross-examination.
39 See para. 5.7 of the 'Code of Practice for Victims of Crime', CPS, May 2010; the police officer completes the MG2 form to apply for special measures.
40 s. 51 Criminal Justice Act 1991.
41 s. 51 Crime and Disorder Act 1998.
42 s. 19 (1) YJCEA 1999.
43 s. 19 (3) YJCEA 1999.
44 The coroner is a doctor or lawyer responsible for investigating deaths in particular situations and can also arrange for a post-mortem examination of the body, if necessary.

(1) The purpose of an investigation [. . .] into a person's death is to ascertain:

(a) who the deceased was;

(b) how, when and where the deceased came by his or her death.

All inquests must be held in public in accordance with the principle of open justice and members of the public and journalists have the right to attend. Whether journalists attend a particular inquest – and whether they report on it – is a matter for them. If any such report is fair and accurate it cannot be used to sue for defamation. The only exception is made with inquests where issues of national security are involved; here the coroner can exclude the public and the media.[45]

An inquest into a death can be held with or without a jury, but must be held with a jury if the senior coroner has reason to suspect that:

a) the deceased died while in custody or state detention;

b) the death was a violent or unnatural one;

c) the cause of death is unknown;

d) the death resulted from an act or omission of a police or prison officer;

e) the death was caused by a notifiable accident, poisoning or disease.[46]

Coroners' courts and inquests usually make orders banning the identification of dead children, even though the name of the deceased child may have already been published in the newspaper.[47] Normally coroners will not impose anonymity since it is one of the principal functions of a coroners' court to establish the identity of a person who has died (see below 5.3.1). The media frequently tries to persuade courts against imposing or renewing child anonymity orders, particularly where small children have been victims of domestic violence and abuse, such as in the Victoria Climbié case in 2005. Media representatives will argue that a child of such tender years would not suffer any ill effects from being named.

During the consultation period for the draft Coroners Bill (2008), clause 30 proposed to give coroners, in particularly sensitive cases, new and extensive powers to prevent publication of the name or any information that might identify the deceased person or any interested persons to the inquest. These would typically be apparent suicides or child deaths. The Ministry of Justice received strong views for and against the bill's anonymity proposals. Groups representing the bereaved were generally supportive of the proposals while the media were opposed. There was no consensus of views among coroners.[48] HM Coroner for Greater Suffolk and South East Essex, Dr Peter Dean stated that:

> . . . public reporting can often be necessary and can itself be the essential route through which public education about unavoidable tragedies can be promoted, but this needs to be balanced against the interests of an individual family and can normally be accomplished equally well without adding to personal grief.[49]

Similarly, Coroner Nigel Meadows stated that there ought to be a sound balancing exercise between the rights of public access and the media to court and inquest proceedings, weighted against intrusion into private family grief. Coroner Michael Singleton argued that the reporting of many inquests

---

45 Rule 17 of the Coroners Rules 1984.
46 Section 7 Coroners and Justice Act 2009 ('where jury required').
47 s. 39 Children and Young Persons Act 1933 does not apply to protect the identity of dead children; and if such an order has been in force, it may be challenged.
48 Source: Ministry of Justice (2009a).
49 Ibid., at p. 8ff ('public responses').

in the local newspaper had represented an unnecessary intrusion into the private grief of many people. However, he anticipated that the vast majority of interested persons would seek directions prohibiting publication and there may be calls for a judicial review of these decisions. Dr Nigel Chapman anticipated that the number of appeals could be 'enormous' if reporting restrictions were imposed in inquests and that the wording of such 'gagging orders' would need to be carefully thought through.[50]

Media organizations, in particular, expressed strong opposition to the proposal to exclude the press from inquests. The PCC, Newspaper Society, National Union of Journalists (NUJ), BBC, ITN and the Society of Editors all expressed their concern about the introduction of an anonymity order or reporting restrictions clause in the bill. They felt strongly that the introduction of reporting restrictions would not be in the public interest and would be against the principle of open justice. The BBC argued that:

> . . . to impose reporting restrictions with a view to shielding bereaved families (and others) from publicity would in effect deprive the public of the ability to receive vital information about matters of serious concern within the community.[51]

The PCC said that the right of journalists to report on inquests is a key feature of an open society in which the public, as a whole, has a right to know what is going on and that there are no cover-ups of unusual or premature deaths. The PCC's Editors' Code of Practice Committee believed that the present Code already fulfilled the objective of ensuring sensitive reporting in such matters.[52] Eventually, the anonymity clause was dropped. The only anonymity awarded in the **Coroners and Justice Act 2009** is to families of UK Special Forces and deceased servicemen and women abroad. Sections 10 and 12 of the 2009 Act guarantee confidentiality for soldiers and their families if they so wish.[53]

See Chapter 10.3.4 →

Many people now obtain their news via the Internet. This method of communication has allowed a remarkable explosion of free speech – of providers of information – usually providing content which can be obtained for free by way of a multiplicity of choice. On 23 February 2010, journalist and blogger Simon Perry was refused entry to the Isle of Wight Coroner's court. Perry, of 'VentnorBlog', a site which publishes local news, was outraged and complained to his trade union, the National Union of Journalists (NUJ). NUJ general secretary Jeremy Dear subsequently wrote to the Isle of Wight Coroner's office expressing 'grave concern' at the decision to ban Simon Perry.[54]

5.3 Reporting on children and young persons in England and Wales

Where children and young persons under the age of 18 are involved in court proceedings these are normally held in private – though accredited reporters may attend and report provided they adhere to the legislation that covers the non-identification of the youngster when evidence is given. It is entirely legitimate to report that 'a 13-year-old Cardiff boy was today accused of causing criminal damage. . .'. A criminal court may prohibit publication by the media of the name, address, school or

---

50 Ibid., at p. 10.
51 Ibid.
52 Ibid., at p. 17.
53 Subject to service law by virtue of s. 367 Armed Forces Act 2006; s. 50 Coroners and Justice Act 2009 amends the Fatal Accidents and Sudden Deaths Inquiry (Scotland) Act 1976.
54 Source: 'NUJ General Secretary calls on coroner to allow blogger in court', by Judith Townend, 25 February 2010, *Journalism.uk*, available at <http://blogs.journalism.co.uk/editors/2010/02/25/nuj-general-secretary-calls-on-coroner-to-allow-blogger-into-court>, accessed 22 November 2010.

any information calculated to lead to the identification of any child or young person (under 18) concerned in criminal proceedings before that court. The power also extends to pictures of the child or young person. The primary legislation is the **Children and Young Persons Act 1933** (CYPA).

The overriding welfare principle of the child is enshrined in section 44 of the 1933 Act, which is that a court, dealing with a child or young person, must have constant regard to the welfare of the young person and must take proper steps to remove 'undesirable surroundings'. Also, if a child is found guilty of an offence, proper provisions are put in place to secure his or her education and training until the school-leaving age. Section 39 CYPA enables any court, including the Court of Appeal, to make an order in relation to 'any proceedings'. But 'any proceedings' does not mean 'any proceedings anywhere': it must mean any proceedings in the court that is making the order. So the Court of Appeal can make an order in relation to any proceedings in the Court of Appeal once they have been commenced. But there is nothing in section 39 to enable the Court of Appeal to make an order in relation to proceedings in the Crown Court.[55]

Sections 21 and 22 of the **Youth Justice and Criminal Evidence Act 1999** (YJCEA) detail some special provisions for child witnesses under the age of 17 (see above 5.2.3). The provisions create presumptions that apply to different categories of child witnesses and concern how they will give their evidence. The provisions state:

- Where there is a child witness in a sexual case involving violence, abduction or neglect, the child witness is deemed to be 'in need of special protection'. In such cases, the court does not have to consider whether the special measure(s) will improve the quality of the evidence; this will be assumed to be the case;
- All child witnesses in need of special protection will have the video recording of their evidence admitted as evidence-in-chief, unless this is excluded by the court on the basis that to admit the video recording would not be in the interests of justice;
- Child witnesses in cases of violence will normally be cross-examined via the live link;
- For all other child witnesses, there will be a presumption that evidence-in-chief will be given by video-recording, if one has been made, and that cross-examination will be via the live link. However, the court must be satisfied that this will improve the quality of the evidence.

Sections 21 and 22 YJCEA 1999 also concern witnesses over 17 years of age. The following must be noted:

- If a court makes a special measures direction in respect of a child witness who is eligible on grounds of youth only and the witness turns 17 before beginning to give evidence, the direction no longer has effect. If such a witness turns 17 after beginning to give evidence, the special measures direction continues to apply;[56]
- If a witness is under 17 when evidence-in-chief or cross-examination (when available) is video-recorded before the trial but has since turned 17, the video-recording is still capable of being used as evidence;
- A witness who is over 17 at the beginning of the trial but who made a video-recording as their evidence-in-chief when they were under 17, is eligible for special measures in the same way that they would be if they were under 17, and the same presumptions apply to them.

---

55 See: *R v Lee (a minor)* (1993) 96 Cr App R 188.
56 s. 21(9) YJCEA 1999.

The House of Lords held in R v Camberwell Youth Court ex p D & others (2005)[57] that the presumption for children in need of special protection did not breach Articles 6 ('right to a fair trial') or 14 ('discrimination') of the European Convention. It also clearly stated that the norm for child witnesses giving evidence was by video evidence-in-chief (recorded) and live link for cross-examination. This applies equally to child witnesses for the prosecution and defence. Where a court exercises its powers (statutory or common law) to allow any name (including an adult) or any other matter to be withheld from the public in criminal proceedings, the court may make a direction as is necessary prohibiting publication of that name or matter in connection with the proceedings.[58]

5.3.1 Limitations of section 39 orders

Section 39 of the **Children and Young Persons Act 1933** was intended to be complementary to section 49 of the 1933 Act, which imposes an automatic restriction on news reports identifying children and young persons involved in youth proceedings.[59] Therefore, the media cannot simply argue that the public have a right to know if such an order has been properly made. Any journalist who publishes any matter in contravention with a section 39 court order is liable on summary conviction under section 39(2) of the 1933 Act, to a maximum Level 5. In ex p. Crook (1995),[60] the appellant journalists challenged a section 39 order which stated that nothing should be published which would lead to the identification of children who were alive and named on the indictment. The indictment included a count of manslaughter of another child of the defendant, whose surviving children were in local authority care. The three young children in this case, for whom the protective order was made, were the alleged victims of cruelty by both parents, charges which were heard together with the allegation of manslaughter in respect of their sibling.

The Court of Appeal, dismissing the appeal, stated that a judge or magistrates, in making the section 39 order, have complete discretion to allow representatives from the media – who have a legitimate interest – to make representations before the order is made. The CA ruled that the original judge had been completely correct in making the section 39 order on receipt of the borough council's report and that any publication would have had an otherwise damaging effect on the surviving children. In making the order, the judge had correctly weighed the children's interest against the freedom of the press to report and had reached the conclusion that the likely harm to the children outweighed the restriction of freedom to publish.

Normally, if a child or young person (under 18) has committed a criminal offence, he or she will be tried summarily by magistrates in a Youth Court. In more serious cases ('grave crimes') a youth may be sent to be tried at a Crown Court (see below 5.3.3). If the young person is charged in conjunction with an adult offender, youth magistrates may consider it necessary in the interests of justice to commit them both for trial to the Crown Court. But the line has to be drawn somewhere. If children are not being included in a prosecution, a section 39 order will not be permitted to protect them from media reporting, despite the strong evidence that any revelation of their family history might seriously damage their well-being. If the prosecution is for manslaughter, only the child witness can be protected if he is giving evidence. If there are other children of the same family involved, the order can be made to protect all of them.

In Mrs R v Central Independent Television (1994),[61] a wife failed to secure an injunction preventing the broadcasting of a programme identifying her husband as a convicted molester of small boys. She

---

57 [2005] UKHL 4.
58 s.11 Contempt of Court Act 1981.
59 The 1933 Act consolidated the Children and Young Persons Act 1932. In the latter Act the equivalent provisions to sections 39 and 49 of the Act of 1933 were all contained in section 81.
60 R v Central Criminal Court ex parte Crook [1995] 1 WLR 139 (CA (Crim Div)).
61 (1994) 9 February 1994, (CA) (unreported).

argued that a broadcast would be prejudicial to the welfare of her five-year-old daughter. The identity of the boys was covered by a section 39 order, but the girl was regarded as too remote from the proceedings and the programme had nothing to do with her care or upbringing. More precisely, the little girl was not within the specific categories covered by section 39. However, the mother could possibly have appealed under the general provision of Article 8 ECHR.

See Chapter
2.6

It was held in *Godwin* (1992)[62] that a section 39 order – originally imposed by Judge Laurie at Southwark Crown Court – was only available where the terms of s. 39(1) **Children and Young Persons Act 1933** relate to a *relevant* child. In this case the newspapers had previously reported the abusing stepfather's (S) name, referring to the victim as 'an 11-year-old schoolgirl'. There was a serious risk of jigsaw identification in that the composite picture would present the identification of that child. The appellants, Caroline Godwin, the *Daily Telegraph*, Mirror Group Newspapers and Associated Newspapers Ltd appealed against the section 39 order under s. 159 **Criminal Justice Act 1988**.[63] The appellants argued that the judge had wrongly interpreted section 39. They further argued that there was no evidence that the naming of the defendant (S) would lead to the identification of the child.

The Court of Appeal quashed the original order in its entirety and substituted a new order with an express restriction on the identification of S, as well as 'the nature of the case against him'. S's daughter was therefore protected during the proceedings and after the conclusion by way of a lifelong anonymity order provided additionally by s. 1 **Sexual Offences (Amendment) Act 1992** ('Anonymity of victims in certain offences'). Glidewell LJ allowed the appeal in *Godwin*, stating that it cannot have been Parliament's intention to allow greater reporting restrictions in an adult court than in a juvenile court. This means that a section 39 order does not empower a court to prevent the naming of adult defendants in general; section 39 orders, are, by their very nature, specifically related to children and young persons under 18. The Court of Appeal made it quite clear in *Godwin* that adult courts do not have greater powers to restrict publicity than juvenile courts.

In *R v Winchester Crown Court Ex p. B (A Minor)* (1999),[64] B, aged 14, applied for judicial review of the trial judge's decision to discharge reporting restrictions and to lift the section 39 order, which had prohibited B's identification.[65] The judge had reasoned that reporting restrictions were no longer necessary on the basis that open justice was essential in a civilized society. Judges Simon Brown LJ and Astill J in the Administrative Court dismissed B's application and reiterated that it was well within the Crown Court's powers to discharge a section 39 order in relation to proceedings on indictment (see also: *R v Central Criminal Court ex parte Crook* (1995)[66]).

In *Re Gazette Media Co Ltd* (2005)[67], the Court of Appeal also considered the scope of a section 39 order where two men, S and L, were being prosecuted (and eventually convicted) for offences contrary to s. 1 of the **Protection of Children Act 1978** and for conspiracy to rape. S was charged with offences of making or distributing indecent photographs of his daughter and with the offence of conspiracy to rape. L was charged with conspiracy to rape and also with offences of making and distributing indecent photographs of a child. In this case, the Middlesborough Recorder had made the section 39, stating:

> . . . no reporting of any proceedings in respect of R v S and L. No identification of the defendant S by name or otherwise the nature of the case against him the identification of the alleged

---

62 *R v Southwark Crown Court Ex parte Godwin and Others* [1992] QB 190 (CA (Civ Div); [1991] 3 WLR 689 at p.196.
63 That section permits a person aggrieved to appeal to the Court of Appeal against 'any order restricting the publication of any report of the whole or any part of a trial on indictment or any such ancillary proceedings'.
64 [1999] 1 WLR 788.
65 B had been sentenced to three years' detention for an offence contrary to s. 1 Criminal Attempts Act 1981.
66 [1995] 1 WLR 139 (CA (Crim Div)).
67 *Gazette Media Company Ltd. & Ors, R (on the application of) v Teeside Crown Court* [2005] EWCA Crim 1983 (CA (Crim Div)).

victim [S's daughter], her age place of abode or any circumstances that may lead to her identification in connection with these proceedings.[68]

Solicitors acting for the *Gazette* wrote to the Recorder complaining about the wording of the section 39 order, citing *Godwin*: that – as a matter of law – the order did not empower a court to prevent the names of defendants from being published. Maurice Kay LJ in *Re Gazette* remarked that it was clear beyond doubt that the order made by the Recorder 'flew in the face of *Godwin*' in that a section 39 order could not add specifics beyond the words of s. 39(1). Therefore, a departure from *Godwin* could not be justified. It was not enough to delete the restriction against the reporting of any proceedings in relation to the defendants and the victim; it was also necessary to delete the express restriction on the identification of S and L and the nature of the case against them.

The additional problem in *Re Gazette* was that the restriction provided by s 1 of the 1992 Act ('Anonymity of victims in certain offences' – see above) was not sufficient to protect the identity of the victim during the proceedings and could be interpreted by the media as 'freedom to report'. While conspiracy to rape was an offence to which s 1 of the 1992 Act applied, other linked offences were not. The order was quashed in its entirety and a new order in conventional *Godwin* terms was substituted.

Additionally, it was submitted by the Attorney General that, while a total embargo on the reporting of the proceedings remained unlawful, the prohibition of the naming of a defendant – so as to protect the interests of a child – was now possible within the remits of the human rights provision of Article 8 ECHR and s. 3 **Human Rights Act**, which requires primary legislation to be compatible with Convention rights.

5.3.2 Naming and shaming of young offenders

As stated, proceedings in the Youth Court are 'in private' and no reporting takes place on children and young persons (either as accused or witnesses) if they are aged 18 and under. However, a section 39 order under the **Children and Young Persons Act 1933** may be lifted by the applying court at any time if the magistrates or the presiding judge feel the matter is in the public interest. This was the case post-conviction in the 'Bulger killers' trial of Robert Thompson and Jon Venables, when the judge lifted reporting restrictions in November 1993 (see below).

Section 49 of the 1933 Act allows the media to publish the name and other full details of a young offender (under age 18) 'in the public interest'. This principle was established in *Lee* (see below). Generally, where young defendants are tried for 'grave crimes' at the Crown Court, the media are free to identity them *unless* the court rules otherwise by making a section 39 order. In *R v Lee (Anthony William) (a Minor)* (1993),[69] an order under section 39 of the 1933 Act was made at the trial of L, a boy aged 14, restricting publication of his identity. On sentencing, the judge lifted the restriction. An emergency order prohibiting identification was made by another judge but was too late to prevent publication in some newspapers. L's lawyers made an application to the sentencing judge to reimpose the order. The Court of Appeal upheld the refusal of the judge to ban the media from identifying a 14-year-old boy convicted of robbery and rape because it would involve 'no real harm to the applicant, and [have] a powerful deterrent effect on his contemporaries if the applicant's name and photograph were published'. This was the first case where the 'naming and shaming' of a young offender was made possible while court proceedings were still active, although Lord Bingham stressed that publicity should not be used as an 'additional punishment' – contrary to the views of successive home secretaries and ministers of justice.

---

68 Ibid., at 138.
69 [1993] 1 WLR 103 (CA (Crim Div)).

The ruling in Lee means that 'any proceedings' for the purposes of a section 39 order does not mean any proceedings anywhere but rather any proceedings in the court making the order. This means the identity of a teenager will normally be protected in the courts. That said, a Leeds Crown Court judge allowed a 16-year-old scout's name to be made public – by refusing a section 39 order – after Owen Tappin had been found guilty of raping a teenage girl in a church hall. The Daily Mail reported in January 2010 that the youth had 'never been in trouble with the law' before and had been 'handed in to police by his father'.[70]

The most notorious case of open court reporting on juveniles concerned child killers Jon Venables and Robert Thompson. The 10-year-old boys had snatched 2-year-old James Bulger during a shopping trip with his mother at the Strand shopping centre in Bootle on 12 February 1993 and had brutally tortured him, leaving the toddler's battered body on a freight railway line, where he died. After the boys had been found guilty of murder on 24 November 1993 by the jury at Preston Crown Court, Morland J lifted the protective section 39 order 'in the public interest'. Thereafter, a media frenzy ensued, resulting in shocking and distressing facts being published about the boys' families and dysfunctional family backgrounds. The two boys were sentenced to be detained at Her Majesty's pleasure[71] with an initial maximum tariff of eight years. The Sun's editor expressed outrage and encouraged a coupon-petition, resulting in nearly 280,000 signatures being handed to the Conservative Home Secretary, Michael Howard, in a bid to increase the time spent in custody by the 'Bulger killers'. The Sun's campaign was successful and in July 1994, the Home Secretary announced that the boys would be kept in custody for a minimum of 15 years, with a possible release date in 2008. The increase of the sentencing term (by a politician rather than a judge) was criticized by the European Court of Human Rights in V v UK; T v UK (1999).[72]

In McKerry v Teesdale and Wear Valley Justices (2000),[73] a 16-year-old boy, with a long record of offending, pleaded guilty at the Youth Court to a 'TWOCing' offence.[74] Upon request by a local newspaper, the magistrates lifted the section 39 order and permitted his identity to be revealed, giving as reasons that the young offender posed a serious danger to the public and had shown a complete disregard for the law. The Divisional Court held that the magistrates' reasons were completely acceptable because 'no doubt the justices had in mind that members of the public, if they knew the appellant's name, would enjoy a measure of protection if they had cause to encounter him'.[75] The court further added that the power to dispense with anonymity 'must be exercised with very great circumspection' and that the public interest criterion must be met.

In the conjoined cases of R (on the application of T) v St Albans Crown Court; Chief Constable of Surrey v JHG (2002),[76] it was held that antisocial behaviour orders were very much in the general public interest and that reporting restrictions would not be granted. In the first case, the court had refused to grant anonymity under section 39 **Children & Young Persons' Act 1933** to an 11-year-old boy (T) in respect of whom an ASBO (Antisocial Behaviour Order[77]) had been made. T sought a judicial review of that decision. In the second case, the court had granted anonymity to 17-year-old twins (J and D) when making an ASBO, with the Chief Constable of Surrey appealing against that decision.

The allegations against T included abuse, minor criminal damage and two assaults, and those against J and D included assault, nuisance, trespass, criminal damage, threatening behaviour and intimidation. T, J and D submitted that, given that antisocial behaviour orders were civil in character, they were less serious than many of the offences in respect of which section 39 applications

---

70 Source: 'Teenager raped by Scout, 16' by Chris Brooke, Daily Mail, 20 January 2010.
71 s. 53 (1) Children and Young Persons Act 1933.
72 (1999) 30 EHRR 121 (ECHR).
73 (2000) 164 JP 355 (DC).
74 s. 12 Theft Act 1968 ('taking a vehicle without the owner's consent').
75 Source: Spencer (2000), p. 468.
76 [2002] EWHC 1129 (Admin) of 20 May 2002 (QBD (Admin).
77 s. 1 Crime and Disorder Act 1998.

were commonly refused in Crown Court proceedings. T submitted that the court had failed to consider relevant matters including his age and improvement in his behaviour, and in J and D's case, the chief constable submitted that the court had considered irrelevant matters, including the impact on members of J and D's families. Reaffirming the ruling in *Lee*, the court applied the principle (of open reporting) in R *v Winchester Crown Court Ex p. B (A Minor)* (1999).[78] The court applied the *Lee*-balancing exercise: that of the public interest test in disclosure of the name versus the welfare of the young person in question. While the court did not have to refer to every factor that might weigh in favour of a section 39 direction, it was necessary for it to briefly summarize the principal factors weighing in favour, even if its decision was that those factors were outweighed by the public interest. The public interest test weighed in favour of disclosure in T *and* JHG, where it could be reported that the individuals were on an ASBO and the neighbourhood could learn about the orders, assisting the police in making the orders effective to prevent future antisocial behaviour.

Newspapers are now permitted to report freely on 'young thugs' who 'terrorize suburbia'. Names are included together with addresses and pictures, as well as details of the ASBOs, particularly where youths are linked to more serious offending. One example was the *Daily Mail's* reporting on Stephen Paul Sorton, 17, Jordan Cunlifffe, 16, and Adam Swellings, 19, who were subsequently found guilty of the murder of Garry Newlove in January 2008.[79]

In an announcement to Parliament in July 2010, Conservative Home Secretary, Theresa May announced that it was now 'time to move beyond ASBOs'. Mrs May ordered a review of the legislation (s. 1 **Crime and Disorder Act 1998**) because police should be able to use their 'common sense' to deal with antisocial behaviour. Punishments should be 'rehabilitative and restorative, rather than 'criminalising', she argued.[80]

Following on from the Strasbourg ruling in the Venables and Thompson case (*V v UK* and *T v UK*), Parliament enacted the **Youth Justice and Criminal Evidence Act 1999** (YJCEA) so that young defendants should not be exposed to intimidation, humiliation or distress in court proceedings.[81] Lord Woolf LCJ reinforced the new legislation by a Practice Direction, stating that:

> . . . all possible steps should be taken to assist the young defendant to understand and participate in the proceedings. The ordinary trial process should, so far as necessary, be adapted to meet those ends.[82]

How then should the media interpret ss. 39 and 49 of the 1933 Act, common law development in child anonymity orders and provisions under the 1999 Act? The question remains whether open disclosure on juvenile offenders is always in the interest of justice (rather than the public interest)? Following the lifelong anonymity order on Jon Venables and Robert Thompson in 2001, this was never going to appease those who believed the public had an absolute right to know the whereabouts of the James Bulger killers (see; *Venables v NGN* (2001)[83]). Even in 2010, Justice Secretary Jack Straw refused to reveal Venables' identity after he had been returned to prison in spite of rampant speculation in the media, encouraged by an emotive campaign involving James Bulger's mother.

See Chapters 2.6.2 → and 2.6.3

---

78 [1999] 1 WLR 788.
79 Source: 'The three young thugs brought fear to suburbia', by Liz Hull and Rebecca Camber, *Daily Mail*, 17 January 2008.
80 Source: 'Moving Beyond the ASBO', speech by Theresa May, Home Office press release, 28 July 2010.
81 Section 48 and Schedule 2 of the 1999 Act amend the Children and Young Persons Act 1933 by allowing a judge or magistrate to lift or amend reporting restrictions. Schedule 2 contains amendments relating to reporting restrictions under the following: Children and Young Persons Act 1933; Sexual Offences (Amendment) Act 1976; S.I. 1978/460 Sexual Offences (Northern Ireland) Order 1978; Sexual Offences (Amendment) Act 1992; S.I. 1994/2795 Criminal Justice (Northern Ireland) Order 1994.
82 See: Practice Direction by the Lord Chief Justice of England and Wales (Woolf LCJ): Trial of Children and Young Persons in the Crown Court of 16 February 2000.
83 [2001] Fam 430.

It is then absolutely right and in the interest of justice that in certain special cases, usually involving child killers, courts uphold section 39 reporting restriction orders, as well as post-release lifelong anonymity orders usually granted by the Family Court Division of the High Court. The decision by Dame Elizabeth Butler-Sloss to grant anonymity to the Bulger killers on their release from prison under licence in 2001 was right and humane in the same way as such an order was granted to 'Mary Bell' and her child. Given that all young murderers have served their sentence, they require new identities and lifelong anonymity from media reporting for their own protection. The raw public and media outrage that followed each of their murder trials was proof enough that their lives might be in danger.

Appearing at the Old Bailey by way of live video link, 27-year-old Jon Venables pleaded guilty on 23 July 2010, after admitting downloading and distributing indecent images of children. Venables, living in Cheshire when the images were found on his computer by a probation officer, was sentenced to two years' imprisonment. James Bulger's mother, Denise Fergus, was at the hearing and said 'justice had not been done'. Mr Justice Bean, sitting at the Old Bailey, said Venables had 'colluded in the harm of children'. However, the judge said it would be 'wrong' for Venables' sentence to be increased because of his previous crime. The judge partially lifted reporting restrictions to reveal Venables had been living in Cheshire at the time of the offences and that the case was dealt with by Cheshire police and the Cheshire probation service.[84]

5.3.3 Sexual offences tried in the Youth Court

Historically, Youth Courts could never accept jurisdiction in a rape case (see: R v Billam (Keith) (1986)[85]). However, recent developments in common law and the wider definition of rape under s. 1 **Sexual Offences Act 2003** now mean that certain rape cases may not fall within the 'grave crime' exception and can appropriately be tried in the Youth Court (see: AG's Reference (No.92 of 2009) (2010)[86]).

Lady Justice Smith in R (on the application of B & others) v The Richmond on Thames Youth Court (2006)[87] contended that magistrates would still have the power to commit a juvenile rape case to the Crown Court but that they could equally accept jurisdiction for such indictable and related sexual offences.[88]

Under the guidelines of the 'Rape Protocol of November 2007', rape cases and other serious sexual offences involving a young offender under 18 are now regularly heard by a circuit judge sitting as a district judge in the Youth Court.[89] This protocol does not alter the test for youth magistrates when determining whether a case is a 'grave crime'; for example, an allegation of sexual touching under s. 3 **Sexual Offences Act 2003**.[90]

In W v Warrington Magistrates' Court (2009),[91] W (aged 13 at the time of the offences) applied for judicial review of the decision by the district judge at Warrington Youth Court not to commit him for trial at the Crown Court on charges of attempted rape of an 8-year-old and sexual assault of a 5-year-old and a 13-year-old. It was held that the district judge had correctly exercised his discretion under s. 24 MCA to summarily try the (then) 14-year-old youth at the Youth Court,

---

84 Source: 'Bulger killer Venables jailed over child abuse images', BBC News online, 23 July 2010.
85 [1986] 1 All ER 985.
86 [2010] EWCA Crim 524 (sub nom R v Brett (Stephen Lawrence) of 3 March 2010) (CA Crim Div).
87 [2006] EWHC 95 (Admin) (QBD) (full citation: R (on the Application of W), R (on the Application of S), R (on the Application of B) v The Brent Youth Court, The Enfield Crown Court, The Richmond on Thames Youth Court [2006] of 13 January 2006).
88 s. 24 Magistrates Court Act 1980.
89 See: Sentencing Guidelines Council's definitive guideline 'Overarching Principles – Sentencing Youths', Sentencing Guidelines Council, November 2009, available at <http://www.sentencing-guidelines.gov.uk>, accessed 22 November 2010.
90 The determination of venue in the Youth Court is governed by s. 24(1)(a) Magistrates' Courts Act 1980, which provides that the youth must be tried summarily unless charged with such a grave crime that long-term detention is a realistic possibility or that one of the other exceptions to this presumption arises.
91 [2009] EWHC 1538 (Admin).

where both the attempted rape and sexual assault cases were tried and W was found guilty of all four offences. W was subsequently sentenced in the Crown Court to imprisonment for public protection (IPP) with a minimum term of two years for the attempted rape, and 12 months' imprisonment to run concurrently for each sexual assault. Accordingly, the District Judge was entitled, in his discretion, to hear all four charges and both cases.

The conviction of two boys aged 10 and 11 for the attempted rape of an eight-year-old girl in May 2010 must rank among the most depressing legal events involving children. Given the new guidelines under the 'Rape Protocol of November 2007' and the court's guidelines for trying children, wherever possible, even for grave crimes in the Youth Court — established in Re.W (see above) — it was even more astonishing that the youngest-ever defendants tried (initially for the rape) appeared before a judge and jury at the Old Bailey. The case involving two unnamed boys provoked a debate over whether juveniles should appear in a Crown Court, either as defendants or witnesses, especially in a sex offence case where they may be too immature to understand the allegations involved. Philip Johnston, commenting in the Daily Telegraph, stated that 'as a nation, we have lost our marbles'.[92]

Saunders J, passing sentence and placing these youngest ever sex offenders on the sex offenders register, conceded that the Old Bailey case would have been dropped if the victim had been an adult, because the evidence the girl gave via videolink was so contradictory. The eight-year-old had told her mother and police that the boys had 'done sex' with her in a field near her home in Hayes, West London, in October 2009. Under cross-examination, she had denied that either boy had raped her, agreeing that they had just been playing a game which one of the boys' barristers suggested amounted to no more than 'doctors and nurses', common among pre-pubescent children.[93]

Senior lawyers and children's charities described the trial as 'horrific' and 'absurd' and the trial judge admitted that the system involving child witnesses was 'far from ideal'. 'Why were the children forced to go through the rape trial?' demanded the Daily Mail,[94] a newspaper not usually sympathetic to 'feral' youths charged with violent offences, such as the attackers in the Edlington case where brothers, aged 10 and 12, stamped on their young victims, attacked them with stones and broken glass and forced one of them to strip and perform a sex act. Writing in The Times, the former Director of Public Prosecutions, Sir Ken Macdonald, asked, 'What sort of people are we? In Court 7 in recent days, we have watched a modern folk tale unfolding before our sheepish eyes. Two very small boys and a little girl of 8 have been playing out, according to the determined strictures of a grand prosecution, a distressing drama of innocence and abuse. Yesterday the little boys were convicted of attempted rape.' He further argued that games of 'You show me yours and I'll show you mine' happen in every playground in the country. 'When did we forget?'[95]

One answer was supplied by Alison Saunders, Chief Prosecutor for the London CPS, who said that the eight-year-old victim had given a clear and compelling account to the police which had been consistent with the medical evidence and with the accounts given by other witnesses. Defending the decision to go ahead with the trial, Ms Saunders said: 'This was never going to be an easy case for a court to hear but that does not absolve the CPS of its duty to prosecute where there is sufficient evidence to do so and a prosecution is in the public interest.'[96]

The child victim in this case was questioned to the point of exhaustion, as in a normal adult rape trial, and the seriousness of the sexual assault conviction, coupled with the entry on the sex

---

92 Source: 'Boys branded criminals for attempted rape: what are we doing to our children', by Philip Johnston, Daily Telegraph, 25 May 2010.

93 Source: 'Branded criminals for "playing doctors and nurses" ', by John Bingham, Caroline Gammell and Martin Evans, Daily Telegraph, 25 May 2010.

94 Source: 'Why were children forced to go through rape trial?', by Rebecca Camber, Daily Mail, 25 May 2010.

95 Source: 'This spectacle has no place in a civilised land,' by Ken Macdonald, The Times, 25 May 2010.

96 Source: CPS Press Release, 24 May 2010.

offender register of the two young boys, was widely regarded as unfair by the media. It also became clear that the person who suffered most during this trial was the victim, in spite of 'special measures' being in place.

◉ FOR THOUGHT

Should children be tried in adult courts?

5.3.4 Youth proceedings in Scotland

Children in Scotland[97] between the ages of 12 and 15 who commit a criminal offence are seldom subjected to the adult system of prosecution and punishment.[98] If a child is found guilty or pleads guilty to an offence which, if committed by someone aged over twenty-one could lead to imprisonment, a Sheriff sitting summarily can sentence the young person to a period of detention in local authority residential accommodation for up to one year.

Practically all young offenders under the age of sixteen are dealt with by the Children's Hearing System (see below 5.3.5) and only around 0.5 per cent are prosecuted in the (adult) criminal courts. Of the few that are prosecuted and found guilty, nearly a third are remitted to a children's hearing for subsequent action. The **Social Work (Scotland) Act 1968** abolished youth courts following the recommendations of the Kilbrandon Report of 1961.[99] Lord Kilbrandon wrote that the Secretary of State for Scotland ought to 'consider the provisions of the law of Scotland relating to the treatment of juvenile delinquents and juveniles in need of care or protection or beyond parental control.[100] It had been the primary conclusion of the Kilbrandon Committee that children who appeared before the criminal courts needed attention from local authorities, rather than the courts, to address their deviant behaviour and that they needed protection rather than state punishment. What followed was the Children's Hearing System, which has been admired across the world.

With regard to reporting restrictions, Scots law differs from English law in that there are generally no reporting restrictions for young persons over the age of 16.[101] Reporting restrictions for young persons under the age of 16 can be lifted under section 47 **Criminal Procedure (Scotland) Act 1995** if a judge believes that the matter is in the public interest; in certain high-profile cases this has to be confirmed by the First Minister. The **Sudden Deaths Inquiry (Scotland) Act 1976** states that no one under the age of 17 can be named in fatal accident inquiries. In an inquiry into the death of a six-week-old boy in 1984, Sheriff Principal Philip Caplan QC ordered that no one, including the parents, must be named for fear of jigsaw identification to protect the three-year-old sister of the dead boy.

Young persons under the age of 16 concerned in criminal or Children's Hearing proceedings, or linked adults, will normally never be named or identified in the Scottish media. In December 2004, the *Glasgow Evening Times* reported that 'a 34-year-old woman has been jailed for six months after leaving her two young children "home alone" while she went on holiday with her boyfriend'.[102]

---

97 In March 2009, Scottish Justice Secretary Kenny MacAskill announced to the Holyrood Government that the age of criminal responsibility would be raised from eight to twelve (s. 52 *Criminal Justice and Licensing (Scotland Act)* 2010).
98 s. 41(1) *Criminal Procedure (Scotland) Act* 1995.
99 See: Kilbrandon (1964).
100 Kilbrandon (1971), p. 128.
101 s. 46 *Children and Young Persons (Scotland) Act* 1937.
102 Source: 'Jail for mum who abandoned kids', *Glasgow Evening Times*, 18 December 2004.

Similar to the section 39 order in English and Welsh courts, a section 47 order is made in Scotland, prohibiting the media from naming the child and any persons or information leading to the identification of that child. The Aberdeen-based *Press and Journal* was acquitted of contempt of court for reporting on (then) 15-year-old Luke Mitchell, who had been arrested by the police, suspected of the murder of his 14-year-old girlfriend Jodi Jones in April 2004.

5.3.5 The Children's Hearing system

The Children's Hearing System began operating fully in 1971. The ethos of the **Social Work (Scotland) Act 1968** had been that a child could only be prosecuted for an offence on the instructions of the Lord Advocate, and that no court, other than the High Court of Justiciary and possibly a Sheriff Court, would have jurisdiction over a child for an offence. The **Children (Scotland) Act 1995** represented the first major reform of Scottish childcare law but largely preserved the Children's Hearing System set up under the 1968 Act; the 1995 Act merely made some procedural alterations and specifies the grounds of referral for a deviant child to a 'Hearing' via a local authority Children's Panel.[103] This meant that each local authority became responsible for Children's Hearings and Children's Panels, staffed largely by volunteers and appointed by the First Minister on the advice of the area's Children's Panel Advisory Committee.

The **Children (Scotland) Act 1995** also specified the grounds for referral to a Reporter.[104] Reporters are independent officials who act as 'gatekeepers' to the Children's Hearing System. Anyone, including parents, teachers and social workers, can refer a child to a Reporter if they think that the child may be in need of compulsory measures of care; though referrals for an alleged offence must come from law enforcement agencies such as the police or Procurator Fiscal. On average there are about 40,000 referrals for criminal offences each year. Those attending a Hearing include the child and any relevant person. The aim is to reach consensus about what should happen to stop the child reoffending. The child and parent or guardian have to agree to a specific order and this has to be done by way of a 'voluntary disposal'. The Hearing may decide that no compulsory measures of care are required but they may place the child under a supervision or non-residential or residential supervision order. There is the right of appeal against the Hearing's decision to a sheriff within 21 days. Where a young person is involved in incest or a sexual offences case, probably involving one or more adults, the media must follow the same rules that apply for children under the age of 16 in that no identification must take place. It is common practice for the Scottish media to report that 'a serious offence against a child' has been committed, rather than mentioning anything about 'incest'.

5.3.6 Media access to family courts

Family courts make far-reaching decisions, such as whether children should be taken into care or put up for adoption or given contact with parents who are divorcing. They also decide on custody and how finances should be split. Under youth court rules, it is unlawful to publish anything that would identify a minor involved in a case, but it is possible to identify adults such as social workers and doctors. The procedure of open media reporting in family court proceedings remains under the

---

103 s. 44(1) Criminal Procedure (Scotland) Act 1995 states that if a child who is under the supervision of the Children's Hearing System is found guilty of, or pleads guilty to, an offence in the High Court, then the court has the option of asking for a hearing to advise them as to disposal. If this occurs in the Sheriff Court then a Hearing must advise on disposal.

104 ss. 52(2)(a) to (l) and ss. 52(2)(i) are concerned with a child who 'has committed an offence' while (j) and (k) are concerned with children involved in alcohol, drugs or substance abuse.

discretion of each court, though divorce proceedings have generally been open to the public and the media (see: *Scott v Scott* (1913);[105] also: *Argyll v Argyll* (1967).[106]

See Chapters
◄ **1.4.1**
and **2.3.3**

Heather Mills, for example, applied for her and Sir Paul McCartney's divorce proceedings to be heard in private. This was ruled out by Mr Justice Bennett, who made the full divorce settlement public by way of online publication. The judgment and divorce settlement of 18 March 2008 revealed that Sir Paul was ordered to pay his former wife a lump sum settlement of £16.5 million.[107] However, the custody and ward proceedings concerning their child Beatrice were subsequently held in private, in spite of the media's application for open reporting and fierce media interest abroad. Proceedings in the family courts have long been under close scrutiny and have presented heated debates regarding *in camera* proceedings. Family lawyers and (mainly fathers') pressure groups have argued about whether this type of jurisdiction, such as wardship proceedings, should not be held in open court.[108]

As long ago as 1991, Professor Eric Barendt remarked that it would be a misconception to approach media freedom as simply a particular exercise of a generally held right. Rather, media freedom should be regarded as an institutional freedom, one that is valued because it advances a fundamental social or political good, such as free speech, by providing a forum for public debate.[109]

Since April 2009 family court proceedings are now effectively open to the public and no longer 'in private'. The idea behind the **Children, Schools and Families Act 2010** was to relax reporting restrictions in individual cases. However, there are still a large number of exceptions which provide judges with orders to prevent or limit reporting in such cases in order to protect the welfare of children. The new regime is subject to continuing controversy on the grounds of uncertainty and being 'rushed through' Parliament in response to media and fathers' pressure groups because parties involved in family court proceedings can apply to exclude the media, arguing that it is in the 'interests of the child' or for the protection of a vulnerable witness.

On 27 April 2009, new rules of court were implemented which provided accredited members of the media with the right to attend most family court cases across all tiers of court, except (for the time being) in placement and adoption proceedings and in judicially assisted conciliation or financial dispute resolution appointments. Announcing the new measures in the House of Commons, then Secretary of State for Justice, Jack Straw, stated:

> . . . it is critical that family courts make the right decisions and the public have confidence they are doing so. A key part of building trust in the system is that people understand how it works. At the same time, we must protect the privacy of children and families involved in family court cases so they are not identified or stigmatised by their community or friends. These plans strike the right balance in providing a more open, transparent and accountable system while protecting children and families during a difficult and traumatic time in their lives.[110]

The continuing absence of any general right to privacy in English law has already been discussed and, likewise, the outer limits of freedom of expression. So that leaves us with an assortment of statutory, common law and equitable rules and ongoing disputes between media pressure and an individual's claim to his or her privacy, particularly acute in family courts.

See Chapters
◄ **2.2.7**
and **2.6**

---

105 See: Viscount Haldane in *Scott v Scott* [1913] AC 417 at 35: 'There it may well be that justice could not be done at all if it had to be done in public. As the paramount object must always be to do justice, the general rule as to publicity, after all only the means to an end, must accordingly yield.'
106 [1967] Ch 301.
107 Source: 'Sir Paul McCartney and Heather Mills divorce: Judge's full ruling to be made public', by Caroline Gammell and Matthew Moore, *Daily Telegraph*, 18 March 2008.
108 For further discussion see: Lowe and Douglas (2006), chapters 10, 12 and 16.
109 Barendt (1991), at pp. 63–4.
110 Source: Justice Secretary, Jack Straw's oral statement in the House of Commons, 6 April 2009.

The privacy of minors has already been discussed in that section 39 of the **Children and Young Persons Act 1933** prioritizes and supports the welfare principle (see above 5.3.1).[111] Coupled with parental responsibility under ss. 1 and 3 of the **Children Act 1989**, and the common law duty of confidentiality regarding children and young persons (under 18), courts can still determine questions relating to the welfare of a minor arising from a proposed exercise of parental responsibility[112] and the minor's welfare by virtue of s. 1(1) **Children Act 1989**.[113]

The court recognized the strict limitations of a parent's right to waive a child's right to privacy in *Re Z* (1996).[114] This case concerned a child who was attending a special educational institution; a TV company wanted to broadcast the child's treatment with the permission of the mother. The decision of Z's mother to waive her daughter's right to confidentiality and seek publicity for Z's treatment and education was an example of 'parental responsibility' under s. 3(1) of the 1989 Act. But the court made a 'section 8' order – also known as a 'prohibited steps order' under s. 8(1) **Children Act 1989** – which enabled the court to act under the welfare principle, preventing the exercise of parental responsibility. The Court of Appeal unanimously held in *Re Z* that the publicity and TV broadcast would damage Z's well-being and future progress, justifying the section 8 order.

 The court also refused to allow the production to go ahead, thereby recognizing the child's own right to privacy under Article 8 ECHR in spite of the fact that mother had argued that the broadcast was 'in the public interest' (see also: *Re. KD (A Minor) (Ward: Termination of Access)* (1988)[115]; *Re W (A Minor) (Wardship: Restrictions on Publication)* (1992)[116]; *Re M & N (Minors) (Wardship: Publication of Information)* (1990)[117]).

Changes brought about by Part 2 of the **Children, Schools and Families Act 2010** aimed to create a more open and visible justice system in the previously privately held family courts by allowing the media access to ensure accountability through professional and public scrutiny of court decisions and thereby increase public confidence in the way the family courts work. Part 2, section 13 ('Authorised news publication') of the **Children, Schools and Families Act 2010** states:

(1) A publication of information is an authorised news publication if the following conditions are met.

(2) Condition 1 is that the information was obtained by an accredited news representative by observing or listening to the proceedings when attending them in exercise of a right conferred on accredited news representatives by rules of court.

(3) Condition 2 is that the publisher of the information –

    (a)   is the accredited news representative,

    (b)   publishes the information with the consent of, or pursuant to a contract or other agreement entered into with, that representative, or

    (c)   has obtained the information from a publication of information which is an authorised news publication.

---

111 See: Bainham and Cretney (1993).
112 'Responsibility' under s. 3(1) Children Act 1989; under s. 10(1)(b) of the 1989 Act, the court can make a 'section 8' order even though no application for such an order has been made to the court.
113 For further discussion see: Ormerod (1995), p. 686.
114 *Z, Re. (A Minor) (Identification: Restrictions on Publication)* [1996] 2 FCR 164 (CA).
115 [1988] FCR 657 (Lord Oliver).
116 [1992] 1 WLR 100.
117 [1990] Fam 211, in which a local newspaper intended to publish a story concerning the removal by a local authority of two wards from a long-term foster home without explanation. The Court of Appeal accepted that there was a clear public interest in knowing more of why the decision to remove had been taken and implemented in this manner. But the welfare of the children dictated that the identity of the children, their previous foster parents, the new foster parents, the parents, the schools and any relevant addresses should not be published.

In addition, the ruling in *Clayton v Clayton*[118] (see below) was reversed. This enabled anonymity to be waived at the end of a case, replacing it by lifelong anonymity – for both parents and children, not just the child alone as before.

❖ KEY CASE   *Clayton v Clayton* (2006)

Facts:

The parents were married in 1997 but separated in 2000. They shared custody of their child, C. The father abducted the child and took her to Portugal. Ultimately the child was returned to the mother and the father served nine months for illegal child abduction. He was permitted to resume contact with his child on release. The parents eventually reached an amicable 'share care' agreement, approved by the court. Hedley J granted an injunction preventing the father until his child was 18 'from discussing or otherwise communicating any matter relating to the education, maintenance, financial circumstances or family circumstances of C'.

The father wanted to publish a book about his experiences and to promote the idea of non-court-based 'shared-care' arrangements between the parents. Controversially he also wanted to take his daughter back to Portugal to make a video-diary about the abduction for a TV programme. His wider agenda was to alert the public as to how the courts dealt with the issues relating to family court proceedings and children when parents separated or divorced. The father sought to discharge the injunction to enable him to identify the child as part of his publicity plans.

The issue before the court was to what extent the father could put in the public domain information about the marital dispute and the custody proceedings concerning their child covered by s. 97(2) **Children Act 1989**, which had been held in private. Another hurdle was s.12 **Administration of Justice Act 1960**, which prohibited the publication of information relating to court proceedings and, if published, would amount to contempt of court.

Decision:

The Court of Appeal ruled that the criminal offence inherent in s. 97 of the 1989 Act only applied to the naming of the child while the proceedings were active and did not apply once they had been concluded. The court took the view that as a penal provision which restricted freedom of speech and bearing in mind the strictures of s. 3 HRA 1998 the provision should be interpreted narrowly and only apply while the proceedings were active.

Potter P observed: 'I do not think that, as a generality, it is right to assume that identification of a child as having been involved in proceedings will involve harm to his or her welfare interests or failure in respect of the child's family or private life' (at para 51). The court stressed that section 12 HRA was to be narrowly construed. Taking into account the father's freedom of speech interest under Article 10 ECHR, he was permitted to write a book about the affair. However, the court told him that he was not to involve his child in the

---

118 [2006] EWCA Civ 878 (CA (Civ Div)).

book project. Potter P observed: 'If the father thinks that an exculpatory account to the world of his discreditable behaviour in abducting C will serve any purpose, he must be free to write about it. What he is not free to do is to involve C in the process' (at para 75).

So, have the family court reforms gone far enough? Changes in legislation were regarded as a great victory by fathers' pressure groups, such as 'Fathers for Justice', who had campaigned for years to open up the closed, secretive world of the family courts. However, journalists would argue that the opening up of the family courts is pointless unless changes to allow the identification of *all* adults in such proceedings are made. Some say the new legislation was rushed through Parliament in the 'wash-up' round before Parliament was dissolved in April 2010 prior to the General Election on 6 May 2010.

The motivation for the opening of the family courts was a call for greater transparency and to counter accusations of secret justice, particularly in care proceedings, often seen as demonstrating the state's power to remove children from their parents' care. But the flurry of media interest soon stopped in all but rare high-profile disputes because a continued restrictive reporting regime by way of sections 11–21 of the 2010 Act makes coverage onerous and arguably meaningless.

Following the ruling on open access to the family courts, there have been a number of reported cases of applications to exclude the press from family hearings. One such case concerned *Re Child X*.

❖ KEY CASE   *Re Child X* (2009)[119]

Facts:
The matter concerned ongoing proceedings about residence and contact in relation to X, the young daughter of the applicant celebrity father. The proceedings had hitherto been heard in private and the parties wished that position to continue. Matters had proceeded on the basis of the case's privacy and the confidentiality of X's exchanges with her doctors, and to withdraw this would constitute a betrayal of trust and present a grave danger to the case's successful outcome. The media applied to attend and report on future hearings in the case pursuant to amendments to the Family Proceedings Rules 1991 by The Family Proceedings (Amendment No 2) Rules 2009.[120]

Decision:
A party applying for the exclusion of accredited media representatives from family proceedings held in private had to satisfy the court that exclusion was necessary in the interests of the child involved. It was incumbent on an applicant applying for *exclusion ab initio* to raise the matter with the court prior to the hearing for consideration of the need to notify the media in advance of the proposed application. Where temporary exclusion during proceedings was sought it was for the hearing judge to balance the competing rights under Articles 8 and 10 ECHR, inviting media representations as necessary.

Granting the application in principle, the President of the Family Court Division, Sir Mark Potter, stated that cases involving children of celebrities are no different to those involving any other children. But the need for the child's protection would similarly be more intense. In Child X's case, the President held that the anonymity order under s. 97(2) **Children Act**

---

119 *Re Child X (Residence and Contact – Rights of media attendance)* [2009] EWHC 1728 of 14 Jul 2009 (Fam).
120 Rule 10.28(4) Family Proceedings (Amendment No 2) Rules 2009.

1989 should continue until the end of the proceedings, on the basis of evidential material before the court. However, at the closure of the proceedings the judge should consider the discontinuation of the order and consider making a lifelong anonymity order on Article 8 ECHR grounds instead (thereby reversing *Clayton v Clayton*). In deciding whether the grounds for exclusion override the media's presumptive right to be present, the court must have regard to whether the press' interests lie in reporting on matters which may well be the object of interest and curiosity but which are confidential or private and do not involve matters of public concern.

The Family Court's decision to exclude the media in *Re Child X* was based on a number of unusual features and therefore possibly unlikely to apply to most other cases involving children. Crucial here was the medical and psychiatric evidence relating to the vulnerability of that child and the likely adverse impact of a media presence on Child X's welfare. There was said to be considerable foreign media interest in the case, which gave rise to a real concern as to how reporting of the details of the case could be prevented. Also significant was the question of duties of confidence on the part of medical and other experts who had not warned the parties and witnesses that their evidence was likely to be heard in the presence of media representatives.

In *Re Child X*, the court gave important guidance about the procedure to be adopted in cases where parties know that they are to apply for exclusion of the media, as Sir Mark Potter said:

> . . . I consider that para 6.4 of the Practice Direction of 20 April 2009 should be read as if there were added at the end of the final sentence in that paragraph the words 'and should do so by means of the Press Association Copy Direct service, following the procedure set out in the Official Solicitor/CAFCASS Practice Note dated 18 March 2005'.[121]

Such a procedure, the court held, was then fully in accordance with the principles applied by Lord Mustill in *Re D* (1996),[122] a procedure sufficient to make disclosure to the media of the case they have to meet when application is made to exclude them from the proceedings altogether. The upshot of *Re Child X* was that the media were deprived of the opportunity to see any informative material upon which to base any decision about seeking an application to vary or discharge the order – which, in reporting terms, would not make good copy.

A study by the Family Law and Justice Division of the Ministry of Justice, which interviewed family court managers in January 2010, revealed that:

- 25 per cent said journalists had attended hearings at their court since the rule change;
- 15 per cent said journalists had attended hearings only once and did not come back;
- 11 per cent said that media attendance had led directly to an article being published.[123]

These statistics suggest that the media is not reporting enough on family court cases because reporting is now so complex that journalists will often not know what they can and cannot report. Local newspaper reporters and those working on 24-hour news bulletins probably do not have the time to apply for lifting of reporting restrictions because they have tight deadlines to meet.

The prospect of journalists being in family courts has led some prominent and high-net-worth individuals involved in family court proceedings to settle out of court because they do not want to

---

121 *Re Child X* [2009] op. cit. at paras 78–81, judgment by the President of the Family Court Division of the High Court, 14 July 2009 (Sir Mark Potter P).
122 Re D (Minors) (Adoption Reports: Confidentiality) [1996] AC 593 (Lord Mustill).
123 Source: Ministry of Justice (2010b).

have their dirty linen aired in public. Media law firm Schillings found that, since the changes in the law, cases have often proved to be more complicated and long because they have to apply for anonymity orders in the now open family courts. This has proved to be potentially more expensive for clients. Family lawyer Rachel Atkins of Schillings commented in *The Times* that the new legislation was a 'misguided and politically-motivated fudge that has understandably satisfied neither side'.[124]

Changes in the law by way of the 2010 Act have added complexity and uncertainty for the media and an additional layer of legal expense for court users and, to a more limited extent, the media. The press has not widely used the new access to hearings because so many different layers of legislation have left reporters and editors unclear about what they can and cannot report. Reporting restrictions – particularly under existing youth justice legislation coupled with provisions under the **Children, Schools and Families Act 2010** – are longer and more complex than before and guidance from the courts remains unclear (see also: *Earl Spencer and Countess Spencer v UK* (1998)[125]).

See Chapter 2.3.7 →

For these reasons, the media has adopted a cautious approach to reporting on family proceedings and matters involving children. Journalists appear not to be interested in regularly attending family hearings, given the reporting restrictions. Family matters, such as divorce or wardship proceedings, take many months and sometimes years to conclude and the press is often unable to attend the many hearings that take place. Additionally, the press is often unaware which hearings are of particular interest: which are likely to unveil details of financial arrangements and which are simply directional. In many cases the media are not permitted access to the documents in these cases, which in turn restricts their ability to follow what is going on.

With the opening of the family courts to the media, a judge will now be required to engage in a balancing exercise as between the Article 10 rights of the press and the Article 8 rights of the child. The factors are then to be weighed in the balance as applicable to particular circumstances of each case. The judge can invite media representations before giving brief reasons for his/her decision.[126] Given the new practice directions and guidelines as set out in the 2010 legislation, the media can now identify expert witnesses who give evidence but they cannot identify social workers or other professionals. The media's right to report family court proceedings, subject to the statutory safeguards, has received judicial support and some senior family court judges have supported the public interest in press reporting. The 2010 legislation on reporting in family court proceedings has left many reporting restrictions on children and young persons unchanged and has possibly increased the uncertainty about what might be reported.

👁 FOR THOUGHT

The **Children, Schools and Families Act 2010** attempted to clarify what the press can and cannot report on family cases but the relevant sections actually appear to limit what can be reported rather than open up the reporting restrictions. Do you agree?

5.4 Special orders and restrictions

There is a long-established principle that, subject to certain exceptions and statutory qualifications, the defendant in a criminal trial is entitled to be confronted by his accuser in court. An application

---

124 Source: 'Family courts: 'the changes were a misguided, politically motivated fudge'', by Frances Gibb, *The Times*, 6 May 2010.
125 (1998) 25 EHRR CD 105 (ECHR).
126 See: para 5.5 of the Practice Direction of 20 April 2009.

for an anonymity order (for either the defendant or the witness in a case) should only be made when, after full consideration of all the available alternatives, a clear view is taken provided by conditions under section 88 of the **Coroners and Justice Act 2009**. It is not possible here to set down guidance that will cover every eventuality. Some cases may be at an early stage of investigation; in others, the question of anonymity may first come to the attention of the Crown Prosecutor after charge. Crown Prosecutors ought to ensure that proper consideration is given to the questions of witness anonymity at the most appropriate time and in a way that does not inhibit the effective progress of the case.

When an application is made to protect the defendant's anonymity, magistrates and judges have to strike a balance under Article 6 ECHR between protecting the defendant's rights to a fair trial and ensuring that his life and safety is protected and that justice will be seen to be done. Many witnesses of all ages experience stress and fear during the police and CPS investigatory process. In order to reduce worries and difficulties about giving evidence at court because of possible witness intimidation, the **Youth Justice and Criminal Evidence Act 1999** (YJCEA 1999) introduced a range of measures that can be used to facilitate the gathering and giving of evidence by vulnerable and intimidated witnesses. These measures are known as 'special measures', and are subject to the discretion of the court. Different presumptions apply to different categories of witness (see above 5.2.3).

5.4.1 Lifelong anonymity orders

The possibility of lifelong anonymity orders for child killers has already been highlighted above but warrants further discussion. The issue was first raised in the 'Mary Bell' case (Re X (1985)[127]), where a lifelong injunction was sought on behalf of the claimant and her daughter. Mary Bell was convicted of manslaughter by diminished responsibility on 17 December 1968 at Newcastle Assizes for killing two boys aged three and four. Her accomplice, known as 'Norma', aged 13, was acquitted. Mister Justice Cusack described Mary as 'dangerous' and sentenced her to be detained in secure accommodation at Her Majesty's Pleasure. After conviction, her name was released to the public, resulting in permanent media interest and applications to lift reporting restrictions.[128]

After conviction Mary (X) spent 12 years in secure units, young offender institutions and subsequently prison. On her release in 1980 she was provided, at her request, with a new identity. There were three major periods when X's identity and whereabouts were either discovered or at risk of discovery by the media. The first was after she formed a settled relationship with a man (the second defendant in Re X), and gave birth to Y on 25 May 1984. Y was made a ward of court five days later. In July 1984 the *News of the World* became aware of the birth of Y and an injunction was granted by Balcombe J in Re X (1985),[129] giving both X and Y anonymity until Y's eighteenth birthday. When Y reached 18, she and her mother applied for a lifelong anonymity order at the family court *contra mundum* preventing the disclosure of their identities, addresses and other information that might identify them.[130]

The President of the Family Court Division of the High Court, Dame Elizabeth Butler-Sloss, granted a lifelong anonymity order on 21 May 2003 (see: *Re X (a woman formerly known as Mary Bell) and others v O'Brien and others* (2003)[131]). Claimants X and Y argued, *inter alia*, that there was a serious risk that their rights under Article 8 ECHR would be breached if the injunctions were not granted. There were, they said, exceptional circumstances, including the young age at which the offences were

---

127 *X CC v A* [1985] 1 All ER 53 (sub nom 'Re X (a minor) (wardship injunction – a woman formerly known as 'Mary Bell').
128 Source: 'On this day' BBC Archive online, 17 December 1968, available at <http://news.bbc.co.uk/onthisday>, accessed 23 November 2010.
129 [1985] All ER 53.
130 For further insight into the original trial and Mary's development see: Sereny (1998) (see also: Chapter 7.5.2).
131 [2003] EWHC 1101 (Dame Elizabeth Butler-Sloss P) (QB).

committed by Mary, the length of time elapsed since the offences were committed, the need to support rehabilitation, the adverse affect of publicity on rehabilitation and X's mental state. It was argued on Y's behalf that her situation was so inextricably linked up with that of her mother that it was not possible to treat them separately. The defendants, who were Y's father and two newspaper publishers, did not oppose the applications.

Granting the lifelong anonymity order, the President stated that such relief was 'exceptional' for reasons already explained in her decision in the *Venables and Thompson* case.[132] Dame Elizabeth stressed that the granting of the relief sought by Mary Bell and her daughter (Y) was not to be taken as a broadening of the principles of the law of confidence nor an increase in the pool of those who might in the future be granted protection against potential breaches of confidence – and that such cases would remain 'exceptional'.[133]

See Chapter 2.6.2 ➜

Following Dame Elizabeth Butler-Sloss' judgment in both the Venables and Thompson and the Mary Bell (*Re X*) rulings, it was then somewhat surprising that Mr Justice Eady granted a lifelong injunction *contra mundum* to protect Maxine Carr – then aged 27 – on 24 February 2005. The order bans publication of any details that could reveal Ms Carr's new identity, including any description of where she resided or the nature of her work. Eady J said that the order was 'necessary' in order to protect Carr's 'life and limb and psychological health'.[134] Carr had been convicted in December 2003 of conspiring to pervert the course of justice. She had provided a false alibi for Ian Huntley in the 'Soham killings' by lying to police about her whereabouts on the weekend in August 2002 when he murdered 10-year-old schoolgirls Holly Wells and Jessica Chapman.

In applying for the lifelong anonymity injunction, the Family Court was told by Ms Carr's QC, Edward Fitzgerald, that she had received threatening letters and a number of women who had been mistaken for her had been threatened or assaulted. The court had a psychiatrist's report which concluded that the risks to her fragile state were very high, supported by statements from the police, the Probation Service and Home Office. Sample comments and threats from internet chatrooms were read out in court and Mr Fitzgerald told the judge that there was an 'overwhelming case' for granting the injunction and that there was 'a real and significant risk of injury or of worse – killing – if the injunction is not granted'.[135] The application was not opposed by the media and was granted.

👁 FOR THOUGHT

Do you think that a family court lifelong injunction on a child killer (*contra mundum*) can prevent the disclosure of his or her new identity and whereabouts in the digital age?

5.4.2 Terrorism trials and control orders

In exceptional cases, it is right that the courts adopt reporting restrictions to protect vulnerable witnesses such as informers. Terrorism cases are now generally prosecuted behind closed doors before a jury on evidence that the defendant knows and is free to challenge the evidence. However, where a defendant is subject to a control order[136] or about to be deported, he may well be tried on

---

132 *Venables and Thompson v NGN* [2001] Fam 430.
133 Re X (2003) EWHC 1101 (QB) at 64 (Dame Elizabeth Butler-Sloss P).
134 Source: 'Maxine Carr wins identity secrecy', *BBC News Online*, 24 February 2005, available at <http://news.bbc.co.uk/1/hi/uk/4295007.stm>, accessed 23 November 2010.
135 Source: 'Maxine Carr wins anonymity for the rest of her life', by Clare Dyer, *The Guardian*, 25 February 2005.
136 s. 1 Prevention of Terrorism Act 2005.

evidence he never sees (known as 'secret evidence'). In Mr Chahal's case, for example, there was no question of secret evidence being used against him.[137] The High Court simply could not look at the material that the Home Secretary used as the basis for his deportation order.

Following the London terrorist bombings in July 2005, the annual report of the House of Commons Home Affairs Committee (2005) reported on the media coverage of terrorism and minority issues.[138] There had been complaints from representatives of the Muslim community that the media coverage of terrorism and Islam had been negative and extreme. Particular concerns were expressed over the use of phrases such as 'Islamic (or Muslim) terrorist', comparing these terms to the term 'Catholic terrorism', one which had never been used during the period of the 'Troubles' in Northern Ireland. Those arrested on terrorism-related charges had also received significant media coverage. Those arrested but later not charged had received only minimal coverage – such as the detention of Iraqi Kurds in Manchester in April 2004, all of whom were later released without charge. The Home Office Committee had noted that the language used by the media had not helped to create the kind of tolerant and inclusive society they would like to see. It was also suggested that the Press Complaints Commission had failed to tackle the issues.[139]

In response to the allegation, various representatives from the media had given evidence before the Home Affairs Select Committee. Among them, the Executive Managing Editor of the *Daily Mail*, Robin Esser, made the point that a high proportion of newsagents were run by Muslims, whose support was crucial for newspaper distribution, and said that the *Mail* would now avoid phrases such as 'Muslim terrorist'. Mr Esser argued that his paper had sought to expose extremists and to emphasize that they were not typical of Islam, including by running pieces written by Muslim leaders.[140]

Media representatives generally recognized that there was a difficulty with reporting the release without charge of suspects whose arrest had been covered in some detail. The BBC acknowledged that 'terrorist arrests in themselves are more newsworthy than somebody who is subsequently released'.[141] The BBC Home Affairs Editor, Mark Easton, admitted that when the extremist cleric Abu Hamza had preached in the street and not in a mosque, he had been on television a 'lot more'. Mr Easton argued that there had been a real news event, but accepted that the availability of pictures had made the story more attractive to national news.[142]

Some Muslim Community witnesses suggested to the Home Affairs Committee that there may have been a concerted government strategy to manage media coverage of terrorism issues, either to divert attention from unwelcome news items or to create a climate of fear. Mr Les Levidow of the 'Campaign against Criminalising Communities' spoke of 'the Government's mass media strategy' to exaggerate and fabricate terrorist threats.[143] Freelance journalist Mr Paul Donovan cited a suggestion that 'terror alerts' were used to divert attention from other political news. This was rebutted by the BBC's Home Affairs Editor, who said, 'I certainly do not believe that there is some kind of coordinated office somewhere in Whitehall trying to change our coverage of terrorism matters.'[144]

How have law enforcement agencies and the courts dealt with reporting on terrorism cases? With the introduction of the **Prevention of Terrorism Act 2005**, all terrorism-related trials were held in secret ('closed hearings'), which arguably goes against the open justice principle, as Lord Chief Justice Taylor emphasized in R v *Keane* (1994):[145]

---

137 See: *Chahal v UK* (1996) 23 EHRR 413.
138 See: House of Commons (2005).
139 Ibid., at para 196.
140 Ibid., at para 203.
141 Ibid., at para 231.
142 Ibid., at para 237.
143 Ibid., at para 238.
144 Ibid., at para 239.
145 [1994] 1 WLR 746.

> . . . we wish to stress that *ex parte* applications are contrary to the general principle of open justice in criminal trials. They were sanctioned in *Davis, Johnson and Rowe* solely to enable the court to discharge its function in testing a claim that public interest immunity or sensitivity justifies nondisclosure of material in the possession of the Crown. Accordingly, the *ex parte* procedure should not be adopted, save on the application of the Crown and only for that specific purpose.[146]

In May 2007, the first big terrorism trial – held in secret – concluded with five men being convicted in the 'Fertilizer bomb plot' (also known as 'Operation Crevice'). Following the 9/11 attacks on the United States and the 7/7 bombings in London, this was one of the most complex trials in legal history, where the accused had been charged with conspiracy to build a massive home-made bomb from fertilizer but were stopped before they could carry out the plan. Only after the conviction of all five defendants was the trial made public. The media was then permitted to report detailed evidence of how Islamist extremism and jihad ideology had developed among the five men, who had been taken overseas to train with the Taleban, mujahideen fighters and members of the Al Qaeda network and how the ringleader of the plot, Omar Khyam, had organized the purchase and storage of 600kg of fertilizer, the key component of a bomb that he had learned to build while at a paramilitary training camp in Pakistan. The public also learnt that the security services and police had spent thousands of man hours of surveillance to smash the conspiracy and bring the men to court.[147]

Closed hearings are now widespread. They are both *ex parte* and *in camera*, where the court considers closed or secret evidence. Closed hearings involve the exclusion of one party, as well as members of the public and the press. It is known that defendants in terrorism trials have been convicted on the basis of 'secret evidence', that is evidence from anonymous witnesses. Secret evidence can now be used in a wide range of cases, including deportation hearings, control orders proceedings, parole board cases, asset-freezing applications, pre-charge detention hearings in terrorism cases, employment tribunals and even planning tribunals. The essential test of whether a case involves secret evidence or not is whether both parties have seen and had an equal opportunity to challenge *all* the evidence that is considered by the court in making its decision.[148] So long as the defendant has disclosure of all the evidence that is used by the court, then no question of the *use* of secret evidence arises.[149]

On 9 February 2007, Sue Hemming, Head of the CPS Counter Terrorism Division, made a statement at a press conference about charges brought against five men arrested in Birmingham on 31 January 2007 in relation to terrorism offences. Three of the five were named: Mohammed Irfan was charged with supplying equipment for use in committing acts of terrorism contrary to s. 5(1) **Terrorism Act 2006** and 'money laundering' for the purposes of funding terrorism, contrary to s. 17 **Terrorism Act 2000**. Amjad Mahmood was charged with the same offences and Parviz Khan was additionally charged with an offence of engaging in conduct to give effect to his intention to kidnap and kill a member of the British Armed Forces, contrary to s. 5 **Terrorism Act 2006**. An unnamed individual was charged with failing to disclose information and assistance in preventing an act of terrorism. One man had been released from custody without charge and another was still held pending further enquiries. She closed her statement by saying:

---

146 Ibid., at 750 (Lord Taylor of Gosforth CJ).
147 See: House of Commons (2009), Part B, pp. 15ff.
148 See: s. 3(1)(a) Criminal Procedure and Investigations Act 1996 (as amended by s. 32 Criminal Justice Act 2003): the prosecution must disclose any material 'which might reasonably be considered capable of undermining the case for the prosecution against the accused or of assisting the case for the accused.'
149 See: *Secretary of State for the Home Department v AHK and others* [2009] EWCA Civ 287 per Clarke MR: 'It follows that the CPR contemplate the court looking at documents produced by only one side, although it is fair to say that this is only in the context of disclosure and not in the context of a document upon which reliance is placed. It may also be added that a judge who looks at particular documents for interlocutory purposes may think it right not to take part in a determination of the merits.'

. . . I would like to remind you [members of the press] of the need to take care in reporting events surrounding these alleged charges. These individuals are only accused of these offences and they have a right to a fair trial. It is extremely important that there should be responsible media reporting which should not prejudice the due process of law.[150]

In *Re. Guardian News and Media Ltd* (2010),[151] the substantive appeals involved five individuals. Four of them, A, K, M and G, were appellants; the fifth, HAY, was the respondent and cross-appellant in an appeal by the Treasury. When the appeals were lodged before the Supreme Court, the individuals' names were concealed by the use of letters, resulting from anonymity orders first made at the outset of the proceedings involving terrorist suspects A, K, M and G. Guardian News and Media Ltd and other members of the press made an application to have the orders set aside to allow for open reporting on these important cases. At that stage, the Supreme Court decided to set aside the order in the case of G, since information concerning his identity was already in the public domain, naming him as Mohammed al-Ghabra. A, K and M, all brothers, had been informed on 2 August 2007 that they were all subject to an asset-freezing order under Article 4 **Terrorism (United Nations Measures) Order 2006**, on the basis that the Treasury had reasonable grounds for suspecting that they might be facilitating the commission of acts of terrorism. HAY's name was added to the list and on 10 October 2005 the Bank of England issued a press release naming HAY as someone who fell within the financial sanctions regime under the Al-Qaida and Taliban (United Nations Measures) Order 2006.

HAY was concerned that his identification would lead to the jigsaw identification of his wife and children, who would suffer adverse consequences. He also feared that the Egyptian authorities would take retributive action against his family members in Egypt. But it was argued by media representatives that press articles about him, his wife and children had appeared since 1999 (see also: *Youssef v Home Office* (2004)[152] which contained details about him). There had also been Al-Jazeera broadcasts about him; yet there was no evidence that any members of his family had been adversely affected in any way. Lord Rodger, in delivering the Supreme Court judgment, concluded that there was no justification for making an anonymity order in HAY's case and he was duly named as Mr Hani El Sayed Sabaei Youssef (or Hani al-Seba'i).

In relation to M's case, M feared that, if his designation as a suspected terrorist was revealed, this might lead to loss of contact, for himself and his children, with the local Muslim community. He also feared that publication of his name would cause serious damage to his reputation. M argued that an anonymity order was needed to protect his privacy rights under Article 8 ECHR. The court considered the impact of publication of M's name in relation to Article 8 and also his reputation as a member of the community in which he lived. As the press were founding their case for setting aside the anonymity order on their Article 10 right, the court had to weigh both human rights articles and examine relevant case law. The question before the court was whether there was sufficient general public interest in publishing a report which identified M to justify any resulting curtailment of his Article 8 right and that of his family to respect for their right to privacy. It was argued that in M's situation, the right to respect his and his family's private life should outweigh the public interest because M would not have an opportunity to challenge the Treasury's allegation, in making the freezing order, that M was facilitating terrorism. An order was made which kept M's identity confidential but otherwise allowed a full report of the proceedings to be published.

The arguments advanced in favour of press freedom and Article 10 were that stories about particular individuals were always more attractive to readers than stories about unidentified people.

---

150 Source: CPS Press Release: 'Five men charged with terrorism offences in Birmingham', 9 February 2007.
151 *Guardian News and Media Ltd and others in Her Majesty's Treasury v Mohammed Jabar Ahmed and others* (FC); also cited as: *HM Treasury v Mohammed al-Ghabra* (FC); *R (on the application of Hani El Sayed Sabaei Youssef) v HM Treasury* [2010] UKSC 1 of 27 January 2010.
152 [2004] EWHC 1884 (QB).

Applying the 'responsible journalism test', the judges recognized that editors knew best how to present material in a way that would interest the readers of their particular publication and so help them to absorb the information. A requirement to report it in some austere, abstract form, devoid of much of its human interest, could well mean that the report would not be read and the information would not be passed on. The approach in *Re. Guardian News and Media Ltd* was welcomed by the media. It encouraged open reporting in sensitive terrorism trials, with possible subsequent control and freezing orders, which were ultimately there to attract a wider readership and inform the public.

By concealing the identities of the individuals it might be argued that the courts were helping to foster an impression that the mere making of the orders justified sinister conclusions about these individuals. The public also had to learn about the complexity of control and freezing orders and, by allowing anonymity orders to exist, the courts were effectively denying the public information which was relevant to a wider debate about how the state was tackling the funding of terrorism. Both M and HAY wanted anonymity in respect of their private and family life on the one hand, while simultaneously inviting the press to report their version of the impact of the freezing orders on them and members of their family. This meant that the public could hardly be expected to make an informed assessment of freezing orders and ancillary orders if they were prevented from knowing who was making these points. The court came to the conclusion that there was a powerful general public interest in identifying all those appearing in court, including M, who was named as Mr Michael Marteen (formerly known as Mohammed Tunveer Ahmed).

In its sixteenth report on 'Counter-Terrorism Policy and Human Rights: Annual Renewal of Control Orders' (2010),[153] the House of Lords and House of Commons Human Rights Joint Committee held the system of control orders to be no longer sustainable in the light of important court judgments[154] (see: *A v UK* (2009)[155]; see also: *Secretary of State for the Home Department v AF and others* (2009)[156]; see also: *Secretary of State for the Home Department v AHK* (2009)[157]). In February 2011 the Government introduced a new regime called 'Terrorism Prevention and Investigation Measures' (or TPIMs), replacing control order curfews with overnight residents' requirements. Lord Carlile argued the new orders provide the same level of public protection.

⊙ FOR THOUGHT

Howard Johnson (2006) argues that – from a media point of view – there needs to be a major reform of the 'chaotic reporting restriction regime in respect of both civil and criminal proceedings'.[158] Do you agree?

5.5 Sensitive court reporting and human rights: analysis and discussion

The freedom of a child to grow up and make mistakes, to act badly and not to have this permanently recorded, is an essential human right recorded in the **UN Convention on the Rights of a**

---

153 House of Lords and House of Commons (2010).
154 Ibid., at para 112.
155 (2009) Application No. 3455/05 [GC], judgment of 19 February 2009 (ECHR).
156 [2009] UKHL 28.
157 [2009] EWCA Civ 287.
158 See: Johnson (2006).

Child. The 1989 Convention was the first legally binding international instrument to incorporate the full range of human rights – civil, cultural, economic, political and social.[159] Article 40 of the UN Convention guarantees the right of a child defendant 'to have his or her privacy fully respected at all stages of the proceedings'. Spencer (2000) argues that many countries have interpreted the Convention differently, but that the UK courts have adopted the role of 'naming and shaming' young offenders as a sanction in the legal system as an additional form of punishment (see: *McKerry v Teesdale and Wear Valley Justices* (2000)[160]; see also 5.3.2 above). Spencer argues further that in countries like Holland and Germany it would be standard practice for the media to suppress the names of young offenders even when they have turned 18.[161]

It is then regarded as a fundamental human right not to disseminate public information concerning a child – such as family court or youth justice proceedings – which may impact on the future behaviour and development of a child. It is for this reason that 'public' proceedings are usually held in private where children are concerned and that the media are prevented from commercializing childhood or child offences. It was held in *V v UK* and *T v UK* (1999)[162] that a Youth Court is best designed to meet the specific needs of children and young persons, even when charged with very serious offences. A trial in the Crown Court with greater formality and an increased number of people involved (including a jury and the public) should be reserved for the most serious adult cases.

As has been argued in previous chapters, Article 8 co-exists with Article 10 ECHR in that the media have a right to freedom of expression. Where the welfare and interest of a child is concerned, the Strasbourg court has sought to protect the privacy of a child under Article 8 and any court can now make an order prohibiting the identification of the child. However, human rights jurisprudence equally states that this power must be used carefully, balancing other interests protected by Articles 6 and 10 of the Convention.

See Chapters
◀ **2.4.2**
and **2.6.1**

Post the incorporation of the Human Rights Convention into UK law by way of the **Human Rights Act 1998**, it can be argued that S's daughter in *Godwin* would also have had the right to respect for her own private life under Article 8, in addition to the terms prescribed by s. 39 **Children and Young Persons Act 1933**. The relationship between Articles 8 and 10 ECHR was considered by the House of Lords in *Re S (A Child) (Identification: Restrictions on Publication)* (2004),[163] where the court did not consider that there was scope for extending the restrictions on freedom of expression beyond what was provided by statute as construed in *Godwin*. It is fair to say that there has been considerable criticism of the use of the 'open justice' principle to justify the naming of the parties in the *Re S (A Child)* case, where it is worth noting that all the facts could have been reported *except* for the identity of the parties.

Although there was no opposition to the granting of a lifelong anonymity order in the Mary Bell case (*Re X* (2003) – see above 5.4.1), the Attorney General has not advanced any public interest argument against the granting of protective lifelong injunctions, as Lord Woolf CJ said in *A v B (a company)* (2002).[164] This means that *any* interference with the freedom of expression, and therein press freedom, has to be justified. In the case of 'naming and shaming' a youth, are the media simply pursuing and pandering to the prurient interests of the public?

The right to open justice is a fundamental principle applicable equally to claimants and defendants. How is this principle justified and how does it interact with the rights of third parties, particularly when no named individual is before the court, or named as a respondent, as was the

159 UN Convention on the Rights of the Child. Document A/RES/44/25 of 12 December 1989.
160 (2000) 164 JP 355 (DC).
161 Source: Spencer (2000), p. 468.
162 (1999) 30 EHRR 121 (ECHR); see also: *Secretary of State for the Home Department, ex parte Venables; R v Secretary of State for the Home Department, ex parte Thompson* [1998] AC 407 (HL).
163 [2004] UKHL 47 (HL).
164 [2002] 2 All ER 545 (Lord Woolf CJ) (QB).

case in the 'John Terry superinjunction' (*LNS v Persons Unknown* (2010))? John Terry's application was made without notice; that is, individuals who might have information or who might have been considering publishing it were not cited as respondents to the application and, as a consequence, were given no notice of it. The application was simply made against '*persons unknown*'. Mr Terry asserted that *any* publication of the information would amount to an actionable breach of confidence and that publication would be a misuse of private information. The judge, while accepting

that there was a real risk that some information about the footballer's illicit relationship would be published, did not think that there was a real threat that intrusive details or photographs would be published.

So, what happens in a case where the applicant does not know who the respondent is but has in mind a number of other individuals whom they intend to serve with the order? Should they be required to ensure that those individuals are given a proper opportunity to make submissions to the court – and, if so, how? Should it be at the time the initial 'without notice' application is made? Or at a later 'on notice' hearing after the order has been made? These are important and difficult issues and not new, because they were commented on by Sir William Blackstone in relation to press freedom during the early part of the nineteenth century, when he said:

> . . . the liberty of the press is indeed essential to the nature of a free state; but this consists in laying no previous restraints upon publications, and not in freedom from censure for criminal matter when published. Every freeman has an undoubted right to lay what sentiments he pleases before the public; to forbid this, is to destroy the freedom of the press.[165]

It can finally be argued that the imposition of reporting restrictions on court proceedings or inquests amounts to a fundamental breach of the principle of freedom of expression (Article 10 ECHR) and is against the principle of open justice. In an age where press freedom and freedom of information are well enshrined in human rights law, there are many who say that any future legislation ought to push for even more openness in the court process and anything that is done which fetters that freedom should be resisted. Arguably, the present situation of court reporting works

well in that there is adequate legislation in place, enhanced by press and broadcasting codes of practice – such as the PPC Code of Practice or the OFCOM regulations – which protect youths, victims of sexual offences and the bereaved.

Perhaps the very concept of a 'superinjunction' gives a misleading impression of always unjustified super-secrecy? Superinjunctions are absolutely necessary in some cases, where valuable and confidential commercial rights need to be protected, and these could be rendered worthless if 'open justice' notions were to be applied without discrimination in all cases. Many members of the public would be outraged if they could not secure a so-called 'superinjunction' to restrain the unauthorized publication of their personal taxation details, for example.

👁 FOR THOUGHT

Are superinjunctions and anonymity orders acceptable in certain cases or do they contravene human rights law? If so, in what circumstances should reporting injunctions and anonymity orders be permitted to derogate from human rights principles?

---

165 Blackstone (1825), Vol. 2 at p. 152.

5.6 Summary of key points

- Section 39 **Children and Young Persons Act 1933** protects children and young persons under age 18 (England and Wales) by requiring court proceedings to be held *in camera*;
- No child or young person under age 18 must be named ior dentified by the media either as a person in proceedings or as a witness;
- Section 49 **Children and Young Persons Act 1933** allows a court to publish the name of a young offender 'in the public interest'.
- Section 1 **Sexual Offences (Amendment) 1992** Act provides lifelong anonymity to victims of sexual offences or indeed anyone who makes an allegation of being a victim whether or not any actual proceedings have been initiated;
- Section 13 **Children, Schools and Families Act 2010** allows media publication of information in the family court by an accredited news representative;
- Section 46 **Children and Young Persons (Scotland) Act 1937** allows media reporting of young persons in Scotland over the age of 16;
- Section 47 **Criminal Procedure (Scotland) Act 1995** allows a judge in Scotland (at times to be confirmed by the First Minister) to lift reporting restrictions on a young person under 16 in the 'public interest'.

5.7 Further reading

Barendt, E. (1991) 'Press and broadcasting freedom: does anyone have any rights to free speech?' 44 C.L.P. 63.

Johnson, H. (2006) 'Family justice: open justice'. *Communications Law*, 2006, 11(5), 171–4.

Lowe, N. and Douglas, G. (2006) *Bromley's Family Law*, 10th Edition. Oxford: Oxford University Press.

Spencer, J.R. (2000) 'Naming and shaming young offenders'. *Cambridge Law Journal*, 2000, 59(3), 466–8.

Chapter 6

Freedom of Public Information

Chapter Contents

6.1 Overview

Campaigners have long argued that too much of what is decided on behalf of the citizenry of Britain is kept under wraps and that everyone has a right to know what details are recorded about themselves in official documents. Similar concerns have also been expressed in relation to access to information at European Union level, which is of course increasingly important to the British people as well. In the UK, discussions and demands for legal reform have related to three separate strands to freedom of information:

- Access to official information, now described as the 'freedom of information regime';
- The type of information that is to remain secret, the so-called 'official secrets regime' and governance of the security services;
- What use can be made of data in relation to individuals, the 'data protection regime'.

The interaction of these separate strands of legal regulation can produce complex legal questions and problems, which will be highlighted in this chapter.

After many years of pressure, the government at last introduced legislation so that information from public bodies should be made public if it is properly asked for. In 2000, the **Freedom of Information Act** (FOIA) was introduced. A similar regime was introduced in Scotland under the **Freedom of Information (Scotland) Act 2002**, which is in some respects broader than the UK Act. The Act was welcomed by those who had campaigned, but not wholeheartedly. There are many exceptions to what information can be disclosed and those in favour of more open government protest that the exceptions are too numerous and too generally specified. It would seem that the role of the investigative journalist – which includes the ferreting-out of what others wish to conceal – is far from dead.

A good example of the release of previously secret information can create major public disquiet, such as the so-called 'Expenses and Allowances' scandal which hit Parliament in 2009 when a dossier of MPs' allowances and expenses was leaked to the *Daily Telegraph*. Much of the information was later made available to the public under the FOIA after some MPs had fought a long battle to prevent disclosure. But the 'official version' under the FOIA was redacted – edited to conceal some detail. However, the *Telegraph* had the scoop of the year by reporting all the facts early, in advance of the 'official' (FOIA) release. As a result, a large number of MPs and some members of the House of Lords had to pay back money which had been wrongly claimed, running into many thousands of pounds in a number of cases. Many representatives argued that their claims had been approved by the relevant parliamentary authorities and were not illegal, which was technically true. However, some MPs were turned into figures of fun. It was revealed that one had claimed 'to have my moat cleaned' (Douglas Hogg MP), another for 'work to a duckhouse' (Sir Peter Viggers). Some had been changing their choice of what was declared to be their 'second home'. There was an abortive attempt to amend the FOIA to exclude MPs' expenses from the ambit of disclosure, but this collapsed when it was seen as a 'political non-starter' (see below 6.3.2).

Members of Parliament and peers serving in the House of Lords were allowed one home in London and another in their constituency, if outside the capital, to make the most of what they could claim from public funds. Also among the host of revelations was the existence of the so-called 'John Lewis' list – based on the prices charged in the upmarket department store of that name. It revealed that MPs were permitted to claim up to £10,000 for a new kitchen, more than £6,000 for a bathroom and £750 for a television on parliamentary allowances.[1] The *Daily Telegraph's* publication over many weeks and the subsequent official version led to a review of parliamentary expenses and allowances and widespread changes in what could be claimed for and by whom. As detailed later

---

1   Source: 'Don Touhig helped FOIA curbs on expenses: MPs' expenses', by James Kirkup, *Daily Telegraph*, 14 May 2009.

in this chapter, some MPs resigned as a result of what had been made public and tens of others decided not to contest their seats in the May 2010 General Election. Four Parliamentarians – three MPs and one peer – faced prosecution in the courts on fraud charges. The *Telegraph* revelations also led to the unprecedented resignation of the Speaker of the House of Commons, Michael Martin MP, who was widely seen as hostile to the disclosures and increased openness.

Another example of a successful FOIA request[2] was the GCSE scandal during summer 2009, when examination watchdog Ofqual, the standards regulator set up by former Labour Education Minister Ed Balls, secretly downgraded the GCSE exam results of thousands of pupils to avoid a damaging public row over grade inflation. FOIA released documents indicating that the GCSE results in science showed a big jump. Just two days before grades were finalized in August, Ofqual's chief executive ordered the independent boards that set and marked papers to cut the number of pupils who would win top grades. This caused huge public embarrassment and brought all GCSE marking and grading into doubt.

It is true that the **Freedom of Information Act 2000** (FOIA) has made the reporting of goings-on in public bodies somewhat easier, as those organizations must disclose information if requested. But many continue to argue that it has not gone far enough, such as access to Prince Charles's frequent correspondence with ministers about Government policies, which are currently protected and ought to be open to public scrutiny.

Freedom of information is inextricably linked to the right of freedom of expression and privacy and therefore to Article 8 ECHR and common law principles. The World Summit on the Information Society (WSIS) declared and affirmed freedom of information and expression as fundamental human rights in 2003, as outlined in Article 19 of the **Universal Declaration on Human Rights**.[3] This includes freedom to hold opinions without interference and to seek, receive and impart information and ideas through any media and regardless of frontiers. The 2004 WSIS 'Declaration of Principles' also acknowledged that 'it is necessary to prevent the use of information resources and technologies for criminal and terrorist purposes, while respecting human rights'.[4]

In this chapter the **Freedom of Information Act 2000** (FOIA) will be discussed in detail, looking at the complexity of the legislation and court action which emerged after appeals to the Information Commissioner and Tribunal had been exhausted. Legal challenges have largely centred on whether an organization is a public authority and whether such an authority may derogate from the freedom of information principle inherent in the Act under section 32 FOIA (see below 6.4). Reference will also be made to the **Data Protection Act 1998** and how the two statutes interact or differ (see below 6.4.3). The question central to the chapter will be whether the FOIA has made a difference to public life (see below 6.5). In the light of the *Bavarian Lager* case,[5] access to EU documents has been given particular priority post the Lisbon Treaty in relation to EU citizens (see 6.4.6 below).

6.2 Historical overview

The legislative struggle in Britain for freedom of information is partly linked to freedom of speech and media freedom, and has already been discussed in Chapter 1. As can be seen from legal

---

2 FOIA request to the Department for Children, Schools and Families by Imran Ghory 23 July 2009.
3 The objective of the World Summit on the Information Society (WSIS) is to formulate a common vision and understanding of the global information society. Its annual action plans facilitate the effective growth of the Information Society and help bridge the digital divide. It is also regarded as an effective means to assist the United Nations in fulfilling those goals. The summits were held in Geneva in December 2003, Tunis in November 2005 and Geneva in May 2010. See <http://www.itu.int/wsis/implementation/2010/forum/geneva> (accessed 23 November 2010).
4 For further discussion see: Klang and Murray (2004), Chapter 15; see also: Weber (2010).
5 See: *Commission v The Bavarian Lager Co. Ltd.* [2009] EUECJ (ECJ).

challenges reported in Chapter 2 such as the 'Crossman Diaries', 'Spycatcher' and David Shayler cases, Britain – along with many other countries – has had a long tradition of secrecy and unwillingness to publish official information.

Until it was reformed in 1989, section 2 of the **Official Secrets Act 1911** made it an offence for any civil servant or public contractor to reveal any information he had learned in the course of his work; an offence which successive governments continued to prosecute well into the 1990s, despite recommendations published in 1972 by the Franks Committee calling for reform.[6] The '**Press Act**' of 1662[7] represented the last occasion on which the censorship of the press was formally and strategically linked to the protection of the economic interests of the Stationers' Company. The Press Act revived the system of censorship for books of all kinds as well as for newspapers. It prohibited the publication of any literary work without prior licence, drawn up by the Star Chamber as a decree in 1637. The 1662 Act set out a comprehensive set of provisions for the licensing of the press and the regulation and management of the book trade. The duty of supervision was assigned to the Secretary of State, the Archbishop of Canterbury and the Bishop of London. In addition, it confirmed the rights of those holding printing privileges (or printing patents) granted in accordance with the royal prerogative. The licensing regime was abolished in 1694 and with it the printing monopoly of the Stationers Company, which led to problems over unofficial or pirate copies, leading, in, turn to the first copyright regime in 1710, **Statute of Anne 1710**.

The historical development which follows in England can largely be linked to freedom of speech and the press (see Chapter 1) and official secret legislation and parliamentary confidentiality (see Chapter 2), which leads to public pressure and a number of attempts to introduce freedom of information legislation. The Labour Party first pledged itself to a Freedom of Information Bill in its 1974 election manifesto, but the uncertain positions of the Wilson and Callaghan governments made progress impossible. In 1978, Liberal MP, journalist and humorist Clement Freud (1924–2009) introduced an Official Information Bill as a private member's bill. The bill would have repealed the controversial catch-all s. 2 of the **Official Secrets Act 1911**, and would have established the right of freedom of information two decades before the 2000 Act as we know it came into force under Tony Blair's government. Freud secured a second reading of the bill despite entrenched opposition in Whitehall; it was some way through its committee stage when the Callaghan government collapsed in 1979. Two years later, Sheffield Labour MP Frank Hooley introduced another Freedom of Information Bill, which was opposed by the Conservative government and defeated at second reading. Another attempt was introduced by Liberal Leader David Steel MP, which was eventually converted into the **Data Protection Act** passed in 1984. This Act gave individuals the right to see information held about themselves on a computer. At the same time, Conservative MP Robin Squire promoted the 'Community Rights Project', which led to the **Local Government (Access to Information) Act 1985**; this Act granted the public wider rights in respect of public authorities, such as public access to council meetings, reports and papers. The **Access to Personal Files Act 1987**, introduced by Liberal MP Archy Kirkwood (now Lord Kirkwood of Kirkhope), gave citizens the right to see manually held social work and housing records about themselves as well as public access to school records.

The **Access to Medical Reports Act 1988**[8] resulted from another private member's bill by Archy Kirkwood MP. The Act gave people the right to see any report produced by their own doctor for an employer or insurance company. In the same year, the **Environment and Safety Information Act 1988** was passed, introduced as a private member's bill by Chris Smith MP, which granted

---

6 See: Official Secrets Act debate in Parliament between Prime Minister Edward Heath and opposition leader Harold Wilson, Hansard, HC Deb 12 December 1972 vol 848 cc 231–4.
7 Printing Presses (the Licensing Act) 1662 (13 & 14 Car.II, c.33) ('The Press Act').
8 As amended by the Access to Health Records Act 1990.

individuals the right to request information from a large number of organizations mentioned in the Act. While the companies are not named, they are defined as bodies that are 'under the control of' a public authority' and generally include those that:

(i)   have public responsibilities relating to the environment;
(ii)   exercise functions of a public nature relating to the environment; or
(iii) provide public services relating to the environment.

In 1991–2 an amended version of the Freedom of Information Bill was reintroduced by Archy Kirkwood and backed by shadow Home Secretary, Roy Hattersley MP, promising a 'Freedom of Information Act' should Labour win the 1992 general election. The bill lasted only 45 minutes in Parliament and did not receive a second reading. At the same time, the Labour front bench published the Right to Information Bill, which was partly based on the Kirkwood bill, but also included proposals to reform the **Official Secrets Act**. But the Conservatives won their fourth general election on 9 April that year, defeating Neil Kinnock and his party.

Though the Conservative government under Prime Minister John Major did not support any freedom of information legislation, cabinet minister William Waldegrave was given responsibility for implementing a more open-style government policy. John Major introduced the White Paper on 'Open Government' and the Right to Know Bill in July 1993, which proposed two new legal rights to information: public access to manually held personal files and to health and safety information. The bill also proposed to reform the **Official Secrets Act 1989**.[9] The 'Code of Practice' which was subsequently introduced relating to government openness and access to public official information was established in April 1994, supervised by the new office of the Parliamentary Ombudsman (The Parliamentary Commissioner for Administration), who, when publishing his first report in 1996, recommended the introduction of a Freedom of Information Act. Though the government rejected this proposal, it accepted that the Code of Practice needed amendment and it introduced an amended Code in February 1997.

When New Labour won the General Election in 1997, they were immediately reminded of their earlier party manifesto promise to introduce freedom of information legislation. However, Home Secretary Jack Straw made it clear that their priority lay in bringing European human rights legislation into UK law, resulting promptly in the **Human Rights Act 1998**. The Labour government's White Paper 'Your Right to Know' had been drafted in 1997, proposing wider public access to information from public bodies such as law enforcement agencies. The White Paper covered the following government departments and public authorities:[10]

- The Department of Health;
- The Department for Education and Employment;
- The Benefits Agency;
- The Employment Service;
- Local councils and local public bodies such as Registered Social Landlords and Training and Enterprise Councils;
- Quangos, nationalized industries and public corporations, such as the Equal Opportunities Commission and the Health and Safety Executive;
- The National Health Service;
- Courts and tribunals;
- The police and police authorities;

---

9   See debates in Parliament, Mr William Waldegrave and Mrs Marjorie (Mo) Mowlam, Labour MP for Redcar, Hansard, HC Deb 15 July 1993 vol 228 cc 1113–26.
10 Source: White Paper, 'Your Right to Know' (Crn 38 18). January 1998.

- The armed forces;
- Schools, further education colleges and universities;
- Public service broadcasters such as the BBC and Channel 4;
- Some private sector organisations carrying out duties on behalf of government;
- Privatized utilities.

It was an aspirational White Paper, offering a freedom of information regime and – at that time – probably the most generous among countries that had introduced such legislation. Robert Hazel from the Constitution and Public Policy Unit at University College London, in his response to the White Paper, called the proposals 'almost too good to be true'.[11] In May 1998, the Select Committee on Public Administration published its report findings on the White Paper and called on the government to introduce freedom of information legislation during its next parliamentary session. The Freedom of Information Bill was drafted and introduced into the House by Labour MP Andrew Mackinlay under the 10-minute rule. It was backed by a slightly amended version in the House of Lords in November of that year by the Conservative peer Lord Lucas of Crudwell, receiving its second reading in February 1999. The Macpherson Report of 1999 into the Stephen Lawrence police inquiry, which made the damning declaration that the Metropolitan Police was institutionally racist, recommended inter alia that the police should be fully and openly accountable to public scrutiny and the only way this could succeed would be by way of freedom of information legislation.

When the **Freedom of Information Act 2000** (FOIA) was ultimately passed, many saw it as a disappointment, with great curtailment of the original proposals in the 'Your Right to Know' White Paper. The range of exemptions and the breadth of grounds on which information could still be withheld caused considerable controversy (see below 6.4.1).

6.2.1 Lessons from abroad: comparative legislation

Clearly, a government's commitment to freedom of information and free speech is a political principle which asserts that members of the public have a right to know what the state is doing and what it knows about them. This usually means a statutory right, where members of the public may inspect their own records held by public authorities as well as examine certain information held by a public body. This right to know has existed in Sweden since the eighteenth century, in the USA since 1966, in France since 1978, in Canada, Australia and New Zealand since 1982 and in the Netherlands since 1991. In the UK, freedom of information was given statutory force by the **Freedom of Information Act 2000** (FOIA).

The Swedish **Freedom of the Press Act 1766**, passed by the Riksdag (Parliament) as the fourth major provision of the Swedish Constitution, may well be regarded as the world's first 'Freedom of Information Act'. The Swedish 'Press Act' not only guarantees freedom of speech and press freedom, but also uniquely grants an individual access to official documents (subject to certain exceptions) which should 'immediately [and free of charge] be made available to anyone making a request'. This provision has survived to this day and any refusal by a Swedish public authority to allow access to official documents may be ultimately appealed to the Supreme Administrative Court. Additionally, Sweden's Parliamentary Ombudsman retains supervisory functions regarding freedom of information.

On 11 October 2006, the Inter-American Court of Human Rights in *Caso Claude Reyes y Otros vs Chile* (2006)[12] affirmed that there is a general right of access to information held by government

---

11 Source: Robert Hazel, Commentary on The Freedom of Information White Paper 'Your Right to Know', December 1997, School of Public Policy, London, available at <http://www.ucl.ac.uk/spp/publications/unit-publications/19.pdf>, accessed 23 November 2010.

12 *Caso Claude Reyes y otros Vs. Chile* [2006] Fondo, Reparaciones y Costas Sentencia de 19 de septiembre de 2006. Serie C No. 151. Corte Interamericana de Derechos Humanos.

and that Chile had violated this right by not having an access-to-information law or other mechanisms to ensure that citizens receive answers to requests. The court requested Chile to adopt measures to ensure 'an adequate administrative process for dealing with requests for information, which sets deadlines for providing the information',[13] and it instructed the Chilean state to train its public officials in the right to information and international standards on exemptions.

In June 2010, the Icelandic Parliament in Reykjavik passed 'freedom of information' legislation that would now permit a high level of protection for journalistic sources and whistleblowers, and – *inter alia* – outlaw 'libel tourism'. The new legislation created a framework which permits and indeed encourages investigative journalism, access to free information and the promotion of free speech. The parliamentary resolution had been drafted by the Icelandic 'Modern Media Initiative' led by Julian Assange, founder of Wikileaks; it read:

> . . . for Iceland to strongly position itself legally with regard to the protection of freedoms of expression and information. Parliament resolves to task the Government with finding ways to strengthen freedoms of expression and information freedom in Iceland, as well as providing strong protections for sources and whistleblowers. In this work, the international team of experts that assisted in the creation of this proposal should be utilized . . . With the goal of improving democracy, a firm grounding will be made for publishing, whilst improving Iceland's standing in the international community.[14]

While the latest Icelandic freedom of information legislation is mainly aimed at improving the nation's own transparency – including the banking system – Iceland hopes to lure internet-based media and data centres to use the country as a base for global free speech. This means that any foreign media outlet can set up an office or server in Iceland and publish from there, covered by Icelandic legislation; a practice already undertaken by WikiLeaks (see below 6.5.1). The new measures aim to counteract challenges to media freedom from other countries. It is quite possible that media organizations will be moving their ISPs to Iceland to prevent them from being searched or seized once the legislation is passed.[15] To some experts on how the Internet is changing media law, the Iceland initiative should be hailed more for its bold thinking than for offering genuine legal protection.

Yet there are still many countries that do not allow the free flow of information or freedom of speech. On 20 June 2010, a Hong Kong publisher announced that he had scrapped plans to publish an insider account of the decision-making behind Beijing's 1989 Tiananmen Square crackdown on pro-democracy student protesters. Bao Pu told *The Guardian* that he had planned to release the memoirs of China's former premier Li Peng, which gives details on events immediately before and after the killing of workers and students in Beijing in June 1989. But the print run of 20,000 copies had been stopped by the publishers because of copyright issues, stating that 'relevant institutions have produced new information about the copyright-holder. We have no choice but to stop right now.' The manuscript would be one of the few accounts of high-level discussions on how China handled the demonstrations in 1989. In the purported memoir, Li claims armed rioters opened fire first at Chinese troops, forcing them to return fire in self-defence.[16] He gives a precise

---

13 Ibid., at para 162 of the judgment.
14 The elusive founder of the electronic whistleblowers' platform Wikileaks, Julian Assange, surfaced from years of hiding, giving press interviews in Brussels at the EU Parliament in relation to 'freedom of information'. Assange is a renowned Australian hacker wanted in the past by US intelligence. Source: 'Icelandic Modern Media Initiative', motion to Parliament on 16 February 2010, available at <http://www.immi.is/?l=en&p=vision>, accessed 23 November 2010.
15 Source: 'New law aims to make Iceland a haven for press freedom', 17 June 2010, *Deutsche Welle*, available at <http://www.dw-world.de/dw/article/0,,5696823,00.html>, accessed 23 November 2010.
16 Source: 'Tiananmen leader's "diary" revealed', by Michael Bristow, *BBC News online*, 4 June 2010, available at <http://news.bbc.co.uk/1/hi/world/asia-pacific/8721953.stm>, accessed 23 November 2010.

death toll for the military action, totalling 313 dead, including 42 students and 23 soldiers. Li also quotes late Chinese leader Deng Xiaoping as advocating martial law, saying his government would try to minimize casualties, but 'we have to prepare for some bloodshed.'[17] The Tiananmen Square crackdown remains an outlawed subject in mainland China and the Chinese government has never provided a credible account nor allowed an independent investigation into the events and fatalities. Bao was able to broach the subject in Hong Kong because the province promised freedom of speech as part of its special semi-autonomous political status even though, in the event, he was thwarted.

6.3 The Freedom of Information Act 2000 (FOIA)

The **Freedom of Information Act 2000** (FOIA) gives UK citizens the right of access to information held by public authorities, similar to practices in Sweden and France.[18] It covers more than 100,000 public bodies including local councils, police forces, primary schools and GP surgeries. The Act grants general rights of access in relation to recorded information held by public authorities. Part 1 FOIA deals with a person's right of access to information held by public authorities and states in section 1 that:

(1) Any person making a request for information to a public authority is entitled –

(a) to be informed in writing by the public authority whether it holds information of the description specified in the request, and

(b) if that is the case, to have that information communicated to him;

Responsibility for freedom of information rests with the Ministry of Justice (MOJ).[19] The 2000 Act requires the MOJ and each public authority to adopt a publication scheme which contains information routinely made available without charge.[20] The Act, which did not come fully into force until 1 January 2005, requires public bodies to adopt 'publication schemes' making certain types of information available and providing public access to this. However, the FOIA does not specify what type of information should be included in such publication schemes. Any person making a request in writing to a public authority for information must, firstly, be told whether the authority holds that information, and, secondly, be provided with that information unless it is excluded from the right's scope under one of a number of exemptions (see below 6.3.2).

Nearly all public authorities covered by the FOIA are also covered by the **Environmental Information Regulations 2004**,[21] which make a number of companies subject to the same obligations. Special 'right to know' rules apply to environmental information which came into force on 1 January 2005 (at the same time as the 'right to know' provisions under FOIA). These Regulations – based on EU legislation – are more generous and the exceptions much narrower than those contained in the main statute of the FOIA 2000. For example, a number of private companies bound by the Regulations are required to release environmental information to the requesting individual and none of the exceptions are 'absolute'. This means that an exception – that is a

---

17 Source: 'Tiananmen Square memoir axed by Hong Kong publisher', Associated Press in Hong Kong, 20 June 2010, *The Guardian*.
18 Two pieces of French legislation provide the right to access government records: (1) Loi no. 78–753 du 17 juillet 1978 de la liberté d'accès au documents administratifs and (2) Loi no 79–587 du juillet 1979 relative à la motivation des actes administratifs et à l'amélioration des relations entre l'administration et le public.
19 At first with the now defunct Department of Constitutional Affairs.
20 See: <http://www.justice.gov.uk/information/publication-scheme.htm>, accessed 23 November 2010.
21 They replace the old Environmental Information Regulations 1992.

lawful reason for withholding information (derogation) – may only be relied on where 'in all the circumstances of the case, the public interest in maintaining the exception outweighs the public interest in disclosing the information' (see below 6.3.2). This puts the applicant in a very strong position when requesting information on, for instance, emissions, substances, energy, noise, radiation or waste released into the environment.

The FOIA is generally regarded as a complex yet extremely useful piece of legislation. Its many exemptions and qualifications have led to an equally complex area of jurisprudence and case law abounds, resulting in a solid body of decisions handed down by the courts and the First Tier Tribunal (FTT) (see below 6.4.2). Since the Act has been in force, there are now sufficient decisions at appellate level for some definitive rulings and greater clarity in relation to the protection of confidential information and the exemption of material held in relation to the media (see below 6.3.2). The media has made extensive use of the FOIA statute and brought many sensitive issues to the fore, such as the *Daily Telegraph's* exposure of parliamentary expenses and the scandal which followed (see above 6.1 and below 6.3.3). Within two months of the statute taking effect, government departments were forced to release over 50,000 files including cabinet minutes, documents from the Prime Minister's Office and accounts of world history from the Foreign and Commonwealth Office. Due to the large volume of requests, many local authorities had to appoint their own information request officer. Wirral Council, for example, had 131 information requests in 2009, ranging from parking tickets to bin collections.

◉ FOR THOUGHT

Your request to the Information Commissioner requiring information on a major bank robbery in Northern Ireland has been refused on 'national security' exemption grounds. Draft a letter to the First Tier Tribunal ('Information Tribunal') challenging the decision.

6.3.1 The Information Commissioner

What type of information one can obtain is ultimately the decision of the Information Commissioner (IC), who also decides whether the information requested might be exempt because of the risk – for instance – of prejudicing international relations.[22] The IC's office is the UK's independent authority under the FOIA, there to uphold information rights in the 'public interest' and promote openness by public bodies and data privacy for individuals. The IC can override a refusal to publish information in the public interest by issuing an enforcement notice following an appeal by the party whose request was refused.

Christopher Graham took up his post as the new Information Commissioner in June 2009.[23] One of his main challenges was to tackle the lengthy backlog of cases that his office (the ICO) had been struggling with; some of them for three years. Many feel that Graham, a former producer for BBC Radio 4's investigative show *File on Four*, at least has a journalist's instinct and understands the frustrations of requesters. Following Mr Graham's appointment, the government extended the list of public authorities for the purposes of FOIA to four further organizations, namely

---

22 The Data Protection Registrar referred to in the Data Protection Act 1984 became the Data Protection Commissioner by virtue of the Data Protection Act 1998. With the coming into force of certain provisions of the Freedom of Information Act 2000, the Data Protection Commissioner became the Information Commissioner.

23 Richard Thomas – appointed CBE in 2009 – was the UK's first Information Commissioner, soon after the organization was first created in 2002.

academy schools, the Association of Chief Police Officers (ACPO), the Financial Ombudsman Service and the Universities and Colleges Admissions Service (UCAS). A 'Campaign for Freedom of Information' (CFOI) study in July 2009 revealed that of the 493 cases still outstanding in the 18 months to March 2008, 46 per cent had been delayed by between one and two years, 25 per cent by between two and three years and 5 per cent by more than three years. One case had been outstanding for almost four years.[24]

For many supporters, the FOIA and the office of the Information Commissioner have radically altered Britain's climate of secrecy for the better and improved openness within national and local government. The revelations about MPs' expenses would not have been available to the *Daily Telegraph* had the parliamentary authorities not been preparing a heavily redacted document for FOIA release. Some have criticized the act as a bureaucratic waste of time and money, with requesters complaining that important information is often redacted or withheld by authorities who are only too aware of the complex rules and exemptions of FOIA legislation. The process is too slow, taking some three to four years, at times, to request information and the appeals process before the Information Commissioner's Office has been swamped with too many cases.

6.3.2 MPs' expenses scandal: Heather Brooke's campaign

Campaigning journalist Heather Brooke filed repeated requests for details of MPs' expenses from 2005 onwards, and so did *Sunday Times* reporter Jonathan Ungoed-Thomas and the *Sunday Telegraph's* Ben Leapman.[25] Ms Brooke spent five years investigating MPs' expenses and became famous via her *Guardian* blog:

> . . . when I first telephoned the House of Commons about expenses, back in 2004, I was working on a book called *Your Right to Know: a citizens guide to using the Freedom of Information Act*. . . . Little did I realize that this simple request to the Commons would end up becoming a five-year investigation, and take me to the High Court and back . . . Eventually, I found someone who dealt with FOIA but when I explained that I was after a breakdown of MPs' expenses, I was met with baffled silence. I did one request for travel information (refused), then for the names and salaries of MPs' staff (this was blocked personally by Speaker Michael Martin) and then finally one for information on second homes. This was in 2006. My request for details on second homes was rejected, but in July that year I took it to the Information Commissioner, Richard Thomas. My request sat in his in-tray for a year. This is not uncommon and, indeed, two other cases seeking similar details on two other MPs had been languishing even longer (requests brought by Ben Leapman from the *Sunday Telegraph* and Jonathan Ungoed-Thomas from the *Sunday Times*). Eventually, our three cases were combined and in June 2007 the Commissioner finally made his decision. It pleased no one: he refused to agree to the publication of receipts but thought the allowance could be broken down into more specific categories.[26]

More than a month after the *Daily Telegraph* began disclosing details of Members of Parliaments' use of public money during the spring of 2009, the House of Commons authorities began to

---

24 Source: 'Information Commissioner and Tribunal Decisions', Campaign for Freedom of Information, 4 January 2010, available at <http://www.cfoi.org.uk>, accessed 23 November 2010.

25 See: Brooke (2010); see also: *The Heather Brooke Story*, BBC TV drama, first shown on BBC4, 30 October 2009.

26 Extract printed with kind permission by Heather Brooke from her *Guardian* blog 'Unsung Hero' in May 2009, available at <www.guardian.co.uk/politics/2009/may/15/mps-expenses-heather-brooke-foi>, accessed 23 November 2010.

release selected documents including claim forms and some receipts. However, personal details, claims relating to security and other information were blacked out, which made it impossible to tell from the documents where MPs had 'flipped' their second homes or claimed for multiple properties in a single year or, more seriously, claimed reimbursement of interest on mortgages that had already been paid off. The House of Commons even tried to amend the **Freedom of Information Act** to remove residential addresses from the scope of the Act. This was done in order to protect the privacy and safety of MPs – this was, however, met with considerable public outcry. The censorship of the documents also prevented the public at the time from seeing that Prime Minister Gordon Brown had claimed reimbursement of his share of the costs of a cleaner whose services he shared with his brother. Other claims, such as that lodged by Douglas Hogg, which included the cost of cleaning his moat, or Sir Peter Viggers for a duck house, do not appear at all.

The Commons had been due to publish its version of the expenses documents by July 2009, but brought forward publication after the *Daily Telegraph*'s full disclosures of all MPs' expenses. The documents covered the three financial years from 2004 to 2005. By June 2009, some twenty MPs had announced they would stand down following the expenses scandal. Maurice Frankel, of the Campaign for Freedom of Information, stated that the released information by Parliament was 'a very poor substitute' for the unedited material' and had it not been for the *Telegraph*'s revelations, the full expenses scandal would never have come to light.[27]

On 17 June 2010, Labour MP Eric Illsley[28] appeared before the City of London Magistrates' Court accused of deliberately overclaiming second home allowances for his home in London between 2005 and 2008 totalling £14,500. Simon Clements, for the prosecution, said Mr Illsley had taken advantage of a pre–2008 House of Commons rule stating MPs need not provide receipts for expenses under £250. Other defendants were Elliot Morley, a fisheries minister under the last Labour government, former Bury North Labour MP David Chaytor, and former Livingstone Labour MP Jim Devine, plus Lord Hanningfield, a Conservative peer, and Lord Taylor of Warwick.

In advance of the plea and directions hearing at the Old Bailey on 11 June 2010, legal analyst and correspondent Joshua Rozenberg – together with a number of media lawyers representing the major newspapers – attended Court One at the Old Bailey to apply for reporting restrictions to be lifted by submitting an 'open justice' argument before Saunders J. Journalists were permitted to attend the hearing but were not permitted to take notes. Saunders J, refusing the four Parliamentarian defendants' argument claiming parliamentary privilege and ordered that they were to stand trial in November 2010.

Mr Rozenberg reports that during the initial hearing in Court One, Mr Justice Saunders confirmed that parliamentary privilege belongs to Parliament and not to its members, citing Article 9 of the **Bill of Rights 1688**. Saunders J explained that the four defendants could not waive that privilege even if they had wanted to. The judge also cited the fundamental principle of separation of powers, now referred to as 'exclusive jurisdiction'.[29]

Lord Pannick QC for the prosecution conceded that the parliamentary expenses scheme and its administration were most probably covered by privilege, but that the Article 9 parliamentary privilege did not cover MPs' expenses claims, to which Mr Justice Saunders responded:

27 Source: 'MPs, expenses published by Parliament with key details removed', by James Kirkup, *Daily Telegraph*, 18 June 2009.
28 The MP for Barnsley Central was returned to Parliament with an 11,000 majority at the general election on 7 May 2010.
29 Source: 'Jurisprudence', by Joshua Rozenberg, Standpoint Magazine, July/ August 2010 at p. 14.

> . . . the fact that it is the submission of the claim form that sets the machinery of Parliament in motion does not make it part of that machinery just as putting a coin in a slot machine does not make the coin part of the mechanism of the slot machine.[30]

The judge's analogy was pragmatic, making the point that a line has to be drawn somewhere as to where parliamentary privilege begins and ends. The judge further added that extending the freedom of expression in Parliament to incidental parliamentary business expenses was stretching the meaning of 'incidental' too far for it to be covered by parliamentary privilege. All four defendants appealed.

David Chaytor, Elliot Morley and Jim Devine, who had attempted to use the 300-year-old law of parliamentary privilege to argue that any case against them should be dealt with by Parliament rather than the courts, all lost their appeals in December 2010 when nine Justices of the Supreme Court dismissed the former MPs' claims, stating that they were not covered by privilege and that they were therefore subject to criminal laws. In January 2011 both Mr Chaytor and Mr Illsley pleaded guilty to defrauding parliament. Mr Justice Saunders sentenced Mr Chaytor to 3 months' imprisonment. A jury at Southwark Crown Court found Tory peer Lord Taylor guilty of falsely claiming parliamentary expenses. Mr Illsley received a 12 months prison sentence and was suspended from the Labour Party.

6.3.3 The Trafigura case: gagging parliamentary questions

The FOIA request relating to the 'Trafigura' scandal, reported in the document called the 'Minton Report', caused considerable disquiet in media circles. All matters concerning the report and the spilling of toxic waste off Ivory Coast had been 'gagged' under a superinjunction against *The Guardian*. This 'gagging order' was then leaked on Twitter and Wikileaks had published the full 'Minton Report'. Twitter also revealed that Trafigura's lawyers had attempted to rely on the *sub judice* rule by preventing the issue from being aired in Parliament. This, in turn, raised issues about the relationship of Parliament and the courts under the **Bill of Rights Act 1688** and parliamentary privilege. Thousands of 'tweets' called into question privileges guaranteeing free speech in Parliament.

The United Nations 'Minton Report' (September 2009) exposed a toxic waste-dumping incident in August 2006, involving the multinational Dutch oil company Trafigura. Truck- and shiploads of chemical toxic waste from the cargo ship *Probo Koala* had been illegally fly-tipped by a Trafigura vessel in 2006 at locations around Abidjan in Ivory Coast. The Minton Report said that tens of thousands of people in Abidjan claimed they had been affected by fumes, reporting serious breathing problems, sickness and diarrhoea. The Ivorian authorities claimed that 15 people had died as a result of inhaling the chemicals as a consequence of the illegal dumping.

Following the online revelations, the High Court gagging order was lifted and senior figures at Trafigura admitted their approach may have been a little 'heavy-handed', insisting it had not been their intention to try to silence Parliament. Trafigura agreed to pay out more than £30m to some 30,000 inhabitants of Abidjan who had been affected by the toxic waste. Trafigura subsequently sued the BBC *Newsnight* programme for defamation, resulting in an out of court settlement by the BBC on 17 December 2009.

While Britain can sometimes seem like a secret state, there are increasing legal powers to access official files and personal information under the **Freedom of Information** and the **Data Protection acts**.

See Chapter
◀ 3.5.2

---

30 Ibid.

6.3.4 Was the 'War on Terror' and the invasion of Iraq by UK forces legal? The FOIA and the Chilcot Inquiry

One of the most controversial political subjects in recent times has been the invasion of Iraq in the Second Gulf War in March 2003, also named by US and UK Governments as the 'War on Terror'. The UK's involvement in Iraq remains a divisive subject and is one that provokes strong emotions, especially for those who have lost loved ones in that country among the military, support staff as well as journalists. Many, including Members of Parliament, have been looking for answers as to why the UK committed to military action in Iraq.

At the time the **Freedom of Information Act 2000** came into force in January 2005, there were some 40 requests to various government departments about the process leading up to the Iraq War. The *Daily Telegraph* pursued the then Attorney General, Lord Goldsmith, as to the legality of the Iraq war. The newspaper revealed that Lord Goldsmith initially believed that invading Iraq without a second United Nations resolution was illegal. There was also a veto in place issued by the Ministry of Justice that cabinet minutes on the issue could not be released. Channel 4 News reported that Elizabeth Wilmshurst – who resigned as deputy legal adviser to the Foreign Office because she thought the invasion contravened international law – revealed Lord Goldsmith's thinking in a section of her resignation letter. She suggested that the Attorney General changed his mind twice before advising Tony Blair that the original UN Security Council resolution 1441[31] could justify war, though many international lawyers insisted at the time that 1441 did not provide satisfactory legal justification. The Foreign Office released Ms Wilmshurst's correspondence under the FOIA. On 13 March 2003, Lord Goldsmith told Downing Street that he was satisfied that an invasion would be legal.

Following public pressure, the government set up an Inquiry which began on 24 November 2009, chaired by Sir John Chilcot. All committee members of the inquiry were Privy Councillors with long and distinguished careers, whether as historians, senior officials or as chairmen of highly respected boards and commissions. Up until then, the government had repeatedly said that an inquiry should be held only after combat troops had left Iraq so as not to undermine their role there. The purpose of the inquiry was to examine the UK's involvement in Iraq, including the way decisions were made and actions taken, and to establish as accurately and reliably as possible what happened and to identify lessons that could be learned. Prime Minister Gordon Brown, in his statement of 15 June 2009, said that he wanted the Committee to publish its report as fully as possible, disclosing all but the most sensitive information essential to UK national security. Gordon Brown told the House of Commons at the time that 'no British document and no British witness will be beyond the scope of the inquiry', though in reality there was considerable concern about the degree of non-disclosure of certain information relating to the decision-making process on the war on Iraq.

In nearly six hours of testimony before the Chilcot inquiry, former Attorney General, Lord Goldsmith, admitted to the inquiry panel that he was first convinced by his American counterparts in February 2003 that military action might possibly be 'legal' and that a second UN resolution would not be necessary. He then clarified his advice days before war broke out in March after senior commanders convinced him that the armed forces 'deserved' a 'yes or no answer'. Lord Goldsmith presented a picture of someone kept out of the loop of key decision-making. The Attorney General at the time of the Iraq War acknowledged that he changed his advice on the legality of the invasion twice in the five weeks leading up the start of the conflict.[32]

---

31 UN Security Council Resolution 1441 (2002) of 8 November 2002 offered Iraq under its leader Saddam Hussein a 'final opportunity to comply with its disarmament obligations' that had been set out in several previous resolutions. Resolution 1441 stated that Iraq was in material breach of the ceasefire terms presented under the terms of Resolution 687 (1991). Iraq's breaches related not only to weapons of mass destruction (WMD), but also the known construction of prohibited types of missiles, the purchase and import of prohibited armaments, and the continuing refusal of Iraq to compensate Kuwait for the widespread looting conducted by its troops during the 1991 invasion and occupation.

32 Source: Iraq Inquiry ('The Chilcot Inquiry into the Iraq War'), Witness Lord Goldsmith, 27 January 2010.

On 29 January 2010, former Prime Minister Tony Blair gave evidence to the inquiry. He was asked how strategy towards Iraq had evolved during six years from September 2002, including key meetings with US President George W. Bush Jnr as well as the diplomatic processes at the United Nations which preceded the invasions in March and April 2003. Tony Blair's testimony concluded on 21 January 2011 with the deterioration of the security situation in Iraq, the high levels of violence in 2006 and 2007 and how the United Kingdom responded to this, followed, finally, by how the British Government provided strategic direction. Sir John asked the fundamental questions which had been raised by most FOIA inquiries: why did Britain invade Iraq, why target Saddam, and was it legal?[33] Tony Blair said:

> . . . well, I think it is unavoidable in a situation where it is that controversial and divisive and it is that – you know, that open to challenge. You see, there actually could have been a major debate about Kosovo and legality; there could have been. There wasn't – because in the end most people went along with the action; they agreed with what we were doing. The truth is that the law and the politics follow each other quite closely, and I think, necessarily in this situation, where we were setting our strategic objectives. You know, we had this strong belief and, as I say, this is my belief now too, that this threat had to be dealt with with a certain amount of urgency. We had our alliance with the United States of America and so on and all the issues to do with Saddam, and then obviously, at the same time, as you are proceeding and strategy is evolving, diplomacy is evolving, you are looking at the issues to do with legality.[34]

Elizabeth Wilmshurst, Deputy Legal Adviser in the Foreign Office until 2003, gave evidence on 26 January 2010. Ms Wilmshust had primary and shared responsibility for Iraq issues from September 2001 together with Sir Michael Wood, then legal counsel, leading up to the Iraq conflict in March 2003. All correspondence would be copied to the Attorney General's office.[35] Ms Wilmshurst spoke about the challenge when the then Foreign Secretary, Jack Straw, did not agree with the legal advice given to him on Iraq by Sir Michael and herself. When the chairman to the inquiry then asked Ms Wilmshurst whether it made a difference that Jack Straw himself was a qualified lawyer, Ms Wilmshurst answered, 'He is not an international lawyer.'[36]

The important question was as to the legitimacy of the Iraq War in relation to the UN Security Council and its resolution 1441. According to Elizabeth Wilsmhurst, it lacked legitimacy, and therefore lacked support from the legal advisers in the Foreign Office. She was then asked about interpretation of Resolution 1441: 'was it the Council or was it individual member states to determine whether there was a material breach sufficient to justify the use of force?'[37] She stated that until 7 March 2003, there appeared to be no difference in opinion between the legal advisers and the Attorney General – simply put, the war on Iraq was illegal. However, Lord Goldsmith appeared to change his mind after that date, which Ms Wilmshurst deeply regretted:

> . . . the Attorney had relied on private conversations of what the UK negotiators or the US had said that the French had said. Of course, he hadn't asked the French of their perception of those

33 Source: The Chilcot Inquiry, Witness Tony Blair, 29 January 2010 at paras 14–18, available at <http://www.iraqinquiry.org.uk/media/45139/20100129-blair-final.pdf>, accessed 23 November 2010.
34 Ibid., paras 7–24.
35 Source: Iraq Inquiry, witness statement by Elizabeth Wilmshurst, 26 January 2010 at paras 3–17, available at <http://www.iraqinquiry.org.uk/media/44211/20100126pm-wilmshurst-final.pdf>, accessed 23 November 2010.
36 Ibid., at paras 8–10.
37 Ibid., at paras 15–19.

conversations. That was one point that I thought actually was unfortunate in the way that he had reached his decision, and the other point that struck me was that he did say that the safest route was to ask for a second resolution. We were talking about the massive invasion of another country, changing the government and the occupation of that country, and, in those circumstances, it did seem to me that we ought to follow the safest route. But it was clear that the Attorney General was not going to stand in the way of the government going into conflict.[38]

It emerged that from 7 to 13 March 2003, the Attorney General's view had evolved from saying that the stronger case was to have the (second) resolution to saying that the better view was the revival argument, which he had previously described as a reasonable case that could be made that the invasion of Iraq would be 'legal'.[39] Mrs Wilmshurst answered:

. . . so far as I was concerned, I mean, I could see that the UK reputation as an upholder of the rule of law and as an upholder of the United Nations would be seriously damaged, at least that's what I foresaw.[40]

Elizabeth Wilmshurst resigned her position on 18 March 2003.

By March 2010, the total amount of money spent on the public inquiry amounted to £2,237,700. This figure included staffing costs, office accommodation and the costs incurred in setting up and running three months of public hearings at the Queen Elizabeth II conference centre in London.[41] The Chilcot Inquiry on the Iraq War began on 24 November 2009 with a brief suspension for the General Election in May 2010 and continued well into 2011.

6.4 Seeking the truth under FOIA: legal challenges

The **Freedom of Information Act 2000** created a statutory right to information held by public authorities. The duties imposed on public authorities are set out in section 1(1) FOIA (see above 6.3) and are essentially twofold:

- a duty to 'confirm or deny' that the requested information exists;[42] and
- a duty to communicate that information.

The right of access to information is a right that is applicable to everybody, and not merely those who have an interest in the information. This right applies to all information held by a public authority.

6.4.1 When is information not released: exceptions under FOIA

The **Freedom of Information Act 2000** (FOIA) includes 23 separate sections of exemptions, which fall into two categories or 'class' exemptions – absolute exemptions and 'public interest' exemptions. *Absolute* exemptions disqualify all information of a certain type from the disclosure

---

38 Ibid. p. 18, paras 1–18.
39 Ibid., at p. 20, paras 10–19.
40 Ibid., at p. 21, paras 18–21.
41 The Inquiry considered the period from 2001 up to the end of July 2009. See: The Iraq Inquiry website:<www.iraqinquiry.org.uk>, accessed 23 November 2010.
42 s. 1(6) FOIA.

regime. The second category of *public interest* exemptions states that information may be exempt subject to a 'prejudice' test.[43]

Absolute exemptions include:

- bodies dealing with security matters and Government intelligence (s. 23 FOIA);
- court records (s. 32 FOIA);
- Parliamentary privilege (s. 34 FOIA);
- information provided in confidence (s. 41 FOIA);
- information whose disclosure is prohibited by law (s. 44 FOIA).

◉ FOR THOUGHT

How far, in your opinion, has the **Freedom of Information Act 2000** played a part in the 'War on Iraq' revelations, as opposed to pure political pressure, resulting in the Chilcot Inquiry?

These exemptions covered by the act are absolute, meaning that if a request is received for information covered by the sections above, there is neither a duty to disclose it nor to confirm or deny that it is held. Moreover there is no need to consider whether there might be a stronger public interest in making the disclosure despite the existence of an exemption. In other words, information is either exempt or it is not.

Class exemptions include court records, any material relating to actual or potential criminal investigations, material relating to audits and national security. More controversially, they also cover material relating to government policy formulation, including background information on which decisions were based. Furthermore, anything else which 'would in the reasonable opinion of a qualified person be likely to prejudice the effect conduct of public affairs' – something again left undefined in the Act and an increasing cause for appeals to the First Tier Tribunal (FTT) and the courts. Exempt information need not be disclosed by the authority. The rights conferred under FOIA are subject to 'procedural' and 'substantive limitations'. Where access is denied, the public authority has a duty to give reason.

Some qualified information that would be in the public interest includes:

- bodies dealing with national security matters (s. 24 FOIA);
- defence (s. 26 FOIA);
- international relations (s. 27 FOIA);
- the economy (s. 29 FOIA);
- law enforcement (s. 31 FOIA);
- formulation of government policy (s. 35 FOIA);
- communications with the Queen (s. 37 FOIA);
- health and safety (s. 38 FOIA);
- legal professional privilege (s. 42 FOIA);
- commercial interests (s. 43 FOIA).

Here follows a brief summary of standard class exemptions of procedural access to 'public interest information':

---

43 The rights contained in s. 1(1) FOIA 2000 are subject to exceptions contained in sections 1 (3), 2, 9, 12, and 14 FOIA.

Section 1(3) FOIA provides that a public authority may refuse to provide information if it is unable to understand what is being asked for. For example, if an inadequately particularized request is made, (i.e. where the public authority reasonably requires further particulars in order to identify and locate the information requested), it is not obliged to provide the information until the further particulars it requires are received, which help to identify and locate the information.

Section 2 explains the effect of the exemptions in Part II of the Act.

Section 9 allows the public authority to charge a fee before section 1 (1) is complied with; the fees notice must be in writing and, once served, the public authority is not obliged to comply with the request for a period of three months.[44]

Section 12 allows a public authority not to comply with a request for information if the cost of compliance exceeds the 'appropriate' limit.

Section 14 provides an exemption if the request for information is vexatious.

Finally, it must be remembered that all exemptions are time-limited, expiring after 30 years when documents containing previously exempt information become historical records, unless the information was specifically exempted from the 30-year disclosure rule, such as sensitive information relating to correspondence by members of the Royal Family; for example the abdication of Edward VIII in 1936 to marry American divorcee Mrs Simpson, which was sealed for 100 years.

◉ FOR THOUGHT

You are seeking disclosure from your local authority on toll charges levied on your local road tunnel and whether the authority is making a profit. The council provides you with information under FOIA which is more than 10 years old. Formulate your request for disclosure to the Information Commissioner stating your grounds for disclosure (see: the 'Merseytravel' case: *Mersey Tunnel Users Association v Information Commissioner*. Tribunal decision of 15 February 2008[45]).

6.4.2 Appeals before the First Tier Tribunal (FTT)

The so-called 'First Tier Tribunal' (FTT) on information rights (formerly the 'Information Tribunal') hears appeals from notices issued by the Information Commissioner under:

● **Freedom of Information Act 2000** (FOIA);
● **Data Protection Act 1998** (DPA);

---

44 Concern has been expressed by human rights lawyers about the charging of fees for access to public information (compared with the Swedish legislation, which grants all freedom of information requests free of charge).
45 Information Tribunal Appeal Number: EA/2007/0052; Information Commissioner's Ref: FS501 36587.

- **The Privacy and Electronic Communications Regulation 2003** (PECR);
- **The Environmental Information Regulations 2004** (EIR) (see: *OFCOM v The Information Commissioner* (2010)[46]).

A panel composed of a Tribunal judge and two other non-legal members – all appointed by the Lord Chancellor – hears appeals at venues across the United Kingdom. These oral hearings are open to the public. When a Minister of the Crown issues a certificate on grounds of national security, the appeal must be transferred to the Administrative Appeals Chamber of the Upper Tribunal once the application is received by the FTT.

The FTT will often require to see information which must be kept confidential from one or more of the other parties to the appeal. Among other things, this can mean that during the hearing the party requesting the information is asked to leave the room. For instance, there will be cases where a person who made a request for information under section 1(1) FOIA is a party to an appeal which examines the application of exemptions to the obligation to supply information. In many cases, the Tribunal will need to see the information which has been withheld in order to reach its decision. However, in cases where disclosure has been refused, it would in most cases undermine the very object of the exemption if the information in question were to be disclosed, during the Tribunal proceedings, to the person who made the request. Such evidence will often also reveal something of the nature of the requested information in a way which would undermine the objectives of the exemption. Equally, it may reveal other information which the Tribunal requires in order to determine the case, but which would be exempt under FOIA; for example, commercially sensitive information that is revealed in documents recording a public authority in consultation with third parties. The legal basis for the Tribunal dealing with confidential information in proceedings was considered in the Ruling in *Sugar v Information Commissioner and the BBC* (2009) (see below 6.4.4).

The Information Commissioner (IC) takes a rather restrictive view of commercial interests when it comes to applying the section 43 exemption of the 2000 Act ('commercial interests'). In his 'FOIA Awareness Guidance' on Commercial Interests (2008),[47] the Commissioner draws a distinction between commercial interests and financial interests, stating that the latter cannot be protected by the application of the section 43 exemption. This approach was called into question in the Information Tribunal decision regarding the Student Loans Company (SLC). In *Student Loans Company (SLC) v Information Commissioner* (2008),[48] the SLC challenged a decision of the Commissioner that it must disclose a training manual used by staff who deal with defaulting borrowers. Among other things, the SLC argued that disclosure would harm its commercial interests under s. 43(2) FOIA, in that the manual would help borrowers to delay or avoid complying with their obligations. The IC contended that the SLC was not participating competitively in the purchase and sale of goods or services and that a detrimental financial effect of the kind feared by the SLC would not constitute prejudice to the commercial interests of the SLC.

When the matter was appealed before the Information Tribunal, it ruled that the IC's approach to section 43 was too restrictive. The Tribunal did not consider it appropriate to tie its meaning directly or indirectly to competitive participation in buying and selling goods or services and to exclude all other possibilities. It held that the word 'commercial' includes debt collection as a commercial activity, even when carried on by a company supported by public funds. The Tribunal ruled that a better approach was to ask itself whether a detriment to the SLC, from the

---

46 [2010] UKSC 3; on appeal from: [2009] EWCA Civ 90.
47 Source: FOIA Awareness Guidance on Commercial Interests the Commissioner, Issue No 5; V3.0, 6 March 2008.
48 EA/2008/0092.

delay and reduction of debt collections and increasing the costs of collections, could fairly be described as prejudicing the SLC's commercial interests. For these reasons, the Tribunal ordered some parts of the manual to be redacted before disclosure.[49] It would be interesting to learn if the Information Commissioner will review or revise his section 43 guidance notes in the light of the above decision.

The Information Tribunal was also challenged in relation to section 32 exemptions ('court records'). In *Dominic Kennedy v IC & Charity Commissioners* (2008),[50] *Times* journalist Dominic Kennedy had requested information concerning the Charity Commission's 2007 inquiry into the Mariam Appeal, a controversial fund set up by former Labour MP for Glasgow Kelvinside, George Galloway (see below 6.4.3). Mr Galloway had set up the Mariam Appeal to help an Iraqi girl suffering from leukaemia. He said that the charitable activities had been well known to the fund's three main backers: Saudi Arabia, the United Arab Emirates and Jordanian businessman Fawaz Zureikat, the appeal's chairman. Mr Galloway had also declared his own travel arrangements on behalf of the appeal to the House of Commons Register of Members' Interests. He described the accusation that he received hundreds of thousands of pounds from Saddam Hussein as a 'lie of fantastic proportions'.[51]

Following the publication of articles by Dominic Kennedy in *The Times* where allegations were made in respect of George Galloway's Mariam Appeal, the Charity Commission opened an inquiry as to whether the Appeal fund had been properly registered as a charity. In total there were three investigative inquiries,[52] one of which established that the objects of the Mariam Appeal were stated to be charitable objects, but that the Appeal was not registered as a charity. Its known income was nearly £1.5 million until its closure in 2003. The results of the first two inquiries were published in June 2004 in a Statement of Results of the Inquiry (SORI). But further information requests by the journalists fell within the terms to be held exempt under s. 32 FOIA.

At the time the Charity Commission was investigating the charitable status of the appeal, Mr Galloway had already started his libel action against the *Daily Telegraph* over its allegations that he received money from the Iraqi regime and that some of the Mariam Appeal funds were used for non-charitable purposes. The newspaper had found documents in Iraq which it said suggested that the MP had been given a percentage of Iraqi oil sales through the oil-for-food programme – which, it calculated, would be worth about £375,000 a year. Mr Galloway strenuously denied the allegations and won his libel action against the *Telegraph*, (see: *Galloway v Telegraph* (2004).[53] Despite repeated requests to the Information Commissioner by Mr Kennedy, the three inquiries' reports and information were not released and were withheld under s. 32 FOIA. This was subsequently supported by the Information Tribunal. The Charity Commission's inquiry into the Mariam Appeal could be said to involve matters of acute public concern. But Mr Kennedy's appeal was dismissed and the Charity Commission's findings are now shelved and the Mariam Appeal file has been closed for 30 years.

See Chapter 3.2.6 →

6.4.3 Section 32 exemptions: *Kennedy v Information Commissioner*

Section 32 has been the most legally challenged part of FOIA; it covers the following absolute exemptions on information filed with or otherwise placed in:

---

49 Redaction is the process of editing requested information to remove exempt or excepted material. When a public authority decides to redact part of the requested information, it must justify each individual redaction by reference to a specific exemption or exception, explaining why it applies. The Information Commissioner has applied this principle when investigating complaints made under FOIA.

50 EA/2008/0083.

51 Source: 'Britain: Antiwar MP George Galloway suspended from Parliament', *Asian Tribune*, 27 July 2007.

52 Under s. 8 Charities Act 1993.

53 [2004] EWHC 2786 (QB).

- the custody of a court or tribunal); or
- served upon or by a public authority, for the purposes of court proceedings (including inquests and post-mortem examinations); or
- placed in the custody of a person conducting an inquiry or arbitration or the purposes of that inquiry or arbitration; or
- created by a court or member of the administrative staff for the purposes of court proceedings; or
- created by a person conducting an inquiry or arbitration for the purposes of that inquiry or arbitration.

It is important to remember that the proceedings for which the document covered by the exemption is held must actually have commenced. The exemption cannot be stretched to cover proceedings which are merely contemplated, although in such cases it may be possible to rely upon the exemption relating to legal professional privilege.[54]

The first issue which the Tribunal in the '*Kennedy*' case (see below) was called upon to determine was whether the word 'document' as it appears in section 32 included electronic documents or merely hard-copy documents. The Tribunal decided that the word should be given an expansive interpretation so as to include both electronic documents and hard-copy documents. The Tribunal further held that section 32 can apply not merely to records relating to ongoing inquiries, but also to inquiries that are closed. In the course of its decision, the Tribunal accepted that it was giving section 32 'a very wide scope', which contrasted with the approach taken by the Tribunal to other exemptions under FOIA. However, it concluded that this was the required result given the need to respect the autonomy of the courts and those bodies that conduct statutory inquiries and arbitrations.

In *Kennedy v Information Commissioner* (2010),[55] *Times* journalist Dominic Kennedy appealed to the Administrative Court of the Queen's Bench Division against the Information Commissioner's and the Information Tribunal's findings in the inquiry information relating to George Galloway and the 'Mariam Appeal' (see above 6.4.2). The Information Commissioner had dismissed a complaint by Mr Kennedy against the Charity Commission's refusal to supply him with any information in answer to his request, dated 8 June 2007. Eventually the Information Tribunal held that all three inquiries fell under the 'exceptions' part of FOIA – which was upheld by the Court of Appeal (dismissing Kennedy's appeal). The relevant parts of section 32 FOIA read:

> . . . (1) Information held by a public authority is exempt information if it is held only by virtue of being contained in –
>
> (a) any document filed with, or otherwise placed in the custody of, a court for the purposes of proceedings in a particular cause or matter;
> (b) any document served upon, or by, a public authority for the purposes of proceedings in a particular cause or matter; or
> (c) any document created by
>
>> (i)   a court, or
>> (ii) a member of the administrative staff of a court for the purposes of proceedings in a particular cause or matter.

---

54 Source: Freedom of Information Act 2000, 'Awareness Guidance No 9' information contained in court records, March 2007.
55 [2010] EWHC 475 (Admin) of 19 January 2010 (QBD).

(2) Information held by a public authority is exempt information if it is held only by virtue of being contained in –

   (a)   any document placed in the custody of a person conducting an inquiry or arbitration, for the purposes of the inquiry or arbitration; or

   (b)   any document created by a person conducting an inquiry or arbitration, for the purposes of the inquiry or arbitration.

(3) The duty to confirm or deny does not arise in relation to information which is (or if it were held by the public authority would be) exempt information by virtue of this section.

(4) In this section –

   (a)   'court' includes any Tribunal or body exercising the judicial power of the State;

   (b)   'proceedings in a particular cause or matter' includes any inquest or post-mortem examination;

   (c)   'inquiry' means any inquiry or hearing held under any provision contained in, or made under, an enactment; . . .

Calvert-Smith J held that the Information Tribunal was correct in holding that the wording of s. 32(2) FOIA had a very wide scope. There was no right under FOIA to disclosure of documents held by public authorities which had been placed in the custody of or created by a person conducting an inquiry; the documents (of the Charity Commission) fell under the absolute exemptions set out under section 32 FOIA, regardless of their content and the consequences of their disclosure, and notwithstanding the public interest in their disclosure.

The Queen's Bench Division effectively dismissed Dominic Kennedy's appeal on a point of law under s. 59 FOIA, against part of the decision of the Information Tribunal of 14 June 2009, by which it largely upheld a decision of the first respondent, the Information Commissioner. It was further held that the exemption would continue to apply for 30 years.[56] Calvert-Smith J further stated that s. 32(2) FOIA had created two exemptions from disclosure of information held by a public authority if it was held only by virtue of being contained in (a) any document placed in the custody of a person conducting an inquiry or arbitration, for the purposes of the inquiry or arbitration, or (b) any document created by a person conducting an inquiry or arbitration, for the purposes of the inquiry or arbitration. Mr Kennedy also sought clarification as to the term and definition of 'document' as being 'something written, inscribed, engraved etc. which provides evidence or information or serves as a record', and suggested that this terminology was obsolete in the digital age. The court agreed and stated that the word 'document' must now include both hard and electronic copies of documents.

❖ **KEY CASE**   *Kennedy v Information Commissioner* (2010)

Facts:
The appellant, Dominic Kennedy (K) appealed against part of a decision of the Information Tribunal upholding a ruling of the first respondent, the Information Commissioner (IC), rejecting a complaint against the refusal of the second respondent, the Charity Commission (C) to supply him with information concerning the Charity and the Mariam Appeal in 2003.

---

56 Subject to the historical records provision in s. 63(1) FOIA.

K was a journalist who had been investigating the Mariam Appeal, set up by Glasgow Labour MP, George Galloway. Following allegations in a newspaper article about the charity, C carried out three separate inquiries under s. 8 **Charities Act 1993**. K made a FOIA request for information concerning the inquiries. C refused to provide any information. C sought a fresh determination from IC, who held that all the information requested was exempt under s. 32 FOIA.

The Tribunal held that s. 32(2) FOIA granted absolute exemption to the bulk of the information that fell within the terms of K's request. The main issues were: (i) whether documents containing information that came into C's custody for the purposes of anything other than the inquiries were covered by s. 32; (ii) the scope of the exemption and in particular whether the exemption applied to documents held following the conclusion of the inquiries; (iii) the meaning of the word 'document' in s. 32.

Decision:
K's appeal was dismissed. (1) As the Tribunal had found, once a public authority placed documents it held prior to an inquiry into its own custody, those documents were within the scope of s. 32(2) where they were only being held for the purpose of the inquiry. (2) The exemption under s. 32 could be waived if the relevant inquiry involved matters of key public concern. As the Tribunal stated, the phrase 'for the purposes of the inquiry or arbitration' qualified the word 'placed' in s. 32(2)(a) and not the word 'held' in the preceding general words to s. 32(2), and subsequent events could not alter the purpose for which a document was placed in custody. The words 'held only by virtue of being contained in' did not limit the exemption. (3) The word document in s. 32(2) included electronic documents and not merely hard-copy documents.

6.4.4 Is the BBC a public body? *BBC v Sugar*

The complex nature of the FOIA is demonstrated by the second Court of Appeal case in *Sugar v BBC* (2008)[57] (and subsequent challenge in the House of Lords), which involved the exemption from disclosure granted to the BBC in relation to material created for the purposes of journalism. The case also illustrates some of the complexities involved in challenging a non-disclosure decision (see also: *BBC v Sugar* (2009)[58] below).

The background to this complex legal challenge covers an initial BBC inquiry, resulting in the 'Balen Report'. The report, an internal BBC document, was compiled in 2004 by a senior journalist, Malcolm Balen, who looked at the Corporation's coverage of the Israeli–Palestinian conflict. It was commissioned by the BBC's former director of news, Richard Sambrook, following allegations of bias from both sides. For example, hundreds of listeners had complained in 2004 when the Middle East correspondent Barbara Plett revealed that she had cried at the death of Yasser Arafat. On the other hand, allegations of pro-Jewish bias even extended to the children's programme *Newsround*. Malcolm Balen viewed many hours of BBC TV and listened to radio news reports from the Middle East, identifying the nature and coverage of the Israeli–Palestinian conflict at the time and the language used by BBC news correspondents on the ground and whether there were any inconsistencies.

Following Mr Balen's inquiry, his report was presented to the BBC's Journalism Board for consideration in 2004. Since the subject matter was of an obviously sensitive nature, and following

---

57 [2008] EWCA Civ 191.
58 [2009] EWHC 2348 (Admin).

the Hutton Inquiry,[59] the BBC's Board of Governors set up a panel, chaired by Sir Quentin Thomas, to provide an external independent review of reporting of Middle East affairs. The 'Thomas Report' was published in April 2006 and concluded there was 'no deliberate or systematic bias' in the BBC's reporting, but said its approach had at times been 'inconsistent' and was 'not always providing a complete picture', which had meant that it was sometimes 'misleading'. Governors signed off the 'Thomas Report' as a further independent review of the Israeli–Palestinian broadcasting coverage by the BBC. The 'Balen Report' was not published but a number of individuals requested copies under freedom of information legislation. On 8 January 2005, a commercial lawyer, Steven Sugar, asked to see Mr Balen's assessment but his request was turned down by the BBC on the grounds that the report directly impacted on the BBC's reporting of crucial world events; furthermore, the Corporation stated that FOI legislation did not apply in this case.[60] The BBC reasoned in its response to Mr Sugar that the 'Balen Report' was an *internal* document aimed at checking its own standards of journalism.

Mr Sugar complained to the Information Commissioner (IC) stating that the BBC – as a public body – was under a duty to disclose the requested information. On 24 October 2005, the IC ruled in favour of the BBC. Mr Sugar subsequently appealed to the Information Tribunal, which ruled in favour of Mr Sugar on 29 August 2006. This meant the BBC should disclose the report and could not derogate under the FOIA.[61] The BBC appealed against the Tribunal's decision. The grounds of appeal before the High Court were as follows: that the Tribunal did not have jurisdiction to hear an appeal from the IC; and, even if it did, the IC's decision had been flawed as a matter of law. On 27 April 2007, High Court judge Davies J backed the Information Commissioner's decision and held that the 'Balen Report' was 'for the purpose of journalism'. Additionally, the judge imposed restrictions on potential appeals to the Information Tribunal in the future, stating, *inter alia*, that the Tribunal lacked jurisdiction.[62]

❖ KEY CASE   *BBC v Sugar* (2009)[63]

Facts:

The BBC had received four separate requests for information about programming contained in the 'Balen Report'. In each case the BBC declined to provide the information requested because the Corporation believed that the report was held 'for the purposes of journalism' and refused to disclose it under the FOIA.

When Mr Steven Sugar complained to the Information Commissioner (IC), claiming that the report was public information and of generally wider interest, the IC upheld the BBC's view and their derogation under FOIA.

Mr Sugar appealed to the Information Tribunal. The Tribunal reversed the IC's decision, concluding that when the work was originally commissioned, it was for predominantly

---

59 On 21 December 2006, former Director General of the BBC, Greg Dyke, told the Information Tribunal that he supported an application by *The Guardian* and 'Open Government' campaigner, Heather Brooke, for the publication of minutes of the special meeting of BBC Governors which took place hours after the Hutton Report had criticized the BBC. Within 24 hours of the report, the BBC governors sacked Mr Dyke and apologized to the government. Gavyn Davies, the BBC's chairman, also resigned; see also: 'Report of the Inquiry into the circumstances Surrounding the Death of Dr David Kelly C.M.G.', by Lord Hutton, House of Commons, 28 January 2004, available at <http://www.the-hutton-inquiry.org.uk/content/report/index.htm>, accessed 23 November 2010.

60 Exact dates are cited here to show the length of time it took for the information to be disclosed and for the IC and the Tribunal to make their decisions.

61 For the purposes of journalism, art or literature within the meaning of Schedule 1, Part VI FOIA.

62 *Sugar v BBC* [2007] EWHC 905.

63 [2009] EWHC 2348 (Admin).

journalistic purposes, but when it was elevated to the Journalism Board as a formal report, it was held for wider public purposes. The Tribunal ruled in Mr Sugar's favour, stating that the Corporation could not derogate under FOIA. The BBC appealed to the High Court against the Tribunal's decision.

Decision:

Allowing the BBC's appeal, High Court judge, Irwin J, held the Information Tribunal was wrong in law when it stated the 'Balen Report' was not covered by the exemption (derogation) under FOIA. The Tribunal's decision was quashed. Irwin J said the Tribunal had failed to properly deal with the evidence presented and that its key conclusions were flawed.

Mr Sugar appealed the High Court decision before the Court of Appeal. On 25 January 2008, the Court of Appeal rejected Mr Sugar's appeal (Lord Buxton J, Lord Lloyd J and Sir Paul Kennedy). The disclosure of the 'Balen Report' was to be prohibited and exempt under s. 44 FOIA. Importantly, the CA rejected the view that the BBC was a public body, which meant the Corporation did not have to disclose information relating to its journalism. However, on 11 February 2009 the House of Lords overturned the Court of Appeal's decision and ruled in Mr Sugar's favour. Their Lordships decided – by a 3:2 vote – that the case should return to the High Court. Lord Phillips said the High Court had been wrong to treat the request as one not regarding a public authority, simply because of the nature of the information. He said the case depended on whether the report itself (and the material therein) fell within the scope of the FOIA. The House of Lords further ruled that the Information Tribunal *did* have jurisdiction and that the High Court must reconsider the case based on the other issues raised in the BBC's defence.

As part of the BBC's appeal to the House of Lords, the Corporation wanted clarification of the law in respect of possible derogation from the FOI statute itself and as to the legal standing of the Information Tribunal[64] and, furthermore, as to whether and how the FOIA was to apply to public service broadcasters.[65] That said, the House of Lords ruling did not necessarily mean that the 'Balen Report' should now be released. Their Lordships asked for further clarification of Freedom of Information legislation and the jurisdiction of the Information Tribunal. For this reason the matter was returned to the High Court.[66]

On 2 October 2009, Irwin, J at the High Court ruled in the BBC's favour. The decision included that the information requested by Mr Sugar was held 'significantly' for the purposes of journalism and was therefore exempt under the FOIA. At the subsequent Court of Appeal hearing on 23 June 2010, Lord Neuberger MR, Lord Moses and Lord Munby JJ upheld the High Court's (second) decision, rejecting Mr Sugar's appeal. The BBC's press release following the (second) High Court judgment in June 2010 included the following statement:

> . . . the BBC's action in this case had nothing to do with the fact that the Balen Report was about the Middle East – the same approach would have been taken whatever area of news output was covered.[67]

This means that – for the time being at least – the 'Balen Report' is not being released. The Court of Appeal judgment of June 2010 has wide implications for the application of the **Freedom of Information Act 2000** to public service broadcasting.

---

64 Now 'First Tier Tribunal'.
65 See: *BBC v Sugar* [2009] UKHL 9; the House of Lords overturned the Court of Appeal decision by a 3:2 majority (Lord Phillips, Lord Hope and Lord Neuberger in favour; Lord Hoffman and Baroness Hale dissenting).
66 For further discussion see: Johnson (2008a).
67 Source: 'BBC Balen report can stay confidential', BBC Press Release, 23 June 2010.

Timeline of the 'Balen Report' controversy

January 2005 – Steven Sugar submits a request to the BBC under FOIA, asking for a copy of the report by Malcolm Balen regarding the BBC's news coverage of the Middle East and in particular of the conflict between Israel and Palestine.

11 February 2005 – BBC responds to Mr Sugar's request, stating that it is under no obligation to disclose the information. The BBC relies on an exception under the Act which allows it not to disclose information 'held for the purpose of journalism, art or literature', claiming that the Balen Report is held for the purpose of journalism.

18 March 2005 – Mr Sugar writes to the Information Commissioner (IC), arguing that the Balen Report is not held for the purposes of journalism.

24 October 2005 – The IC rejects Mr Sugar's request, upholding the view that the Balen Report is held for the purpose of journalism and so falls outside the BBC's obligations under the Act. The IC states that he has no jurisdiction to further consider the issue.

30 December 2005 – Mr Sugar writes to the Information Tribunal to appeal the IC's decision.

29 August 2006 – The Tribunal upholds Mr Sugar's request, saying that the Commissioner did have jurisdiction to consider the issue, and that the Balen Report did not fall within the 'purposes of journalism' exception; the BBC was under duty to disclose the report.

27 April 2007 – The High Court decides that the Tribunal should not have reviewed the case as it did not have jurisdiction, upholding the original decision of the BBC and the IC that the report is 'for the purposes of journalism' and does not have to be disclosed.

25 January 2008 – The Court of Appeal upholds the decision of the High Court.

11 February 2009 – The House of Lords overturns the Court of Appeal's decision by a 3:2 majority (Lord Phillips, Lord Hope and Lord Neuberger in favour; Lord Hoffmann and Baroness Hale against). The original decision of the Tribunal stands and the Balen Report should be disclosed. The BBC can still appeal the Tribunal's decision on a point of law at the High Court.

2 October 2009 – The High Court rules in favour of the BBC (Irwin J). The Balen Report will remain secret and does not have to be disclosed.

23 June 2010 – The Court of Appeal upholds the High Court decision and rejected Mr Sugar's appeal (Lord Neuberger MR, Lord Moses J and Lord Munby J). The Balen Report is for the purposes of journalism and exempt under FOIA.

6.4.5 How does the FOIA differ from the Data Protection Act 1998?

The **Data Protection Act 1998** established a framework of rights and duties which are designed to safeguard personal data.[68] The Act is only concerned with living individuals and so if the subject of the information is dead, then the information cannot be personal data. The **Data Protection Act** applies to a particular activity – processing personal data – rather than to particular people or organizations. This means, if an organization processes personal data, they must comply with the 1998 Act and they must handle the personal data in accordance with the data protection principles.

---

68 The Data Protection Act 1998 gives effect in UK law to EC Directive 95/46/EC ('on the protection of individuals with regards to the processing of personal data and on the free movement of such data'). The 1998 Act replaces the Data Protection Act 1984 and was brought into force on 1 March 2000.

Broadly speaking, if any organization collects or holds information about an identifiable living individual, then it is processing personal data. The scope of the **Data Protection Act** is therefore very wide as it applies to just about everything concerned with individuals' personal details; the legislation applies to both manual and electronic systems.

This framework balances the legitimate needs of organizations to collect and use personal data for business and other purposes against the right of individuals to respect for the privacy of their personal details. The legislation itself is complex but essentially the 1998 Act gives an individual the right to see personal data held on them by public authorities. Data means information which:

(a)   is being processed by means of equipment operating automatically in response to instructions given for that purpose;

(b)   is recorded with the intention that it should be processed by means of such equipment;

(c)   is recorded as part (or with the intention that it should form part) of a relevant filing system (i.e. any set of information relating to individuals to the extent that, although not processed as in (a) above, the set is structured either by reference to individuals or by reference to criteria relating to individuals, in such a way that specific information relating to a particular individual is readily accessible); or

(d)   does not fall within paragraph (a), (b) or (c) but forms part of an 'accessible record'.[69]

Since the coming into force of the **Freedom of Information Act 2000** (FIOA) in 2005, it has become evident that problems have arisen regarding some of the complex exceptions under FOIA and the interplay between the different sections and the **Data Protection Act**. The 1998 Act sets out rules to make sure that personal information is handled properly by 'data controllers', whereas the FOIA covers the 'right to know' about public authorities (see above 6.3.2). If an organization or business is processing personal data, they usually have to notify the Information Commissioner (IC) about this activity (see above 6.3.1). Failure to notify is a criminal offence. The IC's office is required to maintain a register on prescribed data, and the register is available to the public for inspection via its website. The main purpose of notification and the public register is transparency and openness. It is a basic principle of data protection that the public should know (or be able to find out) who is processing personal data, plus other details about the processing (such as why it is being carried out). So notification serves the interests of individuals by helping them understand how organizations process personal data.

There are very often 'grey areas', where data controllers may find it difficult to determine whether or not certain information is subject to the requirements of the 1998 Act. The Office of the Information Commissioner has suggested that in those cases where data controllers are unsure whether or not information comes within the definition of data relevant for the filing system, they should evaluate how accessible the data are by making reasoned judgments. Data controllers should then consider the extent to which a decision not to treat the information as being covered by the Act will prejudice the individual concerned. Where the risk of prejudice is reasonably likely, then data controllers would be expected to err on the side of caution and take steps to ensure compliance.

For example, if information about a particular web-user is built up over a period of time – perhaps through the use of tracking technology – with the intention that it may later be linked to a name and address, that information is personal data. Information may be compiled about a particular

---

69 An 'accessible record' is defined in section 68 of the Act and can be summarized here as a health record, educational record (local education authority schools and special schools only), local authority housing record or local authority social services record.

web-user but without the intention of linking it to a name, address or email address. There might merely be an intention to target that particular user with advertising or to offer discounts when they revisit a particular website without the intention to actually locate that user in the physical world. The Information Commissioner takes the view that such information is, nevertheless, personal data.[70] Should an individual or organization feel that they are being denied access to personal information, they are entitled to contact the IC's office (Office of the Information Commissioner) for help, such as breaches of data protection (known as a 'compliance assessment')[71] (see above 6.3.1).

The IC's office has wide discretion to decide how to undertake a compliance assessment and usually takes the following criteria into account:

- whether the request appears to raise a matter of substance;
- any undue delay in making the request;
- whether the person making the request is entitled to make a subject access request.

The IC's office revealed, for example, that the Ashford and St Peter's Hospitals NHS Trust lost three unencrypted USB sticks containing sensitive patient information in October 2009. Each of the devices contained the full treatment and full diagnosis history relating to a number of cancer patients. The IC set up a full inquiry, resulting in the resignation of the NHS Trust's Chief Executive. The Trust's Controller had to ensure that patients' personal data would be kept securely in future, with appropriate staff training on the **Data Protection Act**.[72]

The **Freedom of Information (Scotland) Act 2002** contains much the same terms as its English and Welsh equivalent – though it is much broader in scope. The case of *Common Services Agency v Scottish Information Commissioner* (2008)[73] concerned the attempts to secure statistics about childhood incidents of leukaemia in the Scottish border area of Dumfries and Galloway in relation to public fear about nuclear processing operations at Chapelcross near Annan and Sellafield in neighbouring Cumbria. Section 38 of the Scottish Act (which is much the same as s. 40 FOIA 'personal information') decided that this was not available.

Here follow some common data protection myths and realities which are in the form of 'for thought' boxes with the answers supplied in the relevant footnotes.

👁 FOR THOUGHT NO.1

The **Data Protection Act 1998** stops parents from taking photos in schools. Is this correct?[74]

---

70 Source: Information Commissioner's Legal Guidance, March 2007, p. 12.
71 See for example: The ICO's Report on the Surveillance Society (2006) compiled by the Surveillance Studies Network. September 2006. Online report available at <http://www.ico.gov.uk/upload/documents/library/data_protection/practical_application/surveillance_society_full_report_2006.pdf>, accessed 23 November 2010.
72 Source: Undertaking by the Data Controller of Ashford & St Peter's Hospitals NHS Trust (not dated), available at <http://www.ico.gov.uk/upload/documents/library/data_protection/notices/ashford_hospital_undertaking.pdf>, accessed 23 November 2010.
73 [2008] UKHL of 9 July 2008.
74 Photographs taken purely for personal use are exempt from the Data Protection Act. This means that parents, friends and family members can take photographs of their children and friends participating in school activities and can film events at school. The Data Protection Act does apply where photographs are taken for official use by schools and colleges, such as for identity passes, and these images are stored with personal details such as names. It will usually be enough for the photographer to ask for permission to ensure compliance with the 1998 Act.

FOR THOUGHT NO.2

A company is never allowed to give a customer's details to a third party. True?[75]

FOR THOUGHT NO. 3

The *Daily Telegraph* reported on 30 September 2005 the case of an 11-year-old girl who sat her flute exam but was unable to find out her result. The exam board cited the **Data Protection Act 1998** and said that only the person who made the application, the flute teacher, could see the results. The original article resulted in several letters in the press blasting the Act. Was this correct?[76]

FOR THOUGHT NO. 4

The case of a car owner trying to find out who damaged his car gained some coverage in the national and local press, including a letter written by Ann Widdecombe for the *Daily Express* in August 2005. It was reported that the car, which was uninsured as it was off the road and out of use, was vandalized on the owner's driveway by a youth. Police apprehended the culprit but refused to release the youth's details to the owner, who wanted to bring civil proceedings against him to repair the damage to his car. The police cited the **Data Protection Act 1998** as the reason. Was this correct?[77]

6.4.6 EU legislation on 'the right to know': the *Bavarian Lager* case

In the European Court of Justice (ECJ)[78] *Bavarian Lager* case[79] (see below), Advocate General Eleanor Sharpston QC opined on the clash between two Regulations concerning the protection of and freedom of access to personal data and information. The Advocate General noted that the two existing Regulations, the 'Access Regulation' 1049/2001 and the 'Data Protection Regulation' 45/2001, contradicted each other, recommending new legislation in this respect to provide individuals with legally enforceable rights; furthermore, that the principles of data protection should

---

75 Where an organization is satisfied that someone asking for information about another person's account is authorized to access it, the 1998 Act does not prevent this. Organizations should be cautious about releasing customers' details. There is a market in personal information and unscrupulous individuals try to obtain information about others by deception. Where a couple are estranged, or parents and an adult child are estranged, one party may try and obtain information by deception. Therefore, organizations must have appropriate safeguards in place to ensure that, if staff decide to reveal a customer's personal details, such as bank account information, they are sure that the person they are speaking to is either their customer or someone acting on their behalf; for example, evidence that the account-holder has given authority.

76 The 1998 Act does not prevent an exam board from giving results to the students or their parents. The decision by this particular exam board was clearly unfair and unnecessary given that the student's mother in this case had to make a subject access request to discover her daughter's exam result – but at least data protection access rights made sure she got the information to which she was entitled.

77 The claim that the Data Protection Act 1998 stops the police from disclosing details of cautioned offenders to the victims of their crime is incorrect. The Act is not a barrier to disclosing relevant details where civil proceedings by the victim are contemplated.

78 Now: the Court of Justice.

79 *Commission v The Bavarian Lager Co. Ltd.* [2009] EUECJ of 15 October 2009 (see also: *Bavarian Lager v Commission* [1999]).

apply to *any* information concerning an identifiable person. These rules should then be consistently and homogeneously applied in all member states to safeguard the protection of individuals' fundamental rights and freedoms with regard to the processing of their personal data within the Community.

❖ **KEY CASE**   The *Bavarian Lager* Case before the European Court of Justice[80]

Facts:

The Bavarian Lager Co. Ltd ('Bavarian Lager') was established in Clitheroe, Lancashire, in 1992 to import bottled German beer into the UK for pubs. British breweries holding rights in more than 2,000 pubs were required to allow the pub managers the possibility of buying beer from another brewery, on condition that the beer was conditioned in casks with an alcohol content exceeding 1.2% by volume, known as 'Guest Beer Provision (GBP).[81] Bavarian Lager could not sell its bottled lager because most of the 2,000 pubs were 'tied' into GBP in exclusive purchasing contracts with breweries. Bavarian Lager lodged a complaint with the Commission in April 1993, arguing that this constituted a measure having an effect equivalent to a quantitative restriction on imports and was therefore incompatible with Article 28 EC.[82]

During the administrative procedure before the Commission, a meeting was held on 11 October 1996 between representatives of the Community and UK administrative authorities and the Confédération des Brasseurs du Marché Commun. Bavarian Lager wanted to take part in that meeting, but the Commission refused. On 15 March 1997, the Department of Trade and Industry announced that the GBP provision was to be amended in order for bottled beer to be sold as GBP. The Commission suspended all Treaty infringement proceedings against the UK.

By fax of 21 March 1997, Bavarian Lager asked the Director General of the Commission ('Internal Market and Financial Services') for a copy of the 'reasoned opinion', and access to the Commission documents concerning the meeting of 11 October1996. That request was refused. Reasons given included that the related documents were 'data protected' because five individuals wished to remain anonymous.

Bavarian Lager, relying on Article 8(1) and (2) of the Charter, and the Access to Documents Regulation 1049/2001 ('the Access Regulation'), argued for 'administrative transparency'. The Commission, in turn, relied on Regulation 45/2001 on 'Data Protection' ('DP', the 'Personal Data' Regulation). The DP requires the person to whom personal data is to be transferred to demonstrate that the transfer is necessary. Bavarian Lager applied to the Court of First Instance[83] for clarification.

When the case reached the European Court of Justice the Commission, supported by the UK, argued that the Court of First Instance had made errors of law in its findings

---

80 Ibid.
81 Under Article 7(2)(a) of the *Supply of Beer (Tied Estate) Order 1989* (SI 1989/2390).
82 See: *Bavarian Lager v Commission* [1999] ECR II-3217(ECJ).
83 Now known as the 'The General Court'. As from 1 December 2009, the date on which the Treaty of Lisbon entered into force, the EU has legal personality and has acquired the competences previously conferred on the European Community (EC). Community law has therefore become *European Union law*. The term 'Community law' will still be used where the earlier case-law of the General Court is being cited. The General Court is made up of at least one judge from each member state.

concerning the application of the exemption in Article 4(1)(b) of Regulation No 1049/2001 and thereby rendered certain provisions of Regulation No 45/2001 ineffective.

Decision by the European Court of Justice:
The Court of Justice set aside the judgment by the Court of First Instance, meaning that Bavarian Lager lost its appeal; the court reached the following conclusions:

1. The CFI had erred in law because it failed to correctly interpret Art 6 'Access Regulation' 1049/2001, i.e. processing personal data by EU institutions[84]; a person requesting access is not required to justify his request and therefore does not have to demonstrate any interest in having access to the documents requested;
2. The 'DP Regulation' 45/2001 requires consideration, whether the applicant has a legitimate ('necessary') interest in receiving the particular personal data; accordingly
3. The Commission had not erred when it decided that Bavarian Lager had not established a legitimate interest in receiving the personal data contained in the documents.
4. The court dismissed the action of Bavarian Lager against the Commission's decision of 18 March 2004, rejecting an application for access to the full minutes of the meeting of 11 October 1996, including all the names, i.e. the data had been lawfully withheld by the Commission. In the absence of the consent of the five participants at the meeting of October 1996, the Commission sufficiently complied with its duty of openness by releasing a version of the document in question with their names blanked out.
5. Since Bavarian Lager was unsuccessful in the appeal, the court ordered Bavarian Lager to pay the costs relating to the appeal, i.e. all Commission appeal proceedings including the Court of First Instance.[85]

Though the *Bavarian Lager* case originally concerned the 'free movement of goods' principle, the main issue before the Court of Justice centred on freedom of information. The Court of Justice made it clear that a fully-fledged system of personal data protection not only requires the establishment of rights for data subjects and obligations for those who process personal data, but also appropriate sanctions for offenders and monitoring by an independent supervisory body.

The Advocate General's opinion appears to favour freedom of information principles but at the same time she warned that personal data needs to be safeguarded – relying on the fundamental principles of Article 6 EU and the **Charter of Fundamental Rights of the European Union** ('the Charter'). The Charter recognizes the primary importance of both the protection of personal data and the right of access to documents. Article 8(1) and (2) of the Charter provide as follows:

1. Everyone has the right to the protection of personal data concerning him or her;
2. Such data must be processed fairly for specified purposes and on the basis of the consent of the person concerned or some other legitimate basis laid down by law. Everyone has the right of access to data which has been collected concerning him or her, and the right to have it rectified.

---

84 See: *Bavarian Lager v Commission* [1999] op. cit.
85 Cases also decided and cited: *Council v Hautala* [2001] ECR I – 9565; *Sweden v Commission* [2007] ECR I – 11389; *Netherlands v Council* [1996] ECR I – 2169 (Case C-58/94). The ECJ ordered the Kingdom of Denmark, the Republic of Finland, the Kingdom of Sweden and the UK to bear their own costs.

To this end measures should be adopted which are binding on the Community institutions and bodies. These measures should apply to all processing of personal data by all Community institutions and bodies insofar as such processing is carried out in the exercise of activities all or part of which fall within the scope of Community law, according to Article 6 of the EU Treaty. Access to documents, including conditions for access to documents containing personal data, is governed by the rules in Article 255 EC.

The *Bavarian Lager* case[86] demonstrates that under the 'Access to Documents Regulation',[87] EU institutions may refuse freedom of access to information where disclosure would risk undermining the protection of the private life of an individual. The 'Data Protection Regulation'[88]states that personal data cannot be transferred to recipients other than Community institutions, unless the recipient organization establishes that the data are *necessary* for the performance of a specific task, carried out in the public interest or subject to the exercise of public authority.

Article 12 of the Council Directive 95/46[89] defines the individual's (or 'data subject's') right to access data. The Directive states that:

> . . . member states shall guarantee every data subject the right to obtain from the controller:
>
> (a)   without constraint at reasonable intervals and without excessive delay or expense: [abbreviated]
>
> . . . communication to him in an intelligible form of the data undergoing processing and of any available information as to their source [abbreviated].

This means that every EU member state's public authority ('the controller') must provide access to requested information within reasonable time intervals (usually interpreted as once a year), without charge and 'without excessive delay', meaning usually within three months.

In her judgment in the *Bavarian Lager* case, the Advocate General ruled that the 'Access to Documents Regulation' established the general rule that the public *may* have access to documents of public institutions of member states. But the Court of Justice equally laid down exceptions by reason of certain public and private interests, particularly in relation to the right of access to a document where the disclosure would undermine the privacy and integrity of an individual. In certain circumstances, however, an individual's personal data may be communicated to the public. Where a request based on the 'Access to Documents Regulation' seeks to obtain access to documents including personal data, the provisions of the 'Data Protection Regulation' become applicable in their entirety, including the provision requiring the recipient of personal data to establish the need for their disclosure (the 'necessity test').

The provisions of the EU data protection legislation also include the ability for the 'data subject' (the individual) to correct any erroneous data. A study by the Finnish Data Ombudsman in 2004 indicated that 60 per cent of data subjects had not received information about when data was gathered.[90] Raento (2006) states that Finnish legislation (**Personal Data Act 1999 (Finland)**) and the Finnish Ombudsman's instructions stress that *some* requests for information on processing can be submitted in a letter or online.[91]

---

86 *Commission v The Bavarian Lager Co. Ltd.* [2009] EUECJ of 15 October 2009.
87 Regulation 1049/2001 of the European Parliament and of the Council of 30 May 2001 regarding public access to European Parliament, Council and Commission documents (OJ 2001 L 145, p. 43).
88 Regulation 45/2001 of the European Parliament and of the Council of 18 December 2000 on the protection of individuals with regard to the processing of personal data by the Community institutions and bodies and on the free movement of such data (OJ 2001 L 8, p. 1).
89 Council Directive 95/46 on the protection of individuals with regard to the processing of personal data and on the free movement of such data.
90 See: Aarnio (2004).
91 See: Raento (2006), p. 408.

In the UK, 'data controllers' are required to appoint a Data Protection Officer under the Data Protection Act, to whom all access requests are to be directed. This provision greatly simplifies practical access requests. But a problem remains for the 'data subject' since they often do not know which file holds their particular data, which could mean they should request *all* data files from the controller in question.

6.5 Has the freedom of information legislation made a difference to public life? Analysis and discussion

Has the **Freedom of Information Act 2000** made a difference to public life? Arguably yes. For many supporters, the FOIA has radically altered Britain's climate of secrecy for the better, and improved openness within national and local government. However, many journalists have criticized the FOIA, calling it a bureaucratic waste of time and money, particularly with the increased challenges before the First Tier Tribunal (FTT). Too much information is still being withheld by authorities who try to hide behind the complex exclusion clauses. At times, the Information Commissioner (IC) has taken years to release information and appeals can take up to four years to process because the IC's office is swamped with cases.

That said, by 2007, around one thousand press stories had been based on disclosures under the UK and Scottish Freedom of Information Acts, covering an enormous range of information being released under the FOIA, revealing the substantial contribution to accountability made by the Act.

Having passed the FOIA in 2000, the Labour government took five years to bring the Act into force. In 2007, Tory ex-Chief Whip David Maclean MP even proposed a private member's bill as an amendment to the FOIA to exempt Parliament from 'freedom of expression'. But the bill died quickly without support from the House of Lords.[92] It is true to say that some ministers and senior officials deny any benefits from the FOIA. Instead, they accuse the Act of impeding the effective work of government, not least because officials face frivolous or time-consuming fishing expeditions from journalists and others.

6.5.1 Should the free flow of information via WikiLeaks be prohibited?

On 28 December 2007, the whistleblower website WikiLeaks released graphic video footage of the slaughter of Iraqi civilians by US helicopter gunships. The incident was filmed from a military Apache helicopter and showed an attack carried out in the Iraqi suburb of New Baghdad in July 2007, when two Reuters journalists, Saeed Chmagh and Namir Noor-Eldeen, were killed. Reuters had been trying unsuccessfully to obtain the video through the **Freedom of Information Act**. Wikileaks obtained and then decrypted the video via anonymous sources within the military.

The film prompted an instant uproar and confrontation between the Pentagon and its defenders, who argued that the rules of engagement had been followed, and critics, who decried the brutality of killing unsuspecting people from the air and the perverse glee of some of the soldiers. In one exchange on the 38-minute video, soldiers in the helicopter watch a US tank on the ground below and one says, 'I think they just drove over a body.' Another chuckles and says, 'Really?' The two can be heard laughing. When a soldier on the ground reports that a small girl in a van on the scene was seriously wounded, a helicopter gunner says, 'Well, it's their fault for bringing their kids into a battle.' The other responds, 'That's right.' After they blow up a building killing people inside, the

---

92 Source: 'Bill curbing FOIA fails to find sponsor in Lords', by Hélène Mulholland, *The Guardian*, 13 June 2007.

gunners can be heard saying 'Sweet' and 'Nice missile'.[93] Following the controversial release of the film by WikiLeaks, the International Federation of Journalists (IFJ) called on US President Barack Obama to open a fresh investigation into the actions of the US army, which was implicated in killings of journalists in Iraq.[94]

On 19 June 2009, WikiLeaks founder Julian Assange released the full report on the corruption that had led to the UK government's taking control of the British overseas territories, the Turks and Caicos Islands (TCI), a popular Caribbean tourist destination and tax haven.[95] Following the corruption allegations made against the Islands' political elite, the British Foreign and Commonwealth Office commissioned Sir Robin Auld to head up a Turks and Caicos Islands Commission of Inquiry. The Report by the Parliamentary Commission inquiry found that foreign property developers had given millions of US dollars in secret loans and payments to senior Islander politicians, including the TIC's former Premier, Michael Misick. A lawsuit in the UK High Court ensued, initially resulting in a *contra mundum* injunction against all media reporting. This injunction was overturned, permitting free reporting on the Commission's findings. The UK government has been in control of the TCI since April 2010.[96]

It was WikiLeaks that had exposed the full Trafigura scandal by releasing the (super)injuncted documents[97] (see above 6.3.3). The website was also instrumental in bringing about the resignation of the Prime Minister of Tanzania, Edward Lowassa, by releasing the (secret) Richmond Parliamentary Committee Report that exposed gross corruption at the highest level of Tanzania's government on 7 February 2008. The website also released the full British National Party membership list for 2007–8 and claimed to have swung the Kenyan presidential election in 2007 by exposing corruption at the highest levels.

See Chapter
1.3.5 →

What, then, of the future? Should the legal system prevent publication on free internet websites like WikiLeaks, that pride themselves on releasing secret government information supplied by international bona fide sources? Julian Assange from WikiLeaks says 'no'. He believes in the totally free flow of information. He highlights some one hundred lawsuits since the website started in 2006; all of which, he states, WikiLeaks has won. On the BBC Radio 4 *Media Show* in June 2010, Assange claimed that WikiLeaks was staffed by only five full-time members and supported by more than ten thousand volunteers. The whistleblower website had released more classified documents than the rest of the world press combined. Assange said: 'That's not something I say as a way of saying how successful we are – rather, that shows you the powerless state of the rest of the media. How is it that a team of five people has managed to release to the public more suppressed information, at that level, than the rest of the world press combined?'[98]

WikiLeaks acts as an electronic dead-drop for highly sensitive or secret information, which is then published in pure and original form. No rewriting is allowed. Created by an online network of dissidents, journalists, academics, lawyers, technology experts and mathematicians from various

---

93 Source: 'Crimes without punishment', by J. Patrice McSherry, *The Guardian*, 14 April 2010.
94 The IFJ works for press freedom by trade union development, working for journalists' rights and social conditions. The organization believes that there can be no press freedom where journalists exist in conditions of corruption, poverty or fear. The IFJ is also a founder of the International News Safety Institute, founded in 2003, which promotes practical action worldwide to increase the safety and protection of journalists and media staff. Source: <http://www.ifj.org/en/pages/press-freedom-safety>, accessed 23 November 2010.
95 Source: 'Big Trouble in Little Paradise: the Turks and Caicos Islands takeover', by Julian Assange, 19 June 2009, available at <http://mirror.wikileaks.info/wiki/Big_Trouble_in_Little_Paradise__the_Turks_and_Caicos_Islands_takeover/>, accessed 30 November 2010.
96 For further discussion see: Smartt (2010); also: Smartt (2008), pp. 200–3.
97 Source: 'Ivory Coast toxic dumping report behind secret Guardian gag', WikiLeaks, 13 October 2009, available at <http://mirror.wikileaks.info/wiki/Ivory_Coast_toxic_dumping_report_behind_secret_Guardian_gag/>, accessed 30 November 2010.
98 Source: Interview with Julian Assange from WikiLeaks on the BBC Radio 4's *The Media Show*, 16 June 2010. Assange is a former physics and pure maths student; as a former computer hacker he has made it his personal quest to reveal governmental corruption around the world.

countries, the website also uses technology that makes the original sources of the leaks untraceable. Within a year of its launch, the site claimed that its database had grown to 1.2 million documents and that by June 2010 some ten thousand secret documents and pieces of information were flooding in daily. The website allows anyone in the world to upload documents that are 'secret'. WikiLeaks' webservers are mostly located in Sweden and Belgium, countries that have generous legislation on freedom of expression and information. Furthermore, the website never reveals its sources of information, backed by these countries' supportive legislation. Assange describes this process as 'principled leaking', and all material is vetted by a team of experts for authenticity. WikiLeaks is essentially an outlaw operation, creating a viral or word-of-mouth buzz with arresting secret intelligence. It has forced itself to the forefront of journalism in the digital age. The website has become a conduit for publishing material under its premise that every person has a right to freedom of information.

With the existence of social networking sites such as Facebook, YouTube or Bebo this raises important issues as to whether privacy and personal data can be realistically protected in the twenty-first century. Websites such as WikiLeaks put the whole area of 'freedom of information' and the complex regime of the FOIA 2000 into question, with its complex applications and class exceptions, where the Information Commissioner has to balance state, individual, corporate and media interests when making an effective decision as to whether to disclose sensitive information or not. In the meantime, someone may well leak the relevant information in any case, either via a social networking site or via a 'whistleblower' site such as WikiLeaks. The MPs' expenses scandal demonstrates this. Most would agree that this was significant and important information which the public had to know. The *Daily Telegraph*'s revelations about the parliamentary expenses 'abuses' were of genuine public interest.

6.6 Summary of key points

- The **Freedom of Information Act 2000** (FOIA) applies to UK government departments – including those operating in Scotland – and public authorities in England, Wales and Northern Ireland. It also applies to the House of Commons, the House of Lords and to the Welsh and Northern Ireland assemblies;
- The FOIA grants wide-ranging right to see all kinds of information held by the government and public authorities;
- Authorities will only be able to withhold information if an exemption in the Act allows them to; even exempt information may have to be disclosed in the public interest;
- Complaints and requests are dealt with by the Information Commissioner (IC), who can order disclosure;
- The **Freedom of Information (Scotland) Act 2002** provides similar rights to information held by the Scottish Executive, Scottish public authorities and the Scottish Parliament, enforced by the Scottish Information Commissioner;
- The **Data Protection Act 1998** (DPA) entitles a person to see personal information held by public or private bodies. The DPA was amended by the FOIA to improve individual rights to see personal information held by public bodies, but the right to information held by private bodies has not been affected;
- The **Official Secrets Act 1989** and the **Security Services Act 1989** created criminal offences for unauthorized disclosures by civil servants and other state officials (see: *R v Shayler* (2003));
- The UK Information Commissioner (IC) enforces these rights across the whole of the UK including Scotland;
- The public authority decides in the first instance whether information is exempt or disclosure is in the public interest, but the individual can challenge its decisions.

📖 6.7 Further reading

Goldberg, D. (2009) 'Freedom of information in the 21st century: bringing clarity to transparency'. *Communications*, 2009, 14(2), 50–6.

Johnson, H. (2008a) 'Freedom of information – confidence and journalism exemptions from Disclosure'. *Communications Law*, 2008, 13(5), 174–6.

Klang, M. and Murray, A. (2004) *Human Rights in the Digital Age*. Oxford: Routledge-Cavendish.

Weber, R.H. (2010) *Shaping Internet Governance: Regulatory Challenges* (in collaboration with Mirina Grosz and Romana Weber). Zürich: Springer.

Chapter 7

Blasphemy, Obscenity and Censorship

Chapter Contents

7.1 Overview

The removal of a photograph of 10-year-old actress Brooke Shields – fully made-up and naked – from Tate Modern's *Pop Life: Art in a Material World* exhibition in September 2009 reopened the debate about how far art should be allowed to go. It raised questions not only about the validity of freedom of expression and perceived morals but most importantly about the social function of art. Richard Prince's image *Spiritual America* risked breaking obscenity law, so the display at Tate Modern was closed and its catalogue withdrawn from sale.[1]

The very same question had arisen in December 1999, relating to ancient blasphemy laws, when a provocative statue of the late Diana, Princess of Wales, as the Virgin Mary was unveiled as part of an exhibition at Tate Liverpool. Part of 'Heaven', a collection of work by artists from around the world, the 15-foot fibreglass figure by Luigi Baggi, showing the Princess of Wales dressed in the traditional robes of the Virgin Mary, was to be part of an exhibition aimed at demonstrating how religious practice and devotion have found outlets in popular culture. It was to explore how celebrity, particularly that of pop singers, royalty and fashion models, had been replacing traditional subjects of Christian worship.

Diana's 'Madonna' statue provoked a storm of controversy and Lord Alton, Professor of Citizenship at Liverpool John Moores University, described the sculpture as 'creepy' and 'deeply offensive'. But the Bishop of Liverpool, James Jones, called the exhibition a reflection of today's society.[2] There was no prosecution in this case and the exhibition went ahead because of the absence of the necessary vilification of Anglican religious icons to constitute blasphemy.

This chapter examines the legal approach to art and literature in the context of English obscenity laws. The intention is to highlight the cultural independence of art, drama and literature in relation to freedom of expression. The chapter also charts the recent abolition of blasphemy laws, though it will still highlight past and relatively recent contemporary issues affecting the relationship between art and law and case law relating to public morality offences.

The common law of 'blasphemy' was abolished by section 79 of the **Criminal Justice and Immigration Act 2008**[3] (see below 7.2.4). Salman Rushdie's controversial novel *The Satanic Verses* (1989) was censored in all Muslim states as well as in India, China and South Africa.[4] On 13 March 1989, a magistrate refused to grant Abdul Hussain Choudhury summonses he had applied for against the novelist and his publishers, alleging the commission of the crimes of blasphemous and seditious libel.[5] The magistrates' court's decision was based on the grounds that blasphemy only pertained to the Christian religion and not to Islam and that there had been no attack on Her Majesty The Queen or the state to constitute seditious libel. The Divisional Court refused an application for judicial review based on the same decision.

See Chapter 3.3.3 →

See Chapter 1.2.2 →

Legal challenges on behalf of an author, artist, playwright or photographer, either during their lives or sometimes by their heirs or publishers after their deaths, are sometimes successful, as evidenced by the fact that books such as D.H. Lawrence's *Lady Chatterley's Lover* or plays such as Michael Bogdanov's *The Romans in Britain* are eventually read or performed. This can be seen as a triumph for freedom of expression, or at least a reflection of the development of cultural and sexual morals and norms in society. While attacks on someone's reputation cannot generally be justified under the

---

1 Source: 'Tate Modern removes naked Brooke Shields picture after police visit', by Charlotte Higgins and Vikram Dodd, *The Guardian*, 30 September 2009.
2 Source: 'Storm over Diana "Madonna" statue', *BBC News Online*, 8 December 1999, available at <http://news.bbc.co.uk/1/hi/uk/555606.stm>, accessed 23 November 2010.
3 In s. 1 Criminal Libel Act 1819 ('orders for seizure of copies of blasphemous or seditious libel') the words 'any blasphemous libel, or' were omitted; in ss. 3 and 4 Law of Libel Amendment Act 1888 ('privileged matters') the words 'blasphemous or' were omitted.
4 See also: Rana (1990).
5 *R v Chief Metropolitan Stipendiary Magistrate, ex parte Choudhury* [1990] 3 WLR 986.

right to free speech – nor words which advocate violence or hatred – different laws have emerged over time in different countries which have struck the balance between what would amount to acceptable speech or artistic limitations on the one hand or a claim to freedom of speech in a democratic and liberal society on the other.

See Chapters
← 2.4.2
and 3

Blasphemy was illegal under common law, covering only irreverence and sacrilege against the Church of England, after a judgment in 1938. The last successful prosecution was in 1977, when Mary Whitehouse of the 'National Viewers' and Listeners' Association' brought her private prosecution against Denis Lemon, editor of *Gay News*, for publishing a poem about a centurion's love for Jesus Christ (see below 7.2.3).

After a brief historical overview of ecclesiastical laws and how they have limited the citizen's rights by finding objectionable or distasteful words or utterings which may have been important to the speaker, there follows a more detailed look at how obscenity legislation has developed (see below 7.2.1 and 7.5.1). There have been some 'entrepreneurs' who have tried to manipulate EU law on 'freedom of movement of goods', such as the 'movement' of pornographic commodities, including 'top shelf' publications which flooded the UK market after the country's entry into the 'common market' in 1973. While British customs authorities tried to stop 'continental filth' entering British shores, decisions by the European Court of Justice held otherwise. The overarching question is: can the state censor art or literature and deem it 'obscene' or should citizens be able to make up their own minds (see below 7.5.3)?

This chapter is essentially concerned with an assessment of blasphemy, obscenity laws and how common law and Parliament have tried to restrain artistic expression over the years. Though blasphemous libel was abolished by the **Criminal Justice and Immigration Act 2008** and seditious, defamatory and obscene libel by section 73 of the **Coroners and Justice Act 2009**, some sections of this chapter will show how writers, playwrights, film-makers and artists have historically fought for freedom of expression, thought and religion.

7.2 Historical overview: blasphemy

Atheist writer and best-selling author Philip Pullman has been repeatedly threatened amid claims that he ought to be 'punished' for blasphemous writings, such as *The Good Man Jesus and the Scoundrel Christ* or *His Dark Materials*,[6] the latter denying that Jesus was the son of God.[7] When the movie *The Golden Compass*, based on his work and starring Nicole Kidman and Daniel Craig, premiered in New York and London in 2007, there were angry demonstrations by Roman Catholics, who attacked Pullman as a 'militant atheist', supported by the wrath of the American Catholic Church, which said the film 'sent out a viciously sacrilegious message, promoting atheism for kids'.[8] The author received scores of letters condemning him to 'eternal hell' and 'damnation by fire'.[9] In his blog, Pullman said:

> . . . my version of the Jesus story doesn't attempt to solve . . . questions, but I hope readers will find it interesting . . . The device of a mysterious stranger starting to chronicle Jesus' acts, and Christ resolving to turn the truth into history, such as the feeding the 5,000 where Jesus waves his food in the air and suggests everyone shares whatever they have.[10]

---

6 Source: 'Philip Pullman threatened by religious zealots over new Jesus Christ book', by Andrew Hough, *Daily Telegraph*, 22 March 2010.
7 See: Pullman (2007).
8 Source: 'The Church vs. the cinema: Philip Pullman's blasphemous materials?', by Ciar Byrne, *The Independent*, 28 November 2007.
9 Source: Catholic Action UK, BlogSpot, available at <http://catholicactionuk.blogspot.com/2007/10/review-of-phillip-pulman.html>, accessed 23 November 2010.
10 Source: 'Jesus and Christ', from Philip Pullman's online blog 14 September 2009, available at <http://www.philip-pullman.com/pages/news/index.asp?NewsID=39>, accessed 23 November 2010.

In April 2010, Mr Pullman was afforded special security by organizers of the Oxford Literary Festival when he appeared at the Sheldonian Theatre. The *Catholic Herald* had condemned Pullman's work as 'fit for the bonfire', while Rupert Kaye, chief executive of the Association of Christian Teachers, had described Pullman's literature as containing 'heresy' and 'blasphemy'.[11]

Historically, blasphemy has invariably been used offensively, not defensively. As Spencer, assessing the Law Commission's review of blasphemy laws of 1981, stated:

> . . . far from being the law under which Christians have defended themselves from persecution, blasphemy is the law with which Christians have made unbelievers suffer in the same sort of way in which evangelising Christians in communist countries are sometimes made to suffer for their beliefs today'.[12]

Blasphemy in English law singularly protects Christianity.[13] There have been a number of attempts to remove or restrict ecclesiastical blasphemy laws and replace them with public order legislation, which were ultimately successful (see: *R v Shepperd & Whittle* (2010)[14]) (see below 7.2.4). While obscenity laws clearly fall within the remit of criminal law and, if infringed, will be subject to prosecution, this was not necessarily the case with blasphemy. The expression of unwelcome sentiments was only redressible if that expression was intended or likely to cause a breach of the peace or unlawful violence; that is, only on the same grounds as apply to any expression of opinion on any subject.

7.2.1 Ecclesiastical restraints and disciplines

The origins of the offence of blasphemy lie in ecclesiastical courts during medieval times. Jurisdiction over blasphemous libel and seditious, obscene and defamatory libel was exercised by the Star Chamber established by the **Statute of Westminster 1275** which '. . . regarded with the deepest suspicion the printed word in general, and anything which looked like criticism of the established institutions of the Church or State in particular'.[15] Blasphemy laws were used extensively to protect the official religion of the state during the Reformation in the sixteenth century — particularly during Tudor times — often resulting in the death penalty. Mary I ordered the burning of Protestant martyrs. Known as 'Bloody Mary', her nickname implies that she was hated throughout the land for the burning of Protestants, such as Archbishop Cranmer, in her quest to restore Catholicism to England (the counter-reformation). Equally, her sister Elizabeth I ordered the burning of Roman Catholic martyrs, although Elizabeth's treatment of Catholics was regarded as rather moderate in comparison with that of Protestants under Mary's reign. Public worship other than Anglicanism was punishable under Elizabeth's rule and penal laws affecting Catholics became increasingly severe.

Once the Star Chamber was abolished in 1641, the Court of King's Bench inherited its criminal jurisdiction, thereby completing the transfer of jurisdiction over the offences into the courts of the common law. The common law courts then took over the jurisdiction of blasphemy and seditious libel with great enthusiasm. Residual jurisdiction developed to control public morals and public decency — though not necessarily directly connected with any religious connotations.

See Chapter
3.3.2 ➔

---

11 Source: 'Association of Christian Teachers Responds to Archbishop of Canterbury's speech on 'Belief, unbelief and religious education', available at <http://www.christian-teachers.org.uk/newscomment/33>, accessed 23 November 2010.

12 See: Spencer (1981).

13 see: *R v Chief Metropolitan Stipendiary Magistrate, ex parte Choudhury* [1991] 1 QB 429.

14 [2010] EWCA Crim 65 (CA Crim Div); where the offenders had produced racially inflammatory material and posted it on a website hosted by a remote server in the USA. It was held that they could be charged and tried in the UK under ss. 19 and 29 Public Order Act 1986.

15 See: van Vechten (1903–04), p. 33.

Dramatist Sir Charles Sedley ('*Sedley's case*') was the first person to be tried at common law for indecency and blasphemy in 1675. He had shown himself naked on the balcony of a house in Covent Garden in the presence of several people and urinated on them. He was indicted at common law for 'outraging public decency'. After his guilty plea, the magistrates' court ruled:

> ... notwithstanding that there was not any Star Chamber, yet they would leave him to know that the Court of King's Bench was the *custos morum* of all the King's subjects and that it was then high time to punish such profane actions, committed against all modesty, when they were as frequent as if not only Christianity but morality also had been neglected.[16]

Sedley's case was cited in *R v Hamilton* (2007),[17] where the defendant appealed his conviction for outraging public decency. Hamilton had surreptitiously filmed up the skirts of women in a supermarket. The offence was only discovered after the films were found during a search of his home for other material. The defendant contended that the offence was not committed since nobody had witnessed the offence. His appeal failed since the proof of the offence of outraging public decency required two elements:

1. The act was of such a lewd character as to outrage public decency; this element constituted the nature of the act which had to be proved before the offence could be established;
2. It took place in a public place and must have been capable of being seen by two or more persons who were actually present, even if they had not actually seen it. This constituted the public element of the offence which had to be proved.

Though not seen, the acts of *Hamilton* were capable of being seen, and had they been seen would have caused the outrage to the possibility of which the offence was directed.

A published attack on a high state official was either prosecuted as seditious or defamatory libel. An attack on the church or its doctrine was generally prosecuted as either a blasphemous or a seditious libel, depending on the taste and offensive description of the lawyer drafting the indictment, as was established in *Taylor's case*.[18] In *Taylor's case* (1676),[19] the court discussed the meaning of blasphemous libel, which they held as an attack on Christian beliefs which would undermine and endanger society:

> ... for to say that religion is a cheat is to dissolve all those obligations whereby the civil societies are preserved and that Christianity is a parcel of the laws of England and therefore to reproach Christianity is to speak in subversion of the law.[20]

The preferred position of the doctrines of the Church of England also extended to causing disturbances at the places of worship of the established church. Section 2 of the **Ecclesiastical Courts Jurisdiction Act 1860** provided that:

> ... any person who shall be guilty of riotous, violent, or indecent behaviour in England or Ireland in any cathedral church, parish or district church or chapel of the Church of England ... whether during the celebration of divine service or at any other time, or in any churchyard or burial ground, or who shall molest, let, disturb, vex, or trouble, or by any other unlawful means

---

16 *Sedley's case* (1675) Strange 168; (1675) 1 Sid 168.
17 [2007] EWCA Crim 2062 (CA Crim Div).
18 See: Jackson (1937), p. 193.
19 (1676) 3 Keb 607.
20 Ibid.

disquiet or misuse any preacher duly authorised to preach therein, or any clergyman in holy orders ministering or celebrating any sacrament, or any divine service, rite, or office, in any cathedral, church, or chapel, or in any churchyard or burial ground, shall, on conviction thereof before two justices of the peace, be liable to a penalty of not more than a level 1 fine for every such offence, or may, if the justices before whom he shall be convicted think fit, instead of being subjected to any pecuniary penalty, be committed to prison for any time not exceeding two months.

This is a good example showing how common law blasphemy became akin to a public order type offence, relating to 'indecent behaviour' and the 'disorder' of established church premises. Many of the common law blasphemy provisions were later incorporated in public order offence legislation. Elliott (1993) canvassed that the common law should be abolished since it interferes with freedom of speech and religion.[21] This eventually happened in 2008 (see also below 7.2.4).

◉ FOR THOUGHT

Why did it take so long to abolish blasphemy laws in the UK? Chart the historical development and compare this with the law of other jurisdictions (see below 7.2.4)

7.2.2 The common law of blasphemy

For more than fifty years before the prosecution in the 'Gay News case',[22] the offence of blasphemy appeared to have become obsolete (see below 7.2.3). In his Hamlyn Lecture in 1949, Lord Denning MR portrayed 'blasphemy' as a 'dead letter', explaining that the law had not been successfully invoked since John W. Gott satirized the biblical story of the entry of Jesus into Jerusalem in a 1921 pamphlet entitled 'Rib Ticklers or Questions for Parsons'.[23] The leaflet was based on a literal interpretation of the prophecy that the King of Zion would come 'riding upon an ass, and upon a colt the foal of an ass'.[24] Gott received the draconian sentence of nine months' imprisonment with hard labour, which he served in 1922 after losing his appeal.[25]

Blasphemy and blasphemous libel were common law offences triable on indictment and punishable by fine or imprisonment. Blasphemy consisted in speaking and blasphemous libel in otherwise publishing blasphemous matter. Libel involved a publication in a permanent form.[26] The crime of blasphemy did not require an intent in the utterer to blaspheme (see: Whitehouse v Lemon (1979)[27]), or to cause a breach of the peace or fear of violence, or even objective likelihood of such happening as a result of the utterance. Nor did it need proof of shock or distress in the person addressed, since the crime could be committed even though that person shared or welcomed the views expressed.[28]

See Chapter 3.2.2 →

Lord Scarman declared in the 'Gay News case', the first prosecution for blasphemy in England since 1922, brought privately by Mrs Mary Whitehouse, that the modern law of blasphemy was correctly formulated in an article of *Stephen's Digest of the Criminal Law*, which stated that:

---

21 See: Elliott (1993).
22 R v Lemon; R v Gay News Ltd [1979] 1 All ER 898 (sub nom 'Gay News case').
23 R v Gott (John William) (1922) 16 Cr App R 87 (CCA).
24 Zechariah 9:9.
25 Cited by Denning (1949), p. 46ff.
26 For further discussion see: Burns Coleman and White (2006).
27 [1979] AC 617 (the decision was by a majority, with Lords Diplock and Edmund Davies dissenting).
28 See: Spencer (1981), p. 810.

. . . every publication is said to be blasphemous which contains any contemptuous, reviling, scurrilous or ludicrous matter relating to God, Jesus Christ, or the Bible, or the formularies of the Church of England as by law established. It is not blasphemous to speak or publish opinions hostile to the Christian religion, or to deny the existence of God, if the publication is couched in decent and temperate language. The test to be applied is as to the manner in which the doctrines are advocated and not as to the substance of the doctrines themselves. Everyone who publishes any blasphemous document is guilty of the [offence] of publishing a blasphemous libel. Everyone who speaks blasphemous words is guilty of the [offence] of blasphemy.[29]

The elements of the offence of blasphemous libel included:

(1)   It has to be established that the publication (production or broadcast) is intentionally published (performed or broadcast);

(2)   There has to be contemptuous, reviling, scurrilous and/or ludicrous material relating to God, Christ, the Bible or the formularies of the Church of England;

(3)   The publication (performance or broadcast) has to be such as tended to endanger society as a whole, by endangering the peace, depraving public morality, shaking the fabric of society or tending to cause civil strife.

What then made blasphemy a crime was that the material was generally threatening to the community or society. This criminal element would be established if what was done or said was such as to induce a reasonable reaction involving civil strife, damage to the fabric of society or their equivalent.

7.2.3 The *Gay News* case

The **Criminal Law Act 1967** repealed the **Blasphemy Act 1697**, and the **Sexual Offences Act 1967** began to decriminalize gay sex. But the '*Gay News* case' confirmed that the apparently obsolete offence of blasphemy was very much alive.

❖ KEY CASE	'The *Gay News* case' (*R v Lemon; R v Gay News Ltd* (1979))[30]

Facts:

In June 1976, Denis Lemon, editor of *Gay News*, decided to include a homoerotic poem by James Kirkup, 'The Love That Dares To Speak Its Name'. The poem, a necrophilic fantasy about the death of Jesus of Nazareth in Issue 96 of *Gay News*,[31] provoked some protest from gay Christians decrying it as 'blasphemous'. Mary Whitehouse,[32] founder and chairman of the National Viewers' and Listeners' Association (NVLA), expressed her outrage in a letter to *The Times*: 'Although broadcasting is exempt from the *Obscene Publications Act 1959*, we are advised that broadcast blasphemy is a common law offence and that, though dormant, the relevant law is still operative.'[33] Following Robert Ward

---

29 [1979] All ER 898 at 924 (Lord Scarman).
30 R v Lemon (Denis); R v Gay News Ltd [1979] QB 10; [1979] AC 617 (HL).
31 Source: Gay News, 3 June 1976, issue 96, p. 26.
32 Mary Whitehouse CBE (1910–2001), was a British campaigner for Christian beliefs, societal values and morality. She focused her efforts on the broadcast media, and later on publications and theatrical productions, where she increasingly became involved in litigation. She was the founder and first president of the National Viewers' and Listeners' Association (NVLA) which later became mediawatch-uk.
33 Source: 'Letters to the editor', The Times, 3 November 1976.

QC's advice, Mrs Whitehouse took out a private prosecution against Gay News Ltd. and its editor on 30 November 1976.[34] The indictment of 9 December read: 'for publishing and distributing a blasphemous libel concerning the Christian religion, namely an obscene poem and illustration vilifying Christ in his life and in his crucifixion.'[35]

The trial opened at The Old Bailey before Judge Alan King-Hamilton QC on Monday 4 July 1977, with John Mortimer QC and Geoffrey Robertson as counsel for the defence and John Smyth representing Mary Whitehouse. The trial judge disallowed expert literary and theological witnesses for the defence and refused to let Mr Lemon explain his intention in publishing the poem. This left two defence witnesses, novelist Margaret Drabble and journalist Bernard Levin, who testified to the good character of the paper and its editor. The only witness for the prosecution was Probation Officer Kenneth Kavanagh, activist against gay rights and head of the 'Parents Advisory Group' concerned with sex education.

On Monday 11 July the jury returned a guilty verdict by a majority of 10 to 2 on both defendants. Gay News Ltd was fined £1,000 and ordered to pay four-fifths of Mary Whitehouse's costs. Denis Lemon was ordered to pay £500 court costs and sentenced to 9 months' imprisonment, suspended for 18 months; he was also ordered to pay the remaining fifth of Mrs Whitehouse's costs (totalling £7,763). Gay News and Denis Lemon appealed against both conviction and sentence on points of law (including misdirection).

Decision (CA):
On 17 March 1977 the Court of Appeal quashed Denis Lemon's suspended prison sentence, but otherwise unanimously rejected all the grounds of appeal (Lord Justice Roskill, Lord Justice Eveleigh and Mr Justice Stocker). Mary Whitehouse's appeal costs were ordered to be paid out of public funds. Gay News Ltd and Denis Lemon accordingly lodged a petition for leave to appeal at the House of Lords.

Decision (HL):
In November 1978 five Law Lords heard the appeal, with Louis Blom-Cooper QC and Geoffrey Robertson QC representing the appellants and John Smyth again appearing for Mary Whitehouse. Their Lordships considered the narrow issue of *mens rea* in relation to blasphemy. The appellants contended that intention to do wrong was an essential ingredient of the crime of blasphemy. The respondent contended that it was not. Their Lordships could not agree on 'intention' (Lord Diplock said yes; Viscount Dilhorne said no; Lord Edmund-Davies said yes; Lord Russell of Killowen said no). The final decision was left to the newest appointee, Lord Scarman, who stated that his approach to the appeal was determined by his desire to see the blasphemy law extended. The appeal was lost.[36]

The House of Lords in 'Gay News' held that in order to secure a conviction for the offence of publishing a blasphemous libel, it was sufficient for the prosecution to prove — for the purpose of establishing mens rea — an intention to publish material which was in fact blasphemous; that is, it was not necessary to prove that the accused intended to blaspheme. Lord Edmund-Davies and Lord Scarman also held that it was not an essential ingredient of the crime of blasphemy that the publication must tend to lead to a breach of the peace. Their Lordships accepted that the offence of

---

34 Under s. 8 Law of Libel Amendment Act 1888.
35 The charge against the distributor Moore Harness Ltd was subsequently dropped.
36 See also: *Whitehouse v Lemon* [1979] AC 617 (HL).

blasphemy could not by its very nature lend itself to any precise legal definition; therefore, national authorities were urged to exercise a degree of flexibility in assessing whether the facts of a particular case fell within the accepted definition of the offence.[37] (See also: *Tolstoy-Miloslavsky v UK* (1996)[38]; also: *Bowman v Secular Society Ltd* (1917)[39]).

In a final attempt to obtain redress, Gay News Ltd and editor Denis Lemon lodged a complaint with the European Court of Human Rights on 7 August 1979, alleging breaches of Article 7 ('no punishment without law'), Article 9 ('freedom of thought, conscience and religion'), Article 10 ('freedom of expression') and Article 14 ('prohibition of discrimination') of the **European Convention**. Announcing their decision on 7 May 1982, the Commission agreed that there had been some interference with freedom of expression, but found that Mary Whitehouse's human rights had been infringed by the blasphemous content of the published poem. Consequently, the Commission declared the case inadmissible to be heard by the full plenum of the Strasbourg court. By April 1983, *Gay News* had ceased to exist, due to its financial problems linked to the lengthy court action defending the case against Mrs Whitehouse. She, in turn, regarded her '*Gay News*' prosecution as one of her greatest victories, upholding public morals and resurrecting the blasphemy laws.

Mrs Whitehouse was not always successful in her actions. She incurred enormous legal costs, for instance, after her private prosecution collapsed against the National Theatre's staging of *The Romans in Britain* in March 1982, and again in 1985 in her action against the Independent Broadcasting Authority (IBA) over the film *Scum*.

7.2.4 Abolition of blasphemy laws

Though there have been no successful prosecutions in recent years, blasphemous libel remained a criminal offence, punishable by either a heavy fine or imprisonment until 2008. There were a number of Law Commission recommendations to abolish the common law of blasphemy, for example in 1981 and 1985, and abolitionists in Parliament wholeheartedly supported the removal of these ancient laws, such as Lord Willis (1978), Tony Benn (1989), Bob Cryer (1990) and Frank Dobson (2001). The Liberal peer, Lord Avebury, argued that the archaic blasphemy laws were utterly contrary to the principle of free speech, when he said in 1995 and again in 2003 that:

> . . . in a free society we must be allowed to criticise religious doctrines and practices, even if that offends some people. While it may be offensive to some Christian believers to hear their beliefs mocked or denied that is equally true of people of other faiths, and of unbelievers, who repeatedly hear atheism equated with a lack of values or immorality. In an open and pluralist society there should be no inhibition to free speech without the very strongest justification, and robust debate should be expected and accepted in religious as in political and other spheres.[40]

In 2008, Lord Lester, Lord Avebury and Dr Evan Harris MP proposed an amendment to the Criminal Justice and Immigration Bill which would, *inter alia*, abolish the common law offences of blasphemy and blasphemous libel. These Parliamentarians held the strong belief that the common law offences of seditious libel and blasphemy were archaic in modern-day Britain and in a multicultural society; furthermore, that the continued existence of these old laws were regularly cited by other common

---

37 Ibid., at para 42.
38 [1996] EMLR 152 (A/323) at para 41.
39 [1917] AC 406 at 454 (Lord Sumner).
40 Source: with kind permission of Lord Avebury from his blog of Tuesday 11 March 2008: 'At 18.15, meeting with (Baroness) Kay Andrews to discuss my amendment to the Criminal Justice & Immigration Bill abolishing blasphemy and the remaining statutory religious offences, dealt with by the Law Commission in 1985 and covered by my Bills of 1995 and 2002, followed by the Select Committee on Religious Offences which reported in 2003. The Government had tabled their own amendment falling a bit short of mine, in that they retained a couple of obsolete Acts I wanted to repeal', available at <http://ericavebury.blogspot.com/search?q=blasphemy+criminal+justice+and+immigration+bill>, accessed 23 November 2010.

law countries as justification for the retention of such anachronistic laws, thereby restricting freedom of expression in, for example, Pakistan, India or Bangladesh.[41] Encouraged by such political pressure to abolish Britain's blasphemy laws, author Philip Pullman and Nicholas Hytner, director of the National Theatre, supported by 'English Pen' (the lobby group for freedom of expression), led 'obliteration' protests to remove the blasphemy laws which only afforded protection to the Church of England. The movement, supported by Salman Rushdie and Hanif Kureishi, lobbied Parliament to repeal these ancient laws which – they argued – had no place in a growing secular society and contravened human rights law.[42]

Success was achieved when the common law offences of 'blasphemy' and 'blasphemous libel' were abolished by section 79 of the **Criminal Justice and Immigration Act 2008**.[43] Moreover, section 73 of the **Coroners and Justice Act 2009** abolished the common law offences of 'sedition', 'seditious libel', 'defamatory libel' and 'obscene libel' in England, Wales and Northern Ireland, leaving 'obscenity' laws intact. The law has now been refocused on inciting religious hatred as a public order offence.[44]

> See Chapter
> 3.3.3 ➡

7.3 Sex in print: obscene publication laws

> See Chapter
> 3.1 on the
> abolition of
> obscene
> libel ➡

'Obscenity' is a rather modern notion, first referred to in 1795 in the *Herculaneum* exhibition.[45] Excavations of the ancient Roman town, buried by the eruption of Vesuvius in AD 79, found a large number of erotic frescoes and pornographic symbols indicative of Roman culture at the time. This resulted in an exhibition about Herculaneum which included a special room for 'obscene' antiquities, including a figure of Pan in a zoophilic relationship with a she-goat.

Scholars debate exactly when 'pornography' emerged in Europe as a recognizable discourse. Kendrick (1997) insists that its emergence is relatively late in the cultural scheme of things: the word 'pornography', he argues, dates only from the 1820s.[46] Darnton (1990), on the other hand, points to French works of the 1740s and emphasizes the crucial influence of materialist philosophy.[47] Traditional bibliographers, represented by Foxon (1965), go back even further and point to Aretino's postures and the Italian 'whore dialogues' of the mid-sixteenth century.[48] The private case collection of the British Library contains a large collection, including contributions from British publishers such as William Dugdale (see below).[49]

Before the **Obscene Publications Act 1857**, the only law against sexually explicit material in Britain was King George III's **Royal Proclamation For the Encouragement of Piety and Virtue, and for the Preventing and Punishing of Vice, Profaneness and Immorality** of 1787. This was the first regulation in England against sexually explicit material and included the suppression of all 'loose and licentious Prints, Books, and Publications, dispersing Poison to the minds of the Young and Unwary and to Punish the Publishers and Vendors thereof'.

---

41 Source: Report Stage amendments of the Coroners and Justice Bill, House of Lords, Official Report, 9 July 2009, cols. 850, Hansard, 14 October 2009.
42 Source: 'Arts lobby raises pressure for blasphemy law repeal', by Jack Malvern, *Sunday Times*, 13 February 2006.
43 In s. 1 Criminal Libel Act 1819 ('orders for seizure of copies of blasphemous or seditious libel') the words 'any blasphemous libel, or' were omitted; in ss. 3 and 4 Law of Libel Amendment Act 1888 ('privileged matters') the words 'blasphemous or' were omitted.
44 See: Part III ('racial hatred') Public Order Act 1986; specifically s. 19 'publishing or distributing written material' and s. 20 'public performance of play'.
45 Herculaneum ('Ercolano' in the Italian region of Campania) was an ancient Roman town destroyed by volcanic pyroclastic flows in 79 AD.
46 See: Kendrick (1997).
47 See: Darnton (1990).
48 See: Foxon (1965).
49 The British Library hosts a private case collection on 'Sex and Sexuality', 1640–1940 ('Literary, Medical and Sociological Perspectives') and 'Erotica', 1650–1900.

Statutory control of offensive or indecent material tended to be treated as a means of controlling a public nuisance under the **Vagrancy Acts of 1824 and 1838** and the **Indecent Advertisements Act 1889**. The 1889 Act – essentially a public order act – covered advertisements and public displays. For such a display to be deemed 'obscene' and 'offensive', it had to be visible to those passing by in the street that the display would cause some disruption to those passing by. Most of these statutory offences were repealed by the **Indecent Displays (Control) Act 1981**, which replaced them with an offence of publicly displaying indecent matter. The 1981 Act, intended to reduce the public display of sexually explicit 'top shelf' magazines, permitted shopkeepers to protect themselves from prosecution by limiting access to indecent material to adults and either charging for access or displaying a warning notice.[50] The 1981 Act was also repeatedly used to remove 'sexy' postcards advertising prostitution from telephone booths. Back in the nineteenth century there were many years during which obscenity laws were hardly applied. Sigmund Freud's *Interpretation of Dreams* (1900), for example, was enjoyed by the educated European middle classes as well as British royalty. Young Queen Victoria and her German husband, Prince Albert, gained a titillating insight into Freud's book, which told them of the sexual motivations that underpinned human behaviour, at the same time as they were amusing themselves with creating naughty sketches of family members and the Royal Household.[51] When a copy of Michelangelo's statue of David was presented to Her Majesty, the authorities provided a detachable plaster fig leaf so that Queen Victoria might not be depraved by the sight of a penis on her visits to South Kensington.

See Chapter ◄ 2.2.6

By the late 1840s, the British Museum had built up its 'secret' collection of pornographic art and publications, and by 1834, London's Holywell Street[52] ('Bookseller's Row') prided itself on some 57 'porn shops', openly displaying popular pornographic literature,[53] including catalogues of erotic etchings, such as *Yokel's Preceptor* published by William Dugdale, containing advice on where to find homosexual lovers in London.[54] It was at this time that the Lord Chief Justice, Lord Campbell, felt that pornography was getting out of hand and encouraging dangerous promiscuity in British society, which led to the proposal of his Obscene Publications Bill.

'Obscenity' had only been tested at common law in the 'Hicklin' – or 'innocent schoolgirl' – test (see: *R v Hicklin* (1868),[55]), establishing that the words 'obscene' and 'immoral' were exclusively applied to sex. The test was whether the publication had a tendency to deprave and corrupt 'upright' members of society, particularly 'innocent schoolgirls', should the publication fall into their hands; as Lord Chief Justice Cockburn articulated:

> . . . the test of obscenity is this: whether the tendency of the matter charged as obscenity is to deprave and corrupt those whose minds are open to such immoral influences and into whose hands a publication of this sort may fall.[56]

Arguably, the 'Hicklin' test did not constitute sufficient safeguards to reputable publishers and authors, as distinct from mere purveyors of pornography. On strict interpretation, it left the publisher to prove that his publications were suitable reading matter for an innocent schoolgirl.

---

50 Art galleries are specifically exempted from the Indecent Displays (Control) *Act* 1981 under section 1(4)(b). The repeal of the previous statutory offences, combined with the exemption of art galleries from the Act's coverage, means that the charge most likely to arise out of an allegedly offensive art show is that of outraging public decency.

51 See: *Albert v Strange* (1849) 64 ER 293.

52 The street ran parallel to the Strand from St Clement Danes to St Mary-le-Strand in Westminster, and was demolished in 1903. The site is now known as Aldwych.

53 William Dugdale's *Antiquities of Warwickshire* can be used as an authority and reference work on Victorian history and the history of Parliament at the time, where, for example, 'pornography' was cited as 'the writings of prostitutes', see: Broadway (2008).

54 William Dugdale (1800–68) was a publisher, printer and bookseller of politically subversive publications and pornographic literature.

55 (1868) LR 3 QB 360.

56 Ibid., at 452 (Cockburn LCJ).

As soon as the **Obscene Publications Act 1857** (also known as 'Lord Campbell's Act') had come into force in September that year, the first arrests were made, including the pornographic publisher William Dugdale (see above), who had published a number of 'pseudo-medical manuals', including *An Essay on Onanism* (1772) by M. Tissot, *La Masturbomanie* (1830), *The Secret Companion: A Medical Work on Onanism and Self-Pollution* (1845) and *On the Use of Night-Caps* (1845) by R.J. Brodie.[57] The procedure for dealing with obscene publications under the 1857 Act fell into several parts. On one hand the law operated in a rather unique way, in that it did not directly concern the author or the publisher, but merely the publication itself and the shopkeeper or retailer who stocked it. Justification of restraint of publications became particularly acute during Queen Victoria's reign around the time she lost her beloved husband in 1861. With ever stricter legislation applied to 'obscene' publications, it could be argued that the Queen wanted to impose her private grief on society by tightening up British morals and standards in public life. Her famous phrase 'we are not amused' was probably never more apt – though scholars like Palmer (1997) argue that the statement could have referred to her opinion on her nine pregnancies.[58]

Where works were seized under the **Obscene Publications Act 1857**, the onus was on the occupier or owner of the premises to give reasons why the works complained of should not be forfeited and destroyed. The author and publisher had no right to be heard and there was also no time limit between the date of the publication of the work complained of and subsequent legal action. This meant that works which had been circulated freely for years could suddenly become the subject of criminal proceedings. There was no uniformity of punishment by way of fines: a magistrate in Lancashire might impose a fine of £400, while his London counterpart on the bench might only fine a bookseller, publisher or printer £10; very often, the author would not be prosecuted at all. In addition there was the **Customs Act 1876**, under which obscene publications and other articles could be seized at the port of entry (see below 7.5.3).

By the mid–1950s, lawyers were becoming increasingly puzzled by the apparent anomalies of the 'Hicklin test', and the inconsistencies of prescribed law such as 'obscene libel' prescribed by the **Obscene Publications Act 1857**. During a parliamentary debate in the House of Commons in 1954, Lieutenant-Colonel H.M. Hyde (MP for Belfast North) speculated why foreign and objectionable material known as 'crime comics or horror comics' were allowed to enter the country unchecked, yet the law permitted a bench of magistrates to order the forfeiture and destruction of other foreign 'obscene' publications such as Bocaccio's *Decameron*, a work which had been regarded as a literary masterpiece throughout the civilized world for more than 500 years.[59] When the **Obscene Publications Act 1959** (OPA) came into force, it modified the law on obscene publications 'to provide for the protection of literature; and to strengthen the law concerning pornography'.[60] Section 1 (1) OPA 1959 provides the 'obscenity' test, in that:

> . . . an article shall be deemed to be obscene if its effect or (where the article comprises two or more distinct items) the effect of any one of its items is, if taken as a whole, such as to tend to deprave and corrupt persons who are likely, having regard to all relevant circumstances, to read, see or hear the matter contained or embodied in it.

The OPA 1959 provides for:

- prosecution; and
- forfeiture.[61]

---

57 For further discussion see: Colligan (2003); see also: Manchester (1988).
58 See: Palmer (1997).
59 Source: Debate on 'obscene publications'. Hansard, 22 November 1954, Vol 533 cc 1012–20.
60 The Obscene Publications Acts 1959: Archbold: 31–63, amended 1964: Archbold: 37–76.
61 See: Archbold: 31–63; expanded under the 1964 Act: Archbold: 37–76.

A prosecution could not be commenced more than two years after the commission of the offence. The 1959 act punishes publication per se and the 1964 act makes the publication 'for gain' a criminal offence.[62]

The **Obscene Publications Act 1964** was designed to:

- penalize purveyors of obscene material by making it an offence under section 2 either to publish an obscene article or to have an obscene article for publication for gain[63]; and
- prevent such articles from reaching the market by way of seizure and forfeiture proceedings under section 3.[64]

The issue of whether a publication, play, picture or film is 'obscene or not' must be tried by jury without the assistance of expert evidence.[65] Section 2 OPA 1959 defines the meaning of 'article', which implies any description of a piece of writing containing or embodying matter to be read or looked at or both. This was later extended and amended to include any sound recording, film or other record such as a video recording or DVD (see: R v Lamb (1998)[66]; also: R v Snowden (2010)[67]).[68] Most importantly, the **Obscene Publications Act 1959** created two defences under section 4:

(1)   The defence of 'innocent dissemination'; and
(2)   The 'defence of public good'.

Section 4 of the 1959 Act reads:

> . . . a person shall not be convicted of an offence against section two of this Act, and an order for forfeiture shall not be made under the foregoing section, if it is proved that publication of the article in question is justified as being for the public good on the ground that it is in the interests of science, literature, art or learning, or of other objects of general concern.

Subsection 2(1)(A) added:

> . . . a moving picture film or soundtrack . . . is justified as being for the public good on the ground that it is in the interests of drama, opera, ballet or any other art, or of literature or learning.

The 'defence of public good' means that a person who publishes any such 'obscene' article, recording or photograph ('the publication') will not be charged with a criminal offence if he can prove that the publication is justified for the public good, such as in the interests of science,

---

62 s.1 Obscene Publications Act 1964, 'Obscene articles intended for publication for gain'.
63 Definition of 'obscene see Archbold: 31–63; definition of 'publishes' see Archbold: 31–72.
64 Section 3(A) OPA 1964, where the article in question is a moving picture film of a width of not less than 16 millimetres, requires the DPP's consent; see: Archbold: 31–74.
65 See: Archbold: 31–68.
66 [1998] 1 Cr App R (S) 77 (CA Crim Div), where the appellant was found in possession of video tapes which he supplied by mail order under s. 2(1) Obscene Publications Act 1959. The recordings showed sadomasochistic scenes, some scenes involving animals. His sentence of five years' imprisonment (to be served consecutively) was upheld. The appeal centred on count 1 of the indictment where Lamb had argued that the content of the video was not obscene.
67 [2010] 1 Cr App R (S) 39 (CA Crim Div), where the appellant pleaded guilty to seven counts of publishing an obscene article and for copying DVDs and 2,840 pornographic DVDs, contrary to s. 2(1) Obscene Publications Act 1959. Fifty-five of the DVDs were categorized as 'obscene', involving activity with animals and other activities involving defecation, vomiting and urination. The DVDs and videos had been sent to 293 customers. His two-and-a-half-year prison sentence was upheld.
68 An amendment in 1977 added erotic films, with the Criminal Justice and Public Order Act 1994 amending the Obscene Publications Act 1857, which thereafter included computer images. It became illegal to transmit electronically stored data which was 'obscene on resolution into a viewable form'. This was mainly to protect children, and covered photographs, and pseudo-photographs linked to paedophilic activity.

literature, art or learning, or is an object of general public concern. In summary, the 1959 Act relates to publication of an obscene article and the 1964 Act strengthened the previous act by introducing the 'possession' element of an obscene publication for gain, covering 'any person having an obscene article for publication for gain', including wholesalers.

There are very difficult jurisdictional issues when material is hosted on the Internet, particularly overseas, as to whether this is within reach of the English criminal law. It will depend on a range of factors including who posted the material on the site, where it is hosted and what the person intends the material to do. If a website is hosted abroad and is downloaded in the UK, the case of R v Perrin (2002) applies.[69] This case was specifically concerned with 'publishing' electronic data under the **Obscene Publications Act 1959** and states that the mere transmission of data constitutes publication. It confirmed the decision in the earlier case of R v Waddon (2000)[70] that there is publication both when images are uploaded and when they are downloaded. The Court of Appeal held in Waddon that the content of US websites could come under British jurisdiction when downloaded in the UK. Section 1(3) **Obscene Publication Act 1959** was duly amended to include electronically stored data or the transmission of such data.

⊙ FOR THOUGHT

Do you not think that the combined effect of sections 1, 2 and 4 of the **Obscene Publications Act 1959** generate an absurd paradox? How can something be justified as being for the 'public good' if its tendency is also to 'deprave and corrupt'?

7.3.1 The saucy seaside postcard: the art of Donald McGill

In July 1954 a trial in Lincoln had a major impact on the popular and lucrative market of the 'saucy' seaside postcard. The artist Donald McGill (1875–1962) had fallen foul of Britain's obscenity laws. Hailed by author George Orwell as a unique British artist, famous for the modern cartoon and seaside comic strip, Orwell wrote in his essay, The Art of Donald McGill in 1941:

> Who does not know the 'comics' of the cheap stationers' windows, the penny or twopenny coloured post cards with their endless succession of fat women in tight bathing-dresses and their crude drawing and unbearable colours, chiefly hedge-sparrow's-egg tint and Post Office red? . . . In general, however, they are not witty, but humorous, and it must be said for McGill's postcards, in particular, that the drawing is often a good deal funnier than the joke beneath it. Obviously the outstanding characteristic of comic cards is their obscenity . . . But I give here a rough analysis of their habitual subject-matter, with such explanatory remarks as seem to be needed:
>
> SEX. More than half, perhaps three-quarters, of the jokes are sex jokes, ranging from the harmless to the all but unprintable. First favourite is probably the illegitimate baby. Typical captions: 'Could you exchange this lucky charm for a baby's feeding-bottle?' 'She didn't ask me to the christening, so I'm not going to the wedding.' Also newlyweds, old maids, nude statues and women in bathing-dresses. All of these are IPSO FACTO funny, mere mention of them being enough to raise a laugh. The cuckoldry joke is seldom exploited, and there are no references to homosexuality.[71]

---

69 (2002) 4 Archbold News 2 (unreported).
70 (2000) 6 April 2000 (unreported).
71 Orwell (1941).

Between 1904 and 1962, McGill produced an estimated 12,000 designs, of which an estimated 200 million were printed and sold. But in 1951 McGill's postcards came under the scrutiny of the newly elected Conservative government, who had decided to crack down on public indecency and what they saw as a decline in public morals after the Second World War. A select committee on censorship was set up to reinforce judgment on public decency and taste by applying the near obsolete **Obscene Publications Act 1857**. Local policing groups were set up, such as the 'Proclamation Society',[72] to judge public performances, literature and artworks. Such busybodies took it upon themselves to check the spread of 'open vice, immorality and obscene publications' which were allegedly contaminating the minds of the young. These 'friendship societies' would inform the police about local bookshops, which would then be raided and prosecuted together with publishers and printers while authors would habitually escape prosecution. During the 1950s, some 167,000 bookshops were censured for the sale of 'saucy seaside postcards', from Cleethorpes to Bournemouth, Blackpool to Brighton.

Donald McGill's trial commenced in Lincoln on 15 July 1954, where he was charged with contravening obscenity laws. McGill's defence essentially posed the question of whether seaside postcards were capable of corrupting the minds and morals of those into whose hands they came, applying the 'innocent schoolgirl' test. He was found guilty and fined £50 with an additional £25 in court costs. The financial burden on McGill and the devastating effect on his future after most of his postcards and drawings had been destroyed under the forfeiture orders of the **Obscene Publications Act 1857** meant that he, like many artists and retailers of 'saucy postcards', went bankrupt.[73] In 1957 McGill gave evidence before the House of Commons Select Committee which was once again considering amendments to the **Obscene Publications Act 1857**. McGill told the Committee that a national system of censorship was open to the vagaries of individual interpretation. The result was the **Obscene Publications Act 1959**, which ironically eased the ban on the saucy seaside postcard. Soon afterwards, McGill died, aged 87, in 1962, and his fan base – with collectors including the Beatles and film director Michael Winner – is still vast to this very day.

7.3.2 Filth or literature? *Lady Chatterley's Lover* and other obscene creative works

Almost every country places some restrictions on what may be published, although the emphasis and the degree of control differ from country to country and at different periods. Books are banned for a variety of reasons. Materials are often suppressed due to the perceived notion of obscenity. Obscenity can apply to materials that are about sexuality, race, drugs or social standing. Over the years, governments have sought to ban certain books by way of legislation which seeks to protect the public from abuse, embarrassment or perceived danger to public security.

There have been a large number of prosecutions under British obscenity laws involving works of literature; not all of them can be mentioned here. Gustave Flaubert's *Madame Bovary* and James Joyce's *Ulysses* were just two classic examples where legislative censorship tried to suppress the novels on 'obscenity' grounds (see also: *R v Calder & Boyars Ltd* (1969)[74]). Published in 1857, Flaubert's *Madame Bovary* was banned on sexual grounds in Italy in 1864 and in the United States in 1954 by the National Organization of Decent Literature. Flaubert was prosecuted and subsequently acquitted for 'offences against public morals' in 1857 under French obscenity laws. James Joyce's *Ulysses*, published in 1918, was banned on sexual grounds and in 1922 some 500 copies of the book were burnt in the USA.

---

72 Later 'The Society for the Suppression of Vice'.
73 Source: 'Naughty but nice. Jolly seaside smut – or should we be taking Donald McGill's postcards more seriously?', by John Russell Taylor, *The Times*, 11 March 2006.
74 [1969] 1 QB 151.

The most high-profile prosecution in the decade which followed the 1959 Act was undoubtedly the unexpurgated Penguin 'Classics' paperback edition of *Lady Chatterley's Lover* by D.H. Lawrence. *Lady Chatterley's Lover* was first published in 1928 in Italy and France. The short novel was immediately banned in Britain on account of the rather descriptive steamy bravura lovemaking scenes between Lady Constance (Connie) Chatterley of Wragby Hall and her gamekeeper Mellors. In 1960, 30 years after D.H. Lawrence's death, Penguin planned to publish *Lady Chatterley's Lover* in the UK. What followed was the most significant literary obscenity trial of the twentieth century, where the publishers were charged under s. 1(1) **Obscene Publications Act 1959** (OPA). The indictment was based on the premise that the novel put promiscuity on a pedestal, and that the majority of the book was merely 'padding' between graphic scenes of sexual intercourse and filthy language.

'Lady C's' trial took place against a changing modern Britain, on the cusp of the first Beatles LP, as the pill went on sale and the promotion of 'free love' and flower power were just a few years away. Penguin called upon a string of expert witnesses to defend the book's literary merit, including several members of the clergy, one of whom remarked that the work 'was a novel and not a tract, and novels deal with life as it is'. On 10 November 1960, the jury acquitted Penguin of all charges.[75] As soon as the verdict was pronounced, London's largest bookstore, W&G Foyle Ltd, reported a run on their bookshop with 300 copies sold in just 15 minutes and orders for 3,000 more copies. The next morning, Foyle's reported a queue of some 400 people – mostly men – wanting to buy 'Lady C', available in paperback for 3s 6d (16p).[76] *Lady Chatterley's Lover* made legal history, highlighting the fact that the rigid British establishment was becoming increasingly out of touch with public opinion on matters of obscenity. The case marked a famous turning point, with a victory for more liberal publishing houses, making prosecutions more difficult and increasingly rare.

The 'trial of Oz' in 1971 became the longest obscenity trial in English legal history, held at the Old Bailey under the auspices of Judge Michael Argyle QC. *Oz* was a short-lived, highly controversial underground magazine that sprang up during the post-*Lady Chatterley's Lover* trial period, deriving its name from the fact that most of the editors came from Australia. *Oz* was not only alternative but openly permissive, advocating sex and drugs as forms of liberation. It was satirically subversive in campaigns against the police, the judiciary and the establishment in general, using four-letter words in a provocative fashion.

In 1971 the editors of *Oz* magazine, Richard Neville, Felix Dennis and Jim Anderson, were found guilty at the Old Bailey of publishing obscene materials concerning Issue 28, the 'Schoolkids' issue. Issue 28 of May 1970, with its French erotic book design cover (*Desseins Erotiques*), contained 48 pages of articles on homosexuality, lesbianism and sadism. Of particular significance was the notoriously explicit cartoon by Robert Crumb, depicting Rupert Bear in a sexual situation ravaging a gypsy granny. What made it worse was that Issue 28 had been largely edited by invited younger readers between the ages of 15 and 18.

John Mortimer (later author of the famous 'Rumpole of the Bailey' series of novels) acted for the defence, but the jury found the defendants guilty of publishing an obscene magazine under the 1959 Act. The sentences were severe: Judge Argyle set out a prison term of 15 months for the editor, Richard Neville, and 12 months and 9 months respectively for his associates. Moral crusader Mary Whitehouse applauded the verdict and the sentence.[77] The Court of Appeal subsequently revoked the sentences with a judgment by Lord Widgery LCJ, where the court recognized 14 errors of law and a large number of errors of fact in the trial judge's summing-up to the jury. *Oz* ceased publication not long after the trial. Williams (1972) argued that the trial's significance was political rather than literary and linguistic.[78]

---

75 See: *R v Penguin Books Ltd* [1961] Crim LR 176.
76 Source: BBC News online 'On this day' 10 November 1960, available at <http://news.bbc.co.uk/onthisday/hi/dates/stories/november/10/newsid_2965000/2965194.stm>, accessed 24 November 2010.
77 See also: Palmer (1971), which contains court transcripts of the actual trial.
78 See: Williams (1972).

In 1976, *Inside Linda Lovelace* ('ILL')[79] became a bestseller; not so much for its literary merit but because of the Director of Public Prosecutions' action against the publishers in respect of obscenity. The jury decided that ILL's steamy descriptions of sexual orgies would not 'deprave and corrupt' the sort of people likely to buy the book and the publishers of ILL were duly acquitted.[80] Everyone thought this would be the last prosecution under UK obscenity laws in respect of written published material. In 1979 a House of Commons Select Committee, chaired by Bernard Williams, recommended that 'the written word' should be excluded altogether from the 1959 Act, as the prosecution of such cases was expensive and rarely successful; not least because of the absurd spectacle of professors of English in court, trying to find literary merit in works when they clearly contained very little. The report was ignored by the new Conservative Government.

The last novel banned under the 1959 Act was *Lord Horror* by David Britton (1989). The controversial author had founded a series of small press magazines in the 1970s specializing in horror fiction, with titles like *Weird Fantasy* and *Crucified Toad*. In 1976, Britton co-founded a small publishing house, Savoy Books, with Michael Butterworth. *Lord Horror* (and its sequels) depicted fascism in carnivalesque fashion in comic-book format, offering a historical fantasy based on the life of the pre-war fascist and wartime traitor William Joyce, better known as 'Lord Haw Haw', who broadcast Nazi propaganda from Germany. Britton himself described *Lord Horror* as 'so unique and radical, I expected to go to prison for it. I always thought that if you wrote a truly dangerous book, something dangerous would happen to you. Which is one reason there are so few really dangerous books around.'[81] Manchester magistrate Derrick Fairclough ordered the forfeiture and destruction of all copies of *Lord Horror* under s. 3(2) of the 1959 Act. The order was overturned by the Court of Appeal in 1992.

7.3.3 The *Lolita* dispute

Vladimir Nabokov's *Lolita* first appeared in Paris in 1955,[82] and has been seen by literary academics in American Studies, such as Giles (2000), as symbiotically intertwined with other American literary classic texts during the Truman and Eisenhower years. Giles reports on the cultural reception of *Lolita* in Britain, which focused on delicate and troublesome questions such as the love of a middle-aged European, Humbert Humbert, for an American nymphet, 12-year-old Dolores Haze. Giles states that the book is more than just a lusty publication of lascivious reputation and provides literary pleasures focusing on the relationship between formal aesthetics, public morality and social power; a comic satire of sex and eroticism in post-war America.[83]

Lolita was the second publishing hit for the Frenchman Maurice Girodias, innovative founder of the Olympia Press in Paris. He had found a gap in the market by publishing erotic and pornographic literature written in foreign languages, such as D.H. Lawrence's *Lady Chatterley's Lover* (see above 7.3.2). Olympia was a radical publishing house with the advanced marketing concept of putting into circulation works of literature that 'establishment' publishers would not dare to print or even accept. It published controversial works largely in English, which attracted little attention from the French censors, such as William S. Burroughs' *Naked Lunch*, Samuel Beckett's *Molloy* and *Watt*, works by the Marquis de Sade and John Cleland's *Fanny Hill*. Apart from Olympia's greatest hit *Lolita*, Girodias found similar publishing success with *Candy*, a 1958 reworking of Voltaire's *Candide* and the *Story of O* by Pauline Réage (the pseudonym of Dominique Aury), one of the earliest works of

---

79 Linda Susan Boreman (1949–2002), better known by her stage name, Linda Lovelace, was an American pornographic actress who was famous for her performance of deep throat fellatio in the enormously successful 1972 hardcore porn film *Deep Throat*.
80 Source: 'Ex-porn star Lovelace dies after car crash', by Leo Standora, *New York Daily News*, 23 April 2002.
81 Source: David Britton in an interview with the Savoy publishing house, available at <http://www.savoy.abel.co.uk/HTML/dave. html>, accessed 24 November 2010.
82 Nabokov (1955); the book was made into a film by Stanley Kubrick in 1962, starring James Mason and Sue Lyon.
83 For further discussion see: Giles (2000).

sadomasochistic erotic fiction to be written by a woman. As the educated British middle classes travelled across to France, the first editions of Olympia Press with their distinctive green covers found their way to UK and American destinations. Olympia Press and Penguin Classics were the forerunners of avant-garde publishing houses whose 'gentleman-pornographer' editors pushed the boundaries of freedom of expression to the limit long before human rights legislation became fashionable.

As soon as Graham Greene got hold of a copy of *Lolita* in the United States, he called the novel the best he had ever read in an interview in *The Times* in 1955. The American edition, published by G.P. Putnam's Sons, sold some 100,000 copies in three weeks. Green's comment in *The Times* provoked an angry response from the editor of the *Sunday Express*, who called *Lolita* 'the filthiest book I have ever read . . . sheer unrestrained pornography'. This just increased the demand for the book. By 1959, Nabokov was experiencing extensive British antipathy to the book. Customs officials had been instructed to seize all copies entering the United Kingdom. George (later Lord) Weidenfeld, Nabokov's publisher, tried to solve the problem of how to publish *Lolita* in the UK at the time the government was debating the Obscene Publications Bill.

Weidenfeld turned to the most famous libel lawyer of his generation, the late Peter Carter-Ruck, whose *Memoirs of a Libel Lawyer* reveal that while he regarded *Lolita* as a 'beautifully written, poignant and tragic' work, he was well aware of its legal risks: 'Obscenity was well to the fore in the minds of the authorities at that time.'[84] Carter-Ruck advised the British publishers and *Lolita*'s author that the book was a fair business risk for publication, subject to the amendment of four sentences.[85] But Nabokov categorically rejected this advice, stating that *Lolita* was a work of art which must not be mutilated. In the event, Carter-Ruck devised a scheme of remarkable cunning in order to circumvent the obscenity laws. He advised Lord Weidenfeld to inform the government by letter of the intention to publish and distribute the book in the UK, but not to post the letter until just before the dissolution of Parliament on 18 September 1959 before the General Election. This had the desired effect that neither the outgoing Conservative Home Secretary Rab Butler[86] nor Prime Minister Harold Macmillan[87] could take any action over *Lolita*. When Parliament reassembled on 27 October 1959, the publication of the book was well in place with its distribution beginning on 6 November. Even though the Conservatives had been returned to power, neither the publishers nor the author ever stood trial for obscenity. However, D.H. Lawrence's *Lady Chatterley's Lover* was prosecuted the following year and so was Hubert Selby's *Last Exit to Brooklyn* in 1968. Both books were eventually cleared for publication, with the Court of Appeal in *Last Exit to Brooklyn* establishing that writers could explore depravity and corruption without necessarily encouraging it.

◉ FOR THOUGHT

Books are controversial because of language, politics, sexuality, or religion. Some books seem to be challenged or banned because of multiple objections from different types of censors. Books are still being banned under UK obscenity laws every day. Try and find out which of the great classics were initially banned and on what grounds; and why we are able to read some of these great classics today.

---

84 Source: Carter-Ruck (1990), pp. 98ff.
85 See also: Doley et al. (2009).
86 Richard Austen Butler (1902–82).
87 Maurice Harold Macmillan, 1st Earl of Stockton (1894–1986) and grandson of a Scottish crofter, Daniel Macmillan, who founded Macmillan Publishing. Harold Macmillan was Prime Minister from 10 January 1957 to 18 October 1963.

7.3.4 Caricatures and satires

The provocative power of caricatures was illustrated by the Muhammad cartoons controversy, which originated from the publication of 12 editorial cartoons by the Danish newspaper *Jyllands-Posten* in September 2005. Newspapers and magazines around the world reprinted the cartoons, leading to a global wave of protests and riots by Muslims who claimed that the caricatures were just another expression of Western colonialism. Questions about the use of archaic blasphemy laws emerged in Danish and German law.[88]

See Chapter 1.6

Today, caricatures and satires are generally dealt with by the tort law of defamation.[89] In *Charleston v News Group Newspapers Ltd.* (1995),[90] the House of Lords considered the digitally enhanced photo montage that showed the faces of two famous Australian actors, Anne Charleston ('Madge') and Ian Smith ('Harold'), of the popular TV series *Neighbours*, superimposed on the nearly naked bodies of others in pornographic poses and agreed with Mr Justice Blofeld's order to strike out the libel action against the publishers of the *News of the World*. Their Lordships, applying the 'bane and antidote' defence, declined to find defamation in *Charleston* because if the readers who did not take 'the trouble to discover what the article was all about, carried away the impression that two well-known actors in legitimate television were also involved in making pornographic films, they could hardly be described as ordinary, reasonable, fair-minded readers'.[91]

See Chapter 3.3.5

English law has taken on a balancing approach between freedom of speech and common law development, whereby each case has to be judged on its own merit and possible impact on modern British society. As Lord Steyn said in the *Bruce Grobelaar* case:

> . . . to curtail the right of a satirist to deploy ridicule to the extent and in the manner in which he chooses would be a far-reaching incursion on freedom of speech. There is no warrant in our legal history, modern principles of public law, convention principles, or policy for such an approach.[92]

As the law of defamation has clarified, hard-hitting satire cannot be defended as honest comment when it is malicious. Satire can be regarded as being libellous if the insults cannot be anyone's honest opinion and if it merely heaps insults on someone. Generally, the satirist or caricaturist ought to employ this genre to criticize a matter of general relevance, which will then afford him the freedom of expression defence in human rights law. This does not defend him if extreme blasphemy or obscenity has been used or where someone's reputation, honour and human dignity has been infringed.

See Chapter 3.4.1

7.4 Censorship of stage productions

Until the **Theatres Act of 1968**, the Lord Chamberlain's Office had control of theatres, including censorship of the production content as well as logistical matters such as the granting of theatre and performance licences. Thereafter, local authorities were granted this power. As the chief official of the Royal Household, the Lord Chamberlain traditionally embodied the express wishes of the monarch. In Elizabethan times, when companies of actors needed patronage to obtain a licence for their productions, the Lord Chamberlain became one such benefactor; apart from licensing, he had

---

88 The Criminal Code of Denmark (§ 140 *Straffeloven*) and of other European States (e.g. Germany with § 166 *Strafgesetzbuch* (StGB)) have blasphemy provisions, but they are applied rarely nowadays. See also: *Otto-Preminger-Institute v Austria* (1995) 19 EHRR 34.
89 See: Rogers and Parkes (2010), para 3.4
90 [1995] 2 AC 65 (HL).
91 Ibid., at 76 (Lord Bridge of Harwich).
92 See: *Grobbelaar v News Group Newspapers Ltd* [2002] UKHL 40 at 38 (Lord Steyn).

direct power of censorship over the stage and public entertainments via the Master of the Revels, a court officer in his service who was granted the right to censor plays. When the Queen's Theatre (now Her Majesty's Theatre) in London's Haymarket burnt down on 17 June 1789, dance master and mortgage holder Giovanni Gallini obtained a licence from the Lord Chamberlain to perform opera at the nearby Little Theatre.

One obstacle facing playwright John Osborne (1929–94) was the office of the Lord Chamberlain – situated in Stable Yard at St James's Palace – which might or might not license his work *A Patriot For Me* (1965) for public performance. Osborne's earlier plays had got through, such as *The Devil Inside* (1950), *Personal Enemy* (1955) and *Look Back in Anger* (1957); but not *A Patriot for Me*, whose treatment of homosexuality culminated in a glittering drag ball which was judged to lie beyond the pale. The Lord Chamberlain's office denied Osborne's production at London's Royal Court Theatre an exhibition licence, demanding multiple cuts which would have resulted in the excision of half the play. Osborne and the Royal Court's director refused, and – denied a licence – the theatre was turned into a private members' club in order to produce the play. *A Patriot for Me* won the *London Evening Standard* 'Best Play of the Year' award when it debuted in 1965, though it made a loss of £16,500.

The **Theatres Act 1968** repealed the **Theatres Act of 1843**, which meant that censorship of theatre productions and plays by the Lord Chamberlain's office was finally abolished. Furthermore, the sovereign could no longer exercise his or her powers by virtue of Royal Prerogative in respect of either granting a theatre licence or halting performances. With the **1968 Theatres Act**, local authorities became the official licensing authorities of plays, exhibitions and demonstrations.[93]

Section 2 of the **Theatres Act 1968** ('Provisions with respect to performances of plays') states that:

(1) For the purposes of this section a performance of a play shall be deemed to be obscene if, taken as a whole, its effect was such as to tend to deprave and corrupt persons who were likely, having regard to all relevant circumstances, to attend it.

(2) Subject to sections 3 and 7 of this Act, if an obscene performance of a play is given, whether in public or private, any person who (whether for gain or not) presented or directed that performance shall be liable –

   (a) on summary conviction, to a fine not exceeding £400 or to imprisonment for a term not exceeding six months;
   (b) on conviction on indictment, to a fine or to imprisonment for a term not exceeding three years, or both.

Section 3 of the 1968 Act provides the 'defence of public good', which means a person, such as a playwright, producer or artist, charged under s. 2 of the Act shall not be convicted of an offence if he can prove that the performance in question could be justified as being 'for the public good' on the ground that it was in the interests of drama, opera, ballet or any other art, or of literature or learning.

7.4.1 Mrs Whitehouse and *The Romans in Britain*

For more than 30 years, Wolverhampton schoolteacher Mary Whitehouse led the charge of the middle-class moralists to purge the 'poison being poured into millions of homes through television

93 Including performances of hypnotism within the meaning of the Hypnotism Act 1952.

. . . if violence is shown as normal on the television screen it will help to create a violent society'.[94] The BBC became her prime target when she constantly complained of the increasing 'blasphemy, bad language, violence and indecency' she saw on television. She became the founder and first General Secretary of the National Viewers' and Listeners' Association in 1965. Mrs Whitehouse became increasingly offended by the emerging late-night satire and by the escalating freedom of material enjoyed by BBC producers under Director General Sir Hugh Greene. Mrs Whitehouse considered the racist humour of 'Til Death Us Do Part, for instance, to be 'entirely subversive to our whole way of life'. She was also happy to fight for the benefits of censorship in the courthouse.

In 1974 she launched an unsuccessful lawsuit against a cinema manager for showing the violent thriller Blow-Out. But she emerged the victor from court in 1977, after suing Gay News for blasphemous libel (see above 7.2.3). Her influence on the setting-up of the Broadcasting Standards Council in 1988 was acknowledged by its first chairman, Lord Rees-Mogg, who credited her with helping ensure that 'the public view was always taken into account'.[95]

In 1980, Howard Brenton's play, The Romans in Britain, was staged at the National Theatre (NT); Sir Peter Hall was the NT's Director at the time. The play depicted a male rape and nudity scene and ran at the Olivier Theatre during the autumn and winter of 1980. The production was never seen by Mrs Whitehouse and met with mixed reviews. On 18 March 1982, Mrs Whitehouse appeared on the verge of winning a private prosecution against the play's director, Michael Bogdanov, for allowing the homosexual rape scene, which centred on a young Celt and Druid priest who was subjected to attempted buggery by a Roman soldier. Charges of gross indecency under s. 12 of the **Sexual Offences Act 1956** ('unnatural offences' and 'buggery') which had been brought against Mr Bogdanov were suddenly withdrawn, after a senior Treasury counsel, representing Attorney General Sir Michael Havers, appeared in court to end the case immediately after the prosecution withdrew its evidence.[96] Mr Bogdanov, who faced up to two years in prison if convicted under the 1956 Act, claimed that the case had been withdrawn because Mrs Whitehouse knew a jury would not rule in her favour. 'Romans in Britain' was a landmark case and alleviated fears in arts circles that a victory for Mrs Whitehouse could have led to a return to severe censorship of theatre productions and subsequent prosecution of performers and directors.

7.4.2 Censorship: *Jerry Springer: The Opera*

One of the last attempts to use censorship and prosecute using blasphemy laws was in 2007 by way of a private prosecution in Green, Regina (on the Application of) v The City of Westminster Magistrates' Court (2007),[97] concerning the theatrical work, Jerry Springer: The Opera. This was a parody of the TV chat show, hosted by Jerry Springer, presenting, as entertainment, dysfunctional people who had lurid – and largely sexual – stories to tell. The second act revolved around the host imagining his descent into hell with characters appearing as Satan, Christ, God, Mary and Adam and Eve, who were treated as chat show guests. Their behaviour and language exhibited considerable excesses.

The stage version of the musical had been performed at London's National Theatre and across the UK between April 2003 and July 2006 and a recorded performance of the play was broadcast by the BBC on 8 January 2005. The show and television broadcast were regarded by many as

---

94 From Mary Whitehouse's famous speech at Birmingham Town Hall on 5 May 1964 in front of 2,000 people, where she demanded that television clean up its act. Her speech triggered a new social movement, the 'Clean-Up TV Campaign'.

95 Source: 'Mary Whitehouse: Moral crusader or spoilsport?' BBC News online, 23 November 2001, available at <http://news.bbc.co.uk/1/hi/uk/763998.stm>, accessed 24 November 2010.

96 Source: Correspondence between the Director of Media Watch UK, John C Beyer and Mark Thompson, Director General of the BBC, 21 February 2005, re. 'Romans in Britain', MediaWatch UK, available at <http://www.mediawatchuk.org.uk/index.php?option=com_content&task=view&id=179&Itemid=124>, accessed 24 November 2010.

97 [2007] EWHC 2785 (Admin).

sacrilegious and the BBC received 63,000 complaints (55,000 before the broadcast).[98] In addition, the broadcasting regulator, Ofcom, received over 16,000 complaints.[99] One of the aggrieved was Stephen Green, the National Director of an evangelical group, 'Christian Voice'. Mr Green brought a private prosecution against the BBC for its broadcast of Jerry Springer, alleging blasphemous libel. In a third-party intervention, human rights group Liberty, on behalf of Stephen Green, challenged the producer of the stage musical Jerry Springer, Jonathan Thoday, along with Mark Thompson, Director-General of the BBC, for broadcasting the show in January 2005.[100]

Summonses against both defendants were sought at Westminster magistrates' court. But the district judge refused to issue the summonses and held that the prosecution was prevented by the **Theatres Act 1968** (the Act had been passed to abolish censorship of the theatre). Section 2(4)(a) of the **1968 Theatres Act** meant that the ancient offence of blasphemous libel was to be distinguished from criminal defamatory libel, which was preserved by the **Theatres Act**. In any case, the district judge held that the target of criminal defamation had to be a living person and Christ could not be regarded as a living human being for these purposes. The gist of defamatory libel was that it exposed the victim to hatred, ridicule or contempt among other people or damaged him in his trade. What's more, given the long delay and the circumstances in which this archaic offence had been invoked, the district judge held that this application by Mr Green bordered on the vexatious – though this was not a reason for her decision. It was a fact that Jerry Springer: The Opera had been performed in public for two years without any violence or even demonstrations which would have formed an essential element of the blasphemy offence.

See Chapter
3.4.1 →

After his unsuccessful attempt in the magistrates' court, Mr Green applied to the Administrative Court for judicial review, seeking a mandatory order requiring the issue of the two summonses refused by the district judge. The applicant relied on the common law of blasphemy principles, alleging that the gist of the blasphemous crime element of Jerry Springer was material relating to the Christian religion and that the material was so scurrilous and offensive that it would undermine society generally, by endangering the peace, depraving public morality, shaking the fabric of society and – particularly in this case – could be a potential cause of civil strife (see above 7.2.2). Mr Green further claimed that no matter what the merits and artistic qualities of this work were, the musical play contained material which was contemptuous and reviling of the Christian religion and thereby constituted the offence of criminal blasphemous libel.

The High Court held that the **Theatres Act 1968** did not apply to the broadcasts by the BBC, because the broadcast was not a live performance given to the viewer by persons present and performing. The **Broadcasting Act 1990** brings television and radio programmes within the purview of the **Obscene Publications Act**, but provides a slightly different 'public good' defence.[101] Agreeing with the district judge, the court held that it was plainly relevant to examine the context in which the words in Jerry Springer were spoken. If a blasphemer were shown to be roundly condemned, then that would lessen and eliminate any offence and any danger to the public. This meant that the play as a whole was not and could not reasonably be regarded as aimed at, or an attack on, Christianity or what Christians held sacred. In any case, there had not been any occasion of 'civil strife' or unrest over the musical's performances for nearly two years. Accordingly, the application for judicial review was refused (see also: R v Gibson (1990)[102]; DPP v Schildkamp

---

98 Source: BBC Press Release, Governors' Programme Complaints Committee finding on complaints against Jerry Springer: The Opera, 30 March 2005, available at <http://www.bbc.co.uk/pressoffice/pressreleases/stories/2005/03_march/30/springer.shtml>, accessed 24 November 2010.
99 Source: 'Watchdog clears BBC on Springer', by Adam Sherwin, The Times, 10 May 2005.
100 Source: 'Sense prevailed over Springer 'blasphemy'', by Mark Thompson, BBC Director General, Daily Telegraph, 6 December 2007.
101 Para 6 of s. 15 Broadcasting Act 1990 contains provisions applicable to broadcasts which are identical to the terms in s. 2(4) Theatres Act 1968 (which applies to plays and musicals).
102 [1990] 3 WLR 595, where the two co-defendants were an artist (Gibson) and the operator of an art gallery (Sylveire). Displayed in Sylveire's London gallery was a work entitled Human Earrings; it consisted of a model's head sporting a pair of earrings, each of which was made out of a freeze-dried human foetus of three or four months' gestation, with a ring fitting tapped into its skull and attached at the other end to the model's earlobe.

(1971)[103]; *Knuller (Publishing, Printing and Promotions) Ltd v DPP* (1973)[104]; *Shaw v DPP* (1962)[105]). The High Court, citing the *'Gay News'* case (R v *Lemon*), not only rejected the charge that *Jerry Springer: The Opera* itself was blasphemous but set out a series of legal arguments (see above) which made it hard to see how any future prosecution for blasphemous libel could succeed, at least against a theatrical producer or a broadcaster. This was a landmark decision.

7.5 Art or obscenity?

A display due to go on show to the public at Tate Modern on 1 October 2009 had to be withdrawn after a warning from Scotland Yard that the heavily made-up naked image of 10-year-old actress Brooke Shields could break British obscenity laws. The work, by American artist Richard Prince and entitled *Spiritual America*,[106] was due to go on show as part of the 'Pop Life' exhibition, but the picture had to be removed from public display after the Metropolitan Police threatened to prosecute Tate Modern's director a day before the exhibition was due to open. The police had raised concerns about the exhibition of possibly indecent and obscene child images and the surrounding legislation.

The two main offence provisions in this area are section 1 of the **Protection of Children Act 1978** and s.160 of the **Criminal Justice Act 1988.** The **Protection of Children Act 1978** addresses certain aspects of the sexual exploitation of children by penalizing the making, distribution, showing and advertisement of indecent photographs of them.[107] 'Advertising' or displaying indecent photographs of children is covered by section 1(1)(d) **Protection of Children Act 1978**.[108] The test to be applied in respect of indecent images of children is whether or not they are indecent; rather unhelpfully, however, the word 'indecent' has not been defined by the 1978 Act. Case law has said that it is for the jury to decide based on the recognized standards of propriety.

Richard Prince's work *Spiritual America* had already been shown at a similar exhibition at the Guggenheim in New York in 2007, without attracting major controversy. The 'Pop Life' exhibition at Tate Modern also included works from Jeff Koons' series 'Made in Heaven' including large-scale photographic images of Koons and the porn model (and Koons' then wife) La Cicciolina having sexual intercourse. There were also works by Cosey Fanni Tutti, who, as part of her artistic practice, worked as a porn and glamour model in the 1970s and then displayed some of the resulting images at the exhibition. None of these works were either criticized or withdrawn. Arguments for the Brooke Shields piece's removal centred on the promotion of sexualization of children. It might have been coincidental, but the removal of the *Spiritual America* image coincided with the conviction of nursery worker Vanessa George, who was found guilty in December 2009 of child abuse and sharing child and baby images on Facebook with the convicted sex offender Colin Blanchard and with Angela Allen – both of whom she had never met. George was trusted for three years by parents and staff at Little Ted's nursery in Plymouth, Devon and had been employed as a classroom assistant in a primary school since 1998, having passed all Criminal Records Bureau (CRB) checks.[109]

---

103   [1971] AC 1.
104   [1973] AC 435.
105   [1962] AC 220.
106   *Spiritual America* depicts Brooke Shields in a photograph of a photograph, originally authorized by Shields' mother for a $450 fee, taken by commercial photographer, Gary Gross, for the Playboy publication *Sugar 'n' Spice* in 1976. Prince used the image as the source material for his own 1983 piece, which he displayed in a shopfront in a rundown street in Lower East Side, New York, borrowing the title from a 1923 photograph by Alfred Stieglitz of a gelded horse. Shields later attempted, unsuccessfully, to suppress the picture.
107   The definition of a child was altered from a person under 16 to 18 years of age by section 45(1) of the Sexual Offences Act 2003 (in force from 1 May 2004); see: Archbold: 31–107a and 31–116.
108   s. 1 Protection of Children Act 1978 covers a wide range of offences concerning indecent photographs and images of children, including the making of 'pseudo-photographs'.
109   Source: 'Vanessa George jailed for child sex abuse', by Stephen Morris, *The Guardian*, 15 December 2009.

Was it scaremongering by Metropolitan Police officers in the light of the armchair paedophilic activity of Vanessa George? On one hand, one could defend Prince's provocative image of young Brooke as a comment on the merciless pursuit of celebrity and the commercialization of minors. On the other, one might find a sexually provocative image of the young girl obscene. Some art critics regarded the image as a profound artistic critique of the sexualization of a child star and the dominant 'sex sells' mentality of the American media market. Was the image of Brooke Shields as a seductress art or obscenity? Prince argued that by using the title *Spiritual America* it would conjure up a sense of unease in a country like the USA that prides itself on its democratic principles and Christian values; yet its consumer market revolves around the over-sexualization of individuals, even if they are teenage girls.

Viewed alongside the indisputably serious and appalling nature of recent internet paedophilic crimes in the UK, one could see the plausible argument why the London CPS had suggested the prosecution of the gallery if the picture of Brooke Shields was not removed. But what about Marcus Harvey's 11ft by 9ft portrait of Moors Murderer, Myra Hindley?[110] The image formed the centre-piece of the Summer Exhibition at the Royal Academy in 1997. The selection of this controversial painting caused an outrage, resulting in the resignation of four distinguished and 'disgusted' Royal Academicians, who objected at the low-resolution image being selected for the prestigious summer exhibition, because the image of 'Myra' was made out of children's stencilled handprints. But the picture was not removed under obscene publication laws. The picture was splattered with ink and eggs on the opening night and had to be protected behind glass.

In August 2008, London 2012 Olympic organizers were embroiled in an embarrassing gaffe after Harvey's image of Myra Hindley was used to promote the Games by event organizers 'Visit London'. The controversial picture was used as part of a three-minute promotion video, shown on a loop at London House, attended by the Prime Minister Gordon Brown, Mayor of London Boris Johnson, Olympics minister Tessa Jowell and Sebastian Coe, chairman of London 2012. The face of the notorious serial killer also flashed up in the background at the official celebration of the Olympic handover in Beijing.[111] Marcus Harvey was no doubt thrilled that his picture of the serial killer was not withdrawn from the Royal Academy and was (even if inadvertently) used to promote Britain's cultural heritage. Some critics said that Harvey had created a very powerful image. Others argued that he had sensationalized the serial killing of children. The Royal Academy obviously thought it worthy to be recognized as artistic brilliance, since they had no intention of having the picture removed. In legal terms this could be seen to create double standards compared with the removal of the Brooke Shields image at Tate Modern. Which brings us to the 'margin of appreciation' (see below 7.5.2).

The **Coroners and Justice Act 2009** (which came into force on 1 February 2010) created a new offence of 'possession of a prohibited image of a child'.[112] The definition of 'pornographic' (in relation to child images) is set out in subsection 62(3):

> . . . an image is 'pornographic' if it is of such a nature that it must reasonably be assumed to have been produced solely or principally for the purpose of sexual arousal.

It is for the jury to determine whether this threshold has been met. Arguably, art and literature should be timeless in their ability to stimulate comment and reflect social morale. The media may be obsessed with paedophilia but it does not necessarily mean that art is.[113]

---

110 The 'Moors murders' were carried out by Ian Brady and Myra Hindley between July 1963 and October 1965 in the Greater Manchester area. The victims were five children aged between 10 and 17: Pauline Reade, John Kilbride, Keith Bennett, Lesley Ann Downey and Edward Evans, at least four of whom were sexually assaulted. The murders are so named because two of the victims were discovered in graves dug on Saddleworth Moor.

111 Source: Myra Hindley painting taints London 2012 celebrations', by Ashling O'Connor, *The Times*, 25 August 2008.

112 Chapter 2 of the Coroners and Justice Act 2009, sections 62–9 (England, Wales and Northern Ireland); ss. 62 (2) to (8) set out the definition of a 'prohibited image of a child' in that 'an image must be pornographic and must be grossly offensive, disgusting or otherwise of an obscene character'.

113 For further discussion see: Kearns (2000).

FOR THOUGHT

What makes a piece of art like Richard Prince's image of young naked Brooke Shields 'obscene' compared with the image of Moors Murderer Myra Hindley by Royal Academician Marcus Harvey?

7.5.1 What is the test for indecency? The 'Mapplethorpe' controversy

Freedom of expression carries with it an obligation to protect minors, covered by the **Obscene Publications Act 1959**, embracing plays, books, photographs, magazines as well as, inter alia, films, displaying or describing sexual activities and controversial contemporary art. The late Robert Mapplethorpe (1946–89) is one of the most controversial photographers of all time. The American artist was known for his large-scale, highly stylized black and white portraits of frank homosexual eroticism and much of his work depicts nude males with erections and sadomasochistic sex. When the Mapplethorpe retrospective 'Robert Mapplethorpe: The Perfect Moment' first appeared in Philadelphia shortly after his death from AIDS in 1989, under the curatorship of Janet Kardon, the images were widely criticized by the art world for their obscenity.

'The Perfect Moment' triggered large-scale controversy about the public funding of artworks when it was about to be exhibited at the Corcoran Gallery of Art in Washington, DC in July 1989. Seven of the 175 photographs were censored and deemed obscene, resulting in the arrest of Dennis Barrie, the Cincinnati Contemporary Arts Centre director, on 7 April 1990, because he had been publicly displaying these images for some twelve years in museums and galleries. The Protestant Reverend Donald E. Wildmon had seen a museum catalogue, featuring Piss Christ, a photograph of the Crucifixion immersed in a yellow liquid, which had subsequently resulted in Barrie's arrest. The charges were only withdrawn after the exhibition was cancelled.

In 1997–8, the University of Central England was involved in an obscenity controversy when an art book was confiscated from the university's library. The book in question was Mapplethorpe, published by Jonathan Cape in 1992. A postgraduate art student had borrowed the book from the university library for her thesis on 'obscenity and art'. She had taken a photo of two Mapplethorpe images in the book, one of them featuring two males in 'S & M' outfits, with one male urinating into the mouth of the other. She had taken the film to Boots the Chemist to be developed, and the shop had informed West Midlands Police because of the seemingly offensive and unusual nature of the images. On 21 October 1997, police officers from West Midlands paedophile and pornography unit seized the book – the only copy in the library. The university's Vice Chancellor, Dr Peter Knight, was then interviewed under caution with a view to prosecution, alleging that the book's contents and material were likely to 'deprave' and 'corrupt' under the **Obscene Publications Act 1959**. The university was informed that the book would only be returned if two images illustrating homosexual and sadomasochistic sex acts were removed. In March 1998, the University Senate voted to support the Vice Chancellor's position of refusing to comply. Nearly a year after the Mapplethorpe book had been seized by police officers, the Crown Prosecution Service announced on 30 September 1998 that they would not prosecute the university's Vice Chancellor. The CPS concluded that the book would not tend to 'deprave or corrupt a significant number of those who are likely to read it'. Robert Mapplethorpe's controversial book was returned, in a slightly tattered state, and restored to the university library.[114]

114 Sources: PornWars, Panorama, BBC1, 2 November 1998; BBC World Service, Witness, 10 December 2009; BBC Radio 4, In living memory: The Mapplethorpe Affair, 9 December 2009, broadcast at 11am.

Fritscher (2002) argues, that in the HIV-AIDS driven times of the late 1980s and early 1990s, gay art was censored and silenced particularly harshly during the Reagan years (1980–8) and also during the Republican presidency of George Bush (1988–92) in the USA, thus advocating 'family values'. By 1990, Senator Jesse Helms had proposed a 'National Endowment for the Arts' (NEA) Appropriations Bill which affected future NEA grantmaking procedures. The NEA Act subsequently prohibited funding for projects that were deemed 'obscene'. Senator Helms objected most specifically to aestheticizing Mapplethorpe's 1970s' images of ancient uncloseted homoeroticism which revealed a culture of homomasculinity rather than a straight American pop culture.[115] Had the Mapplethorpe photos, depicting leather-clad male-on-male sadomasochism, been shot by a woman or a heterosexual male, the photographs may well never have been censored. Mapplethorpe's homosexuality was therefore a keystone of his work's vulnerability.

7.5.2 The 'margin of appreciation': blasphemy and freedom of expression in human rights law

Legislation in England and Wales prohibits obscene publications, performances, and photographs by way of the **Obscene Publications Acts 1959** and **1964**. The Convention rights to freedom of expression set out in Article 10 ECHR may be used to claim that the obscenity legislation is incompatible with the Convention. Any restriction of freedom of expression that is imposed by national law must be capable of objective justification as being necessary in a democratic society for one of the purposes set out.

The so-called 'margin of appreciation' enables EU member states to have a degree of latitude to decide law and social policy in the light of their own cultures and values. It was established in *R v Handyside v UK* (1976)[116] that:

> . . . sharing the view of the Government and the unanimous opinion of the Commission, the court finds that the Obscenity Acts 1959 and 1964 have an aim that is legitimate under Article 10(2) ECHR, namely, the protection of morals in a democratic society.[117]

The majority of the Commission agreed that the ECtHR had only to ensure that the UK courts acted reasonably, in good faith and within the limits of the margin of appreciation left to contracting states by Article 10(2), stating that:

> . . . there was no uniform conception of morals. State authorities were better placed than the international judge to assess the necessity for a restriction designed to protect morals.[118]

In the expression 'necessary in a democratic society', the word 'necessary' is not synonymous with 'indispensable', but implies the existence of a pressing social need.

Though some might think that the application of blasphemy and obscenity laws might be archaic, they can nevertheless be justified and considered necessary in democratic societies of EU member states where Christianity is the main religion, though it ought to be stressed that their application is increasingly rare in Europe. In spite of human rights legislation, such as freedom of expression (Article 10 ECHR) and religion (Article 9 ECHR), some member states will have a wider margin of appreciation in making restrictions against items concerning matters of religion, morals

---

115 See: Fritscher (2002).
116 (1976) 1 EHRR 737 (ECHR).
117 Ibid., judgment at para 46.
118 Ibid., at para. 2.

or personal beliefs than others. National authorities, rather than the courts, may well decide in the appropriate forum what protection is necessary.[119]

Various 'obscene publications' laws in the UK and other countries also prohibit film and video releases. Most laws are quite vague in this area and generally only apply to anything which might encourage criminal activity by those watching the films, especially if it encourages violence or sexual violence.

Otto Ludwig Preminger (1905–86), an Austro-Hungarian film director, directed over 35 Hollywood films and was most famous for his 'film noir'. His most famous film was possibly *Fallen Angel* (1945), featuring Alice Faye, Dana Andrews, Linda Darnell and Charles Bickford. Several of his films pushed the boundaries of censorship by dealing with taboo topics (in the USA) such as drug addiction (*The Man with the Golden Arm*, 1955), rape (*Anatomy of a Murder*, 1959) and homosexuality (*Advice and Consent*, 1962). The case of *Otto-Preminger-Institut v Austria* (1994)[120] concerned the seizure and forfeiture of a film, due to be screened at a private film club before an informed adult audience.[121] The film, *Council of Love* (*das Liebeskonzil*), was based on a nineteenth-century play in which the Eucharist is ridiculed and God the Father is presented as a senile, impotent idiot, the Virgin Mary as a wanton woman who displays erotic interest in the devil and Jesus Christ as a low-grade mental defective given to fondling his mother's breasts.

The Austrian Constitutional Court in Vienna held the film to be blasphemous because it contained provocative and offensive portrayals of the objects of veneration of the Roman Catholic religion and therefore the withdrawal of the film was not held to be in violation of Article 10 ECHR. This was confirmed by the Strasbourg Court, which ruled that the Austrian authorities had not overstepped their 'margin of appreciation'.[122] For this reason the film was never allowed to be publically shown in predominantly Roman Catholic Austria (the role of the British Board of Film Classification (BBFC) will be explained further in Chapter 10.6.2).

Examining the ECtHR judgment in *Jersild v Denmark* (1994) (see below),[123] the Strasbourg Court made no reference to the doctrine of the 'margin of appreciation' and found that the repressive measures taken under the criminal law against the applicant journalist violated his right to freedom of expression.

See Chapter ◀ 2.3.1

❖ KEY CASE   *Jersild v Denmark* (1994) ECHR

Facts:

On 31 May 1985 the Danish *Sunday News* Magazine (*Søndagsavisen*) published an article describing the racist attitudes of members of a group of young people, calling themselves 'The Greenjackets' (*grønjakkerne*), at Østerbro in Copenhagen. In the light of this article, the editors of the *Sunday News* Magazine decided to produce a documentary on the Greenjackets. The applicant, Mr Jens Olaf Jersild, a Danish journalist, contacted representatives of the group, inviting three of them, together with Mr Per Axholt, a social worker, to take part in a TV interview. During the interview, the three Greenjackets made abusive and derogatory remarks about immigrants and ethnic groups in Denmark. The edited film – lasting only a few minutes – was broadcast by Danmarks Radio on 21 July 1985 as part of the Sunday news magazine programme. The documentary feature included

---

119 For a more detailed discussion see: Brems (1996).
120 [1994] ECHR 26 (Case No 13470/87) 20 September 1994 (ECHR).
121 Judgment by the European Court of Human Rights of 20 September 1994 with the result of the immediate withdrawal by the Austrian Constitutional Court, of the film, *The Council of Love*, which infringed Art 10 ECHR (Urteil vom 20. September 1994, A/295-A EGMR Einziehung des Films Das 'Liebeskonzil', verstößt nicht gegen Art. 10 EMRK).
122 [1994] ECHR 26 judgment at para 56.
123 (1994) 19 EHRR 1.

avowed racist views. In their statements the youths described black people as belonging to an inferior subhuman race ('. . . the niggers . . . are not human beings. . . . Just take a picture of a gorilla . . . and then look at a nigger, it's the same body structure. . . . A nigger is not a human being, it's an animal, that goes for all the other foreign workers as well, Turks, Yugoslavs and whatever they are called').

Following the programme, no complaints were made to the Radio Council or to Danmarks Radio, but the Bishop of Ålborg complained to the Minister of Justice. Subsequently, the three youths were convicted for making racist statements and Mr Jersild for aiding and abetting them in making racist comments in a public place.[124] Mr Jersild, but not the three Greenjackets, appealed against the City Court's judgment to the High Court of Eastern Denmark (Østre Landsret), but his appeal was rejected and his conviction was upheld by the Danish Supreme Court.

Decision:
The ECtHR jointly dissented with the opinion and judgment of the Danish Supreme Court. Judges Gölcüklü, Russo and Valticos stated, 'We cannot share the opinion of the majority of the Court in the Jersild case.' The ECtHR held that Mr Jersild's right to freedom of expression had been infringed and that he was not a racist. He had a valid defence in the making the programme.

It is interesting that the Strasbourg court in *Jersild* did not show any concern or sensibility towards vulnerable groups in the face of racial abuse compared with its judgment in the *Otto Preminger* case, where the Catholic population of the tiny Tyrol region was very much taken into consideration over the offending film. Were the religious sensibilities so fundamentally different in character in the satirical film by Otto Preminger to the 'nigger' quote in the Danish documentary by Jersild? Why did the ECtHR not apply the 'margin of appreciation' in the *Jersild* case? [125]

In March 1996, The British Board of Film Classification (BBFC) refused a video classification certificate[126] to British film-maker Nigel Wingrove for his 18-minute video *Visions of Ecstasy* on the grounds that it infringed the criminal law of blasphemy (subsequently upheld by the UK Video Appeals Committee). The BBFC declared that it must have regard to the Home Secretary's 'Letter of Designation', by which the Board were entitled to refuse to classify works which were obscene or 'which infringe other provisions of the criminal law.' 'Other provisions' included blasphemy and the Board drew upon the '*Gay News*' judgment.[127] For this reason, the video work became subject to the law of blasphemy for the *manner* of its presentation which would – according to the BBFC – give rise to outrage at the unacceptable treatment of a sacred subject. In his defence, Mr Wingrove cited a particular scene in the film, where the sixteenth-century Carmelite nun, St Teresa of Avila, experienced powerful ecstatic visions by fantasizing about lying on top of a dead Jesus Christ, still nailed to the cross, and bringing him back to life with her caresses. Wingrove said that this scene allegorized St Teresa's sexualized relationship with Christ through 'celestial orgasm'; an argument clearly not appreciated by the BBFC.

See Chapter 10.7.2 →

Visions became the third blasphemy trial in the twentieth century: the first case involved Mr J.W. Gott,[128] sentenced to nine months' imprisonment with hard labour for his 'Rib Ticklers'

---

124 Under Article 266 (b) of the Danish Penal Code.
125 For a detailed discussion see: Mahoney (1997).
126 Under the Video Recordings Act 1984.
127 [1979] 1 All ER op cit at 927–928.
128 *R v Gott (John William)* (1922) 16 Cr App R 87 (CCA).

publication in 1921 (see above 7.2.2), and the second prosecution was in 1977, when Denis Lemon, editor and publisher of *Gay News*, was prosecuted and convicted for printing James Kirkup's poem (see above 7.2.3). In November 1996 the Strasbourg Court rejected Nigel Wingrove's application by seven votes to two, that his right to freedom of expression could be justified under Art 10(2) ECHR, that Mr Wingrove's right had not been curtailed as a consequence of the banning of *Visions* (see: *Wingrove v UK* (1997[129])), moreover, that Mr Wingrove ought to have foreseen that the film would be considered blasphemous under the criminal law and that domestic law provided adequate protection against arbitrary interference with individual rights. The ECHR held in *Wingrove* that the aim of domestic blasphemy laws was a legitimate one, being in accordance with Article 9 ECHR, which provided for freedom of religion, thought and conscience, even though it only protected the religious feelings of Christians and not those of other faiths.

The Strasbourg rulings in *Wingrove* and *Jersild* do not offer a clear and consistent approach to the protection of free speech, as Lord Lester noted when he described the *Wingrove* judgment as a 'timorous ruling' and the ECHR as 'vacillating in its commitment to free speech'.[130] The concept of the 'margin of appreciation' has become rather slippery and elusive, and as human rights law has evolved and the UK blasphemy laws have been repealed, the Strasbourg court appears to have used the 'margin of appreciation' as a substitute for coherent legal analysis in relation to freedom of expression, particularly where art, literature and film are concerned.[131]

7.5.3 'Europorn' and free movement of 'top-shelf' goods

The relevance of this topic relates to the importing and subsequent distribution of publications of alleged indecent and obscene content. Scholars of European Union (Community) law are well aware of the rules relating to the abolition of 'measures having equivalent effect to quantitative restrictions' (MEQR), which have been central to the development of the single European (common) market for decades. Articles 28 and 29 EC (ex 30–34 EC[132]) were designed to eliminate barriers such as the abolition of customs duties, pecuniary restrictions, MEQRs and trade discriminatory practices, which might be capable of hindering the flow of goods from member state to member state. This was challenged in two UK cases which involved obscene publications and indecent articles: *Henn & Darby*[133] and *Conegate*.[134] The principal provision for derogation from Articles 28 and 29 (ex 30–34) EC is Article 30 (ex 36) EC, which provides that a member state can impose restrictions or prohibitions on imports and exports on grounds of public morality, public policy and public security.

'Entrepreneurs' Maurice Donald Henn and John Frederick Ernest Darby began to try to take advantage of EU law soon after the UK had joined the 'common market' in the mid–1970s in order to import top-shelf magazines and other pornographic goods from 'the continent'.[135] In the first criminal action challenging EU law and the UK's derogation from the 'free movement' principle, defendants Henn and Darby argued they were entitled to bring in such 'merchandise' from the European mainland for their personal use and that of their 'friends', and that domestic laws were not only outdated but also contravened the spirit of the Treaty of Rome.[136]

---

129 (1997) 24 EHRR 1 (case No. 17419/90) 25 November 1996 (ECHR).
130 Source: 'British Censors Versus Freedom of Speech', *Evening Standard*, 27 November 1996.
131 See also: Council of Europe (1996); also: Lester (1993).
132 The Treaty of Amsterdam (1997) amended the Treaty on the European Union (TEU or 'Maastricht Treaty', 1992), the Treaties establishing the European Communities and certain related acts. It came into force on 1 May 1999. The Treaty of Amsterdam (1997) renumbered or abolished the original Treaty of Rome (1957) (EC) articles. The Amsterdam Treaty introduced a uniform system of citation of the provisions of the original four Treaties (ECSC, Euratom, EC, EU) to assist the judgments of the European Court of Justice and the opinions of the Advocates General. Judgments and opinions delivered before 1 May 1999 are still cited with the old EC treaty articles.
133 *R v Henn; R v Derby* (Case 34/79) [1979] ECR 3795 (ECJ).
134 *Conegate v Customs and Excise Commissioners* [1985] (C-121/85) ECR 1007 (ECJ – 4th Chamber).
135 For further discussion see: Bernard (1996).
136 The Customs Consolidation Act 1876 prohibited importation of indecent and obscene materials and the Customs and Excise Act 1952 established the criminal offence for evading the prohibition.

❖ **KEY CASE**   *R v Henn; R v Darby* (1980)

Facts:

Maurice Henn and John Darby were operating a pornographic films and 'top shelf' magazine mail order business in the UK with imports from Denmark, Germany and Sweden. On
14 October 1975, a truckload arrived at the port of Felixstowe from Rotterdam containing
a large consignment of a 'sexually explicit nature'. HM Customs and Excise officers had
monitored previous operations. Both Henn and Darby were subsequently indicted for
importing 'indecent and obscene' goods contrary to s. 42 **Customs Consolidation Act
1876**, s. 304 **Customs and Excise Act 1952** and the **Obscene Publications Act 1959**. Their
trial started at Ipswich Crown Court on 17 May 1977. The court heard about the detailed
and explicit sexual activities of the films and referred to the magazines as containing
photographs of naked under-age girls engaged in adult sexual activities. One magazine
advertised for models for acts of buggery. Both men pleaded 'not guilty', arguing that
the 1952 Act contravened EU law under Article 28 EC (now 30 EC). The UK invoked
Article 36 (now 30) EC to justify the seizure of pornographic goods because they would
'deprave and corrupt' UK citizens on the grounds that they were 'indecent and obscene'.

Henn was sentenced to 18 months' and Darby to two years' imprisonment. Both appeals
were rejected by the Court of Appeal Criminal Division on 9 November 1978. The House of
Lords referred the case to the European Court of Justice (ECJ) on 29 January 1979 for
preliminary ruling, to seek clarification on the conflict of UK customs laws with the 'free
movement' principle in respect of obscene publications and pornographic goods.

Decision:

Advocate General Lord Warner opined that the UK had contravened Article 28 EC. He
stated that a member state should apply the same criteria to 'home-produced' goods –
including pornographic publications – as to foreign imports. The UK appeared to tolerate
'home-produced' 'top shelf' literature and prohibited foreign imports from EU member
states, which amounted to a 'quantitative restriction' on imports. Unless there was a valuable reason to derogate from the free movement principle, the UK was duty bound to
change its laws in line with EU law.

But the ECJ added that if it felt that the goods were deemed 'indecent and obscene' under
domestic legislation, the UK could derogate from the 'free movement' principle. However,
the UK should then apply this principle to its own nationally published goods of the same
(pornographic) nature. For this reason, Henn and Darby's appeals were dismissed and
their convictions upheld.

Henn and Darby lost their appeal but similar questions concerning free movement of (pornographic) goods were asked a few years later of the House of Lords in *Conegate*, when a number of
life-size inflatable dolls were seized and confiscated on import at Heathrow Airport from Germany
in October 1982. The two *Conegate* consignments were described on the import documentation as
'window display models', though it was hard to imagine that the 'Love Love dolls,' 'Miss World
Specials' and 'Rubber Ladies' could really be used for this purpose. The consignment was accompanied by some 'sexy vacuum flasks'. Customs inspection officers took the view that these goods were
indecent and obscene within the meaning of s. 42 of the **Customs Consolidation Act 1876**.
Uxbridge magistrates duly ordered the forfeiture of the goods, upheld on appeal by Southwark

Crown Court. Importers Conegate argued that any law prohibiting the importation of such products was an infringement of Article 28 EC (now 30), while the UK invoked Article 36 (now 30) EC justifying the seizure and forfeiture of the articles within the scope of 'public morality'.[137]

The ECJ held that, in principle, it was for member states to determine what laws should be enacted to protect public morality within their jurisdiction, and since the UK was unable to satisfy this requirement, because similar products were already lawfully sold within its territory, the UK's restriction on importation could *not* be justified under Article 36 (now 30) EC. The Advocate General noted that the **Obscene Publications Act 1959** was not at issue in this case and formed the view that a prohibition of imports could not be justified in Community law on the ground of public morality *unless* a broadly comparable standard was accepted for imports and domestic production (see also: *Adoui and Cornuaille v Belgian State and City of Liège* (1982)[138]). This meant that a member state would have to show that the national measure really did have the effect of protecting public morality.

The conflicting ECJ decisions in *Henn & Darby* and *Conegate* have been the subject of severe criticism in that they do not assist standards of control in European member states, nor do they clarify the varied and different measures in parts of the UK, such as the Isle of Man or Scotland, which have applied different prohibitions on imports of obscene goods under the ancient 1876 Act. In England and Wales, for instance, there are controls on displays and prohibited goods such as 'blow-up dolls' though – following the *Conegate* ruling – they could have easily been sold in Boots the Chemist.[139]

The *Conegate* case is an important decision because the ECJ took a different approach in respect of public morality from that taken in *Henn & Darby*. In *Conegate* the UK courts had simply taken a more lenient approach vis-à-vis domestic goods. The ECJ held that the domestic courts' decision to ban imported German pornographic goods was unacceptable because the UK court was clearly giving different treatment to domestically produced products, which was irrational. This meant an arbitrary discrimination within the meaning of the second sentence of Article 36 EC.

In summary, a member state may not rely on grounds of public morality within the meaning of Article 30 (ex 36) EC in order to prohibit the importation of certain goods on the ground that they are indecent or obscene when its domestic legislation contains no prohibition on the manufacture and marketing of the same goods on its territory.

7.6 Indecency or freedom of expression? Analysis and discussion

There appears to be a general theme in English public morality law that everything in art or literature that sufficiently adversely affects certain moral scruples and the sensibilities of the ordinary decent citizen would traditionally be prosecuted under the two most prominent offences concerning blasphemy and obscenity. Immediately on the coming into force of the **Obscene Publications Act 1959**, the publishers of D.H. Lawrence's *Lady Chatterley's Lover* were prosecuted – though at trial found not guilty – for the 'unacceptable' erotic portrayals. Nearly twenty years later, Denis Lemon, editor

---

137 The High Court posed its questions in the light of the conclusion in Case 34/79 R v *Henn & Darby* (Case 34/79 [1979] ECR 3795 (ECJ) that a prohibition on imports justifiable on the ground of public morality and imposed for that purpose could not, in the absence of lawful trade in the same goods within the member state concerned, constitute a means of arbitrary discrimination or a disguised restriction on trade between member states within the meaning of the second sentence of Article 36 EEC.

138 [1982] ECR 1665 (ECJ).

139 Under the Indecent Displays (Control) Act 1981. Under the Local Government (Miscellaneous Provisions) Act 1982, if a local authority decided to adopt Schedule 3 to the Act, then premises could not be used as a sex shop *unless* a licence had been granted; even then the use is subject to compliance with the conditions laid down by the local authority. In fact the definition of a sex shop meant the use of premises for a business which consisted to a significant degree of selling, hiring, exchanging, lending, displaying or demonstrating sex articles or the like. The result was that someone such as an ordinary newsagent whose business largely consisted of selling ordinary newspapers, books and so on, was not subjected to the licensing requirement when Schedule 3 was adopted.

of *Gay News*, was successfully prosecuted for the violation of blasphemy laws which centred on a poem by James Kirkup, complete with an illustration that evoked images of homosexual behaviour with the body of Christ.

One can safely assume that works of literary merit such as *Lolita* or *Lady Chatterley's Lover* would hardly be prosecuted today. Truly obscene material is easily peddled via the Internet on a daily basis and societal attitudes and values have changed over time. One man's literary genius is another's excuse for hatred, such as witnessing Muslim anger at the Danish cartoons in *Jyllands-Posten* about the Prophet Muhammad. It is one of literary history's abiding curiosities that *Lolita's* publication can be accredited to a man whose tactical adroitness later made him one of the most famous libel lawyers, namely Peter Carter-Ruck.[140]

Edwards (2000) examined the contemporary application of obscenity law by police, prosecutors and the courts by presenting her findings of the first national study into pornography trials in English Crown Courts in an international psychological journal. Her findings demonstrated that only five cases in a six-month period were fully considered by a jury during the 1997–8 study. Only one conviction resulted in a six months' prison sentence, from which Edwards concluded that the 'obscenity' offence was virtually obsolete.[141]

7.6.1 Proportionality regarding contemporary tastes and standards

Looking back at the history of the culture wars, concerning censorship under blasphemy and obscenity, one can find some of the bravest standard-bearers for freedom of expression. John Milton's 1644 *Areopagitica* remains one of the most forceful English publications supporting the freedom to publish. It claims that killing a book is as bad as killing a man, for 'who kills a man kills a reasonable creature, God's image; but he who destroys a good book kills reason itself, kills the image of God, as it were, in the eye'. We then move forward to the 1960s, when the authorities tried to ban the Penguin publication of *Lady Chatterley's Lover* under the **Obscene Publications Act 1959**.

Some people have suffered for their artistic free expression. On 7 October 2006, Anna Politkovskaya was shot in the lift of her Moscow apartment block. The Russian journalist and author had won international recognition for her passionate reporting work on the conflict in Chechnya in which she sought to expose human rights abuses. Detained on occasion by the Russian military, the *Novaya Gazeta* special correspondent was famous for her book *The Dirty War*, a collection of articles mainly about the second Chechen conflict which began in 1999. Her last article, published on 28 September 2006, was a condemnation of pro-Kremlin militias operating in Chechnya as part of Moscow's so-called Chechenization policy. Then there was the public poisoning and killing (so far unsolved) of Alexander Litvinenko in London in November 2006, who was about to publish his book denouncing the alleged terror tactics of the KGB in provoking the second Chechen war. That book, *Blowing Up Russia: Terror from Within* was promptly and permanently banned in his native land.

Modern politicians in fragile multicultural societies seek control over material that 'offends' by organizing parliamentary lobbies to change the laws. Many liberal-minded people feel glad that British laws passed over recent decades forbid inflammatory racist speech, writing and images, such as the glorification of the Second World War by Holocaust-denier David Irving, who was imprisoned under Austrian law for his inflammatory speech and publications in 2006.

Given the freedom of the Internet, it is becoming increasingly difficult to determine what may realistically corrupt public morals. There is now a vast network of hi-tech censorship that all but violent criminals support, such as Operation Ore, which aimed to eradicate child pornography on the Internet. The extension of police and online surveillance powers is ever increasing.

See Chapter 10.6 →

---

140 See the obituary of Peter Carter-Ruck, *Daily Telegraph*, 22 December 2003.
141 See: Edwards (2000).

Censorship is at its most dangerous if those who orchestrate it cannot clearly explain th reasons for the decisions they make. When a piece of art or literature is withdrawn under obscenity laws by the authorities, it can be argued that at that stage censorship becomes repression and a curtailment of freedom of expression. When pictures like that of Brooke Shields by Richard Prince are withdrawn, the public no longer have the option of judging for themselves whether the image is obscene or not. Given that the common law offences of 'obscene libel, 'sedition' and 'seditious libel' were abolished by s. 73 **Coroners and Justice Act 2009**, there seems to be no good reason to maintain or revive associated offences in the 1959 statute with their unduly complex mechanism of prosecution. It might therefore be a good initiative to abolish the redundant **Obscene Publications Act 1959**.

FOR THOUGHT

Would you agree that the **Obscene Publications Act 1959** with its archaic 'deprave and corrupt' test is no longer realistic as an appropriate measure for determining obscenity in art and literature and that the defence of 'public good' only confuses juries? What should be the alternative?

7.7 Summary of key points

- s. 1 **Criminal Libel Act 1819** covered 'orders for seizure of copies of blasphemous or seditious libel' (now abolished);
- The **Obscene Publications Act 1857** ('Lord Campbell's Act') was the first major piece of obscenity legislation in Britain, making the sale of obscene publications and materials a statutory offence; the Act gave the (magistrates') courts power to seize and destroy offending material ('forfeiture and destruction order');
- s. 42 **Customs Consolidation Act 1876** prohibits the import of indecent and obscene material, such as obscene prints, paintings, photographs, books, cards, lithographic or other engravings, or other indecent or obscene articles;
- ss. 3 and 4 **Law of Libel Amendment Act 1888** covered 'privileged matters' and 'blasphemous' libel (now abolished);
- The **Obscene Publications Act 1959** (OPA) reformed the law on the publication of obscene materials, previously governed in common law by the 'Hicklin' test (*R v Hicklin* (1868)), also known as the 'innocent schoolgirl test', which had no exceptions for artistic merit or the public good; the act is concerned with the offence of *publishing* obscene material (it repealed the common law offence of 'obscene libel' of the **Obscene Publications Act 1857**);
- s. 1 OPA 1959 covers the test to determine if something is 'obscene';
- s. 2 OPA 1959 covers the actual prohibition of publishing 'obscene material';
- s. 2(1) OPA 1959 creates the offence of 'publishing an obscene article', replacing the common law offence of 'obscene libel';
- s. 4 OPA 1959 provides two defences: (1) the defence of 'innocent dissemination' and (2) the 'defence of public good';
- The **Obscene Publications Act 1964** covers wholesalers, or any person having an obscene article for publication for gain;
- s. 1 **Protection of Children Act 1978** covers the taking, making, distribution, showing or possession with a view to distributing any indecent image of a child; this offence or an offence contrary to s. 160 **Criminal Justice Act 1988** should be charged instead of an 'obscene publications' offence where the material concerned includes indecent images of children (defined as being persons under the age of 18);

- s. 1(1) **Indecent Displays (Control) Act 1981** makes it an offence to publicly display indecent matter in shops; s. 1(2) covers 'any matter which is displayed . . .' or is 'visible from any public place';
- Part III, ss. 17–29 **Public Order Act 1986** define and punish public order offences concerning racial hatred and racially inflammatory publications;
- The **Criminal Justice and Public Order Act 1994** amends OPAs 1959 and 1964 covering computer images as 'publications'; making it illegal to transmit electronically stored data which is obscene on resolution into a viewable form; this covers photographs and pseudo-photographs of children;
- s. 71 **Criminal Justice and Immigration Act 2008** increased the maximum penalty for conviction on indictment for obscene publications to five years' imprisonment;
- s. 79 **Criminal Justice and Immigration Act 2008** abolished common law offences of 'blasphemy' and 'blasphemous libel';
- ss. 62–69 **Coroners and Justice Act 2009** created a new offence in England, Wales and Northern Ireland of possession of a prohibited 'pornographic' image of a child, i.e. grossly offensive, disgusting or otherwise of an obscene character;
- s. 73 **Coroners and Justice Act 2009** abolished the common law offences of 'sedition', 'seditious libel', 'defamatory libel' and 'obscene libel' in England, Wales and Northern Ireland.

📖 7.8 Further reading

Burns Coleman, E. and White, K. (2006) *Negotiating the Sacred in Multicultural Societies: Blasphemy and Sacrilege in a Multicultural Society.* Canberra: University of Australia National University Press.

Council of Europe (2010) 'Blasphemy, insult and hatred – Finding answers in a democratic society'. *Science and Technique of Democracy* No.47. Brussels: Council of Europe Publication.

Doley, C., Starte, H., Addy, C., Helme, I., Griffiths, J., Scott, A. and Mullis, A. (eds) (2009) *Carter-Ruck on Libel and Slander.* London: Butterworths.

Edwards, S.M. (2000) 'The failure of British obscenity law in the regulation of pornography'. *Journal of Sexual Aggression: An international, interdisciplinary forum for research, theory and practice*, Volume 6, Issue 1, 2000: 111–27.

Elliott, D.W. (1993) 'Blasphemy and other expressions of offensive opinion.' *Ecclesiastical Law Journal*, 1993, 3(13), 70–85.

Gilvarry, E. (1990) 'Mapplethorpe retrospective sparks pornography debate'. *Law Society Gazette*, 1990, 87(33), 10–11.

James, J. and Ghandi, S. (1998) 'The English law of blasphemy and the European Convention on Human Rights'. *European Human Rights Law Review*, 1998, 4, 430–51.

Kearns, P. (2000) 'Obscene and blasphemous libel: misunderstanding art'. *Criminal Law Review*, 2000, Aug, 652–60.

Lester, Lord of Herne Hill (1993) 'Freedom of Expression'. In: Macdonald, R. J., Matscher, F. and Petzold, H. (eds) (1993) *The European System for the Protection of Human Rights.* Dordrecht: Martinus Nijhoff, pp. 465–81.

Manchester, C. (1988) 'Lord Campbell's Act: England's first obscenity statute'. *Journal of Legal History*, 1988, 9(2), 223–41.

Routledge, G. (1989) 'The Report of the Archbishop of Canterbury's Working Paper on Offences against Religion and Public Worship'. *Ecclesiastical Law Review*, 1989, 1 Ecc LJ (4) 27,31.

Samuels, A. (2009) 'Obscenity and pornography'. *Criminal Law and Justice Weekly*, 2009, 173(12), 187–9.

Chapter 8

Copyright I: Intellectual Property Law

Chapter Contents

8.1 Overview

Intellectual property rights is a collective term that covers – *inter alia* – copyright. Intellectual property (IP) or 'copyright' law exists to protect the creator or author of an original piece of work, so that others can be prevented from copying or 'pirating' it. Some IP rights are automatic; some have to be registered. The basic idea behind IP is to ensure that a work is not copied or used without permission and to protect the economic rewards (known as 'royalties') of the creators and authors of the works.

The meaning of 'property' can vary and includes designs, films, photos, literature, inventions, etc. Generally, 'property' must be in a fixed or concrete form. The next chapter deals with the recording of material such as music or speech.

The basic rights of copyright include: the right to copy the work; the right to issue copies of it to the public; the right to rent or lend copies to the public; the right to perform, show or play the work in public; the right to communicate the work to the public; the right to make an adaptation of the work.

It is an established principle that copyright is territorial in nature; that is, that protection under a given copyright law is available only in the country where that law applies; in the UK, the main legislation which covers IP law is the **Copyright, Designs and Patents Act 1988** (CDPA – also known as the 'Copyright Act'). It is important, though, to note that because of the impact of the international treaty in the form of the **Berne Copyright Convention**, foreign authors are given 'national treatment' in the UK and have the same rights before a UK court as a domestic author does. For example, a French author can sue for an unauthorized translation into English and the sale of that translated work if sold without authorization in the UK.

This chapter looks firstly at the historical development of intellectual property law, which originated in English law as a result of the abolition of state licensing of books in 1694 by way of the abolition of the Stationers' Company ('Stationers'), the state printing monopoly based in London. This had largely resulted from pressure from London publishers facing a flood of unauthorized 'pirate' copies from provincial and Scottish printers. Parliament then enacted its first copyright statute, the **Statute of Anne 1710**, which, in turn, was extended and reformed over the years, resulting in the principal acts being the **Copyright Act 1911** and the **Copyright Act 1956**.

The chapter then gives a detailed rundown of the main international conventions that govern IP legislation, specifically copyright covered by the **Paris**[1] and **Berne Conventions** and the **World Intellectual Property Treaty** (WIPO)[2] and the **World Trade Organization Trade Related Intellectual Property Agreement** (TRIPS). The main principle of the Paris (1883) and Berne (1886) Conventions was that they established for authors' rights, effectively reciprocity establishing the notion of intellectual property being a *property* right in the same sense that land or chattels were, in contrast with the typical common law perception that the author's right is merely a polite description of a commercial monopoly (see below 8.3).

Copyright is the means by which an author, lyricist, sculptor or other artist makes a living from their creativity. This means that people who create, produce or invest in an original creative work should be the ones who receive the rewards in the form of payment or royalties, i.e that they are the rights owners (see below 8.4.4). Copyright provides that the rights holder determines whether and how copying, distributing, broadcasting and other uses of their works take place. For instance, copyright legislation encourages talented composers and performing artists to create musical works

---

1 The *Paris Convention* essentially deals with industrial property rights, such as patents and trademarks; see Chapter 9.8.
2 The Berne Convention and WIPO also protect related rights such as sound recordings, broadcasts, translations of works and adaptations; see Chapter 8.5.1.

and record companies and music producers to invest in that talent. This chapter covers statutory provision, remedies and defences (see below 8.10.3 and 8.11).

While this and the next chapter concentrate mainly on the music industry, general principles of copyright will be highlighted, applicable to literary, musical or artistic works. Case law from English, Scots and European jurisdictions will demonstrate the intricate legal challenges in this area of law, demonstrating the complexities which are involved when representing an international recording artist – such as Bob Dylan – who may well be recording with different labels during his lifetime, in different countries and with the added complications of the varying degrees of copyright duration (see below 8.6).

Statutory copyright law is supplemented by contract law which will govern IP legislation, such as licensing rights or the sale of copyright as an intangible right. These intangible rights can include the assignment of copyright, the exclusivity of a recording contract to record primarily with one record company and the transfer of such rights (see below 8.9). Intellectual Property (IP) law in its broader sense covers industrial rights, such as patents[3] and trademarks.

See Chapter
← 9.4

See Chapter
← 9.8

Equitable and criminal remedies available to the UK courts have not really deterred piracy and copying of MP3 music files, DVDs or films and therefore the government and the European Commission face constant demands for the law to be strengthened. Possible defences or 'permitted acts' – as they are known in the CDPA 1988 – include fair dealing (reviews, news reporting, criticism, etc.), research and private study (see below 8.10.3)

This chapter further analyses present and future European copyright legislation in the form of 'media sans frontières' initiatives which have encouraged harmonization of the modern copyright environment across Europe, brought about by technological innovation such as the Internet (see below 8.12.1).

8.2 The origins of copyright: historical overview

Copyright law has two basic functions, a property function and an authenticity function, both seeking to establish who is the author of a work. As the history of copyright shows, the property function is now widely accepted in international copyright law – though this was not always the case. The author is then regarded as the single source and is held responsible for this work. Related moral rights which developed much later were introduced with the CPA 1988, establishing that the work must be attributed to the author (the economic owner of copyright) and must not be changed or altered in any way. For example, a manuscript can only be amended, deleted or modified by contract.

The origins of copyright are closely related to the development of printing, which enabled rapid production of copies of books at relatively low cost. The Stuarts (1307–1603) and the Tudors (1485–1603) used their prerogative to grant exclusive patents for publishing books, particularly law books.[4] The growth of literacy created a large demand for printed books, and the protection of authors and publishers from unauthorized copying was recognized as increasingly important in the context of this new means of making works available to the public. During the sixteenth century,

---

3 The European Patent Convention 2000 (EPC) covers this area of law as a treaty agreement. The 14th edition of the EPC of 2009 contains the texts of the 'Convention on the Grant of European Patents and its Implementing Regulations', the 'Protocol on the Interpretation of Article 69 EPC', the 'Protocol on Centralisation', the 'Protocol on Recognition', the 'Protocol on Privileges and Immunities', the 'Protocol on the Staff Complement and the Rules relating to Fees', together with an extract from the 'Revision Act of 29 November 2000' and the decision of the Administrative Council of 28 June 2001, on the transitional provisions under Article 7 of the Revision Act. The World Trade Organization (WTO) in Geneva largely looks after legislation on and registration of trademarks under the 'Uruguay Round Agreement'.
4 For further discussion see: Pfeifer (2008).

the printers, known as 'stationers', formed a collective, called the Stationers' Company. It was provided with the power to require all lawfully printed books to be entered into its register and only members of the Stationers could enter books into the register under the **Licensing Act 1662**. This meant that stationers had considerable monopolies and thereby provided the licensing system,

See Chapter 3.3.2 →

with state backing, giving their members sole rights over particular titles. Failure to register a book or title prevented an action for damages against an infringer, but did not invalidate copyright.

There was no equivalent arrangement for Scotland. How could the works of Sir Walter Scott (1771–1832), the Scottish historical novelist and poet, who was also popular throughout Europe, be safeguarded if his works could not be protected under registration?[5] This anomaly in the law was only really solved in common law after the decision in *Walter v Lane* (1900),[6] and with the **Copyright Act of 1911** (see below 8.2.2).

The abolition of the Stationers' system in 1694 led to major problems of pirate or unauthorized copies, particularly of the very popular almanacs of the time containing predictions and prophecies, such as physician Francis Moore's almanacs (*Old Moore's Almanac*) which contained weather predictions and promoted the sale of his pills. In Elizabethan times, almanacs were bestsellers and Stationers' Company records from the late seventeenth century show sales approaching 400,000 copies each year. Prices were modest – an almanac ranged from 2d to 6d – which meant that anyone able to read could learn from it.[7]

8.2.1 Statute of Anne 1710[8]

Following the abolition of state licensing and the monopoly of the Stationers' Company, the question soon arose as to the rights of the author and who could be defined as an author. In general terms – but also for copyright purposes and all terms of recognition – a named author was seen to be the central organizer, writer and promoter of his own literary or musical works. Authorship meant that he would be allowed to engage in contractual terms with promoters and publishers of his original material. But this was a problem since intellectual property was, by its very nature, an intangible right. How could a work's originality be protected from being copied?

The right to 'copy' introduced by the **Statute of Anne** came after nearly three centuries of print technology, during which monarchs and the Stationers' Company had the right to censor radical literature. 'Booksellers' were essentially both publishers and distributors – bearing in mind the economic interest of printers and booksellers. With the right to copy under the **Statute of Anne**, booksellers were able to operate a system of restrictive trade practices. Initially the statute gave only a limited period of protection. When this ran out publishers sought to argue that this meant a perpetual copyright which gave them an inherent monopoly and licence to print with everlasting effect. The London booksellers, for instance, exercised a tight control over the market for perpetual copyrights, thereby restricting trade and competition.[9] This principle was eventually clarified and rejected at common law by the House of Lords in their decision in *Donaldson v Becket* (1774)[10] (see below). Their Lordships firmly ruled that copyright was entirely a statutory creation. From 1695 onwards, the licensing system gradually disappeared and certain rules began to emerge that

---

5 For detailed discussion of copyright and Scottish literature and folk traditions see: Cornish (2009).
6 [1900] AC 539 (HL).
7 See: Capp (2004).
8 8 Anne (c. 19), with the full title as 'An Act for the Encouragement of Learning, by vesting the Copies of Printed Books in the Authors or purchasers of such Copies, during the Times therein mentioned.'
9 For further discussion see Baloch (2007).
10 (1774) 2 Bro PC 129 (HL).

stationers could not reprint each other's titles, which meant that titles lasted indefinitely. On the other hand, if a title was reprinted or copied by someone, the author had no redress in law.

In 1707 the Parliaments of England and Scotland were united as a result of the Acts of Union. The new Parliament was able to change the laws regarding publications by introducing an important piece of legislation in the form of the **Statute of Anne 1710**, the first copyright statute. The statute introduced the concept that an author was the first owner of copyright and, furthermore, the principle of a fixed term of protection for published works. The act also brought about the depositing of nine copies of a book to specified libraries in the country. The effect was that, after the lapse of a certain period, the privilege enjoyed by the Stationers to make and distribute copies of work reverted back to the 'originator' of the work, who then had the right to assign the privilege to another publisher.

From 1769 onwards, the Court of King's Bench began to accept that a civil right of action arose at law if a copyright had been infringed under the **Statute of Anne**, which amounted to a breach of property. This in turn gave rise to damages. Chancery would grant equitable injunctions protecting 'out-of-time' books against illegal copying (see: *Millar v Taylor* (1769)[11]). But in spite of the Acts of Union, the Scottish courts refused to find any equivalent right for illegal copying of texts since intellectual property was not recognized as 'property'. For many years a person could be prosecuted for the theft of another man's chattel, but not for stealing or copying his poem or song sheet.[12] It was affirmed by Lord Kames in *Hinton v Donaldson* (1773)[13] that there was no foundation for literary copyright either in natural law or the law of nations. Nor was any vestige of such a right to be found in the law of Scotland, which only complicated matters in relation to intellectual property 'across the border'.

The effect of *Hinton v Donaldson* was that any unpublished information, such as a speech or manuscript, was essentially secret and abstract information and not regarded as 'property', with the result that it could easily be stolen or copied. If someone's piece of paper with his doctoral thesis synopsis or findings was found left on a photocopier, no trespass was established and therefore no infringement such as theft could be prosecuted if a student helped himself to that document in order to copy or make use of it (see: *Oxford v Moss* (1979);[14] *R v Absolon* (1983)[15]).

In *Donaldson v Becket* (1774),[16] the House of Lords had to decide on the question of whether an author, after the expiration of the statutory protection given by the **Statute of Anne**, had a perpetual right of literary property at common law. The following question was put to their Lordships: whether at common law an author of any book or literary composition had the sole right of first printing and publishing the same for sale, and could bring an action against any person who printed, published and sold the same without his consent? This question was decided in the negative.

Caird v Sime (1887)[17] – another Scottish case – established the right of a professor to restrain the publication of lectures orally delivered in his classroom, when Lord Halsbury said:

> . . . it is not denied, and it cannot in the present state of the law be denied, that an author has a proprietary right in his unpublished literary productions. It is further incapable of denial that that proprietary right may still continue notwithstanding some kind of communication to others.[18]

---

11 (1769) 4 Burr 2303.
12 See: Ormerod and Williams (2007), paras 1.18–1.24.
13 (1773) Mor 8307 (Lord Kames).
14 [1979] Crim LR 119.
15 (1983) The Times, 14 September 1983 (unreported).
16 (1774) 2 Bro PC 129.
17 (1887) LR 12 App Cas 326 (HL).
18 4 Burr. 2303 published under the separate title in 1770 of 'Literary Property' (Lord Halsbury).

And Lord Watson added:

> . . . the author of a lecture on moral philosophy, or of any other original composition, retains a right of property in his work which entitles him to prevent its publication by others until it has, with his consent, been communicated to the public.[19]

Caird v Sime finally established that the law of property exists in intangible works, such as literature, songs or lectures, irrespective of implied contract or breach of duty. Consequently, the Sheriff in this case ordered all copies of the publications concerned to be delivered up by the plagiarist thief. The House of Lords' decision in *Caird v Sime* affirmed *Albert v Strange* (1849),[20] which stated that whoever copies or publishes an unpublished work without consent is stealing the author's copyright – a proprietary right. The motive or intention on the part of the defendant was then wholly irrelevant.

The **Statute of Anne** provided the conceptual skeleton for copyright law for centuries to come. This had economic consequences, affirmed in *Donaldson v Becket*. Furthermore, the statute served to promote competition in the publishing business by restricting monopolies and recognizing the author as the holder of the right to authorize copying.[21]

8.2.2 The Copyright Act 1911

In 1893 Earl Rosebery[22] became the successor to Gladstone as Liberal prime minister. He gave rousing speeches which were, in turn, reported in *The Times*. Reporters from the newspaper took down shorthand notes of his speeches by way of 'stenography' and later transcribed them, adding punctuation, corrections and revisions to reproduce the speeches, verbatim, which were subsequently published in *The Times*. *The Times* then claimed copyright on the reports, which became the issue in *Walter v Lane* (1900).[23] Their Lordships held that copyright subsisted in the shorthand writers' reports of the public speeches as original literary works. The speeches were made by the Earl of Rosebery in public when reporters were present. Lord Rosebery was the author of his speeches. The shorthand writers were the authors of their reports of his speeches. They spent effort, skill and time in writing up their reports of speeches that they themselves had not written.

Worth noting is that *The Times* – as the journalists' employer – owned the copyright in the shorthand version of the Rosebery speeches. These had been consolidated into a book. Equally worth mentioning is that had Lord Rosebery so wished, he could have prevented the (re)publication of his speeches for breach of his own literary copyright in the original speeches. However, such an action could not have stopped a derivative copyright arising in the shorthand version and *The Times* could have sued third parties who copied the material without their consent. *Walter v Lane* is still good law and was confirmed in *Express Newspapers v News (UK)* (1990)[24] and *Sawkins v Hyperion Records Ltd* (2005).[25] *Walter v Lane* defined the long life of copyright and what could be defined as a 'literary work' for copyright purposes, which eventually resulted in the **Copyright Act 1911** which, in turn, specified the term 'original' for the purpose of a literary work. With the advancement of technology an added crucial characteristic of the **Copyright Act of 1911** was that it also granted copyright to producers of sound recordings (phonograms), an approach which was then followed

---

19 2 Brown P. C. 129; 4 Burr. 2408 (Lord Watson).
20 (1849) 64 ER 293.
21 See also: Deazley (2008).
22 Archibald Philip Primrose, 5th Earl of Rosebery (1847–1929) was a Liberal statesman and prime minister, also known as Lord Dalmeny.
23 [1900] AC 539 (HL).
24 [1990] 1 WLR 1320 (Sir Nicolas Browne-Wilkinson VC).
25 [2005] EWCA Civ 565.

in American and Australian copyright legislation. This new right gave an investor who organized a sound recording or 'phonogram' complete exclusivity in the marketplace. Moreover, title did not have to be traced back to the original author or creator of the works, which was an added bonus for new entrepreneurs. Protection extended only to the copying and the public performance of the recording, not to other recordings or uses of the musical work or the spoken text. The length of the term marked the difference: authors were allowed life plus 50 years for their published works; the producers of recordings only 50 years from making the master copy.

Creative works are afforded copyright protection only if they are original. The classic statement on the meaning of originality in this context is that of Peterson J in *University of London Press Ltd v University Tutorial Press Ltd* (1916):[26]

> . . . the word 'original' does not in this connection mean that the work must be the expression of original or inventive thought. Copyright Acts are not concerned with the originality of ideas, but with the expression of thought, and, in the case of 'literary work', with the expression of thought in print or writing. The originality which is required relates to the expression of the thought. But the Act does not require that the expression must be in an original or novel form, but that the work must not be copied from another work – that it should originate from the author.[27]

8.2.3 The Copyright Act 1956

The **Copyright Act 1956** introduced no substantive amendments to the 1911 Act, but was significant for the development of the phonogram industry.[28] The 1956 Act extended copyright to related and 'neighbouring rights' in sound recordings (phonograms) and who would qualify for these rights. Though musical and dramatic performers had not been well supported by law in the past, it was the **Dramatic and Musical Performers' Protection Act 1925** which imposed criminal sanctions on those who made recordings of dramatic and musical performances without the performers' consent. The law in this respect was consolidated and extended over the years, notably to encompass literary dramatic musical and artistic works in the **Dramatic and Musical Performers' Protection Act 1958**. The **Copyright Act of 1956** extended copyright to sound recordings, cinematographic works (films) and broadcasts. As well as record producers, there were other entrepreneur investors in the phonogram, entertainment and film industry who were now going to be protected under the 1956 Act. The 1911 Act had not extended sound recording rights to the reciter, actor or musician who performed the work, but to the enterprise that made the recording. Initially, there was strong opposition from the recording labels to the 1959 Act, which conferred neighbouring rights on performers. For example, the label now had to compromise and settle by contract with performers what their future earnings would be in the form of royalties. The label, in turn, would then be contracted to organize and market the recording by way of licensing IP rights which followed from that.

In *Robertson v Lewis* (1976),[29] the House of Lords' principle in *Walter v Lane* (1900) (see above 8.2.2) was discussed in relation to facts that more closely resembled the earlier case. The claimants had published a song, based on an arrangement of two Scottish airs and a Gaelic song. The court found that the claimants were not entitled to copyright in the underlying musical work. The court placed considerable weight on the fact that published copies of the song stated that the music was

---

26 [1916] 2 Ch 601.
27 ibid., at 608 (Peterson J).
28 The established definition of 'phonogram' is provided by Article 3 b) Rome Convention as 'any exclusively aural fixation of sounds of a performance or of other sounds'.
29 [1976] RPC 169; a case decided in 1960 but not reported until 1976.

'arranged' by the claimant and it was said that the arrangement involved insufficient originality to attract copyright in its own right. The claimants, relying on *Walter v Lane*, argued that they had copyright in the printed record of the music that they had published. But Mr Justice Cross found that they had failed to establish infringement. Cross J expressed the view that, following the introduction in the 1911 Act of the express requirement of originality, it was arguable that *Walter v Lane* was no longer good law.[30]

8.3 International copyright legislation

Prior to the **Berne Convention** (and to a lesser degree the **Universal Copyright Convention** (UCC) – see below 8.3.2), copyright law only applied at national level, meaning that outside the author's home country there was very little protection for his original or artistic work. For works to be protected outside the country of origin, it was necessary for the country to conclude bilateral agreements with countries where the works were used. By the mid-nineteenth century, there existed only some bilateral agreements among some European nations. But they were neither consistent nor comprehensive and it is fair to say that the English concept of copyright mainly protected economic concerns.

8.3.1 The Paris Convention 1883

The **Paris Convention for the Protection of Industrial Property** of 20 March 1883 ('the Paris Convention') established basic levels of protection and reciprocal recognition for so-called 'industrial property', which excluded the predominantly aesthetic works covered by the **Berne Convention**.[31] It was designed to increase foreign patenting opportunities and established the national priority approach whereby national treatment was granted to all subscribing nations. Essentially, French copyright law applies to anything published or performed in France, regardless of where it was originally created. The **Paris Convention**[32] covers all types of industrial property, such as patents, trade marks and unfair competition. Article 1 of the Convention makes specific reference to the protection of 'utility models, industrial designs, trademarks, service marks, trade names, etc'. The **Paris Convention** covers industrial property in the broadest sense and applies not only to commerce and industry, but also to agricultural, 'extractive industries' and the manufacture of natural products, for example, wines, grain, tobacco leaf, fruit, cattle, minerals, mineral waters, beer, flowers, flour, etc. An applicant from one contracting state who files a patent application in another contracting state can use his first filing date as the effective filing date in another contracting state, so long as the applicant files another application for the patent within a year from the first filing.

See Chapter
9.8 →

8.3.2 The Berne Convention 1886

The **Berne Convention for the Protection of Literary and Artistic Works** ('the Berne Convention'[33]) – essentially based on the principles of the **Paris Convention** – was signed on 9 September 1886 in the Swiss town of Berne and became the first international agreement to unify

---

30 Ibid., at 171–2 (Cross J).
31 See: Paris Convention; Stockholm text 1967, Articles 1(2) and 1(3) Paris Convention.
32 The Paris Convention was revised at Brussels on 14 December 1900, at Washington on 2 June 1911, at The Hague on 6 November 1925, at London on 2 June 1934, at Lisbon on 31 October 1958 and at Stockholm on 14 July 1967, and amended on 28 September 1979.
33 The Berne Convention of 9 September 1886, completed at Paris on 4 May 1896, revised at Berlin on 13 November 1908, completed at Berne on 20 March 1914, revised at Rome on 2 June 1928, at Brussels on 26 June 1948, at Stockholm on 14 July 1967, and at Paris on 24 July 1971, and amended on 28 September 1979.

a system of copyright protection.[34] The principal aim of the **Berne Convention** was to help creators gain protection for their works. This meant that the creation of a work in fixed form (written or recorded on a physical medium) gave the author automatic right in the work without having to register it.

The **Berne Convention** created automatic copyright in works as soon as they were created, asserted and declared. The minimum term of protection was the lifetime of the author and 50 years after his death.[35] This provided the author of a work, as well as the first two generations of his descendants, with the necessary copyright protection with the following exceptions:

1.	For photography the minimum term was 25 years from the year the photograph was created;
2.	For cinematography the minimum term was 50 years after first showing, or, if the work was never shown, 50 years from the creation date.[36]

The **Berne Convention** has been revised a number of times. The Stockholm revision in 1967 was a response to technological change and included giving newly independent developing countries access to works for the purpose of national education, further enhanced by the 'Paris Revision Conference' in 1971.

Taking the most recent text of the **Berne Convention**,[37] one finds, inter alia, the following important passages which provide for *exceptions* to the author's right, and therefore deal with conflict of laws:

Article 2(4) Legal and administrative texts and translations

It shall be a matter for legislation in the countries of the Union to determine the protection to be granted to official texts of a legislative, administrative and legal nature, and to official trans-lations of such texts;

Article 2(8) News

The protection of this Convention shall not apply to news of the day or to miscellaneous facts having the character of mere items of press information;

Article 2bis Lectures and speeches

(1) It shall be a matter for legislation in the countries of the Union to exclude, wholly or in part, from the protection provided by the preceding Article political speeches and speeches delivered in the course of legal proceedings;

(3) Nevertheless, the author shall enjoy the exclusive right of making a collection of his works mentioned in the preceding paragraphs;

Article 9(2) Reproduction

It shall be a matter for legislation in the countries of the Union to permit the reproduction of such works in certain special cases, provided that such reproduction does not conflict with a normal exploitation of the work and does not unreasonably prejudice the legitimate interests of the author;

34	The original signatory countries comprised: Belgium, France, Germany, Italy, United Kingdom, Switzerland and Tunisia, further joined by Luxembourg in 1887, Monaco in 1889, Norway in 1896, Morocco in 1917, Portugal in 1911, the Netherlands in 1912 and Romania in 1927.
35	Article 7 (1) Berne Convention.
36	Note: These are the minimum terms of protection. Countries are free to provide longer terms of protection under national law. In the UK, for example, the standard period of protection is 70 years from the death of the author.
37	Completed at Paris on 24 July 1971 and amended on 28 September 1979.

Article 10 (1) Quotations

It shall be permissible to make quotations from a work which has already been lawfully made available to the public, provided that their making is compatible with fair practice, and their extent does not exceed that justified by the purpose, including quotations from newspaper articles and periodicals in the form of press summaries;

Article 10bis Free uses of works of newspaper/online articles, news and broadcasts

(1) It shall be a matter for legislation in the countries of the Union to permit the reproduction by the press, the broadcasting or the communication to the public by wire of articles published in newspapers or periodicals on current economic, political or religious topics, and of broadcast works of the same character, in cases in which the reproduction, broadcasting or such communication thereof is not expressly reserved. Nevertheless, the source must always be clearly indicated; the legal consequences of a breach of this obligation shall be determined by the legislation of the country where protection is claimed;

(2) It shall also be a matter for legislation in the countries of the Union to determine the conditions under which, for the purpose of reporting current events by means of photography, cinematography, broadcasting or communication to the public by wire, literary or artistic works seen or heard in the course of the event may, to the extent justified by the informatory purpose, be reproduced and made available to the public;

Article 11bis Dramatic and musical works and public performances

(1) Authors of dramatic, dramatico-musical and musical works shall enjoy the exclusive right of authorizing:

  (i) the public performance of their works, including such public performance by any means or process;
  (ii) any communication to the public of the performance of their works;

Article 17 Circulation, presentation and exhibition of works

The provisions of this Convention cannot in any way affect the right of the Government of each country of the Union to permit, to control, or to prohibit, by legislation or regulation, the circulation, presentation, or exhibition of any work or production in regard to which the competent authority may find it necessary to exercise that right.

Though the 'public interest' defence is commonly used in the UK, the **Berne Convention** does not explicitly permit this defence when someone's copyright has been infringed, so it would not necessarily be justifiable if an author's copyright has been infringed to argue that the copying was 'for the greater good of society' (see: *Gartside v Outram* (1856);[38] also: *Beloff v Pressdram Ltd* (1973)[39]). In other words, the Berne Convention does not expressly permit the public interest defence to copyright infringement, whereas UK copyright law will take the public interest defence into account (see: *Ashdown v Telegraph Group Ltd.* (2001)[40]).

The **Universal Copyright Convention of 1952** (UCC),[41] first created in Geneva, was an alternative to the **Berne Convention 1886**, because some countries disagreed with certain aspects of the **Berne Convention**, most notably the United States, who at the time only provided protection on a

---

38 (1856) 26 LJ Ch 113.
39 [1973] 1 All ER 241.
40 [2001] Ch 685 (Ch D).
41 The Universal Copyright Convention (UCC), Law (Approval) revised at Uruguay on 6 November 1992, No. 16.321.

fixed-term registration basis via the Library Of Congress and required that copyright works must always show the copyright symbol ©. The UCC ensures that international protection is available to authors even in countries that would not become parties to the **Berne Convention. Berne Convention** countries also became signatories of the UCC to ensure that the work of citizens in **Berne Convention** countries would be protected in non-**Berne Convention** countries. The US finally signed up to the **Berne Convention** on 1 March 1989 and now only requires registration for work first published in the US by US citizens.

The **Berne Convention** and the UCC impose general rules and formalities for UK copyright protection in addition to the UK 'Copyright Act' (**Copyright, Designs and Patents Act 1988 – CDPA**). While the CDPA does not acknowledge the © copyright symbol, the UCC does, though it is fair to say that the UCC is of limited importance today since most countries are now part of the union of the **Berne Convention**.

Although the **Berne Convention** has been subject to numerous changes, it still possesses the same distinguishing feature it had some 125 years ago: it is an agreement by its signatory states that the private and proprietary rights of their domestic authors should be both respected and enforceable in the courts of all the assigned member states. Today, the **Berne Convention** is administered by the World Intellectual Property Organization (WIPO – see below) and comprised 164 contracting parties in 2011.

In recent years, the accession of countries to the **Berne Convention** has grown rapidly, with copyright protection being a crucial part of the new global trading system. However, the WIPO Convention system including the **Berne Convention** lacks effective sanctions for failure to properly enforce and implement the Conventions. The Agreement on the 'Trade Related Aspects of Intellectual Property Rights' (the TRIPS Agreement – see below) incorporates the substantive provisions of the Paris Act of the **Berne Convention**, highlighting the importance now attached to copyright protection by many countries. TRIPS is potentially more effective because trade sanctions through the World Trade Organization (WTO) can be taken against members who do not effectively enforce copyright law or respect the rights of owners and authors of other WTO member states.

In summary, the **Berne Convention** requires member nations to offer the same protection to authors from other member countries that it provides to its own nationals – so-called 'national treatment'. It also sets out a common framework of protection and specifies minimum protection levels that are required.

8.3.3 Performers' rights: the Rome Convention 1961

The **Rome Convention 1961** was the first to address the related rights of producers of phonograms and performers. The convention was created at a time when few countries had legislation to protect all three categories of beneficiaries: the protection of performers, the protection against rebroadcasting and the fixation of performances for broadcasting purposes, where the performers' consent to broadcasting was left to national law.

See Chapter
9.3

The convention began to take shape at a diplomatic conference in Rome in 1928 with the aim of revising the **Berne Convention**, taking into account technological advancement in the phonogram industry. It was around the same time that the International Labor Office (ILO) began to take an interest in the status of performers as employed workers, which included performers and producers of phonograms who were, at that time, not protected under existing copyright legislation.

In 1960 a committee of experts from the United International Bureaux for the Protection of Intellectual Property (BIRPI),[42] the United Nations Educational, Scientific and Cultural Organization

---

42 The predecessor organization to WIPO.

(UNESCO) and the ILO met at a summit in The Hague to draft a new convention. This became the **Convention for the Protection of Producers of Phonograms Against unauthorized Duplication of their Phonograms** ('the Rome Convention'), signed on 26 October 1961.

The **Rome Convention 1961** recognizes the existence of contractual arrangements for the use of performances, stating that performers cannot be deprived of the ability to control by contract their relations with broadcasting organizations. The meaning of 'contract' in this context includes collective agreements and decisions of arbitration boards. The Convention also allows discretion to member states in respect of the participation of more than one performer in a performance.[43] Article 8 **Rome Convention** provides that if several performers participate in the same performance, the manner in which they should be represented in connection with the exercise of their rights may be specified by each contracting state. Article 12 provides discretion to states in 'secondary use' of phonograms. This controversial area of law provides that if a recording published for commercial purposes is used directly for broadcasting or any communication to the public, an equitable remuneration is paid by the user to the performers, the producers or both. At the same time Article 12 does not grant an exclusive right either to performers or producers of phonograms in respect of secondary use of a phonogram. By providing for a single remuneration only, this has established a kind of non-voluntary licence. Article 12 does not specify that payment of remuneration is mandatory for either beneficiary; it states only that at least one of them should be paid for the use, and that, in the absence of agreement between these parties, domestic law may establish conditions for sharing of the remuneration.

See Chapter
9.3.2 →

Like the **Berne Convention**, the **Rome Convention** guarantees performers, producers of phonograms and broadcasting organizations the same rights in domestic law as well as the other contracting states.[44] Article 5 **Rome Convention** states that each contracting state shall grant national treatment to producers of phonograms if any of the following conditions is met:

(a) the producer of the phonogram is a national of another contracting state ('criterion of nationality');

(b) the first fixation of the sound was made in another contracting state ('criterion of fixation');

(c) the phonogram was first published in another contracting state ('criterion of publication').

This means that producers of phonograms are entitled to national treatment if they are nationals of another contracting state if the first fixation was made in another contracting state ('criterion of fixation'), or if the phonogram was first or simultaneously published in another contracting state ('criterion of publication'), as illustrated in the *Bob Dylan* case[45] (see below 8.8.1).

Broadcasting organizations are entitled to national treatment if their headquarters are situated in another contracting state[46] or if the broadcast is sent out from a transmitter situated in another contracting state, irrespective of whether the initiating broadcasting organization was situated in a contracting state.[47] Contracting states may declare that they will protect broadcasts only if both the condition of nationality and of territoriality are met in respect of the same contracting state. The **Rome Convention** does not protect against cable distribution of broadcasts.

The minimum term of protection under the **Rome Convention** is 20 years from the end of the year in which:

---

43 Article 7(2) Rome Convention.
44 Article 2(1) Rome Convention.
45 See: *Sony Music Entertainment (Germany) GmbH v Falcon Neue Medien Vertrieb GmbH* (C-240/07) [2009] ECDR 12.
46 Article 5 'criterion of nationality' Rome Convention.
47 Article 6 'principle of territoriality' Rome Convention.

(i)   the fixation was made, as far as phonograms and performances incorporated therein are concerned; or

(ii)   the performance took place, as regards performances not incorporated in phonograms; or

(iii)   the broadcast took place.[48]

The **Rome Convention** was pioneering because it set elaborate standards of related rights protection at a time when very few countries had any legislation to protect performers, producers of phonograms and broadcasting organizations.

8.3.4 Trade-related IPs: 'the TRIPS Agreement' of 1994

The 'Agreement on Trade-Related Aspects of Intellectual Property Rights' (TRIPS), concluded in 1994 as part of the Uruguay Round of negotiations under the former GATT,[49] contains provisions on copyright protection. It provides that member countries shall comply with the 1971 Paris Act of the **Berne Convention**.[50]

The TRIPS Agreement[51] provides a right in respect of commercial rental of copies of computer programmes and audio-visual works. Furthermore, that data compilations are protected as original creations, regardless of whether the compilation exists in machine-readable or other form, and without prejudice to protection under copyright or otherwise of the material included. TRIPS also states that copyright protection extends to expressions (but not to ideas, procedures, methods of operation or mathematical concepts). TRIPS requires that the laws of member states make clear that computer programs are protected as literary works under that convention. The duration of protection is 50 years following the death of the author. There is one exception: that no rights or obligations are created in respect of moral rights. TRIPS essentially states that individual IP rights can be exchanged between member states across the world, particularly developing countries, independent from privileges obtained from governments, ensuring that they operated under a rule of law (here: private law).

While TRIPS provides a relatively flexible framework of protection of trade secrets under the 'minimum standard of protection' imposed by Article 39 TRIPS, the national and international legislative and judicial authorities enjoy a certain degree of freedom with respect to how they implement the protection of trade secrets (i.e. undisclosed confidential information). This means some uncertainty exists over the issue of the existence and extent of an exclusivity period during which the 'test data' may not be used. This does not appear to be imposed by Article 39.

> ### ◉ FOR THOUGHT
>
> How useful is the TRIPS Agreement to a new solo artist or pop group in relation to 'unfair commercial use' by third parties, such as the making of a pilot recording (known as 'test data')?

---

48 Article 14 *Rome Convention*.

49 The General Agreement on Tariffs and Trade (GATT) was negotiated during the UN Conference on Trade and Employment and was the outcome of the failure of negotiating governments to create the International Trade Organization (ITO). GATT was formed in 1947 and lasted until 1994; it was replaced by the World Trade Organization in 1995.

50 Articles 1 to 21 TRIPS.

51 Agreement on Trade-related Aspects of Intellectual Property Rights (TRIPS), Annex 1C to the Agreement establishing the World Trade Organization (WTO).

8.3.5 The World Intellectual Property Organization (WIPO) and the WIPO Treaty

The World Intellectual Property Organization (WIPO) was established in Stockholm by the WIPO Convention on 14 July 1967 (amended on 28 September 1979). WIPO's main purpose is to encourage creative activity with a mandate from its member states to promote the protection of intellectual property throughout the world. WIPO's International Bureau is based in Geneva and had 184 contracting signatory states at the time this book was published. Membership is open to any state that:

(i)   is a member of the Paris Union ('the Paris Convention') for the Protection of Industrial Property, or of the Berne Union ('the Berne Convention') for the Protection of Literary and Artistic Works;

(ii)   or is a member of the United Nations, or of any of the United Nations' specialized agencies, or of the International Atomic Energy Agency, or that is a party to the statute of the International Court of Justice;

(iii)   or is invited by the WIPO General Assembly to become a member state of the organization.

WIPO provides a range of services for owners and users of intellectual property, including international registration services, which enable applicants to seek protection for their patents, trademarks or designs in multiple countries by filing a single application. WIPO maintains an IP classification system and database. The modernization of WIPO legislation is ongoing, including the **WIPO Performances and Phonograms Treaty** of 20 December 2006 and the **WIPO Broadcasters Treaty** of 8 March 2007, the latter providing protection against signal theft on an international level. WIPO's 'Arbitration and Mediation Center' offers alternative dispute resolution services for private parties involved in international IP disputes, including so-called 'cybersquatting', where an internet domain name is in dispute.

WIPO has cultivated multi-voiced consultations towards an instrument concerned with proprietary protection. Together with UNESCO in 2003, it brought about a convention aimed primarily at preserving and enhancing both tangible and intangible elements of indigenous cultures,[52] resulting partly in the 'Convention on Rights in Traditional Cultural Expressions' of 2005, which affords individual copyright to 'any forms in which traditional culture and knowledge are expressed' provided that they are characteristic of the community's culture and social identity and cultural heritage.[53] This effectively means the introduction of community musical rights in cultural material. But who will claim the rights in digitization of such works? On the one hand there is now free access to folk and indigenous music and cultures; on the other, producers are likely to claim their own IP on sound recordings if they have found a musical gem. Why else would a producer or label wish to invest in the recordings and production of traditional folk songs, groups or dances such as the music of the *Sardanes*, the music for the Catalan circle dance, or finding the Tyrol's next top yodelling idol in the 'yodel off' organized by the Tyrolean Tourist Board?

There appears to be an abundance of global IP legislation and conventions that protect musical works.[54] In addition, performers and producers of phonograms enjoy protection under the **WIPO**

---

52 United Nations Educational, Scientific and Cultural Organization, Convention for the Safeguarding of the Intangible Cultural Heritage, which was adopted in 2003 and came into force in 2006.

53 Source: World Intellectual Property Organization, Convention on the Protection of Traditional Cultural Expressions (GRTKF/IC/9/4, 2005). For further information, see WIPO's Inter-Governmental Committee on Intellectual Property and Genetic Resources, Traditional Knowledge and Folklore, 13th Session, 13–17 October 2008.

54 TRIPS; Berne Convention for the Protection of Literary and Artistic Works of 28 September 1979; WIPO Copyright Treaty (WCT) of 20 December 1996; Copyright Universal Convention of 6 September 1952, Articles 9 et seq.

Performers and Phonograms Treaty (WPPT).[55] The WIPO Treaty harmonized the exchange of the music trade at international level, even though some conflicts still exist at World Trade Organization (WTO) level, regarding international copyright law which relates to musical works in particular.[56]

It is, then, for savvy IP and entertainment lawyers to sort out legal processes for enforcing copyrights and IP rights through the maze of the above conventions and international treaties, linked to domestic copyright law.

8.4 The Copyright, Designs and Patents Act 1988 (CDPA)

Under the **Copyright Act 1911** (and arguably under the 1956 Act), a literary work did not enjoy the status of 'work' for the purposes of potential copyright protection unless it had been reduced to writing or some other material form. The **Copyright, Designs and Patents Act 1988** (CDPA or 'the UK Copyright Act') introduced an immediate copyright which exists automatically in original literary, dramatic, musical or artistic works. 'Literary work' means any work, other than a dramatic or musical work, which is written, spoken or sung, and accordingly includes tables, compilations, computer programs and databases.[57] 'Dramatic work' includes dance or mime and 'musical work' means a work consisting of music, *exclusive* of any words or action intended to be sung, spoken or performed with the music.[58] Copyright does not subsist in a literary, dramatic or musical work *unless* and *until* it is recorded, in writing or otherwise.[59] The expression of general or common ideas cannot be protected – for example, no one could lay claim to the generic concept of battles in outer space. Similarly, character names cannot usually be copyrighted, although they can be registered as trademarks to distinguish them as a separate brand such as 'James Bond'. Illustrations or original images of those characters can also be protected. Copyright also applies to the World Wide Web, which is regarded as a publishing medium ('the publisher'), where copyright will be created automatically once an item or photo is published.

See Chapter ◄ 9.8.1

8.4.1 Fundamental principles

The purpose of the **Copyright Act** is to protect the rights of creators to be paid for, and to control the use of their works and to address the needs of users who want access to material protected by copyright. The balance is achieved by providing the creator with statutory rights. These are limited by 'exceptions' for the benefit of certain users (e.g. educational establishments).

The categories covered by the **Copyright, Designs and Patents Act 1988** (CDPA – 'the UK Copyright Act') are:

1. Literary, dramatic and musical works;
2. Databases;
3. Artistic works;
4. Sound recordings and films;
5. Broadcasts and cable programmes (and certain satellite programmes);
6. Published editions.

---

55 Adopted in Geneva in December 1996; WPPT came into force on 20 May 2002.
56 For example the dispute between the US and China in which Japan joined as a third party (among other countries) which was initiated on 10 April 2007.
57 s. 3(1) CDPA.
58 Ibid.
59 s. 3(2) CDPA.

Under the CDPA, copyright arises automatically when an original literary, dramatic, musical or artistic work is created, provided it is either written down or otherwise recorded in some material form. This means there is no form of official registration of copyright in the UK. 'Recorded' also includes the digital medium, storage on a computer hard drive or memory stick, as well as digital music recordings. A copyrighted work under UK copyright legislation is relatively easy to prove within the CDPA and does not need to meet such stringent standards of novelty and rigours as an invention needs in order to satisfy patent laws or trademarks. Section 4(1)(a) CDPA even provides that artistic works, including photographs, are protected as copyright works 'irrespective of artistic quality'.

See Chapter 9.8 →

A higher standard is applied by the courts where derivative works are concerned, particularly in the digital age of so-called 'recreative' works. These are works that have been derived from, and which purport to be perfectly accurate copies of, antecedent works that were created at an earlier point in history. They can comprise, for example, ancient religious scholarly works, old compositions or music scores and paintings. The recreative author engages in reproducing the work and it is this process which may or may not be defined as 'copying'. This will depend on what raw materials he has to copy from, what sources of information are available to him to help him accurately identify all the expressive contents of the antecedent work that need to be faithfully reproduced, and what tools and resources are available at his disposal to facilitate the execution of his recreative enterprise. In what form that copying takes place will vary significantly in each case. Recreative derivative works are then identical to the antecedent works from which they were copied. The test for breach of copyright will depend on whether there is a material difference between the original works and the derivative work.[60]

The production of the work may involve the exercise of genuine intellectual skill, labour and effort by the creator, in which he may well be excluded from copyright breach, as the House of Lords held in *Walter v Lane* (1900), where the newspaper reporter's published report (taken from his shorthand notes and transcribed) of a public speech by Lord Rosebery was a copyrightable work (see above 8.2.2). An author of a work also has the right not to have a work which he has *not* created falsely attributed to him.[61]

The fundamental principles underlying the **Copyright Act** – covering England, Wales, Scotland and Northern Ireland – are summarized in the following sections of the CDPA:

Section 1(1): Copyright is a property right which subsists in accordance with this Part in the following descriptions of work –

(a) original literary, dramatic, musical or artistic works . . .

Section 2(1): The owner of a copyright in a work of any description has the exclusive right to do the acts specified in Chapter II as the acts restricted by the copyright in a work of that description.

Section 4(1): In this part 'Artistic work' means (a) graphic work, photograph, sculpture or collage, irrespective of artistic quality.

Section 9(1): In this part 'author' in relation to a work means the person who creates it.

Section 16(1): The owner of the copyright work has . . . the exclusive right to do the following acts in the United Kingdom –

---

60 For further discussion see: Pila (2010).
61 s. 80(7) CDPA.

(a) to copy the work

Section 16(2): Copyright in a work is infringed by a person who without the licence of the copyright owner does, or authorises another to do, any of the acts restricted by the copyright.

Section 20(1) The communication to the public of the work is an act restricted by the copyright.

Section 20 (2) References in this Part to communication to the public by electronic transmission, and in relation to work include –

(b) the making available to the public of the work by electronic transmission in such a way that members of the public may access it from a place and at a time individually chosen to them.

The Act also covers 'related rights' which include performers', producers' and broadcasting organizations' rights.[62]

Under s. 16 CDPA, the copyright owner has the exclusive right to copy the work, issue copies to the public, rent or lend the work to the public, perform the work in public, communicate the work to the public and make an adaptation of the work. 'Performance' includes a dramatic performance (including dance and mime), a musical performance, a reading or recitation of a literary work, or a performance of a variety act or any similar presentation.[63]

Section 20 CDPA makes the communication to the public an act restricted by the copyright. Communication to the public includes making it available by electronic transmission in such a way that members of the public may access it from a place and at a time individually chosen by them. Section 20 prohibits communication 'to the public' via the Internet and safeguards copyrighted work that is made available online without the author's consent, for example, offering a film for download via a website, transmitting a film via cable or wireless technology or streaming a film via the web or emailing a digital file. The exact interpretation of the meaning 'to the public' is left to be interpreted by the courts.

A considerable number of changes have been made to the law in this area since the enactment of the CDPA in 1988. Most of these have resulted from secondary legislation amending the 1988 Act in order to implement EU Directives in the field, namely:

- Directive 91/250/EEC on the legal protection of computer programs;
- Directive 92/100/EEC on rental and lending rights and on certain rights related to copyright in the field of intellectual property;
- Directive 93/83/EEC on the coordination of certain rules concerning copyright and rights related to copyright applicable to satellite broadcasting and cable retransmission;
- Directive 93/98/EEC harmonizing the term of protection of copyright and certain related rights;
- Directive 96/9/EC on the legal protection of databases;
- Directive 98/84/EC on the legal protection of services based on, or consisting of, conditional access; and
- Directive 2001/29/EC on the harmonization of certain aspects of copyright and related rights in the information society.

---

62 Part II CDPA 'Rights in Performances', amended by The Performances (Moral Rights, etc.) Regulations 2006.
63 s. 180(2) (a)–(d) CDPA.

Other changes have arisen from the **Copyright (Visually Impaired Persons) Act 2002**[64] and **The Copyright, etc. and Trademarks (Offences and Enforcement) Act 2002**,[65] and from various legislation since 1988 in areas outside copyright. EC legislation has also led to the introduction of 'publication right' and 'database right' in UK law (see above). These changes necessitated a considerable number of consequential amendments throughout the legislation, too numerous to be indicated by footnotes in this text.

In many cases, previous references to 'broadcasts or cable programmes' as species of copyright works have become references simply to 'broadcasts' (as redefined), and references to the act of 'broadcasting or inclusion in a cable programme service' have become references to 'communication to the public'. However, this is not always so, and readers are advised to consult the legislation as amended online if they need to determine the precise position previously on provisions now referring to 'broadcasts', 'broadcasting' or 'communication to the public and other amendments to the CDPA 1988.

8.4.2 The protection of literary, dramatic, musical and artistic works and joint ownership

Under the CDPA 1988, a literary work is defined as 'any work, other than a dramatic or musical work, which is written, spoken or sung'.[66] This means that copyright cannot subsist in a literary work which is merely spoken or sung, unless and until it is recorded, for example in writing or recorded in other form.[67] On that basis, the 1988 Act introduced a change which impacted significantly on the principle established in *Walter v Lane* (see above 8.2.2).[68]

'Artistic works' can mean graphic work, a painting, drawing, map, engraving, etching, lithograph, woodcut or similar work; a photograph, sculpture or collage, a work of architecture, such as either a building or a model of a building, or a work of artistic craftsmanship – irrespective of artistic quality.[69] Generally the author of the work is the first owner of copyright. If there are two or more authors of a work, they jointly have first ownership of copyright. In relation to sound recordings, this is the producer.[70] In commercial films the principal director and producer are usually joint authors. The author of a broadcast is the person who made it. The publisher of a typographical arrangement of a published edition is the author of it and so on.

It is important to distinguish ownership of a physical product with the ownership of the copyright embodied within it. For example, the purchase of a pop music DVD does not mean that the purchaser owns the copyright in the musical work within it or the copyright in the sound recording. Therefore purchasing a DVD alone does not entitle the purchaser to copy the work or do any other acts which are restricted to the copyright owner. The same goes for the purchase of a book – it does not mean that the purchaser owns the copyright of the manuscript.

See Chapter 9.7.6 →

---

64 This came into force on 31 October 2003; this statute removes barriers to equal access to information for people with sight loss; the UK Copyright Act (CDPA) has to be applied equally to the creation of 'accessible' copies required by a person with a visual impairment as much as to anything else, particularly in areas of activity such as education and public libraries.

65 This Act amends the criminal provisions in intellectual property law, more specifically the law relating to copyright, rights in performances, fraudulent reception of conditional access transmissions by use of unauthorised decoders and trademarks. The Act brings about some rationalization of these criminal provisions by removing some of the differences. The three areas in which rationalization is provided by the Act are maximum penalties for certain offences in intellectual property law, police search and seizure powers relating to offences and court orders on forfeiture of illegal material that may have been seized during investigation of offences. The Act does not make any changes to the scope of criminal offences in intellectual property law so that the type of behaviour that can give rise to an offence remains the same (see also Chapter 8.10.3).

66 s. 3(1) CDPA.

67 s. 3(2) CDPA.

68 For further discussion of copyright in the spoken word and the origins of authorship, see Gravells (2007).

69 s. 4 CDPA.

70 s. 5(1) CDPA.

The right to be identified as the author of dramatic, musical or artistic work is defined in sections 77 and 78 CDPA. The right has to be asserted by the author in order to have effect. Section 77(4) states that:

The author of an artistic work has the right to be identified whenever –

(a) the work is published commercially or exhibited in public, or a visual image of it is broadcast or included in a cable programme service;
(b) a film including a visual image of the work is shown in public or copies of such a film are issued to the public; or
(c) in the case of a work of architecture in the form of a building or a model for a building, a sculpture or a work of artistic craftsmanship, copies of a graphic work representing it, or of a photograph of it, are issued to the public.

Where two or more people collaborate in creating a work and their individual contributions are not distinct, they are joint authors of that work ('joint authorship' or 'joint ownership'). However, where two or more persons collaborate but it is possible to determine the separate parts attributable to each author, it will not be a work of joint authorship. In *Ray v Classic FM* (1998),[71] Robin Ray (1934–98)[72] brought an action against Classic FM, alleging infringement of his copyright in five documents containing his proposals for categorizing the tracks on the classical music radio station's recordings and in a catalogue created by him over a five-year period. Robin Ray was one of the first executives hired by the start-up commercial classical music radio station, Classic FM, with which he remained associated from 1991 to 1997. He undertook the mammoth task of drawing up a list of 50,000 pieces of classical music, and rating them for popular appeal, which became the basis for the Classic FM playlist. This list proved to be extremely attractive to similar popular classical music radio stations in other countries. Ray's legal dispute centred on the question as to who was entitled to the copyright in the playlist and ratings. Classic FM claimed joint authorship of the works on the basis that Mr Ray had simply put into writing ideas initiated by the radio station's representatives at a series of meetings concerning the contents of the catalogue and its categories. The Chancery Division upheld Mr Ray's claim, that in order to be a joint author for the purposes of s. 10 CDPA, a *significant* creative contribution as an author had to be made to the production of the work which was not distinct from that of the other author with whom there was a collaboration. The contribution had to be something which was incorporated into the finished work and protected by copyright. Since copyright did not subsist in the ideas, but in their written expression (known as 'penmanship'), a joint author had to do more than contribute ideas and had to participate in the writing or be the creator of the work. Although penmanship did not have to be exercised, a joint author had to have a direct responsibility for what ended up on paper, which was equivalent to penmanship. The court observed that Mr Ray had not merely written down the ideas of Classic FM's representatives, but was solely responsible for the five documents, the catalogue and ideas contained in it. Robin Ray was duly awarded copyright in the five documents.

The decision in the *Robin Ray* case set out several factors to consider when deciding upon ownership:

---

71 [1998] ECC 488 (Ch D).
72 From 1965 he was the chairman of the BBC's *Call My Bluff*; he was also a regular panel member on the BBC's classical music series, *Face the Music* from 1966 onwards. Ray was able to recognize all kinds of musical pieces, including the composer, opus and Köchel number for Mozart pieces.

1. Commissioning in itself is not indicative of ownership;
2. The agreement may state ownership in the work;
3. A contractor is entitled to retain copyright in the absence of any terms to the contrary;
4. The usual contractual rules will be applied. Conditions/terms must be:

    i)   reasonable and equitable;
    ii)   necessary to effect business efficacy;
    iii) obvious;
    iv)   clearly expressed;
    v)   not contradictory to other express terms.

8.4.3 What do Spandau Ballet and Procul Harum have in common?

In the *Spandau Ballet* case,[73] the court ruled that to be a joint owner of copyright the parties must have *substantially* contributed to the song's creation, not just to its interpretation. As per Parker J:

> . . . There is a vital distinction between composition or creation of a musical work on the one hand and performance or interpretation of it on the other.[74]

So, if a drummer just adds a short drum loop, this would not make any material difference to the song, and would not justify the claim that the song was co-written. However, one could argue that the performable arrangement produced by a group would constitute a separate copyright for the new arrangement.

In the landmark case of *Fisher v Brooker* (2009),[75] the House of Lords asserted the joint ownership and copyright in the famous song 'A Whiter Shade of Pale' (released on 12 May 1967), eventually granted to Mathew Fisher of the 1960s group Procul Harum. Crucial in this case was that Mr Fisher made his claim some forty years after the song's release.

❖ **KEY CASE**   *Fisher v Brooker* (2009)

Facts:

On 7 March 1967, the original members of Procul Harum, namely Gary Brooker, Bobby Harrison, Ray Royer and Dave Knight, entered into a recording contract ('the licence') with Essex Music Ltd ('Essex'). Shortly after, Matthew Fisher ('the claimant') joined the band as Hammond organist. The licence gave the label the right to manufacture, sell, lease, otherwise use or dispose of the band's performances. In other words, Essex could exploit any recording made by the band under the **Copyright Act of 1956** 'absolutely'.

'A Whiter Shade of Pale' ('the song') became an instant worldwide hit after the recording was released as a single by the Decca label on 12 May 1967. The band had registered the song with the Performing Rights Society (PRS) and the Mechanical Copyright Protection Society (MCPS) on 17 March 1967.

---

73 *Hadley v Kemp* [1999] EMLR 589.
74 Ibid., at para 589 (Park J).
75 [2009] UKHL 41 (HL).

The claimant had crucially composed the familiar organ solo at the beginning of the song and he raised the question of his having a share in the rights of the song with Brooker and the band's manager Keith Reid at the time of the recording. But he was rebuffed. Mathew Fisher left the band in 1969. In 1993 Essex's rights were assigned to Onward Music Ltd.

During April 2005, the claimant notified the respondents, Gary Brooker, 'Essex' and Onward Music, of his intention to claim his share of the musical copyright in the song. After his claim was rejected, Mr Fisher began legal proceedings on 31 May 2005. At the High Court, the respondents argued that the claimant was far too late, nearly forty years, in claiming the copyright for joint owner- and authorship of the song. They asked the court for laches and to strike out the claim under the doctrines of estoppel. After a number of cross appeals, the case reached the House of Lords in 2009.

Decision:
Giving reasons, their Lordships declared that Matthew Fisher was joint owner of copyright: 'Mr Fisher's instrumental introduction – the organ solo – is sufficiently different from what Mr Brooker had composed on the piano to qualify in law, and by quite a wide margin, as an original contribution to the work.'[76]

Their Lordships held that it did not matter that the claimant had not asserted his joint authorship and copyright for such a long time. His claim was still valid even after 40 years and could not be defeated by equitable remedies. The fact that the respondents had derived substantial financial benefits from the song far outweighed any detriment resulting from the claimant's delay. Their Lordships revoked the respondents' licence to exploit the song, awarding Mr Fisher a 40 per cent share in royalties, backdated to the date of his original claim in 2005.

Fisher v Brooker set the precedent for any other claims of this kind where an artist wishes to assert his rights in a song or recording during his lifetime. The court ruling meant that Mathew Fisher (and his heirs) could receive royalties in the song – at least from the point of assertion of the claim but not from the date of composition. For the various royalty collecting societies, such as the PRS (Performing Rights Society) and the MCPS (Mechanical Copyright Protection Society), it meant that they had to amend their records and backdate the royalties payable to Mr Fisher to the start of his legal action.

See Chapter ◀ 9.3.2

8.4.4 Economic rights, royalties and performers' rights

In March 2010, EMI was being sued in the US for alleged non-payment of royalties in an action brought against the British record label by a company in Tennessee that oversees payments to music writers, namely Bluewater Music Services. The music copyright administrator filed a lawsuit against EMI Music (North America) involving dozen of songs by artists including Chris Le Doux and the Doobie Brothers. The songs were used in compilations and sold as mobile telephone ringtones. Disclosure of the action came just a few weeks after Pink Floyd won a court claim against EMI that prevented the record company from selling single downloads of the band's albums on the Internet.

---

76 Ibid., at 42.

Pink Floyd had gone to the High Court in London to seek clarification of its contract with EMI, which was last negotiated in 1998–9, before the expansion of music online. The ruling was an additional blow for EMI, owned by Guy Hands' Terra Firma, a private equity group, which lost £1.7bn in 2009.[77]

Intellectual property rights underpin the economic theory by which the owner of a copyright can make money from his published work, song or picture by way of royalties. Royalty payments (or 'royalties') are usage-based payments made by one party (usually the licensee) to another (the licensor) for ongoing use of an asset, such as an intellectual property right. Royalties are typically a percentage of gross or net sales derived from the sale of a book, music score, music CD or music download.[78] A royalty interest is the right of the author or creator of the work to collect a stream of future royalty payments, used in the publishing and music industries to describe a percentage ownership of future production or revenues from a given licence agreement.[79]

The CDPA expresses the economic rights of a copyright owner as a series of 'restricted acts' that only the copyright owner can do or authorize, such as granting consent to a performer to perform his music,[80] or permission to a publisher to 'exploit' a book by way of a publication licence. These restricted acts are set out as follows:

1. Copying or reproduction right;[81]
2. Issuing or distribution right;[82]
3. Lending and rental rights;[83]
4. Public performance right;[84]
5. Communication right (including broadcasting right);[85]
6. Adaptation right (including translation right).[86]

Breaches of these rights are called primary infringements, a strict liability offence, where the claimant does not have to prove intention, recklessness or carelessness. This means that purely innocent breaches may be actionable. A further group of 'secondary infringements' such as selling, importing, providing premises for infringing performances or equipment to produce infringing items are set out in sections 22 to 27 CDPA. In such instances, the claimant must prove actual or constructive knowledge on the part of the defendant that they either knew or ought to have known that they were committing an infringing act.

The landmark case of *Grisbrook v MGN Ltd* (2009)[87] examined how far licence terms can be implied when technology has moved on beyond what the legislators of the **Copyright Act** initially intended or even imagined. When freelance photographer Alan Grisbrook began working for the *Daily Mirror*, the World Wide Web did not exist and there were certainly no online editions of newspapers. There was little time or need for written commission agreements and his celebrity photos were simply verbally commissioned by editors. It was then understood that if Mr Grisbrook's photos were not used for a particular edition, they would go into the *Mirror*'s photo library of back

---

77 Source: 'EMI sued over failure to pay royalties on songs by Doobie Brothers', *Observer*, 28 March 2010.
78 For royalty advice and collections for artists and singer-song-writers see: Universal Music Group: <http://www.umusicpub. com/artistswriters_newsignings.aspx>, accessed 24 November 2010.
79 For further detailed authority on the publishing industry see: Owen (2007).
80 Part II CDPA 'Rights in Performances; Chapter 1, sections 180ff: Rights conferred on performers and persons having recording rights.
81 s.17 CDPA.
82 s.18 CDPA.
83 s. 18A CDPA.
84 s. 19 CDPA.
85 s. 20 CDPA.
86 s. 21 CDPA.
87 [2009] EWHC 2520 (Ch D).

copies. Little did Alan Grisbrook know that some twenty years later, his 'exclusive' photos of celebrities would appear on the newspaper's website, easily and publically accessible to the world at large via the Internet. Alan Grisbrook's work was first commissioned in 1981 to provide photographs for the *Daily Mirror's* Diary page. For the next 16 years he supplied the *Mirror's* publishers, Mirror Group Newspapers (MGN), with hundreds of photographs, many of which made the front page. Most of the photos were of celebrities or other well-known individuals, and many of the photographs were taken late at night, showing the person concerned emerging from a restaurant or nightclub.

❖ **KEY CASE**　　　*Grisbrook v MGN Ltd* (2009)

Facts:

Between 1981 and 1997 photojournalist Alan Grisbrook supplied hundreds of photographs of celebrities to MGN, publisher of the *Daily Mirror* newspaper. There was no written contract between Grisbrook and MGN; all pictures had been commissioned verbally by editors. All used and unused photos went into MGN's archives and Mr Grisbrook was paid whenever a photograph was used. It was acknowledged that Mr Grisbrook had retained copyright in the photos and had licensed MGN to use the material in this way. MGN had a hard-copy picture library of more than 30 million photographs, transparencies and negatives. If the picture appeared as part of a reproduction of a newspaper page ('rag-out'), the photographer would not be due a further fee. MGN subsequently developed a digital picture library called FastFoto, containing more than a million images. Mr Grisbrook's complaint centred on the online FastFoto library.

In 1998, Mr Grisbrook commenced proceedings to recover unpaid licence fees amounting to £161,000.[88] In 1999, he complained that 191 of his images were included in the website. In 2002, in a consent order resulting from Grisbrook's 1998 and 1999 actions, MGN undertook not to infringe copyright in his photographs. Grisbrook subsequently found his material was still being used on some of MGN's websites: 6,000 original photographs, negatives and transparencies and 2,000 images on the FastFoto system. MGN removed some of the material, but refused to remove the images from websites that offered complete back issues of the publications.[89]

In 2008, Mr Grisbrook commenced proceedings for breach of a court undertaking, arguing that the publication of this material amounted to a copyright infringement and was, therefore, in breach of the undertaking that MGN had given. He sought an order for imprisonment of the officers of MGN, and sequestration of MGN's assets. MGN argued that the licence originally granted by Grisbrook permitting publication in the newspaper also extended to subsequent reproduction of the published material, including archiving and making it publicly available via its website. MGN relied on the defence of public interest under s. 171(3) CDPA.

---

88 Mr Grisbrook's counsel cited *Ray v Classic FM* (see above 8.4.3), where Mr Justice Lightman had taken the 'minimalist' approach following decisions of the House of Lords in *Liverpool CC v Irwin* [1977], and the Court of Appeal in *Philips Electronique v BSB* [1995].

89 The MGN websites included: mydailymirror.com, launched in June 2006 enabling users to buy *Daily Mirror* front pages in the form of posters, T-shirts or greetings cards; arcitext.com, launched in February 2006 allowing subscribers to access the *Daily Mirror* archives as pdf documents which reproduce part of the newspaper as it was printed; and mirrorarchive.co.uk, launched as a test site in April 2007 but intended to be the commercial equivalent of arcitext.com.

Decision:

The Court found that the implied licence did not extend to the exploitation of Mr Grisbrook's photos on back issue websites; this, therefore, amounted to an infringement of copyright. Nevertheless, because it was a difficult question, and one not contemplated at the time the licence was granted or when the consent order was made, MGN was entitled to take a different view. There had been no deliberate breach of the undertaking.

In these circumstances, the Court refused Mr Grisbrook's application, holding that although MGN's actions amounted to infringement of copyright, that right could be adequately protected by a declaration of infringement. Contempt proceedings were not appropriate for the resolution of disputes of this kind.

In the light of the *Grisbrook* judgment, authors of creative works ought to study their agreements with publishers of newspapers (including online editions) carefully.

FOR THOUGHT

How would you advise photographer Alan Grisbrook now when he is asked by a commissioning editor of a news organization (which also has an online edition) whether she can use his photo of a famous celebrity to accompany a front page story? Formulate the standard terms for him.

A composer can grant a recording label the rights to his performances;[90] if recordings are made without his consent or that of the performer, this creates a new action relating to the use of illicit recordings.[91] Rights are also conferred on a performer ('performers' rights') by the provisions of Chapter 3 of Part II CDPA.[92] Performers' moral rights include the right to object to derogatory treatment of their performance.[93] A 'performance' is defined by the CDPA as:

(a)   a dramatic performance (which includes dance and mime);
(b)   a musical performance;
(c)   a reading or recitation of a literary work; or
(d)   a performance of a variety act (or any similar presentation).[94]

An author's or performer's rights are infringed by a person who, without his consent:

(a)   makes a copy or recording of the whole or any substantial part of a qualifying work or performance (directly from the live performance);
(b)   broadcasts live the whole or any substantial part of a qualifying performance; or
(c)   makes a copy or recording of the whole or any substantial part of a qualifying work or performance (e.g. directly from a broadcast of the live performance).[95]

---

90 ss. 181–184 CDPA.
91 ss. 185–188 CDPA.
92 ss. 205 A–F CDPA ('rights in performances' and 'moral rights').
93 s. 205F CDPA.
94 s. 205 F CDPA.
95 s. 182 CDPA.

The Court of Appeal's judgment in the *Sawkins* case[96] caused great concern in the music industry. The case centred on musical scholar, Dr Lionel Sawkins,[97] the world's leading authority on Lalande's musical works.[98] One question before the court in *Sawkins* was what actually constituted 'music' in copyright terms. Was it the sound or the scores from which music was played? This is because the **UK Copyright Act** does not specifically define 'music'.

The crucial question in the *Sawkins* case was whether copyright can subsist in modern performing editions, such as those produced by Dr Sawkins. At the same time, concern was raised that relatively small recording labels, such as Hyperion Records, would be deterred in future from recording rare or obscure music only listened to by niche markets if they were faced with an additional financial burden. Furthermore, would a mere editor of a published (music) edition be granted the elevated status of 'original' composer by overly generous copyright rules?

In 2001, Dr Sawkins had completed three modern performance editions of Lalande's works after spending hundreds of hours making changes and corrections to the existing musical records and notations of Lalande's original works. The editions covered *Te Deum Laudamus* (1684), *La Grande Piece Royale* (1695) and *Venite Exultemus* (1701). The Sawkins' editions contained information in conventional modern musical notation with indications and directions for performers which affected the sounds they produced while playing their instruments, as well as the combination of sounds heard by listeners hearing the performance. Dr Sawkins' had sought to reproduce faithfully Lalande's music in the form of an accurate edition close to the composer's original intentions.

Hyperion Records then produced a CD of early French music, including Lalande recordings of performances using the Sawkins scores. The record label had paid Dr Sawkins a one-off ('killer') fee for providing the performing editions, but refused to pay him any subsequent royalties on the basis that an editor was not entitled to copyright in a performing edition of non-copyright music. Dr Sawkins claimed that his performance editions were *original* musical works with a separate copyright under s. 3 CDPA. Hyperion's counter argument was that Sawkins' works were merely transcriptions of Lalande's music, and continued to deny Dr Sawkins any royalties because they claimed that he had not created *original* musical works within the meaning of the **UK Copyright Act**.

Discussions in the Court of Appeal revolved around possible commercial results of this case, especially as to who actually obtains money from the licence fee. Would the royalties go to the scholar who prepared the performing edition? *Sawkins* ultimately defined 'music' as 'combining sounds for listening to' as opposed to mere noise; a landmark case for composers and musical scholars.

The Court of Appeal held that there had been a breach of s. 77 CDPA, because the Hyperion music CD did not identify Dr Sawkins as the author of the performing editions. Dr Sawkins had clearly spent hundreds of hours making the performing editions, which therefore satisfied the requirement of an 'original' work in the copyright sense. The subsistence of copyright involved an assessment of the *whole* work in which copyright was claimed (see also: *Ladbroke v William Hill* (1964)[99]). Lord Justice Mummery rejected Hyperion's argument that musical copyright could only

---

96 See: *Sawkins v Hyperion Records* [2005] EWCA Civ 565 (CA Civ Div).
97 Dr Lionel Sawkins, a Principal Lecturer in music at the Roehampton Institute in London prior to retirement in 1985, is acknowledged to be a world authority on the music of the French composer Michel-Richard de Lalande. In 2001 the French Government made him an Officier de L'Ordre des Arts et des Lettres. He was twice invited to act as Conseiller Artistique for festivals of music by Lalande in Versailles in conjunction with the Centre de Musique Baroque. Dr Sawkins devoted much of his retirement to preparing editions of Lalande's compositions and of the 22 currently on sale or hire, he has prepared 19. His editions of Lalande (and other Baroque composers such as Lully, Rameau and Royer) have been performed all over the world, and recorded on several different labels.
98 Michel-Richard de Lalande (1657–1726) was the principal court composer of two French kings during the seventeenth and eighteenth centuries. Lalande composed a number of *grands motets* – sacred music written for performance by single voices, choirs and orchestral groups. Few of Lalande's original manuscripts have survived.
99 [1964] 1 WLR 273.

be secured by composition in the form of notes on the score, stating that 'Hyperion's arguments ignored the fact that the totality of the sounds produced by the musicians are affected, or potentially affected, by the information inserted in the performing editions produced by Dr Sawkins'.[100] This meant that the sound on the CD was not just that of the musicians playing music composed by Lalande; on the contrary, in order to make that sound, the musicians had to play from Dr Sawkins' scores in order to 'make music'.

Lord Mummery summarized his reasons why Dr Sawkins' editions were original musical works and therefore entitled to copyright protection in their own right:

(a)   He (Dr Sawkins) originated the performing editions by his own expert and scholarly exertions;
(b)   The editions did not previously exist in that form;
(c)   The contents of his editions affected the combination of sounds produced by the performers; and
(d)   the resulting combination of sounds embodied in the CD was music.

The court awarded damages to Dr Sawkins both for infringement of his copyright and for infringement of his 'moral rights', i.e. the right to be identified as the author of the edition. Furthermore, Hyperion Records were ordered to notify Dr Sawkins and seek his permission before any future exploitation of his work could take place.[101]

In addition to receiving royalties for songwriting and CD sales, performing rights royalties are paid to a songwriter, composer or publisher whenever their music is played or performed in **See Chapter 9.3.1 →** any public space. These royalties are collected on behalf of the record label and/or the producer by the PRS.

FOR THOUGHT

What about the performance editions of the Lalande compositions made by Dr Sawkins? What if an unauthorized sound recording was made of the orchestral performance of Dr Sawkins' music performance score edition of Lalande's works, could Dr Sawkins assert copyright in them as 'original' musical works? How would you advise Dr Sawkins?

8.5 Musical works

Can a recording artist or publishing author protect his name, a song or title by copyright? It depends. Copyright may or may not be available for titles, slogans or logos, depending on whether they contain sufficient authorship. In most circumstances copyright does not protect names. Does an artist or performer need to register his work or sound recording to be protected? Not really, because copyright protection is formality-free in countries party to the **Berne Convention** (see above), which means that protection does not depend on compliance with any formalities such as registration or deposit of copies.

---

100 *Sawkins* [2005] EWCA Civ 565 (CA Civ Div) at 32 (Mummery LJ).
101 The trial took place in May 2004 and lasted six days. Mr Justice Patten gave judgment in favour of Dr Sawkins on 2 July 2004. That judgment was unanimously upheld by the Court of Appeal (Lords Justice Mummery, Mance and Jacob) following a two-day hearing in March 2005. Dr Sawkins was represented by Carter-Ruck and Counsel Richard Arnold QC (in the Court of Appeal only) and Andrew Norris. Carter-Ruck and Andrew Norris acted under conditional fee agreements backed by after-the-event insurance. Source: Press release by Carter-Ruck, 19 May 2005.

Mechanical rights royalties are different and are paid to the songwriter, composer or publisher (the author of copyright) when music is reproduced as a physical product. These royalties are collected by the MCPS.

Copyright is the foundation upon which the music business is built. This intellectual property right gives the creator, owner or author of the work exclusive rights over how it is published, distributed and adapted. Copyright legislation encourages talented composers and performing artists to create musical works, and record companies and music producers to invest in that talent. Copyright is essential in the music business to ensure that creators, artists and producers are adequately protected and compensated for the use and sale of their creative works. Though the original creator ('author') of a piece of work is protected by the **Copyright Act**, IP legislation remains essentially weak in the UK, in spite of additional EU legislation. Civil and criminal remedies available to the UK courts have not really been sufficient to deter piracy and copying of MP3 music files and DVDs.[102]

In order to understand the various levels of copyright, it is important to distinguish between the copyright in a song in terms of music publishing and copyright in the sound recording of that song, where the copyright holder is usually the (music) producer. These are two different copyrights and carry different durations. 'Sampling' is dealt with as 'third party' copyright.

One of the longest-running lawsuits in the US has been between the indie singer-songwriter Aisha and pop superstar Madonna (*Aisha v Madonna* (2005)[103]). A former child prodigy in her native Jamaica, Aisha Goodison, claims that Madonna has hacked into her online song catalogue and has plagiarized her work, thereby breaching US copyright law. In her Miami lawsuit, Aisha called Madonna a 'chronic copyright infringer and plagiarizer'. Aisha claimed, for example, that titles such as 'Like A Virgin,' 'Vogue', 'Justify My Love,' and songs such as 'Ray Of Light' and 'What It Feels Like For A Girl' were originally written by her. Madonna's recording label, Warner Bros, was also being sued as co-defendant for allegedly allowing the intellectual property theft. Aisha alleged that Warners allowed such 'misconduct' to continue because of the substantial profits made from Madonna's success.

8.5.1 Sound recordings and rights in performances

Sound recordings of, for instance, films, are known as 'derivative works', that is they derive from works which themselves are copyrighted (film sound track). These are covered by section 5 CDPA, meaning:

(a) a recording of sounds, from which the sounds may be reproduced; or

(b) a recording of the whole or any part of a literary, dramatic or musical work, from which sounds reproducing the work or part may be produced, regardless of the medium on which the recording is made or the method by which the sounds are reproduced or produced.[104]

A sound recording or film is 'released' when it is first published, broadcast or included in a cable programme service, or in the case of a film or film soundtrack, the film is first shown in public. Copyright protection in sound recordings and broadcasts exists in UK copyright law for 50 years from the end of the calendar year in which they are first broadcast (see below 8.6).

---

102 For further details see: Harrison (2008).
103 *Aisha Goodison & Sonustar v Madonna Ciccione; Madonna Richie & Time Warner AOL; Warner Bros Records and Others* [2005] District of Florida, Case No: Civ-05-22618, 14 October 2005.
104 s. 5(1) CDPA.

Live performances are often recorded or transmitted and may be sold for a profit, for example a live recording of a comedy act. While separate copyright subsists in the recording of the performer, the performance itself is also IP protected. The performance then gives rise to performer's rights which – in turn – are covered by the term 'dramatic performances', which include dance and mime, musical performances, readings and recitations of literary works and variety acts. Circus acts can also be included and certain sporting events, such as ice dancing. A 'recording', in relation to a performance, means a film or sound recording, and must be:

(a)   made directly from the live performance;
(b)   made from a broadcast of the performance; or
(c)   made, directly or indirectly, from another recording of the performance.[105]

The rights conferred to the performer or recording artist are independent rights in copyright (and moral rights), relating to any work performed or any film or sound recording of, or broadcast of the performance, and therefore have independent obligations arising on behalf of third parties. All these rights include the right to carry out any of these acts with a substantial part of the work. The performance (or part thereof) is then assessed qualitatively in order to establish the economic interest (royalties) in the performance of the work (see above 8.4.4). A performer's rights are infringed by a person who, without consent, makes a copy of a recording of the whole or any substantial part of a qualifying performance (other than for his private or domestic use).[106]

8.5.2 Exclusive rights

In December 2008, Warner Music Group ('Warners') ordered the video-sharing site YouTube to remove its exclusive recording artists James Blunt, Madonna and Led Zeppelin because of a disagreement over royalties. Warners argued that the Google-owned company had not been willing to accept contractual terms which would fairly and appropriately compensate the recording artists, songwriters, labels and publishers for their copyrighted works.[107]

A granting of an 'exclusive licence' means the copyright owner grants a person, recording company or publisher permission to exercise a particular right exclusively (even to the exclusion of the copyright owner themselves). An exclusive licence can be limited in the rights given and the time period and firmly falls within the realms of contract law. An exclusive licence must be made in writing. For its correct form, this contract must be signed by or on behalf of the copyright owner who in turn authorizes the licence – to the exclusion of all other persons, including the person granting the licence – to exercise a right which would otherwise be exercisable exclusively by the copyright owner.[108]

The recording right in relation to performers is covered by sections 185 to 188 CDPA. Here the **Copyright Act** deals with exclusive recording rights of a performer and the record company, where the label is entitled to the exclusion of all other persons (including the performer) to make recordings of one or more of his performances with a view to their commercial exploitation.[109] This section of the CDPA essentially deals with the problem of 'bootlegging', which is the making of unofficial or unauthorized taped recordings of live performances and the making of pirate copies which, in turn, would breach the record company's sound recording copyright.[110] Exclusive

---

105   Ibid.
106   ss.182A–D added by SI 1996/2967; s.182A(1A) added, by SI 2003/2498.
107   Source: Warner Music Group news website, available at <http://www.wmg.com/newsdetails>, accessed 24 November 2010.
108   s. 92(1) CDPA.
109   s. 182D(8) CDPA, added by SI 2006/18.
110   Under s. 5 CDPA.

recording rights are then 'assigned' to one label ('the qualifying party') by way of an assignment or licence (contract law). Both parties then have the benefit of an exclusive recording contract and all recordings and performances will then be subject to exclusive commercial exploitation; this means with a view to the recordings being sold or let for hire, or shown or played in public.[111]

It is worth noting that an exclusive licensee has the same right in title (to sue in their own name) as the copyright owner in this respect. Therefore, the exclusive licence holder can also take action for copyright infringement without joining the copyright owner to the action – which is what some of the famous labels regularly do against samplers and online file-sharers, such as EMI, Warners or Sony. An exclusive licence holder has the same rights against a successor in title who is bound by the licence as he has against the person granting the licence.[112]

Is UK copyright law compliant in relation to defences or permitted acts? Article 9(2) of the **Berne Convention** introduced the 'three-steps test', which imposes on signatories to the treaty constraints on the possible limitations and exceptions to exclusive rights under national copyright laws. The 'three steps' clause was subsequently included in several international treaties on Intellectual Property (IP) such as the TRIPS Agreement, the WIPO Copyright Treaty, the EU Copyright Directive and the WIPO Performances and Phonograms Treaty (see above 8.3).

The 'three-steps-test' is now defined by Article 13 TRIPS:

> . . . members shall confine limitations and exceptions to exclusive rights to certain special cases which do not conflict with a normal exploitation of the work and do not unreasonably prejudice the legitimate interests of the rights holder.

'Three steps' then imposes limitations on exclusive copyrights which are confined to certain special cases that do not conflict with a normal exploitation of the work and do not unreasonably prejudice the legitimate interests of the author. The 'three steps' test is seen as the most enduring of standards affecting copyright limitations. Its application outlines the delicate balance between exclusive rights and sufficient breathing space for the free flow of ideas and information. The problem is that at no point is this mentioned in the **UK Copyright Act** (CDPA 1988), though the UK argues that the defences are balanced in such a way as to satisfy the general requirement. Some would argue that this is not the case.

8.6 The duration of copyright

The original copyright legislation – that copyright subsists for 50 years from the death of the author – was superseded by EU legislation which states that all musical, literary, dramatic and artistic works have a 70-year duration of copyright after the author's death.[113] As part of the EU harmonization process on copyright, Article 1 of Directive 2006/116[114] states that:

> . . . the rights of an author of a literary or artistic work within the meaning of Article 2 of the *Berne Convention* shall run for the life of the author and for 70 years after his death, irrespective of the date when the work is lawfully made available to the public.

The duration of copyright in a broadcast or cable programme expires at the end of the period of 50 years from the end of the calendar year in which the broadcast was made or the programme was

---

111 s. 185 CDPA.
112 s. 92(2) CDPA.
113 s. 12 CDPA ,as amended by the Duration of Copyright and Rights in Performances Regulations 1995 (SI 1995 NO. 3297).
114 On the 'Term of Protection of Copyright and Certain Related Rights Enforcement Directive' of 12 December 2006 ('the harmonization Directive').

included in a cable programme service. Where the work has originated from outside the European Union or the author is not an EU national, the situation is slightly different. In this situation, the copyright will normally last for as long as the work attracts copyright protection in the country of origin or the EU, whichever is the shorter. If, for instance, the copyright in Costa Rica might be the lifetime of an author plus 120 years, the Costa Rican author would only receive lifetime copyright (and royalties) plus 70 years in any EU member state. What is important is the country where the work was first published.[115]

In the case of unpublished works or where the author is unknown, it can be quite difficult to work out the exact term of protection. The following explanation provides some detail about what might affect the term of copyright. In general, unpublished manuscripts will be protected by copyright until at least the end of the year 2039. In the case of unpublished works where the identity of the author is unknown, but where there is every ground to presume that he is a national of a country of the **Berne Convention**, it becomes a matter for legislation in that country to designate the competent authority which shall represent the author and shall be entitled to protect and enforce his rights in the countries of the Union.[116] For older unpublished works, the situation is more complicated, but for any literary, dramatic or musical work that was still unpublished at 1 August 1989, or which was created from 1 August 1989 to 31 December 2005, the term of protection lasts at least until the end of 2039.[117]

For artistic works, other than photographs and engravings and works of unknown authorship, that were created before 1 January 1996, the term of protection even for unpublished works is life of the author plus 50 years after his death, but that term of protection may have been extended or revived from 1 January 1996. For literary, dramatic, musical and artistic works created on or *after* 1 January 1996, the term of protection does not depend on whether or not the work is published so the term of protection is as set out generally for these works.[118] Thus, even if the work is only published for the first time in the last year of copyright protection, copyright will still expire at the end of that year. However, publication rights may apply to works that are published for the first time after copyright has expired. For engravings and anonymous or pseudonymous artistic works of all types, other than photographs, which were created before 1 January 1996 and, if created before 1 August 1989, were unpublished at that date, the term of protection lasts at least until the end of 2039. The duration of copyright in photographs is dependent upon when the photograph was taken.

The **Copyright Designs and Patents Act 1988** cannot be retrospective, that is, it only covers works that have been created since 1 August 1989 when the act came into force. For works created *before* that date, one has to refer to the previous copyright legislation (see above 8.2.3). However, the EC 'Duration of Copyright and Rights in Performances Regulations 1995' was retrospective and harmonized the situation regarding the length of copyright protection for existing works irrespective of when they were created.

There are several different categories under which different materials are classified in the **1988 Copyright Act** and subsequent amendments and additions by way of EU legislation. Here follows a summary of duration of copyrights:

i. Literary, dramatic, musical or artistic works

Seventy years from the end of the calendar year in which the last remaining author of the work dies. If the author is unknown, copyright will last for 70 years from the end of the

---

115 See Article 5 Berne Convention 'rights guaranteed outside the country of origin and in the country of origin'.
116 Article 15(4) Berne Convention.
117 See also: s. 93 CDPA for copyright to pass 'under will' with unpublished work; see also s. 169 CDPA 'anonymous unpublished works'.
118 See also: s. 191E CDPA 'performer's property right to pass under will with unpublished original recording'.

calendar year in which the work was created, although if it is made available to the public during that time, (by publication, authorized performance, broadcast, exhibition, etc.), then the duration will be 70 years from the end of the year that the work was first made available.

ii. **Sound recordings and broadcasts**

Fifty years from the end of the calendar year in which the work was created, or, if the work is released within that time: 50 years from the end of the calendar year in which the work was first released.

iii. **Films**

Seventy years from the end of the calendar year in which the last principal director, producer, author or composer dies. If the work is of unknown authorship: 70 years from end of the calendar year of creation, or if made available to the public in that time, 70 years from the end of the year the film was first made available.

iv. **Typographical arrangement of published editions**

Twenty-five years from the end of the calendar year in which the work was first published.[119]

v. **Broadcasts and cable programmes**

Fifty years from the end of the calendar year in which the broadcast was made.[120]

vi. **Crown copyright**

Crown copyright will exist in works made by an officer of the Crown. This includes items such as legislation and documents and reports produced by government bodies. Crown copyright will last for a period of 125 years from the end of the calendar year in which the work was made. If the work was commercially published within 75 years of the end of the calendar year in which it was made, Crown copyright will last for 50 years from the end of the calendar year in which it was published.

vii. **Parliamentary copyright**

Parliamentary copyright will apply to work that is made by or under the direction or control of the House of Commons or the House of Lords and will last until 50 years from the end of the calendar year in which the work was made.

How does one establish which authors are still in copyright since there is no national register for copyright works in the UK? Certain interest groups have been formed to look after common interests, negotiate licences and collect fees – so-called 'collecting agencies'.

See Chapter 9.3

The table below outlines the major categories and their lifetimes:

Literary Works	Written works. Includes lyrics, tables, compilations, computer programmes, letters, memoranda, email and web pages.	Author's life plus 70 years after death. Anonymous/corporation authors: 70 years from year of publication (see above for special rules for unpublished works).
Dramatic Works	Plays, works of dance and mime, and also the libretto of an opera.	Author's life plus 70 years after death.
Crown Copyright	All works made by Her Majesty or by an officer or servant of the Crown in the course of his or her duties	Published work: 50 years from the end of the year when first published. Unpublished work: 125 years beyond the year it was created.

---

119 s. 15 CDPA.
120 s. 14 CDPA.

Parliamentary Copyright	All works made by or under the direction or control of the House of Commons or House of Lords.	Mostly 50 years beyond year it was created. Exceptions include bills of parliament.
Musical Works	Musical scores.	Author's life plus 70 years after death.
Artistic Works	Graphic works (painting, drawing, diagram, map, chart, plan, engraving, etching, lithograph, woodcut) photographs (not part of a moving film), sculpture, collage, works of architecture (buildings and models for buildings), and artistic craftsmanship (e.g. jewellery).	Author's/creator's life plus 70 years after death.
Computer Generated Works	Literary, dramatic and musical works.	50 years from first creation or 50 years from creation if unpublished during that time.
Databases	Collections of independent works, data or other materials which (a) are arranged in a systematic or methodical way, or (b) are individually accessible by electronic or other means.	Full term of other relevant copyrights in the material protected. Also, there is a database right for 15 years (this can roll forward).
Sound Recordings	Regardless of medium or the device on which they are played.	50 years from first recording.
Films	Any medium from which a moving image may be reproduced.	70 years from death of whoever is the last to survive from: principal director, producer, author of dialogue, composer of film music.
Broadcasts	Transmissions via wireless telegraphy through the air (not via cable or wires), includes satellite transmissions.	50 years from when broadcast first made.
Cable Programmes	Services via cable.	50 years from when broadcast first made.
Published Editions	The typography and layout of a literary, dramatic or musical work.	25 years from first publication.

8.6.1 Moral rights and related rights

Linked to UK copyright legislation are 'moral' rights, covered by Chapter IV of the CDPA 1988. Section 80 CDPA deals with the author's right to object to derogatory treatment of his work. Moral rights normally exist for as long as copyright exists in the work. Moral rights involve the right to claim authorship of a work, protect the work from harm and distortion and ultimately protect the creator's reputation. Importantly, the author retains these rights even after assigning any economic rights in the work to a publisher, film or recording company. As a property right, with economic value, it can be transferred to a third party (i.e. spouse or heirs). Moral rights may be waived but cannot be assigned or passed on after the author's death.[121]

As already stated, the CDPA 1988, EU legislation and international treaties give the creators of literary, dramatic, musical and artistic works, sound recordings, broadcasts, films and typographical arrangements of published editions special moral rights to control the ways in which their material may be used. The rights cover broadcast and public performance, copying, adapting, issuing, renting and lending copies to the public. This means the creator has the right to be identified as the author and to object to distortions of his work.

Section 79 CDPA makes some interesting exceptions. Moral rights do not extend to computer programs, the design of a typeface or any computer-generated work. Furthermore, the right does not apply to publications in a newspaper, magazine or periodical, or an encyclopaedia, dictionary, yearbook or other collective work of reference, or a work in which Crown copyright or parliamentary copyright subsists (such as Hansard).[122]

Related rights are a term in copyright law and have developed alongside copyright. They include those of performing artists in their performances, producers of phonograms in their recordings and those of broadcasters in their radio and television programmes. Related rights tend to be of a more limited nature. They are usually of shorter duration and are used in opposition to the term 'author's rights'. Related rights are primarily a result of technological development and generally concern the exploitation of works. The first organized support for the protection of related rights came from the phonogram industry, which sought (and gained, at least in countries following the common law tradition) protection under copyright law against unauthorized copying of phonograms (i.e. records, CDs etc.) under copyright.

Section 103 CDPA deals with remedies for infringement of moral rights, actionable as a breach of statutory duty owed to the person entitled to the right. In such infringement proceedings of the right conferred by section 80 ('right to object to derogatory treatment of work'), the court may, if it thinks it is an adequate remedy in the circumstances, grant an injunction on terms prohibiting the doing of any act unless a disclaimer is made, in such terms and in such manner as may be approved by the court, dissociating the author or director from the treatment of the work.

8.6.2 Paternity and integrity rights

An author's right of paternity is to be identified in his work when it is published commercially, as defined by s. 175 CDPA. In order for the right to be exercised, it must be asserted, arguably weakening the value and strength of the paternity right. Paternity rights – as with moral rights – do not apply to computer programs, computer-generated works or the design of typefaces. These rights also do not extend to works where copyright was originally vested in the author's employer because an employer, having paid for the creation of the work, should have total freedom to exploit the work; a controversial topic for university lecturers who like to have their academic publications attributed only to them, rather than jointly (or solely) to the higher education institution.

Assertion of the right of paternity is a statement in writing by the author that he wishes to be named on all copies of the work. The signing of a manuscript would not be construed as assertion because it merely identifies the author and does not explicitly state his intentions to be identified. A letter, though not a legal document, is sufficient, as long as the author makes his desire to assert his right of paternity clear to the recipient. Anyone who has notice of the written paternity statement will be bound by it. In the case of an assignment or licence, a statement must be attached to it stating that the author wishes to assert his right and thus be named on all copies of the work. The

---

121 s. 86 CDPA.
122 ss. 79(6) and (7) CDPA.

right may also be asserted in relation to the public exhibition of an artistic work by securing that when the author or other first owner of copyright parts with possession of the original, the author is identified on the original or copy (or the frame or mount of that picture).[123] The right may be asserted at any time. Infringements are covered by s. 78(5) CDPA which provides court action and remedies.

Identifying the copyright holder may be straightforward or may require some detective work, and particular care must be taken when obtaining an image from a website or search engine such as 'Google Images' (they only cache a copy and the thumbnail page does not display any copyright warning). Copyright lawyers have started to serve notices on people who use the original image without giving ownership details and some people have incurred large bills by assuming 'Google Image' thumbnails may be freely used. Usually, work displayed on most websites will be associated with a user or domain owner, who can be approached via metadata which identifies the rights owner and gives contact details.[124]

Even if a photo appears to be an 'orphan work', it is still someone's copyright and is unsafe to use since copyright persists for 70 years after the death of the photographer. Though it might be all right to use very old photos, some of these, such as portraits of famous composers, may still be owned by agencies or trusts who hold the image under licence. Equally, sometimes the credited author will not be the copyright owner because they have assigned copyright to someone else but retained their moral right to be identified as the author.

8.6.3 False attribution and passing off

Section 84 CDPA deals with 'passing off' and the false attribution of a work. In order to satisfy the originality criterion for the purposes of copyright subsistence, the author of the work must first establish that the work originated from him or her. Therefore, 'originality' must be distinguished from 'novelty'. The work must be an independent creation, but it need not be an invention in the sense of striking uniqueness, ingeniousness or novelty. In other words, the author must show that the work and its underlying ideas, facts or information expressed therein originate from him.

In *Clark v Associated Newspapers Ltd* (1998),[125] the claimant, an MP and an author with an established reputation, Mr Alan Clark, invoked two rights to protection from false attribution of authorship: the statutory right under s. 84 CDPA 1988 and the common law right under the law of passing off. It was for the judge – Mr Justice Lightman – to exercise his discretion whether a substantial body of readers of the *Evening Standard* had been or were likely to be misled 'more than momentarily and inconsequentially' into believing that the claimant was the author of the articles and whether the claimant, as an author with an established goodwill, had suffered or was likely to suffer damage in consequence.

During and after the General Election in 1997, articles had appeared as a weekly column in the *Evening Standard* (written by Peter Bradshaw), headed 'Alan Clark's Secret Election Diary' and 'Alan Clark's Secret Political Diary', next to a photograph of the claimant. The articles were parodies of Mr Clark's well-known diaries, published in 1993.[126] The format of the parodies was such as to deceive a substantial number of readers into attributing their authorship to Mr Clark. The court granted an injunction to Mr Clark to restrain the defendant from publishing any further such 'diaries' in the *Evening Standard*.

123 s. 78(3)(a) CDPA.
124 There is an extension for the Firefox web browser called EXIFviewer which will display IPTC and EXIF metadata.
125 [1998] All ER 6 (Ch D).
126 See: Clark (1993). Alan Clark's published diaries cover the period 1983 to 1992 after he left the House of Commons, describing the government (and downfall) of Prime Minister Margaret Thatcher.

The court was assisted by the evidence of witnesses who had seen or read the articles, and of experts as to the features of the market for newspapers and other published works. The test was that rational men had been deceived and the question before the court was whether by the adoption of the format chosen the defendant had succeeded too well in making the articles look real, and Lightman J reached the conclusion that it had. The claimant had a substantial reputation as a diarist and his identity as author of the articles would plainly be of importance to readers of the *Evening Standard* in deciding whether to read the articles. That was reflected in the choice of format adopted and most particularly in the design of the heading, which was calculated to exploit the public recognition enjoyed by the claimant and the public interest which any diary written by him could be expected to generate. The consequent identification of the claimant as author was not sufficiently neutralized to prevent a substantial number of readers being deceived. The problem in this case lay in the format adopted by the 'diarist' Peter Bradshaw, who was in clear breach of s. 84 CDPA in that the (headings) of the articles contained a clear and unequivocal false statement attributing their authorship to the claimant and Mr Clark was accordingly entitled to relief in respect of the commission of the statutory tort.

The court made it clear that the judgment was no bar to publication of parodies. But the 'vice' in this case lay in the format of the articles. Lightman J concluded that the defendants, Associated Newspapers, the editor Max Hastings and Mr Bradshaw, had committed the common law tort of passing off and the statutory tort of false attribution of authorship.

8.7 Copyright works and free movement

Some implications of counterfeiting and piracy can mean that these practices provide a source of revenue for organized crime and pose risks to the public. Counterfeiting practices impact on the sustainable development of the world economy, causing significant financial loss for holders of IP rights and for legitimate businesses by distributing infringing material and therefore undermining legitimate trade. The EU has acknowledged these implications by addressing legislation to counteract these illegal practices and by encouraging member states to include measures which include the digital environment.

8.7.1 Film

Film piracy cost the UK economy £614 million pounds in lost revenues from fake DVD sales and illegal downloads in 2009, according to a report commissioned by the film industry body 'Respect for Film'. The report, commissioned from Oxford Economics, called for new measures, including tighter regulations on car boot sales, bans on cameras in cinemas and legislation to tackle illegal file-sharing.[127] Since the film industry is a significant contributor to the UK's economy, such a drain on growth is clear copyright theft, making copyright enforcement one of the most challenging areas which the government seeks to tackle.

See Chapter 9.3

Copyright in the film sector is particularly complex because of the many layers involved and the fact that there is no single creator of a film. Copyright exists in each of the following strata of a film:

- Artistic – i.e. the set designs used in the film;
- Dramatic – if the film is based on a dramatic work, dance or mime material (see: *Norowzian v Arks Ltd. and Others* (1998)[128] – see below);

---

127 Source: Oxford Economics (2009).
128 [1998] EWHC 315 (Ch).

- Literary – within the source material and the original screenplay;
- Musical – the soundtrack of the film, including both musical score and any lyrics;
- Film – the images in the 'first fixation' of the film;
- Sound recordings – the physical recording of the soundtrack;
- Broadcasts and cable usage – for sale of the underlying material and film for other exploitation;
- Performance – any live interpretation of the film;
- Published editions – within the typographical layout of the page for any published versions of the screenplay.

In 1998 film-maker Mehdi Norowzian launched an unsuccessful lawsuit in the High Court Chancery Division, seeking remuneration for the use of techniques and style from his short film which he made in 1992, called Joy. In Norowzian,[129] Mr Justice Rattee had to first decide whether the Joy sequence constituted a 'dramatic work' within the meaning of s. 1(1) CDPA in order to decide whether an advertising clip for Guinness breached Mr Norowzian's copyright. Mr Norowzian further claimed that his film clip of Joy fell under s. 3 CDPA, as a 'work of dance or mime', which entitled him to being the maker of it and therefore the 'author' within the meaning of sections 9 and 11 of the 1988 Act.

In 1994, drinks giant Diageo had launched the successful Guinness advertising campaign on TV and cinema screens, promoting the stout with a film clip called Anticipation. Mr Norowzian claimed that Anticipation was a copy of his Joy dance sequence clip and that the makers of the Guinness advert had breached his copyright. Anticipation portrayed a man who, having been served by a barman with a pint of Guinness, waits for the frothing liquid in his glass to settle, and, while he waits, carries out a series of dance movements. Was Anticipation a copy of Joy under s. 17(2) CDPA? Rattee J concluded that Joy was neither a dramatic work nor a recording of a dramatic work; therefore Anticipation did not infringe copyright.

The Court of Appeal clarified the earlier judgment in Norowzian (1998);[130] and held that a film was protected as a dramatic work subject to copyright law, but not the artistic techniques demonstrated in it. While their Lordships did not criticize the original trial judge, they stated that the standards applied by the law in different contexts vary a great deal in precision and by applying different standards and factors when weighing up what constitutes a 'dramatic' work.[131] In any case section 5 CDPA did not specifically define 'film' – it merely states that it is a 'recording on any medium from which a moving image may by any means be produced'.[132]

As has already been pointed out, copyright is an unregistered right and arises automatically on the creation of the material, provided that the material is original and that the work must be recorded in permanent form. The copyright in a film lasts for 70 years from the end of the calendar year in which the last principal director, producer or author of the screenplay dies (or composer in the case of the film's soundtrack or recording). If the work is of unknown authorship, copyright is 70 years from the end of the calendar year of creation, or if made available to the public in that time, 70 years from the end of the year the film was first made available. Copyright does not subsist in a film (or sound recording) which is a copy taken from a previous film (or sound recording).[133]

Copyright law makes the producer and the principal director of a film joint first-owners of copyright, although in practice the director will often assign his interest in the copyright to the production company or financiers. The producer must ensure that all underlying rights in the film,

---

129 [1998] EWHC 315.
130 See: Norowzian (Mehdi) v Arks Ltd. and Guinness Brewing Worldwide Limited (No 2) [1999] EWCA Civ 3014 (CA).
131 Ibid. (Buxton LJ, Nourse LJ, Brooke LJ).
132 s. 5(1) CDPA.
133 s. 5(2) CDPA.

including in the screenplay itself, have been acquired by assignment before they will be able to raise finance for the film. Assignments of rights must be in writing, signed by both parties (although technically they only have to be signed by the assignor) and should include rights to exploit the film (or underlying material) in every imaginable manner, including in ways that have not yet been invented at the time of the assignment (see below 8.9.1). While an idea for a film cannot be protected by copyright, the title of a film might be protected in limited circumstances. Titles most certainly qualify for trademark registration and may therefore be protected (a search of the US Copyright Office, UK and EU Trademark Offices will quickly establish already registered film names and titles).

It is worth mentioning that not all films are commercial productions; home movies, mobile phone pictures, camcorder images and so on can also constitute 'film' – but have a shorter period of protection of 50 years from when they are made.[134] For instance, if a party films an important or traumatic event – such as the assassination of US President John F Kennedy in Dallas in 1963 – and a news agency wants to use that film footage, they may not be able simply to use the whole film without consent.

Before a film producer seeks financial backing for his film, he must acquire the following rights, which determine the producer's right to exploit the work as a film:

- to adapt the work in the form of a screenplay;
- to reproduce the work in the form of a film;
- to exhibit the work;
- to broadcast the work or include it in a cable service programme;
- to issue copies of the work in the form of a film to the public;
- to rent or lend copies of the work in the form of a film to the public.

When commissioning an original work, the producer will need to acquire similar rights but must be aware of the agreement between PACT[135] and the Writers' Guild,[136] which sets out standard terms for such contracts.

Concerns have been raised when dealing with adaptations of plays or books in the making of a film. With either original or adapted works, the film producer needs to ensure that all ancillary rights are acquired[137]; these are:

- to adapt the work for television, radio or live performance on stage;
- to publish the screenplay in the form of a book of the film;
- to adapt the work in the form of a synopsis or treatment for promotional purposes;
- to copy the work in the form of a remake, sequel or prequel to the film;
- to produce a soundtrack album;
- to use the copyright owner's name and likeness;
- merchandizing rights.

When dealing with character merchandizing and image rights, the law regarding the protection of an individual's image is not as well developed in the UK as in the USA. Where image rights laws (or

---

134 s.13 CDPA.
135 PACT is the UK trade association representing and promoting the commercial interests of independent feature film, television, digital, children's and animation media companies: see <https://www.pact.co.uk>, accessed 24 November 2010.
136 The Writers' Guild of Great Britain was established in 1958. Its mission is to ensure that writers of all media are properly represented; it is affiliated to the Trades Union Congress: see <www.writersguild.org.uk>, accessed 24 November 2010.
137 s. 21 CDPA.

'rights of publicity') exist, they generally establish an individual's right to control and benefit from the commercial use of their image. In Europe, image rights are usually limited by overriding human rights law, such as Article 10 ECHR, the right to freedom of expression and free speech. Image protection is only available where the image is being exploited commercially rather than for purposes of artistic expression. Since films are both artistic and commercial endeavours, there is a significant amount of grey area here.

The exploitation of artistic works used in films was addressed in *Lucasfilm v Ainsworth* (2010).[138] The case goes back to artistic drawings and a clay model made in 1976 of a 'military style storm-trooper helmet' by designer Ralph McQuarrie. Andrew Ainsworth produced over 50 stormtrooper helmets for the film *Star Wars* in 1977, having applied 'two-dimensional sculpturing techniques' to the original design, which, in UK copyright law, is regarded and recognized as 'artistic works' under s. 4 CDPA. Mr. Ainsworth began selling replicas of the helmet. Lucasfilm claimed that Mr Ainsworth had breached US copyright and trademark laws, obtaining a default judgment in California with a US$ 20m fine against him. Mr Ainsworth counterclaimed to enforce his own copyright in the helmet. The complex case does not only centre on whether the three-dimensional object was a 'sculpture for the purposes of s. 4 CPDA, but also on the conflict between the UK, the US and EU law. On the latter issue, the judge held that the principles underlying the **Brussels Convention on Jurisdiction and the Enforcement of Judgments in Civil and Commercial Matters** (1968)[139] recognized a distinction between title (for land) and validity and registration aspects (for registrable intellectual property rights) on the one hand and trespass/infringement on the other, and that where the subsistence of a foreign copyright was not in issue, the English court could determine questions of its infringement if it were appropriate to do so having regard to the doctrine of *forum conveniens*.[140] The UK courts held that US copyright subsisted in the helmet and had been infringed by the defendant. Furthermore, it held that the US default judgment was not enforceable in England.

Most importantly, they held that the *Star Wars* helmet belonged to Lucasfilm and Mr Ainsworth was required to assign any such copyrights to them. There followed a number of cross-appeals on this issue. Eventually, in December 2009, Lucasfilm's appeal failed in the UK Court of Appeal. Jacob LJ postulated an extremely narrow view of the justiciability of foreign intellectual property actions. He held that there was no copyright in the 'helmet sculpture', nor could this be enforced in the United States. This meant that Mr Ainsworth's cross-appeal partly failed and partly succeeded to the extent that the Court of Appeal rejected the original judge's direct enforcement of US copyright. This meant that there was no financial remedy for the George Lucas empire to compensate it for the modicum of selling which Mr Ainsworth managed to achieve in the US. Mr Ainsworth was, however, warned that were he to seek any further selling into the USA, he would be in breach of US copyright laws.

This case raises difficult questions in foreign IP law in relation to UK and EU copyright legislation. Under the traditional rules of jurisdiction *forum conveniens* might resolve those difficulties (see also: *Owusu v Jackson* (2005)[141]; *Equitas Limited v Allstate Insurance Company* (2008);[142] *Skype Technologies v Joltid Ltd* (2009)[143]; *Catalyst v Lewinsohn* (2009)[144]). Lucasfilm was before the Supreme Court in March 2011.

Any claims concerning image rights in the UK will be made under either copyright or trademark related legislation, such as 'passing off' regarding the unauthorized use of a person's image or

---

138 [2010] 3 WLR 333 (CA Civ Div).
139 *Civil Jurisdiction and Judgments Act* 1982, Sch. 1 (as substituted), Article 2: see post, para 123. Under the Brussels Regulation this is reflected in Article 22. However, matters of infringement or alienation of the patent and the validity, infringement and alienation of unregistered intellectual property (such as copyright, in issue here) are all outside Article 22.
140 For further discussion see: Rogerson (2010).
141 [2005] (C-281/02) ECR I-1383 (ECJ).
142 [2008] EWHC 1671.
143 [2009] EWHC 2783 (Ch).
144 [2009] EWHC 1964 (Ch).

photo. Image rights are usually subject to separate negotiations in contract and are strictly commercial endeavours. The tort law of defamation also covers abuse of image rights in the UK, where the claim would be that the use of the image lowered the estimation of that person in the eyes of a reasonable person or has caused him to be open to public ridicule. Personalities can also protect themselves from abuse of image rights by registering their names as a trademark. In August 2007, pop star Britney Spears filed an application for her son, 'Sean Preston', as a US Trademark Application term[145]. Britney filed the application to safeguard her own intention to brand her children's clothing range.[146]

See Chapter
◀ 3.3.1

Since 1996, UK law has determined that anyone who performs in a film has rights in their own performance, and consent must, therefore, be obtained from all performers that their performance may be used. These rights extend to 50 years after the year in which the performance occurred. Performers also benefit from moral rights in much the same way as authors. This means that the distortion or modification of a performance, say, on YouTube or the Internet in general, might give rise to a claim for infringement of the protection against derogatory treatment.

Moral rights exist for authors of material, including films (see above 8.6.1). In a film the moral right grants the film director ownership of the material, thereby also conveying integrity rights which allow him to insist that his work is not treated in a derogatory way. Sometimes these moral rights are waived in the UK, but they cannot be waived in other parts of Europe, such as France.

Film music rights exist in the actual composition of a piece of music as well as in the form in which it has been produced and recorded. In addition, a separate copyright exists in the lyrics of a song (see above 8.5.). It is important that all rights in all the music used in the film are cleared as early as possible; this includes incidental music or background music.

Then there are separate copyrights in costumes, props and works of artistic craftsmanship, such as the scenery or backdrops. Some costumes may not fall under IP law, but may attract 'design rights' which arise automatically on the creation of the item. The person who commissioned the article is the first owner of this design right, which lasts for 15 years from the year of creation. American costume designer Colleen Atwood (born 1948), for example, has had numerous Oscar Academy Award nominations and awards for movies such as *Chicago* in 2002 and *Memoirs of a Geisha* in 2006. All her costume designs are copyright protected and Atwood's costumes created for Barnum's Circus in 2005 were also trademark protected.

Commercial products in films are generally covered by trademark law, which protects a product's brand image and reputation in the marketplace. There is increasing product placement in large film productions, such as the James Bond franchise, which may, in turn, finance the movie. Producers ought to take particular care when dealing with major brands such as Aston Martin or BMW. Large corporations will often pursue legal action against even the smallest perceived breaches of their copyright or trademark rights, in order to ensure that they are not deemed to have 'acquiesced' to such activity.[147] Under the EU Audiovisual Media Services Directive 2008/48/EC product placement can now take place on television services in the EU. Product placement has now also been permitted in the UK in certain specified circumstances.

See Chapter
◀ 10.8

---

145 Under 'Goods & Services' – IC 025. US 022 039, clothing includes: shirts, T-shirts, under shirts, night shirts, rugby shirts, polo shirts, cardigans, jerseys, pants, overalls, track suits, play suits, vests, fleece vests, pullovers, snow suits, etc.

146 The trademark registration reads: Owner: Britney Brands, Inc. Corporation Louisiana c/o Davis Shapiro Lewit Montone & Hayes 689 Fifth Avenue New York New York 10022. Mark Drawing Code: (4) Standard Character Mark. Design Serial Number: 78894490. Filing Date: May 26, 2006.

147 Source: Lockley, Dorsey & Whitney, Skillset, The Sector Skills Council for Creative Media. available at <http://www.skillset.org>, accessed 24 November 2010.

👁 **FOR THOUGHT**

Where should a case be decided – as in the *'Star Wars'* case (above) – when intellectual property is protected in the UK but infringed in another state? Can *forum conveniens* solve problems of overlapping jurisdictions? Or would this lead to inconsistent judgments in the international sphere of copyright?

8.7.2 Broadcasts

Originally the CDPA 1988 divided broadcasting into two categories: broadcasts (section 6) and cable programmes (section 7 CDPA). Cable programmes were defined by the 1988 Act as 'any item included in a cable programme service' and a 'cable programme service' meant a service which 'consists wholly or mainly in sending visual images, sounds or other information by means of a telecommunications system, otherwise than by wireless telegraphy, for reception'.[148] Copyright in cable programmes was the same as in general broadcasts: 50 years from the end of the calendar year in which the cable broadcast was made.[149] As a result of changes in EU law this distinction no longer exists, repealing section 7 CDPA: cable programmes are no longer treated as a separate category but subsumed under the general concept of broadcasting.

A 'broadcast' is defined by the 1988 Act as 'a transmission by wireless telegraphy of visual images, sounds or other information' which:

a.   is capable of being lawfully received by members of the public; or
b.   is transmitted for presentation to members of the public;
c.   and references to broadcasting shall be construed accordingly.[150]

The context of broadcasting is now extended to satellite and digital transmission, and any related system which includes reception of a broadcast relayed by means of a telecommunications system.[151] Copyright in broadcasts exist for 50 years from the end of the calendar year in which the broadcast was made. Additionally, the **Broadcasting Act 1990** states that there is a duty to provide advance information about programmes by the service provider, who, for the purposes of the Act, is 'the publisher' in relation to programming schedules.[152]

There has been much controversy regarding whether hypertext links between websites on the Internet, which allow users to surf from one site to another, are infringing copyright. In the case of *Shetland Times v Wills* (1997),[153] the legal effect of hypertext links was considered for the purposes of copyright law. The case involved two Scottish newspapers and their online editions, with both their editors based in the Shetland Islands. Former student rector of Edinburgh University, Dr Jonathan Wills, former editor of the *Shetland Times*, began to publish the *Shetland News* after falling out with Robert Wishart – owner of the *Shetland Times*. Dr Wills also operated a website for his newspaper, *Shetland News*, using news headlines as the means of access to its stories. From 14 October 1996, the *Shetland News* incorporated in its website certain news headlines copied verbatim from the *Shetland Times* site. The *Shetland News* page included *Shetland Times* headlines as hypertext links and by clicking

---

148 s. 7(1) CDPA.
149 s. 14 CDPA.
150 s. 6(1) CDPA.
151 ss. 6(2)–(4) CDPA.
152 ss. 176, Schedule 17 of the Broadcasting Act 1990.
153 [1997] SLT 669.

on these a person would be directed to the relevant stories on the *Shetland Times* website, bypassing the front page of that site altogether.

The *Shetland Times* objected primarily because the links enabled browsers to bypass the front pages which contained advertising. The *Shetland Times* feared that their advertising revenue would accordingly be reduced. The *Shetland Times* alleged copyright infringement in two separate acts:

1. Their website was a 'cable programme service' in terms of s. 7 CDPA, and the use of the *Shetland Times'* headlines in the *Shetland News* site constituted an infringement of copyright under s. 20 CDPA.

2. The headlines attracted copyright protection as original literary works and by storing the headlines by electronic means the *Shetland News* had infringed copyright in them subject to s.17 CDPA. The Court of Session accepted that linking to another website does not involve copying material but simply providing a means of access to the other site. The only material which had been copied was the text of the various headlines.

The Scottish Court of Sessions held that there was an arguable case for the subsistence of both copyrights. Its decisions that a website is a 'cable programme service' could have far-reaching consequences (beyond copyright law) for the regulation and development of the Internet. The court held that the headlines could in fact attract copyright protection despite the *de minimis* rules. On these findings Lord Hamilton granted an interim interdict.[154] The case was settled before a full proof could be heard on the facts and for the moment there is no authority to determine whether or not hypertext links constitute a restricted act for the purposes of copyright law.

The implications of the *Shetland Times* case for website requirements are of some significance. Much of the information gathered on websites will fall into the category of compilation, either as anthologies of material, or as expressions of raw data. Since most (news) websites now use hyperlinks to other sites, copyright protection is therefore doubtful. But headlines in hyperlink texts might attract copyright, as Lord Hamilton stated in the *Shetland Times* case.

However, to some extent this case now has only historical value as a result of the introduction of the 'communication right' under section 20 CDPA, which protects works distributed on the World Wide Web without the need for the complexities involved in the *Shetland Times* case. On the other hand this view may contradict general copyright law, which denies copyright to titles and slogans. But the creation of a headline does involve skill and labour, particularly in 'red tops' where the reader's attention is often drawn to the story by the headline, which will thus provide entertainment and ultimately sales. The *Sun's* famous headline 'Freddie Starr Ate My Hamster' of 13 March 1996 must have been one of the most perfect headlines and would certainly have been classed as an 'original literary work' and thereby would have attracted copyright protection.

⊙ FOR THOUGHT

What if the *Shetland Times* case had decided that hyperlinks did infringe copyright? How could this have affected the intrinsic nature of news online websites and the World Wide Web in general? Does the abolition of the separate concept of the cable programme and the introduction of the new communication right under section 20 CDPA (as amended) mean the *Shetland Times* case is of only historic importance?

---

154 An 'interdict' is a Scottish Court order similar to an injunction, which prohibits the person named in the order from taking any action specified in the order. An interdict can be obtained quickly on an interim basis (known as 'interim interdict'). A person who breaches an interdict is liable to be held in contempt of court. This could bring a penalty of up to two years in prison. A fine can also be imposed.

8.7.3 Typographical arrangements of published editions

Protection for typographical arrangements was introduced after the invention of photolithography in the early twentieth century. The process of photolithography enabled commercial printing based on photographic images of a published edition of a work. The artistic development was a great improvement in typographical design, associated with the Arts and Crafts movement between 1880 and 1920. A new font could be registered as a design but the typographic layout of a book could not be protected, even though it may have involved considerable skill and effort.

Publishers were concerned that the skill and labour which had gone into the typographical design of fine editions of classical works could be appropriated by other publishers who used photolithography to make facsimile copies. At the time, publishers reproduced classic literary works that had fallen out of copyright, as the duration for protection had elapsed, for example with Gilbert and Sullivan's works. It is worth noting that even if the work reproduced is out of copyright – such as Shakespeare's works – a new edition with original typographical layout will have its own new and separate copyright. Other publishers were readily able to directly and exactly copy the works and sell those copies in competition with the original publisher. Due to the state of the law at the time, the publisher had no right of recourse against the competitor who had copied their typographical arrangement.

See Chapter 9.2.1 →

The Publishers' Association made representations to the Departmental Committee on International Copyright, asking it to recommend that a copyright in typography should be created by an amendment to the **Berne Convention**. The Committee was sympathetic but nothing came of the representations until after the Second World War, when protection for these typographical arrangements was first introduced by s. 15 **Copyright Act 1956**, later transposed into s. 8 of the **Copyright, Designs and Patents Act 1988** (CDPA), which defines these as 'published editions'. The legislative intention was to protect high-quality editions of classic works such as Jane Austen novels or Beethoven symphonies.

The 'edition' is the product between the covers which a publisher offers to the public. The edition is treated as the whole of what is published for the purposes of assessing whether infringement has taken place. In a typical publication, copyright subsists both in the content of a work and also in the typographical arrangement and design elements of the work. Typographical arrangement covers the style, composition, layout and general appearance of a page of a published work. A 'published edition' of the whole or part of one or more literary, dramatic or musical works and the exclusive right to reproduce the typographical arrangement of the published edition is owned by the publisher.[155] Published editions do not have to be original but they will not be new copyright works if the typographical arrangement has been copied from existing published editions. Copyright in the typographical arrangement of a published edition expires 25 years from the end of the year in which the edition was first published.

In *Newspaper Licensing Agency Ltd. v Marks and Spencer Plc* (2001),[156] Lord Hoffmann traced the history of this copyright. He attributed it to two developments in the publishing industry, one artistic and the other technological. One of the issues in this case was whether copyright in a typographical arrangement subsists in the arrangement of each and every item in a newspaper or other publication or in the publication as a whole. The House of Lords determined that it subsisted in the latter.

8.8 Media 'sans frontières': EU harmonization legislation

The CDPA was amended by EU legislation in the form of the Regulation of 1995 on the Duration of Copyright and Rights in Performances, the Regulation of 1996 on Copyright and Related

---

155 s. 9(2)(d) CDPA.
156 [2001] UKHL 38 (HL).

Rights,[157] and Directive 2006/116 EC on the Term of Protection of Copyright and Certain Related Rights Enforcement ('the harmonization Directive'), relating to the protection of copyright and related rights. Most importantly, EU legislation provides the 70-year rule. This means musical, literary, dramatic and artistic works are now protected by a 70-year duration of copyright *after* the death of the author.[158] In the case of a work of joint authorship, the term of 70 years is calculated from the death of the last surviving author.[159]

The terms of the 'harmonization' Directive 2006/116 apply in situations where the work or subject matter at issue is protected in at least one EU member state under that state's national legislation on copyright and related rights, even if the holder of such rights is a national of a non-Member State. In other words, if the work of a right holder outside the EU is prior to the effective date of 1 July 1995, and is covered by copyright protection under the national provisions of at least *one* EU member state, the provision will automatically extend to all other member states, irrespective of whether the right holder can claim direct protection under international treaties or the national provisions of the member state in which protection is sought. The 'test' case invoking the 'harmonization' Directive was the 'Bob Dylan' case (see below 8.8.1),[160] which marked the precedent for harmonization rights of performers and producers.

An EU Recommendation of April 2009 proposed to extend the term of copyright protection for performers and sound recordings to 95 years. The extended term would enable performers to earn royalties for a longer period of time throughout their lifetime. The Recommendation would also benefit record producers, who would generate additional revenue from the sale of CDs, music DVDs and commercial music downloads such as iTunes. As part of the proposed 'extended copyright' legislation, there would be a 'use it or lose it' clause in the performers' contracts which would typically link performers' rights to their record companies, allowing performers to get their rights back if the record producer does not market the sound recording during the extended period. In this way the performer would be able to either find another record label or producer willing to sell his music or to do it himself, something that is now made possible via the Internet.[161]

8.8.1 The 'Bob Dylan' case: Sony Music Entertainment (Germany) GmbH v Falcon Neue Medien Vertrieb GmbH (2009)

The European Court of Justice's decision in the *Bob Dylan* case is regarded by entertainment lawyers as a major victory for a recording label (here: Sony, Germany) which holds the (related) rights of the producer of phonograms in recordings. There was an added complication in this case. Not only had copyright run out in the Dylan recordings (which is why Falcon records thought they were free to 'grab' the old releases) but under Art 7(2) Directive 2006/116, if the holder of a sound recording right was not a Community national, then without prejudice to international obligations, the term of the right could be no longer than that which was applicable in the country of which the rightholder was a national. Thus, if the right holder was a national of country X and under the laws of country X protection was 30 years from 'fixation' (publication), the protection granted in the EC community could not extend beyond 30 years. The ECJ effectively said that Art 10(2) and Art 7(2) were dealing with different situations. Thus, the ECJ ruled that, provided that, as of 1 July

---

157 EU Regulation 96/2967 on Copyright and Related Rights.
158 Specifically Directive 2006/116 EC on the 'Term of Protection of Copyright and Certain Related Rights Enforcement Directive' of 12 December 2006.
159 Art 1(2) Directive 2006/116
160 *Sony Music Entertainment (Germany) GmbH v Falcon Neue Medien Vertrieb GmbH* (C-240/07) [2009] ECDR 12.
161 Source: Press Release of the European Commission of 23. 4. 2009 on the 'Proposal for a European Parliament and Council Directive amending Directive 2006/116 of the European Parliament and of the Council on the term of protection of copyright and related rights' (SEC(2008) 2287, SEC(2008) 2288).

1995, a right holder who was a national of a non-member state was protected in at least one member state, then the copyright was 'revived' under Art 10(2).

> ❖ **KEY CASE**
>
> The *Bob Dylan* case (*Sony Music Entertainment (Germany) GmbH v Falcon Neue Medien Vertrieb GmbH* (2009))[162]

Facts:

German record label Falcon had distributed two CDs containing recordings of original US performances by Bob Dylan from 1964 to 1965, including 'Blowin' in the Wind', 'Gates of Eden' and 'The Times They Are A-Changin''. Sony (Germany) held the related rights. Article 85 of the German Copyright Act (*Urheberrechtsgesetz*)[163] states that the producer of an audio recording (phonogram) has the exclusive right to reproduce and distribute the recording, meaning that companies are simply holders of the producer's rights of phonograms. In German law, these rights expire 50 years after production of the audio recording – which the Falcon label seized after expiry.

The German courts argued that under the Convention for the Protection of Producers of Phonograms against Unauthorized Duplication of their Phonograms, in force both in the USA and Germany, protection could only be claimed in relation to work created after 1 January 1966, the date when the German Copyright Act came into force. Sony claimed that the UK's **Copyright, Designs and Patents Act 1988** grants protection to phonograms before 1 January 1966 and also extends to phonograms of US producers. For this reason, Sony claimed that Dylan's albums were also protected in Germany, relying on Article 137f **German Copyright Act** and Art. 10(2) of the EU 'harmonization' Directive 2006/116.[164]

Sony argued that, even if copyright on the Dylan recordings expired prior to 1 July 1995, protection would still continue as long as the right existed under the law of another EU member state or related contracting party to the agreement on the European Economic Area (EEA) on that date.

The claim to copyright proceedings between Sony and Falcon reached an impasse at final appeal at the German Federal Court of Justice (Bundesgerichtshof), which, in turn, referred the case to the ECJ for a preliminary ruling on the interpretation of the 'copyright harmonization' Directive.

Decision:

Referring to the ECJ's judgment in the *Phil Collins* case,[165] Advocate General Ruiz-Jarabo Colomer cited the principle of non-discrimination and equal rights amongst member

---

162 [2009] ECDR 12 (C-240/07) (ECJ).

163 Article 85 (1) 'The producer of an audio recording shall have the exclusive right to reproduce and distribute the recording. If the audio recording has been produced by an enterprise, the owner of the enterprise shall be deemed the producer. The right shall not subsist by reason of the reproduction of an audio recording. (2) The right shall expire 50 years after publication of the audio recording.'

164 Initially called Directive 93/98, which was later codified by Directive 2006/116 on the term of protection of copyright and certain related rights.

165 *Collins (Phil) v Imtrat Handelsgesellschaft mbH* (C-92/92); *Patricia Im- und Export Verwaltungsgesellschaft mbH v EMI Electrola GmbH* (C-326/92) [1993] ECR I-5145.

states on literary works, artistic works and related rights. This meant that Sony could claim protection of Dylan's albums in Germany on the basis that they were still protected under UK legislation, by way of the 'harmonization' Directive 2006/116, even though they had at no time been directly protected under the provisions of the **German Copyright Act**.

The case set the precedent in the application of EU Directive 2006/116 in the harmonization of related copyright of performers and producers. The ECJ held that such was sufficient for copyright to 'revive'. It is worth noting that the ECJ was not ruling on the inapplicability of Art 7(2) of the Directive, but merely stating that it was irrelevant to the interpretation of Art 10(2). Thus, it may be the case that copyright is revived under Art 10(2) but disapplied under Art 7(2) if the right holder who is a national of a non-member state cannot demonstrate that he has commensurate equivalent protection in the country of which he is a national.[166]

8.9 Commercial contracts: stamping your authority on copyright

Though the original author of a piece of work is protected by the **UK Copyright Act**, some would argue that the copyright legislation remains essentially weak in spite of additional European 'harmonization' laws because there are enforcement problems, particularly with digital reproduction. But for major commercial firms it could be argued that the law is (too) strong.[167] It is therefore absolutely essential that all parties seek proper legal advice prior to entering into contract negotiations involving intellectual property rights. Naturally, each party will respectively seek to acquire the ownership rights that will often be the central focus of negotiations (known as the 'deal-breaker').[168] Key issues will be monitoring misuse and using effective enforcement methods such as trading standards cooperating with HM Revenue and Customs to confiscate (and destroy) infringing items at the point of entry into the UK.

8.9.1 Exploitation of copyrighted work: licensing agreements and assignments

Licensing schemes and assignments of copyright are stated within the scope of the **UK Copyright Act**, namely Chapter V of the CDPA 1988. Assignments tend to be more popular in the United States, whereby artists will assign their copyright to a publishing company. An assignment is an outright transfer of ownership of rights by the copyright owner (e.g. the songwriter) to someone else, which usually covers the life of the copyright: 70 years from the end of the year in which the original author and owner of copyright dies. The requirements for a valid express assignment are set out in section 90 CDPA; but fortunately for many the law recognizes in addition to express statutory assignments equitable implied assignments based on the circumstances or conduct of the parties. For sound recordings and performer's rights it is 50 years from the end of the year in which the recording was released or the performance made.[169]

The CDPA also allows a copyright owner to agree to assign the copyright in works that he will create in the future. When such works come into existence they will automatically transfer to the

---

166 For further discussion, see: Traub (2009).
167 For further details see: Cornish (2010).
168 For further discussion see: Miller, Vandome and McBrewster (2009).
169 Sections 12 and 13A CDPA.

assignee in the agreement. Where insertions into the contract are required to establish rights over the copyright work, only the grant of licensing will be implied. Otherwise an appropriate assignment will be required. The same goes for literary and dramatic works.

The following circumstances may give rise to the need for assignment:

i) The right to use the material;
ii) The right to exclude the author from using the material;
iii) The right to enforce copyright against third parties.

Factors to be considered when determining the likelihood of assignment should include:

a) The fee;
b) Duration of assignment;
c) The impact of assignment upon the author/creator;
d) Was there an intention for the author to retain first ownership?

Section 90(1) CDPA states that copyright is transmissible by assignment, by 'testamentary disposition' or by operation of law, as personal or moveable property.

It is possible to license a right instead of assigning it. In granting a licence, the copyright owner merely gives another person permission to use that right for the particular purpose as agreed in the licence terms, such as publishing the book from a given manuscript or to make a CD from a particular sound recording or live performance. Licensing is more flexible than an assignment as it is possible to license multiple copyrights to many people simultaneously, such as multiple music publishers. This is known as a non-exclusive licence (see also 8.5.2). A licence granted by a copyright owner is binding on every successor in title to his interest in the copyright, except a purchaser in good faith for valuable consideration and without notice (actual or constructive) of the licence or a person deriving title from such a purchaser. The licensor can then do anything with the work as he sees fit.[170] This practically means that a music publisher, for example, may do anything with a composer's script, such as issue an abridged or electronic version. The same is true of book manuscripts.

Licensing schemes for public performances of sound recordings are firmly grounded in conventional contract law, particularly in relation to 'related rights'. A recording company does not need to ask the artist's opinion on the cover sleeve of the CD, for instance, unless this is specifically recorded in the terms of the licence agreement. Famous recording artists who have exclusive licences with, for example, Warner Brothers, will insist as part of their contract deal that they receive special treatment, such as a specific photographer or hairdresser for the cover sleeve of the album (now including downloads and merchandise). Decca–Universal artist Ute Lemper was adamant that her album sleeve cover photo could only be taken by Helmut Newton in the pose of Marlene Dietrich.

A principle of de minimis will be presumed in respect of licensing requirements and that an entitlement would be intended for such an arrangement. The scope of the licence ought to be limited in respect of those opportunities as envisaged by the parties at the time of the agreement. New exploitation and/or unexpected opportunities will not be considered to be included within such scope.

What about implied assignments and licences? Given the often hurly burly world of real commercial practice, parties do not always enter into the appropriate statutory written assignment, which can cause injustice later and frustrate the real intentions of the parties. In certain circumstances English law recognizes an implied assignment or licence.

---

170 s. 90(4) CDPA.

The *Dr Martens'* case[171] involved the UK manufacturers Griggs, who operated under licence from the owners of the Dr Martens Boot. Part of the licensing arrangements allowed Griggs to use the 'Dr Martens' trademark. Griggs commissioned an advertising agency to combine the Dr Martens logo with their own 'Airwair' mark to create a single trademark. The agency in turn secured the services of a freelance designer. This led to a bitter IP dispute concerning ownership of the new combined logo: 'Dr Martens Airwair'. The agency claimed copyright in the new mark and assigned copyright to Griggs. Griggs, in turn, claimed a beneficial right to the new mark. But the original designer argued that there was no original assignment to the advertising agency of the copyright in the mark and so maintained first copyright ownership.

In *Dr Marten's*, the agreement between the agency and the original designer failed to take account of the copyright ownership, albeit that there was no dispute as to the author retaining the legal title and first ownership status of the logo. However, the court ruled that the equitable and beneficial ownership resided with Griggs, because the commercial value of the logo would be with Griggs and not the designer. This would be due not to the labour, skill and effort involved in its creation, but to the use of the logo upon the goods sold under both the Dr Martens trademark and their own 'Airwair' trademark. The Chancery Court further held that the right to exclude others from using the combined 'Dr Martens Airair' logo clearly stayed with Griggs, and could not be enforced by the designer. This meant that Griggs would be fully entitled to benefit from the assignment of the work. In addition, the court presumed that the granting of a licence in this case would have been a perpetual, exclusive licence that would equate to the granting of an assignment. In the event of any infringement proceedings it would not be expedient for Griggs to join the designer in proceedings, nor could Griggs bring infringement proceedings against any use made by the designer. It was decided, therefore, that the implied term within the contract between the advertising agency and the designer was that legal ownership would be assigned to Griggs. This case clearly sets out the erroneous nature of silent contracts and removes the incorrect presumption that many parties rely upon.

Nowadays, record labels try to persuade recording artists to sign '360°' licence deals so that they can exploit the artists' recordings commercially, including touring and merchandise. Record labels traditionally pay for the recording and mixing of albums and tend to underwrite new acts' touring costs to help raise their profile and sales. In addition they fund the manufacturing, packaging and distribution of the recordings.

⊙ **FOR THOUGHT**

What happens if it can be proved that a company is guilty of copyright infringement? What do you need to prove in relation to the company's director/s or secretary?

8.10 Copyright infringements

In April 2006, after a three-week hearing in the High Court, Peter Smith J rejected claims that Dan Brown's best-selling novel *The Da Vinci Code* breached the copyright of an earlier book. Michael Baigent and Richard Leigh had sued publishers Random House, claiming that Mr Brown's book 'appropriated the architecture' of their book, *The Holy Blood and the Holy Grail*, published in 1982 by the same publishing house. The claimants said Mr Brown — whose book has made him the highest-paid author in history — had 'hijacked' and 'exploited' their book, which took them five years to

---

171 See: *Griggs Group Ltd. v Ross Evans* [2003] EWHC 2914 (Ch).

create. The judge said that a comparison of the language in *The Holy Blood and the Holy Grail* and *The Da Vinci Code* did show some limited copying of the text but that this did not amount to copyright infringement. The claimants were ordered to pay 85 per cent of Random House's legal costs, estimated at £1.3m.[172]

If a person carries out any of the 'restricted acts' without the authorization of the copyright owner, this constitutes copyright infringement, an act of strict liability where *mens rea* is not an issue.[173] Restricted acts include:

- to issue copies of the work to the public;
- to perform, show or play the work in public;
- to broadcast the work;
- to make an adaptation of the work or do any of the above in relation to an adaptation.[174]

That said, court actions offer civil and criminal remedies sufficient to deter piracy and copying of MP3 music files, DVDs or films though prosecutions have so far been rare. Possible defences include permitted acts, fair dealing (reviews, news reporting, criticism, etc.) and research and private study (see below 8.11).

If the owner of the copyright in an original work believes that his work has been copied or pirated, he can enforce these rights in the administrative courts. The courts usually use equitable remedies, such as 'specific performance'. They can also issue a warrant for an inspection of the copiers' premises for evidence of production or possession of the copied or 'pirated' goods. There could be an interim injunction (or interdict in Scotland) to stop the illegal activities (see below 8.11.1). The copyright owner's rights are not limited by the amount of work used. If he believes that a 'substantial part' of his work is being copied or broadcast, this will still constitute an infringement of the work. A substantial part is assessed qualitatively and could be a very small part of the work if that part was distinctive and thus substantial (see below 8.10.4).

8.10.1 Secondary infringements

The copyright owner is also able to take action against persons who subsequently deal with an infringing copy or who facilitated the infringement itself. These acts are known as acts of secondary liability and are covered by sections 22 to 26 CDPA. Section 23 CDPA includes the copyright in a work which is infringed by a person who, without the licence of the copyright owner:

(a)   possesses it in the course of a business;
(b)   sells or lets it for hire, or offers or exposes for sale or hire;
(c)   in the course of a business exhibits it in public or distributes; or
(d)   distributes it otherwise than in the course of a business to such an extent as to affect prejudicially the owner of the copyright, an article which is, and which he knows or has reason to believe is, an infringing copy of the work.

In relation to secondary liability, it must also be shown that the person who conducted those restricted acts knew or had reason to believe that he was infringing copyright. This becomes an issue when, for instance, counterfeit DVDs are sold at car boot sales by third parties.

---

172   Source: 'Brown wins Da Vinci Code case', *The Guardian*, 7 April 2006.
173   Chapter II of the CDPA.
174   s. 16 CDPA.

New regulations amending the CDPA 1988 which came into force on 31st October 2003[175] have introduced the ability for copyright owners (and certain licensees) to take infringement proceedings against anyone who circumvents technological measures – such as copy control devices which have been applied to a work – or who removes or alters electronic rights management information associated with a work or imports or sells devices for these acts to be done.

⊙ FOR THOUGHT

As an entertainment lawyer, how would you advise your client – the copyright owner – who wants to take action in relation to acts of secondary liability against a person who conducts restricted acts within the provision of the **Copyright Act** (CDPA)? How realistic is it to trace the person who conducted the original infringement (the acts of primary liability), and how would you go about it?

8.10.2 Criminal offences

Some acts of copyright infringement also constitute a criminal offence and therefore criminal proceedings can be brought by the copyright owner or Trading Standards authorities. UK copyright law allows for criminal prosecution where there is deliberate intent or passing off in a commercial context. A person commits an intellectual property offence if he knew or had reason to believe that he was conducting any of the acts (defined by statute) with an infringing article or that his actions would cause an infringement.

Criminal liability for making or dealing with infringing articles is covered by section 107 CDPA, which states that a person commits an offence who, without the licence of the copyright owner:

(a) makes for sale or hire; or
(b) imports into the UK otherwise than for his private and domestic use; or
(c) possesses in the course of a business with a view to committing any act infringing the copyright; or
(d) in the course of a business –

  (i)   sells or lets for hire; or
  (ii) offers or exposes for sale or hire; or
  (iii) exhibits in public; or
  (iv) distributes; or

(e) distributes otherwise than in the course of a business to such an extent as to affect prejudicially the owner of the copyright.
(f) an article which is, and which he knows or has reason to believe is, an infringing copy of a copyright work.[176]

The courts can also order damages for loss of financial rewards (e.g. royalties) and recognition of the work[177] (see below 8.11.2). Criminal copyright prosecution allows for imprisonment and fines

---

175 EU Regulation 2003/2498 on Copyright and Related Rights Regulations and EU Regulation 2003/2426 on Privacy and Electronic Communications Regulations.
176 s. 107(1)(a)–(e) CDPA.
177 ss. 17–21 CDPA.

and infringing goods may be seized (see below 8.11.4). It is important to understand that even if a criminal prosecution succeeds, a separate civil case will be necessary to recover financial losses caused by the infringement (see below 8.11.2). However, the difficulty of proving intent and the higher standard of proof ('beyond reasonable doubt') required for a criminal prosecution means that copyright infringement is almost always dealt with as a civil procedure with the aim of recovering damages.

In March 2010, the Crown Prosecution Service (CPS) dropped its case against a teenager who was arrested and charged with illegally uploading music files to a file-sharing website. Matthew Wyatt, then 17, of Stamford, Lincolnshire, was arrested by Cleveland Police in 2007 for allegedly uploading three record albums and a single to OiNK,[178] a members-only BitTorrent tracker file-sharing site which operated from 2004 to 2007. The site allowed active members to find other people on the Web who were prepared to share files – enabling users to get hold of free music. Users were asked to make a donation, although it was not necessary for them to do so to invite friends to join the site. Following a two-year investigation by the International Federation of the Phonographic Industry (IFPI)[179] and the British Phonographic Industry (BPI),[180] the site was shut down by British and Dutch police. Police found almost US$300,000 (£183,580) in the site owner's PayPal account and that he received $18,000 (£11,000) a month in donations from people using his website.[181] OiNK founder Alan Ellis, then 26, had been found not guilty of conspiracy to fraud during his jury trial in January 2010. He had operated the site from his flat in Middlesbrough from 2004 until it was closed down in a police raid in October 2007. In that time OiNK facilitated the download of 21 million music files.

Ellis was the first Briton to be charged with illegal file-sharing. Wyatt was charged with distributing copyrighted material, a criminal offence that carried a maximum ten-year custodial sentence. This was the first time the CPS had acted as proxy for a private prosecutor. When the CPS decided at the last minute not to continue its prosecution, the main reason may have been that this action could have been better dealt with by the civil courts or trading standards.

Running a BitTorrent (file-hosting) site can be a lucrative business. According to the Musicians' Union, 87 per cent of their members earn less than £16,000 a year and 90 per cent of PRS for Music members earn less than £5,000. Some copyright holders, like music publisher Paul Harris (ReverbXL), would prefer that torrent sites invested their profits in technology that ensures no copyrighted material is linked on their servers. Harris and many other musicians have demanded action from the government, asking that their songs are properly protected so that the artist can

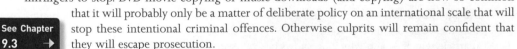

receive due royalties. Labels are losing huge sales while tracks are downloaded illegally through sites like OiNK. Despite the conviction of The PirateBay in Sweden, similar sites are still operating, breaching music copyright daily.

See Chapter 9.5.6 →

Trading standards or the police do not generally follow up infringements and with the CPS dropping the case against Matthew Wyatt (above), there is little motivation for copyright infringers to stop. DVD movie copying or music downloads (and copying) are now so common that it will probably only be a matter of deliberate policy on an international scale that will stop these intentional criminal offences. Otherwise culprits will remain confident that they will escape prosecution.

See Chapter 9.3 →

---

178 The site was called 'OiNK's Pink Palace' (frequently written as 'OiNK').
179 IFPI represents the recording industry worldwide, with a membership comprising some 1,400 record companies in 66 countries and affiliated industry associations in 45 countries. IFPI's mission is to promote the value of recorded music, safeguard the rights of record producers and expand the commercial uses of recorded music in all markets where its members operate.
180 Established in 1973, the BPI is the representative voice of the UK recorded music business. BPI members account for approximately 90 per cent of all recorded music sold in the UK, and globally the UK's recorded music market is the third biggest.
181 Source: 'Free music site cleared of fraud', BBC News Online, 5 January 2010.

8.10.3 Defences and permitted acts

The CDPA allows a number of uses of copyright works *without* the permission of the copyright owner in certain specific circumstances. There are two distinct types of permitted acts: fair dealing and exceptions (see below 8.10.4 and 8.10.5). It is an offence to perform any of the following acts without the consent of the owner:

- Copy the work;
- Rent, lend or issue copies of the work to the public;
- Perform, broadcast or show the work in public;
- Adapt the work.

As stated previously, the author of a work or a director of a film may also have certain moral rights:

- The right to be identified as the author.
- The right to object to derogatory treatment.

8.10.4 Fair dealing

Fair dealing (or 'fair use', 'free use' or 'fair practice') sets out certain actions that may be carried out, but would not normally be regarded as copyright infringement. The fair dealing exceptions are fairly limited, covered by sections 28 and 29 CDPA. The idea behind this is that if copyright laws are too restrictive, it may stifle free speech and news reporting, or result in disproportionate penalties for inconsequential or accidental inclusion. Fair dealing describes acts which are permitted to a certain degree without infringing the work; these acts are:

- Private and research study purposes;
- Performance, copies or lending for educational purposes;
- Criticism and news reporting (see: *Time Warner v Channel 4* (1994)[182]);
- Incidental inclusion;
- Copies and lending by librarians;
- Acts for the purposes of royal commissions, statutory enquiries, judicial proceedings and parliamentary purposes;
- Recording of broadcasts for the purposes of listening to or viewing at a more convenient time ('time shifting'), including podcasts and BBC iPlayer;
- Producing a back-up copy for personal use of a computer program;
- Playing a sound recording for a non-profit-making organization, club or society.

Fair dealing acts differ from other exceptions to copyright in that these involve an assessment as to whether the dealing is fair. In determining this issue the courts have considered the following questions.

Firstly, is the person really using the work for the stated purpose? For example, if an entire work has been used and it is followed by two lines of vague review, this will not constitute criticism and review. If the use has not been for one of the stated purposes, it will not fall within 'fair dealing' and as such any use without permission will be an infringement. If the work has been used for one of the stated purposes, the court will then consider whether the use of the work was fair in all the circumstances. Such an assessment will involve a number of factors and will depend upon the particular circumstances of each case.

---

182 [1994] EMLR 1 of 22 October 1993 (CA).

Secondly, has the (alleged) copyright infringer availed himself of the 'fair dealing' exception? And if so, has he provided a sufficient acknowledgement alongside his work? Has he demonstrated a visible and prominent notice which amounts to a sufficient acknowledgement to the copyright owner (with the exception of reporting current events or news – see below)?

In *Fraser-Woodward Limited v (1) British Broadcasting Corporation (2) Brighter Pictures Ltd.* (2005),[183] the High Court (Chancery) provided further guidance on the application of the fair dealing defence for review and criticism (see below). The issues concerning 'fair dealing' were: (1) whether the use of 14 photographs of Victoria Beckham and her family in a television programme was for the purposes of criticism and review; (2) whether the dealing was fair; (3) whether there was sufficient acknowledgement of the author within the meaning of s.178 CDPA; and in relation to two of the photographs whether the use amounted to incidental inclusion. A number of useful cases were cited in *Fraser-Woodward v BBC* which ought to be studied separately. While *Ashdown v Telegraph Group Ltd.* (2001)[184] was authority for the proposition that the criticism must be of a work or another work, it was held not sufficient in this case to criticize anything to invoke 'fair dealing'; there was no requirement that the criticism and review contain specific reference to the work in question.

❖ **KEY CASE**   *Fraser-Woodward Limited v (1) British Broadcasting Corporation (2) Brighter Pictures Ltd (2005) (High Court – Chancery Division)*

Facts:

The case concerned the use by the BBC and Brighter Pictures of 14 'off-guard' photos of the Beckham family, taken by Jason Fraser, during the making of a TV programme, *Tabloid Tales*, presented by Piers Morgan. Fraser-Woodward Ltd sued for copyright infringement seeking flagrancy damages. The BBC and Brighter Pictures argued that the photos fell within the fair dealing defence under s. 30 CDPA 1988. They argued that the programme included criticism of the photos and the tabloid press in general. Mr Fraser argued that there was no fair dealing and that there was no sufficient acknowledgement.

Decision:

The Court held, dismissing the claim, that in respect of all but one of the photographs the use was for the purposes of criticism and review of other works, namely the tabloid press and magazines. Mann J referred to Walker LJ's judgment in the *Pro Sieben* case,[185] that the defence of fair dealing should be interpreted liberally. Mann J also confirmed *Hubbard v Vosper* (1972),[186] that there could be no limitations on the extent of commentary capable of amounting to 'criticism' for the purpose of the defence. Any review or criticism should be considered in its context. He held that, on the facts the programme, it did include criticism of the photographs themselves. Importantly, the Court found that the reproduction of the photographs did not prejudice the legitimate interests of Mr Fraser. The fact that he does on occasion license his photographs for use in television programmes, and without apparently significantly undermining his ability to license the pictures elsewhere, contradicted his evidence that undue damage to their value was inevitable from their use in the BBC show. Overall, Mr Justice Mann held that there was not 'excessive use' of the

---

183 [2005] EWHC 472 (Ch).
184 [2001] Ch 685 (Ch).
185 See: *Pro Sieben Media AG v Carlton UK TV Ltd* [1999] FSR 160 at p. 162 (Walker LJ) (CA).
186 [1972] 2 QB 84; concerning review of a literary work on Scientology as authority for the proposition that the criticism or review.

photographs to negative the fair use. The photographs were used by the defendants purely for the purpose of criticizing tabloid journalism and the methods employed by the tabloid press and celebrities such as the Beckhams to exploit stories to their advantage.

This decision in *Fraser-Woodward v BBC* also provides guidance as to the meaning of sufficient acknowledgement, in respect of which there is very little case law. *Sillitoe v McGraw Hill Book Co* (1983)[187] is not authority for the proposition that any identification must be express. All that is required is that it is an identification. It is simply not enough to say that the author can be identified if you look hard enough; authorship acknowledgement must be more apparent than that. In the end, it is a question of fact and for the courts to decide whether there has been an identification.

The ruling in respect of 'fair dealing' in *Fraser-Woodward v BBC* means that the scope of the defence now stretches not only to criticism and review of other copyright works, but will also cover criticism of works that may not be protected by copyright at all or are unpublished or identified with any specificity, such as the tabloid press in general. The key requirement for the defence to apply is that the author/s of the allegedly infringing material must demonstrate a genuine intention to criticize or review, rather than a desire to compete with the copyright work or to reproduce the copyright work simply to advance or promote their own product or service (see also: *IPC Media Ltd. v News Group Newspapers Ltd.* (2005)[188]).

8.10.5 Exceptions

There are a number of general exceptions in the **Copyright Act** for a variety of purposes, covered by sections 30–76 CDPA. Broadly these are:

- Educational exceptions – such as examinations; dramatic performances;
- Research and private study – no more than 1 per cent of the work can be copied;
- Library and archiving exceptions – e.g. making copies for use in non-commercial research, or for archiving material;
- Public administration – e.g. parliamentary or judicial functions; public information; law reports etc.;
- Incidental inclusion of the copyright work – e.g. the filming of a documentary which incidentally includes a passing car playing copyright music;
- Lawful use of a computer program or database – such as making back-up copies;
- Timeshifting – e.g. a person is allowed to make a copy of a broadcast for private and domestic use to watch or listen to at a more convenient time; or for educational purposes.

8.11 Remedies

The court will order remedies for infringement of copyright depending on the circumstances, such as how flagrant was the infringement and what benefit did the defendant gain from the infringement? Did that person carry out one of the restricted acts without the copyright owner's permission?

---

187 [1983] FSR 545.
188 [2005] EWHC 317 (Ch).

8.11.1 Injunctions

Injunctions (or Scottish interdicts) are granted to enforce a legal or equitable right. Accordingly, a grant presupposes the existence of such a right. Injunctions are made by a court and usually require a person to do or refrain from doing specified acts, although they may also require a person to positively do something to prevent what would be unlawful conduct leading to damage to the claimant, such as 'delivery up' of a plagiarized manuscript or music score.

Injunctions are discretionary remedies, which can be positive or negative. If the loss or damage sustained by the claimant was to be satisfactorily compensated by an award of money, then it is said that damages are an adequate remedy, and an injunction will not be available unless the case presents exceptional circumstances. Injunctions may be granted on an interim or perpetual basis. Instances of use in commercial and intellectual property law include:

1. Infringement of intellectual property rights (including copyright, designs, trademarks, patents and breaches of confidence);
2. Passing off;
3. Unlawful use of trademarks;
4. Enforcing the terms of an exclusive licence;
5. Trespass to goods;
6. Publication of libellous (defamatory) material;
7. Statements that damage a business;
8. Groundless threats for alleged infringement of certain intellectual property rights.

Types of injunctions include:

*   Interim (or preliminary) injunction which may be granted to maintain the status quo between the parties leading up to the final hearing of the dispute;[189]
*   Special interim injunction (or 'freezing orders' or 'freezer') and search orders (historically called 'Mareva orders' and 'Anton Piller' orders respectively) which (i) restrains a party from removing from the jurisdiction assets located there; or (ii) restrains a party from dealing with any assets whether located within the jurisdiction or not;[190]
*   Final Injunctions, when the parties' rights are finally determined; these injunctions may be awarded 'in perpetuity' (e.g. for trademark infringements);
*   Mandatory and prohibitive injunctions require the defendant to take positive steps to reverse the effects of some wrongful act or to cease an omission that causes the defendant damage; they are prohibitory in nature to require the defendant to stop some wrongful conduct;
*   Discretion in awarding injunctive relief whereby the defendant will remain liable in damages provided the losses suffered are proved in the litigation.

Scottish actions and interdicts will be cited as follows. In *Gleneagles Hotels Ltd. against Quillco 100 Ltd. and Toni Antioniou* (2003),[191] an intellectual property action concerning trademark infringement, Lord Nimmo Smith granted the following interim interdicts on 11 February 2003 on behalf of the pursuers, Gleneagles Hotels. They read as follows:

> . . . For interdict against the defenders or either of them, their employees or agents or anyone on their behalf or acting under their instruction from infringing or continuing to infringe the pursuer's rights in United Kingdom trademarks in the word 'GLENEAGLES' . . . and that by

---

189 See: Part 25 Civil Procedure Rules (52nd update of March 2010) 'Interim Remedies'.
190 Ibid., 25 (f) Civil Procedure Rules.
191 (2003) Outer House, Court of Sessions (Case No: A 372/03) 1 April 2003 (unreported).

using the name 'GLENEAGLES FILM STUDIOS' and/or the Gleneagles Film Studios sign comprising the words 'GLENEAGLES FILM STUDIOS' and depicting a glen and an eagle in substantially similar form (a) in the course of developing and/or marketing a hotel, conference facilities, timeshare lodges, golf courses, club house and restaurant facilities at Aberuthven, Perthshire or any of the foregoing, and (b) in the course of developing and/or marketing a film studio complex and/or housing at Aberuthven, Perthshire aforesaid and (c) causing, directing, procuring, assisting or enabling others to do any of the above acts; and for *interdict ad interim*;

. . . For interdict against the defenders or either of them, their employees or agents or anyone on their behalf from passing off as those of the pursuer the services provided by, and the business operated by, the defenders, and that by promoting or advertising the 'Gleneagles Film Studios' development at Aberuthven, Perthshire under the GFS name or GFS sign similar to the said GFS sign in the Appendix hereto; and for interim interdict.

(See also: *Alan Mackie T/A 197 Aerial Photography against Nicola Askew, Largsholidaylets.co.uk* (2009)[192] for copyright infringement of a website).

Other court orders may include:

- an order directing a party to prepare and file accounts relating to a dispute;
- an order directing any account to be taken or inquiry to be made by the court; and[193]
- an enforcement order in intellectual property proceedings making the continuation of an alleged infringement subject to the lodging of guarantees.[194]

8.11.2 Damages

In April 2005 the clothing chain Monsoon took legal action against the discount retailer Primark (owned by Associated British Foods – ABF) for the alleged breach of the design rights pertaining to a number of items of clothing. Monsoon's legal action concerned specific design rights in a zigzag linen skirt, a curved panelled skirt, tropical floral print swimwear, girls' corduroy trousers, children's striped scarf and poodle and heart socks. The 'zigzag' skirt, for instance, sold for £44 in Monsoon and for just £11 in Primark. The case was settled in early 2004 when Primark paid £23,000 damages to Monsoon for selling replicas of a girl's dress and top. Monsoon argued in both actions that the sale of these items was damaging to the Monsoon brand. The company had already had to defend itself against allegations of copying designs. Primark has also been involved in similar disputes in the High Court with clothing retailers H&M over the appropriation of designs and motifs on a range of adult and children's clothing.

A landmark ruling followed in 2007 which may have marked the end of counterfeited goods, such as perfumes, cosmetics and cut-price clothes. *L'Oréal v Bellure* (2006)[195] concerned the 'smell-alike' copies of luxury perfumes, such as L'Oréal, Lancôme and Laboratoire Garnier products, all of which were manufactured in Dubai by Belgian company Bellure, who, in turn, claimed that the articles were not imitations in the sense of being counterfeits. L'Oréal and others claimed that Bellure took unfair advantage of their own product names, packaging and brand image.

Lewison J (Chancery Division) found Bellure to have infringed L'Oréal's trademark, and that it had taken unfair advantage of L'Oréal's reputation within the UK; in effect, trying to pass off its

---

192 (2009) Sheriffdom of South Strathclyde, Dumfries and Galloway, 11 August 2009 (Case No: SA1251/08) (unreported).
193 Ibid., 25(n)–(p) Civil Procedure Rules.
194 Article 9 Directive 2004/48.
195 L'Oréal SA ; Lancôme Parfums et Beauté & CIE; Laboratoire Garnier & CIE v Bellure NV; North West Cosmetics Ltd., HMC Cosmetics Ltd; Malaika Investments Ltd., Sveonmakeup.co.uk; Starion International Ltd. [2006] EWHC 2355 (Ch).

own brand as that of L'Oréal's. L'Oréal relied upon s.10 (1) and (3) **Trademarks Act 1994**, which state that:

(1) A person infringes a registered trademark if he used in the course of trade a sign which is identical with the trademark in relation to goods or services which are identical with those for which it is registered.

(3) A person infringes a registered trademark if he uses in the course of a trade in relation to goods or services a sign which:

(a) is identical with or similar to the trademark, where the trademark has a reputation in the UK and the use of the sign, being without due cause, takes unfair advantage of, or is detrimental to, the distinctive character or repute of the trademark.

See Chapter 9.8.2 → The High Court ruled in favour of L'Oréal, which had claimed that Bellure was copying its brand by producing 'smell-alike' perfumes that were packaged to look like L'Oréal (see also: *L'Oréal SA v eBay France SA* (2009)[196]; also: *L'Oréal SA v eBay International AG* (2009)[197]).

Companies which specialize in copied goods have savvy lawyers who advise them on a daily basis on how close to the copyright infringement line they can get without crossing it. However, the *L'Oréal v Bellure* ruling is seen by the clothing and cosmetics industry as groundbreaking in deterring future copying of the genuine articles.

Most commonly, damages are awarded for loss of royalties or loss of profit. The calculation is usually based on the licence fee, or alternatively on the equitable remedy of an account for profits which focuses on the illegal gains of the defendant as opposed to the damages suffered by the claimant. Exemplary (or punitive) damages can be made, though they are rarely awarded in the UK. These are compensation awards in excess of actual damages – a form of punishment awarded in cases of malicious or wilful misconduct or breach of copyright. Section 97(2) CDPA provides some forms of damages in copyright infringement actions:

. . . the court may in an action for infringement of copyright having regard to all the circumstances, and in particular to –

(a) the flagrancy of the infringement, and
(b) any benefit accruing to the defendant by reason of the infringement,

award such additional damages as the justice of the case may require.

For much of the time, copyright infringements go undetected and many creative people and organizations complain that there is little point in their endeavours if they go unrewarded. The massive scale on which copyright is ignored means that prosecuting every infringement is just not practical. It is argued that only a series of high-profile successful cases will dissuade the copiers.

8.11.3 Delivery up

As previously stated, the copyright owner is able to take civil as well as criminal action for copyright infringement. There are a number of remedies available.[198] An order for 'delivery up' is made under section 99 CDPA, where a person has an infringing copy of a work in his possession, has made

---

196 (2009) (RG 07/11365) Tribunal de Grande Instance, Paris, jugement de 13 May 2009 (unreported).
197 [2009] EWHC 1094 (Ch).
198 ss. 96–100 CDPA 'Rights and remedies of the copyright owner'.

copies of the particular design or copyright work or has adapted the work for making copies, knowing or having reason to believe that the work was an original by the right-holder.

The owner of the copyright in the work may apply to the court for an order that the infringing copy or article be 'delivered up' to him.[199] The infringing articles may also be seized and destroyed[200] (see below 8.11.4). Delivery up is usually part of a default judgment (i.e. without a trial or where a defendant has failed to file either an acknowledgment of service or a defence). On an application for judgment for delivery up of goods where the defendant will not be given the alternative of paying their value, the evidence must identify the goods and state where the claimant believes the goods to be situated and why their specific delivery up is sought.[201]

8.11.4 Right to seize and search orders

The 'right to seize' enables the police and other agencies such as trading standards, collecting agencies and anti-piracy units to enter a property in order to seize the infringing articles. Trading Standards (or the police) usually apply to the magistrates' court to obtain a search warrant in order to seize infringing articles.[202] An 'Anton Piller' or 'search' order is a court order requiring a defendant to grant access to property and/or premises and to allow the claimant to conduct a search for evidence that may be easily disposed of upon notice of legal proceedings.[203] The 'Anton Piller' order was established in *Anton Piller KG v Manufacturing Processes Ltd. and Others* (1975),[204] which involved an action for copyright infringement and misuse of confidential information.

Until that time there was no such court order. No constable or bailiff could knock at the door and demand entry to inspect papers or documents. The householder could simply shut the door and refuse entry; a principle established in the leading case of *Entick v Carrington* (1765).[205] But the order sought in *Anton Piller* was not simply a search warrant which would authorize the police or the claimants' solicitors to break down the defendant's door. Orders available at that time were right of entry orders but had to be made with the *permission* of the defendant. If permission was not granted, the claimant would be guilty of contempt of court.[206] The search order applied for in *Anton Piller* was an order without notice to the defendants (*ex parte*).

❖ **KEY CASE**   *Anton Piller KG v Manufacturing Processes Ltd* (1975)

Facts:

Since 1972, German manufacturers of frequency converters for computers, Anton Piller KG (the claimants), had, as their agents in the UK, a company called Manufacturing Processes Ltd, which was run by Mr A.H.S. Baker and Mr B.P. Wallace (the defendants). Piller supplied the English company with extensive confidential information about the machines, including a manual showing how they work, and drawings which were subject to copyright. Piller claimed that the defendants were in secret communication with other German manufacturers and were giving them confidential information about the claimants' power units and details of a new converter, the disclosure of which could be most damaging to the claimants.

---

199   s. 99 (1) CDPA.
200   s. 100 (1) CDPA.
201   This Practice Direction supplements Criminal Procedure Rules Part 12.
202   s. 109 CDPA.
203   Now covered by the Civil Procedure Rules 2010 (53rd update), Practice Direction 31A, Rule 31.12 'Specific disclosure or inspection of documents'.
204   [1975] EWCA 12 (Civ Div).
205   (1765) 2 Wils 275.
206   Ibid., as per Lord Denning MR.

In order to prevent the disposal by the defendants, before discovery in an action of documents in their possession relating to the claimants' machines or designs, the claimants applied *ex parte* for an interim injunction to restrain the defendants from infringing their copyrights and disclosing confidential information and for an order to enter the defendants' premises to inspect all such documents and to remove them into the claimants' solicitors' custody. Brightman J granted the interim injunction but refused to order inspection or removal of documents. The claimants appealed.

Decision:
The appeal was allowed, on the basis that in most exceptional circumstances, where claimants had a very strong prima facie case, actual or potential damage to them was very serious and there was clear evidence that defendants possessed vital material which they might destroy or dispose of so as to defeat the ends of justice before any application *inter partes* could be made. The court had inherent jurisdiction to order defendants to 'permit' claimants' representatives to enter defendants' premises to inspect and remove such material; and in the very exceptional circumstances the court was justified in making the order sought on the claimants' *ex parte* application.

Ormond LJ in *Anton Piller* stated that the granting of such a search order was extremely rare and should only be made when there was no alternative way of ensuring that justice is done. The judge specified three preconditions that must be satisfied prior to the making of a search order:

1.   There must be a strong prima facie case;
2.   The potential or actual damage to the claimant must be serious;
3.   There must be clear evidence that the defendants have documents or articles in their possession that would give rise to liability, and there must be a real possibility that these would be destroyed prior to the hearing of application by notice.

Most importantly, the 'Anton Piller' search order is applied for to the court without notice (i.e. *ex parte*) to the defendant. These search orders are normally applied for where the claimant alleges that important documents have been stolen, copied or counterfeited ('piracy'). The same goes for freezing orders.[207] If the court grants such an order, it will usually order a close examination of company accounts alongside the search (and freezing) order.

8.12 The expansion of copyright exceptions: analysis and discussion

When the author of this book bought her first Beatles single, she did not envisage a time when Paul McCartney would be a pensioner. In 2006, Sir Cliff Richard lost his battle in the UK to extend copyright in some of his early rock 'n' roll singles – recorded at Abbey Road studios in 1958 – such as 'Move It'. Hailed as Britain's Elvis Presley at the time, Sir Cliff is now attempting at European Commission level to extend copyright in sound recordings to 95 years. The Beatles would also be in a similar situation from 2012, the fiftieth anniversary of their first hit single, 'Love Me Do'.

---

207 Such orders are now referred to as 'search orders' and are dealt with in s. 7 Civil Procedure Act 1997 (as amended) and Part 25 Civil Procedure Rules (52nd update of March 2010) 'Interim Remedies'.

At present, under s. 13(1) CDPA, Cliff Richard's and the Beatles' hits are subject to the 50-year rule. This also means that many other famous and living recording artists' copyright on their recordings will come to an end and that royalties to these musicians will stop. Furthermore, it means that the rights to the songs that are out of copyright can be easily seized on by the cheaper labels now sold in all supermarkets.

In 2005, Gordon Brown – then Labour Chancellor of the Exchequer – commissioned the former Financial Times editor Andrew Gowers to advise on the future of copyright in the digital age.[208] The Gowers Review (2009)[209] rejected the proposals that copyright of recorded music should extend from 50 to 70 or even 95 years (as the EU had suggested). Gowers' recommendations were taken up by the Intellectual Property Office (UK-IPO), resulting in the consultation document 'Taking Forward the Gowers Review of Intellectual Property: Proposed Changes to Copyright Exceptions' in 2009. At the same time, the then Labour Culture Secretary, Andy Burnham MP, urged Parliament not to tamper with the 50-year copyright term.

The Gower consultation report provoked an overwhelming response from more than 4,500 members of the music industry demanding 'fair play for musicians'. Among the most famous respondents were Robbie Williams, Robert Plant and Roger Daltrey. This was soon followed by the EU Parliament's passing the new 70-year copyright term. At the same time a new fund for session musicians was established in the form of a 20 per cent share in record sales to complement the broadcast royalty. This now allows artists to renegotiate 50-year-old recording contracts which, in turn, contain the 'use-it-or-lose-it' clause to restore unissued or deleted recordings to the owner-ship of the artist.

The EU Parliament's extension to the 70-year copyright term in recorded music is also known as the 'Beatles Copyright Extension', designed to prevent the Fab Four's first hits losing copyright protection in 2012. This extended copyright arrangement was naturally welcomed by Sir Paul McCartney and EMI Records. EMI released digitally remastered version of the Beatles' studio albums in September 2009, after a nearly 22-year wait. The 14-disc album box set features the track listings and artwork as they were originally released in the UK, including Magical Mystery Tour. In November 2010, the band's albums and entire back catalogue were also made available on iTunes, selling more than 450,000 Beatles albums within the first seven days of the digital download release. 'Hey Jude' reached the UK top 40 and EMI said that two million Beatles singles had been downloaded within one month.

One of the most fervent lobbyists, Feargal Sharkey, formerly of the punk group The Undertones and now head of the industry group UK Music (an umbrella organization representing the collec-tive interests of the UK's commercial music industry), declared, 'I am especially pleased that the announcement focuses on the "invisible" members of our industry ... who could derive real benefits from this move at a time in life when their earning power would be severely dimin-ished.'[210] But the EU legislative proposals still lack the force of law since the EU Council has not yet ratified the proposals.

Over the past decade, there have been revolutionary changes in technology. The Internet sits alongside devices ranging from MP3 players and e-readers, to vast online electronic music and literature libraries, all made possible by inexpensive broadband which allows efficient user-friendly

---

208 Andrew Gowers (born 1957) was editor of the Financial Times from 2001 to 2005. In December 2005, he was commissioned by Chancellor Gordon Brown to lead an independent review of intellectual property rights in the UK, known as the 'Gowers Review of Intellectual Property'. In June 2006, Mr Gowers joined Lehman Brothers in London as head of corporate communications, and stayed until the collapse of the firm in 2008. In autumn 2009, Gowers joined BP as head of media relations. He was responsible for handling the oil company's media response to the Deepwater Horizon oil disaster on 20 April 2010 when an explosion on the Deepwater Horizon drilling rig killed 11 men and sent millions of gallons of oil gushing into the Gulf of Mexico.

209 Source: HM Treasury (2009).

210 Source: Feargal Sharkey speaks at Music Week Conference', 4 June 2009, UK Music website, available at <http://www.ukmusic. org/events/143-feargal-sharkey-speaks-at-music-week-conference>, accessed 25 November 2010.

downloads. Ultra-fast broadband, already available in countries like South Korea, allows the sending or receiving of two hundred MP3 music files, an entire *Star Wars* DVD or the complete digitized works of Charles Dickens in a matter of minutes. This technology has meant that file-sharing has become an increasing problem for artists and authors. Will the world of recorded music and literature be destroyed by piracy and illegal downloads or can new sources of revenue and funding be found to punish illegal downloaders? Promoting the cross-border exchange of intellectual assets –

See Chapter 9 →

such as music or literary manuscripts – is not only about adopting, implementing and enforcing copyright (IP) laws. There needs to be a coherent and multidisciplinary policy setting which promotes the safe creation, exchange and transfer of intellectual assets.

The impact of intellectual property protection has been analysed and measured from a legal perspective in relation to the various international treaties (e.g. **Paris** and **Berne Conventions**; TRIPS and WIPO) and domestic legislation in form of the **UK Copyright Act**. But from an economic perspective, it is unclear whether the level and efficiency of the protection of IP rights in a given country (the host country) significantly affects the decision of foreign companies to invest in that country and that artist or author. Protectionism may also come into play, resulting from import and export control regulations which may not affect the music trade within the EU, but could be excessively restrictive on trade to and from other countries, depending on political decisions and multilateral negotiations and agreements.

8.12.1 The three-steps test on copyright reform

The Berne and TRIPS conventions' 'three-steps test' was invoked as a justification for refusing certain exceptions to copyright invoked by the French Parliament during the passage of the DADVSI bill (*Loi sur le Droit d'Auteur et les Droits Voisins dans la Société de l'Information*)[211] through the French Parliament. DADVSI was to implement, *inter alia*, the 2001 EU Copyright Directive, in turn implementing the 1996 WIPO Treaty (see above 8.9.2). Most of DADVSI focused on peer-to-peer (P2P) file sharing and the criminalization and prevention of digital rights management (DRM) and their protection

See Chapter 9.4 →

measures. DADVSI has also been referred to as 'iTunes' (or 'iPod') law because it significantly hampers free software and music downloads and restricts the making of copies of copyrighted works for private use. Apple and other US software houses relentlessly protested against the new French legislation – though French legislators do not view it in this way. DADVSI, though initially controversial because of its highly technical terms (similar to the passing

See Chapter 9.6.2 → **on 'HADOPI'**

of the **Digital Economy Act** in the House of Lords in 2009), was eventually adopted by both houses of the French Parliament in June 2006, including the controversial 'three strikes and you're out' principle permitting disconnection of a person's Internet connection.

The three-step test may prove to be extremely important if any nation attempts to reduce the scope of copyright law (unless the Word Trade Organization (WTO) decides otherwise). Currently, exceptions to copyright protection are not clearly defined and require modification and adequate trade sanctions which can be properly enforced. To ensure there are proper incentives for companies to continue investing in the creation, production, promotion and marketing of sound recordings, it is vital that international treaties and national laws continue to grant producers of sound recordings various longevity rights in those recordings. These rights should include the exclusive right to commercially copy the recordings and to distribute/import/export those copies. Depending on the country you live in, these rights may be called copyrights, or 'related' or 'neighbouring' rights. These are separate to any rights that may subsist in the music or the lyrics that are being

---

211 Translation: 'legislation on authors' rights and related rights in the information society'.

recorded. It is these rights that enable law enforcement bodies to take criminal action against those who copy and distribute music without the permission of the record companies that invested in producing it. They also allow record producers to take civil actions to recover compensation for damages suffered as a result of music piracy. While there are often other laws or regulations that are broken by music pirates (e.g. tax laws and trademark laws), the rights of music producers under copyright or related/neighbouring rights laws are the fundamental basis for the illegality of music piracy.

The 'three-step test' had not played a great role in copyright debates in the UK until the implementation of EU legislation on intellectual property by way of the 'harmonization' directive and various international treaties on copyright.[212] Senftleben (2004) investigated the development, structure and function of the three-step test in international copyright law and its application in the twenty-first century. He questioned whether the test would be fit for purpose in a future copyright system in line with international harmonization rules governing copyright law by demonstrating the test's impact on different types of limitations, such as private use privileges and the US fair use doctrine. Senftleben found that organizations lobbying on behalf of right-holders now frequently reinforce arguments against the expansion of copyright exceptions by suggesting that any such change would, or might, be incompatible with the 'three-step test', and would accordingly contravene international and European law.[213]

The extent to which international musical (and other published) works are now protected is largely similar at the global level. However, there still exist substantial differences in the scope of protection at national level and, confusingly, within EU legislation, such as the liability of Internet Service Providers (ISP) in relation to music downloads and piracy. ISP responsibility, then, appears to be the key to internet copyright infringements. The possibility of blocking 'offending sites' and redirection to official sites does exist but requires cooperation internationally. Difficulties of IP protection, law enforcement against piracy and the cross-border flow of musical works within the enforcement of copyright law and the various international conventions is potentially flawed – for example in relation to China. There will be differences between national regulations particularly in respect of moral rights for which the TRIPS minimum standard of protection does not apply.

FOR THOUGHT

Can the traditional balance between grants and reservations of copyright law be recalibrated along the lines of the 'three-step test' in order to meet current and future needs in an ever-emerging information society? What could be the unforeseen obstacles in new IP legislation and implementation in the UK?

8.13 Summary of key points

● The **Statute of Anne 1710** introduced right of copy of the author of the work who had the right to assign the privilege to another publisher after the licence to the Stationers' Company had expired;

---

212 See: Directive 91/250 on the legal protection of computer programmes; Art 6(3); Directive 92/100 on rental rights and certain rights related to copyright in the field of intellectual property; Art 10(3) (codified under Directive 2006/115, art 10(3)); Directive 96/9 on the legal protection of databases; Art 6(3) Directive 2001/29 on the harmonization of certain aspects of copyright and related rights in the information society, Art 5(5).

213 For further discussion see: Griffiths (2010).

- The **Copyright Act 1911** granted copyright to producers of sound recordings (phonograms);
- The **Berne Convention 1886** created automatic copyright in works as soon as they were created, asserted and declared. The minimum term of protection is the lifetime of the author ('creator of the work') plus 50 years after his death;
- The **Rome Convention 1961** was the first convention that addressed related rights, i.e. guarantees performers, producers of phonograms and broadcasting organizations the same rights in domestic law as well as the other contracting states; the minimum term of protection is 20 years;
- The World Intellectual Property Organization (WIPO, 1967) encourages and promotes creative musical activity across the world and seeks to protect IP; WIPO provides international registration and classification services of IP, including patents, trade marks and designs in multiple countries by filing a single application; WIPO has no effective method of enforcing other international copyright conventions (see: TRIPS);
- The **TRIPS Agreement** ('Agreement on Trade-Related Aspects of Intellectual Property Rights', 1994) provides a right on commercial retail of copies of computer programs and audiovisual works;
- TRIPS extends copyright protection to expressions (but not to ideas, procedures, methods of operation or mathematical concepts);
- TRIPS protection is 50 years following the death of the author;
- TRIPS allows for trade sanctions to be taken against World Trade Organization (WTO) members who do not provide effective enforcement of copyright law and tolerate piracy and counterfeiting;
- Copyright exists automatically in original literary, dramatic and musical works, sound recordings, films and broadcasts as well as the typographical arrangement of published editions;
- There is no form of official registration of copyright in the UK;
- Section 3(1) **Copyright, Designs and Patents Act 1988** (CDPA) includes the digital medium, i.e. storage on a computer hard drive and digital music recordings;
- Section 4(1)(a) CDPA provides that artistic works, including photographs, are protected as copyright works 'irrespective of artistic quality';
- Section 11 CDPA defines the 'first owner' of copyright as the author of the work; with the major exception of employee works which belong to the employer (in the absence of a contractual provision to the contrary) if created in the scope of the employment;
- Section 3A CDPA ('the database copyright') provides for publishers and broadcasters the development of 'databases' as original works; databases constitute the author's own intellectual creation;
- *Copyright and Database Regulations 1997*[214] cover unfair extraction rights for non-original databases;
- Copyright exceptions are covered by sections 30–76 CDPA, including educational exceptions, research, library and archiving purposes, public administration;
- Related rights are rights which ensure that right-holders (e.g. writers, composers, lyricists, performers or record producers) get a share of the money earned from the commercial use of their creations;
- A licence granted means the owner keeps the copyright to his works; the owner gives the licensee permission to do certain things for a specified period of time;
- An assignment is an outright transfer of copyright and ownership of rights from the owner ('the assignor') to someone else ('the assignee'); the assignor no longer owns the rights once these have been assigned;

---

214 EC Regulation 97/3032 on Copyright and Rights in Databases.

- An exclusive deal means that the artist can only record with the particular label and not with another recording company;
- Duration of copyright in literary, dramatic, musical or artistic works is the life of the author plus 70 years from the end of the year in which the author dies;
- Duration of copyright in sound recordings, live performances, film, broadcasts and cable programmes is 50 years from the end of the year in which the recording was released, if released within 50 years of it being made or the performance was made;
- The EU 'harmonization' Directive on copyright and related rights in the information society (2001/29/EC) reflects technological developments arising from the WIPO and TRIPS treaties on copyright.

8.14 Further reading

Cornish, W. (2010) *Intellectual Property: Patents, Copyrights, Trademarks and Allied Rights.* 7th Edition. London: Sweet & Maxwell.

Cornish, W. (2009) 'Conserving culture and copyright: a partial history'. *Edinburgh Law Review,* 2009, 13(1), 8–26.

Deazley. R. (2008) *Rethinking Copyright: History, Theory, Language.* Northampton, Massachusetts, USA: Edward Elgar Publishing Ltd.

Gravells, N.P. (2007) 'Authorship and originality: the persistent influence of Walter v Lane'. *Intellectual Property Quarterly,* 2007, 3, 267–93.

Griffiths, J. (2010) 'Rhetoric & the "Three-Step Test": copyright reform in the United Kingdom'. *European Intellectual Property Review,* 2010, 32(7), 309–12.

Harrison, A. (2008) *Music: The Business. The Essential Guide to the Law and the Deals.* 4th Edition. London: Virgin Books.

Miller, F.P., Vandome, A.F and McBrewster, J. (eds) (2009) *Intellectual Property: Government-granted Monopoly, Exclusive Right, Copyright, Trademark, Patent, Industrial Design Right, Trade Secret, History of Patent Law, History of Copyright Law.* Beau Bassin, Mauritius: Alphascript Publishing – VDM Publishing House Ltd.

Owen, L. (ed.) (2007) *Clark's Publishing Agreements: A Book of Precedents.* 7th Edition. Haywards Heath: Tottel Publishing

Pedley, P. (2008) Copyright Compliance: *Practical Steps to Stay within the Law.* London: Facet Publishing.

Pfeifer, K-N. (2008) 'The return of the commons: copyright history as a helpful source?' *International Review of Intellectual Property and Competition Law,* 2008, 39(6), 679–88.

Phillips, J. (2009) *Copyright in the UK and the European Community.* London: Butterworths.

Pila, J. (2010) 'Copyright and its categories of original works'. In: *Oxford Journal of Legal Studies,* 2010, 30(2), 229–54.

Rogerson, P. (2010) 'Conflict of laws: foreign copyright jurisdiction'. *Cambridge Law Journal,* 2010, 69(2), 245–7.

Senftleben, M. (2004) *Copyright, Limitations and The Three-Step Test: An Analysis Of The Three-Step Test In International And EC Copyright Law.* The Hague: Kluwer Law International.

Chapter 9

Copyright II: Entertainment Law

Chapter Contents

9.1 Overview

The media is heavily dependent on the use of copyrighted works, such as the radio industry in relation to recently issued recordings. Obtaining appropriate authorization to broadcast such works is therefore crucial. In the form of some case studies, this chapter will focus on the development of the phonogram (recording) industries and the technological developments which have led to possible industry copyright infringements, such as internet piracy, music downloads and sampling. It also touches on other intellectual property (IP) violations in other industries, such as book publication, films, games and downloads, which can impact on the media; for instance, where television broadcasters will need copyright authorizations to show modern films.

The chapter then focuses on the advance of information technology (IT) and how the development of the Internet has impacted on invention, innovation, research and design. Though there is legislation in place which supposedly protects creators' IP rights and prevents others from using their inventions, designs or other creations, it is fair to say that economic rights in the form of royalty payments to artists and authors have dramatically reduced since music downloads via peer-to-peer file sharing (P2P) have become increasingly easy (see below 9.5.4).

The emergence of online music distribution services – both illegal and legal – has created challenges for the music industry and the various royalty-collecting and performance rights societies. Music tracks are virtually accessible anywhere in the world through the Internet (see below 9.5.7). The complex issue of music piracy will also be discussed. Piracy is subject to rather confused copyright legislation and rights management, traditionally organized at the national level. In recent years, the issue has received particular attention from EU institutions. This chapter focuses on recent domestic legislation in form of **The Digital Economy Act 2010** (see below 9.7.2) as well as actions taken at international and European Parliament level (see below 9.6.1 and 9.7.3).

Another challenge is the advent of e-books and e-readers such as the Apple iPad and Amazon's Kindle, where many books (and indeed newspapers and magazines) are now available digitally. The 'Google library book project' has undertaken the Herculean task of doing just this, and will also be discussed in this chapter (see below 9.7.5). But how will the digitization of copyrighted works affect legislation and fairly reward authors in future? The controversial issue of 'orphan books' – not defined in the **Digital Economy Act 2010** – will be addressed and how 'author-unknown' works should be operated and administered in future, particularly with the advent of e-books (see below 9.3.3).

Both Chapter 8 and this chapter outline the basic social objectives of intellectual property protection, which is essentially the protection of the right holder in form of literary, dramatic, image and musical copyright. The chapter closes with specific areas of industrial property rights, namely patents and trademarks. They are generally exclusive rights – subject to a number of limitations and exceptions – aimed at fine-tuning the balance between legitimate interests of right holders and of users (see below 9.8).

Having intellectual property laws is not enough. They have to be enforced, covered, *inter alia*, by the **Copyright, etc. and Trade Marks (Offences and Enforcement) Act 2002**, existing criminal law and – at international level – Part 3 of the TRIPS Agreement (see below 9.8.2). Then there is the rather controversial 'Anti-counterfeiting Treaty' being sponsored by the G8 Group of nations ('ACTA Treaty 2010').[1] In March 2010 the EU Parliament rebuked the ACTA Treaty by a remarkable vote of 633 to 13, stating that the substance of the treaty was 'fatally flawed'.

---

1 The aim of the ACTA negotiations (launched in 2008) is to provide an international framework that improves the enforcement of IP laws, by improving international standards as to how to act against large-scale infringements of copyright, often conducted by criminal organizations. At the time of publication, the negotiating parties of ACTA were Australia, Canada, the EU, Japan, Korea, Mexico, Morocco, New Zealand, Singapore, Switzerland and the USA, i.e. mainly the 'demand side' of IP protection. The ultimate objective is that large emerging economies, where IP enforcement could be improved, such as China or Russia, will sign up to the global ACTA pact. Though led by the EU Commission, member states participate in the negotiations. With the entry into force of the Treaty on the Functioning of the EU (TFEU), trade policy falls under the ordinary legislative procedure and trade-related agreements such as ACTA require consent of the EU Parliament.

Right owners often forget that the human rights of the alleged infringers have to be protected too – as cited in relation to the ACTA proposals (and the **Digital Economy Act 2010**) for a so-called 'three strikes and you're out' approach, where infringers would be automatically cut off after three occasions of downloading infringing material have been proved. (see below 9.8.2).

9.2 Phonograms and the recording industry

The music industry is a complicated business with a number of representative sectors and components interacting to make it work. The music industry worldwide was worth £30 billion in 2006, with the UK being Europe's largest music market (the world's third largest) with around 10.4 per cent of world record sales in 2005.[2] Over the past decade, there have been revolutionary changes ranging from the Internet and MP3 players to e-readers and vast online electronic music and literature libraries. All have been made possible by inexpensive broadband, which allows fast, efficient and user-friendly downloads.[3] Today, an estimated 95 per cent of all digital music is downloaded. Research by the International Federation of the Phonographic Industry (IFPI[4]) found that around 40 billion music files were downloaded without payment in 2008 and that 70 per cent of all music consumed in the US, UK, France and Germany in 2009 came through digital channels, while revenues from digital platforms in those countries accounted for only 35 per cent of revenues.

Mobile handset manufacturers Nokia and SonyEricsson started offering music services bundled with mobile phones in 2008. The launch of the Apple iTunes service – which made accessing paid-for downloads much easier – hugely increased demand. Later came streaming services such as Spotify, allowing listeners to enjoy unlimited music from the Internet – the music is played from servers and not downloaded. The advertising-supported option is free. With no advertising it is currently available for £10 a month (see below 9.5.7).

The UK is also the world's fourth-largest music publishing market providing ten per cent of worldwide revenues and is second only to the USA as a source of repertoire. Record companies ('the record label') are the main developers of musical talent. About 23 per cent of label revenue is reinvested in 'talent spotting', that is the signing and developing of new artists through their A&R (artist and repertoire) departments. Record labels enable artists, through advances in royalties, sales and marketing support, to be able to have a musical career. If one purchases sheet music of, for instance, Elton John's 'Song for Guy', this gives the right to use each single copy purchased, but it does not grant the right to photocopy additional copies, nor to perform the work in a live public performance, nor to record the work, nor to broadcast a recording or live performance. The process is covered by mechanical copyright protection and licensing, whereby the cost of the sheet music is expected to cover approximately half of the total licensing expenses required to put on a public performance (see below 9.3.2).

The minimum protection guaranteed by the **Rome Convention 1961** to performers is to sanction performances without their consent. It is important to remember that the performer of the song has rights as well as the writer of the song (note: a performer's rights ought not to be confused with the performance right in copyright law). This expression was used in order to allow

---

2 Source: IFPI (International Federation of the Phonographic Industry) Annual Report 2010: 'Music How, When, Where You Want It – But Not Without Addressing Piracy', by John Kennedy the then Chairman & Chief Executive, IFPI, available at <http://www.ifpi.org/content/library/DMR2010.pdf>, accessed 5 February 2011.

3 The terms upload and download often create confusion, as their definitions depend on the exact context. Download and upload refer to the transfer of information between computers. The person/computer sending the information refers to the transfer as an upload, while the person/computer receiving the information refers to it as a download.

4 IFPI (International Federation of the Phonographic Industry) represents the recording industry worldwide with some 1,400 members in 72 countries and affiliated industry associations in 44 countries. See also: IFPI Annual Report 2011 and CEO Frances Moore's personal statement. <www.ifpi.org>.

countries like the UK to continue to protect performers by virtue of penal statutes, determining offences and penal sanctions under public law, such as the **Copyright Acts of 1911 and 1956**. Under the **Rome Convention**, record producers ('producers of phonograms') have the right to authorize or prohibit the direct or indirect reproduction of their recordings ('phonograms'). The Convention also provides for the payment of equitable remuneration for broadcasting and communication to the public of phonograms.[5]

See Chapter
◄ 8.3.3

Under section 5(1) **Copyright, Designs and Patents Act 1988** (CDPA), the 'author' of a sound recording ('musical works') or a film is the producer, though it is commonly accepted that the copyright owner will be the person who made the arrangements for the recording to be made – typically a record label. It is then through advances in royalties, sales, marketing support and more recently 360-degree branding that a recording artist is able to have a musical career (see below 9.7.6).

Can a recording artist protect his name or the song by copyright? It depends. Copyright may or may not be available for titles, slogans or logos, depending on whether they contain sufficient authorship. In most circumstances copyright does not protect names, though a wrongful attribution of authorship or a performance may give rights under s. 84 CDPA or in the tort of 'passing off' (see: *Clark v Associated Newspapers Ltd* (1998)[6]).

See Chapter
◄ 8.6.3

Does an artist or performer need to register his work or sound recording to be protected? Not really. Copyright protection is formality-free in countries party to the **Berne Convention**, which means that protection does not depend on compliance with any formalities such as registration or deposit of copies. It exists immediately it is created. However, the various performance rights and collecting agencies and the Musicians' Union (MU) tend to differ. Commonly, authors do insert a small 'c' in a circle (©) – sometimes with the date – to warn people that the work is in copyright, but this is a matter of practice, not a legal requirement, in the UK.

9.2.1 Gilbert and Sullivan in America

Chapter 8 introduced the reader to the origins of copyright, closely related to the development of printing, which led to the rapid production of copies of sheet music at relatively low cost. Though the **Copyright Acts of 1911 and 1956** generally safeguarded the artist's rights in the UK, international law did not grant automatic copyright to the author in another country, such as America. Above all, there were no statutes in the late nineteenth century that governed public performances; and therefore there were no penalties for infringement. This led to widespread copying and 'passing off' of creative works, particularly those originating in English-speaking countries.

The famous British lyricist W.S. Gilbert and composer Arthur Sullivan[7] were particularly hard hit by the lack of statutory copyright and performance right protection. Their operettas were regularly performed throughout the United States during the 1870s, but they were never paid any royalties at the time for their earlier operatic productions of HMS *Pinafore* (1877). A Boston musician and composer, George Lowell Tracey, an American citizen, travelled to London in order to see a performance of *Princess Ida*, and subsequently created his own pirate copy of the piano score. Tracey then owned the legal copyright in the piano 'arrangement' in the United States as an American citizen and therefore Gilbert and Sullivan had no protection against any unauthorized performance whatsoever.

Gilbert and Sullivan had assigned the *Iolanthe* performance rights to Richard D'Oyly Carte[8] in 1879, who had also arranged the operetta's opening performance at London's Savoy Theatre.[9] Carte,

---

5 Article 10 Rome Convention.
6 [1998] All ER 6 (Ch D).
7 Librettist lyricist William Schwenck Gilbert (1836–1911) and composer Arthur Seymour Sullivan (1842–1900).
8 Representing the vision of British impresario Richard D'Oyly Carte (1844–1901), the D'Oyly Carte Opera Company was launched after Carte split from the Comedy Opera Company in July 1879.
9 See also: Ainger (2002).

in turn, tried to stop the unauthorized simultaneous performances of *Iolanthe* in American's North East by taking legal action against some of the theatre producers. But the circuit court in Maryland found that *Iolanthe*'s performances were not copyright-protected in American law. The producer at the Standard Theater in New York had hired John Philip Sousa, leader of the Marine band in Washington, to arrange his own orchestral accompaniment to *Iolanthe* (see: the *Iolanthe* case, 1883[10]).

The court in *Iolanthe* decided that the work's score was not an integral part of the dramatic work. This was in spite of the fact that the *Iolanthe* libretto was a published work and therefore copyright-protected (and quite profitably). But the piano score and performances in form of the full orchestra version could not be protected, with the conclusion that in order to retain common law copyright, one could not publish *any part* of an opera. This was an unsatisfactory result for Gilbert and Sullivan, who then never received a single dime for the early performances in America. The unsuccessful outcome of the *Iolanthe* case finally ended Gilbert and Sullivan's hopes of protecting the right of public performance via common law.

The reason for the lack of copyright protection for the operatic duo was that the US was not party to the **Berne Convention** (1886) at the time. It was not until 1989 that the USA signed the Berne Convention, though they were already party to the 'weaker' **Universal Copyright Convention** (UCC).

Sound recordings and works of architecture gained protection under the **Copyright Act of 1911**; the act introduced a new arrangement for calculating the term of copyright, thereby introducing economic rights. The 1911 Act abolished common law copyright protection in unpublished works, apart from unpublished paintings, drawings and photographs.

Iolanthe was not recorded until 1951, when Decca Records took up the challenge under the musical direction of Isidore Godfrey.[11] HMV (His Master's Voice) had already made nine acoustical recording 'samples' of *HMS Pinafore*, *The Mikado* and *The Yeomen of the Guard* in 1907–8, and the subsequent invention of electronic recordings allowed far higher fidelity, which then prompted D'Oyly Carte and HMV to re-record all the operettas.[12] 'Nipper' the dog, used by HMV on their record label since 1899, became one of the most famous trademarks in history.

9.2.2 Music publishing

Traditionally there are a number of categories of 'performers' involved in the process of music composition and exploitation. Some are direct copyright holders, others indirect. At the start of the creative process there is the person who is responsible for writing the music: the composer of the music and the lyricist of musical works (remember that there are two separate copyrights here – musical in the notes and literary in the words). Copyright law recognizes them as the 'authors'. The second stage involves the musicians or singers of the 'song' or melody and lyrics composed by the authors. These are the 'performers', covered by a separate regime of performers' rights.[13]

In recordings, the phonogram producers (or 'record producers') finance the performance and will normally own a sound recording copyright and a recording right in relation to the performers used, in the sense that they may provide finance and recording studio facilities.[14] Each record label will try to secure an exclusive contract with the artist or group. For example, the Beatles recorded

---

10 *Carte v Ford and another* (1883) Circuit Court, District of Maryland, 21 February 1883 (sub nom 'the Iolanthe case') 'Dedication of opera by publication of uncopyrighted score and libretto'.
11 Isidore Godfrey (1900–1977) was musical director of the D'Oyle Care Opera Company for 39 years, from 1929 to 1968. He conducted most of the company's performances during that period.
12 Source: Marc Shepherd has compiled an excellent online discography covering all Gilbert and Sullivan's *Mikado* recordings: http://gasdisc.oakapplepress.com/mik.htm
13 See: Part III CDPA.
14 See: ss. 185–188 CDPA.

their albums at Abbey Road Studios exclusively with EMI. Tom Jones also used to record with EMI ('What's New Pussycat?' and 'Delilah'), and then left for the Island Record label ('Praise & Blame'); Decca Records have their own classical, jazz and crossover artists, like Wynton Marsalis (blues trumpet), Rollando Vilazón (tenor), and the Three Tenors, José Carreras, Plácido Domingo and Luciano Pavarotti, (1935–2007).

The reproduction of the recorded materials has traditionally been on vinyl and, later, CD. Authors, performers and producers are each given 'performers' rights' for their creative works (related rights). The record label, by way of licence, will then be able to control the exploitation of the works. Indirect copyright holders comprise the music publishers, who are not directly involved in the creative process of the works. Their task is to support the authors and ensure that the musical works and scores are exploited by making sure that the repertoires are provided to the public and that the rights holders are granted their copyright; this includes all productions such as musicals or operettas performed by amateur societies.

See Chapter
← 8.5.1

9.2.3 Music Publishers Association (MPA)

Traditionally, publishers were also responsible for the printing and selling of sheet music. Between 1868 and 1877, Richard D'Oyly Carte, for example, wrote and published his own music compositions, as well as several comic operas, such as *Doctor Ambrosias – His Secret* (1868) and *Opera Comique* (1871) with his father's music publishing company (see 9.2.1 above).[15] Mechanical reproduction of a song or a recording (i.e. sheet music) covered the making of multiple copies and was undertaken by well-known music publishers, such as Breitkopf und Härtel (German music publishing in Leipzig[16]), Chappell Music (now the music publishing arm of Warners), Harry Fox Music Publishing (HFA) and the Hartenshield Group for choral and chamber music. Over recent years, physical music publishing activities have decreased as the revenues generated are minor compared to, say, book publishing revenues.[17]

The Music Publishers Association (MPA) has a worldwide catalogue of printed music and links to publishers (digitally and in hard copy). The MPA can act as a link between a performer seeking permission to photocopy printed music or perform it and the copyright owner, that is the songwriter/s. All recordings must be licensed, even non-commercial recordings. In the UK this is covered by the MCPS (see below 9.3.2).

9.3 Performing rights and collecting societies

Individual intellectual property right holders in music cannot easily enforce their statutory claims to exclusive usage and remuneration. Since the middle of the nineteenth century, composers and publishers have responded by creating collective bodies, so-called collecting societies, which monitor musical activity in a given territory and collect and distribute royalties accordingly. These societies, first established in Western Europe, operate on two principles: the principle of *reciprocity*, linking monopolistic national societies; and the principle of *solidarity*, making a collecting service available to all rights holders at roughly the same rate. Created for the administration of music rights, the societies' emergence is a consequence of the development of copyright, which in the

---

15 Sources: 'Music and Musicians, *The Daily News*, 12 April 1895; 'Original Correspondence, *The Era*, 10 September 1871.
16 Important and prominent publishers dating back to 1725 when Bernhard Christoph Breitkopf brought out a Hebrew Bible as their first major publication. Works published subsequently included those by composers Telemann, Leopold Mozart, Haydn and Bach. 'Härtel' was added to the name when Gottfried Christoph Härtel took over the company in 1795. By the latter half of the 1700s, all major composers wanted to have 'Breitkopf' publish their works.
17 Source: Wallis et al. (1999).

eighteenth century had already established its legal roots under the influence of the law of nature that was flourishing throughout Europe.

Collecting societies established themselves during the mid-nineteenth century when French composers realized the benefits of operating collectively when licensing public places to use their music. The '*propriété littéraire et artistique*' had already been recognized in France by two laws from the revolutionary period dated 1791 and 1793. Prussia passed its first 'copyright' law on 11 June 1837, '*Gesetz zum Schutze des Eigenthums an Werken der Wissenschaft und Kunst in Nachdruck und Nachbildung*' (legislation for the protection of intellectual ownership of scientific and artistic works against reproduction and copying), one of the most comprehensive and advanced laws protecting intellectual property in central Europe at the time.[18]

In 1847, the French popular chanson composer Ernest Bourget visited the Paris Concert Café 'Ambassadeurs', whose orchestras regularly played his music. When the waiter presented the composer with the bill for the sugared water that he and his colleague had consumed as the fashionable luxury drink of the period, Bourget refused to pay, claiming that the orchestra had repeatedly played his music – without paying him anything. Bourget took the café owner to court and on 8 September 1847, the Tribunal de Commerce de la Seine prohibited the owner from playing any further works by Bourget unless the composer consented. The Ambassadeurs' owner lost his appeal on 26 April 1849 at the Cour d'Appel de Paris and was sentenced to pay compensation to Monsieur Bourget, thereby establishing one of the first royalties cases.[19] During the following decades, composers and music publishers in other counties formed collective syndicates. Pierre Proudhon and Mikhail Bakunin formed the first syndicate for composers and music publishers in Spain during the 1930s.[20]

Collecting societies are in charge of the repertoire of the various rights holders. They monitor the use of it, negotiate the conditions for licensing agreements and commercial use, collect royalties and distribute them to the various rights holders. Collecting societies enjoy considerable market power since their collective practice is largely standardized, such as using the same tariffs, licensing conditions and distribution rights in the repertoire. This system guarantees a certain level of solidarity among rights holders and strengthens the rights of relatively unknown or niche authors and artists, who can expect the same level of protection as popular performers or song writers. Administrative fees are the main source of income of the collecting agencies. In general, fees are charged to the collecting societies' members for the services of collecting the income from the users (collection fee), and allocating such revenues to rights holders (allocation fee).[21]

That said, there will be those artists who prefer to manage their own conditions and royalties. In any case, certain rights generally have to be managed by right holders individually, such as the right to make an adaptation of a work or the use of music for the purposes of synchronization of films, commercials, ringtones or 'viral' marketing use on social networking sites. If anything, artists ought to ensure that the moral rights in their work are adhered to, including integrity rights of their original composition. Collecting agencies have tried to stop the practice of author-managed works.

See Chapter 8.6.1 →

These days, collecting and performance rights societies administer a considerable proportion of composers' and music publishers' rights. Most importantly, collecting societies ensure that right holders are rewarded through licensing agreements by way of royalties for the use of their music by commercial users including radio and television broadcasters, record companies, music service providers and music retailers. They act on behalf of their individual members in the negotiation of licensing agreements with commercial users who wish to avail themselves of music by copying,

---

18 See: Kreile and Becker (2001).
19 For further discussion see: Gillieron (2006).
20 See: Koempel (2007).
21 See: Ficsor (2003).

broadcasting or sampling music or by making it available on the Internet, such as YouTube or Spotify (see below 9.4 and 9.5.7).

Several countries have different forms of royalty collection. Some record labels and their artists have exclusive rights of reproduction ('private copying') and reprographic reproduction and therefore different rights to remuneration covered by EU legislation.[22] As well as copyright law the societies are subject to competition law to prevent them abusing their monopoly rights as there is usually only one society in relation to a particular area.[23] Many countries are subject to supervision by expert tribunals, such as the Copyright Tribunal in the UK.[24] Such courts or tribunals have the power to adjust collection schemes and the levels of licence fees, if these are regarded as unreasonable. Additionally, the **Berne Convention** provides harmonizing legislation in the countries of the Berne Union to determine the conditions under which certain exclusive rights may be exercised.[25] In general, the Convention provides for mandatory collective management of rights of subscribing countries to the Berne Union.

See Chapter
← **8.3.2**

Where a right is not provided for an exclusive right of authorization but rather by a mere right to remuneration, the so-called 'Article 12 rights' of performers and producers of phonograms comes into play. Article 12 **Rome Convention** reads as follows:

> . . . if a phonogram published for commercial purposes, or a reproduction of such phonogram, is used directly for broadcasting or for any communication to the public, a single equitable remuneration shall be paid by the user to the performers, or to the producers of the phonograms, or to both. Domestic law may, in the absence of agreement between these parties, lay down the conditions as to the sharing of this remuneration.

Some collecting societies traditionally apply social and cultural deductions when collecting royalties. These deductions are gathered into funds and dedicated to a number of services of social or cultural benefit to their members, such as pension schemes, assurances, sponsoring of cultural events, etc. The original model was introduced by CISAC (Confédération Internationale des Sociétés d'Auteurs et de Compositeurs), the International Confederation of Societies of Authors and Composers, founded in 1926.

After the Second World War, royalty deductions were limited to a maximum of ten per cent of all remunerations collected. This created an international solidarity among members of collecting societies and among repertoires. As deductions were applied on all royalties collected domestically (including those related to foreign repertoires), large foreign repertoires contributed to increase social and cultural revenues in favour of the domestic repertoire and CISAC and members. CISAC has imposed complete reciprocity: if one collecting society decides to deduct, the other collecting society is also fully entitled to do so.

Today, CISAC is an international performance rights organization that coordinates the protection of its member creators' rights, with its headquarters in Paris and regional offices in Budapest, Buenos Aires and Singapore. The organization counted 225 different authors' societies from 118 countries in 2010 and indirectly represents more than 2.5 million creators within all the artistic repertoires: music, drama, literature, audio-visual, graphic and visual arts. The UK singer-songwriter Robin Gibb of Bee Gees fame was President of CISAC in 2010 and Mexican film-maker Alfonso Cuarón Vice President. CISAC collected international royalty payments of €7.14 billion in

---

22 See: EC Council Directive No. 92/100/EEC of 19 November 1992, on Rental Rights and Lending Rights and on Certain Rights Related to Copyright in the Field of Intellectual Property which introduced such a right in favour of the authors and performers – the 'unwaivable right to equitable remuneration' in respect of the rental of phonograms and audio-visual works into which their works or, respectively, performances have been incorporated.

23 See: Articles 101 and 102 TFEU (Treaty on the Functioning of the European Union 2008), preventing abuse of a dominant position.

24 See: ss.116–149 CDPA.

25 Article 11bis(2) and Article 13(1) Berne Convention.

2009.[26] It sees itself as voicing the opinion of the international community of creators as well as operating the system of collective administration that promotes their rights.[27]

Since there is now a great deal of cross-border representation of artists and performers, collecting societies have created different categories of rights (to existing copyright) under one umbrella, referred to in the industry as the GEMA categories (Gesellschaft für musikalische Aufführungs- und mechanische Vervielfältigungsrechte: Society for musical performing and mechanical reproduction rights). GEMA is the society for musical performing and mechanical reproduction rights which originated in Germany.[28] GEMA, in turn, is a member of the BIEM (Bureau International des Sociétés Gérant les Droits d'Enregistrement et de Reproduction Mécanique : International bureau of societies administering the rights of mechanical recording and reproduction). BIEM is an organization that coordinates statutory licence agreements and is based in Neuilly-sur-Seine, France (presently representing 44 societies from 42 countries). Virtually every international performing rights society has now entered into some form of reciprocal representation agreement with its world counterparts and practically all GEMA countries are also members of CISAC.[29]

Importantly, fully developed collective management systems may grant 'blanket licences' for the use of the entire world repertoire of works or other protected subject matter which they manage. In practice, one collecting society would never grant an entire repertoire to the world at large. Article 18 of EC Directive 2001/29 ('The Information Society Directive') states that:

> . . . this Directive is without prejudice to the arrangements in the Member States concerning the management of rights such as extended collective licences.

Most commonly, there will be a system of bilateral reciprocal representation agreements in the case of performing rights. The 'guarantee-based system' involves the following elements:

(i)   The legality of authorizing the use of works not belonging to the organization's repertoire covered by statutory copyright law and/or common law;

(ii)   The organization guarantees that individual rights owners will not claim anything from users to whom blanket licences have been granted and, if they still try to do so, that such claims will be settled by the organization; any user will be indemnified for any prejudice and expense caused to him as a result of justified claims by individual owners of rights; and

(iii) The organization guarantees that it treats rights owners who have not delegated their rights to it in a reasonable way, taking into account the nature of the right involved.

The alternative to the 'guarantee-based system' is the so-called 'extended collective management system'. The collecting agency is authorized by the various rights holders to manage their rights collectively. Rights holders have the opportunity to 'opt out' from the collecting system, in which case they will take care of their own rights and remuneration management – a model understandably not favoured by collecting agencies.

Each collecting society relates to a specific form of exploitation of musical works and the conditions under which such exploitation is permissible. These categories result mainly from the

---

26 Source: CISAC Press Release at the General Assembly, Bilbao, 11 June 2010; see also: CISAC Annual Report 2009.

27 CISAC's mandate follows ISO standards and in turn delivers the ISAN system of voluntary numbering and metadata system for the identification of audio visual content (International Standard Audiovisual Numbers – ISAN). In order to assign IPMP (Intellectual Property Management and Protection) numbers on a worldwide scale the CISAC secretariat has been appointed by the ISO as Registration Authority for IPMP (MPEG-4, Part 1 – ISO/IEC 14496–1) in July 2001.

28 The reference to the GEMA categories was notably relied on by the EU Commission in its 1971 GEMA Decision. See Decision of June 2, 1971 (IV/26 760–GEMA) [2971] OJ L134/15.

29 For full and detailed discussion see: Dehin (2010).

day-to-day activities of collecting societies and are broadly used in the music industry. In particular:

1. **Mechanical reproduction rights** which define the author's (or creator's) right to authorize the sound recording of his work;
2. **Public performance rights** which authorize the public performance of the works; these reflect the fee authors and publishers are entitled to when a musical work is performed 'live', or via broadcasts, or as background music in shops, bars, hairdressers, restaurants, etc.

The two main royalty collecting societies in the UK are the Performing Rights Society (PRS) and the Mechanical Copyright Protection Society (MCPS). PRS and MCPS represent the rights owners and obtain rights clearances. MCPS and PRS entered into an operational alliance in 1997 and rebranded in January 2009 as 'PRS-MCPS' (http://prsformusic.com), now the largest UK collecting society. The alliance became one of the founding members of UK Music, an industry-wide body representing all aspects of the music business in September 2008, headed by Feargal Sharkey (see below 9.5).

9.3.1 Public performance rights: the Performing Rights Society (PRS)

The PRS regulates the public performance and communication rights in relation to music and literary copyright in musical works (but not the performance of these by singers etc.).[30] The PRS provides a performance licence for live performances and live broadcast of a musical work. Public performance rights may be licensed directly from the copyright owner by way of a direct request or from the collection society PRS directly (or the BMI in the United States[31]).

Any person or business wishing to play copyrighted music in public will require the consent by way of a licence from either the copyright owner or the collecting society to do so. If the person does not obtain the required licence, they run the risk of infringing copyright. Businesses typically applying for music licences include fitness clubs, cinemas, shopping centres, funeral parlours, providers of wedding functions and medical premises. Royalties are then distributed to the artist, creator or producer by the PRS.

9.3.2 Mechanical reproduction rights: The Mechanical Copyright Protection Society (MCPS)

The distinction between mechanical and performing rights arose at a time where the exploitation of musical works occurred mainly in the public arena – that is in live performances – from the mid-nineteenth century onwards. A mechanical licence is a broad term that refers to the reproduction for distribution or sale of musical compositions in the form of sound recordings. Any time an artist or producer produces a recording of a composition which they do not control, they need a mechanical licence. There are a large number of legal challenges in this area of musical copyright and piracy.

In February 1971, for example, Bright Tunes Music Corporation ('Bright Tunes'), then copyright holder of the song 'He's So Fine', composed by Ronald Mack, brought a copyright infringement action in the US District Court for the Southern District of New York (SDNY) against a former member of The Beatles, George Harrison, and also against related entities, 'Harrison Interests',

---

30 A performer can prevent someone from making a recording of their live broadcast; see: ss. 181–184 CDPA.
31 Broadcast Music, Inc. (BMI) collects licence fees on behalf of songwriters, composers and music publishers and distributes them as royalties to those members whose works have been performed: <http://www.bmi.com/licensing>.

alleging that the Harrison composition, 'My Sweet Lord', infringed Ronald Mack's composition. In late November 1975, Allen Klein (on behalf of ABKCO[32]) offered to pay Bright Tunes $100,000 as a settlement. Bright Tunes made a counter-offer demanding $148,000 and 40 per cent of the writers' and publishers' royalties earned in the US. The parties were unable to reach an agreement and the matter proceeded to trial. After a number of cross-appeals, the US Supreme Court found copyright infringement in favour of Mr Mack[33] (applying: *Warner Brothers v American Broadcasting Companies* (1981)[34]; also: *Sheldon v Metro-Goldwyn Pictures Corp.* (1936)[35]; also: *Northern Music Corp. v Pacemaker Music Co.* (1965)[36]).

With the onset of the digital age, the distinction between the two rights (mechanical and performance) has become increasingly blurred and it is for economic rationalization reasons that the MCPS and PRS joined forces, now operating as one performing rights society. Mechanical rights royalties are different and are paid to the songwriter, composer or publisher when music is reproduced as a physical product (such as sheet music) or for broadcast or online downloads such as iTunes. The mechanical licence royalties are collected by the MCPS.

Many prominent performers, including L.L. Cool J, Biz Markie and Massive Attack have been sued for allegedly using uncleared 'samples' by contravening 'needle time' restrictions.[37] SST records[38] charged UK samplist DJ Norman Cook $1,000 for sampling California-based band Negativland's record called 'Michael Jackson' on the Fatboy Slim CD *Better Living Through Chemistry* (released in the US by Astralwerks in 1996). Subsequently, Coca-Cola unwittingly used Fatboy Slim's version of the song in its advertising campaign and also breached copyright. It was later established that Negativland 'appropriated' the song from an unlicensed record of a 1966 religious church recording in Concord, California.

Negativland were themselves sued in 1991 by Island Records over a song called 'U2'. Island argued that the record was packaged so that consumers might think it was a song called 'Negativland' by the band U2, rather than the other way around. SST agreed to delete the record, but Negativland scored a public relations success when founder member Mark Hosler called U2 guitarist 'The Edge' and asked him to help pay the group's legal costs in the suit. The Edge expressed his sympathies but no cheque was forthcoming. Interestingly, in 2008, Mark Hosler was invited by the 'Digital Freedom Campaign' – a fair use advocacy group that is dedicated to defend the rights of artists, consumers and innovators – to travel to Washington, DC as a 'citizen lobbyist' to speak with various members of Congress about Negativland's work.[39]

While musical and performance copyright needs to be protected, licence fees can prove prohibitive to many musicians and may outweigh the artistic merit in using a sample or song cover (see below 9.4). Nowadays, digital music services involve a combination of mechanical rights (storage of the digital musical work on a hard disk) and performing rights (the musical work is made available to the public on a website). So a performing artist needs to obtain several licences from several entities, each holding either the performing or the mechanical rights. The mechanical licence is usually limited to one configuration, such as a physical CD or album, as opposed to a

---

32 Founded in 1960, ABKCO Music and Records is one of the world's leading independent entertainment companies. It owns a prestigious repertoire catalogue, including compositions and recordings by Sam Cooke, The Rolling Stones, Bobby Womack, The Animals, Herman's Hermits, Marianne Faithfull and The Kinks.

33 See: *ABKCO Music Inc. v Harrisongs Music, Ltd.* [1983] [1983] US Court of Appeals, Second Circuit November 3, 1983 722 F.2d 988; 221 USPQ 490.

34 [1981] 654 F.2d 204; 211 USPQ 97 (2d Cir. 1981).

35 [1936] 81 F.2d 49, 54, 28 USPQ 330, 335 (2d Cir. 1936).

36 [1965] 147 USPQ 358 (SDNY 1965).

37 See: s. 135A (5) CDPA: 'needletime' means the time in any period (whether determined as a number of hours in the period or a proportion of the period, or otherwise) in which any recordings may be included in a broadcast.

38 SST Records is an American independent record label formed in 1978 in Long Beach, California by musician Greg Ginn. The company was initially called Solid State Transmitters, through which Ginn sold electronics equipment.

39 Source: *Negativland News*, 27 October, 2008, available at <http://www.negativland.com/news/?cat=5>, accessed 25 November 2010.

digital download, which is different again from a mobile phone ringtone. Almost all publishers require a separate licence for each use.

Under the present copyright system (both in the US and in UK/EU law) any phonogram or 'phono recording' is subject to both a copyright for the sound recording and a copyright for the written song itself. The mechanical licensing for entire repertoires involves paying the composition copyright owners for the right to re-record a song, and is mostly handled by the Harry Fox Agency in the United States, the Canadian Mechanical Rights Reproduction Agency (CMRRA) in Canada, the MCPS in the UK and the GEMA authorities Europe-wide (see above).

The rise of global media corporations combined with digital production and distribution technologies has seriously undermined the principles of collecting societies. Wallis et al. (1999) concluded that the present structure of music copyright is likely to collapse, skewing the distribution of revenues in favour of big corporate players and global musical producers if there is no institutional intervention.[40]

9.3.3 Orphan works

The very nature of orphan works (or 'author-unknown works') is complex and arguably not adequately covered by the **Digital Economy Act 2010**. Orphan works are defined as where the copyright owner cannot be identified or traced and section 43 of the 2010 Act makes some provision for 'other persons' to be authorized to use or license such works. It is not clear whether collecting societies can lay claim to represent orphan works and license e-books or online distribution.

Collecting societies, particularly with published literary works, have argued that orphan works schemes should be limited to licensing bodies which represent rights holders (such as the ALCS – The Authors' Licensing and Collecting Society – for book or journal publications[41]). It is highly likely that collecting societies will become 'foster parents' to orphan works and will collect royalties until and unless an author or creator is found. Any future or dormant stakeholders are covered by the provision of section 43 of the 2010 Act and the section also allows any licensing body to run orphan works schemes. Once a collecting agency has become the authorized body of an orphan work it is obliged to carry out diligent searches to trace the copyright owners before it becomes the licensing body for the orphan work.

Section 43 also amends the definition of 'book' in the **Public Lending Right Act 1979**. The 1979 Act pre-dated the advent of audio and e-books and interpreted 'books' only in printed format. Section 43 extends the definition to works that are in sound-recorded or electronically-recorded format, so long as they consist mainly of written or spoken words or still pictures. Generally 'books' must have an international standard book number ('ISBN') code under the PLR (Public Lending Rights) payment scheme. Audio- and e-recorded books or plays are therefore new and unique creations, which makes the producer of this new and different format unique in copyright terms (different from the printed volume). It is for this reason that section 43 amends the definition of 'author' as well, extending eligibility for PLR to a wider category of rights holders including digitized copies. Public lending rights have been extended by section 43 and are now available to all rights holders living inside the European Economic Area (EEA) and to non-EEA rights holders. This means that they remain able to license or assign their rights to public libraries (and other bodies including prison libraries) independently.

Photographers have been particularly worried that the orphan works provision in section 43 makes it easier for their work to be considered 'orphan'. They fear that their work will be stripped

---

40 See: Wallis et al. (1999).
41 Source: 'ALCS Lobbying Activities on the Digital Economy Bill', available at <http://www.alcs.co.uk/Authors--rights/Lobbying-and-submissions/The-Digital-Economy-Bill.aspx>, accessed 25 November 2010.

of metadata (which identifies them as copyright owners) and be used without payment; or that their photographic work may be used in an objectionable manner, thereby depriving them of their moral rights (see: *Ray v Classic FM* (1998)[42]). The nervousness of photographers about the 'orphan' provision is understandable as photographic works are particularly vulnerable to being used without permission via the Internet. It is hoped that an EU Regulation or secondary legislation to the **Digital Economy Act 2010** will follow, which may strengthen the position of photographers by creating a structured framework for them within a legal copyright context. Such regulation would enable photographers to claim compensation for any unauthorized use of their work or to stop exploitation by way of an injunction.

There has been a call for greater clarity about the treatment of royalties generated from the use of orphan works. The 2010 Act introduced a power for the Secretary of State to make regulations by way of secondary legislation which would cover the treatment of royalties generated from the use of *all* orphan works. Specifically, the Secretary of State is enabled to make regulations covering the administrative costs that the licensor of an orphan work can charge; how long royalties must be held for the absent copyright owner of the orphan work; and what happens to those royalties if the copyright owner does not come forward after a certain period of time.

As long as the use of the orphan work is licensed by an authorized scheme there is no question of any liability in the event of the copyright owner coming forward, as the use of the work will have been authorized by the licence, in the same way that it would have been under a licence from the copyright owner themselves. Similarly, the copyright owner who turns up to find that their work has been used in the belief that it was orphan would have no claim for infringement as long as the use was licensed.

9.4 Acquiring rights from third parties: who sampled whom?

Building on past works is part of the essence of songwriting, but copyright law views songwriting as the genesis of a new song with no ties to previous lyrics or melodies. Many classical composers based their compositions on folk music and previous works. Bela Bartók's works, for instance, are based on Hungarian folk music and Dvořák's 1893 Symphony No. 9 *From the New World* quotes 'Swing Low Sweet Chariot'.[43] Yet the pop group DNA was forced to settle out of court in 1990 by paying a relatively small fine of £4,000 for a remix of Suzanne Vega's 1981 song 'Tom's Diner'.[44]

The golden rule of music licensing for an artist and producer begins with the knowledge as to which licences exist and how to obtain them. Is the work in the public domain? Is the artist using a composition or a sound recording, or both? Is he creating a cover song? Is he sampling an existing recording? Or is the work out of copyright? Knowing the difference between compositions and sound recordings is key to determining the necessary licence and can be a headache for any budding artist, who may incur high legal costs from copyright violations. The short answer is: unless the artist or producer controls the composition or sound recording, he will need a licence to use it.

As has been demonstrated above, compositions (the underlying structure of the song, including melodies, lyrics, chords, etc.) and sound recordings (the fixed master recording and/or audio file) are two separate copyrights. Compositions are often called 'publishing rights', while recordings are 'master rights'. Music publishers and songwriters control the publishing rights, and record labels and recording artists (if they own the label) own and control the master rights.

---

42 [1998] ECC 488.
43 Source: Schwartz and Childs (1992).
44 Source: Beaujon (1999).

The issue of copyright, licensing and royalty payments becomes complicated when portions of music are used or reused as part of a different song, advertisement or ringtone, known as 'sampling'. In sampling the artist is creating a *derivative* work, which requires negotiation as there is no standard rate and will require direct contact with all parties involved, usually by way of a collecting agency such as PRS-MCPS. But this system is far from perfect and there is a fundamental problem with data collection. The collection societies try and distribute royalties accurately and fairly, but many outlets, such as radio stations or other broadcasting outlets such as bars or clubs, do not always report every song played or sampled. Strictly speaking, if a band or DJ wishes to sample a song, the artist should get paid by either beats per minute or bars in the music score to be sampled.

'Mechanical royalties' (to the publisher) are usually based on the amount of 'phonorecords' sold; that is, sales based on sound recordings determined by the record companies through 'Sound Scan' and other reporting systems. While US mechanical royalties are calculated on a 'penny basis' per song, other countries might base mechanical royalties on percentages. The current statutory rate for a US copyright is 9.1¢ per song. The PRS-MCPS system grants a mechanical licence for the entire record based on a percentage of the wholesale or retail price, regardless of the number of songs. Public performance monies collected by the organization depend on their survey and consensus of how many times the song is played, when, where and at what time of day, and on what type of medium. Each collecting society has its own unique monitoring and survey systems and detection techniques based on random survey, census, sampling, or digital detection method. The difficulty remains how the various layers of collecting organizations track all of the music and samples accurately so that royalty monies are correctly paid to songwriters and publishers, because each of the organizations uses slightly different systems and methods for calculations.

Michael Jackson's songs have been sampled on 95 songs by other artists and the Red Hot Chilli Peppers in eight other songs. Eminem's single 'Beautiful', for instance, used the rock band Queen and singer-songwriter Paul Rodgers' single 'Reachin' Out/Tie Your Mother Down'. Sampling is different to 'covering' (or 'covers'), where typically one artist sings the song of another artist. Samples can be a few bars of a song or a distinct sound recording like the guitar entry to Led Zepplin's 'Whole Lotta Love'.[45] Sampling is typically done with a 'sampler', which could be a piece of hardware or a computer program. The technique of sampling probably dates back to the late 1970s, when a Jamaican-born DJ in the Bronx named Kool DJ Herc began playing the 'break' in a rock, soul, funk or even Latin song over and over by switching between records, while MCs[46] would 'rap' over the beat they created. From rap's inception to the present day, many rap beats contain parts of recognizable songs, such as Run DMC's 1986 hit 'Walk This Way' which borrows a guitar riff, drum beat and chorus from rock band Aerosmith.[47]

Using a sample means the use of a pre-recorded track – for example, Van Halen's 'Jump' – in a new recording or rap mix. In this case, the artist, MC or DJ needs to clear both the sound recording copyright with Van Halen's record label as well as the mechanical licence from the music publisher in order to legally use the underlying composition.[48] Sampling may also fall foul of the composer's moral rights if it distorts his work in the sample.[49]

The process of sampling inherently infringes the copyright in the underlying and original composition and sound recording. Even if a rap artist or DJ wishes to use only a couple of beats, this process will involve either licensing the sample from the copyright holder/s or asking the artist or right holder for permission (or both). The US District Court for the Southern District of New

---

45 1969 7" single US: Atlantic 45-2690. Bonham, Jones, Page, Plant, Dixon.
46 MC (Master of Ceremonies) is a music artist and/or performer who usually creates and performs vocals for his own original material. This must not be confused with a DJ (Disc Jockey) who plays party music and creates music mixes.
47 Source: Sanjek (1992).
48 See: McLeod (2004).
49 See: ss. 79–82 CDPA.

York decided in *Grand Upright Music Ltd. v Warner Bros. Records, Inc.* (1991)[50] that rapper Biz Markie had violated the copyright of Gilbert O'Sullivan's 'Alone Again (Naturally)', which Markie had sampled in his song 'Alone Again' on his album *I Need A Haircut* (Cold Chillin', 1991). The track 'Alone Again' was subsequently not included on Markie's audio CD since, after his unsuccessful lawsuit, he was told by the court to remove it from the album. Nor could he make it available in MP3 format.

Sampling artists are, then, at the mercy of large record labels and music publishers, who have whole legal departments devoted to finding out 'who sampled whom'.[51] Cover songs have always been popular, and are now witnessing a resurgence as tribute albums and 'best of' CDs or digital-only releases are issued by record labels to cash in on artists like the Beatles or Rolling Stones before copyright in their songs expires.

If a sampling artist is being confronted by the legitimate copyright holder in a legal challenge, he can possibly use the *de minimis* defence, which means the sample used was small enough so that the rights holder cannot claim that he 'owned' the sampled section. This constitutes 'fair use' of the original. Alternatively, the defendant MC or DJ could claim that the sampling was done in parody, which also amounts to 'fair use' (see: *Twentieth Century Music Corp. v Aiken* (1975)[52]). If a sampler was considered a musical instrument rather than a copying device, then the use of a sample would be more similar to 'covering' the sound than duplicating it. In this case, a sample would constitute covering a small segment of a song and therefore would be subject to compulsory royalty rates.[53]

Two early US cases imply that the size of the borrowed portion could determine whether or not IP infringement occurred. In *Boosey v Empire Music Co.* (1915),[54] the Southern District Court of New York ruled that six similar notes or more constituted copyright infringement; while in *Northern Music Corp. v King Record Distribution Co.* (1952),[55] the same court indicated that the use of more than four bars constituted an infringement.

In addition to mechanical licensing for covers, a song also has a public performance right that derives from the section of copyright that applies to performing a composition in public. Only the underlying composition copyright holders receive income from performance rights societies. Most artists who use a sample licence pay either a flat fee or a royalty calculation based on the number of copies of their new work sold. A more popular song or artist demands a higher licensing fee, as when Puff Daddy sampled The Police's 'Every Breath You Take' for his 'I'll Be Missing You'. When The Verve, a 'Britpop' rock band from Wigan, scored their first major global hit with 'Bitter Sweet Symphony' in 1997 and sold 1.8 million copies of their album *Urban Hymns* in the UK alone, the band and their record label, Virgin, were faced with a major legal challenge at the time the band won the title of 'best British group' at the 1998 Brit Awards. In writing the song 'Bitter Sweet Symphony', Verve singer, Richard Ashcroft, had used a sample of The Rolling Stones' hit song 'The Last Time', originally recorded and performed by the Andrew Oldham Orchestra in the early 1960s.[56] Andrew Loog Oldham was the Stones' original manager. Though the Stones' subsequent manager Allen Klein initially refused to license 'The Last Time' to The Verve, Verve manager Jazz Summer eventually persuaded Klein to allow the group to use the sample. One of the conditions imposed on the band was that Mick Jagger and Keith Richards receive the songwriting credit for the title. This way, Klein also received the copyright to the (new) composition in The Verve song.

---

50 *Grand Upright Music Ltd. v Warner Bros. Records Inc.* [1991] 780 F. Supp. 182 (SDNY 1991).
51 To check who samples whom see: <www.whosampled.com> (accessed 25 November 2010).
52 [1975] 422 US 151.
53 See: Hampel (1992).
54 [1915] 224 F 646 (SDNY1915).
55 [1952] 105 F Supp 393 (SDNY 1952).
56 The Andrew Oldham Orchestra was a musical side project in the mid-1960s, created by Andrew Loog Oldham, the original producer/manager of The Rolling Stones. There was no actual orchestra per se. The name was applied to recordings made by Oldham using a number of session musicians, including members of the Rolling Stones.

When Nike used 'Bitter Sweet Symphony' in their 'I can' commercial for the Super Bowl XXXII on 25 January 1998, The Verve's (commercial) hit also boosted album sales of *Urban Hymns* in the USA. The Verve subsequently gave $175,000 of that profit to charity.[57] But that was not all. The Verve faced another legal challenge in 1999, when Andrew Loog Oldham (by that time living in Bogota, Columbia) served a writ on The Verve and their label Virgin. At the High Court in London, Oldham claimed that he owned the recording rights of the orchestral version of 'The Last Time', not Decca (the Stones' original record company). He sued Virgin and The Verve for using the sound recording, demanding a million pounds in royalties. In their defence, the band and Virgin said that they had paid royalties to Decca Records for the song, in the honest belief that Decca owned the recording of Mr Oldham's version of the song. But Oldham and music publishers ABKCO successfully argued that too much of 'The Last Time' had been sampled by The Verve. The Verve's lead singer, Richard Ashcroft, had to cede authorship of 'his' song and all publishing and royalty rights to ABKCO and Mr Oldham.[58] In an interview with *New Musical Express* in 2008, Mr Loog Oldham joked about the legal battle with The Verve and how Richard Ashcroft 'should have known better' and that the band had just used too much in the sample song.[59]

Is sampling illegal? Yes, contrary to popular belief and practice, sampling of an original copyrighted song without permission by the right holder is illegal. Unauthorized sampling actually violates two potential legal rights. First, the minute an Inc, for instance, samples a portion of someone's song, this constitutes a violation of the copyright in the song itself. Secondly, sampling violates the sound recording copyright, usually owned by the record label or recording artist. Thus, sampling without prior permission subjects the illegal copier to a copyright infringement both of the original author (or publisher) and the record company. It is worth noting that sampling may also infringe the moral rights of the author or creator of the work in the UK and Europe (but not the US), whereby the creator may object to derogatory treatment of their work.[60]

9.4.1 Public performance licences: The Phonographic Performance Ltd (PPL)

'Public performance' occurs whenever sound recordings are played outside the domestic or family circle. Whenever a sound recording is played in a commercial environment, even if only one person can hear it, it becomes a public performance and a fee is payable to PPL. If a business plays music videos, they will be required additionally to apply for a VPL licence (Video Performance Ltd). The VPL licence fees are assessed according to the number and size of the screens upon which music videos are played. The PPL issues different types of licences according to businesses type and size, typically including cinemas, shopping centres, funeral parlours, dental practices or gyms. If they do not obtain the required public music licence, they risk copyright infringement and prosecution. Each business must register and pay a fee to the music licence collecting agency PPL (Phonographic Performance Ltd.). PPL issues different licences for different businesses and the sound recordings or music videos used. The various categories comprise, for instance, educational establishments, health and fitness, holiday parks, offices and factories, shops and stores and public transport. Aerobics and dance teachers need their own PPL licence, depending on the size of groups and venues.[61]

Many services broadcast online, whether as an online-only radio service, or as a simulcast of an AM/FM or DAB broadcast. For this reason, PPL issues two separate licences for non-interactive

---

57 Source: 'Nike deal sweetens US prospects of British band', by Alice Rawsthorn, *Financial Times*, 6 April 1998.
58 Source: 'Who's Suing Whom: Bitter Symphony as The Verve is sued by Oldham', by John Willcock, *The Independent*, 11 January 1999; also: 'Verve Sued Again Over Pop Tune', by Chris Ayers, *The Times*, 9 January 1999.
59 Source: 'Rolling Stones' manager derides The Verve', *NME News*, 7 October 2008.
60 See: Article 6bis Berne Convention 1886 (as amended).
61 Fees increase pro rata from £15.74 per band of 1,000 persons up to £151.71 (August 2010).

online radio, the 'PPL Small Webcaster Licence' for small-scale services, and the 'PPL Standard Webcaster Licence'.

9.4.2 Licensing background music

How many licences does a business need? It can be confusing as to whether one needs a PRS/MCPS or PPL licence in order to play music in public. This issue was addressed in Re. *Phonographic Performance Ltd* (PPL) (2009),[62] where an action was brought by the 'British Beer & Pub Association' (BBPA) and the British Hospitality Association (BHA) against PPL for charging additional fees for background music since 2005. PPL had demanded from the hotel and catering businesses that they needed two licences, one for public performances (PRS) and another for phonographic playback (background music) from PPL. This had brought in additional subscription fee revenue of about £20 million for PPL.

In Re. PPL, Kitchin J held that the PPL could not charge a separate licence fee for playing background music of sound recordings because the businesses in question had already paid their PRS fees; a second music licence was therefore not necessary. Based on the Chancery Court's decision, Mr Justice Kitchin stated that there was nothing in ss. 125–128 **Copyright, Designs and Patents Act of 1988** to suggest that separate royalties ought to be charged for playing background music, since that was covered by 'public performances'. The case had first been decided by the Copyright Tribunal; Kitchin further ruled that the Tribunal had only limited jurisdiction in this respect, with no power under s. 128B CDPA to order back payments in respect of users who used sound recordings not contained in a broadcast. He therefore ordered that PPL pay back all overcharged licence fees to the hoteliers and pub landlords.[63] Re *Phonographic Performance Ltd* was a landmark victory for the hospitality industry, who can now play background music with just one music licence.

What about viral marketing – a new online trend to promote a particular product simply by 'word of mouth' – a social networking site or tweets? The viral marketing trend is being defined as the utilization of pre-existing social networks to produce increases in brand awareness or to achieve other marketing objectives by identifying individuals with high social networking potential. Viral marketing has become a cheap and cost-effective online buzz to promote a particular product or idea.

In 2002 (three years before YouTube's birth), BMW launched a short internet video clip entitled *The Hire*, starring British actor Clive Owen. More than 11 million viewers initially 'tuned' in, though in order to view the clip, one had to register on the BMW website. More than two million registered, providing the German car manufacturer with an enormous (free) database and future clientele for marketing the new Z3 sports car. Though one cannot really tell how many of those clicks were converted into sales, an estimated 100 million viewers clicked on the video in the first four years.[64] *The Battle for Milkquarious* – a short online rock opera released on YouTube in February 2010 – was an aggressive viral marketing videospot by the California Milk Processor Board promoting the 'Got Milk' campaign.[65]

In July 2010, MJ (Morgan Jane) Delaney availed herself of the 'viral marketing' medium when she release her title 'Newport' (Ymerodraeth State of Mind)' on YouTube. Arguably, this 'spoof' unashamedly breached copyright law. MJ claims that her short video clip, promoting the Welsh city

---

62 *Phonographic Performance Ltd v The British Hospitality Association* [2009] EWHC 175 (Ch).
63 See: Copyright Tribunal Refunds' applications the PPL website, available at <http://www.ppluk.com/en/Music-Users/Copyright-Tribunal-Refunds>, accessed 25 November 2010.
64 'The Hire' can be viewed on YouTube, under 'BMW Films', available at <http://www.youtube.com/watch?v=rIHGT8vWleQ>, accessed 25 November 2010.
65 Source: 'Battle for Milquarious', YouTube, 26 February 2010, available at <http://www.youtube.com/whitegoldiswhitegold>, accessed 25 November 2010.

of Newport, is a 'parody' of Alicia Keys' and Jay-Z's 'Empire State Of Mind'.[66] More than 100,000 people rushed to view the 'Newport' clip on the video-sharing website within the first 48 hours after its debut release, apparently with enthusiastic support from twitter queen Lily Allen and retweet-support from Welsh actor-comedian Rob Brydon and Radio 2's show host Claudia Winkleman. The internet sensation featured Newport rapper Alex Warren and singer Terema Wainwright. The music video was littered with witty one-liners, among them the city's twinning with Guangxi Province in China ('There's no province finer'). Instead of the Manhattan skyline as a backdrop to their video, scenes from the Welsh town were featured. MJ Delaney told Sky News that the video music clip was merely an 'in-joke' with her boyfriend and that she had not even contemplated getting a music rights licence. However, her 'joke' probably amounted to copyright infringement. YouTube was forced to take the Newport viral down by EMI.

Viral marketing is now used as a tool on all social networking sites, including Twitter, PayPal, Facebook, MySpace and Flickr, spreading brand names across the social media landscape, often accompanied by music. 'Virals' have become a powerful tool for advertisers, who are increasingly leaving TV advertising for online marketing spots made possible via streaming media such as YouTube. So does it need a music or video licence?

The cheap social marketing tool 'virals' rely on 'spreading the word' about a product or idea and hoping it continues to grow – and if it uses music video clips or brief samples, like the 'Newport' rap, it will require a music licence, because, in copyright terms, virals plagiarize existing music without paying the original artists any royalties. Artists like MJ Delaney might argue, however, that her music video clip is a 'new creation' and therefore does not breach copyright laws – alternatively, she could argue that it was a parody of the original song. That said, she should have paid a licence fee to one of the collecting societies for the song or at least asked Jay Z and Alicia Keys for permission to 'sample' their song.

9.5 Artists in revolt

From 2009 onwards, a number of pop stars declared war on peer-to-peer (P2P) file-sharing, including Gary Barlow of Take That, James Blunt and prominent music promoter and X-Factor-creator Simon Cowell.[67] Singer Lily Allen voiced strong concerns via her blog spot about Internet piracy, calling all file-sharing illegal and claiming that her number one enemies are millions of people all over the world who download her music without paying for it.[68] Björn Ulvaeus from the pop group Abba commented in September 2009:

> . . . 'Thank you for the music, for giving it to me'. Is this the song of the grateful downloader? It makes me angry when those who want to get round copyright on the Internet evoke a faceless and immensely powerful 'intellectual property industry' as their main enemy just because it suits them.[69]

Some artists have a different view, such as Radiohead, Pink Floyd and Blur. They believe that free releases of new singles via YouTube help artists attract a new generation of fans, on the basis that more revenue is generated by live acts and concerts. It is difficult to establish at what point music

66 Source: 'Jay-Z and Keys Spoof is YouTube hit', YouTube, 30 July 2010, available at <http://www.youtube.com/watch?v=maNgAxUnJ8I>, accessed 25 November 2010.
67 See: 'Simon Cowell has called in cops after Leona Lewis' new track was leaked on to the Internet,' *Sun*, 19 August 2009.
68 Source: Lily Allen campaigns against music piracy, *Daily Telegraph*, 21 September 2009.
69 Source: 'Filesharing is defended by gigging performers, but who pays the songwriter?' Björn Ulvaeus, guest commentator, *Times Online*, 12 September 2009.

downloads become illegal and the international debate surrounding music downloads, encouraged by famous pop stars, continues.

9.5.1 Physical music piracy

The Office of Fair Trading (OFT) and Trading Standards commonly use the term 'piracy' to describe the deliberate infringement of copyright on a commercial scale, including activities that cause commercial harm. In relation to the music industry it refers to unauthorized copying. Piracy falls into four categories, namely physical music piracy, counterfeits, bootlegs and internet piracy. Physical music piracy is the making or distribution of copies of sound recordings on physical carriers without the permission of the rights owner whereby the packaging of pirate copies may or may not be different from the original. Pirate copies are often compilations, such as the 'Greatest Hits' of a specific artist, or a compilation of a specific genre, such as dance tracks or hip hop, and can extend to music videos, films and games.

9.5.2 Counterfeiting

Counterfeits are an example of physical piracy. They are recordings made without the required permission from the artist or publisher, which are then packaged so that they resemble the original as closely as possible. The original artwork is reproduced on sophisticated copiers, including trade marks and logos. This is likely to mislead the consumer into believing that they are buying the real thing.

9.5.3 Bootlegs

Bootlegs are unauthorized recordings of live performances. They are duplicated and sold without the permission of the artist, composer, producer or record company. The first bootlegged recordings can be traced back to 1969, when Bob Dylan gave his first live concerts. By the early 1980s the bootleg industry in Germany and the Netherlands was thriving. Music industry experts claim that there were about 30,000 illegal Dylan bootleg recordings in Italy alone, claiming that the bootleg industry is the most serious form of piracy.[70] It can be argued that in some cases bootlegging serves a useful cultural service. Some of the early recordings of the great opera singer Maria Callas, for example, in her live performances at La Scala Opera House in Milan only exist now – and are sold 'officially' by record companies – because of the illicit activities of members of the audience and technicians!

It is interesting to note that Bob Dylan recently released his own official edition of a 'bootleg' series (Volumes 1–9). Volume 9 (2010), for example, features the legend's studio recordings from 1962 to 1964, also known as the 'Witmark' and 'Leeds' demos in mono format, never previously released on CD; just one way to extend copyright in his recordings and thereby increase royalties. For die-hard Dylan enthusiasts there now exists a large collection of previously buried treasure brought to light in a cornucopia of unissued material, including demo recordings, outtakes and coffee-house recordings, such as the legendary 1966 Royal Albert Hall appearance.

9.5.4 Piracy and file-sharing: is it legal?

The advent of personal computers has made it easy and convenient for someone to convert media in a physical/analog or broadcast form into a universal, digital form (also known as 'ripping'). The

---

70 See: Heylin (1994).

original may or may not be copyright. Combined with the Internet and file-sharing tools, it has become very easy to make unauthorized copies for distribution of (copyrighted) digital media. Research by the International Federation of the Phonographic Industry (IFPI) found that around 40 billion music files were downloaded without payment in 2008. According to the BPI's Chief Executive Geoff Taylor, there were around six million active file-sharers in the UK in 2008 and an estimated 95 per cent of all digital music was downloaded.[71]

What is the law on file-sharing? File-sharing is not in itself illegal. On file-sharing or peer-to-peer (P2P) networks the files being shared are held on members' computers and those who want a particular game, music track or video get bits of it from anyone else who has it via the Internet. It only becomes illegal when users are sharing content, such as music or films, which are protected by copyright legislation.

Can the Internet Service Providers (ISPs) be held to account for illegal file-sharing, P2P downloads and internet piracy? How can a fair balance be struck between allocating responsibilities to the end user and the (music) industry? In August 2008 a British woman, who put a game on a file-sharing network, was successfully sued at London's Patents County Court by the game's creator, Topware Interactive, and ordered to pay damages of £16,000. Isabella Barwinska from London had shared a copy of Dream Pinball.

Topware Interactive had started its campaign against pirates of Dream Pinball in early 2007 after legal action forced 18 British internet firms to pass on details of suspected pirates that it had identified. Davenport Lyons, the law firm acting for Topware, sent out about 500 letters to identified persons in the UK who had made the game available via file-sharing networks such as 'eMule', 'eDonkey' and 'Gnutella'. In the letters the lawyers had asked for a payment of £300 as a 'settlement' figure that would head off further legal action. Some of those accused of sharing the game chose to fight the legal action and it was in one of these contested cases that Topware Interactive won its claim for damages.[72] The test case opened the floodgates for litigation against thousands of other Britons suspected of sharing games online.

A Hertfordshire couple in their 60s were horrified to receive a letter from Davenport Lyons in November 2008, accusing them of downloading a hardcore gay porn movie. The 20-page 'pre-settlement letter' from the lawyers, acting on behalf of German pornographers, insisted the couple pay £503 to their clients for the 115-minute film Army Fuckers, which featured 'Gestapo' officers and 'Czech' farmers, or face court action. The lawyers also sent out similar demands to other individuals for a German gay porn film with an even more offensive title.[73] By March 2010, the Solicitors Regulation Authority[74] was investigating the London-based law firm, Davenport Lyons (and others) for complaints received by the consumer group Which that a number of 'online victims' had been bullied and harassed for being wrongly accused of illegal file-sharing.[75]

Owners of films, music and computer games need to protect their rights and prevent illegal copying. But many of these letters are sent to people who have no idea what a download is and are innocent. If all of the recipients of these settlement letters paid up, the film producers would be raking in £12.5 million per year, which would make the porn film industry even more profitable. A German company called DigiProtect claims the users are breaking copyright law and is demanding £500 to settle out of court. A 20-page legal letter lists the name of the film involved along with the time and date of the alleged download. Michael Coyle from Southampton-based solicitors Lawdit

---

71 Source: 'The role of record labels in the digital age'. Extract from the speech by BPI Chief Executive Geoff Taylor on 20 June 2008.
72 Source: 'Game sharers face legal crackdown', BBC News Online, 19 August 2008.
73 Source: 'Porn bill for couple who can't download', by Tony Levene, The Guardian, 29 November 2008.
74 The Solicitors Regulation Authority (SRA) regulates more than 110,000 solicitors in England and Wales, as well as registered European lawyers and registered foreign lawyers. The SRA is the independent regulatory body of the Law Society for England and Wales.
75 Source: 'Law firm investigated over claims that it bullied alleged filesharers', by Bobbie Johnson, The Guardian, 5 March 2010.

was acting on behalf of hundreds of people who received legal papers in the post in 2010. Allegations against the Hertfordshire couple were eventually dropped.[76] Michael Coyle said: 'The cynical lawyer in me would say this is a money-making exercise. If you send out 10,000 letters and ask for £500 each time, you only have to get half to pay up and you've made a significant amount of money. Because it is porn, the person who's being accused won't want to go to court and is more likely to pay up to make the matter go away even if they are completely innocent.'

In September 2010 the UK's Information Commissioner (IC), Christopher Graham, told the BBC that the firm behind a leak of thousands of Sky Broadband customers' personal data could face a fine of half a million pounds. The list, produced by ACS:Law, contained the names and addresses of more than 5,300 people alleged to be illegally sharing adult films online. Mr Graham said that ACS:Law had 'a number of questions to answer', such as: 'how secure was this information and how was it so easily accessed from outside?' The Information Commissioner has significant power to take action and can levy a fine of up to half a million pounds on companies that flout the Data Protection Act.

See Chapter
6.3.1 →

The documents appeared online after users of the message-board '4chan' attacked ACS:Law's website relating to its sending thousands of letters to alleged net pirates, asking them to pay compensation of about £500 per infringement or face court. Armed with IP (internet protocol) addresses – which can identify the internet connection used in any copyright infringement – ACS lawyers could then apply for a court order to get the physical address of the broadband licence holder from the service provider whose network has allegedly been used for the file-sharing. The leak contained around 1,000 confidential emails, including personal correspondence between Andrew Crossley – who runs ACS:Law – and work colleagues, as well as lists of potential file-sharers and information on how much the firm had made through its anti-file-sharing activities. The leaked unencrypted document also contained personal details of more than 5,300 BSkyB Broadband subscribers alongside a list of adult videos they may have downloaded and shared online. A BBC investigation in August found a number of people saying they were wrongly accused by ACS:Law of illegal file-sharing.[77]

The **Digital Economy Act 2010** gives ministers, court authorities and OFCOM the power to disconnect illegal file-sharers and permits courts to block websites containing copyright-infringing material. The music and games industries have welcomed the Digital Economy Act and its 'cut-off' measures as a step in the right direction. The Internet Service Providers' Association (ISPA), on the other hand, is 'outraged' about the new legislation that grants the High Court powers to force ISPs to block websites containing 'substantial' amounts of copyrighted material; particularly if the rights holder demands redress, regardless of whether the website has any knowledge of the actions of its users (see below 9.7.2). While BPI chief, Geoff Taylor, welcomes the 2010 Act with great enthusiasm, he states that the law enforcement agencies such as OFCOM will have to pay particular attention to non-P2P piracy so that the wrong people will not be victimized.

9.5.5 The 'Napster' case

Napster became the first online song-swapping file share service, based in the USA, attracting more than 60 million users in 2000. Created by Shawn Fanning while he was studying at Northeastern University in Boston, the service was so named after Fanning's unusual hairstyle. Napster's technology allowed people to share their MP3 music files with other Internet users, thereby bypassing the commercial music licensing market and avoiding buying CDs. The service operated between June 1999 and July 2000, when Napster was accused of violating US copyright legislation, namely the **Digital Millennium Copyright Act** (DMCA) (see below 9.7.3).

---

76 Source: 'Cash demand over 'porn downloads', BBC *Newsbeat* broadcast, 5 December 2008.
77 Source: 'ACS:Law could face £500,000 fine for porn list leak', by Daniel Emery, BBC *News online*, 28 September 2010.

The lawsuit was filed jointly by the Recording Industry Association of America (RIAA), AOL, Time Warner, Bertelsmann, EMI, Vivendi Universal and Sony. Heavy metal band Metallica and rap artist Dr Dre sued in separate legal actions, demanding, *inter alia*, that some 60,000 pages be removed from Napster containing the artists' names. In May 2000, San Francisco Judge Marilyn Hall Patel ruled that Napster was guilty of copyright infringement and for trading copyrighted music without permission. Napster was not entitled to claim protection under the DMCA, because the company did not transmit, route or provide connections for infringing material through its system. Napster was ordered to pay damages and the service was shut down in July 2000 by way of a court injunction. While appealing against the court's decision, Napster's chief executive, Konrad Hilbers, tried to reach an amicable settlement with the companies concerned. This involved licensing agreements.

In January 2002, Napster's brand and logo were registered as trade marks. Napster then launched a legal file-swapping service as a free beta test version to a selected 20,000 users with more than 100,000 music files on a subscription basis. Shawn Fanning assured the courts that 98 per cent of the code behind the program had been rewritten, adding a music player, chat rooms and instant messaging to the service.[78] There is no doubt that Napster paved the way for decentralized P2P file-sharing and distribution programs. These have become increasingly difficult to control and have made internet piracy relatively easy.

9.5.6 The '*Pirate Bay*' case

The event that took the issue of copyright to the fore in Sweden − a country with the highest penetration of high-speed broadband fibre-optic connections in Europe − was the *Pirate Bay* case, where its owners were jailed in 2009. The Swedish-based company The Pirate Bay (TPB) had offered 'BitTorrent' file-sharing of music, films and TV shows since 2003. On 17 April 2009, the Stockholm district court (Tingsrätt) found four men behind TPB guilty of Internet piracy. After a 13-day trial, judge Tomas Norström and three *namndeman* (a jury with extended powers) found Peter Sunde, Gottfrid Svartholm Warg, Fredrik Neij and Carl Lundström guilty of 'assisting in making copyright content available', that is having made 33 copyright-protected files accessible for illegal file-sharing via the TPB website.[79]

The Stockholm court found that by providing a website with search functions, upload and storing capabilities and contacts between file-sharers, TPB had made it very easy to commit illegal 'copyright' acts. The four accused used as a defence the fact that they did not actually 'host' any files, but this was not acceptable to the Stockholm judge, who sentenced all four to one year's imprisonment.[80] Resulting from a parallel civil legal action, the four men were ordered to pay 30 million Swedish kronor (£3m) in damages to copyright holders for lost sales, including 17 media and record companies such as Warners, MGM Pictures, Columbia Pictures, Twentieth Century Fox Film, Sony BMG, Universal and EMI. The Pirate Bay was shut down by a court order and their appeal to the Swedish Court of Appeal was dismissed. The TPB appellants had demanded a retrial on the grounds that the Stockholm Tingsrätt judge was biased in that he was a member of several copyright protection agencies in Sweden.[81]

By January 2010, The Pirate Bay was up and running again; firstly from a server in Ukraine and then from a Dutch data centre called 'CyberBunker', based in an old nuclear facility some 120 miles

---

78 The new service offered standard MP3 music files and 'nap' files, which are MP3s with the addition of a protective layer that prevented them being copied off the host computer or burned onto CDs. There was also a 'buy' button, linking the service to the music retail site CDNow, owned by Bertelsmann.

79 Source: 'Artist hoppar av Pirate bay-åtalet', *Svenska Dagbladet*, publicerad Tobias Brandel, 17 April 2008.

80 Prosecutor's charges against the four defendants in Swedish: Internationella åklagarkammaren Stockholm, 31 January 2008, available at <http://www.idg.se/polopoly_fs/1.143041!stamningsansokanpb.pdf>, accessed 25 November 2010.

81 Source: Reuters 'Swedish court says Pirate Bay judge not biased. 25 June 2009.

south-west of Amsterdam. Following the *Pirate Bay* case, the Swedish government brought into force the EU Intellectual Property Enforcement Directive,[82] which demands that ISPs turn over traffic data to copyright holders who are trying to track down filesharers.

The Swedish Pirates Party, which campaigns for patents to be scrapped and copyright to last just five years instead of 70, trebled its membership to more than 45,000 after April 2009. The 'Pirates' even managed to secure a seat in the European Parliament by securing 7 per cent of the national vote during the June 2009 elections. The support the Pirates Party received from the Swedish voters demonstrates just how difficult it is for copyright owners and performers to convince the public that illegal file-sharing can be equated to a criminal activity or a civil wrong!

Sweden is not alone in seeing political parties capitalize on public unrest over tighter governmental controls on Internet use. The German 'pirate party' (Piratenpartei Deutschland) won close to one per cent of the EU election vote; though the group failed to secure an EU parliamentary seat, it passed the threshold for public funding. Registered 'pirate parties' now exist in Austria, Denmark, Finland, Poland and Spain. The Pirate Party UK was officially registered on 30 July 2009; its manifesto covers copyright, patent law and freedom of speech.

Internet pirates now tend to move away from EU member states to new 'cyber' territories, such as China or Ukraine, to avoid prosecution for illegal file-sharing. This change is rooted in the evolution of 'bulletproof hosting' by websites that are seemingly impervious to legal threats and blocks using non-EU countries with less stringent IP legislation. These bulletproof services are generally linked to illegal activities – including online child pornography – and are very popular with criminal groups, spammers and file-sharing services.[83]

9.5.7 Spotify: the online music-streaming jukebox

In October 2009, *Spotify*, the online music-streaming jukebox based in Sweden, added offline music content to its desktop version, meaning that one can listen to music 'live' via the Internet as well as download and store around 3,000 tracks on a PC.[84] Spotify also launched its application ('app') for the Apple iPhone that allows users to temporarily download music. Users can create a playlist while connected to the Internet, but then choose to sync them with a computer and then listen to the songs offline. This service is only available to premium subscribers, who pay £10 per month for their music (Spotify already allows users to listen to music offline via an application on their mobile phones).[85]

Spotify grants the user a limited, non-exclusive, revocable licence to make personal non-commercial use of the 'Spotify Software Application'; this includes a right to download the music as a 'stream' of media content made available in the UK (the site hosts similar services in other countries, namely France, Finland, the Netherlands, Norway, Spain and Sweden). The Swedish music streaming service is looked on as a rival to Apple's iTunes store because of its wide-ranging, free library of millions of songs. The next generation, already available in South Korea, allows the sending or receiving of 200 MP3 music files in five minutes, an entire *Star Wars* DVD in three minutes or the complete digitized works of Charles Dickens in less than ten minutes.

The question is: is it legal? Seemingly so, though songwriter and producer Pete Waterman thinks that streamed music services online are 'scandalous', stating that 'these streaming business models are a disgrace, they devalue our artists, they damage this country economically, culturally

---

82 EU Directive 2004/48 on the enforcement of intellectual property rights.
83 Source: 'Internet pirates find "bulletproof" havens for illegal file sharing', by Bobbie Johnson, *The Guardian* 'Technology' section, 5 January 2010.
84 Spotify uses a piece of software that allows online users to play any music on demand. It keeps a secret cache on your PC and uses that to serve music to other users, known as 'legal BitTorrent' for music.
85 Source: 'Spotify offers PC music downloads', *BBC News Online*, 1 October 2010.

and morally.'[86] All the music on Spotify has been licensed from and delivered by labels or other rights holders. If an artist asks the server how their music ended up on Spotify, it can turn out that the artist's music has been licensed and delivered by a label or aggregator without the artist knowing about this. Spotify has negotiated deals with necessary rights holders in all of their launch countries (see above), and has agreed royalties, based on how frequently an artist's or producer's music is played. All the metadata (name of album, track, artist, etc.) is delivered by the relevant record label or aggregator.

Digital warehouses or music 'aggregators' are the core of the digital media business. They hold licensed content in various formats for distribution to media and retail businesses. Here are a few of the big music aggregators:

- Apple (iTunes)
- Napster
- Nokia Music (Nokia Music Store)
- Digital Distribution Domain (Musimob)

The Internet has given us access to a wide range of social networks, allowing us to share experiences and swap songs or films. This means that file-sharing has become an increasing problem for artists or authors. Will the world of recorded music and literacy be destroyed by piracy and illegal downloads or can new sources of revenue and funding be found as an alternative to punishing illegal downloaders?

9.6 Regulating the collecting societies

As has already been described above, there are a number of collecting society models throughout Europe as well as in the United States and Canada. Some collecting societies only control public performance rights while others also control the reproduction rights. The Performing Right Society (PRS), for example, looks after an assignment from the composer or music publisher regarding their performing rights in musical and literary works and the Mechanical Copyright Protection Society (MCPS) acts on behalf of its members for the purpose of administering the 'mechanical' (music publishing) rights and distributes royalties to its members after deducting a commission fee (see above 9.3.1 and 9.3.2). GEMA administers both the public performance and the mechanical right based on a representative contract. This can be confusing and it has been suggested that the European Commission should establish a unified model of collective rights management. There are also differences in domestic law in the administration of collecting societies resulting from different approaches to intellectual property. In Germany, for instance, a composer may not assign copyright (§ 29 *Urheberrechtsgesetz* – UrhG), while this is expressly permitted under UK law if done in writing.[87]

The ongoing policy question for domestic and EU governments around collecting societies has been to develop a workable model that meets the primary objective, which is to protect authors' and creators' copyright and safeguard the economic interests of writers, composers, producers and music publishers. At the same time, works should be accessible for commercial use by developing effective distribution models that protect copyright and the ability for right holders to collect accurate royalties and rewards. This model should be represented by collecting societies supported by workable EU legislation.[88]

---

86 Source: 'A bum note for rock 'n' roll', by Justin Stoneman, *Sunday Times, Culture* Supplement, 3 January 2010, p. 27.
87 s. 90 CDPA.
88 For further discussion see: Koempel (2007).

9.6.1 EU legislation on regulating performing rights societies

The impact of the Internet and digital technologies has been on national, regional and international copyright agendas for some time. For example, the European Commission's Green Paper on Copyright in the Knowledge Economy (2007)[89] looked at the long-term future of copyright policy in the knowledge-intensive areas. The UK Government continues to lobby the European Commission over internet piracy, backed by a strong 'UK Music' lobby, including U2 manager Paul McGuinness, former lead vocalist of The Undertones Feargal Sharkey, Pink Floyd drummer Nick Mason and singers Annie Lennox and Tom Jones. At the heart of the debate is who should bear the burden of policing and protecting the music industry. Lord Mandelson, on behalf of the UK Government, and former EU Commissioner for Information Society and Media, Viviane Reding, believe that it should be the Internet Service Providers (ISP) who operate a 'three strikes' policy, whereby anyone found illegally downloading music repeatedly should be given a 'red card' and eventually cut off from the Internet. ISPs have argued that they are only 'hosting' websites and have refused to become the internet police. On the other side of the musical spectrum is a group of musicians, the Featured Artists Coalition (FAC), who claim that despite the damage that file-sharing does to sales of their records, it can also encourage people to buy concert tickets and merchandise.[90]

In 2010 regulator Ofcom was given the power to disconnect persistent illegal file-sharers. Ofcom's duty is to secure a significant reduction in unlawful file-sharing by imposing two specific obligations: notification of unlawful activity and, for repeat infringers, a court-based process of identity release and civil action. This facility has eased the burden on ISPs.

See Chapter 10.4.4 →

In October 2005 the European Commission published a Recommendation[91] concerning the cross-border collective management of copyright and related rights for legitimate online music services, addressed to all member states and existing collecting societies. The (non-mandatory) Recommendation suggests models of best practice including transparency, governance, accountability and efficiency to achieve the main objective, which is to protect rights holders' copyright. The Recommendation facilitates online music licensing services across the EU, including sub-publishing arrangements of online rights. In other words, the Recommendation proposes a streamlining of collective rights management via the creation of a unified online rights 'hub' that delivers maximum value and efficiency of licensing and royalty distribution to rights owners by way of a pan-European licence.

Another controversial challenge has been that of digital rights management (DRM), a generic term for access control technologies that can be used by hardware manufacturers, publishers and copyright holders to impose limitations on the usage of digital content and devices. DRM restricts certain content by overriding some of the user's wishes, such as preventing the user from burning (or 'ripping') a copyrighted song to a CD. Microsoft's Windows Vista operating system, for example, had an inbuilt DRM scheme which disabled and degraded content. DRM technology is contentious because it inhibits uses of digital content which is not desired to be copied by the rights holder. DRM systems are backed by Article 11 of the **WIPO Copyright Treaty 1996**, which requires nations party to the Treaty to enact laws to allow DRM technologies. The US-DMCA legislation criminalizes the production and dissemination of DRM technology that allows users to circumvent technical copy-restriction methods. The French Parliament adopted DRM technology as part of its DADVSI law. DRM has been employed in the past by Sony, Amazon, Microsoft, AOL and the BBC – though most providers and software houses are now stepping back from DRM use (except for films and games).

---

89 COM 2007 724 final of 20.11.2007.
90 Source: 'Musicians hit out at plans to cut off Internet for file sharers'. *Times Online*, 10 September 2009, by Patrick Foster, Media Correspondent: http://entertainment.timesonline.co.uk/tol/arts_and_entertainment/music/article6828262.ece
91 Commission Recommendation of 18 October 2005 on collective cross-border management of copyright and related rights for legitimate online music services (2005/737/EC).

There are a number of online commercial providers that offer online DRM copyright tools to the global publishing market, such as ACAP (Automated Content Access Protocol). ACAP is an online provider for the use of publishing content in any language on the Internet. The service provider enables the copyright terms, conditions and permissions that would routinely be read by a 'human' in the offline environment to be read and unambiguously interpreted by the machines that replace the human in the online environment. ACAP puts content on the net and assures the rights holder that third parties can no longer exploit that content without appropriate permission.[92]

Rights holders may well argue in favour of DRM since the device prevents unauthorized duplication of their work and maintains their artistic integrity as well as ensuring continued revenue streams. But the Electronic Frontier Foundation argues that DRM systems are anti-competitive and essentially restrict the use of online material. The lobby group further argues that the presence of DRM violates existing private property rights by restricting a range of legal user activities and devices (such as a digital audio player). Steve Jobs – co-founder and chief executive of Apple – opposes DRM for music and the iTunes Store now offers DRM-free songs, but has kept DRM on video content. Key issues around DRM – such as the right to make personal copies, provision for persons to lend copies to friends, provision for service discontinuance, hardware agnosticism, contracts for public libraries, and customers' protection against one-sided amendments of the contract by the publisher – have not been fully addressed by any 'harmonizing' EU legislation.

9.6.2 The French graduated response: HADOPI – the 'Creation and Internet' law

How has digital copyright protection been addressed across Europe? In July 2007, the Court of First Instance in Belgium issued a decision in a copyright infringement case brought by the Belgian music collecting society SABAM against an ISP, Scarlet (formerly known as Tiscali). In its decision, the court ordered Scarlet to install filtering software within six months to prevent the ISP's users from accessing unauthorized music downloads via peer-to-peer (P2P) systems; and to remove copyrighted music from its network.[93]

The Belgian decision in SABAM v Tiscali (Scarlet) appears to be the first time that a European court considered whether ISPs can be required to monitor or filter the activities of their users in order to stop file-sharing on P2P networks. The Belgian decision generated a substantial amount of criticism. Was the technology available to employ such filtering systems? Who should pay for it? How should one resolve the competing claims of rights holders as to their intellectual property and intermediaries (ISPs) as to their responsibility for traffic passing across their networks and – at the same time – protect end-users' right to privacy?

In January 2008, the Swiss file-sharing service 'RapidShare' was dealt a blow by the German district court (Landgericht) in Hamburg, whereby the author-licensing association GEMA had filed a claim against RapidShare for the uploading of copyrighted content.[94] The court ruled that the site must take responsibility for copyright infringement, even when the material in question was uploaded by its members. The case sent a clear message to any German-language service providers which might gain financial benefit from unlawful uses of copyrighted works.

On 29 January 2008, the European Court of Justice handed down its decision in the case of *Promusicae v Telefónica* (C–275/06).[95] The ECJ looked at the various European Directives currently in

---

92 Source: 'Solutions to address the challenges of communicating digital rights and permissions', available at <www.the-acap.org>, accessed 25 November 2010.
93 *SABAM (La Société Belge des Auteurs, Compositeurs et Éditeurs) v S.A.Tiscali (Scarlet)* [2007] (N° 04/8975A) Tribunal de la première instance de Bruxelles a l'audience publique du 18 May 2007; décision de 29 juin 2007.
94 Oberlandesgericht Hamburg, Urteil v. 02.07.2008 – Az.: 5 U 73/07 – *Haftung von Rapidshare IV*.
95 Source: Press release No 5/08 of 29 January 2008 of the European Court of Justice in the judgment of court in Case C-275/06: *Productores de Música de España (Promusicae) v Telefónica de España SAU*.

force on the question of copyright, the enforcement of IP rights and e-commerce plus the human rights legislation on the right to privacy under Article 8 ECHR. The Court confirmed that while Community law does not require member states to implement in their national laws an obligation to disclose personal data in the context of civil proceedings in order to ensure the effective protection of copyright, it does not preclude it either. The Court also underlined how important it was that the authorities and courts of the member states should not only interpret their national law in a manner consistent with the Directives, but also make sure that they do not rely on an interpretation of them which would be in conflict with fundamental rights or other general principles of Community law, such as the principle of proportionality.

In April 2009, the French upper legislative house, le Sénat, passed new copyright legislation in the form of la loi HADOPI (haute autorité pour la diffusion des œuvres et la protection des droits sur l'Internet). HADOPI forms a progressive yet graduated response strategy to combat and punish internet piracy. It requires ISPs to monitor their subscribers' use of copyrighted works on their networks and implement progressively more severe punishments to repeat offenders, culminating in suspension or termination of their internet accounts. The HADOPI legislation also established an agency for monitoring compliance and addressing disputes. The agency has the powers to send warning letters to file-sharers and ultimately cut them off. Though welcomed by EU Commissioner Reding, France's HADOPI has not found overall support from other EU member states.

On 25 August 2009, the Utrecht District Court ordered the Dutch website Mininova to remove all files on its server that point to copyrighted works, or face a fine of up to five million Euro. Mininova – similar to Sweden's Pirate Bay – had one of the largest indexes of 'BitTorrent' files. The action was brought by Stichting Brein, an organization funded by copyright-holder groups.[96] The Dutch court found that Mininova was inciting users to infringe copyrights while at the same time profiting from advertising on the site. Mininova's defence was that it was impossible to find and remove bit torrents that point to copyrighted materials. Unlike The Pirate Bay, Mininova had already been in the process of removing files when it received the 'takedown' notice from copyright holders. The court said that Mininova should have known that commercially made films, games, music and TV series are copyrighted and that these works are only copyright-free in exceptional cases. Ignorance was no defence.

There have been a number of differing legal approaches in Europe with France's HADOPI legislation presenting the most aggressive strategy, requiring its ISPs to monitor their subscribers' use of copyrighted works where repeat-downloading music pirates are either cut off or suspended from internet use. The ECJ's decision in *Promusicae v Telefonica* may be seen as striking the right balance between fundamentally competing rights. Meanwhile the **Digital Economy Act 2010** proposes the UK's solution to the problem, having passed responsibility to the regulator Ofcom.

The Belgian Court decision in *SABAM v Tiscali* (Scarlet) was appealed on 28 January 2010, following the *Promusicae* decision. The Belgian court of appeal held that there were no sufficient remedies for an existing infringement and that there was no sufficient legal guidance provided by Belgian legislation which specifically gave injunctive relief to order filtering and blocking devices, preventing future copyright infringements. This question was referred back to the ECJ.

In conclusion, there is – to date – no unified legislation across EU member states in the form of definite 'harmonization' legislation to either discourage copyright infringement or to discourage P2P file-sharing. Clearly, common Europe-wide answers to these issues are needed. The European Court of Justice (ECJ) should be asked to rule on these issues as soon as possible.

---

96 LJN: BJ6008, Rechtbank Utrecht, 250077 / HA ZA 08-1124, 25. 8. 2009.

FOR THOUGHT

Is the cutting-off of someone's internet connection a breach of human rights?

9.7 Codifying cyberspace: towards legislation to protect authors and artists from piracy?

The creative industries believe illegal file-sharing is almost endemic while the UK Government has set a target of reducing the problem by at least 70 per cent in the next two or three years, as cited in the *Digital Britain Report* (2009).[97] Nine bodies representing the creative industries, among them the Federation Against Copyright Theft (FACT)[98], and five trade unions, including the Musicians' Union (MU), have in the past expressed a desire for the government to force ISPs to warn repeat online infringers, to throttle the speed of their broadband connection and to ultimately disconnect persistent illegal file-sharers.

The British Phonographic Industry (BPI)'s Chief Executive, Geoff Taylor, strongly supports the above pressure groups, believing that ISPs should become the internet police and adopt the 'three strikes' legislation, similar to the French HADOPI law. At his speech to an audience at the 'London Calling 2008 – the future of digital media' conference, he said:

> . . . the rules of economics are seen to have broken down some time around 1998 when Internet protocols finally snapped the pernicious link between the words 'intellectual' and 'property'. No one in the record companies that I know opposes a business model which, for certain uses, provides music to the consumer 'free at the point of consumption'. It is simply not sustainable to believe that basic rules of civilised society, including respect for the law and for property rights, can just be suspended or ignored in the virtual world. Those rules exist and are supported in our society for good reason. It is becoming more and more clear that citizens, as much as creators, require protection from crime, fraud, abuse and other risks in the online world. Almost everyone now recognises that mass filesharing of music is against the law, is seriously damaging the music sector in this country and that urgent action must be taken. We (the BPI) believe that where ISPs have information that customers are using their broadband service to distribute music illegally, then they have a legal and a social responsibility to prevent it from happening again. We are engaging in a dialogue with ISPs that are willing to talk to us, and with Government, which has committed itself to enacting legislation to require ISPs to take action to deal with illegal activity on their networks, unless a voluntary agreement is swiftly found.[99]

The computer software, film and games industries have also sustained serious financial damage because of illegal copiers, downloaders and vendors of these commodities. A new police unit was set up in 2006, dedicated to combating film piracy and tracing organized criminal networks

---

97 HM Department for Culture, Media and Sports (DCMS) and Department for Innovation, Business and Skills (BIS) (2009).

98 FACT's primary purpose is to protect the UK's film and broadcasting industry against counterfeiting, copyright and trademark infringements. Established in 1983, FACT works closely with Police, Trading Standards, HM Revenue & Customs, the UK Border Agency and the Serious and Organised Crime Agency (SOCA). Its key areas include online piracy, hard goods piracy, organized criminal networks and detection of illegal recording in cinemas.

99 Source: 'The role of record labels in the digital age'. Extract from the speech by BPI Chief Executive Geoff Taylor on 20 June 2008.

sustaining the manufacture and distribution of counterfeit film, games and software products.[100] The Metropolitan Police's 'Economic and Specialist Crime Command' unit (working in partnership with FACT) investigates those individuals and organizations accruing sizeable criminal profits under the **Proceeds of Crime Act 2002**.

The video games industry has been particularly hard hit by piracy. Nintendo, one of the biggest gamemakers and developers, sold more than 30 million Nintendo DS systems in 2009, bringing lifetime sales of the popular portable console to in excess of 70 million. However, Nintendo lost nearly $1 billion due to pirated software for the Wii and DS in 2007.[101] Since then, the gamemaker has been urging the US and other governments to combat piracy by taking a more aggressive stance on copyright theft. In February 2009, Nintendo filed its own lawsuit – along with 53 other DS software companies – against pirated software purveyors, namely two companies importing and selling pirated copies of 'R4 Revolution' for DS devices (also known as 'game copiers' or R4 cartridges). Game copiers are designed to bypass security protection measures on Nintendo DS consoles, enabling users to download illegally pirated games and store them on a single chip. The devices can be used to store and load multiple titles. The lawsuit was filed at the Tokyo District Court, seeking to ban the importation and sale of 'R4 Revolution' for DS and similar software emulation devices in Japan based on the Japanese **Unfair Competition Prevention Act**.

The court ruled in favour of the game companies and made it illegal to import and sell the R4. Nintendo welcomed the ruling, and said it had brought the legal action against two retailers, Playables Limited and Wai Dat Chan, on behalf of the thousands of video game studios that depend on legitimate sales of games for their financial survival. But, in spite of repeated warnings requesting their discontinuation, vendors were ignoring requests, forcing renewed legal action. This sent the message to the 'pirates' and vendors of illegal software that legal action has been meaningless and that injunctive action has been ignored. It appears that clever pirates will invariably hack into the dual-screened handheld DS devices and that game publishers in Japan (and elsewhere in the world) will either have to develop even better anti-piracy technology or file another lawsuit.

There followed an interesting twist in the above legal action. In July 2010, London's High Court ruled that 'game copiers', namely 'R4 cartridge' devices, can no longer be imported, sold or marketed in the UK. Following the successful but highly ineffective lawsuit in Japan (above), companies that sold the cartridges argued that they simply allowed users to easily play home-made games. More than 100,000 game-copying devices were seized in the UK alone were between 2007 and 2009. The UK ruling followed a similar judgment in the Netherlands in early July 2010, in which The Hague District Court ruled that 11 Dutch online retailers acted unlawfully by importing and selling game copiers for use with the Nintendo DS and modification chips for use with the Wii.[102]

The theft of intellectual property is an important issue for the video games industry and the Dutch and UK judgments have assisted trading standards and police piracy crime unit teams in actively pursuing and stopping other individuals who deal in game-copying devices and software.

---

100 Under s. 107(1) CDPA, a person commits an offence who, without the licence of the copyright owner

(a) makes for sale or hire, or
(b) imports into the United Kingdom otherwise than for his private and domestic use, or
(c) possesses in the course of a business with a view to committing any act infringing the copyright, or
(d) in the course of a business –
    (i) sells or lets for hire, or
    (ii) offers or exposes for sale or hire, or
    (iii) exhibits in public, or
    (iv) distributes, or
(e) distributes otherwise than in the course of a business to such an extent as to affect prejudicially the owner of the copyright, an article which is, and which he knows or has reason to believe is, an infringing copy of a copyright work.

101 Source: 'Nintendo DS shatters sales record', *Wired* Magazine online, 15 September 2008, available at <http://www.wired.com/gamelife/2008/09/npd-nintendo-ds>, accessed 25 November 2010.

102 Source: 'Nintendo DS R4 cartridges ruled illegal', by Nick Cowen, *Daily Telegraph*, 29 July 2010.

9.7.1 Licensing copyright for digital music, films and books

Should Internet Providers (ISP) be more proactive, as Geoff Taylor from the BPI suggests? It is true that ISPs now routinely monitor traffic sent over their network – primarily for maintenance and security purposes – and it should therefore be relatively easy to keep an eye on traffic sent using file-sharing programmes. But is it technically more difficult to establish exactly *what* is being shared and by whom?

Content rights owners often monitor websites which offer links to copyright content and then obtain the Internet Protocol (IP) address of the online computer being used to share that data. While most countries have their own national copyright law, globally they operate – as previously discussed – within an international framework established by a number of copyright agreements such as the **Berne** and **Rome Conventions**, the WTO-TRIPS Agreement and the WIPO Internet Treaties. These multilateral treaties allow not only the protection of rights holders but also the monitoring of illegal P2P file-sharing, such as that of the UK Internet Watch Foundation (IWF). Additionally, domestic legislation, such as the UK **Copyright Act** (CDPA), will protect, for example, a US copyrighted work which is published or made available in the UK, provided certain basic qualifying conditions have been met. Furthermore, there are a series of EU 'harmonizing' regulations and directives, notably the **Information Society Directive**[103] – implemented into UK law in 2003.

See Chapter 8

See Chapter 10.6.1

These international and regional instruments establish certain parameters and limits on the ability to make changes to national copyright laws. Furthermore, modern web-based technologies have global reach and are not bound by national frontiers. The management of rights on an international basis where, for example, permissions are needed to use music in a pan-European service is an emerging area requiring attention. The European Commission's Green Paper on Copyright in the Knowledge Economy[104] of 2007 attempted to structure the copyright debate as it relates to scientific publishing, the digital preservation of Europe's cultural heritage, orphan works, consumer access to protected works and the special needs of the disabled to participate in the information society.

9.7.2 Digital Britain: the Digital Economy Act 2010

Lord Mandelson's *Digital Britain* Report of 2009 referred to a 'guidepath' of how Britain could sustain its position as a leading digital economy and society.[105] Apart from modernizing and upgrading the UK radio and broadcasting infrastructure, the *Digital Britain* Report stated that piracy of intellectual property for profit could and must not be tolerated and would be treated as theft, vehemently pursued through the criminal courts. The report became the blueprint for the *Digital Economy Bill* which, in turn, became the **Digital Economy Act 2010**.

Following Lord Mandelson's proposal to suspend the internet accounts of those who engage in persistent file-sharing, the music and film industries voiced some concern that the proposed legislation might well target the 'soft underbelly' of file-sharing, namely teenagers who are doing it because they are either apathetic or believe they can get away with it; furthermore that this drastic legislation would potentially criminalize a whole generation of music fans.

The **Digital Economy Act 2010** received Royal Assent during the 'wash up' period in April 2010 before the dissolution of Parliament to make way for the General Election on 6 May 2010. The act centres on four main objectives:

---

103 EC Directive 2001/29 on the harmonization of copyright and related rights in the information society.
104 COM 2007 724 final of 20.1.2007.
105 HM Department for Culture, Media and Sports (DCMS) and Department for Innovation, Business and Skills (BIS) (2009).

1) To advance and modernize the UK's competitive digital communications infrastructure;

2) To support the UK's creative industries by taking action to tackle online copyright infringement ('piracy') and to strengthen the framework for the creation of successful business models;

3) To support local and regional news in the UK and update licensing arrangements;

4) To improve public confidence in digital activities by providing security of the communications network.

In more detail, the 2010 Act covers the following provisions:

i) **Ofcom** – to require the sectoral regulator to carry out an assessment of the UK's communications infrastructure every three years;

ii) **Online infringement of copyright** – to tackle online copyright infringement (piracy) by placing obligations on Internet Service Providers (ISPs) to work with rights holders and, if necessary, to take technical measures against infringing subscribers. It also provides a power for the Secretary of State to introduce regulations for rights holders to seek a court injunction to prevent access to specified online locations for the prevention of online copyright infringement;

iii) **Internet domain registries** – to provide reserve powers in respect of efficient and effective management and distribution of internet domain names;

iv) **Channel 4 Television Corporation** – to adjust the corporation's functions from a focus on traditional broadcast activities to include provision of public service media content on other platforms, including the Internet;

v) **Independent television services** – to enable future alterations of the Channel 3 and Channel 5 licences;

vi) **Digital radio** – to provide arrangements for digital switchover by making changes to the existing radio licensing regulatory framework;

vii) **Access to electromagnetic spectrum** – to allow for the charging of periodic payments on auctioned spectrum licences, and confer more proportionate enforcement powers on Ofcom;

viii) **Video games** – to make changes to how video games should be classified in the UK; e.g. age ratings of computer games must be on the same statutory footing for ratings of 12 years and above;

ix) **Public lending rights (PLR)** – to extend PLRs to non-print books;

x) **Copyright penalties** – changes to levels of penalties for copyright infringement.

The most drastic measure in the **Digital Economy Act 2010** is the disconnection of broadband customers who are deemed to be infringing[106] copyright laws without first being given the opportunity to plead their innocence before a court. This was passed to Ofcom on the legal basis that the regulator can send out warning letters to illegal file-sharers as well as monitor online traffic.[107] Before the 2010 Act had come into force law firms, acting on behalf of game and software companies, had begun sending out threatening letters to alleged online illegal file-sharers, demanding compensation money for their clients. Law firms sending threatening letters to homes prior to the **Digital Economy Act 2010** relied on the existing **Copyright, Designs and Patents Act 1988**, which allows media companies to take civil action and seek damages against people allegedly breaching their copyrights.

See Chapter 10.4.3 →

---

106 The statutory definition of an 'infringing copy' is contained in s. 27(2) CDPA 1988.
107 For further discussion see: Koempel (2010).

Gill Murdoch and her husband Ken MacKinnon received a threatening lawyer's letter, which arrived at their Inverness home on 12 April 2008. Solicitors Davenport Lyons, acting on behalf of gamemakers Atari, demanded that the couple pay an immediate £500 for allegedly making available a copy of the computer game *Risk II* so that it could be pirated across the Internet. The couple, aged 56 and 68 respectively, were stunned, not least because neither plays computer games. They told Dan Sabbagh from the *Media Guardian*, 'We're not into things like that. We like to walk our dog, or cycle or garden – we don't use the Internet for anything other than for Googling information.'[108] Davenport Lyons insisted that the couple had a Wi-Fi connection and it may have been used by someone else. The couple denied this and, sure of their innocence, reported the solicitors to the local trading standards and consumer watchdog organization Which?, that fought off the claim on the couple's behalf following months of hostile correspondence with Davenport Lyons. After considerable adverse publicity, Atari pulled out and sent letters of apology to wrongly targeted customers, including the couple from Inverness.[109]

In November 2009, ACS:Law applied to the Royal Courts of Justice requesting that several ISPs provide details of customers linked to suspect IP addresses. The law firm was acting on behalf of a little-known company called MediaCAT, which has the right to pursue legal actions against anybody pirating any pornographic film owned by companies producing pornographic material, such as the one owned by adult entertainment magnate David Sullivan, co-owner of West Ham football club. ACS:Law also sent some 6,500 demands for payment, taking over some of Davenport Lyons's caseloads, with an expansion in 2010 to send out 50,000 to 60,000 warning letters following new measures provided by the **Digital Economy Act 2010**.

As soon as the 2010 Act came into force, media and entertainment law firms began sending out thousands of letters to suspected illegal file sharers. Soho firm Gallant Macmillan completed a mailshot to 2,000 individuals in July 2010, claiming that they infringed dance music label The Ministry of Sound's copyright after downloading and sharing music, typically demanding around £350. It followed in the steps of ACS:Law, who had also sent thousands of letters demanding compensation from alleged file-sharers. The Ministry of Sound's move marks an intensification of the legal battle against file-sharers. Some recipients of the letters, concerned about forking out huge damages, actually paid up. Others complained to 'Which?' and local trading standards authorities.[110]

The idea behind the **Digital Economy Act** is to make it clear that ISPs, Ofcom or rights holders have to notify users of alleged P2P file-sharing infringement and can issue 'warning letters' on a 'three strikes' basis, thereby demanding damages, take-down notices and eventually cutting the infringer off from his server. Legal critics say that the process is complicated and expensive, and that the only penalty that can be levied is a fine. Unless a user confesses to illegally downloading a file or a court order is obtained to seize a computer and the file is then located on its hard drive it is hard to see how such an action will succeed. ISPs have denied responsibility, stating that they are merely temporarily 'hosting' connections and services. Broadband providers like O_2 are not interested in disconnecting their users and have left it to regulator Ofcom to deal with Internet pirates under the recent statutory powers to monitor, disconnect and prosecute with the support of the Culture Secretary.

There are potential grounds for appeal once the measures under the 2010 Act are enforced. Firstly, there is a serious risk of arbitrary enforcement touching on civil liberties. Secondly, there is the question of proportionality and reasonableness, because suspending web access to persistent offenders is a draconian step and diminishes freedom of expression and potentially disenfranchises citizens where e-Government has become the norm.

---

108 Source: 'Digital Economy Act likely to increase households targeted for piracy', *Media Guardian*, 12 April 2008.
109 Source: 'City couple triumph in illegal computer download battle', by Helen Paterson, *The Inverness Courier*, 31 October 2008.
110 Source: 'File sharers targeted with legal action over music downloads', by Miles Brignall, *The Guardian*, 17 July 2010.

Are injunctions and take-down notices the right step towards protecting the publishing, entertainment and games industry in order to safeguard copyright? Or have these industries failed to develop services and devices that will stop file-sharing infringement or alternatively pay-to-use services?

> ### ◉ FOR THOUGHT
>
> How enforceable are the solicitors' threatening letters, demanding money from (alleged) illegal file-sharers and downloaders of, say, dance music or games? How well has the **Digital Economy Act 2010** been drafted and how easy is it to define the legal basis for disconnection from your server? How well will the 2010 Act stand up to appeals?

9.7.3 The US Digital Millennium Copyright Act 1998 ('the DMCA')

The **Digital Millennium Copyright Act** (DMCA)[111] is a US copyright law that implements two 1996 WIPO treaties; it criminalizes the production and dissemination of technology, devices or services intended to circumvent measures, such as digital rights management (DRM), which control access to copyrighted works.[112]

The DMCA's 'anti-circumvention provisions' changed the remedies for the circumvention of copy-prevention systems (also known as 'technical protection measures') and require that all analog video recorders have support for a specific form of copy prevention created by 'Macrovision' (now known as 'Rovi Corporation'). The DMCA also criminalizes the act of circumventing an access control, whether or not there is actual infringement of copyright itself. Most importantly, the DMCA extended and increased the penalties for copyright infringement on the Internet. Title II of the Act – the 'Online Copyright Infringement Liability Limitations Act' or 'OCILLA' – creates a safe harbour for online service providers (OSPs, including ISPs) against copyright liability. This practically means that if US ISPs (or OSPs) adhere promptly to the requirement to block access to allegedly infringing material or remove such material from their systems – after receiving notification from a copyright holder or a performing rights society – ISPs will not be liable. OCILLA then provides a safe harbour from liability to their users and service providers. However, s. 1201(c) of Title II does not change the underlying substantive copyright infringement rights, remedies or defences in US law.

The DMCA is silent in relation to websites that contain hyperlinks to infringing material. There have been a few US lower-court decisions which have ruled against linking in some narrowly prescribed circumstances. One is when the owner of a website has already been issued with an injunction against posting infringing material on their website and then links to the same material in an attempt to circumvent the injunction. One such case was *Intellectual Reserve (IR) v Utah Lighthouse Ministry (ULM)* (1999),[113] a religious organization that often criticized the plaintiff's Mormon religion. IR won an injunction against ULM to stop them posting its copyrighted *Mormon Church Handbook of Instructions*. ULM's response was to simply link to other websites which held a copy of the copyrighted works. These websites did not have permission to host the copyrighted book. The court

---

111 United States Pub. L. No. 105–304, 112 Stat. 2860 (28 October 1998).
112 Passed on 12 October 1998 by a unanimous vote in the US Senate, signed into law by President Bill Clinton, the DMCA amended Title 17 of the US Code to extend the reach of copyright, while limiting the liability of the providers of online services for copyright infringement by their users.
113 See: *Intellectual Reserve, Inc. v. Utah Lighthouse Ministry, Inc.* United States District Court, D. Utah, Central Division, 6 December 1999.

found ULM's linking to be 'contributory infringement' and therefore it granted a preliminary injunction preventing ULM from linking to the copyrighted *Church Handbook of Instructions*. The court found that ULM's linking to the unauthorized material was likely to be found 'contributory infringement' of IR's copyright. Therefore, it granted a preliminary injunction preventing ULM from linking to the sites in question.

In *Lenz v Universal Music Corp.* (2008),[114] the US District Court for the Northern District of California ruled that copyright holders must consider fair use before issuing takedown notices for content posted on the Internet. Stephanie Lenz had posted on YouTube a home video of her children dancing to Prince's song 'Let's Go Crazy'. Universal Music Corp. ('Universal') sent YouTube a takedown notice pursuant to the DMCA, claiming that Lenz's video violated their copyright in Prince's song. Lenz claimed 'fair use' of the copyrighted material and sued Universal for misrepresentation of a DMCA claim. The court held that, in violation of the DMCA, Universal had not in good faith considered fair use when filing a takedown notice.

ISPs in the United States have made it clear that they do not wish to become the 'internet police', reiterating that they merely see themselves as 'conduits' or 'wires' for internet traffic that provide content to the end user. It is not in their commercial interest to disconnect their users. For this reason ISPs are reluctant to accept content-related liability, touching on legal areas such as libel, fraud, obscenity and copyright infringement.

FOR THOUGHT

The film and music industries have made it clear that they want a commitment to stop file-sharing and that the responsibility for doing so should firmly rest with Internet Service Providers (ISPs). Can and should P2P file-sharers be disconnected if they are in fact 'sharing' their connection in a household?

9.7.4 E-readers and iPads: the death of the book publishing industry?

The Public Lending Right (PLR) was introduced in the UK via the **Public Lending Act 1979** to compensate authors for the activities of libraries. This provision has been extended to e-books and audio books under s. 44 **Digital Economy Act 2010** ('power to make consequential provision'). The provision also changed the definitions of 'book' and 'author' – as originally defined under s.5(2) **Public Lending Right Act 1979** – to extend to online digitized provisions, such as e-readers, iPads and electronic publishing.

9.7.5 The Google Book Search project

The digitization of copyrighted works is now fully advanced with e-readers flooding the market where students of law, for example, are able to read more or less parts of every textbook via the Google book project. How can copyright legislation be applied fairly to adequately reward authors? Is the present legal framework still fit for the digital age? Will the current set of legal rules give consumers across Europe access to digitized books without paying for them? Will it guarantee fair remuneration for authors? Will it ensure a level playing field for digitization across Europe or is there still too much fragmentation following national borders? What could be the contribution of

---

114 *Lenz (Stephanie) v Universal Music Corp; Universal Music Publishing, Inc., and Universal Music Publishing Group* [2008] Case Number C 07-3783 JF, Filed 20 August 2008 in the United States District Court for the Northern District of California San Jose Division.

a European digital library as suggested by the former EU Commissioner for Information Society and Media, Viviane Reding?

One of the most controversial and bitterly fought cases has been that involving the 'Google Book Search' project. The multinational Internet search engine Google has hosted and developed a number of internet-based services and products, one of them being the 'Google Books' search engine. Since August 2004, Google has been digitizing copies of books, initially only works in the USA, which were most commonly compilations of books which were out of print or difficult to access – thereby making them accessible via its search engine. From 2005, Google scanned books held in US libraries on an enormous scale, focusing initially on works in the public domain but then extending their scanning to works in copyright to which they attached an 'opt-out model' rather than a system of up-front rights clearance. Google subsequently entered into partnership agreements with certain publishers, the idea being to promote sales of books.

The Authors Guild and the Association of American Publishers issued separate legal proceedings against Google, announcing a 'landmark settlement' on 28 October 2008 (*Authors Guild v Google*) ('The Settlement Agreement'). Though the settlement took place in the United States, it is not limited to US authors and publications, but applies to books and 'inserts'[115] published and/or distributed in the US prior to 5 January 2009, which may include many works authored by UK and European Community writers. This means that UK and all other EU authors, their heirs and successors are potentially part of the 'class' to which the Google Settlement applies. Each author and/or publisher was given the opportunity in 2009 to submit claims for financial recompense. The 'Settlement' website provides a link to a database listing works that are potentially covered by the Settlement.[116] In order to account for the books or inserts scanned prior to the opt-out date (i.e. 5 January 2009), *Google* agreed to make available funds of no less than $45m for claims.[117]

Challenges to Google's original classification of a work are based on tests set out in the Settlement to identify a work as being 'in print'. Will each author really go to the trouble of studying the complex 'Google Settlement' website closely in order to chase his royalties? Or will the publishers pass on the (Google) royalties to their authors? Studying the Google Settlement more closely (online), it can be noted that the publishing contract contains no author rights reversion mechanism, nor does it stipulate (other) applicable terms upon which the book remains 'in print'. How does the Google Settlement measure 'in print'? Is it by reference to units sold? If, for example, more than 50 per cent of income for a work comes from the Book Rights Registry, this income will not be relevant, nor will the fact that a work has been included in a database or that information on it appears in search engine results. This could mean, in practice, that textbook royalties, for example, could decrease.

Many UK and EU authors have actively participated in the Settlement by registering claims against their works. Authors who did not wish to be included had the opt-out chance until 5 January 2010. Authors can also send a request to their publisher requesting the reversion to the author of rights in their book by sending a 'Change Status Notice' to the Book Rights Registry (with a copy to the publisher). The 'Change Status Notice' must affirm that the author believes that the book is no longer 'in print' so that the work can be deemed to be 'author controlled'. Under the US class action Google Book Settlement, it was agreed between Google, authors and publishers that

---

115 'Inserts' are distinct parts of text included within books, such as forewords, poems or quotations from other books, graphic works or illustrations. Claims in respect of inserts apply only in cases where the author/owner of the insert is a distinct person from the rights holder of the book in which it appears.

116 See: The Google Settlement website which covers the 'Google Book Search Copyright Class Action Settlement', available at <www.googlebooksettlement.com>, accessed 4 February 2011.

117 Source: The Google Settlement, op cit. For each work claimed against, minimum rates of $60 (books), $15 (inserts), $5 (partial inserts) apply. The money attaches to the digitized content, so multiple claims for exactly the same text appearing in multiple volumes will not attract multiple payments. If total claims are less than $45m, further payments will be made: up to $300 per book, up to $75 per insert.

authors could receive 63 per cent of the online revenue generated by Google with digitized books. Arguably, it can only be a matter of time before Google makes the works commercially available. Though this can be challenged by rights holders individually, it is a complex process since this has to be done under US legislation.

The European Commission believes that more should be done to open access to books that are either out of print or orphan works, and the promotion of digital libraries should be on the agenda of decision-makers all over the world (not only in Europe). Governments should pay special attention to adequate regulation of private agreements that lead to new online libraries or e-publications. The new EU Information and Digital Affairs Commissioner, Neelie Kroes, has suggested a similar solution to the Google Books project to be made available in the EU. Commissioner Kroes stated in her report 'A Digital Agenda for Europe' (2010)[118] that the Commission needs to ensure a regulatory framework which paves the way for a rapid roll-out of services, similar to those made possible in the United Sates by the Google Settlement. The Commission is working on a Regulation that would improve models of new publications available online and an adequate formula to remunerate such creations with the proposed extension of copyright duration to 95 years.

How will the future of Europe's copyright framework stand up to the digitizing of orphan works and out-of print copies, works which represent the vast majority of European library collections (around 90 per cent)? Commissioner Kroes firmly believes that orphan works, out-of-print books and compendia must be recovered and 'given a new lease of life'.

If the EU Parliament succeeds in bringing forward such legislation, it could lay the foundation for a new generation of cultural growth in Europe. The EU copyright reforms intend to sustain honest consumers, innovative internet entrepreneurs and support creative authors, where any piracy and illegal file-sharing infringement would be adequately policed with tough and durable enforcement models.[119]

👁 FOR THOUGHT

What steps should publishers take, as part of the publishing contract with the author of a work, to publish a new edition of a book in respect of the Google Book Settlement?

9.7.6 Are 360-degree deals the answer to free music downloads? New business models in the recording industry

While digital music sales have increased, CD sales have fallen dramatically since 2005. Record companies' profit margins have been savaged by piracy and CD burning. Labels such as Sony, EMI, Warners and Universal are desperate to earn profits elsewhere, with many successful artists such as Radiohead releasing their new songs for free online. Record labels are now looking for solutions that will enable them to continue being viable enterprises.

How are songwriters, artists and authors going to be protected when ISP applications such as Spotify make uploads of whole album recordings freely available as downloads? How are authors, artists and performers going to support their creativity when they are not receiving the necessary rewards for their intellectual originality in the form of royalties? Most performing artists (and

---

118 COM (2010) 245 final, Brussels, 19 May 2010.
119 For further detailed discussion see: Colston and Galloway (2010).

authors) strongly believe they have a right to make money from their creative work and deserve payment in royalties.

For record labels, the new '360° deals' mean they can still earn revenue if album sales continue to slide, like a hedge fund against a declining CD market. For artists, the deals may mean that labels are more committed to their cause, because if an artist makes money in any of his ventures, such as tours and merchandise, the label makes money too. Aside from financial benefits, some say the changing label–artist relationship could re-energize the music industry.

The likes of Madonna and Jennifer Lopez have become recognized brands in themselves; linked to their brand is a multi-million dollar industry involving clothing, make-up, movies and mobile phone ringtones. In a historic two-album deal, EMI Music reportedly paid the heavy metal group Korn $15 million in 2005 for a percentage of the band's touring, merchandise, publishing and licensing revenue. Warner Brothers' deal with the US rock band My Chemical Romance includes part of their merchandise sales and Interscope Records signed LA's Pussycat Dolls, launching a series of ventures with the group, including a Las Vegas nightclub and a cosmetics line.[120]

The Strategic Advisory Board for Intellectual Property (SABIP) looked at 'offline' copyright infringement and online piracy. Its 2009 findings and subsequent report revealed how consumers obtain films, music and games for free. Following on from the 'Gowers Report' ('Gowers Review of Intellectual Property', 2006), SABIP was set up as a 'quango' by the Labour Government to partner the Intellectual Property Office. Their remit was to provide a strategic overview of the Government's intellectual property (IP) and to develop a workable strategy to understand the economic value of IP.

SABIP's review concluded that policy-makers urgently needed a better understanding of how consumers behave in both the online and offline digital environment. The report also showed that consumers were more interested in factors such as price, quality and availability of material, rather than its legal status, and that the digital world needed to be looked at from a new perspective. This would include consumer choice rather than criminal behaviour, where some artists even claimed that file-sharing leads people to buy more of the legally available products. As part of the new coalition governmental policy on quangos, the (new) Department for Business, Innovation and Skills dissolved SABIP in July 2010.[121]

FOR THOUGHT

How many people buy counterfeit DVDs, CDs or video games? How many people illegally download music without paying for it online? What information would you provide as a policy adviser to a minister in the Department for Business, Innovation and Skills to tackle piracy threats to the recording and publishing industries?

9.8 Patents and trademarks

It is important to remember that media industries aree affected by other IP rights in addition to copyright and performers' rights. These include so-called industrial property rights, covering inventions or brand names, which can be patented, or product logos, which can be registered as trademarks (or if not registered protected by the common law tort of passing off). Governments and

---

120 Source: 'Korn, MCR cut new deals to combat sinking CD sales', Rolling Stone magazine, 27 October 2005.
121 Source: 'Dissolution Statement' by SABIP: http://www.sabip.org.uk/home/press/press-release/press-release-20100719.htm

parliaments have given creators these rights as an incentive to produce ideas that will benefit society as a whole.[122]

Under the TRIPS Agreement, industrial designs must be protected for at least 10 years to a maximum of 20 years (in the case of patents), so that owners of protected designs are able to prevent the manufacture, sale or importation of articles bearing or embodying a design which is a copy of the protected design. In fact, in the UK registered designs can be protected for a maximum period of 25 years and unregistered designs for a period of 15 years.[123] Industrial property can be divided into two main areas:

1. **The protection of distinctive signs**; in particular trademarks (which distinguish the goods or services of one undertaking from those of other undertakings) and geographical indications (which identify a good as originating in a place where a given characteristic of the good is essentially attributable to its geographical origin).

The protection of such distinctive signs aims to stimulate and ensure fair competition and to protect consumers, by enabling them to make informed choices between various goods and services. The protection may last indefinitely, provided the design in question continues to be distinctive.

2. **Types of industrial property that protect and stimulate innovation, design and the creation of technology**. In this category fall inventions, protected by patents, and industrial trade secrets.

The social purpose is to provide protection for the results of investment in the development of new technology, thus giving the incentive and means to finance research and development activities. The extent of protection and enforcement of these industrial property rights varies widely around the world as IP and industrial designs are vitally important in trade and international economic relations. The World Trade Organization's (WTO) TRIPS Agreement covers a series of internationally-agreed trade rules for IP rights which attempt to narrow the gaps in the way these rights are protected around the world and to bring them under common international rules.

See Chapter
◄ 8.3.4

9.8.1 Definition and legislation

A patent is a title granted by the state to the creator or owner of an invention, which entitles the inventor to prevent others from manufacturing, using, selling and, in some cases, importing the technology without his permission for a specified period of years (TRIPS states 20 years for inventions). Patent protection must be available for both products and processes, in almost all fields of technology. Plant varieties must be protectable by patents or by a special system, such as the breeder's rights provided by the convention of the International Union for the Protection of New Varieties of Plants (UPOV).

To stop a patent owner from abusing his rights – for example by failing to supply the product on the market – governments can issue 'compulsory licences', allowing a competitor to produce the product or use the process under licence. If a patent is issued for a production process, then the rights must extend to the product directly obtained from the process. Under certain conditions, alleged infringers may be ordered by a court to prove that they have not used the patented process.

Trademarks are signs that distinguish goods or services from one business from those of other businesses. Trademarks are registered to ensure that no one else has registered a mark which is the

---

122 See also: Sterling (2008), p. 779.
123 See: Registered Designs Act 1949 (as amended) and Part III CDPA 1988.

same or similar to the one which is proposed for goods or services. This is usually done by searching the Trademark Register of each country. Section 1 of the Trademarks Act 1994 defines trademarks as:

> . . . any sign capable of being represented graphically which is capable of distinguishing goods or services of one undertaking from those of other undertakings.
>
> A trademark may, in particular, consist of words (including personal names), designs, letters, numerals or the shape of goods or their packaging.

Section 2 of the 1994 Act defines a 'registered trademark' as:

> . . . a property right obtained by the registration of the trademark under this Act and the proprietor of a registered trademark has the rights and remedies provided by this Act.

One can obtain a Community Trademark via the Office for Harmonization in the Internal Market (OHIM), a European Union agency responsible for registering trademarks and designs that are valid in all 27 member states (subject to some substantive requirements), which makes national marks less important.[124]

TRIPS additionally defines what types of signs can be eligible for protection as trademarks and what the minimum rights conferred on their owners must be. Service marks must be protected in the same way as trademarks used for goods, and marks that have become well known in a particular country enjoy additional protection.

A place name is sometimes used to identify a product. This 'geographical indication' identifies the product's special characteristics, such as 'Champagne, 'Scotch' or 'Roquefort', and the TRIPS Agreement contains special provisions for such (food) products. But the Agreement also states that place names must not be misused so that the public cannot be misled, nor should this practice lead to unfair competition by way of registration of geographical indications, such as for wines.

In relation to EU legislation, signs and trademarks may only be invoked if they are of more than 'mere local significance'.[125] 'Local' in the context of EU standards covers a wider scope than it might have under national law. An individual assessment must be made on the particularities of each case and cannot be based on geographical criteria alone. An important element is the intensity of the marketing and the volume of sales made. The amount of population concerned is also a criterion to be taken into account.

See Chapter 8.3.5 → The basis for protecting integrated circuit designs (or 'topographies') in the TRIPS agreement is the Washington Treaty on Intellectual Property in Respect of Integrated Circuits (also part of WIPO). In respect of topographies the protection is available for at least ten years.

OHIM, as the 'EU Trademark Office', checks for evidence to substantiate that a trademark or design does not exist before registration and also checks for provisions on passing off in case of a domestic legal challenge, as was the case in the *Frankie Goes to Hollywood* (see below). OHIM will analyse the various requirements under both the national law (such as the UK **Trademarks Act 1994**) as far as the conditions for passing off are concerned and EU legislation, such as the **Council Regulation on Community Trademark** of 2009 and the implementing Council Regulation 40/94 on Community Trademark.

---

124 OHIM website: <http://oami.europa.eu>, accessed 25 November 2010.
125 Art. 8(4) of the EC Regulation 2868/95 of 13 December 1995 implementing Council Regulation 40/94 on the Community trademark (CTMR).

❖ **KEY CASE**   *Gill v Frankie Goes To Hollywood Ltd* (2008)[126]

Facts:

'Frankie Goes to Hollywood' (FGTH) was a band formed in Liverpool in the early 1980s, consisting originally of band members Holly Johnson (vocals), Paul Rutherford (vocals; keyboard), Peter Gill (drums), Mark O'Toole (bass guitar) and Gerard (Jed) O'Toole (guitar). The group's debut single 'Relax' was banned by the BBC in November 1983, as 'obscene' and topped the singles charts for five weeks. T-shirts bearing the slogan 'Frankie says . . .' became very popular. In 1984, Gerard O'Toole left the band and was replaced by Brian Nash. After a gig at Wembley Arena in 1987 Holly Johnson left the group, citing musical estrangement. The band split up and the name 'FGTH' was not in use until 2003 when the five members were approached by a TV show, *Bands Reunited*, with a view to reforming in order to perform on the programme for a charity concert for the Prince's Trust in 2004. Holly Johnson refused to take part or rejoin the band. He had embarked on a solo career.

In January 2004, Holly Johnson registered a company under the name Frankie Goes To Hollywood Ltd ('Frankie') and sought to register the words as an EU Community trademark[127] in respect of goods and services in Classes 9, 16, 25 and 41.[128]

The opponents (Peter Gill, Mark O'Toole, Gerard O'Toole and Paul Rutherford) filed an opposition to this application, which was based on earlier rights resulting from their previous use of the name 'Frankie Goes to Hollywood' in relation to goods listed in the application. It was the contention of the opponents that, by virtue of the identity of the applied-for trademark with the opponents' earlier unregistered name, they were entitled to common law protection under the law of passing off. Additionally, the opponents noted a great similarity of the goods and services in respect of which registration was sought and the existence of the original FGTH goods, and that there was likelihood of confusion between the new trademark applied for and the earlier mark. The application to oppose the new trademark registration was filed under s. 5(4) **Trademarks Act 1994**, which states that a trademark shall not be registered if its use is liable to be prevented by the law of passing off. The Trademark Registry upheld the opposition and the hearing officer gave the following reasons:

(a) While the director of the applicant company (Holly Johnson) was credited as being the originator of the name, this in itself did not confer upon him, as inventor of the name, any rights in respect of its use as a trademark;

(b) The band was seen as a partnership at will, in respect of which any goodwill generated by the five members of the band during the 1980s in connection with commercial activities would vest in the partnership itself, rather than giving each member, or any individual member, a discrete right of ownership over the partnership assets in order to enforce that right against other members. This position was maintained

---

126 [2008] ETMR 4 (Case B 849 069). Office for Harmonisation in the Internal Market (Opposition Division) 27 July 2007.

127 The application claims priority from UK trademark application no.2359948 filed on 2 April 2004.

128 The classifications included, *inter alia*, in class 9: apparatus for recording & transmission; CDs; CD-ROMs; DVDs; computer software; mouse mats; mobile phone accessories; sunglasses; in class 16: printed publications; periodicals; books; magazines etc.; calendars; in class 25: clothing; footwear; headgear; belts etc. and in class 41: the provision of online publications and digital music (not downloadable) from the Internet; audio and video recording services; live concerts; TV & radio; photography; interactive information provided online from computer databases or the Internet.

when the band dissolved in 1987 as there were no formal arrangements made as to the distribution of partnership assets at that time;

(c) The reformed band, performing without the director of the applicant company (Holly Johnson) in 2004, constituted a new partnership.

Decision:

The Opposition Division ruled that the opposition would be upheld. Under Art. 8(4) of Regulation 40/94, the opponents' mark must be used in the course of trade. In this case, the director of the applicant company had not used the name outside the period of his membership of the band in respect of the goods and services covered by the application. This meant that Holly Johnson, director of the new company, could not make use of the goodwill and reputation that was still vested in the original band partnership trademark. Therefore, the use of the name by the director of the applicant company would amount to a mis-representation from which damage would inevitably follow. Therefore the opposition succeeded (cited authorities: *SAXON Trademark* (2003);[129] *Harrods Ltd v Harrodian School* (1996);[130] *Barlow Clowes International Ltd (In Liquidation) v Eurotrust International Ltd* (2005)[131]).

The main issue in Frankie Goes to Hollywood centred on the law of 'passing off' – particularly of a non-registered trademark, in respect of s. 5(4) **Trademarks Act 1994**. The issue was that the original band had been using their band logo 'Frankie says . . .' on its merchandise throughout the 1980s, but this had never been registered as a trademark. Put succinctly, to succeed in a 'passing off action' the proprietor of a non-registered trademark must demonstrate the following:

●   That the (opponent's) goods or services have acquired a goodwill or reputation in the market and are known by some distinguishing feature;
●   That there is a misrepresentation by the (applicant) (whether or not intentional) leading or likely to lead the public to believe that services offered by the (applicant) are services of the (opponent);
●   That the (opponent) has suffered or is likely to suffer damage as a result of the erroneous belief engendered by the (applicant's) misrepresentation.[132]

Millett LJ defined 'passing off' in Harrods Ltd v Harrodian School Ltd. (1996)[133] as follows:

. . . It is well settled that (unless registered as a trademark) no one has a monopoly in his brand name or get up, however familiar these may be. Passing off is a wrongful invasion of a right of property vested in the plaintiff; but the property which is protected by an action for passing off is not the plaintiff's proprietary right in the name or get up which the defendant has misappropriated but the goodwill and reputation of his business which is likely to be harmed by the defendant's misrepresentation.[134]

Former lead singer and founder of FGTH, Holly Johnson, argued in court that he had devised the original band name, after being inspired by a painting of Frank Sinatra that appeared in a book

---

129 [2003] EWHC 295 (Ch).
130 [1996] RPC 697.
131 [2005] UKPC 37.
132 See: Keeling, Llewelyn and Mellor (2010).
133 [1996] RPC 697.
134 Ibid., at 791 (Millett LJ).

called *Rock Dreams* by Guy Peellaert, but admitted that he had never registered the name as a trademark. Therefore, the EU Trademark Office did not dispute that Mr Johnson originated the name, but ruled that the mere act of inventing a name does not, in itself, bring the inventor any rights. It then followed that the use of the non-registered trademark 'Frankie Goes to Hollywood' was 'of more than mere local significance', in that the original band members (the opponents in this action) could show that the (original) band 'Frankie Goes to Hollywood' was very successful both in the UK and other European countries in the period between 1984 and 1987, and that its music continues to be very popular. It was for this reason that the Trademark Office prevented the registration of a subsequent new Community trademark, bearing the very same name. This would certainly have been a case of 'passing off' of the old trademark already in existence (though never registered).[135] It was for these reasons that Holly Johnson's application for a new trademark was refused. The only way that band names can be protected, as pop groups break up or re-form, is by way of contract, licensing agreement or assignment procedures.

9.8.2 Criminal provisions for IP and trademark infringement

As has already been discussed in Chapter 8.9, the owner of a copyright, patent or other form of intellectual property right can issue a licence for someone else to produce or copy the protected trademark, work, invention or design. At the same time, the TRIPS Agreement recognizes that the terms of a licensing contract could restrict competition or impede technology transfer. It says that, under certain conditions, governments have the right to take action to prevent anti-competitive licensing that abuses intellectual property rights. It also says that governments must be prepared to consult each other on controlling anti-competitive licensing.

One such lawsuit involving unfair competition and trademark infringement[136] concerned the famous American-born Greek opera soprano Maria Callas, who died on 16 September 1977. Her surviving estate wanted to register her name as a trademark posthumously for her special jewellery, which she wore for her performances of *Tosca* in 1956 at the New York Metropolitan Opera. Made of nearly 200 tear-shaped Swarovski crystals, worth approximately $85,000, the original jewellery set – tiara, earrings and necklace – was created specifically for Callas by the Atelier Marangoni in Milan, Italy. The Italian company wanted to register their jewellery as the 'Maria Callas' collection but her surviving estate opposed the trademark application. The US Trademark Office found – following a ruling in the highest Italian court – that anyone could now use the trademark label 'Maria Callas'.

In general, intellectual property – including industrial property – laws give private rights that can be enforced by the owners of the rights using civil remedies. Part 3 of the TRIPS Agreement states that governments have to ensure that IP rights can be enforced under their laws and that the penalties for infringement are robust enough to deter further violations. Procedures must be fair and equitable, and not unnecessarily complicated or costly. They should not entail unreasonable time limits or unwarranted delays. Applicants involved should be able to ask a court to review an administrative decision or to appeal a lower court's ruling.

TRIPS describes in some detail how enforcement should be handled, including rules for obtaining evidence, provisional measures, injunctions, damages and other penalties. It states that courts have the right, under certain conditions, to order the disposal or destruction of pirated or counterfeit goods, covering wilful trademark counterfeiting or copyright piracy on a commercial level. All governments that have signed up to TRIPS have agreed to ensure that owners' IP rights

---

135 [2008] ETMR 4 at 97–99.
136 Re. MC MC S.r.l, Application No. 79022561 (26 September 2008), US Trademark Office.

must receive the assistance of police, trading standards and customs authorities to prevent imports of counterfeit and pirated goods.

Increasingly, states are resorting to criminal law to enforce civil rights. This means that imprisonment is more likely in repeat offence cases. But this also means that public enforcement bodies, such as local authority trading standards, will have to bear the costs of enforcement. The key issue in a criminal action (unlike in civil cases) is that *mens rea* will be required in that the prosecution will have to show that the defendant knew or ought to have known he was committing an infringing act beyond all reasonable doubt.

The main objective of the **Copyright, etc. and Trademarks (Offences and Enforcement) Act 2002** is to remove some of the discrepancies between the nature of IP offences. Maximum penalties under the 2002 Act include an unlimited fine and/or up to 10 years' imprisonment to reflect the seriousness of these crimes and to bring the penalties into line with existing ones for similar trademark offences.[137] The following four areas of IP law are covered by the **Copyright, etc. and Trademarks (Offences and Enforcement) Act 2002** concerning criminal offences in relation to the making for sale or hire or dealing with the following types of illegal material:

- Copies of material that is protected by copyright, such as music, films and computer software, that have been made without the authorization of the copyright owner, i.e. infringing or pirate copies, and articles that are specifically designed or adapted for making infringing copies of copyright material.[138]
- Copies of recordings of performances that have been made without the authorization of the performer(s) or a person having recording rights in the performance, i.e. illicit or bootleg recordings.[139]
- Devices or other apparatus, including software, that allow people to access encrypted transmissions without paying the normal fee for their reception, i.e. unauthorized decoders for conditional access transmissions where the transmissions can be either broadcasts, including satellite broadcasts, cable programme services or information society services.[140]
- Goods, packaging or labels bearing a trademark that has been applied without the consent of the trademark owner, i.e. counterfeit goods, and articles that are specifically designed or adapted for making unauthorized copies of a trademark for use on such goods and other material.[141]

The 2002 Act provides maximum penalties for the above-named offences and grants additional police search and seizure powers relating to these offences; the act also makes provision for court orders on forfeiture of illegal material that may need to be seized during investigation of offences.

Section 2 of the 2002 Act allows the police to obtain search warrants for all the offences in section 107(1) and (2) CDPA, including those only triable in the magistrates' courts.[142] These provisions are in addition to any powers available to the police as a result of the **Police and Criminal Evidence Act 1984** (PACE).[143]

---

137 Section 1 of the 2002 Act raises the maximum penalty for conviction on indictment for the offences referred to in sections 107(4), 198(5) and 297A(2) in Parts I, II and VII CDPA 1988.

138 See the offences in s.107(1) and (2) in Part I CDPA.

139 See the offences in s.198(1) in Part II CDPA.

140 See the offences in s. 297A in Part VII CDPA.

141 See the offences in s. 92 *Trademarks Act* 1994.

142 The equivalent provision in section 200 of Part II of the 1988 Act is applied to all the offences in section 198(1) by this section. Equivalent search warrant provisions are introduced by section 2 for the offences in section 297A of Part VII of the 1988 Act.

143 The existing search warrant provisions in sections 109 and 200 PACE allow a justice of the peace (or in Scotland, a sheriff or justice of the peace) to grant a warrant where information/evidence on oath leaves him satisfied that there are reasonable grounds for believing that an offence has been or is about to be committed and there is evidence of this on the premises.

Section 3 reproduces in Part I of the **Copyright, Designs and Patents Act 1988** provisions corresponding to those in ss. 97 and 98 **Trademarks Act 1994,** allowing forfeiture of infringing goods. Section 3 provides forfeiture provisions for goods infringing copyright, i.e. infringing copies and articles specifically designed or adapted for making such copies. Section 97 relates to forfeiture in England, Wales and Northern Ireland; s. 98 is a modified version relating to forfeiture in Scotland.

Section 4 of the 2002 Act introduced forfeiture provisions, very similar to those in section 3, into Part II CDPA in respect of goods that infringe rights in performances, i.e. illicit recordings.

Section 5 of the 2002 Act introduced forfeiture provisions, very similar to those in section 3, into Part VII CDPA in respect of devices that permit fraudulent reception of conditional access transmissions, i.e. unauthorized decoders used to access transmissions such as satellite television without payment.

Section 6 provides for search warrant and seizure provisions corresponding to those that are introduced or amended by section 2 for Parts I, II and VII CDPA 1988 for the offences in s. 92 **Trademarks Act 1994** relating to counterfeit goods and articles for making them.[144]

In Scotland, the forfeiture provisions apply where a person has been convicted of one of these offences or on application by the procurator fiscal. The court can order destruction of goods or release to another person with conditions. Broadly similar provision is introduced by section 3 into Part I of the 1988 Act. The Act does not make any changes to the scope of criminal offences in IP law, so that the type of behaviour that can give rise to an offence remains the same.

See Chapter 8.10.2

The proprietor of a registered trademark can only succeed in a claim for trademark infringement under Article 5(1) of EU Directive 89/104 (1989), if he satisfies six conditions:

(a)   there must have been the use of a sign by a third party;
(b)   that use must have been in the course of trade;
(c)   such use must have been without the consent of the trademark proprietor;
(d)   the allegedly infringing use involved the use of a sign which was identical to the trademark;
(e)   that sign was used in relation to goods or services which were identical to those for which the trademark was registered; and
(f)   that use affected, or was liable to affect, the functions of the trademark, in particular its essential function of guaranteeing to consumers the origin of the goods or services.

9.8.3 E-commerce and online auction providers

Are online providers and auction 'houses' such as eBay liable for IP infringements committed by their users? This was the question raised by the Chancery Court with reference to the European Court of Justice (ECJ) in the landmark case of *L'Oréal v eBay* (2009).[145] The central questions in this case were: did eBay (Europe) itself commit infringements by using trademarks in relation to infringing goods? Or was eBay simply a 'hosting' ISP and therefore not liable for copyright infringement as a mere auction site?

What does the e-commerce Directive[146] say about the legal aspects of hosting (auction) websites and their liability towards either counterfeited or IP-infringing goods? Key provisions of the e-commerce Directive are summarized in Article 14 ('Hosting'), which states:

144 This section also extends to the Isle of Man, since the Trademarks Act 1994 also does.
145 [2009] EWHC 1094; [2009] ETMR 53 (Ch) 22 May 2009.
146 EC Council Directive 2000/31.

... where an information society service is provided that consists of the storage of information provided by a recipient of the service, member states shall ensure that the service provider is not liable for the information stored at the request of a recipient of the service, on condition that:

(a) the provider does not have actual knowledge of illegal activity or information and, as regards claims for damages, is not aware of facts or circumstances from which the illegal activity or information is apparent; or

(b) the provider, upon obtaining such knowledge or awareness, acts expeditiously to remove or to disable access to the information.

The auction website eBay is as an 'online marketplace', operating some 21 websites in eight languages, which display listings of goods for sale posted by users and which enable buyers to purchase such goods from sellers.[147] The databases on which live listings are stored are not divided by country, but are housed in four locations in the United States. eBay's software platform comprises about 30 million lines of code divided into some 237 sub-systems. Most of the software is bespoke. eBay Europe was launched in October 1999, and today can count around 16 million active listings on the site at any one time. An average of around 1.3 million listings is posted each day, rising to a peak of over 4.5 million at Christmas eBay operates both auction-style and fixed-price listings.

The largest online auction provider in the world, eBay has appeared as a defendant five times before four different national courts for its role in facilitating the sale of counterfeit products on its site. In the French Court, eBay was held liable in three different lawsuits for 'committing gross negligence' by not fulfilling its obligation to make sure that its activity did not generate illegal acts. The Paris Grand Tribunal imposed an obligation on eBay because it was held to provide not merely a hosting service but also acted as a broker and was therefore subject to the common regime of civil liability (see: *L'Oréal SA v eBay France SA* (2009)[148]).

The French judgment stands in marked contrast to that of the Belgian Court. In the *Lancôme* case, the role of eBay was seen as being a mere 'host', with no obligation to monitor the information hosted on its website and therefore no liability for any IP infringement or any other form of illegal nature that the online auction house was not aware of. If it did become aware of any illegal acts, the duty was to promptly remove the information from the site (see: *Lancôme Parfums et Beaute & Cie v eBay International AG* (2008)[149]).

In a similar action, the US court, applying the DMCA legislation (see 9.7.3), limited eBay's responsibility, and only made the site liable if eBay had specific knowledge of any trademark infringements. If the site did have knowledge of any infringement, its responsibility was confined to taking down the objectionable items. The court did not say that eBay was under a general obligation to pre-emptively remove items based on generalized knowledge that they might host counterfeit goods (see: *Tiffany (NJ) v eBay Inc* (2008)[150]).

The decision by the German Bundesgerichtshof in 2008 is probably the most interesting one; it sits between the French, Belgian and US extremes. In the *Rolex Counterfeit Watches* case, the Bundesgerichtshof classified an online auction provider is an 'interferer' and therefore subject to the duty to examine, thereby preventing infringements. This means the online auction house must,

147 eBay Inc was founded in 1995 under the name AuctionWeb. It changed its name in 1997. It was listed on the NASDAQ stock exchange in 1998. In 2008 eBay Inc's revenue was $8.54 billion and its income was $1.78 billion. At the time of the L'Oréal court case in 2009, eBay had over 300 million registered users, of which about 84 million were active. More than 125 million active listings appear on eBay's websites at any given time. On average about 7.3 million new listings are posted each day, although this can rise to 12 million new listings a day.
148 (2009) (RG 07/11365) Tribunal de Grande Instance, Paris, jugement de 13 May 2009) (Unreported).
149 (2008) (A/07/06032) Belgium, Comm. Bruxelles, 28 May 2008.
150 (2008) (No.04 Civ. 4607) Southern District of New York, July 14, 2008; Tiffany (NJ) Inc v eBay Inc 576 F Supp 2d 463 (SDNY 2008).

once it is informed of a clear trademark infringement, promptly remove the infringing item from its website and ensure that similar trademark infringements will not reoccur (including repetitions of infringement of the same brand name) (see: Bundesgerichtshof judgments in the Rolex cases against ricardo.de AG in: *Internet Auction III* (2008); *Internet Auction II* (2007); *Re. Internet Auctions of Counterfeit Watches* (2005)[151]).

It could be said the German ruling is the fairest in allocating responsibilities between the trademark owners and online auction providers. The Belgian and US decisions place all responsibilities of combating IP infringement on the trademark owner whereas the German decision imposes on the online auction provider a duty, upon notification of a clear trademark infringement, to use reasonable measures to remove the infringements and to employ subsequent filtering checks.

L'Oréal v eBay (2009) became the test case in the UK, (see below) where the Chancery Court referred the 'e-commerce' harmonization questions to the European Court of Justice (ECJ) with no clear satisfactory solution. The English High Court held that eBay was not liable, which was generally reported in the UK media as a victory for eBay. As the ECJ ruling in the case has been inconclusive, there is no answer to third-party liability in relation to trademark infringement relating to linked sites and link marks online.

Given that the key aspects of European trademark law are supposed to have been harmonized by an EC Directive,[152] and that there is also an EC Directive harmonizing the liability of ISPs,[153] European courts ought to be in a position to give the same answers to the questions raised. To date they have not.

FOR THOUGHT

Which legal position should be adopted? The German *Bundesgerichtshof* decision in the Rolex cases, which limits the liability of an online auction provider by exempting it from trademark infringements which cannot be detected by reasonable means? Or the French *Tribunal de Grande Instance* ruling, which places the entire responsibly on the online auction house and requires the provider to filter out items based on mere suspicion of an IP infringement?

9.8.4 The *L'Oréal v eBay* case[154]

In this action the Chancery Court (with reference to the European Court of Justice – ECJ) had to determine whether the sellers had sold goods which infringed the claimants' trademarks in that they were:

(i)   counterfeit;
(ii)   non-European Economic Area (EEA) goods;
(iii) tester products that were not intended for resale; or
(iv)   products which, being unboxed, would have damaged the reputation of claimants' trademarks.

---

151 The Bundesgerichtshof held that, assuming they had used the signs in the course of trade, the sellers had infringed Rolex's trademarks; but that Ricardo had neither infringed the trademarks nor participated in infringement by the users. Accordingly, Rolex's claim for damages was dismissed.

152 EC Directive 2006/116 on the 'Term of Protection of Copyright and Certain Related Rights Enforcement Directive' of 12 December 2006 ('the harmonization Directive').

153 Directive 2000/31 on certain legal aspects of information society services, in particular electronic commerce, in the Internal Market Arts. 13, 14, 15 [2000] OJ L178/1.

154 *L'Oréal SA v eBay International AG* [2009] EWHC 1094 (Ch).

The UK court asked the ECJ to determine whether the defendants (eBay) and linked companies were jointly liable for the infringements committed by their users in selling infringing goods (i.e. joint tortfeasors). The claimants were all cosmetics companies bringing claims for trademark infringement against three defendant companies which facilitated the online auction and sale of goods, as well as seven individual sellers of cosmetic products which, the claimants maintained, infringed a number of Community trademarks and UK trademarks of which they were the proprietors.[155]

L'Oréal made three principal claims against eBay Europe. The first was that eBay Europe was jointly liable for the infringements allegedly committed by the fourth to tenth defendants (companies which traded in L'Oréal and Lancôme products online). L'Oréal's second claim was that eBay Europe were primarily liable for use of the link marks (a) in sponsored links on third party search engines and (b) on the site, in both cases insofar as such use was in relation to infringing goods. The third claim was that of the products purchased via eBay, 17 were adduced in evidence, with L'Oréal' claiming that two of them were counterfeit and that the remaining 15 had not been marketed in the European Economic Area (EEA) by them (they were consignments for the American market). L'Oréal further argued that the products were unboxed and simply 'testers'; further that the defendants had employed copyright-protected images and text in their listings of goods for sale on the eBay sites without their permission.

L'Oréal also argued that hyperlinks (link marks) at the top of the sponsored link led to a page from the eBay Express site showing a search for 'matrix hair' and 'magie noire' which brought up 48 items from international sellers and that all of these were to infringing goods. The basis of this allegation was that the country or region stated was the United States in all cases and the items were priced in sterling. L'Oréal contended that, so far as the auction-style listings were concerned, eBay did in fact conduct an auction. eBay disputed this and L'Oréal accepted at least that eBay's activities differ from those of traditional auctioneers. L'Oréal claimed that each of the fourth to tenth defendants infringed one or more of the trademarks by using signs identical to the trademarks of goods to those for which the trademarks are registered. These claims all concerned the Lancôme marks.[156] In providing the online facility for sellers to sell infringing products it would make eBay and the other defendants joint tortfeasors.

In their defence, eBay argued that they had set up systems and policies which discouraged the sale of infringing products and which enabled trademark owners, by notifying them, to have the webpages on which allegedly infringing products were sold taken down.[157] eBay also argued that they were merely fulfilling the function of an ISP ('hosting site') and were not involved in the sale of infringing goods, relying on Article 14 of Directive 2000/3 (the e-commerce Directive). eBay submitted that, as a matter of law, eBay Europe were under no duty or obligation to prevent third parties from infringing L'Oréal's (or anyone else's) registered trademarks. The online trading house also argued that it attempts to prevent or at least minimize infringements, in particular through the VeRO programme which filters infringing goods, such as counterfeit watches by Rolex. eBay further submitted that the companies procuring the (allegedly counterfeited) goods (the fourth to tenth defendants) had sold a large proportion of items previously via eBay without complaint from the cosmetic companies. Counsel for eBay Europe submitted that in reality L'Oréal's claim of joint tortfeasorship was a thinly-disguised attack on eBay's business model.

---

155 L'Oréal divided the trademarks into two groups for the purposes of their claims. The first group, referred to as 'the Lancôme Marks', consisted of Lancome, Renergie, Definicils and Amor Amor. The second group, referred to as 'the Link Marks', consisted of Definicils together with the remaining trademarks not included in the first group.
156 The complaint against the fourth defendant concerns advertisements and offers for sale for 'Lancome Maquicomplet Concealer Light Buff RRP £18.50', sold on 23 November 2006; 'Lancome Renergie Microlift Active Redefining Treatment', sold on 23 November 2006; and 'Lancome Definicils Full Size Black Mascara Waterproof', sold on 5 December 2006.
157 eBay Europe pleaded defences under ss. 10(6) and 11(2) *Trademarks Act* 1994 (though these were not pursued at trial).

In summary, Mr Justice Arnold's judgment in the UK *L'Oréal v eBay* case simply means that eBay was not a joint tortfeasor for the sale of counterfeit products online. The judge's reasoning was that under English common law, a defendant would only be a joint tortfeasor if he intentionally procures and shares a common design. Mere knowledge and involvement, including facilitating the infringement, was insufficient to render one liable as a joint tortfeasor.[158]

An important point raised in *L'Oréal SA v eBay* was that of sponsored links and 'link marks'. If a user clicks on a search engine such as Google using one of the link marks, this will cause a sponsored link to the site to be displayed. The user will then be taken to a display of search results on the site for products by reference to the link mark. eBay Europe, for example, chooses the keywords based on the activity on the site. The sponsored link (to a business) pays a certain amount for each click-through of each keyword, and in turn, receives revenue via eBay.

It was this aspect which was referred to the ECJ by the UK Chancery Court for a preliminary ruling. The question centred on the scope of infringement of Article 5(1) of EC Directive 89/104, which approximates the laws of the member states relating to trademarks. The problem is that the Directive does not specifically define the use of a trademark by third parties; it only covers the use of a trademark sign in relation to the proprietor's goods.

In this respect, the ECJ did not come to a conclusive decision. It held that EU trademark law had not been completely harmonized in respect of copyright and trademark infringement via hyperlinks and link marks. Since there has been no pronouncement by the ECJ on this issue to date, there is no clear answer about sponsored links, including the main third party search engines such as Google, MSN and Yahoo and purchased keywords link marks triggered by eBay.

What was really at the heart of the *L'Oréal* case? Was it not – as Counsel for eBay Europe argued – an attack on eBay's business model? Mr Justice Arnold agreed with Counsel on this, stating that this claim came close to the heart of the issue. It is a fact that eBay (and other online auction houses) have created a new form of trade and a business model which is highly successful. But it also carries with it a higher risk of infringement than more traditional methods of trade. That said, copyright and industrial property rights are at increased risk and it could be argued that the high profits which eBay (and others) make from their sites oblige them to ensure that IP rights are not infringed.

The UK court ruling was that, as a matter of common law, eBay Europe was under no legal duty or obligation to prevent infringement of third parties' registered trademarks. Since Article 11 of the EC Enforcement Directive is not clear on third-party duty obligation with regard to future infringements as a result of online auction site operation, there is, as yet, no liability for past infringements on the ground of joint tortfeasorship. In view of the current uncertainty over this area of law, the ECJ's response to the *L'Oréal* case does not provide *acte clair*.

👁 FOR THOUGHT

Are eBay (or similar online auction websites) under a duty to prevent third parties from IP infringing because they are under a duty not to participate in a common design to infringe? Should eBay – having participated in hyperlinked sites (link marks) – prevent third parties from infringement?

---

158 *L'Oréal* [2009] EWHC 1094 (Ch) at 381–2 (Arnold J).

9.8.5 The future of the digital agenda: analysis and discussion

The Internet is borderless, but where online markets are concerned, many layers of legislation persist. This is particularly true in Europe and is stifling competitiveness in the digital economy. It is perhaps not surprising that the EU is falling behind in markets such as media services, both in terms of what consumers can access and the business models that can create jobs.

Most of the recent successful internet business models, such as Google, eBay, Amazon and Facebook, originated outside of Europe and therefore mostly operate outside EU law. Despite the body of key single-market legislation in Europe on e-Commerce, e-Invoicing and e-Signatures, transactions in the digital environment are still too complex, with inconsistent implementation of the rules across EU Member States.

Authors and creators of works are faced with considerable uncertainty about their rights and legal protection for their intellectual property with different duration rights. The EU Commission is taking action in the following areas:

1) Simplify copyright clearance, management and cross-border licensing by enhancing the governance, transparency and pan-European licensing for (online) rights management by legislating a framework Directive on collective rights management;

2) Create a legal framework to facilitate the digitization and dissemination of cultural works in Europe by issuing a Directive on orphan works to conduct a dialogue with stakeholders with a view to further measures on out-of-print works;

3) Review and harmonize collective rights management to allow right holders to benefit from the full potential of the digital market, including measures to promote cross-border and pan-European licences;

4) Make online and cross-border transactions straightforward.[159]

As technology continues to develop, film producers, recording companies, games manufacturers, publishers and authors will become increasingly affected by piracy. There is an urgent need for greater copyright guidance for rights holders but also for the end user. Simply cutting peer-to-peer file-sharers off from the Internet will not solve the problem. Many quickly reappear. Or will savvy media and entertainment lawyers make a fast buck by pursuing individual file-sharers in the courts?

Widespread online and offline copyright infringement (whether wilful or unwitting) under-lines the need for media companies to better explain to consumers what they can and cannot do with the products they bought or 'illegally' downloaded. Maybe there should be more copyright guidance for rights holders rather than issuing a list of 'don'ts'. However, it is a fair bet that many infringers know perfectly well that what they are doing is illegal and still continue. Law enforcement is about as effective in some areas as in the old Wild West.

9.9 Summary of key points

- PRS-MCPS are collecting societies that ensure that composers, songwriters and publishers are paid royalties when their music is used in live performance, on TV or radio, CDs and DVDs, downloads, streams, etc.;
- PPL licenses music for business use;
- Piracy falls into four categories: physical music piracy, counterfeits, bootlegs and Internet piracy;

---

159 Source: European Commission (2010).

- The **Digital Economy Act 2010** provides for the disconnection of broadband customers who are deemed to be infringing copyright laws without first being given the opportunity to plead their innocence before a court;
- Section 1 **Trademarks Act 1994** defines a registered trademark as a property right that is obtained by the registration of the trademark;
- EEC Directive 89/104 (1989) approximates the laws of EU member states on trademarks, encompassing all types of indicators of source, including designs and the shape of goods and their packaging;
- EC Directive 2000/31 is the 'e-Commerce Directive' (2000) which relates to the liability of ISPs and electronic commerce; it ensures the continued free flow of information on the Internet and the development of e-commerce; the e-Commerce Directive grants certain exemptions to online intermediaries under the conditions set out in Articles 12 to 15;
- EC 'Community Trademark Regulation' (CTMR – Regulation 207/2009) provides registration of EU-wide trademarks at OHIM in Alicante, Spain, covering all 27 member states – on the same terms as a party can obtain a national trademark in the UK;
- The US **Digital Millennium Copyright Act 1998** (DMCA) criminalizes the production and dissemination of technology that allows users to circumvent technical copy-restriction methods;
- The **Copyright, etc. and Trademarks (Offences and Enforcement) Act 2002** provides for criminal offences in relation to the making for sale or hire or dealing with types of illegal material:

  1) Copyrighted material including music, films and computer software, that have been made without the authorization of the copyright owner (i.e. pirate copies);
  2) Copies of recordings of live performances that have been made without the authorization of the performer(s);
  3) Copying devices and software that allow people to access encrypted transmissions without paying the normal fee for their reception;
  4) Goods, packaging or labels bearing a trademark that has been applied without the consent of the trademark owner;

- To prove trademark infringement certain following conditions must be satisfied; these are:

  1) there must have been the use of a sign by a third party;
  2) that use must have been in the course of trade;
  3) such use must have been without the consent of the trademark proprietor;
  4) the allegedly infringing use involved the use of a sign which was identical to the trademark;
  5) that sign was used in relation to goods or services which were identical to those for which the trademark was registered;
  6) or the use of an identical or similar mark on identical or similar goods/services and consumer confusion is likely to result;
  7) or the use of an identical or similar mark on similar or dissimilar goods/services and this is taking unfair advantage or is detrimental to the reputation of the owner of the registered mark;
  8) that use affected, or was liable to affect, the functions of the trademark, in particular its essential function of guaranteeing to consumers the origin of the goods or services (Directive 89/104 Art. 5(1)(a) (1989));
  9) The defendant cannot bring himself with an available defence such as use of his own name which might be identical to the trademark or is validly using the mark in a legal comparative advertisement.

📖 9.10 Further reading

Colston, C. and Galloway, J. (2010) *Modern Intellectual Property Law*. 3rd Edition. London: Routledge.

Cook, T. (2010) *EU Intellectual Property Law*. Oxford: Oxford University Press.

Dehin, V. (2010) 'The future of legal online music services in the European Union: a review of the EU Commission's recent initiatives in cross-border copyright management'. *European Intellectual Property Review*, 2010, 32(5), 220–37.

Ficsor, M. (2003) 'Collective Management of Copyright and Related Rights at a Triple Crossroads: should it remain voluntary or may it be "extended" or made mandatory?' Copyright Bulletin No 3, December 2003. United Nations, Educational, Scientific and Cultural Organization (online publication): available at http://portal.unesco.org/culture/en/ev.php-URL_ ID=14935&URL_DO=DO_TOPIC&URL_SECTION=201.html, accessed 25 November 2010.

Gordon, S. (2008) *The Future of the Music Business. How to Succeed with the New Digital Technologies. A Guide for Artists and Entrepreneurs*. 2nd Edition. San Francisco, CA: Backbeat Books (Hal Leonard Corporation).

Harrison, A. (2008) Music: *The Business. The Essential Guide to the Law and the Deals*. 4th Edition. London: Virgin Books.

Hildebrand, L. (2009) *Inherent Vice: Bootleg Histories of Videotape and Copyright*. Durham, North Carolina, USA: Duke University Press.

Keeling, D.T., Llewelyn, D. and Mellor, J. (2010) *Kerly's Law of Trademarks and Trade Names*. 15th Edition. London: Sweet & Maxwell.

Koempel, F. (2007) 'If the kids are united'. *Journal of Intellectual Property Law & Practice*, 2007, 2(6), 371–6.

Music Managers Forum (2003) *The Music Management Bible. 2nd Edition*. London: Sanctuary Publishing Ltd.

Passman, D.S. (2008) *All You Need to Know about the Music Business*. 6th edition. London/New York: Penguin.

Smartt, U. (2004) 'Stay out of Jail: Performance, Multimedia and Copyright Laws'. Leslie Hill and Helen Paris: *Guerrilla Performance and Multimedia*. 2nd Edition London/New York: Continuum.

Sterling, A. L. (2008) *World Copyright Law*. 3rd Edition. London: Sweet & Maxwell.

Chapter 10

Regulatory Bodies and Self-Regulation

Chapter Contents

10.1 Overview

This book closes with its final chapter on regulators and 'quangos' that were in existence following the General Election in 2010. While the topic may be a little dry, it is important to understand the principles behind self-regulation in relation to the UK media and communications industries. The merits and disadvantages of regulatory bodies will be discussed in relation to the alternative – court action – and whether voluntary regulatory powers are sufficient to deal with wrongdoers. For comparative purposes, the chapter includes a look at the statutory Irish Press Council and its Press Ombudsman (see below 10.3.7).

In the UK three models of regulation are used:

● Industry self-regulation, e.g. the Press Complaints Commission (PCC) and the Advertising Standards Authority (ASA) in relation to non-broadcast advertising (though now a co-regulatory regime as the Office of Fair Trading has back-stop powers in relation to false and misleading advertising if the voluntary self-regulatory system fails; see: **Consumer Protection Unfair Trading Regulations 2008**);
● Co-regulation, a combination of industry self-regulation with oversight by a statutory body (e.g. PhonepayPlus and the ASA in relation to broadcast advertising);
● Statutory regulation control by a statutory body, such as the Office of Communications (OFCOM) in relation to, for example, complaints about taste and decency, privacy and unfairness in relation to broadcasters; see: **Communications Act 2003**).

The best-known regulators in the UK are the non-statutory Press Complaints Commission (PCC), regulating the print press and their online content, and the statutory body Ofcom (the Office of Communications), which oversees broadcasters and telecommunications providers. Day to day oversight of internet content is now regulated by Ofcom (under the **Digital Economy Act 2010**). The Association of Television on Demand (ATVOD), which falls under the Ofcom 'umbrella', co-regulates the editorial content of UK video-on-demand services that fall within the statutory definition of 'On Demand Programme Services'.[1]

The model for self-regulation of the print press appears straightforward: the PCC has drawn up a *Code of Practice* which is updated from time to time (see below 10.3.4). Possible breaches of the Code are considered by the PCC, which, in turn, makes rulings in the form of adjudications and enables resolution of complaints, imposing sanctions if necessary, though there is no provision of compensation to individuals who suffer as a result of the breach of the code (see below 10.3.6). The main difference between the PCC and Ofcom is that the latter is a statutory body, set up under the **Communications Act 2003**, whereas the PCC has no statutory basis, a contentious issue discussed in this chapter. Ofcom has a more effective range of sanctions (see below 10.3.8).

In recent years there have been problems over premium rate phone lines (known as 'Premium Rate Telecoms Services' or PRS), mainly used by TV and radio quiz shows and competitions, horoscopes, technical helplines and adult chat lines and all charging very high rates. This chapter looks at the role of self-regulator PhonepayPlus (formerly known as ICSTIS) and its guidelines and enforcement services. PhonepayPlus operates under a co-regulatory regime overseen by Ofcom, the statutory body which acts as a back-stop if the voluntary system proves ineffective (see below 10.4.5).

Some regulators have come and gone, depending on governmental preference and policy issues. The regulation of the film, games and commercial video industry is covered by the British Board of Film Classification (BBFC), a self-regulatory body with some statutory recognition such as the **Video Recordings Act 1984** and the legacy of Mrs Mary Whitehouse. The impact of new media

---

1 s. 368A Communications Act 2003.

in general, and the Internet in particular, continues to dominate the thoughts of those involved in the regulation of audio-visual material (see below 10.6.2 and 10.6.3).

The chapter closes with a final look at European legislation and how the European Commission has addressed the digital age in the form of its 'media sans frontières' legislation (see below 10.8.1).

10.2 Quangos: the reasons behind regulators

It is argued by the new Conservative–Liberal coalition that came into power in May 2010 that millions of pounds could be saved by reducing the number of 'quangos' (quasi-autonomous non-governmental organizations) and by cutting the pay of senior staff in those public bodies. This was the pre-election pledge by the then Conservative opposition leader (and now Prime Minister) David Cameron in July 2009. Speaking on BBC Breakfast Television at the time Mr Cameron set out a three-point plan to overhaul organizations such as Britain's broadcasting regulator, Ofcom. Following the broadcast, a row broke out between Conservatives and the then governing Labour Party, after the Tory Leader promised he would cut back on Britain's 790 quangos, 68 of which were led at the time by executives earning more than (then) Prime Minister Gordon Brown's £194,000 salary, amounting to a total of around £34 billion per year. But how much does the ordinary member of the public actually know about regulators and government quangos? Take Ofcom, the media and telecoms regulator, with its 873 staff, a budget of £142 million and paying its chief executive nearly £400,000 in 2010.

Quangos and regulators are public bodies operating at arm's length from government, but for which ministers are ultimately accountable. In the case of Ofcom it is the Department of Culture, Media and Sport (DCMS). Ministers are usually responsible for appointments, subject to scrutiny by an appointments review body under a Code of Practice to avoid such things as conflicts of interest. For example, the government could not appoint media mogul Rupert Murdoch unless he were to dispose of his media interests. Major players in the UK regulatory field include London Transport, the Environment Agency and pay review bodies.

The Nolan committee, chaired by Lord Nolan, was set up in 1994 under the Conservative Government, at the request of Prime Minister John Major, to examine standards of public life in the wake of allegations that MPs were asking Parliamentary questions for cash and other accusations of sleaze. The Committee concentrated on Members of Parliament, Ministers and Civil Servants, executive quangos and NHS bodies. The Committee concluded:

> . . . we cannot say conclusively that standards of behaviour in public life have declined. We can say that conduct in public life is more rigorously scrutinised than it was in the past, that the standards which the public demands remain high, and that the great majority of people in public life meet those high standards. But there are weaknesses in the procedures for maintaining and enforcing those standards. As a result people in public life are not always as clear as they should be about where the boundaries of acceptable conduct lie. This we regard as the principal reason for public disquiet. It calls for urgent remedial action.[2]

Nolan recommended that all appointments should be subject to independent scrutiny, that merit should be the overriding principle governing appointments and that all public bodies should follow a code of conduct. The post of commissioner for public appointments was created in the wake of the Nolan report and first held by Dame (now Baroness) Rennie Fritchie. Her role was to regulate, monitor and report on the public appointments process. However, only 12,500 of the total 35,000 public body appointments came under her remit at the time.

---

2 See: House of Commons (1994).

Does the ordinary citizen actually know that he can contact the Press Complaints Commission (PCC) if his privacy has been invaded by a newspaper? How much is actually known about the self-regulators such as the Internet Watch Foundation (IWF) or the even more obscure existence of the prime-time, pre-pay phoneline regulator PhonepayPlus? While all regulators have elaborate websites, are freely accessible and offer free advice, it is arguably not well known by ordinary citizens that these authorities exist and offer free alternative redress to going to court in areas of privacy, defamation, harassment, obscenity, violence or child pornography.

Once the Conservatives were in power, Mr Cameron promised that policy work would be returned to Whitehall departments to ensure there was greater parliamentary accountability via ministers. Those quangos that would survive would only carry out purely administrative functions, with ministers taking responsibility for serious performance failures. He vowed in 2009 that Ofcom would be one of those quangos.[3]

It could be argued that, if the advantages of regulators are generally speed and dealing with public complaints out of court, the downside of self-regulation is that these authorities tend not to have legal powers in the form of injunctions, fines or damages (apart from Ofcom). Traditionally, non-statutory regulatory authorities could not be challenged in the administrative courts by way of judicial review, though Lord Woolf stated in the *Ian Brady* case,[4] when the Moors Murderer challenged an adjudication by the PCC, that any exercise of jurisdiction over the PCC 'would be reserved for cases where it would clearly be desirable for this court to intervene'.

The newsreader Anna Ford also tried to seek judicial review in a PCC decision, but the courts could see no justifiable basis for interfering with a self-regulatory body.[5] However, if the actions of a voluntary regulator impinge on the rights of the subjects of the decision, particularly their human rights such as freedom of expression or privacy rights, then it is likely that the courts will intervene, which could meant that the strict demarcation between non-statutory (self- or voluntary) and statutory regulators is breaking down.

The regulators' ability to hand out 'informal' advice and publish decisions, commentaries and adjudications tends to alleviate most complaints from 'ordinary' people, leaving only a handful of complaints, which tend to be from celebrities or royalty who, mostly accompanied by their lawyers, attempt to use the regulators as a first step to gain privacy by trying to protect their reputation.

10.3 Regulating the print press: objective journalism

From time to time, events occur which cause questions to be asked about the methods used by journalists and press photographers to gather material for publication. In January 2007 there was persistent harassment by photographers of Kate Middleton, HRH Prince William's girlfriend and future wife amid speculation that an engagement was about to be announced.[6] Then, in the same month, Mr Clive Goodman, a reporter employed by the *News of the World*, was jailed following his conviction for conspiracy to intercept communications, including some involving the Royal Family, without lawful authority, which led to *The Guardian*'s and PCC's (separate) investigations into clandestine recording devices and unethical undercover journalism (see below 10.3.5). A further event was the release of the Information Commissioner's list of publications that employed journalists who had had dealings with a particular private investigator known to have obtained personal data by illegal means (see below 10.3.6). These events gave rise to renewed doubts about whether the

---

3 Source: 'Tories pledge to cut back quangos', BBC Breakfast, 6 July 2009; see also: 'David Cameron plans to save millions by cutting quangos', by Nicholas Watt, *The Guardian*, 6 July 2009.
4 R v PCC ex parte Stewart-Brady [1997] EMLR 185.
5 See: R v PCC, ex parte Anna Ford [2002] EMLR 5, 31 July 2001 (Unreported) (QBD).
6 See: *Miss Kate Middleton v The Daily Mirror*. PCC adjudication 5.4.2007.

press was overstepping the mark in the methods used to obtain information and the question of whether press regulation was working in its present form.[7]

The democratic model of freedom of expression acknowledges the pre-eminence of political speech and sees a pedagogical role for the media. Many journalists are committed to the principle of objectivity and make an effort to report news free of bias. Schudson (2003) states that one of the fundamental underpinnings of the Anglo-American model of journalism is the notion of 'objectivity', which the American sociologist described as 'a kind of industrial discipline [for journalists]'.[8]

But does objectivity in journalism really exist? Every journalist knows when undertaking his training that the fundamental basis of journalism is based on the classic model of inquiry: 'Who, What, How, Where, When and Why?' But this seemingly simple principle, which is based on objectivity, can become extraordinarily problematic in practice. Journalists, like any other human beings, have a set of prejudices and other views that can affect their objectivity. That said, they ought to have a set of professional values and expectations which affect their daily work. The ideal scenario should be that a journalist, when going about a news story or documentary investigation, should be able to put aside his own personal beliefs, feelings, politics and prejudices and become genuinely objective in the coverage of the story. But in practice, he may well have to adhere to the editorial policy of the news organization he works for, which permeates the paper, online copy or broadcast. The need for a pay cheque may override ethical concerns the journalist may hold.

Take the classic example of the Rupert Murdoch UK media empire, which covers not only The Times, the Sun and the News of the World newspapers (and online editions) and Sky News on TV, but also Fox News and the Wall Street Journal in the United States, making the Murdoch News Corporation one of the largest media conglomerates in the world. Parts of the Murdoch assets are now also run by members of his family. His son James Murdoch oversees assets such as News International (British newspapers), Sky Italia (satellite TV) and Star TV (satellite TV in Asia) and his daughter Elisabeth Murdoch runs Shine, a 'top tier' independent production company that includes Kudos, which produced the TV series Life on Mars.

In August 2010, Rupert Murdoch gave $1m to help Republicans in that year's US mid-term elections. Clearly Mr Murdoch uses his wealth and media muscle to promote his ideas, backing Tony Blair and the Labour Party in the 1997 UK General Election and Barack Obama in the US in 2008. For a time the White House limited Fox News journalists' access on the grounds that the channel was more interested in 'unrelenting propaganda' against the Obama administration than in reporting the news. The organization's self-promotion constantly repeats the phrase 'fair and balanced'.[9]

During the summer of 2010, Rupert Murdoch announced that he would merge his main company, News Corp with BSkyB, a UK satellite broadcaster in which it already had a minority stake. While a price had yet to be set and the acquiescence of the shareholders secured, News Corp was lobbying the EU Commissioners to win pre-clearance for the deal on competition grounds, even though the deal may well fall foul of EU competition law governing media diversity. Ofcom indicated that they would review Mr Murdoch's proposal under concurrent powers they hold with the Office of Fair Trading in relation to media competition matters under the **Enterprise Act 2002** and the **Communications Act 2003**.

Murdoch's British media empire had been at the centre of a political storm since 2009, with newly emerging allegations in September 2010 that illegal phone-hacking had taken place at his tabloid newspaper, the News of the World. Much attention focused on the role of David Cameron's former media adviser, Andy Coulson, who was editor of the paper at the time of the alleged hacking, yet continued to deny any knowledge of it. This raised broader questions about Mr Murdoch's

---

7 For further discussion see: Gaber (2009).
8 See: Schudson (2003), p. 82.
9 Source: 'Murdoch $1m donation may not prove bias', by Mark Mardell, BBC News Online, 18 August 2010.

powerful grip on the UK media industry and laid bare the extent to which British politicians are intimidated by him, a state of affairs which some regard as profoundly unhealthy. As the 'Coulson saga' played out, Mr Murdoch continued to work on the consummation of the BSkyB deal which would increase his power still further (see below 10.3.8). Mr Coulson resigned as the Prime Minister's press chief on 21 January 2011, whilst Culture Secretary Jeremy Hunt referred the aquisition of BSkyB to the Competition Commission.

It goes without saying that any journalist who wants to work for the Murdoch empire will need to adhere to the policies and editorial line of that media corporation which, during the last General Election, for example, was anti-Labour and pro-Conservative. The Sun's editor wrote shortly before the General Election in April 2010 that Gordon Brown's 'ailing Labour Party was in disarray'.[10]

Wainwright v The Home Office [2003][11] confirmed that the UK does not have an established law of privacy (see also: *Kaye v Robertson* [1991][12]). Individuals seeking to protect their private lives from media intrusion have instead brought their grievances to the courts via a number of creative means such as the law of confidence, defamation, Article 8 ECHR, breach of copyright and the **Data Protection Act 1998**. In the absence of any privacy legislation, the UK courts have been left to develop this area to such an extent that Sedley LJ said in *Douglas v Hello! Ltd* [2001],[13] 'we have reached a point at which it can be said with confidence that the law recognizes and will appropriately protect the right of personal privacy'.[14]

See Chapter 2.2.7 →

See Chapter 2.4.3 →

The conflict between an individual's right to privacy and the media's claim to freedom of expression have been discussed at length in Chapters 1 and 2 of this book. Do we really have the right to share someone's private life in public? Recent case law from both the UK and the Strasbourg Human Rights Courts seems to suggest otherwise. There was Naomi Campbell's victory in the House of Lords against the *Daily Mirror*[15] and Princess Caroline's victory in the Strasbourg court[16]. Since the *Campbell, Princess Caroline von Hannover* and *Max Mosley* cases, journalists have become more astute about protecting genuinely private matters, such as medical information or rehabilitative treatment details, which – though said by some to be in the public interest – are to be kept totally private.

See Chapter 2.4.5 → **and 2.4.6**

Then there were the applications for superinjunctions applied for by ingenious lawyers on behalf of famous individuals and public figures, such as footballer John Terry, who tried to 'gag' the media in early 2010 by attempting to prevent news about his illicit affair with his best friend's girlfriend.[17] In this area of law, the courts became more astute and generally followed the ruling in *Campbell*, saying that the Naomi Campbell privacy case meant that the law must not be misused.

See Chapter 2.7.1 →

The head of Britain's 2012 Olympic bid, Lord Sebastian Coe, tried to bar two Sunday papers from reporting details of his affair with Vanessa Lander around the same time in 2004 that Naomi Campbell's case was heard before the Law Lords. He pleaded with the courts by way of superinjunction to be left alone, but the courts denied him the right to privacy and details of his private life and his 10-year affair with Ms Lander became public. Ms Lander revealed that she had had an abortion after falling pregnant by the Olympic gold medallist in May 1996. At the time, the papers said, Lord Coe's then wife Nicola was expecting their third child. Lord Coe was unable to persuade the High Court to grant him an injunction to prevent the publication of an article about his

10 Source: 'Brown's blown it', by Tom Newton Dunn (Political Editor); further stories on the same day by Kevin Schofield and Alex West, *Sun*, 17 April 2010.
11 [2003] UKHL 53 (HL).
12 [1991] FSR 62.
13 [2001] QB 967.
14 Ibid., at 134 (Sedley LJ).
15 *Campbell v Mirror Group Newspapers Ltd* [2004] 2 AC 457 (HL).
16 *von Hannover v Germany* (2005) 40 EHRR 1 (ECHR).
17 *John Terry (previously referred to as LNS) v Persons Unknown* [2010] EWHC 119 (QB).
18 Source: 'My 10 year affair with Lord Sebastian Coe', by Suzanne Kerins, *The Sunday Mirror*, 30 May 2004.

extra-marital affair with Vanessa Lander and her terminated pregnancy. The *Sunday Mirror* claimed to have taken 'no pleasure in exposing the failures of one of our greatest living athletes'.[18]

Nevertheless, as unhappy as the paper may have been with the unintended consequences of its 'kiss-and-tell' feature, the newspaper's revelations about the peer's love life and the alleged abortion of Lord Coe's love-child sat uncomfortably with the Law Lords' decision in *Campbell*. By using the successful *Campbell* appeal, Lord Coe seemed to misunderstand the significance of that judgment: Naomi Campbell's right to seek drug treatment privately is rather different from Lord Coe's requesting a superinjunction to avoid loss of reputation. Mr Justice Fulford could not agree to Lord Coe's request for an injunction, stating that Ms Landers' right to free speech, and the *Sunday Mirror's* right to tell its readers about the habits of those in the public eye, outweighed Lord Coe's right to privacy. Had Lord Coe and John Terry succeeded in their requests for an injunction, this could have been a celebratory day for adulterers[19] (see: *Coe v Mirror Group Newspapers* [2004][20]).

It is in areas such as these, where most claimants lack the financial resources of the likes of John Terry or Lord Sebastian Coe, that the scope of the law is out of reach for many. It is at this point that the ordinary citizen should be able to turn to the free advice of self-regulatory bodies, like the PCC, which may be of more use in spite of their limitations and lack of compensatory powers.

10.3.1 Historical overview

The idea of a UK press complaints commission was originally based on the Swedish model of the Press Council (Pressens Opinionsnämnd), enshrined in law since 1776 and promoting 'freedom of speech' principles with constantly updated legislation since then. The Swedish Press Council is a statutory body, governed by the Swedish print media, tasked with determining whether the actions of a newspaper are in line with good journalistic practice. Complaints regarding the practices of the print and online media can be reported by members of the public to the Press Ombudsman (Pressombudsmannen), who determines whether a complaint should be brought before the Press Council. The Council then determines whether the offending publication shall pay damages for having breached good journalistic practice.[21] The first Swedish Pressombudsmannen was Lennart Groll from 1969 to 1980.

10.3.2 The model of self-regulation

Self-regulation of the British print press began with the Press Council in 1953, a voluntary body that aimed to maintain high ethical standards of journalism and to promote press freedom. The origins of the Press Council go back to 1947 when the Labour government established a Royal Commission under the chairmanship of Sir David Ross to review and advise Parliament on the finance, control, management and ownership of the press. When the Commission reported on its findings in 1949 it recommended the establishment of a self-regulatory press council.

However, during the 1980s a small number of publications failed in the view of many to observe the basic ethics of journalism. This in turn reinforced a belief among many members of Parliament that the Press Council, which had lost the confidence of some in the press, was not a sufficiently effective body. Some believed that it would be preferable to enact a law of privacy and right of reply as well as to set up a statutory press council wielding enforceable legal sanctions.[22] Given the serious implications of such a course of action, the Conservative Home Secretary Douglas Hurd appointed a Departmental Committee in 1989 under (later Sir) David Calcutt QC to consider

---

19 See also: 'The complete history of the Love Rat; Rod Liddle's extra-marital antics have kept the public entertained of late, but has he really taken brazen philandering to its limits?', by Adrian Turpin, *The Independent*, 17 July 2004.

20 (2004) 29 May 2004) (Unreported) (QBD).

21 See: Falkheimer (2002).

22 For further discussion see: Rampal (1981).

the matter. The Committee's task was to consider what measures were needed to give further protection to individual privacy from the activities of the press and improve recourse against the press for the individual citizen.[23]

The Calcutt Report on 'Privacy and Related Matters' (1990) did not suggest new statutory controls but recommended that a 'Press Complaints Commission' ought to replace the Press Council. The new commission was given just 18 months to demonstrate 'that non-statutory self-regulation can be made to work effectively. This is a stiff test for the press. If it fails, we recommend that a statutory system for handling complaints should be introduced.'[24] Members of the press responded with vigour to the Calcutt Report, acting with great speed to set up their own self-regulator in the form of the Press Complaints Commission (the PCC) in 1991.

Five years later, in July 1995, the Conservative Secretary of State for National Heritage, Virginia Bottomley, reported the findings of the Select Committee on 'Privacy and Media Intrusion' to the House of Commons, that a case had not been made out to enact a privacy law as a form of civil remedy for media intrusion into a person's privacy.[25] The Labour MP for Islington and Finsbury, Chris Smith, asked Mrs Bottomley why a criminal offence had not been introduced specifically designed to prevent physical intrusion from bugging devices planted by the press which seriously invaded a person's private property.[26] The Secretary of State's response was non-committal, stating that it was up to the press regulator, the PCC, to keep its journalists in check by way of adherence to their Code of Practice.

In 2003, a Parliamentary Select Committee on 'Culture, Media and Sport' considered whether some form of statutory regulation of the print press ought to be introduced since there had been too many calls for the abolition of the PCC. Giving evidence to the Select Committee, Mr Justice Tugendhat QC had stated that 'no new laws are necessary because recent changes in the law have already cured the defect in English law. I agree with the PCC that there is no need to introduce new legislation at the present time.'[27] Tugendhat J based his views on the statutory provisions of the **Human Rights Act 1998**, the **Data Protection Act 1998** and the **Protection from Harassment Act 1997**, as well as common-law decisions in *Campbell* [2002][28], *A v B* [2002][29] and the Strasbourg court's ruling in *Peck* [2003][30] (see below). In other words, no new laws were necessary because recent changes in the law had already cured the defect in English privacy law.

❖ KEY CASE   *Peck v UK* [2003] (ECHR)

Facts:

On the evening of 20 August 1995, Geoffrey Dennis Peck,[31] suffering from depression, attempted suicide in Brentwood High Street by cutting his wrists with a kitchen knife. The incident was caught on CCTV installed by Brentwood Borough Council. The CCTV operator alerted the police, who arrested Mr Peck for possession of a dangerous weapon. He was released without charge.

On 9 October 1995, Brentwood Council issued two CCTV photographs of Mr Peck to *CCTV News* with an article promoting neighbourhood safety, entitled: 'Defused: the partnership

---

23 See: House of Commons (1990).
24 Ibid.
25 House of Commons (1995).
26 Ibid., at 1326.
27 Source: House of Commons – Department of Culture, Media and Sport (2003). Supplementary memorandum submitted by Mr Michael Tugendhat QC. Comment on the Supplementary Memorandum submitted by the PCC, 16 June 2003, at para 501.
28 [2004] 2 AC 457 (HL)
29 [2002] EWCA 337 (QB).
30 *Peck v UK* (2003) 36 EHRR 719 (ECHR).
31 Born 1955 in Brentwood, Essex.

between CCTV and the police prevents a potentially dangerous situation'. The *Brentwood Weekly News* front page of 12 October 1995 showed a clear photograph of Mr Peck's face and the *Yellow Advertiser*, with a circulation of 24,000, published a similar article and photo of Mr Peck entitled 'Gotcha' publishing a follow-up article on 16 February 1996, entitled 'Eyes in the sky triumph'. A number of people recognized Mr Peck.

Anglia TV showed the 'Peck' CCTV footage on 17 October 1995 though his face was pixelated; the average audience was 350,000 at the time. The same council CCTV footage – with Mr Peck's face not pixelated – was also shown on BBC TV's national *Crime Beat* on 11 March 1996, with an average of 9.2 million viewers. Friends and family recognized him.

Mr Peck objected to the media and on 25 April 1996 complained to the Broadcasting Standards Commission (BSC) about the *Crime Beat* broadcast, claiming his right to privacy had been infringed under Article 8 ECHR and that he had received unfair and unjust treatment. On 13 June 1997, the BSC upheld both complaints.

On 1 May 1996, Mr Peck complained to the Independent Television Commission (ITC). The ITC found that the applicant's identity was not adequately obscured and that the ITC Code had been breached. Following an apology by Anglia TV, no further action was taken.

On 17 May 1996, Mr Peck complained unsuccessfully to the PCC about the newspaper articles. Mr Peck applied to the High Court for leave to apply for judicial review on 23 May 1996, which was rejected, as was his appeal to the Court of Appeal. He subsequently lodged an application with the European Commission of Human Rights on 22 April 1996 under Art 8 'right to privacy'.

Decision:

The Human Rights Commission ruled that the disclosures by Brentwood Council of the CCTV material to *CCTV News*, the *Yellow Advertiser*, Anglia TV and BBC TV were not accompanied by sufficient safeguards and therefore breached the applicant's private life in violation of Article 8 ECHR. The Court also found that the refusal of judicial review had deprived Mr Peck of an effective remedy in relation to the violation of his right to respect for his private life and the right to proper redress. The ECtHR commented, *inter alia*, on the lack of legal power of the said regulators, namely the BSC, ITC and PCC, in that they were unable to award damages to the applicant or indeed punish the print press and broadcasters.

Finding that the applicant had no effective remedy in domestic legislation, the Commission concluded that there had also been a violation of Article 13 ECHR, 'right to effective remedy'. The Court awarded Mr Peck €11,800 (non-pecuniary damages) and €18,075 (costs and expenses).

The problem in Mr Peck's case was that the issue of CCTV and authorities invading his privacy had arisen before the HRA 1998 legislation had come into force in the UK. Otherwise he would have had a sound claim not only against the local authority but also against the regulators – most probably under the common law of confidentiality – as recognized in *A v B* and additionally under the **Data Protection Act 1998**. Mr Peck could also not appeal the PCC's decision because the PCC was not a recognized statutory body and not party to the European Convention at the time.

When the Department for Culture, Media and Sport launched another inquiry into the possible discontinuation of press self-regulation in 2007, its report concluded that the PCC should continue, since there were now sufficient safeguards in statutory and common law to support private individuals if they could not be granted satisfactory redress by the regulator. Citing the words by Sedley LJ in *Douglas v Hello! Ltd*,[32] chairman Mr John Whittingdale MP (Conservative, Maldon and East Chelmsford) said that there was now a 'qualified right to privacy' in English law where individuals could seek redress against the media by way of the **Human Rights Act 1998**.[33]

The PCC continues to face criticism for being 'toothless'. How effective is the press regulator really in dealing with serious media intrusion into people's private lives? There was extensive media intrusion with relentless press coverage into the lives of Gerry and Kate McCann following the disappearance of their daughter Madeleine while on holiday in Portugal in May 2007. There was harassment and defamation of a prime suspect, Robert Murat. Neither the McCanns nor Mr Murat were helped by the PCC, so they sought 'proper' legal redress via the High Court in the tort of defamation, with the result that four national newspaper groups had to apologize to Robert Murat in July 2008 for publishing false allegations about him over claims that he was involved in the abduction of Madeleine McCann. Murat received £600,000 in libel damages from News International, Mirror Group Newspapers, Express Newspapers and Associated Newspapers.[34]

The Express Newspapers' titles, including the *Daily Express, Daily Star* and *Sunday Express*, were made to apologize to Kate and Gerry McCann for wrongly suggesting that the couple were responsible for Madeleine's death, by printing front-page apologies and paying a settlement of £550,000 damages.[35]

Then there were the reported suicides by a number of young people in Bridgend, Wales in 2008. None of the victims' families were particularly helped by the PCC in spite of its subsequent inquiry into the reporting of the suicides. The story made global news, including a feature in US magazine *Vanity Fair* which reported on a 'suicide epidemic' in a small Welsh town:

> Since January of 2007, 25 people between the ages of 15 and 28 have killed themselves within 10 miles of here, all by hanging, except for one 15-year-old, who lay down on the tracks before an oncoming train after he was teased for being gay. This isn't just a series of unrelated, individual acts. It's an outbreak – a localized epidemic – of a desire to leave this world that is particularly contagious to teenagers, who are impressionable and impulsive and, apparently in Bridgend, not finding many reasons for wanting to stick around. It represents, if the official statistics are to be believed, a fivefold increase in Bridgend's young-male suicide rate in three years.[36]

The media asked itself: were the youthful suicides caused by an Internet cult? Was it simply the malaise of boredom in a remote town with high unemployment and nothing to do? The 'cluster suicides' became the subject of frantic media reporting, with the cumulative effect of incessant journalistic 'inquiries' made of grieving family members resulting in unintended distress. The press was accused of an increased glorification of suicide, with stories presented in a way that was apparently romanticizing suicides and thereby seriously influencing vulnerable young people with the 'Werther' effect.[37]

---

32 *Douglas v Hello! Ltd* [2001] 2WLR 992.
33 Source: House of Commons – Department of Culture, Media and Sport (2007).
34 Source: 'Madeleine McCann: Newspapers pay out £600,000 to Robert Murat', by Oliver Luft and John Pluckett, *The Guardian*, 17 July 2008.
35 Source: 'Papers paying damages to McCanns', *BBC News Online*, 19 March 2008.
36 Source: 'The Mystery Suicides of Bridgend County', by Alex Shoumatoff, *Vanity Fair*, 27 February 2009.
37 The Werther effect is based on the psychiatric phenomenon of 'copycat' cluster suicides, largely among young people after a widely publicized suicide. The term is derived from Goethe's novel *The Sorrows of Young Werther (Die Leiden des jungen Werthers)*, the story of a young artist who shoots himself after an ill-fated love affair. Following its publication in 1774 there was a series of reports of young men in Germany who took their own lives in the same way, which led to the book being banned.

After the PCC received a colossal number of complaints from the public, expressing their concern over the suicide media coverage, which was often accompanied by graphic images illustrating suicide methods, the regulator set up an inquiry into the investigation and reporting on suicides. The PCC Report revealed a complex web of public anxieties in Bridgend which had gone far beyond the scope of the press regulator. There were additional concerns about broadcasters and foreign media as well as complex societal issues. The PCC concluded that it was a 'cumulative jigsaw effect of collective media activity, which became a problem only when the individual pieces were put together', and found that no clause of the PCC Code had been breached.[38]

The February Report of 2010 by the Culture, Media and Sport Committee on 'Press Standards, Privacy and Libel' concluded:

> . . . The Human Rights Act has only been in force for nine years and inevitably the number of judgments involving freedom of expression and privacy is limited. We agree with the Lord Chancellor that law relating to privacy will become clearer as more cases are decided by the courts. On balance we recognise that this may take some considerable time. We note, however, that the media industry itself is not united on the desirability, or otherwise, of privacy legislation, or how it might be drafted. Given the infinitely different circumstances which can arise in different cases, and the obligations of the Human Rights Act, judges would inevitably still exercise wide discretion. We conclude, therefore, that for now matters relating to privacy should continue to be determined according to common law, and the flexibility that permits, rather than set down in statute.[39]

Even so, the government did not make any changes to the PCC, nor did they suggest that the PCC ought to be placed on a statutory footing. The only suggestion made was that the Code of Practice ought to be amended to include a requirement that journalists notify the subject of their articles prior to publication and guidance for journalists and editors on pre-notification be included in the PCC's *Editors' Codebook*. However, the PCC ruled out making pre-notification mandatory, as this was not 'in the public interest'.[40]

During a February 2010 debate in the House of Commons on 'Press Standards, Privacy and Libel', the PCC was again criticized for being ineffective on the issue of use of phone-tapping and clandestine recording devices, particularly by the *News of the World*.[41] At the same time, Justice Secretary Jack Straw and Lord Lester proposed that the libel laws and press regulation ought to be reformed by way of the Defamation Bill and also in the light of the *Max Mosley* case.

See Chapter
◀ 2.4.5

10.3.3 The Press Complaints Commission (PCC)

The PCC came into being in January 1991 following the Calcutt Report (see above 10.3.1). The PCC is an independent self-regulatory body which deals with public complaints about the editorial content of newspapers and magazines (and their websites). The main role of the PCC is to handle complaints, by administering and upholding a Code of Practice. Where possible, the PCC uses mediation to resolve complaints to the satisfaction of the individual concerned. It exercises its powers of critical adjudication where this is either not possible or not appropriate. The Commission comprises 17: 7 industry representatives from across a range of newspapers and magazines, and 10 lay members who are drawn from a variety of backgrounds not associated with the press. The Board of the Commission has one permanent sub-committee which reports

---

38 Source: Press release by the PCC on the 'reporting on suicides' of 9 March 2009.
39 Source: House of Commons (2010a) Culture, Media and Sport Committee. Second Report on Press Standards, Privacy and Libel at p. 67 of 24 February 2010: http://www.publications.Parliament.uk/pa/cm200910/cmselect/cmcumeds/362/36202.htm
40 For further discussion see: Bingham, pp. 455–62.
41 Source: House of Commons (2010a), at page 58.

to it, the Business Sub-Committee, comprising the PCC Chairman and three lay members, who – together with the PCC Director – monitor PCC finances and scrutinize the annual budget. The Commission is supported by a small Secretariat (of 15), who have no background in journalism.

An Appointments Commission is formally responsible for appointing new members of the Commission, as well as the PCC's Charter Commissioner and Charter Compliance Panel. The Charter Commissioner deals with complainants who believe their complaint has been mishandled. The Appointments Commission comprises the Chairman of the PCC, the Chairman of 'PressBof' (The Press Standards Board of Finance[42]) and three public members, who are appointed separately and are not members of the PCC.

The Editors' Code of Practice Committee ('the Code Committee') is a separate committee made up of regional editors who produce a formal Code of Practice ('the Code') for the Commission to administer which reflects the experience of the Commission itself, and has its own chairman. The Code has been subject to numerous changes since it was first drawn up in 1991. The PCC does not determine the wording of the Code; that is the responsibility of the industry, using input from, for example, the National Union of Journalists (NUJ) and practitioners in the field. The Code is reviewed on an annual basis using public consultation (via a call for submissions) in order to take account of changes in public attitudes. All publishers and editors who are members of the PCC commit themselves to abide by the Code and to ensure secure and adequate funding of the PCC.[43]

The PCC says of itself (on its website) that it offers a service which is both 'quick and free' and that 'it costs nothing to complain to the PCC – you do not need a solicitor or anyone else to represent you', thanks to the commitment of the newspaper industry, which self-regulates through tough and effective sanctions without being a burden on the taxpayer. It is true that most disputes are resolved amicably and quickly by the PCC, which states that nine out of 10 complaints are resolved, taking on average about 35 working days to do so (excluding complaints where no breach of the Code is established, or no further action is required).

The Commission is informed of all complaints submitted although only a comparatively small number are discussed in detail at monthly board meetings. The course of a complaint handled by the PCC will depend on whether it is deemed to fall within the scope of the Code, whether a breach is apparent and whether the complainant and the editor of the publication concerned reach an informal settlement brokered by the PCC. The Commission takes the final decision about all complaints, in particular those referred to it for adjudication. Commission members also function as directors of the PCC, so have ultimate responsibility for the management of the Commission.

Only a quarter of the population supports the view that the PCC should publicize its views about published stories without first contacting the individual they feature; 58 per cent disagreed or strongly disagreed that such an approach would be proper.[44] Bearing in mind that around 3,000 citizens complain annually to the PCC, the Commission adjudicates on only a relatively small number of cases, although mediation (conciliation) is apparently on an upward trend, reaching 787 cases in May 2010.[45] In 2009, some 738 complaints concerned possible ethical breaches of the

42 PressBof ensures that the Commission does not receive its income direct from industry members, which protects its independence on individual cases. PressBof also appoints the PCC Chairman and nominates the editorial members of the Commission.

43 See also: *The Governance of the Press Complaints Commission: An Independent Review* published in July 2010. The Governance Review Panel consisted of: Chairman Vivien Hepworth (Executive Chairman of Grayling), Stephen Haddrill (Chief Executive of the Financial Reporting Council), Dr Elizabeth Vallance (Chairman of the Institute of Education; PCC Appointments Commission) and Eddie Young (former Group Legal Adviser of Associated Newspapers). Report available at <http://www.pcc.org.uk/assets/441/Independent_Governance_Review_Report.pdf>, accessed 26 November 2010.

44 The full results – which were also part of the 2010 public polling – can be accessed at <http://www.pcc.org.uk/assets/111/PCC_Survey_2010.pdf> (accessed 26 November 2010).

45 See biannual complaints reports and statistic, available at <http://www.pcc.org.uk/cases/monthlysummaries.html>, accessed 26 November 2010.

'Editors' Code of Practice' (compared to 678 in 2008). Of those complaints, 609 were amicably settled; the rest were successfully mediated by the Commission.[46]

Topping the charts for complaints in 2009 were the *Daily Mirror*, *Daily Mail* (including the *Mail on Sunday*) and *Heat* and *Loaded* magazines, with typical complaints such as:

> ...a woman complained to the Press Complaints Commission that an article headlined 'Wanted! The Epic Boobs girl!', published in the February 2010 edition of *Loaded*, intruded into her privacy in breach of Clause 3 (Privacy) of the Editors' Code of Practice. The complaint was not upheld.[47]

Two in three complaints were about 'accuracy' in reporting and one in five related to intrusion into privacy.[48]

10.3.4 The PCC's Editors' Code of Practice

Crucially, the 'Code' spells out polices and sanctions for journalistic breaches, such as invasion of privacy, harassment by the press and subterfuge. In considering complaints, the Commission and its secretariat apply the Code and its 16 clauses setting out the standards to which editors and their staff should work. The terms of the Code and the manner of its application are strengthened by a preamble which states that 'it is essential that an agreed code be honoured not only to the letter but in the full spirit' and that the Code 'should not be interpreted so narrowly as to compromise its commitment to respect the rights of the individual'. The preamble also requires editors and publishers to 'take care to ensure [that the Code] is observed rigorously by all editorial staff and external contributors, including non-journalists, in printed and online versions of publications'. The Code's provisions therefore extend more widely than might at first appear, to cover freelancers, photographers and eyewitness reporters.

The PPC's Code of Practice has been revised a number of times, particularly in respect of privacy (clause 3), harassment (clause 4) and the protection of children and young persons (clause 6). The most controversial area of the code is clause 10, which deals with clandestine recording devices and subterfuge. The provisions of the Code may be overridden if it can be demonstrated that there is a public interest in doing so. The last revision of the Code of Practice was in January 2011. Its main aspects cover:

1 **Accuracy**
   The press must take care not to publish inaccurate, misleading or distorted information, including pictures. Any inaccuracy, misleading statement or distortion must be corrected with a possible apology.

2 **Opportunity to reply**
   There must be a fair opportunity for reply to inaccuracies.

3 **Privacy**
   This is similar to Article 8 ECHR where everyone is entitled to respect for his or her private and family life, home, health and correspondence, including digital communications. Editors are expected to justify intrusions into an individual's private life without consent. It is unacceptable to photograph individuals in private places without their consent. The Code defines 'private places' as 'public or private property where there is a reasonable expectation of privacy'.

---

46 Source: PCC Annual Report 2009 'Key Statistics', available at <http://www.pcc.org.uk/review09/downloads/PCC_Review_B2.pdf>, accessed 26 November 2010.
47 *A woman v Loaded*. PCC adjudication of 11.5.2010.
48 Source: Press Complaints Commission Annual Report 2009.

4   Harassment

Journalists must not engage in intimidation, harassment or persistent pursuit e.g. by telephoning or photographic pursuit.

5   Intrusion into grief or shock

Enquiries and approaches to those suffering grief and shock must be made with sympathy and discretion. Publications must be handled sensitively. When reporting suicide, care should be taken to avoid excessive detail about the method used.

6   Children

A child under 16 must not be interviewed or photographed on issues involving their own or another child's welfare; a parent or guardian must be present.

7   Children in sex cases

Children under 16 who are victims or witnesses in cases involving sex offences must not be identified.

8   Hospitals

Journalists must identify themselves and obtain permission from a responsible executive before entering non-public areas of hospitals or similar institutions to pursue enquiries.

9   Reporting of crime

Relatives or friends of persons convicted or accused of crime should not generally be identified without their consent, unless they are genuinely relevant to the story.

10   Clandestine devices and subterfuge

Journalistic material must not be acquired by using hidden cameras or clandestine listening devices; or by intercepting private or mobile telephone calls, messages or emails; or by the unauthorized removal of documents or photographs; or by accessing digitally-held private information without consent.

11   Victims of sexual assault

Victims of sexual assault must not be identified.

12   Discrimination

There must not be any prejudicial or pejorative reference to an individual's race, colour, religion, gender or sexual orientation, unless genuinely relevant to the story.

13   Financial journalism

Journalists must not use for their own profit financial information they receive in advance of its general publication, nor should they pass such information to others, e.g. in relation to shares or securities and their performance.

14   Confidential sources

Journalists have a moral obligation to protect confidential sources of information.

15   Witness payments in criminal trials

There must be no payment to a witness once court proceedings are 'active' as defined by the **Contempt of Court Act 1981**.

16   Payment to criminals

Payment or offers of payment for stories, pictures or information, which seek to exploit a particular crime or to glorify or glamorize crime in general, must not be made directly or via agents to convicted or confessed criminals or to their associates.[49]

There are occasions when the Commission decides that an important matter of principle is involved and that it should issue a formal ruling to amplify and publicise the issue – as in the Bridgend suicide reporting inquiry. In a complaint in which a breach of the Code is disputed by the publication concerned but is nonetheless upheld in an adjudication by the PCC, the regulator has one sanction

---

49 For updates on the Code see: <www.pcc.org.uk> (accessed 5 February 2011).

which it can impose: a requirement upon the publication to publish the Commission's criticisms in full and with due prominence. All adjudications, whether or not they uphold a complaint, are published by the PCC on its website, as are summaries of cases resolved through conciliation.

Complaints to the PCC must be made *ex post facto*, that is as soon as the damage is done. In the adjudication *Desbrow v The Scotsman*,[50] the Scottish newspaper had taken four months to reply to a straightforward complaint by Mr Desbrow of Kirkcudbrightshire. The Commission adjudicated that the newspaper had breached the Code and adjudicated in favour of the complainant. Though the PCC claims that its Code provides 'powerful sanctions', the Commission has no legal enforcement powers. This means that, if an editor wishes to contravene or ignore an adjudication or an order of restraint not to publish, there are no enforcement powers for the Commission.

Each year, clauses 3 ('privacy') and 15 ('accuracy') are the most challenged parts of the Code. In *David and Victoria Beckham v Sunday Mirror*,[51] the Commission's adjudication ordered the offending newspaper either to provide 'on-the-record corroborative evidence' or, in the absence of such evidence, offer the complainants an opportunity to reply. The paper had alleged that the famous couple had marital difficulties, suggesting that 'It's all over' and that 'Posh' (Victoria Beckham) was threatening to end the marriage. The Commission decided to take no action.

There have been suggestions that the PCC takes complaints lodged by members of the Royal Family particularly seriously. This is strongly denied by the current chairman Baroness Buscombe, although it could be said that the former chairman, the Rt Hon Lord Wakeham, was more protective of the Royal Family when it was PCC policy to 'give the Royal Princes as much privacy as possible, while at the same time allowing the press and the public legitimate access to them'.[52] That meant no interviewing or photographing and no long-lens photos or harassment at the time when young princes William and Harry were under the age of 18.

Following the untimely death of 33–year-old singer Stephen Gately of pop band Boyzone on 10 October 2009 in Mallorca, the PCC received more than 23,000 complaints from the public about an opinion piece written by the *Daily Mail* columnist Jan Moir on 13 October. The article was published the day before Gately's funeral in Dublin with the original headline on the *Mail*'s website: 'Why there was nothing "natural" about Stephen Gately's death'. This was later amended in the printed edition and online to: 'A strange, lonely and troubling death.' Moir told her readers that Gately's death after a drunken night out in Mallorca 'strikes another blow to the happy-ever-after myth of civil partnerships'.

The public outcry about Moir's article was fuelled by widespread discussions on social networking sites like Twitter, and resulted in the highest number of complaints the PCC had ever received about a single article. Justifying its public interest responsibility, the Commission got in touch with Gately's family. The Commission also asked the *Daily Mail* editor, Paul Dacre – a PCC board member – to supply a response. In a new *Daily Mail* piece on 23 October 2009, Jan Moir expressed regret over her original column, though she stood by her earlier assertion that the circumstances surrounding the pop star's sudden death were 'more than a little sleazy' and that there was 'nothing natural' about Gately's death. The PCC's decision not to uphold the public complaint against the *Daily Mail* over its publication of Jan Moir's article caused great controversy. The adjudication made the point that one of the primary functions of a self-regulatory system is to defend freedom of speech. The PCC endorsed the newspaper's view that it must allow its journalists freedom of speech, which includes offensive views by its columnists. The PCC's director, Stephen Abell, said the article contained flaws, but the Commission had decided 'it would not be proportionate to rule against the columnist's right to offer freely expressed views about something that was the focus of public attention'.[53]

---

50 Mr Darrell Desbrow v The Scotsman. PCC adjudication of 9.10.2003.
51 David and Victoria Beckham v Sunday Mirror. PCC adjudication of 16.11.2003.
52 Source: Extract from a speech given by the Rt Hon Lord Wakeham, Chairman of the PCC entitled, 'Prince William and Privacy', delivered at St Bride's Institute, Fleet Street on Wednesday 28 June 2000.
53 Source: Press release by the PCC on 17 February 2010.

The PCC remains under constant criticism for performing inadequately amid claims that the search for an alternative system has become urgent. The Jan Moir decision may not have weighed in the press regulator's favour. In May 2010, the PCC received 55 complaints about a 'kiss and tell' story in the *Mail on Sunday*, revealing details of a covertly recorded conversation between the former Labour minister, Lord Triesman, and Melissa Jacobs, an economics graduate, who claimed, *inter alia*, to have had a six-month affair with the peer. Undercover reporters had found out that Lord Triesman had told Ms Jacobs, over coffee, that Spain and Russia – two of England's main rivals to stage the soccer World Cup in 2018 – were suspected of corruptly colluding. Radio phone-ins and websites, including the online version of the newspaper, were bombarded with complaints from England fans, who questioned whether a story based on private comments and journalistic subterfuge should have ever entered the public domain. Football fans complained to the PCC that by publishing details of Lord Triesman's conversation with Ms Jacobs, the *Mail* had seriously undermined England's bid to host the 2018 World Cup finals. The peer immediately stepped down from his role as FA chairman.[54] The PCC did not investigate or admonish the newspaper editor for breaching clause 10 of the Code.

◉ FOR THOUGHT

Do you think that Jan Moir's article about Stephen Gately violated the PCC Code in relation to intrusion into grief, accuracy and discrimination? Or was she just exercising her journalistic right to 'freedom of expression'?

10.3.5 Clandestine devices and subterfuge

The most controversial area of the Code has been clause 10, which deals with clandestine recording devices and subterfuge. The 2004 version of the PCC Code read:

> . . . the press must not seek to obtain or publish material acquired by using hidden cameras or clandestine listing devices; or by intercepting private or mobile telephone calls, messages or emails; or by the unauthorised removal of documents or photographs.

A report by the then Information Commissioner (IC), Richard Thomas, entitled 'What Price Privacy', suggested that journalists were increasingly contravening section 55 of the **Data Protection Act 1998** by obtaining information via illicit means, such as phone tapping or using private detectives in order to dig up stories at any price.[55] The IC's investigation, supported by the police, had uncovered evidence of a pervasive and widespread media industry devoted to the illegal buying and selling of information.

See Chapter
6.4.5 →

On 26 January 2007, the *News of the World's* (NOW) Royal Editor, Clive Goodman, was sentenced to four months in prison after pleading guilty to intercepting phone messages from Prince William's voicemail. His co-conspirator, Glenn Mulcaire, a private investigator, also pleaded guilty to a further five counts of unlawful interception of communications under s. 1 **Regulation of Investigatory Powers Act 2000** (RIPA), which says:

> . . . it shall be an offence for a person intentionally and without lawful authority to intercept, at any place in the United Kingdom, any communication in the course of its transmission by means of –

---

54 Source: 'Fans protest as bid to host World Cup falls prey to the oldest trick in the book', by Cahal Milmo, *The Independent*, 18 May 2010.
55 See: Information Commissioner's Office (ICO) (2006a).

(a)   a public postal service; or

(b)   a public telecommunication system.

Those counts related to the Liberal Democrat MP Simon Hughes, supermodel Elle Macpherson, publicist Max Clifford, football agent Skylet Andrew and Gordon Taylor, chief executive of the Professional Footballers Association. Mulcaire was sentenced to six months' imprisonment. The clandestine recordings had come to light in the 'Blackadder' column of the News of the World on 6 November 2005, revealing how Prince William had consulted doctors over a pulled knee tendon and had postponed a mountain rescue course. Hardly anyone from the Royal Household knew about this.

Prosecutor David Perry QC told the court that Goodman and Mulcaire had hacked into a total of 609 people's mobile phone voicemails and that the newspaper had paid Mulcaire more than £100,000 a year for his services. Goodman, in turn, had paid Mulcaire £12,300 in cash between 9 November 2005 and 7 August 2006, hiding Mulcaire's identity by using the code name 'Alexander' on his expenses claim.[56] Sentencing judge Mr Justice Gross described Goodman and Mulcaire's behaviour as 'low conduct, reprehensible in the extreme' and added that 'neither journalists nor private security consultants are above the law. This case was not about press freedom; it was about a grave, inexcusable invasion of privacy.'[57]

After the trial, NOW editor Andy Coulson promised a substantial donation to the Prince's charities by way of an apology and later resigned. He was replaced by former Sunday Mirror editor Colin Myler (who resigned from the Mirror Group in 2002 after an article in the Sunday Mirror caused the collapse of a trial against Leeds footballers Lee Bowyer and Jonathan Woodgate. The paper was fined £75,000 for contempt of court).[58]

See Chapter ◄ 4.6.2

Following the 'Goodman' scandal, the PCC launched its own inquiry into journalistic practices and possible breaches of clause 10 of its Code. Following the investigation into clandestine practices and subterfuge, the Commission promptly revised clause 10 in 2007, accompanied by a number of recommendations to editors and publishers to ensure that phone message tapping and other clandestine devices were strictly against the spirit of the Code and contravening human rights legislation (see: Malone v UK [1984][59]). Clause 10 now reads:

i) The press must not seek to obtain or publish material acquired by using hidden cameras or clandestine listening devices; or by intercepting private or mobile telephone calls, messages or emails; or by the unauthorised removal of documents or photographs; or by accessing digitally-held private information without consent.

ii) Engaging in misrepresentation or subterfuge, including by agents or intermediaries, can generally be justified only in the public interest and then only when the material cannot be obtained by other means

But the problem did not go away. The Guardian continued its campaign to stamp out dirty journalistic practices.[60] The paper reported on 9 July 2009 that phone tapping and subterfuge was still going on at the News of the World, in spite of the PCC changing its clause 10 and increased legislation in form of data protection and the **Regulation of Investigatory Powers Act 2000** (RIPA). Following the Guardian allegations, the PCC launched another inquiry into phone tapping and subterfuge. The Commission examined two issues: firstly, whether it had been misled by News International

---

56 Source: 'Clive Goodman sentenced to four months', by Chris Tryhorn, The Guardian, 26 January 2007.
57 Source: 'Pair jailed over royal phone taps', BBC News Online, 26 January 2007.
58 Source: 'Media 100: Colin Myler', The Guardian, 9 July 2007.
59 (1984) 7 EHRR 14; see also: Malone v Metropolitan Police Commissioner [1979] 1 Ch 344.
60 Source: 'Timeline: News of the World phone-hacking scandal', The Guardian, 9 November 2009.

(publishers of News of the World) in 2007 in relation to the 'Goodman' phone hacking scandal and secondly, whether the NOW still employed and indeed condoned clandestine practices in 2009.

The regulator's findings caused outrage in certain editorial circles since the Commission found 'no evidence' that it had been 'materially misled' by News International.[61] Guardian editor Alan Rusbridger accused the PCC of not interviewing a single witness in the 'Goodman' case, nor had the PCC inspected any further documents other than those already supplied and inspected by the police in their 2005–6 investigation. Speaking on BBC Radio 4's Today programme, Rusbridger also said that questioning Colin Myler was rather pointless, since he had only been recently appointed as News of the World editor.[62]

The News of the World phone-hacking affair refuses to go away and Labour MP Chris Bryant and former Deputy Prime Minister John Prescott are seeking judicial review of perceived failures by the Metropolitan Police in relation to their investigations of the matter. A special TV documentary, Dispatches, on Channel 4 in October 2010 examined the allegations that, during Andy Coulson's time as editor of News of the World, phone hacking was a routine practice at the paper and allegedly carried out with his knowledge. The programme revealed that News Group Newspapers – part of the Murdoch empire – had paid £1 million to three people to settle legal actions after they had their phones hacked by reporters. Responding to The Guardian's and Dispatches' revelations, Andy Coulson issued a statement insisting he was unaware of any of the illegal activities that took place at the paper while he was editor: 'I took full responsibility at the time for what happened on my watch but without my knowledge.'[63] Demands increased that Andy Coulson ought to resign his post as the Prime Minister's public relations advisor which he did in January 2011.

Leading media lawyer, Geoffrey Robertson QC, has frequently attacked the existence of the PCC when he says that 'the most satisfactory reform of the PCC would be its abolition', questioning whether its 'lay' members really are 'lay' and truly represent ordinary members of society. In a Guardian blog debating the continued existence of the press regulator, Mr Robertson wrote in November 2009:

> . . . the PCC tries to function as a poor person's libel court, but why should the vilified poor have to resort to an amateur set of adjudicators who can award them no compensation or damages – not even their bus fare home – and cannot direct newspapers to publish any correction prominently? The PCC's worst feature has been its propagandistic claim that it has raised standards of journalism – which it has not, other than perhaps the reporting of the royal family, over whom it is obsessively protective. It goes to extravagant lengths to deter people from asserting their legal rights.[64]

Mr Robertson also attacked the PCC for not stamping out bad journalistic behaviour and suggested that the self-regulator is standing in the way of suitable privacy legislation. He has urged editors to follow the example set by Private Eye editor Ian Hislop, who has never joined the PCC and refuses to do so.[65]

Some have suggested that it is time to appoint a Press Ombudsman – already employed in Sweden and Ireland – as a statutory alternative to the PCC. Others have proposed that the PCC could

---

61 Source: PCC's Report on phone message tapping allegations of 9 November 2009, available at <http://www.pcc.org.uk/news/index.html?article=NjAyOA==>, accessed 26 November 2010.
62 Source: Alan Rusbridger, comment on BBC Radio 4's Today programme, 9 November 2009.
63 Source: 'Tabloids, Tories and Telephone Hacking', Dispatches, Channel 4, 5 October 2010. Political journalist Peter Oborne investigated the News of the World's working relationship with the police, claiming undue influence together with claims of intimidation against politicians, exploring the broader links between News International and the government.
64 Source: 'What should be done with the PCC?', by Geoffrey Robertson QC, The Guardian, 23 November 2009.
65 Source: Geoffrey Robertson's speech at the joint event of English PEN and Index on Censorship at the Free Word Centre, London, 10 November 2009; see: <http://www.englishpen.org/aboutenglishpen/campaigns/reformingthelibellaws/penindexlibelreportlaunch/>, accessed 26 November 2010.

raise its public profile by overhauling its governance and demonstrating that it might appoint genuine 'lay' members of the public to its board and by making the process of pursuing complaints clearer.

FOR THOUGHT

Does self-regulation by the press offer sufficient protection against unwarranted invasions of privacy? And if so, how?

10.3.6 PCC adjudications

Approximately half of all complaints on which the PCC has sufficient information to allow it to form a view are found to fall outside the scope of the Code, in which case a letter is sent to the complainant and the case is merely recorded by the Commission. Of those cases that are deemed to fall within the scope of the Code, the Commission secretariat finds an apparent breach in about 65 per cent. In such cases, the secretariat contacts the editor of the publication concerned; if the editor accepts that a breach has occurred, he may offer to resolve the complaint by a process of mediation through the PCC. Remedies secured through conciliation may include a published or a private apology, undertakings about future conduct, confirmation of internal disciplinary action, *ex gratia* payments or donations to charity.

Of those cases in which the Commission secretariat finds an apparent breach of the Code (possibly 20 to 25 per cent of all complaints received), a substantial number – about a third or more – are neither resolved through conciliation nor adjudicated formally by the board of the Commission. Such cases include complaints in which the PCC concludes that no breach has in fact occurred. There are also cases in which an editor accepts that a breach has occurred and conciliation is not achieved but the PCC deems that no major principle is at stake and that a ruling can be issued without a formal adjudication by the PCC Board.

One high-profile complaint came from the former Royal Butler to Princess Diana, Paul Burrell, who complained about the accuracy of an offending article in the *News of the World*.

❖ KEY CASE   *Mr Paul Burrell v News of the World*[66]

Facts:

Paul Burrell complained to the PCC that an article published in the *News of the World* of 15 June 2008, headlined 'Burrell: I had sex with Diana', was in breach of Clause 1 (Accuracy) of the Code. The article reported that Ron Cosgrove, Mr Burrell's brother-in-law, said that Paul Burrell had once said he had sex with Princess Diana. Mr Burrell strongly denied the allegation and said that the newspaper should have sought comment from him before going ahead with the article.

The newspaper argued that it had credible evidence to publish the story, dating back to 1993 from three independent sources, providing the NOW with two of Mr Cosgrove's affidavits. The NOW did not reveal the other sources. The paper's editor stated that it did not

---

66 PCC adjudication of 15.6.2008.

seek to publish the complainant's denial because he was a 'self-confessed and notorious liar', quoting the coroner at the Diana inquest in 2008.[67]

The principal task for the PCC was to consider whether the newspaper had taken care not to publish misleading information in the way it had presented the story, such as: were readers misled by the omission of Mr Burrell's comment? Would readers conclude from the article that the royal butler had sexual relations with Princess Diana?

Decision:

The Commission could not make a finding of fact as to whether the alleged conversations between Mr Burrell and Mr Cosgrove ever took place, since the information came from the recollection of a 15-year-old conversation, and was not corroborated on the record by anyone outside Mr Cosgrove's immediate family; the other sources remained anonymous. The PCC stated that Mr Burrell's denial of the allegations should have been made clear in the article, since the claims about him were significant and substantial, particularly since the publication was very prominent. Mr Burrell should have been able to put his side of the story and the readers could have made up their own minds as to the value of his comments.

Mr Burrell's complaint was upheld.

In 2008, Professor Sir Roy Meadow complained that a comment piece in The Times, headlined 'A moving response to our family justice campaign', was inaccurate and misleading.[68] His complaint centred on Clause 1 ('Accuracy').[69] The journalist's point was that the complainant's submission of statistics-based evidence in the Sally Clark case, when he was not a statistician, was an example of his going beyond his remit, and that other women had won their appeals against similar 'cot death' murder convictions, based also on the misleading statistical evidence of Sir Roy on 'Sudden Infant Death Syndrome' – simply, that he had misled the jury in the Sally Clark case.[70] As a means of resolving the complaint by Sir Roy, The Times invited the Professor to submit a letter for publication outlining his concerns, but the complainant rejected the offer. The PCC did not uphold Professor Meadow's complaint, stating that The Times piece was an opinion piece and that the columnist's interpretation of the 'cot death' cases was accurately based on the appeal judgments, including those in other cases.[71] Above all, they held that the piece had been in the public interest.

Following the Alfie Patten 'boy dad' story in the Sun, the PCC received a large number of complaints about alleged press payments to children and their parents. The Commission launched another detailed investigation. The story concerned Alfie Patten, who had been falsely accused of fathering a child aged 13.[72] Following its investigation into payments to the families of Alfie Patten

---

67 Coroner Lord Justice Scott Baker oversaw the six-month inquest at London's High Court (2 October 2007 to 7 April 2008). The jury returned a majority verdict that Princess Diana and her companion Dodi Al Fayed were unlawfully killed due to the gross negligence of their driver, Henri Paul, and the paparazzi.

68 Source: 'A moving response to our family justice campaign', by Camilla Cavendish, The Times, 17 July 2008.

69 Professor Sir Roy Meadow v The Times. PCC adjudication of 17. 7. 2008.

70 Solicitor Mrs Sally Clark was convicted in 1999 of killing her 11-week-old son Christopher in December 1996 and eight-week-old Harry in January 1998 (the 'cot death' case). Her first appeal against the convictions failed in 2000, but the second succeeded and she was acquitted in 2003, when three Appeal Court judges ruled that Mrs Clark's conviction was 'unsafe', based on Professor Sir Roy Meadow's evidence during her trial. Expert witness Professor Meadow (for the prosecution) told the jury that the probability of two natural unexplained cot deaths in a family was 73 million to one. At appeal, the Royal Statistical Society and other medical experts disputed that figure, stating that the odds of a second cot death in a family were around 200 to one. The GMC found Sir Roy guilty of serious professional misconduct in July 2005; he was struck off the medical register. Sally Clark died on 16 March 2007.

71 Angela Cannings served 18 months after being wrongly convicted of killing her two sons. Donna Anthony served six years after being wrongly convicted of killing her son and daughter. Trupti Patel was cleared of killing three of her children.

72 Source: 'Exclusive: Baby-faced boy Alfie Patten is father at 13', by Lucy Hagan, Sun, 13 February 2009.

and Chantelle Stedman for stories about the background to the birth of Chantelle's baby Maisie, the PCC published its report providing guidelines on payments to parents for their children's stories and paying special attention to children's welfare.[73] In particular, it said, editors should ask themselves three questions:

1. Is the payment alone responsible for tempting parents to discuss a matter about their child that it would be against the child's interests to publicize? If so, only an exceptional public interest reason could justify proceeding with the arrangement.
2. Is there any danger that the offer of payment has tempted parents to exaggerate or even fabricate the information?
3. Is the payment in the child's interest?

The Commission did not find that the the the *Sun*, the *People* and the *Mail on Sunday* had breached Clause 6 (iv) of the Code ('interviews with children').

10.3.7 The Press Council of Ireland and the Press Ombudsman

For the purpose of comparison, it is worth looking at another regulatory authority, such as the Press Council of Ireland to examine whether press regulation ought to be put on a statutory footing. In spite of substantial opposition from the Irish print press, the Republic began to establish its own press regulator from 2003 onwards. The new statutory body, the Press Council of Ireland, came into force on 1 January 2008. The Council's first Chairman was Professor Thomas Mitchell, former Provost of Trinity College Dublin.[74]

When the Irish Legal Advisory Group (LAG) embarked upon law reform for Ireland – including the law on defamation and privacy – their terms of reference prioritized 'bringing the law into line with the law of other states' by pinpointing the areas of law in need of change.[75] Apart from setting up the Irish Press Council, the LAG felt that the change in privacy and defamation laws was spurred on by a realization that the Republic's legislation in this respect was anachronistic and incognizant of the democratic model as practised in other democratic countries such as Sweden, Germany and Australia. The LAG noted that no law had ever been struck out on the basis of the constitutional right to free speech until 2007 (see: *Dillon v DPP* [2007][76]).

Nagle (2009) comments that, in the history of Irish freedom of expression, jurisprudence reveals that there has never been any explicit recognition of an ideology which framed any 'free expression' guarantee.[77] Nagle further states that this failure to recognize a formula for media freedom has done a disservice to the free speech rights of media organs, especially when confronted with the tort of defamation: free speech has had to bow to the right to a good name.[78]

The Irish Press 'Code of Practice for Newspapers and Periodicals' ('the Irish Press Code') has some rather similar elements to the PCC's Code of Practice, but has innovatively taken aspects from the 'Statement of Principles' of the Australian Press Council, the 'Publishing Principles' of the German Press Council and the 'Ethics Code' of the US-based 'National Conference of Editorial Writers'.

The Press Council of Ireland and the Office of the Press Ombudsman are independent regulatory statutory bodies. The Office of the Press Ombudsman receives complaints from members of the

---

73 Source: 'Press Complaints Commission and Payment to Parents for Material about their Children'. PCC Report of 2 July 2009.
74 For further discussion see: McGonagle and Barrett (2007).
75 Source: Press Release, 'Consultation Conference on Defamation', by the Legal Advisory Group, University College Dublin, 1 December 2003, LAG Report, p. 2, available at <http://www.justice.ie/en/JELR/Pages/Consultation_conference_on_defamation>, accessed 26 November 2010.
76 [2007] IEHC 480.
77 Bunreacht na hÉireann art.40.3.2°.
78 See: Nagle (2009).

public, considers whether they are valid, and then seeks to resolve them by conciliation to the satisfaction of everyone involved. Where conciliation is not possible, the Ombudsman will make a decision based on the 'Code of Practice for Newspapers and Periodicals'. He has the option of referring some significant or complex complaints directly to the Press Council for decision. Both services are free of charge. The professional and ethical standards are those set out in the Irish Press Code. The fundamental principle enshrined in the Code is 'freedom to publish', based on Article 10 ECHR, which includes news and comment 'without fear or favour' – as long as the article is in the public interest.

The Code places a duty on all members of the press to maintain the highest professional and ethical standards. The 10 main principles of the Irish Press Code include:

- Principle 1 – Truth and accuracy;
- Principle 2 – Distinguishing fact and comment;
- Principle 3 – Fairness and honesty;
- Principle 4 – Respect for rights;
- Principle 5 – Privacy;
- Principle 6 – Protection of sources;
- Principle 7 – Court reporting;
- Principle 8 – Prejudice;
- Principle 9 – Children;
- Principle 10 – Publication of the decision of the Press Ombudsman and Press Council.

A decision of the Irish Press Ombudsman can be appealed to the Press Council of Ireland only where grounds are stated and reasonable cause is shown, either in relation to significant new information or to any error in procedure or in the application of the Principles of the Code of Practice. Mere disagreement with the Ombudsman's decision cannot be grounds for appeal. The Press Council decides, in the first instance, on whether the appeal is admissible, and, if it is admitted, on the appeal itself.

❖ **KEY CASE**   *O'Donoghue and the Sunday World*[79]

Facts:
An article in the *Sunday World* on 17 January 2010 republished information from the public record about Wayne O'Donoghue's trial five years earlier in the context of a forthcoming TV documentary by RTE's *Scannal* about the trial. The article also revealed the location of Mr O'Donoghue's UK university and the course he studied, the first name of his girlfriend and six identifiable photographs of her. He complained under Principles 3 ('fairness and honesty') and 5 ('privacy') of the Code.[80]

In its response to the privacy complaint, the newspaper said that it had not published the details of the complainant's UK residence nor the full name of his girlfriend. The *Sunday World* also defended its publication on the grounds that the complainant had a criminal conviction for manslaughter and widespread publicity had surrounded that trial, because it believed there were significant and important questions that remained unanswered, and

---

79 Decision of the Irish Press Council of 23 July 2010.
80 Source: 'Wayne's Girl: Child killer O'Donoghue finds love with sexy British student'; [with reference to the photograph]: . . . 'this is the stunning English girl who has found love in the arms of child killer Wayne O'Donoghue. Sara, from Bolton, has fallen head over heels for the convicted criminal – despite knowing about his conviction for killing schoolboy Robert Holohan five years ago this week', *SundayWorld* cover story, 17 January 2010.

because it believed that the complainant should have been charged in relation to other matters. The newspaper also said that photographs of Mr O'Donoghue were freely available on the Internet, with no privacy claimed and no restriction on viewing. Wayne O'Donoghue appealed the decision of the Press Ombudsman to the Press Council of Ireland.

Decision:

The Council held that the newspaper's defence was not a sufficient justification for the publication of the private information concerned, as the information published had no relevance to, or bearing on, such matters. Neither was the publication justified in the public interest, defined in the Preamble to the Code of Practice as a 'matter capable of affecting the people at large so that they may legitimately be interested in receiving and the press legitimately interested in providing information about it'. His complaint regarding the breach of Principle 5 was upheld. But Mr O'Donoghue's complaint about Principle 3 (harassment) was not upheld or supported by any evidence that refuted the newspaper's account of its reporter's actions, which said that the journalist attempted to speak to Mr O'Donoghue on one occasion.

Coad (2005) argues that both the PCC and the Irish Press Council's concerted efforts of democratic independence and self-regulation bear significant shortcomings and 'alarming procedural opaqueness'.[81] John Horgan, former chairman of the Irish Labour Court, has been very critical of the Irish Press Council, whom he also calls 'opaque' and 'toothless'. Horgan was asked in 2007 to become a founding member of the Irish Press Council. But he soon argued with the Committee for not demonstrating enough 'judicial' independence. Horgan had asked that the Commission include dissenting views in its adjudications, allowing for minority views to be expressed. When the (nearly formed) Irish Press Council did not agree to Mr Horgan's suggestions, the two sides parted company, upon which John Horgan vented his anger in the *Irish Times*, writing:

> . . . the new Press Council needs to establish its credibility, and it does nothing to achieve that by holding up a facade of unanimity where such may not exist. This was a unique opportunity to demonstrate exemplary openness and transparency. The Press Council above all should be the last one to suppress minority or dissenting opinions for the sake of collegiality.[82]

This means there is only a lay majority of one in the Irish Press Council plus the independent chairman when adjudicating a citizen's complaint. The Council cannot make financial compensation awards either, though it may order apologies and/or retractions.

⦿ FOR THOUGHT

Do you think that the PCC is a proper regulator or do you agree that the Commission has 'no teeth'? Compare the PCC's powers with those of the Irish Press Council, Ofcom or the Information Commissioner (IC) in relation to powers to investigate, call for evidence or impose sanctions.

---

81 Coad (2005).
82 Source: 'Press Council's suppression of dissenting voice forced me to quit', by John Horgan, *Irish Times*, 12 May 2008.

10.3.8 Press self-regulation or privacy legislation?

Where does this leave the PCC? Some say that the Commission is the cornerstone of self-regulation, to which the print industry has made a binding commitment in that all editors, photographers and publishers who subscribe to the PCC and therefore the Code have to ensure that it is observed by all editorial staff and external contributors. Others say that the PCC is toothless and lacks any powers to impose any penalties or legislative sanctions and that the PCC's Code is pure window dressing.[83]

In its report 'Self-Regulation of the Press' (2007) the House of Commons Culture, Media and Sport Select Committee found that the PCC had become 'a more open body' providing 'a better service to complainants'.[84] The PCC stated in its Annual Report (2010) that it was proud of its record in increasing the proportion of complaints resolved through conciliation between the complainant and the publication concerned.

One question remains: how can the PCC realistically punish its journalistic miscreants when it has no real power to sanction an editor who continues to contravene its Code? All the PCC can do is to demand that an offending publication print an apology and publish a relatively small outcome of its adjudications, following complaints from members of the public. *Daily Mail* editor Paul Dacre strongly denies that editors take no notice of the PCC.

⊙ FOR THOUGHT

If the Westminster Parliament allows self-regulation of the press to continue via the PCC, should the existing law on unauthorized disclosure of personal information be strengthened?

10.4 Regulating the communications industry

In many places in the world television, radio and the Internet are now the main sources of news and information. Democracy demands a plurality of service providers to enable access by viewers and listeners to a wide range of sources and views. Equally, it is accepted best practice in many countries that an independent broadcasting industry should have an independent regulatory system to license and oversee the industry. Arguably, proper delegation of responsibilities to an independent regulatory body set up by statute not only creates faith in the fairness of the licensing process but also removes governments from the potential political controversy which can be associated with the grant of licences. Additional legislation is now required by the Audiovisual Media Services Directive (AVMSD),[85] which amended and renamed the Television without Frontiers Directive, providing less detailed but more flexible regulation. AVMSD modernized TV advertising rules to better finance audio-visual content (see below 10.7).

Sometimes, broadcasting-related intellectual property issues, defamation disputes or trademark infringements also come under the auspices of a broadcasting regulator, although, in most industrialized democratic countries, such disputes are generally dealt with by law and the relevant courts. It would be unlikely and very costly for a broadcasting regulator to develop and retain the necessary in-house expertise to deal with such disputes.

It is well known that Eastern European countries before the fall of Communism, such as the German Democratic Republic (GDR), Poland, Czechoslovakia and Hungary, struggled with not

---

83 For further discussion see: Carney (2008).
84 Source: House of Commons – Department of Culture, Media and Sport (2007).
85 EC Directive 2007/65 on the 'Audiovisual Media Services Directive' (AVMSD) of 11 December 2007.

having an independent media. The state controlled newspapers, radio and TV. In East Germany, for instance, it was against the law to view West German TV. But it was, in fact, impossible to monitor and police who was watching West German ARD or ZDF TV shows since the state could not control or regulate what was broadcast in the ether. Some experts would say that it was West German TV advertising the plenty of capitalism that eventually toppled the Berlin Wall and reunified Germany. Today, relatively new democracies such as the Czech Republic, Poland and Bulgaria have struggled to ensure that their broadcasting regulators are sufficiently independent to refute allegations of government interference and political pressure.

Despite the controlling commercial interests of politicians in the media in a few Western democratic states, leading to accusations of some interference, most countries have enjoyed independent broadcasting and regulation, free from overt political manipulation and with relatively inexpensive licensing regimes that encourage diversity, equality and freedom of expression.

10.4.1 Broadcasting regulations

The broadcasting and communications sector broadly comprises the following areas of regulation:

- Broadcasting equipment, such as cameras and recording transmission equipment;
- Data transmission networks and associated cables and ducts;
- Equipment and software that supports fixed and mobile communications, such as telephone lines, video and satellite communications;
- Services, such as communications network providers and ISPs, systems integration, communications software, research and development.

A range of factors play a significant role in shaping this sector with key drivers in the telecoms, radiocomms and broadcasting equipment sector, including:

- Globalization of the market for the manufacture and design of components, leading to major international players buying smaller, innovative businesses;
- New markets opening up as more countries develop a taste for technology;
- Consumers and businesses viewing interaction with telecoms, radiocomms and broadcasting as an everyday experience;
- Advances in the mainstream use of technology, such as digital technology, broadband and high definition;
- Technology convergence bringing new innovative products to market along with improved performance;
- The historic state broadcasting monopoly which existed in most Western European countries, often into the 1980s and 1990s (in the UK from 1927 to 1954 – this monopoly was vested in the BBC, which continues to occupy a special position in the regulatory framework; the UK was one of the first European countries to dismantle this monopoly by the introduction of commercial broadcasting in 1954 via ITV, now legally know as Channel 3 or more commonly ITV1).

The UK communications watchdog, Ofcom, has concurrent powers with the competition regulator the Office of Fair Trading (OFT) on issues relating to anti-trust and cartel behaviour, although the OFT has sole responsibility for deciding whether mergers are anti-competitive (see below 10.4.3).

10.4.2 Statutory powers: the Ofcom Broadcasting Code

Areas covered by any broadcasting or regulatory standards normally include the following areas and guidelines:

- Protection of minors;
- Offence to human dignity;
- Protection against harm, e.g. flashing lights; on-air hypnosis;
- No encouragement of behaviour which is harmful to health or safety;
- No incitement to crime and disorder;
- No incitement to hatred, contempt, racial hatred or on grounds of national or ethnic origin, colour, religion, sex, sexual orientation, age or mental or physical disability;
- Separation of advertising and programming.

👁 FOR THOUGHT

You have been asked to set up an independent broadcasting regulator in a newly democratized state. What, on a practical level, are the considerations and practical obstacles to setting up such a regulator?

10.4.3 Ofcom

Ofcom (the Office of Communications) – also known as the 'media watchdog' – operates in the UK under statute, namely the **Communications Act 2003**, which outlines the regulator's general responsibilities. The Act specifically highlights the furtherance of citizens' interests and the advancement of modern technology in line with consumers' needs.

The **Communications Act 2003** is a considerable piece of legislation with 411 sections and 19 schedules. Many sections involve the incorporation of EU legislation relating to telecommunications and 'borderless' broadcasting. Ofcom's principal duties are listed in section 3(1) of the Act, which reads:

> . . . it shall be the principal duty of Ofcom, in carrying out their functions;
>
> (a) to further the interests of citizens in relation to communications matters; and
> (b) to further the interests of consumers in relevant markets, where appropriate by promoting competition.

Anything in the Act which is inconsistent with EU legislation has been overridden by section 4 of the Act, such as section 4(4) which requires the regulator to pay attention to 'the desirability of encouraging the availability and use of high-speed data transfer services throughout the United Kingdom'.

The creation of Ofcom in 2003 replaced the Broadcasting Standards Commission (BSC), the Independent Television Commission (ITC) and the Radio Authority, the regulators that previously dealt with complaints against broadcasters. From 25 July 2005, Ofcom operated under a single Broadcasting Code applicable across the UK communications industry. In 2005, Ofcom issued a Broadcasting Code for TV and Radio which provides a framework for standards of content, such as protection of the public from offensive or harmful material,[86] in line with EU legislation.[87] Two code regulations, for example, are that children under the age of 18 must be protected[88] and that the inclusion of advertising which may be misleading, harmful or offensive on TV or radio is prevented.[89]

---

86 s. 319(2)(f) Communications Act 2003 ('Ofcom's Standards Code').
87 The 2005 Code gave effect to a number of EC Directives relating to television: including Directive 89/552/EEC, as amended by EC Directive 97/36/EC ('sans frontières').
88 s. 319(2)(a) Communications Act 2003.
89 s. 319(2)(h) Communications Act 2003.

The regulator describes its responsibilities as falling into six main areas. These are:

1. ensuring the optimal use of the electro-magnetic spectrum;
2. ensuring that a wide range of electronic communications services are available throughout the UK, including high-speed data services;
3. ensuring a wide range of TV and radio services of high quality and wide appeal;
4. maintaining plurality in the provision of broadcasting;
5. applying adequate protection for audiences against offensive or harmful material;
6. applying adequate protection for audiences against unfairness or the infringement of privacy.

Ofcom has other responsibilities, such as shaping public policy in the future of broadcasting and new media. Apart from watching over correct allocation of broadband width and ISP-compliance, Ofcom also allocates and administers radio frequencies and bandwidths under its periodic 'spectrum trading process', the relevant legislation being the **Wireless Telegraphy Act 2006**.

Section 355 of the **Communications Act 2003** obliges the regulator to carry out periodic reviews and reallocation of (local) radio licences. Part of the remit involves the character of the service, the quality and range of programming and the amount of local content. Part of the recent reallocation process involved the 'Channel 69' radio bandwidth, with the result that Ofcom cleared the 800 MHz band so it could sell more bandwidth to mobile phone companies and generate revenue of gargantuan proportions. Channel 69 was duly auctioned off in 2009, causing some public disapproval. A passionate protest followed from the amateur dramatics and live entertainment sectors (so-called 'programme-making and special events users' or PMSE), all of whom used Channel 69. Ofcom then moved all its PMSE users to Channel 38, which meant that local sports events, conferences and amateur dramatic groups were forced to discard their old radio microphones and invest in new equipment at their own expense.[90]

The **Digital Economy Act 2010** covers online infringement of copyright, particularly in music, film and video games. Sections 3 to 16 **Communications Act 2003** require Ofcom to report on media content, such as infringement of copyright. Ofcom is also responsible for the specification of the procedural and enforcement aspects of these obligations through the approval or adoption of legally binding codes of practice.

Section 2 of the **Digital Economy Act 2010** inserted new sections 124A to 124N in the **Communications Act 2003** and puts in place obligations on ISPs to meet the criteria set out in the Broadcasting Code. Sections 17 and 18 enable regulations to be made about the granting by a court of injunctions requiring service providers to block access to websites that are used, or are likely to be used, to infringe copyright. Section 134C **Communications Act 2003** requires Ofcom to report on matters specified by the Secretary of State relating to internet domain names when requested to do so. These matters might include the management and distribution of Internet domain names by registries and the misuse of domain names or the use of unfair practices by registries, end users of domain names or their agents (known as registrars) (see below 10.8).

See Chapter
← 9.7.2

Section 264 of the 2003 Act requires Ofcom to report at least every five years on the fulfilment of the public service remit for television by public service broadcasters, namely television services provided by the British Broadcasting Corporation (the BBC), Channel 4, Sianel Pedwar Cymru (S4C), Channel 3 services, Channel 5, Channel 6 and the public teletext service. The public service remit involves the provision of a balanced diversity of high-quality content, which meets the needs and interests of different audiences in the UK.[91] Under the new section 264A of the 2003 Act, Ofcom is

---

90 Source: 'Digital dividend: clearing the 800 MHz band'. Ofcom 800 MHz Statement of 30 June 2009, available at <http://stakeholders.ofcom.org.uk/consultations/800mhz/statement>, accessed 26 November 2010.

91 Paragraphs (b) to (j) of section 264(6) of the 2003 Act provide detailed public service objectives underpinning this remit. According to these objectives, examples of public service media content would include content that reflects, supports and stimulates cultural activity in the UK and content that facilitates fair and well-informed debates on news and current affairs.

required to consider the wider delivery of public service media content on other platforms, such as the Internet and video-on-demand programme services, and review the extent to which such content contributes towards the fulfilment of the public service objectives defined in section 264(6)(b) to (j).

By the time the Conservative Party conference went ahead in Birmingham in October 2010 it was more than a year since David Cameron had made a speech in which he said that Ofcom would be stripped of its policy-making functions under a Conservative government. The Conservative–LibDem coalition's leaked document, tersely earmarking Ofcom to merge with 'Postcomm', made grim reading.[92]

What is to become of Ofcom? Some would argue that the regulator has already stopped making policy and that the Government may well change the broadcasting regulator's terms of reference in line with new EU legislation. But it could take several years to change the statutory remit of the regulator. These years could not be more crucial in the evolution of communications in the UK. Nevertheless, Ofcom is a substantial net contributor to the public purse. In the financial year 2008–9 the regulator received £81 million from the government, and handed back £223 million in receipts from spectrum management by regulating the competition in the Internet broadband and mobile phone market. Ofcom has helped to spread broadband provision across the UK and has curtailed the monopoly held by British Telecom (BT). When the regulator brought broadcasters to book over bogus phone-in competitions and game shows and thereby raised its public profile, it became directly and helpfully involved with the public (see below 10.4.5).

When Ofcom published its discussion paper on 'net neutrality' in June 2010, it chose to define the terms of debate as narrowly as it possibly could, noting that 'questions of fundamental rights and industrial and public services policies are beyond the scope of this discussion document as they are matters for government'.[93] At the same time the Ofcom document states that policy discussions will take place during the EU Commission debates on the topic.

It is too early in the legislative period to tell whether Ofcom will be a casualty of the Government's plans to cut back the quangos. It remains to be seen whether the UK broadcasting regulator will retain its technical functions, such as licensing the spectrum, but could lose its public policy role, such as deciding the future of regional news or Channel 4 or BSkyB.[94]

10.4.4 Ofcom adjudications and decisions

An important role arising from Ofcom's remit is to consider and adjudicate on, inter alia, fairness and privacy complaints, whereby recent case law has confirmed and recognized Ofcom's (and the PCC's) role in privacy issues, such as Douglas v Hello! Ltd [2001].[95] Similarly to the PCC, Ofcom offers an alternative route to litigation.[96] Section 392 of the **Communications Act 2003** gives Ofcom the power to punish for breaches of the Code and impose penalties as it sees fit. Before determining how to publish, the regulator must consult the Secretary of State (for Culture, Media and Sport).[97]

There have been a number of prominent Ofcom adjudications in recent regulatory history. One concerned the 'Shilpa Shetty' incident on Channel 4's Celebrity Big Brother in January 2007. The broadcast had been created and produced by Brighter Pictures, part of Endemol UK, and was broadcast by the Channel Four TV corporation on its Channel 4 service. The fifth in the series of Celebrity Big Brother was broadcast in January 2007. Disagreements between the 'housemates' had developed; in particular, between Indian film actress and model Shilpa Shetty and the late Jade Goody, famous for being one of the first Big Brother contestants, as well as Jo O'Meara, former lead singer of the pop

---

92 Source: 'Quango list shows 192 to be axed'. BBC News online, 14 October 2010.
93 Source: 'Traffic Management and "net neutrality": Ofcom discussion document of 24 June 2010.
94 s. 231 Communications Act 2003 ('Replacement of Channel 4 licence').
95 [2001] QB 967.
96 For further discussion see: Epworth (2005) .
97 s. 392(6) Communications Act 2003.

group S Club 7, and *Playboy* model and former Miss Great Britain, Danielle Lloyd. During the 26-week series, which ran until 28 January 2007, Ofcom received over 44,500 complaints about alleged racist bullying of Ms Shetty.

Following Ofcom's investigation into the 'Shilpa Shetty' affair, the regulator found that there were three events that had breached the Broadcasting Code, where Channel 4 had failed to handle the material appropriately and had not adequately protected members of the public from offensive material; these were:

1. Remarks about cooking in India by the housemates (transmitted 15 January 2007);
2. Danielle Lloyd's comment: 'I think she should fuck off home' (transmitted 17 January 2007);
3. Jade Goody's comment: 'I couldn't think of her surname. Why would I be talking to someone like that, I don't know what her surname is. What is it? Shilpa Cookamada, Shilpa whatever Rockamada, Shilpa Poppadom' (transmitted 18 and 19 January 2007).

In particular, Ofcom found that Channel 4 had breached Rule 1.3 ('protection of children from offensive and unsuitable material') and Rule 2.3 ('offensive material') of the Code. Channel 4 was subsequently fined £1.5 million, which was 5 per cent of the broadcaster's qualifying revenue at that time.[98]

Another important investigation concerned the 'prank' played by Russell Brand and Jonathan Ross on their BBC Radio 2 shows on 18 and 25 October 2008 involving a series of messages left on the answerphone of the former *Fawlty Towers* star Andrew Sachs, who had played 'Manuel' in the 1970s sitcom series. It is of course important not to forget that radio is regulated as well as television by Ofcom, though generally less intensively. When Mr Sachs cancelled a scheduled broadcast appearance on the late night Ross–Brand radio show, Russell Brand and Jonathan Ross swore on air and left lewd messages on the actor's answering machine, telling him that Brand had had sex with his granddaughter. Immediately after the radio broadcast, the BBC only received two complaints. But Mr Sachs' agent, Meg Pool, enraged about the contents of the broadcast, contacted BBC Radio 2's controller Lesley Douglas on 23 October 2008, asking for an unreserved apology to Mr Sachs and his family. Ms Pool was also contacted by the *Mail on Sunday* for comment. On 26 October, the *Mail on Sunday* reported that 'the BBC could face prosecution over obscene phone calls to Andrew Sachs', which resulted in more than 27,000 public complaints to the BBC and Ofcom.

On 28 October 2008 Ofcom began its inquiry into the 'Ross–Brand affair' and on 3 April 2009 found the BBC in breach of the Broadcasting Code, namely Rule 2.1 ('generally accepted standards must be applied in all programmes'); that there had been a lack of clarity about the exact role in the programme of a senior figure at the agency that represented Russell Brand, such as the executive producer who represented the independent production company. Additionally, there had been a failure by the Controller of BBC Radio 2, Lesley Douglas, who had given the go-ahead for the programme which included the offensive telephone recordings. Ofcom also ruled that there had been a general compliance failure by the Executive Producer to sign off the necessary compliance forms for the said programmes on 18 and 25 October 2008. Furthermore, that there had been a general lack of clarity about who had editorial oversight of the series. Ofcom also ruled that rule 2.3 of the Broadcasting Code had been breached ('offensive material must be justified by the context') in that the radio broadcast had been gratuitously offensive, humiliating and demeaning. Rule 8.1 had also been breached (the standard requiring 'adequate protection for members of the public from unwarranted infringements of privacy'), in that the offensive broadcast had seriously infringed Mr Sachs' privacy and that of his family. For the Rules 2.1 and 2.3 breaches Ofcom imposed a fine of £70,000 on the BBC, and for Rule 8.1 an additional £80,000 was ordered for the contraventions.[99]

---

98 See: Adjudication of Ofcom Content Sanctions Committee – Channel Four Television Corporation in respect of its service Channel 4 of 24 May 2007.
99 Source: 'The Russell Brand Show', Ofcom Broadcast Bulletin Issue number 131, 6 April 2009.

Following Ofcom's findings, Russell Brand resigned from the BBC on 29 October 2008. Lesley Douglas, Radio 2's controller resigned on 25 November. Mark Thompson, Director General of the BBC, made a public apology for the serious breach of editorial compliance that had allowed grossly offensive material to be broadcast; he also apologized to Andrew Sachs and his family. Clearly, Ofcom's investigation into the 'Ross–Brand affair' had identified a general weakness in managerial control and compliance within the public sector broadcaster and the Broadcasting Code.

In July 2010, Radio presenter Jon Gaunt lost his High Court 'freedom of expression' challenge against Ofcom. Gaunt was represented by the human rights group Liberty. Mr Gaunt challenged Ofcom's decision which upheld complaints about a talkSPORT radio interview in which he described a local councillor as a 'Nazi' and an 'ignorant pig' (see: *Gaunt and Liberty v Ofcom* [2010][100]). The radio interview on 7 November 2008 was with Michael Stark, the then Cabinet Member for Children's Services for Redbridge London Borough Council, about the council's controversial proposal to ban smokers from becoming foster parents on the ground that passive smoking has a propensity for harming foster children. The radio show host Jon Gaunt, who had himself been in care as a child and had then had foster parents, strongly opposed this proposal. He wrote a highly critical newspaper article published in the *Sun* on 7 November 2008 on this topic under the head-line 'Fags didn't stop my foster mum caring for me'. The article was expressed in forceful and colourful language. It expressed great appreciation for foster parents generally and Mr Gaunt criti-cized Redbridge Council as 'health and safety Nazis', referring to a 'master race philosophy' by Redbridge Social Services, whom he called 'The SS'. But the High Court did not hold this article as unduly offensive.[101]

On the same day, 7 November, at around 11am, Jon Gaunt conducted a live interview with Mr Stark on talkSPORT radio. After carefully reviewing the transcript of the interview, the High Court stated that the first part of the radio interview had been reasonably controlled. Mr Gaunt had then asked Mr Stark about existing foster parents who only ever smoke in the open air. Mr Stark explained that the council would not drag children away from existing foster parents, but that smoker parents would not be used in the future, the trouble being that 'such people do smoke in the house', to which Mr Gaunt responded, 'So you are a Nazi, then?' After Mr Stark protested, Mr Gaunt reiterated, 'No you are, you're a Nazi', with the interview degenerating into an unseemly slanging match. When Mr Stark protested that the insult, as he saw it, was probably actionable, the claimant, Jon Gaunt, replied, 'Take action if you wish', saying 'You're a health Nazi.' Mr Stark asked him just to shut up for a moment, and said in effect that the conditions of those in care were better than they had been. Jon Gaunt regarded this as an offensive insult to his own upbringing and called Mr Stark 'you ignorant pig' and, a little later, a 'health fascist' and an 'ignorant idiot'. About an hour after the broadcast, Jon Gaunt broadcast an apology, saying, 'The councillor wants me to apologize for calling him a Nazi. I'm sorry for calling you a Nazi.' Jon Gaunt was immediately suspended and the radio station terminated his contract without notice by letter, dated 17 November 2008.

Ofcom was asked to investigate the matter under the Broadcasting Code, after the regulator received 53 complaints from listeners. Ofcom issued its finding on 8 June 2009, stating that Mr Gaunt had breached rules 2.1 and 2.3 of the Code.[102] The regulator also expressed concern that talkSPORT's compliance procedures did not appear robust enough to deal with problematic material being broadcast live. They recommended that the broadcaster should retain control over all output to ensure that presenters apply generally accepted standards and protect members of the public adequately from the inclusion of material which is offensive or harmful.

---

100 [2010] EWHC 1756 (QBD).
101 Ibid., judgment at para. 3 (Blair J).
102 Rule 2.1 of the Code provides that generally accepted standards must be applied to the contents of television and radio services so as to provide adequate protection for members of the public from the inclusion in such services of harmful and/or offensive materials. Rule 2.3 provides that, in applying generally accepted standards, broadcasters must ensure that material which may cause offence is justified by the context. Such material may include, among other material, offensive language.

Mr Gaunt took legal action against Ofcom, claiming that its decision breached Article 10 ECHR; that is, it was an unlawful interference with his freedom of expression. His claim was supported by Liberty. Mr Millar QC, on behalf of the claimant, submitted that Ofcom's findings were a 'disproportionate interference with the claimant's freedom of expression' for which there was no pressing social need and that Ofcom's reasons were insufficient to justify the interference under Article 10(2) ECHR[103] (see for this approach: R v Shayler [2003][104]). As to 'offensive expression', Mr Millar drew attention to Handyside v UK [1976],[105] where the Strasbourg Court said that freedom of expression was not applicable only to inoffensive material, but also to that which offends, shocks or disturbs the state or any sector of the population. He argued that without pluralism, tolerance and broadmindedness there is no democratic society. Restrictions must therefore be proportionate to the legitimate aim pursued.

Mr Anderson QC, for Ofcom, submitted that the regulator's ruling did not interfere with the claimant's human rights since his employers had allowed the broadcaster a rather robust freedom of expression where Jon Gaunt had been able to express his own views on live radio. Mr Anderson referred to the judgment of Collins J in the Ken Livingstone case,[106] where the judge said that Mr Livingstone was not to be regarded as expressing a political opinion, attracting a high level of protection, when he indulged in offensive abuse of an Evening Standard journalist outside a city hall reception. The facts of that case were different, but the general point made was that gratuitous offensive abuse cannot be regarded as the expression of political opinion.

The High Court agreed. It did not see Ofcom's finding as an interference with Mr Gaunt's freedom of speech but ruled that the 'ignorant pig' comment and the continued bullying and insulting of the Redbridge councillor had amounted to gratuitous and offensive abuse and therefore breached the Broadcasting Code. Mr Justice Blair dismissed Jon Gaunt's judicial review application, stating that the regulator was justified in its conclusion:

> ... the broadcast was undoubtedly highly offensive [to Mr Stark] and was well capable of offending the broadcast audience. . . . The essential point is that the offensive and abusive nature of the broadcast was gratuitous, having no factual content or justification.[107]

Mr Gaunt was refused permission to appeal. Ofcom's chief executive, Ed Richards, said after the judgment:

> ... we were perfectly happy for this case to be taken to court to review the way in which we interpret our statutory duties. We are very pleased that the High Court has recognized that we came to the right decision in this case. This is a thorough endorsement of our judgment in what was a difficult case. Parliament has given Ofcom the duty of applying generally accepted standards to television and radio services, which we always aim to do in a way that respects the important principles of freedom of expression whilst at the same time protecting audiences from unjustified offensive and harmful material.[108]

To which Jon Gaunt replied that he was preparing to take his legal battle – in conjunction with Liberty – to the European Court of Human Rights.

---

103 [2010] EWHC 1756 at para. 17.
104 [2003] 1 AC 247 at paragraph 23 (Lord Bingham) and paragraph 61 (Lord Hope).
105 (1976) 1 EHRR 737 at para. 59 (ECHR).
106 Livingstone v Adjudication Panel for England [2006] HRLR 45.
107 [2010] EWHC 1756 at paras. 38 and 39.
108 Source: 'High Court backs Ofcom's judgment in Jon Gaunt case', Ofcom press release, 13 July 2010, available at <http://consumers.Ofcom.org.uk/2010/07/high-court-backs-Ofcom%e2%80%99s-judgment-in-jon-gaunt-case>, accessed 26 November 2010.

10.4.5 Private telecoms providers and PhonepayPlus

Recent TV phone-in scandals have highlighted a relatively unknown regulator, namely PhonepayPlus. The UK is one of the world's leading markets for PRS (Premium Rate Telecoms Services), which provide services via fixed or mobile telecoms lines. The industry had approximately 40,000 services in operation in 2007, with an estimated revenue of £1.6 billion. Callers are typically charged a premium rate on their phone bill (around £1.50 per minute on BT lines) when participating in quiz shows or TV phone-ins – with mobile phone charges being much higher. Premium rate goods and services provided by PRS typically include phone-in competitions, adult entertainment chat lines or radio and TV advertising, all using premium rate dialling codes, characteristically beginning with 0900 or 0871, plus the five-digit SMS code for mobile phone services, such as 82828 VOTE. PhonepayPlus also regulates all '118' directory enquiry services and interactive digital TV. One reason for the popularity of PRS is that it provides a reasonably secure and anonymous way of making payments for goods and services purchased remotely.

PRS is a well-known source of fraud and scams. Examples include prize competitions where lengthy calls are made for non-existent prizes, SMS prompts that lead to expensive premium rate calls or internet diallers which invisibly download themselves on to personal computers, then reconfigure the PC's internet connection settings so as to call a premium rate number. This is said to facilitate the main income revenue of unscrupulous PRS services.

The BBC became engulfed in controversy over its use of calls on some of its shows. In 2008, the Corporation was fined a record £400,000 for a number of transgressions – BBC 6 Music's *Liz Kershaw Show*, for instance, had faked competitions in recorded programmes which then went out later 'as live'. The competitions in the recordings had fake winners, so people paying for calls at the time of broadcast had no chance of winning. On the *Clare McDonnell Show* (BBC 6 Music) in September 2006, a production team member created fictitious winners because there were not enough real winning entries for a competition. The BBC's children's flagship show *Blue Peter* was fined £50,000 by Ofcom in spring 2007 after a staff member's child visiting the studio was asked to pose as a phone-in competition winner. In the *Comic Relief* programme in March 2007, a caller who successfully answered a question in a competition for a celebrity prize turned out to be a member of the BBC production staff. Other programmes with similar scams were BBC1's *Sports Relief* in July 2006, BBC1 Scotland's *Children In Need* in November 2005, TMi on CBBC and BBC2 in September 2006 and the World Service's *White Label Show* in April 2006.

On 18 July 2007, Ofcom published its major findings into the PRS phone-in scandals and how (if at all) the regulator had handled public complaints. The inquiry was led by Richard Ayre, a non-executive member of the Ofcom Content Board (and former Deputy Chief Executive of BBC News). Ofcom's report exposed the shocking scams relating to PRS in television and radio quiz shows and game programmes, many hosted by the BBC. The Report concluded that there had been a 'systemic failure' in the way broadcasters operated premium-rate lines during their phone-ins. Ofcom recommended that new licence obligations should be imposed on broadcasters, making them directly responsible for consumer protection and PRS compliance. The report also suggested that both television and radio broadcasters should ensure independent, third-party verification of PRS activity, typically quiz, psychic and adult chat services, which all rely heavily on interaction with viewers using PRS.

ICSTIS was replaced by a new regulator, PhonepayPlus in December 2007, with Ofcom still in overall control over PRS under the **Communications Act 2003**.[109] PhonepayPlus receives its main income from a funding levy from the industry (a flat percentage charge on activity, which was 0.48 per cent in 2009). The balance of funding comes from fines and administrative charges and from interest accrued.[110] The watchdog carries out the day-to-day regulation of the PRS market on Ofcom's behalf.

---

109 For background on ICSTIS see: Pimlot (2007).
110 Source: PhonepayPlus Ltd, Report and Financial Statements for the year ending 31 March 2009.

PhonepayPlus has its own Code of Practice. The 2008 Code set the following standards for its PRS providers:

- clear and accurate pricing information;
- honest advertising and service content;
- appropriate and targeted promotions.[111]

PhonepayPlus investigates complaints and has the power to fine companies, bar access to services and order refunds. The regulator can also bar the individual person behind a company from running any PRS under any company name on any telephone.[112]

When PhonepayPlus took over, the regulator received more than 8,000 complaints in 2007–8, a 108 per cent increase on the previous year. This resulted in new guidelines in relation to the use of marketing lists, consumer opt-in requirements and strict adherence to 'stop' commands.[113] In its annual report of 2009, PhonepayPlus promised to review and strengthen its Code of Practice and sanctions policies and to work more closely with Ofcom. Ofcom also recommended that PhonepayPlus adhere more rigorously to the EU regulatory framework, such as the Unfair Commercial Practices Directive[114] and the Consumer Protection Cooperation Enforcement Regulations,[115] detailing the EU Telecoms Framework.

The Unfair Commercial Practices Directive prohibits any misleading or aggressive marketing; it provides a general ban on unfair commercial practices throughout the EU. The Directive also contains specific provisions preventing exploitation of vulnerable consumers, such as children. The Regulation on Consumer Protection Co-operation amended the **Enterprise Act 2002** and established a network of public authorities with powers to cooperate and share information with each other for the purposes of enforcing the collective interest and protection of consumers' interests. It empowers citizens to use speedier procedures and provides access to justice where local enforcement authorities can apply to a magistrate to obtain a warrant for search and seizure. Enforcement of the rules is the task of national consumer protection authorities, regulators and courts which, in turn, should boost consumer confidence and make it easier for business and regulators to carry out cross-border trading.

Attempting to keep its promise, PhonepayPlus launched an investigation in January 2010, after game-playing iPhone and smartphone users complained about 'surprise' premium-rate call charges. Complaints to the watchdog focused on a free-to-download, advertising-supported game called *BubbleWrap*, developed by Orsome New Zealand and available via Apple's App Store. *BubbleWrap* came with an embedded advert engine from 'AdMob' which encouraged users to tap on the ad to visit a website. The 'app' particularly appealed to children. As their eager fingers strayed on to an advertisement link at the bottom of the screen, this sometimes resulted in premium rate calls at £1.50 a minute, with parents being faced with increased mobile phone bills. A warning should appear before such charges are levied but had failed to do so (in any case, would children know what it meant?). Developers and ad companies blamed a software update of which they say they were unaware. At the time of going to print, this issue had not yet been resolved.

Mobile phone systems and services have become very complex, making the assigning of legal responsibility in such cases very difficult for the regulator to solve and adjudicate. It is also clear that

---

111 For a complete version of the 11th Code of 28 March 2008, incorporating ss. 120 and 121 Communications Act 2003, see <www.PhonepayPlus.org.uk/upload/PhonepayPlus_Code_of_Practice.pdf> (accessed 26 November 2010).
112 A list of barred PRS service providers or individuals that have been found in breach of the PhonepayPlus Code of Practice can be found on their website: at <www.PhonepayPlus.org.uk/upload/barred-SPs.pdf> (accessed 26 November 2010).
113 Source: PhonepayPlus Ltd, Report and Financial Statements for the year ending 31 March 2009.
114 EC Directive on Directive 2005/29/EC concerning unfair business-to-consumer commercial practices in the internal market of 11 May 2005 ('The Unfair Commercial Practices Directive'); amending Directive 84/450/EEC, Directives 97/7/EC, 98/27/EC and 2002/65/EC and EC Regulation No 2006/2004.
115 EC Regulation 2006/2004 on cooperation between national authorities responsible for the enforcement of consumer protection laws of 27 October 2004 ('Consumer Protection Cooperation Enforcement Regulations').

even some large content providers, such as Apple (famous for control), cannot always control what happens with smartphone applications.

10.5 Obscene and violent content online

It appears that the 'Twittersphere' – a term coined by *Guardian* editor Alan Rusbridger – has become a most effective promotional device where information can be posted in just 140 characters, seemingly ignoring court injunctions and gagging orders. Meanwhile, on 20 June 2009 YouTube, the powerful social networking and video-sharing site, revealed the killing of a young woman by Iranian Police. The world watched in horror as the 27-year-old music student Neda Agha-Soltan died, filmed on a mobile phone camera. The 90-second sequence showed how she was hit by a sniper's bullet during a protest against Iranian President Ahmadinejad. The YouTube footage became a 'citizen journalism' sensation, with Neda becoming a martyr figure and a symbol for the student opposition to the Iranian Government. In February 2011, the Supreme Court announced that it now allows 'live text based communications' (i.e. tweets) as 'content' for journalists.

There is no doubt that social networking sites like Twitter, MySpace or Facebook have become powerful promotional and democratic tools. But who controls their violent, offensive or obscene content?

10.5.1 The Internet Watch Foundation (IWF)

In January 2010, a child advocacy group sent out leaflets warning of the arrival of a so-called 'sex offender' in Florida, namely Pete Townshend, the legendary guitarist of the 1960s rock group The Who. Florida activists were outraged that the 64-year-old rocker would perform with The Who at the half-time show during the Super Bowl on 7 February 2010 in Miami.[116]

Mr Townshend had received a caution from UK police in 2003 after he admitted using his credit card to view images on a child porn website. He had also been placed on the sex offenders register for five years. His defence at the time was that he was undertaking online research to write his memoirs, after himself being abused as a boy. The Internet Watch Foundation reported that Mr Townshend had been 'incredibly foolhardy, naive and misguided' to enter such a website. Vice chairman and media lawyer, Mark Stephens, told the BBC: 'It is wrong-headed, misguided and illegal to look at, or download, or even to pay to download paedophiliac material and if you do so, you are likely to go to prison.' Mr Stephens also noted that Mr Townshend had admitted a criminal offence, and if he was prosecuted it would be for the court to decide his motives in doing so, concluding, 'What he has done is incredible naivety at best.'[117]

In advance of the Miami Super Bowl in February 2010, the 'Protect Our Children' pressure group lobbied the Florida police force and the attorney general, asking them to reject Townshend's visa. The campaign failed and some hundred million people watched on TV as the New Orleans Saints pulled off an extraordinary 31–17 win over the Indianapolis Colts, being entertained by the iconic British rock band during the interval. Singer Roger Daltrey and guitarist Pete Townshend, the two surviving original members of The Who, appeared on stage at the Sun Life Stadium in Miami and played a nearly 12-minute set that included 'Pinball Wizard' and 'Won't Get Fooled Again'.

The Internet Watch Foundation (IWF) was established in 1996 as an independent regulator which monitors child sexual abuse and obscene and violent content hosted on websites worldwide. The establishment of the IWF pre-empted the introduction of formal regulatory action and legislation

---

116 Source: 'Pete Townshend labelled "sex offender at large" as Miami residents protest at him performing at Super Bowl with The Who', by Jacqui Goddard, *Daily Mail*, 29 January 2010.
117 Source: 'Townshend "wrong" over child porn', *BBC News Online*, 12 January 2003.

of the internet industry in the 1990s and it has since worked hard to ensure the right balances are drawn between freedom of expression and protection from criminal internet content. Self-regulation is the principle on which the IWF operates, based on a multi-stakeholder partnership. The IWF is funded and backed by the EU as well as major ISPs, mobile phone operators and manufacturers, content service providers, filtering companies, search providers, trade associations and the financial sector.[118] Each of the 90 member organizations nominates a representative to participate in the 'IWF Funding Council' in order to contribute to policy development and strategic planning. This model of self-regulation strives to meet the demands placed upon it by evolving technology, industry growth and media, public and government scrutiny.

IWF's core function is to provide an internet hotline for the public to report their accidental exposure to criminal online content. For example, the **Protection of Children Act 1978** (as amended by the **Sexual Offences Act 2003** and **Coroners and Justice Act 2009**) makes it an offence to take, make, permit to be taken, distribute, show, possess with intent to distribute, and advertise indecent photographs or pseudo-photographs of children under the age of 18. The 'making' of such images includes downloading, that is, making a copy of an indecent image of a child on a computer. Accessing such content online is a serious criminal offence in the UK.[119]

Chapter 2 of the **Coroners and Justice Act 2009**[120] has additionally strengthened the regulators' powers prohibiting the possession of indecent images of children. Section 62 ('possession of prohibited images of children') reads:

(1) It is an offence for a person to be in possession of a prohibited image of a child.

(2) A prohibited image is an image which –

    (a) is pornographic . . . and
    (c) is grossly offensive, disgusting or otherwise of an obscene character.

The self-regulator has extensive search and punitive powers to investigate and punish both servers and users who engage in the uploading or downloading of paedophilic content.[121] The IWF's remit covers three types of internet content:

1. Child sexual abuse content hosted anywhere in the world;
2. Criminally obscene content hosted in the UK;
3. Incitement to racial hatred content hosted in the UK.

Additionally, the regulator's governing body sees itself as giving advice to those working in the IT industry who may inadvertently become aware of potentially illegal websites. The following pieces of legislation largely shape and govern the IWF:

- **Coroners and Justice Act 2009**;[122]
- **Criminal Justice and Immigration Act 2008**;

---

118 IWF is an incorporated charity. Charity No.1112398, see: <http://www.iwf.org.uk> (accessed 26 November 2010).
119 For a comparison of English, US and Canadian law and law enforcement in relation to child pornography on the Internet see: Akdeniz (2008).
120 ss. 62–69 Coroners and Justice Act 2009.
121 Under s. 39 and Schedule 11 Police and Justice Act 2006.
122 Section 69 Coroners and Justice Act 2009 ('indecent pseudo-photographs of children: marriage etc.') further defines and amends the following legislation: (1) In section 1A Protection of Children Act 1978 ('making of indecent photograph of child etc.: marriage and other relationships'), after 'photograph', in each place it occurs, insert 'or pseudo-photograph'; (2) In section 160A Criminal Justice Act 1988 ('possession of indecent photograph of child etc.: marriage and other relationships'), after 'photograph', in each place it occurs, insert 'or pseudo-photograph'; (3) In Article 15A Criminal Justice (Evidence, etc) (Northern Ireland) Order 1988 (S.I. 1988/1847 (N.I. 17)) ('marriage and other relationships'), after 'photograph', in each place it occurs, insert 'or pseudo-photograph'; (4) In Article 3B of the Protection of Children (Northern Ireland) Order 1978 (S.I. 1978/1047 (N.I. 17)) ('marriage and other relationships'), after 'photograph', in each place it occurs, insert 'or pseudo-photograph'.

- **Sexual Offences Act 2003**;
- **Civic Government (Scotland) Act 1982**;
- **Protection of Children Act 1978**.

As already discussed, it is difficult to make an ISP fully responsible for violent, racially offensive, paedophilic or obscene content, since they will argue that they are a 'mere conduit' or 'host', relying on Art 19 of the 'e-Commerce Directive' (2000/31/EC), which reads:

> . . . where an information society service is provided which consists of the storage of information provided by a recipient of the service, the service provider . . . shall not be liable for damages or for any other pecuniary remedy or for any criminal sanction as a result of that storage where –
>
> (a) the service provider –
>   (i) does not have actual knowledge of unlawful activity or information and, where a claim for damages is made, is not aware of facts or circumstances from which it would have been apparent to the service provider that the activity or information was unlawful; or
>   (ii) upon obtaining such knowledge or awareness, acts expeditiously to remove or to disable access to the information, and
> (b) the recipient of the service was not acting under the authority or the control of the service provider.

Article 17 (1) of the 'e-Commerce Directive' appears to exempt the service provider from strict liability, stating:

> . . . where an information society service is provided which consists of the transmission in a communication network of information provided by a recipient of the service or the provision of access to a communication network, the service provider . . . shall not be liable for damages or for any other pecuniary remedy or for any criminal sanction as a result of that transmission where the service provider –
>
> (a) did not initiate the transmission;
> (b) did not select the receiver of the transmission; and
> (c) did not select or modify the information contained in the transmission.

For the purposes of sentencing those convicted of offences involving indecent photographs or pseudo-photographs of children, the indecent images are categorized under the so-called 'Oliver' guidelines according to levels of seriousness (see: R v Oliver [2002][123]).

(i) images depicting erotic posing with no sexual activity;
(ii) sexual activity between children, or solo masturbation by a child;
(iii) non-penetrative sexual activity between adults and children;
(iv) penetrative sexual activity between children and adults; and
(v) sadism or bestiality.

This being an either-way offence, the above levels determine whether the cases are heard either at the magistrates' or the Crown Court. The magistrates take the decision at mode of trial stage as to where the case should be tried, according to the 'Oliver' guidelines on the seriousness of the (child) images.

---

123 (2002) Judgment of 21 November 2002, *The Times*, 6 December 2002 (Unreported).

Once the IWF has detected illegal activity on someone's server, the details of the URL and the registered owner's details are passed on to the relevant law enforcement agency, who can further investigate the hosting of illegal content in the UK or abroad. The main agencies are:

- The Child Exploitation and Online Protection Centre (CEOP);
- The Virtual Global Taskforce;
- The Serious Organised Crime Agency (SOCA);
- The Metropolitan Police Paedophile Unit;
- The West Midlands Police Hi Tech Crime team;
- The Greater Manchester Police Abusive Images Unit;
- The National Hi-Tech Crime Unit Scotland (NHTCUS).

Since 2004, the IWF has created a blacklist of unsuitable URLs which is not made public. Lilian Edwards, Professor of Internet Law, has expressed strong opposition to the IWF's practices, writing: 'The Government now potentially possesses the power to exclude any kind of online content from the UK, without the notice of either the public or the courts.'[124] She demands that the IWF blacklist be made available for public scrutiny and observes that such 'guarded conduct' by the regulator suggests that more may be going on behind the scenes than the public is aware of.

The IWF's research report of 2009 found, by entering the word 'bestiality' into an internet search engine, that one of the most prolific websites showing humans engaged in sex acts with animals was hosted in Denmark. The regulator expressed disappointment that there were no reciprocal arrangements in place to combat criminally obscene content in that country or indeed any cross-border agreements at that time.[125] One major problem remains: most of the websites displaying sexually abusive images of children are hosted in far-away economically deprived regions such as the former Soviet Union, Thailand or Malaysia, countries in which offenders are virtually impossible to pursue and punish under existing legislation.

While child sexual abuse images hosted abroad remain available, the UK internet industry has voluntarily agreed to block access to them using a list provided by the IWF. The regulator believes that blocking is the best solution as a short-term disruption tactic which can help protect internet users from stumbling across illegal images. This gives the regulator more time to instigate the necessary processes to have the images and the URL removed.

👁 FOR THOUGHT

Does self-regulation by an organization like the Internet Watch Foundation (IWF) pose a threat to civil liberties? Should one not be able to view *any* material on the Internet in the privacy of one's own home?

10.6 Film, video and games censorship

The means of regulating sexually explicit and violent material has been debated for decades. Arguments over what denotes a masterpiece or an obscenity in film, image or literature abound. Are the controversial images by Robert Mapplethorpe photographic masterpieces or obscene and

---

124 See: Edwards (2009).
125 Source: IWF memorandum submitted to the Culture, Media and Sport Committee, July 2008, available at <http://www.iwf.org.uk/accountability/consultations/culture-media-and-sport-committee>, accessed 30 November 2010.

See Chapter
7.3.2 →
explicit homoerotic images which must be banned from university libraries? Should J.D. Salinger's *The Catcher in the Rye* (1951) and D.H. Lawrence's *Lady Chatterley's Lover* (1960) be boycotted in school libraries?

Deciding where to draw the line when regulating sexually explicit and violent material relates to the degree of control exercised by a society. Film and games regulators in each country have to decide at both ends of the spectrum where to place minimal restrictions on access to these images, who can watch them and what is appropriate for adults. They can then decide for themselves what is appropriate. That said, censorship of a film, song, play or book can draw attention to the material at issue, thereby making it even more popular. The BBC has frequently banned songs with 'naughty' lyrics or films with either raunchy or defamatory themes. In 1969, for example, 'Auntie Beeb' banned 'Je t'aime . . . moi non plus' by Serge Gainsbourg and Jane Birkin because of the song's licentious lyrics, which were deemed far too inflammatory for *Top of the Pops* during the Woodstock era. Frankie Goes to Hollywood also had their knuckles rapped by Radio 1 DJ Mike Read, who

See Chapter
9.8.1 →
declared 'Relax' 'overtly obscene' and banned the single from his radio show in 1984 for its 'unwelcome' sexual overtones: 'Relax don't do it, when you want to go to it. Relax don't do it, when you want to come . . .' Predictably, both records were huge hits.

The British Board of Film Classification (BBFC – originally the British Board of Film Censors) has, from time to time, rejected foreign films even though they were openly released in their countries of origin, with sexual topics generally being the norm for rejection, such as *The Best of the New York Erotic Film Festival*, rejected in April 1975, or *Confessions of a Blue Movie Star*, a 1978 West Germany documentary by Wes Craven and Andrzej Kostenko. The 1969 film *99 Women* (*Der Heiße Tod / 99 donne / 99 mujeres*) by Jesus Franco, released in Liechtenstein, Spain, Italy and West Germany, was rejected for its 'soft-core' women-in-prison lesbian nature with 'nasty torture sequences'. *The Awakening of Emily*, an Ann Summers production of 1976 featuring Koo Stark, was rejected by the BBFC for its sex scene of two women in a shower in 1983. Prince Andrew was dating the actress at that time but the relationship ended after it emerged that Ms Stark had appeared in the soft porn film.

The BBFC has habitually banned prison films that feature women, such as *Deported Women of the SS* (*Le deportate della sezione speciale SS*), a 1976 Italian prison film by Rino Di Silvestro, or *Barbed Wire Dolls* (*Frauengefängnis*), a 1975 Swiss prison drama by Jess Franco, featuring 'caged women'. *Bamboo House Dolls* (*Nu ji zhong ying*), a 1974 Hong Kong film by Chin Hung Kuei, was banned by the BBFC because of its sensitive topic featuring a Japanese women's POW camp. In 1996, Westminster Council banned *Crash* by David Cronenberg, first premiered at the 1996 London Film Festival and initially permitted by the BBFC. When Westminster Council demanded cuts to certain parts of this sexually violent film – solely for screenings in Westminster – the distributors declined, and the film was therefore banned from screens in the West End, including Leicester Square. However, cinemagoers could easily see the film in neighbouring Camden, where the council allowed the film to play uncut with its BBFC certificate.

10.6.1 *The Mary Whitehouse Experience* and *The Exorcist*

The Mary Whitehouse Experience was a topical comedy show devised by Bill Dare, starring young Cambridge graduates David Baddiel, Robert Newman, Hugh Dennis and Steve Punt. It began on BBC Radio 1 in 1988 and was moved from its Friday lunchtime slot to a late-night slot in 1989 because of its 'raunchiness'. It then moved to BBC TV in 1990, produced by the same company as *Spitting Image*, running for 13 episodes. The show mixed stand-up comedy monologues with sketches and impressions. The show was named after Mary Whitehouse, the prominent campaigner for

See Chapter
7.2.3 →
and 7.4.1

public morality who made it her life's quest to highlight public decency and the moral decline of television standards – particularly at the BBC. Mrs Whitehouse became the first General Secretary of the 'National Viewers' and Listeners' Association' in 1965. The first chairman of the subsequent BSC (Broadcasting Standards Council), Lord Rees-Mogg, credited Mrs Whitehouse for her influence on the setting-up of the Council in 1988 and for ensuring that the public view was always taken into account.

Mrs Whitehouse threatened legal action a number of times, including against famous BBC titles such as *Monty Python's Flying Circus*, *The Kenny Everett Television Show* – with its skimpily-clad dance troupe, Hot Gossip, run by Arlene Phillips – and *Doctor Who*. Not surprisingly, she also threatened to take the BBC to court over the 'Whitehouse Experience', demanding an alternative title, such as 'The William Rees-Mogg Experience' (see also: *Whitehouse v Lemon* [1979][126]). But the BBC staunchly kept the title and the show became a massive hit, particularly with its famous sketch 'History Today', where Newman and Baddiel played two old historians who discussed an important historical issue in a very childish fashion.

When the film *The Exorcist* opened in America on 26 December 1973, the response was immediate and extraordinary. It is based on the book by William Peter Blatty, published in 1971, and depicts a riveting demonic possession and subsequent exorcism of a young girl in Washington DC. Despite much press attention in advance of the film's release, the 'Classification and Ratings Administration' of the Motion Picture Academy of America (MPAA) granted *The Exorcist* an uncut 'R' rating ('for strong language and disturbing images'), allowing minors to view the film if accompanied by an adult. MPAA President Jack Valenti pointed out that *The Exorcist* contained 'no overt sex' and 'no excessive violence', a conclusion echoed by the generally cautious Catholic Conference, which rated the film 'A-IV', an adult classification meaning that the film was 'moral, but may offend some [adult] viewers'. Yet Washington police barred persons under the age of 17 from showings of the movie in spite of the MPAA's 'R' rating. Eventually, Marvin Goldman, head of the KB Theater chain, which owned the Cinema Theater in DC where the movie was first shown, told the *Washington Post* that he would comply with the [MPAA] ruling, stating that the movie should have been rated X (no one under 17 admitted) in the first place.[127] Walter Cronkite devoted a full 10 minutes of his legendary CBS news programme to 'The Exorcist Phenomenon' and the history of demonic possession.

The film struck a unique chord with audiences around the world. In Milan, the crowd at a packed news conference refused to leave a museum where the film's Director, William Friedkin, and technical advisor Father Thomas Bermingham were answering questions about *The Exorcist*. In Rome, the film made the national news when a sixteenth-century church across the street from a cinema where the film premiered was struck by lightning, causing an ancient cross to plummet from its roof onto the pavement below. At a preview screening in New York, one audience member had to be helped out after becoming dizzy, provoking a wave of press reports of fainting, vomiting and other hysterical reactions. By the time *The Exorcist* came to the UK, rumours of its traumatizing power had grown to such proportions that the St John Ambulance Brigade were standing by for the first showings around London.

But *The Exorcist* was immediately banned by the BBFC, due to Mrs Whitehouse's urging them to prohibit it. She called the film 'outright nasty – blasphemous and evil', despite the fact she had never seen a frame of it. She purely relied on adverse media coverage such as Stanley Kaufmann's comment in *New Republic*: 'This is the most scary film I've seen in years – the only scary film I've seen in years . . . If you want to be shaken – and I found out, while the picture was going, that that's what I wanted – then *The Exorcist* will scare the hell out of you.'[128] The British film board eventually granted an 'X' certificate to *The Exorcist* in January 1974, which allowed over-18s to view without cuts or alterations.

At the Golden Globe awards of 1974, *The Exorcist* picked up awards for Best Film, Best Director (William Friedkin), Best Screenplay (William Peter Blatty) and Best Supporting Actress (Linda Blair),

126   [1979] AC 617.
127   Source: 'Exorcist: No One Under 17 Admitted', by Tom Shales, *Washington Post*, 4 January 1974.
128   Kaufmann's quote in *New Republic*, as quoted in Travers and Reiff (1974), pp. 152–4.

while the Oscars that year generated 10 nominations including Best Picture, Best Screenplay (Blatty) and Best Sound. In box-office terms, the movie became the biggest-grossing hit in Warner Brothers' history, nearly trebling the $34m gross of the studio's previous record holder, *My Fair Lady*.[129]

Even after Mrs Whitehouse officially retired in 1994, she continued to vent her spleen well into her nineties from her nursing home, against the 'crassness' of the BBC in particular. Tainted with an image as a blue-rinse reactionary, Mrs Whitehouse endured years of mockery. In her book *Whatever Happened to Sex*, she explained that as a happy family woman she had nothing against sex, but only against its exploitation in the media.[130] After Mrs Whitehouse's death in 2001, complaints to the Independent Television Commission (ITC)[131] about taste and decency rose by 50 per cent. In 1999, Mrs Whitehouse's crusade was taken up by Tory frontbencher Ann Widdecombe. More than 10 years later, in October 2010, Miss Widdecombe emerged as an unexpected star when she appeared in the popular BBC TV series *Strictly Come Dancing*. As she took to the dance floor with partner Anton du Beke, bookmakers slashed her odds of winning the show from 100:1 to 12:1, placing her ahead of Felicity Kendal at 14:1.

10.6.2 The British Board of Film Classification (BBFC)

As the British Board of Film Classification (BBFC) approaches its 2012 centenary as an independent regulator and censor of film, video,[132] DVDs and video games,[133] the regulator is regarded as one of the most trusted and highly regarded non-governmental organizations in the UK, funded by the film, DVD and games industries. The board was set up in 1912, then known as the British Board of Film Censors, with the aim of bringing a degree of uniformity to nationally acceptable film standards. From the mid-1920s on, it became general practice for local authorities to accept the decisions of the board. The BBFC rejects, bans or passes films (as well as DVDs and some video games). It may alter film categories under its own licensing jurisdiction, even though the film may have been given a different category in another country (see *The Exorcist* above).

Today, the BBFC rates about 10,000 pieces a year. Local authorities have the power to decide under what circumstances films are shown in cinemas, but they nearly always choose to follow the advice of the BBFC. Over the past 15 years, the board has rejected fewer films; for example, *Murder-Set-Pieces* in 2008 and *Terrorists, Killers And Other Wackos* in 2005, that is, films which generally include clips of real torture and execution.

The 'film censor' keeps a fascinatingly accurate statistical record online, dating back to 1931, showing detailed descriptions of each film, DVD etc., with censorship comments. In 2010, for example, of 407 films censored, five had to be cut (1.2 per cent), compared with 1983, when the board cut 123 of the 514 submitted films (24 per cent) – the highest censorship rate in 20 years.[134] Since 2000, the BBFC has operated under a series of published guidelines, which regulate the basis of its work and include public consultation exercises, the last being in 2004. As the board has

---

129 Source: 'Entertainment: The Exorcist – hype or horror?', Mark Kermode, BBC Radio 1 online, 2 November 1998.
130 Source: 'Mary Whitehouse: Moral crusader or spoilsport?' BBC News Online, 23 November 2001, available at <http://news.bbc.co.uk/1/hi/uk/763998.stm>, accessed 26 November 2010.
131 The ITC ceased to exist on 18 December 2003 and its duties were assumed by Ofcom (the Office of Communications), the new communications sector regulator. Ofcom inherited the duties of the then five existing regulators, namely The Broadcasting Standards Commission (BSC), the Independent Television Commission (ITC), Oftel, the Radio Authority and the Radiocommunications Agency.
132 In addition there are the Video Packaging Regulations 1985 and the Statutory Instruments S.I. No.911 that brought the Video Recordings (Labelling) Regulations 1985 into UK law on 12 June 1985.
133 Computer games are generally exempt from legal classification in the UK but under the Video Recordings Act 1984 (as amended) some games can lose this exemption and are required to be classified by the British Board of Film Classification. Exemption is usually lost because of grossly violent or sexual content or because the game disc contains video footage that is not part of the game.
134 Source: BFC statistics for works processed in 2010 (films), available at <http://www.bbfc.co.uk/classification/statistics>, accessed 26 November 2010.

developed different sections of its classification process, standards and censorship have changed with evolving pieces of legislation in line with public opinion and changing morality.

When T.P. O'Connor was appointed President of the BBFC in 1916,[135] one of his first tasks was to give evidence to the Cinema Commission of Inquiry, set up by the National Council for Public Morals of the time.[136] He summarized the board's policy by listing 43 grounds for a film's exclusion or rejection; some of the topics included:

- The irreverent treatment of sacred subjects;
- Drunken scenes carried to excess;
- Vulgar accessories;
- The modus operandi of criminals;
- Nude figures;
- Indecorous dancing;
- Excessively passionate love scenes;
- Realistic horrors of warfare including scenes and incidents calculated to afford information to the enemy;
- Subjects dealing with India in which British Officers are seen in an odious light;
- Scenes laid in disorderly houses.

Today, the BBFC is governed by several pieces of legislation, the most significant being the **Video Recordings Acts** (VRA) of 1984 and 2010, which particularly affect classification standards. The 1984 Act requires all 'video works' (films, TV programmes, video games, etc.) which are supplied on a disc, tape or any other device, capable of storing data electronically, to be classified by the BBFC, unless they fall within the definition of an exempted work. Section 4A of the 1984 VRA requires 'special regard' to be given to the likelihood of video works being viewed in the home and to any harm that may be caused to potential viewers or, through their behaviour, to society by the manner in which the work deals with criminal behaviour, illegal drugs, violent behaviour or incidents, horrific behaviour or incidents, and human sexual activity, particularly when video works deal with:

(a)   criminal behaviour;
(b)   illegal drugs;
(c)   violent behaviour or incidents;
(d)   horrific behaviour or incidents; or
(e)   human sexual activity.

The **Video Recordings Act 2010** repealed and then brought back into force parts of the **Video Recordings Act 1984**.[137] The reintroduction of the 1984 act was deemed necessary after Parliament forgot to notify the European Commission in August 2009 of the (original) existence of the 1984 act.[138] This meant neither the 1984 nor the 2010 VRA were initially in accordance with Directive 98/34/EC.[139]

The **Digital Economy Act 2010** additionally passed responsibility for games ratings to the Video Standards Council, particularly for those video games that include violence or encourage

---

135 President from 11 December 1916 to 18 November 1929. Thomas Power O'Connor (1848–1929), known as T. P. O'Connor, was a journalist and Irish nationalist, as well as a Member of Parliament at Westminster for nearly 50 years.
136 Source: National Council for Public Morals (1917).
137 s. 1 Video Recordings Act 2010 ('Repeal and revival of provisions of the Video Recordings Act 1984'): sections 1 to 17, 19, 21 and 22 of the Video Recordings Act 1984, cease to be in force.
138 See: House of Commons, Parliamentary debate of 6 January 2010, Hansard, column 181–209.
139 EC Directive 98/34/EC laying down a procedure for the provision of information in the field of technical standards and regulations and of rules on Information Society services of 22 June 1998.

criminal activity. Video games with specific themes or content – such as the *Grand Theft Auto* series – must also be submitted to the BBFC to receive a legally binding rating in the same way as videos. In considering all these issues, the BBFC needs to be mindful of the possible effect not only on children but also on other vulnerable groups.

Since 1988, Trading Standards Officers have had the power to seize illegal video works, now also including DVDs, Blu-rays and video games. The BBFC provides evidence to the Office of Fair Trading (OFT) to help secure convictions under the terms of the **Video Recordings Act 1984** (VRA). In doing so, the BBFC usually issues a 'Certificate of Evidence' under the VRA 1984 (or the **Criminal Procedure (Scotland) Act 1995**). This evidence is admissible in court as 'standalone' evidence and does not require anyone from the BBFC to attend as a witness.

The **Obscene Publications Acts 1959 and 1964** made it illegal to publish a work in the UK which is regarded as 'obscene' in content (as a whole). The film, DVD, game, etc. must have the

See Chapter 7.3 →

tendency to 'deprave and corrupt', unless the 'publication' can be justified as being for the 'public good' on the grounds that it is in the interests of science, art, literature or learning or other objects of general concern.

The **Public Order Act 1986** makes it illegal to distribute or play to the public a recording of images or sounds which are threatening, abusive or insulting if the intention is to stir up racial hatred or hatred on the grounds of sexual orientation. Images and sounds which are threatening if the intention is to stir up religious hatred are also prohibited.[140]

There are two acts which cover animal welfare issues in films. The **Cinematograph Films (Animals) Act 1937** renders it illegal to show any scene 'organised or directed' for the purposes of a film that involves the cruel treatment of any animal. Section 1 ('production of films involving cruelty to animals') reads:

> . . . No person shall exhibit to the public, or supply to any person for public exhibition (whether by him or by another person), any cinematograph film (whether produced in Great Britain or elsewhere) if in connection with the production of the film any scene represented in the film was organised or directed in such a way as to involve the cruel infliction of pain or terror on any animal or the cruel goading of any animal to fury.

The **Animal Welfare Act 2006** makes it illegal to show or publish a recording of an animal fight which has taken place in the UK since 6 April 2007. This is to combat illegal dog fighting (and the breeding of dangerous dogs for fights), habitually filmed and uploaded by criminals on to YouTube.

10.6.3 Film classification and censorship

BBFC examiners normally view video and DVD submissions on their own ('solo viewing'). Films for cinema release, video games and pornography submissions are classified in teams of two. Controversial works, such as extreme reality material, is viewed in teams of three. Games are measured by the regulator's IT department, who assess how long examiners will need to play the game by viewing all its video elements.

Many films and videos are submitted in foreign languages – most notably Hindi and Cantonese – and examiners with linguistic skills then view these works. Where the work is in a language not spoken by any of the examiners and there are no subtitles, the Board will use an interpreter, who will sit alongside the examiner or team. BBFC examiners log the following details:

---

140 s. 22 Public Order Act 1986.

- General context: plot, characters, outline of individual scenes;
- Timings of classification moments, including camera angles, type of shots, on- and off-screen moments;
- Bad language, sex and drug references, etc.

The BBFC then examines the overall tone of a film, DVD or video game and assesses how these may affect the classification of each.

A 'U' ('Universal') film should be suitable for audiences aged four years and over, allowing very mild bad language, such as 'damn' and 'hell'; for example, the 1964 Walt Disney film, *Mary Poppins*, featuring Julie Andrews and Dick van Dyke.

A 'PG' (Parental Guidance) film should not disturb a child aged around eight. There may be mild bad language, such as 'shit' or 'son of a bitch', and violence is only acceptable in a historical or fantasy setting. An example would be the 2007 film, *Mr Bean's Holiday*, starring Rowan Atkinson, or *Michael Jackson's This Is It* (see below), released following the legendary pop singer's death in June 2009.

❖ **KEY CASE** — BBFC film classification of 'MICHAEL JACKSON'S – THIS IS IT'

Certificate PG

Feature film directed by Kenny Ortega

The cast includes: Michael Jackson, Kenny Ortega, Orianthi

Columbia Pictures Corporation Ltd

Classified 27 October, 2009 as PG

The film – released after the pop legend Michael Jackson died on 25 June 2009 – is a documentary charting the singer's rehearsals for 50 forthcoming concerts which had been scheduled at the O2 Arena in London. The film shows dancers auditioning for the chance to perform with Michael Jackson on stage. The film contains very brief sight of a dancer holding up a knife during the rehearsals for another song but the weapon is not focused upon. Also featured is some occasional theatrical violence, including a scene in which a character jumps out of a window in slow motion to avoid being shot with a machine gun, along with a brief fist fight. The film contains some mild suggestive dancing, and occasional sight of dancers grabbing their crotches. We see clips of zombies rising from graves, blood splashing down the screen to reveal the song title and a subsequent sight of a ghost screaming and laughing as it hangs from chandelier with a rope around its neck. In this sequence such imagery is very theatrical and clearly portrayed within a fantastical scenario, but it was felt to go beyond the level of intensity that would be acceptable at U. Therefore, the film was classified PG for containing infrequent scary scenes.

Consumer Advice: Contains infrequent scary images

No one under 15 is allowed to see, buy or rent a certificate '15'-rated film, DVD or video game. This classification generally includes strong violence, frequent strong language such as 'fuck', and brief scenes of sexual activity or violence are permitted – so are discriminatory language and drug-taking. A games example would be *Castlevania Lords of Shadow* (August 2010), which contains 'strong bloody violence'.

No one under 18 is allowed to see a certificate '18'-rated film in the cinema, or to rent or buy the DVD or video game. '18'-rated films or games are essentially adult works, and generally include very strong violence and/or sexual activity with frequently strong language such as 'cunt'. The regulator occasionally orders cuts to '18' films or games, particularly where the material is in breach of criminal law, such as portraying extremely violent or dangerous acts or illegal drug use, causing potential harm to public health or morals. Examples include the games series, *Grand Theft Auto* (GTA) or the film *A Clockwork Orange* (see below).

10.6.4 Regulating screen violence: *A Clockwork Orange*

Stanley Kubrick's 1971 film *A Clockwork Orange*, based on an adaptation of Anthony Burgess' novel of 1962, is a dark satirical film depicting Alex (Malcolm McDowell), a charismatic delinquent who engages in ultra violence, including rape, performed to Beethoven's music. Alex leads horrific gang violence with 'the droogs'. This controversial film worried the government to such an extent that before the film's general release in January 1972, Home Secretary Reginald Maudling arranged a private viewing of the film. The BBFC had passed the film with an 'X' rating, requiring no cuts (the age bar for an 'X'-rated film had just been raised from 16 to 18). With the film's general release, the BBFC had advised the distributors, Warner Brothers, that the film portrayed 'an unrelieved diet of vicious violence and hooliganism'.[141]

Kubrick became a target for hate mail and abusive phone calls after a number of rapes and murders in the early 1970s were linked to the film, including a sex attack in Lancashire carried out by a gang chanting the Gene Kelly song 'Singin' in the Rain'. This resulted in Stanley Kubrick secretly withdrawing the film by arranging with Warners that the film would just be allowed to die off quietly, after further allegations that *A Clockwork Orange* was inspiring young people to copy its scenes of violence.

Shortly before the film's re-release, Stanley Kubrick died on 7 March 1999, aged 70. The BBFC had already granted the film's uncut version a certificate '18'. Crucially, the director's widow, German-born actress and painter Christiane, retained all consultation rights on the re-released *A Clockwork Orange*. In the film a large floral oil painting by Christiane can be seen during the famous 'Singin' in the Rain' home scene. The American film director Kubrick had moved to England in 1962 to film *Lolita*, his motivation being that the UK would prove to have laxer censorship laws. He settled in England, making a large number of films including *Dr Strangelove* with Peter Sellers, *2001: A Space Odyssey* and *Eyes Wide Shut*.

See Chapter 7.3.3 →

It has been difficult for the government to create new regulations and statutory provisions for internet-based, audio-visual services including film downloads, DVDs and interactive internet-based games, particularly those that display an extraordinary amount of screen violence. There is a fine line between privacy – and what can be viewed or played in one's own home – and the continuation of freedom of expression.

Can screen violence really lead to actual violence? This has been the question that legislators and regulators have asked themselves for years. Dr Guy Cumberbatch, Chartered Psychologist and Director of The Communications Research Group, undertook extensive research in this field. In a report to the Video Standards Council (2004), Cumberbatch established that screen violence *does* influence children's behaviour, particularly their style of play, which changes in line with the

---

141 Source: BBFC censorship comments of 1971, available at <http://www.bbfc.co.uk/AFF022201>, accessed 30 November 2010.

programmes they watched on TV, or DVD or the video games they played. He gave the examples of *Power Rangers, Ninja Turtles* and *Spiderman.*[142]

FOR THOUGHT

How far should film and games censorship go?

10.7 The Advertising Standards Authority

In August 2010 an advertisement for an animal charity working in Afghanistan was banned by the Advertising Standards Authority (ASA). The advert featured a photo of an Afghan man, a donkey and a British soldier and promoted the charity's work treating livestock in Helmand province. The advert's text read:

> . . . Saving her [the donkey's] life means his [the soldier's] just got easier . . . to many farming families in Afghanistan, the well-being of their animals can be the difference between life and death. Desperation is what fuels this war and the simple act of helping their donkey can help prevent entire families from being drawn into this terrible conflict. Hearts and minds can be won over by simple, practical help. SPANA provides veterinary care and training which helps local people to look after their livestock. Ultimately, our brave British servicemen and women can benefit from the care which you help us provide.

The Society for the Protection of Animals Abroad (SPANA) claimed that a family's loss of their animals and consequently their livelihood meant they were more likely to be drawn into the conflict in Afghanistan and said that donations to support the charity's veterinary work with farmers in Helmand would ultimately benefit British troops in Afghanistan. The ASA stated that they had not seen evidence that showed a direct correlation between the work of SPANA and the effects on the lives of British servicemen and women, and adjudicated that the advert was offensive and exploited British troops to obtain donations. The ASA ruling was that the advert for SPANA was 'likely to mislead' by suggesting that donations ultimately benefited British troops and told the charity they must never use this advert again in its current form.[143]

The ASA has been the advertising watchdog for over 50 years. It is an independent self-regulatory body and has dealt with some 26,433 complaints in 2008, after which 2,475 adverts were changed or withdrawn. The regulator also watches over sales promotions, direct marketing and online advertisements in the UK. Its powers include stopping misleading, harmful or offensive advertising, ensuring that sales promotions are run fairly, and reducing unwanted commercial mail (by post, email or SMS). The advertising regulator also resolves problems with mail-order purchases.

Anyone can complain to the ASA free of charge and its self-regulatory value is founded on EC directives, including those on misleading and comparative advertising.[144] The ASA's self-regulation is accepted by the Department of Business, Innovation and Skills (formerly the Department for Business, Enterprise and Regulatory Reform) and the Office of Fair Trading (OFT) as a first line of control in protecting consumers.

---

142 See: Cumberbatch (2004).
143 Source: ASA Adjudication on 'The Society for the Protection of Animals Abroad' (SPANA) of 18 August 2010, Complaint Ref: 123003.
144 Directives 2005/29/EC and 2006/114/EC.

The ASA essentially has two committees, the Committee of Advertising Practice (CAP) and the Broadcast Committee of Advertising Practice (BCAP), whose main functions are to provide advice and guidance to the industry. The regulator distinguishes between 'non-broadcast' (e.g. print press or online) and 'broadcast codes' (e.g. radio and TV).[145] This means there are essentially two codes of practice, which cover all traditional mediums in addition to new media (e.g. mobile phones, handheld computers, Personal Digital Assistants (PDAs)), but also electronic kiosks, electronic posters and computer games – all of which can carry advertising.

The ASA has been designated by Ofcom as the co-regulator for advertising appearing on Video-on-Demand (VOD) services (from 1 September 2010). Ofcom acts as a backstop regulator, which means the ASA can refer cases to Ofcom if advertising continues to appear despite an ASA adjudication against it. Ofcom can then take immediate action on serious breaches of the ASA rules, for instance by using its legal powers to order the immediate suspension of an advertisement accompanied by a fine. Not all VOD advertising is subject to the ASA's regulation, however. Only advertisements on services that are subject to statutory regulation will be affected.[146] Services as defined by the **Communications Act 2003** are required to notify the Association for Television on Demand (ATVOD) that they are operating.[147]

The ASA codes lay down rules for advertisers and media owners. The main aim of the codes states that advertisements must be responsible and must not mislead or offend. There are specific rules that cover advertising to children, adverts for alcohol, gambling, motoring, health and financial products (see below sample adjudications in 10.8.1).

The 'British Code of Advertising, Sales Promotion and Direct Marketing' (the CAP Code) is a rulebook for non-broadcast advertisements, sales promotions and direct marketing communications,[148] supervised and enforced by the Committee of Advertising Practice (CAP). Some rules in the CAP Code go beyond content, for example those that cover the administration of sales promotions, the suitability of promotional items, the delivery of products ordered through an advertisement and the use of personal information in direct marketing. Editorial content is specifically excluded from the Code, though it might be a factor in determining the context in which marketing communications are judged. The CAP Code supplements the law and fills gaps and, as with most of the other regulators' codes, provides an easier way of resolving disputes than by civil litigation or criminal prosecution. Non-compliance with the CAP code may result in Office of Fair Trading action under the Consumer Protection from Unfair Trading Regulations 2008[149] or the Business Protection from Misleading Marketing Regulations 2008 (BPR).[150]

The ASA codes are generally revised every two years, subject to full public consultations, generally attracting around 30,000 responses from consumers, industry, government, charities and other interest groups. The last code came into effect on 1 September 2010. The latest consultation in 2009 took note of increasing complaints about online adverts, particularly pop-ups, including viruses and online fraud of some less than scrupulous brands. Other public complaints centred on 'viral' obtrusive advertising through Bluetooth, 3G phones and text messages, such as third-party advertising in the form of nightclub or health club promotions. A particular area of concern and special monitoring is online gambling, where the ASA provides seminars for advertisers with

145 For online publication of all codes see: <http://bcap.org.uk/The-Codes.aspx> (accessed 26 November 2010).
146 For a list of regulated services, see: <www.atVOD.co.uk> (accessed 26 November 2010).
147 s. 368A Communications Act 2003.
148 A new Appendix has been included in the CAP Code, which applies to video-on-demand (VOD) aspects of advertisements that are subject to statutory regulation under the Communications Act 2003 (as amended).
149 The Consumer Protection from Unfair Trading Regulations 2008 of 26 May 2008 (No. 1277) ('The Unfair Trading Regulations'); see also: EC Directive on Directive 2005/29/EC concerning unfair business-to-consumer commercial practices in the internal market of 11 May 2005 ('The Unfair Commercial Practices Directive').
150 The Business Protection from Misleading Marketing Regulations 2008 (BPR) of 26 May 2008 ('Trade Descriptions') which prohibit businesses from advertising products in a way that misleads traders and set out conditions under which comparative advertising to consumers and business is permitted.

adherence to the 'Gambling Advertising Codes', designed to protect young and vulnerable people while allowing responsible advertising of betting and gaming services to flourish.

Advertising campaigns increasingly cross national boundaries. The European Advertising Standards Alliance (EASA), founded in 1992 and based in Brussels, brings together national advertising self-regulatory bodies and organizations representing the advertising industry in Europe. Today, EASA comprises around 130 representatives from all sectors of the advertising industry under one charter, based on a 'Statement of Common Principles and Operating Standards of Best Practice', and represents some 22 countries. The Alliance operates a cross-border complaints procedure, known as the *Blue Book*.[151] The *Blue Book* is published every three years and contains a comprehensive overview of the scope and activities of the self-regulation systems in advertising. *Blue Book* 6 covers the following key areas:

● Self-regulatory systems in Europe, including national advertising codes and legislation as well as statutory and self-regulatory structures;
● Analysis of key issues in advertising, including advertising to children, food and alcohol advertising, digital marketing communications and green claims;
● Complaints statistics;
● International self-regulatory rules contained in the 'Consolidated Code of the International Chamber of Commerce'.

On 9 February 2010, the then Labour Culture Secretary, Ben Bradshaw, announced in Parliament that product placement would be allowed on TV and radio in the UK. In a written ministerial statement Mr Bradshaw said the new regime would 'provide meaningful commercial benefits to commercial television companies and programme-makers while taking account of the legitimate concerns that have been expressed'. He said that, apart from Denmark, the UK was the only European Union member state that had yet to allow television product placement or express a firm intention to do so.[152] The regulation of video-on-demand services and product placement on commercial radio and TV is shared by the ASA and Ofcom. While product placement is the '*dernier cri*' in advertising during the programming for films, drama, sports and light entertainment, the embedded marketing of branded goods will be banned from children's, religious, current affairs and consumer affairs programmes. Generally banned products include cigarettes and other tobacco products, medicinal products, alcoholic drinks, salty foods and gambling services.

10.7.1 Examples of adjudications

The ASA's activities include investigating and adjudicating on complaints. The vast majority of advertisers, promoters and direct marketers comply with the Code. Those that do not may be subject to sanctions. Adverse publicity may result from weekly published ASA rulings via its website. Decisions are subject to independent review by the Administrative Division of the High Court. When the ASA feels a complaint is justified, it can take action with the licence holder concerned and the regulator's Broadcast Committee of Advertising Practice (BCAP) can additionally investigate a challenge with the licence holder if it finds a potential breach. If a complaint is upheld, the commercial is usually immediately withdrawn, or in rarer cases amended. In more serious cases, Ofcom can apply sanctions to licensees who frequently break the rules, by issuing a formal warning. They can also request a broadcast correction or statement of findings or impose a penalty which

---

151 For its sixth edition *The Seminal Guide to Advertising Self-Regulation – The Blue Book* was launched in Sofia, Bulgaria in April 2010.
152 Source: Written Ministerial Statement on Television Product Placement, 9 February 2010, available at <http://webarchive. nationalarchives.gov.uk/+/http://www.culture.gov.uk/reference_library/minister_speeches/6624.aspx>, accessed 26 November 2010.

may include a fine or the shortening, suspending or taking-away of a station's licence to broadcast (see above 10.4.3).

❖ **KEY CASE** — **ASA Adjudication on British Telecommunications plc Complaint 8 August 2010. Ref: 122359**

Advertisement:
During July 2010 a national press advert for BT fibre optic broadband showed a burst of light. Large text in the middle of the light burst stated: 'BT Infinity. The birth of the instant Internet'. Text next to the light burst stated: 'Upload and share high-quality photos and videos instantly; download your favourite music instantly; enjoy multiple websites and online content instantly; stream HD movies and TV shows instantly.' Text at the bottom of the advert next to the BT logo stated: 'New fibre optic broadband BT'.

Issue:
Four complainants challenged whether the use of the word 'instantly' was misleading because they understood that while BT Infinity might be faster than other broadband services, there would still be some delays to the service.

Response:
British Telecommunications plc (BT) said the headline claim 'Instant Internet' referred to the time it would take a user to get online. They said because their fibre optic broadband allowed users to do that in less than a few seconds, they did not believe this claim was problematic. They said streaming HD content such as from BBC iPlayer could take between three and four seconds to start and would then stream constantly. BT believed consumers would know that the word 'instant' did not mean the complete absence of any delay or zero seconds, especially in the context of broadband and the Internet. They did not believe consumers would feel misled if they knew the speeds offered by their fibre optic broadband.

Assessment:
The ASA considered that consumers would understand the claims 'upload and share high-quality photos and videos instantly', 'download your favourite music instantly', 'enjoy multiple websites and online content instantly' and 'stream HD movies and TV shows instantly' etc. to mean that BT's fibre optic broadband could deliver the listed activities straight away, or with no noticeable delay. The advert breached CAP Code clauses 3.1 ('Substantiation') and 7.1 ('Truthfulness').

Action:
The advertisement must not appear again in its current form.

❖ **KEY CASE** — **ASA Adjudication on Coca-Cola Great Britain 1 August 2007 Complaint Ref: 28111**

Advertisement:
The TV advert for the sports drink 'Powerade' featured a man who was training for his first triathlon. The advert showed different scenes of him riding his bicycle on the road. It

appeared to be either early morning or dusk; the vehicles shown in some scenes had their headlights on.

Issue:

The complainant challenged whether the advert could be seen to condone behaviour prejudicial to health and safety, because the cyclist was not wearing reflective clothing and was not shown to have lights on his bicycle.

Response:

McCann Erickson, on behalf of Coca-Cola, said that this man was training for his first triathlon in a 'fly on the wall'-style 'documentary' which was part of a series filmed during the afternoon in late March, but said the lack of lighting equipment made it seem as though it was later in the day. They were assured that safety precautions were taken when filming the advert. The Broadcast Advertising Clearance Centre (BACC) said they did not consider that the advert was suggestive of danger, nor did they consider that the scenes depicted in the advert were in breach of the Highway Code and they had approved it on that basis.

Assessment:

The ASA said that viewers would not be aware of the lighting aspect and were likely to believe that the advert was filmed in the early morning or at dusk. The advert could give the impression that reflective clothing or lights were not required when cycling in conditions of poor visibility. The ASA expressed concern that the advert could be seen to condone hazardous cycling. The advert breached CAP Broadcast (TV) Advertising Standards Code rule 6.7 ('Health and safety').

Action:

Coca-Cola must not use this advertisement again.

❖ **KEY CASE**   **ASA Adjudication on Bacardi-Martini Ltd 30 July 2008 Complaint Ref: 59713**

Advertisement:

The TV advert for Bacardi rum opened with the image of a bottle labelled 'Bacardi Superior'. Droplets of liquid splashed against it as it vibrated to the bass beat of a club track before disintegrating into the liquid, which then transformed into the shape of a man. The beat developed into a full-blown dance track; the virtual figure began to move and was joined by another; a deep red-coloured liquid figure in the shape of a woman. They danced energetically opposite each other as liquid splashed between and around them before fusing together and reforming into a glass of Bacardi and cranberry. The advert closed with the image of a bottle of 'Bacardi Superior' and the text in white, 'made to mix', and in red, 'with cranberry'. Then, 'enjoy Bacardi Superior Rum responsibly . . .'.

Issue:

One viewer challenged the provocative nature of the couple's dancing, as to whether it linked alcohol with sexual activity or success.

Response:
Bacardi UK said they had taken great care to select appropriate music and had undertaken consumer research to determine the likely response to it. They pointed out that no people were used in the advert and the image merely represented two liquids, which were present throughout the advert, combining to form a new drink. Bacardi said it was clear from research undertaken on the artist who provided the music that the target audience for that genre was aged over 25 years of age.

Assessment:
The complaint was not upheld. The ASA said the figures were surreal and ambiguous and there was nothing in their movement or interaction to suggest sexual activity. The liquid surroundings were likely to be interpreted by viewers as being representative of the product, Bacardi as a mixer. The following codes were investigated under CAP ('Broadcast') TV Advertising Standards Code rules 11.8.1 (c) and 11.8.2 (e) ('Alcoholic drinks'); the ASA found no breach.

10.8 ICANN: The Internet Corporation for Assigned Names and Numbers

For as long as the Internet has been around – coming up to about 40 years – '.com' has been the assumed default extension for websites. Very soon, new extensions to the World Wide Web will be taking shape where 'extension subscriptions' will be for sale with a new domain name service. It has already been possible to drop the 'www' for most URLs. Shortly, there will be new networks and search engines that will direct the user more efficiently to sites, making the .com traffic less important. This will affect the security of internet users as the Domain Name System (DNS) and domain name registration are presently being reallocated.

ICANN, the Internet Corporation for Assigned Names and Numbers, regulates the Internet's core directory of domain names and numbers. It is a private not-for-profit corporation established in California, working under an agreement with the US Department of Commerce in Washington DC. At the top of the hierarchy is an entity called IANA, the Internet Assigned Numbers Authority, operated on behalf of the Commerce Department. In September 2009, contracts with ICANN came to an end and controversy arose as to the control and regulation of country-code domain names ending in .uk, .fr and .eu. ICANN promptly moved ahead with plans to expand the number and type of internet addresses available, particularly in relation to domain name suffixes such as .com, .org and .net.

Former EU Commissioner Viviane Reding announced in May 2009 that the Commission had repeatedly called for more international supervision of the Internet, and argued strongly that the supervision of the Internet should not be regulated and security controlled by a single country, namely the United States, but demanded joined-up regulation globally by other governments. While Madame Reding welcomed the original Clinton administration's decision to privatize domain names and addresses, she refuted the idea that a single department in Washington should regulate the World Wide Web.[153]

After the EU Commission's ongoing complaints about American dominance of the Internet, President Obama finally gave in, agreeing that ICANN should relinquish *some* control over the way the World Wide Web is run in November 2009. This means that some foreign governments are now

---

153 Source: EU Commissioner Reding's weekly video message on the theme 'The Future of Internet Governance: Towards an Accountable ICANN', of 4 May 2009: http://ec.europa.eu/commission_barroso/reding/video/text/message_20090504.pdf

more in charge of DNS system administration – though key aspects are still regulated by the US Department of Commerce, such as the Security and Stability Advisory Committee (SSAC), chartered by the ICANN Board of Directors. SSAC originated in the aftermath of 9/11 and comprises a group of volunteer technical experts which reviews and monitors security issues and incidents relating to the Internet's naming and address allocation systems.

One main area is 'phishing', where criminals register domain names so they can 'phish' or lure victims to websites where the criminal will trick visitors into disclosing bank or credit card information or making bogus purchases. The SSAC studies such malicious uses of domain names and issues reports, recommending ways domain name registration service providers can reduce the number of malicious domain name registrations.

It was Commissioner Reding's intention that internet governance ought to be high on the agenda of all governments, who then share principles, norms, rules, decision-making procedures and best practice, first established under the 'Tunis Agenda for the Information Society'.[154] But it is unavoidable that there will be internet security issues from time to time, such as the Estonia ISP disaster where the country's servers were hacked into in May 2007, causing a diplomatic clash with Russia.

Due to ICANN's globalization and international security regulation there are now powerful combined plans to allow web users to use addresses with names in Chinese, Arabic or other alphabets other than Latin, which will enable the World Wide Web to reach out to societies that have so far not been touched by the Internet. The most contentious issue remains to reach the critical mass in emerging economies such as China. The ICANN Board of Directors continues to roll out more Internationalized Domain Names (IDNs), making it easier for everyone to use the Internet.[155] The latest countries and territories included in September 2010 were able to use their national scripts. People from these areas are now able to type their non-Latin scripts in the top-level domain (TLD) part of an internet address name which follows the dot, such as dot-cn or dot-org; these are:

Country	ccTLD	Script	IDN ccTLD
Thailand	.TH	Thai	ไทย
Occupied Palestinian Territory	.PS	Arabic	فلسطين
Tunisia	.TN	Arabic	تونس
Jordan	.JO	Arabic	الاردن

Meanwhile the UK organization Nominet continues to regulate and handle the day-to-day running of some eight million '.uk' domain names. Nominet UK was founded by Dr Willie Black in 1996 when its predecessor, the Naming Committee, was unable to deal with the volume of registrations then being sought under the .uk domain. Nominet is a not-for-profit company and its members are shareholders without the right to participate in the profits of the company. Anyone can become a member, but most members are ISPs who also act as registrars and self-regulators.

Nominet's research has highlighted that British internet users are six times more likely to choose a .uk rather than a .com address when looking for information via an internet search engine. Nominet's Annual Report of 2009 reported a net growth of 762,674 domains, making it the third largest domain name provider in the world behind .com and .de. Its income increased by 9 per cent to £19.8 million.[156] Nominet works closely with the UK Government and plays a key role in international internet governance and policy development. They liaise with ICANN and the EU Commission on legislation regarding the worldwide domain name registry, governance and security.[157]

---

154 See: The Tunis Agenda for the Information Society. Document: WSIS–05/TUNIS/DOC/6(Rev.1)-E 18 November 2005, available at <www.itu.int/wsis/docs2/tunis/off/6rev1.pdf>, accessed 26 November 2010.
155 See ICANN 'Final Implementation Plan', 8 August 2010, available at <http://www.icann.org/en/topics/idn/fast-track/idn-cctld-implementation-plan–16nov09-en.pdf>, accessed 26 November 2010.
156 Source: Nominet Annual Report and Accounts of 2009, available at <http://www.nic.uk/digitalAssets/45046_report-and-accounts2009.pdf>, accessed 26 November 2010.
157 Source: Nominet, August 2010: <www.nic.uk>, accessed 26 November 2010.

FOR THOUGHT

Is it possible to regulate the whole of the Internet? What should be done about social networking sites and the language used in chatrooms, where users regularly upload images which they share with others worldwide?

10.8.1 Media 'sans frontières': codifying cyberspace or self-regulation in the digital age?

The international audio-visual landscape has changed significantly with the impact of technological developments in the information society. New players and platforms have emerged, boosting or requiring more content production for emerging markets. The EU is tasked with encouraging its member countries to cooperate in conserving and safeguarding cultural heritage of European significance, including TV, cinema and film.[158]

Since 1989 the European Union has issued legislation which governs the audio-visual sector across all EU member states. Linked in rationale to restrictions on overseas ownership are rules which set quotas for domestic programme production. Where trade areas have been established, these quotas are often extended. All signatory states to the 'Television Without Frontiers Directive' (TVWF)[159] agreed to European production quotas providing minimum broadcasting standards. Article 2a TVWF states that:

> . . . member states shall ensure freedom of reception and shall not restrict retransmissions on their territory of television broadcasts from other member states for reasons which fall within the fields coordinated by this Directive.

Article 4.1 of the Directive states:

> . . . member states shall ensure where practicable and by appropriate means, that broad-casters reserve for European works . . . a majority proportion of their transmission time, excluding the time appointed to news, sports events, games, advertising, teletext services and teleshopping. This proportion, having regard to the broadcaster's informational, educational, cultural and entertainment responsibilities to its viewing public, should be achieved progres-sively, on the basis of suitable criteria.

The TVWF Directive was updated in 1997,[160] covering media access to major sporting events, tele-shopping and promoting EU products.[161]

The 'Audio Visual Media Services Directive' (AVMSD)[162] has now largely replaced the 'sans fron-tières' Directive, additionally covering public service broadcasters like the BBC.[163] The AVMSD covers all services with audio-visual content irrespective of the technology used to deliver the content. The

---

158 Article 151(2) EC Treaty.
159 EU Directive 89/552 EEC on Transfrontier Television 'Television without Frontiers Directive' (TVWF).
160 Directive 97/36/EC amended Council Directive 89/552/EEC 'Television without Frontiers' (above) concerning the pursuit of television broadcasting activities.
161 The Commission ordered that Directive 2007/65 had to be transposed into domestic legislation by the end of 2009.
162 EC Directive 2007/65 on the 'Audiovisual Media Services Directive' (AVMSD) amended EU Directive 89/552/EEC 'Television without Frontiers Directive' (TVWF) and includes the pursuit of television broadcasting activities including on-demand services of 11 December 2007.
163 EU Directive 2007/65/EC on the 'Audiovisual Media Services Directive' (AVMSD) amended EU Directive 89/552/EEC 'Television without Frontiers Directive' (TVWF) and includes the pursuit of television broadcasting activities including on-demand services of 11 December 2007.

rules of the Directive apply irrespective of whether one watches news or other audiovisual content on TV, on the Internet or on one's mobile phone. However, taking into account the degree of choice and user control over services, the AVMSD makes a distinction between linear (television broadcasts) and non-linear (on-demand) services. The AVMSD also modernized TV advertising rules to better finance audio-visual content, including teleshopping, product placement and sponsorship.[164]

EU law has been modified to cover services delivered over the Internet in order to combat internet piracy and to monitor mass-market advertising on TV and the Internet in the 'pay per click' society. As the global recession gathers pace, advertisers are keen to extend their product placement and it remains to be seen whether this new form of advertising will provide better value for money and extend the content producers' ambitions beyond e-commerce and internet service operations to TV and radio programmes. All BBC programmes remain advertising free.

While the AVMSD created a level playing field in Europe for emerging audiovisual media, it also sought to safeguard and preserve cultural diversity, protect children, consumers and media pluralism, and combat racial and religious hatred.[165]

10.8.2 Does regulation infringe freedom of expression? Analysis and discussion.

On 5 July 2010, in an exclusive interview with the *Daily Mirror* – his first public interview in 10 years – the pop star Prince declared the Internet dead! Prince said:

> . . . the Internet's completely over. I don't see why I should give my new music to iTunes or anyone else. They won't pay me an advance for it and then they get angry when they can't get it.[166]

The star explained that he would only release a new album in CD format and that there would be no downloads anywhere in the world because of his ongoing battles against internet copyright abuses. Prince banned YouTube and iTunes from using any of his music and even closed down his own official website. Prince also criticized the advent of gadgets and 'apps'.

Anderson and Rainie ('The Pew Report – 2006') believed, from a survey of technology thinkers and stakeholders conducted in 2005, that the Internet would continue to spread in a 'flattening' and improving world. Furthermore, that the Internet would provide 'low-cost networks of billions of devices' by 2020.[167] While the Internet has brought global freedom to communicate and exchange ideas, its growth has introduced difficulties too – for instance, the expression on social networking sites and blogs of personal opinions, with the risk therein of misinformation, defamation and harassment. There is also the ability to search the World Wide Web for content of pretty well any extreme nature, ranging from the sexual to the political.

That said, the number of free web access providers has declined sharply in recent years, as the industry has seen a number of players consolidate or go out of business. Much reliable content is now only available via paid-for services, such as *The Times, Reuters Business News* and the investor's profile, *The Wall Street Journal* or smartphone applications. History will judge whether Rupert Murdoch's decision to charge for access to online web-based archive material in relation to *The Times* and *The Sunday Times* will be successful.

What regulation there is must reflect that the Internet is widely used and extremely beneficial. Over-regulation can impair and limit the growth of the information society. Judicial review of

---

164 Article 3e AVMSD.
165 Source: 2009/C 257/01 Communication from the Commission on the application of State aid rules to public service broadcasting. Official Journal of the European Union, C 257, Vol 52, 27 October 2009.
166 Source: 'Prince – world exclusive interview', by Peter Willis, *Daily Mirror*, 5 July 2010.
167 See: Anderson and Rainie (2006).

regulation can potentially restrict free speech. If regulators are put in place by governments, they should be left to conduct their own standard of strict scrutiny.

Article 10 ECHR protects not only the substance of ideas and information expressed, but also the form in which they are conveyed. Journalistic freedom covers possible recourses to a degree of exaggeration, or even provocation. However, even where a statement amounts to a value judgment, the proportionality of an interference may depend on whether there exists a sufficient factual basis for the impugned statement, since even a value judgment without any factual basis to support it may be excessive (see: *Dichand v Austria* [2002][168]; also: *Monnat v Switzerland* [2006][169]).

Freedom of expression is fundamental to the functioning of democracy. This applies especially to the communication of opinions and argument about policies which all levels of government pursue, including those made in radio and TV broadcasts (see: R *(Animal Defenders International v Secretary of State for Culture, Media and Sport* [2008][170]).

In December 2008, the European Court of Human Rights handed down its judgment in the case of *TV-Vest & Rogaland Pensjonistparti v Norway*.[171] The Court found that the application of a blanket ban on advertising for political parties violated Article 10 ECHR. The Norwegian TV channel, TV Vest – located in Stavanger in the County of Rogaland – had been fined in September 2003 by the Norwegian Media Authority NOK 35,000 under s. 10(3) of the **Norwegian Broadcasting Act 1992** and s. 10(2) of the Broadcasting Regulations, for violating the prohibition on political advertising in TV broadcasts. The broadcast concerned three advertising slots for the Norwegian Pensioners Party during the run-up to the local and regional elections in 2003. TV Vest appealed against the decision to Oslo City Court (Oslo tingrett), stating that the prohibition in the Broadcasting Act was incompatible with the right to freedom of expression under Article 10 ECHR. The City Court upheld the Media Authority's decision in February 2004, supported by the Norwegian Supreme Court in November of that year. Christos Rozakis, President of the (First Section) of the European Court of Human Rights, held that there had been a violation of Article 10, stating that there had not been a:

> . . . reasonable relationship of proportionality between the legitimate aim pursued by the prohibition on political advertising and the means deployed to achieve that aim. The restriction which the prohibition and the imposition of the fine entailed on the applicants' exercise of their freedom of expression cannot therefore be regarded as having been necessary in a democratic society, within the meaning of paragraph 2 of Article 10, for the protection of the rights of others, notwithstanding the margin of appreciation available to the national authorities.[172]

The judgment in the *Norwegian Pensioner* case has caused great controversy and will no doubt have consequences for political advertising in other countries who have signed up to the European Convention on Human Rights.

Freedom of political expression includes not only the inoffensive, but also the irritating, the contentious, the eccentric, the heretical, the unwelcome and the provocative, provided it does not tend to provoke violence (*Redmond-Bate v DPP* [199][173]). But in *Otto-Preminger-Institut v Austria* [1994],[174] the Strasbourg court included as an obligation under Article 10.2 to avoid – as far as possible – expressions that are gratuitously offensive to others.

---

168 (2002) (App. No. 29271/95) of 26 February 2002 (ECHR).
169 (2006) (Application no. 73604/01) of 21 September 2006 (ECHR).
170 [2008] 1 AC 1312 at para. 27 (Lord Bingham).
171 See: *TV Vest AS & Rogaland Pensjonistparti v Norway* (2008) (Application no. 21132/05) Judgment of the 11 December 2008 (ECHR).
172 Ibid., at para 78 (Christos Rozakis, President, ECHR).
173 (1999) 163 JP 789.
174 [1994] ECHR 26 at para. 49 (ECHR).

In human rights adjudications, the Strasbourg jurisdiction has primarily been concerned with whether the claimant's human rights have been infringed (for example 'freedom of speech' under Article 10 ECHR). The ECtHR is not concerned with domestic administrative matters, such as whether a broadcasting or press regulator took human rights law properly into account in its adjudication. It is a domestic court's role to assess for itself the proportionality of the democratic principle of freedom of speech versus other areas of the Convention, such as a person's right to privacy or whether a person has been defamed.

It is accepted that Strasbourg jurisprudence does not protect gratuitous abuse unrelated to a topic being discussed (on the radio for example), but this is a very limited exception to the broad protection of political expression. For this reason, the regulatory body's decision in the *Jon Gaunt* case may well be incompatible with the Convention Article 10.

The existence of a discretionary area of judgment means that such decisions can only be made by a domestic court of law, rather than a regulator which may not have full statutory powers. In this context, it is submitted that the courts should not regard a regulatory authority as better able than jurisprudence to assess what are 'generally accepted standards', such as the Broadcasting Code or the PCC's Editors' Code for the print press (see: R (SB) v Governors of Denbigh High School [2007][175]; also: *Belfast City Council v Miss Behavin' Ltd* [2007][176]; also: R (Nasseri) v SSHD [2010][177]). It is then up to regulators to introduce safeguards into their codes of practice which express responsibilities. As Lord Walker said in the *ProLife* case, in practice the obligation to avoid offensive material is interpreted as limited to what is needlessly or gratuitously shocking or offensive[178] (see: *Murphy v Ireland* [2000][179]). A regulator ought to strike a fine balance between the parameters of indecent, obscene and violent material and sensitive issues such as ethics and morals, existing legislation and the effective monitoring of the service, without being too prohibitive.

Regulation of the Internet, the games and film industries, telecommunications and media pose ongoing challenges to governments. Where should the line be drawn between regulating indecency and obscenity, freedom of expression and, ultimately, the autonomy of end-users? If an adult signs up to an adult pornographic website or views a 'porn movie' streamed in the comfort of his own home, should there be only minimal control over what he chooses to view? The EU has developed guidelines in that respect by trying to provide adequate protection for the young and vulnerable in society in the form of regulatory standards by meeting a multicultural definition of indecency on the one hand and upholding fundamental freedom of expression principles and the right to privacy on the other.

While the international community is fast promoting the transfer of technology and information, there appear to be a number of different policies and laws in place across Europe and the United States, each attempting to regulate, control and curtail the Internet and fast-advancing new media technology. Has legislation been passed too late? Is internet governance now dominated by the private sector? The Internet is highly robust, dynamic and geographically diverse and can be seen as a positive as well as negative tool. It remains to be seen whether the World Wide Web can really be legally controlled and regulated.

Because the UK Government believes that a balance needs to be struck between media harassment and the need for a free press, especially investigative journalism, it has consistently refused to set in stone a privacy law, preferring to rely on media regulations and common law. The House of Lords said as much in the *Naomi Campbell* case.

---

175 [2007] 1 AC 100.
176 [2007] 1 WLR 1420.
177 [2010] 1 AC 1 (HL).
178 R (ProLife Alliance) v BBC [2004] 1 AC 185 at 121 (Lord Walker).
179 (2000) 38 EHRR 13 (ECHR).

> ### ◉ FOR THOUGHT
>
> What form of regulation, if any, should apply to EU-wide provision of news? How can the 'Television Without Frontiers Directive' (TVWF[180]) assist?

10.9 Summary of key points

- The PCC (the Press Complaints Commission) is an independent self-regulatory body which deals with complaints about the editorial content of newspapers and magazines (and their websites);
- The PCC's Code of Practice sets the benchmark for professional and ethical standards for all members of the print press (and their online editions);
- Ofcom (the Office of Communications) is the communications regulator for the television and radio sectors, including web-based television-type services, non-linear on-demand services, fixed-line telecoms and mobile phone services, plus the airwaves over which wireless devices operate;
- PhonepayPlus regulates the premium rate phone companies and services under a Code of Practice under the general oversight of Ofcom (co-regulation);
- The Internet Watch Foundation (IWF) is the independent regulator which monitors child sexual abuse and obscene and violent content hosted on websites worldwide;
- The British Board of Film Classification (BBFC) regulates and censors a combination of film, video, DVD and video games;
- The **Freedom of Information Act 2000** gives citizens the right of access to information held by public authorities;
- The **Data Protection Act 1998** gives an individual the right to see personal data held on them by public authorities;
- EU Directive 89/552 'Television without Frontiers Directive' (TVWF – 'sans frontières') created the conditions for the free movement of television broadcasts within the EU;
- EU Directive 97/36/EC amended the 'Television without Frontiers' Directive (above) concerning the pursuit of television broadcasting activities;
- Directive 2007/65, the 'Audiovisual Media Services Directive' (AVMSD), covers video-on-demand services and modernized TV advertising rules.

📖 10.10 Further reading

Akdeniz, Y. (2008) *Internet Child Pornography and the Law: National and International Responses.* Aldershot: Ashgate.

Carney, D. (2008) 'Self Regulation of unlawful newsgathering techniques'. *Communications Law* (Comms. L.) 2008, 13(3) 76–81.

Coad, J. (2005) 'The Press Complaints Commission: are we safe in its hands?' *Entertainment Law Review*, 2005, Vol 16, Issue 7, 167–73.

Cumberbatch, G. (2004) 'Villain or victim? A review of the research evidence concerning media violence and its effects in the real world with additional reference to video games.' A report prepared for The Video Standards Council.

Davies, M. (2010) 'The demise of professional self-regulation? Evidence from the 'ideal type' professions of medicine and law'. *Professional Negligence*, 2010, 26(1), 3–38.

---

180 EU Directive 89/552 EEC on Transfrontier Television 'Television without Frontiers Directive' (TVWF).

Edwards, L. and Waelde, C. (2009) *Law and the Internet'*. 3rd Edition. London: Hart Publishing.

Fenwick, H. and Phillipson, G. (2006) *Media Freedom under the Human Rights Act*. Oxford: Oxford University Press.

Gaber, I. (2009) 'Three cheers for subjectivity: or the crumbling of the seven pillars of traditional journalistic wisdom'. *Communications Law*, 2009 14(5), 150–6.

Garzaniti, L. (2009) Telecommunications, Broadcasting and the Internet: EU Competition Law and Regulation. 3rd Edition. London: Sweet & Maxwell.

Nagle, E. (2009) 'Keeping its own counsel: the Irish Press Council, self-regulation and media freedom'. *Entertainment Law Review*, 2009, 20(3), 93–9.

Robertson, G. and Nicol, A. (2007) *Media Law*, 5th Ed. Chapter 14 'Media Self Regulation'. London: Penguin.

Schudson, M. (2003) *The Sociology of News Media* (Contemporary Societies by Alexander, G.C. (ed.). New York: W.W. Norton & Co.

Bibliography

Aarnio, R. (2004) 'Tietosuojavaltuutetun katsaus vuoteen 2003', Tietosuoja, 2: 28–31.

Ainger, M. (2002). Gilbert and Sullivan: A dual biography. Oxford: Oxford University Press.

Akdeniz, Y. (2008) Internet Child Pornography and the Law: National and international responses. Aldershot: Ashgate.

Anderson, J.Q. and Rainie, L. (2006) The Future of the Internet. Washington, DC: Pew Internet & American Life Project ('The Pew Report').

Andrew, C. (2009) The Defence of the Realm: The authorized history of MI5. London: Allen Lane.

Atkin, W.R. (2001) 'Defamation law in New Zealand "refined" and "amplified"', 30 Common Law World Review 237.

Aubrey, W.H.S. (orig. 1895 – reprint 2007) The Rise and Growth of the English Nation, with Special Reference to Epochs and Crises: A history of, and for, the people. Whitefish, MT: Kessinger Publishing.

Bainham, A. and Cretney, S. (1993) 'Children', The Modern Law: 409–413.

Baloch, T.A. (2007) 'Law booksellers and printers as agents of unchange', Cambridge Law Journal, 66(2): 389–421.

Barber, N.W. (2003) 'A right to privacy?' Public Law, Winter: 602–610.

Barendt, E. (1989) 'Spycatcher and freedom of speech'. Public Law, PO 204.

Barendt, E. (1991) 'Press and broadcasting freedom: Does anyone have any rights to free speech?' 44 CLP 63.

Barendt, E. (2007) Freedom of Speech (2nd edn). Oxford: Oxford University Press.

Barendt, E. (2009) Media Freedom and Contempt of Court: Library of essays in media law. London: Ashgate.

Barendt, E., Lustgarten, L, Norrie, K. and Stephenson, H. (1997) Libel and the Media: The chilling effect. Oxford: Clarendon Press, p.1032 (referred to in Reynolds [2001] 2 AC 127).

Barnum, D.G. (2006) 'Indirect incitement and freedom of speech in Anglo-American law', European Human Rights Law Review, 3: 258–280.

Barsby, C. and Ashworth, A.J. (2004) 'Juries: Contempt of Court Act 1981, s. 8. Case comment', Criminal Law Review, Dec: 1041–44.

Beaujon, A. (1999) 'It's not the beat, it's the Mocean', CMJ New Music Monthly, April: 25.

Bentham, J. (1843) 'Draft of the Organization of Judicial Establishments'. The Works of Jeremy Bentham, Published under the Supervision of His Executor, John Bowring, 11 volumes, 1838–1843. Edinburgh: W. Tait.

Bentham, J (1843, reprinted 2001) 'The anarchical fallacies', The Works of Jeremy Bentham, Published under the Supervision of His Executor, John Bowring, 11 volumes, 1838–1843. Boston, MA: Adamant Media Corporation.

Bernard, N. (1996) 'Discrimination and Free Movement in EC Law', International and Comparative Law Quarterly, 45: 82–108.

Bilton, M. (2003) Wicked Beyond Belief: The hunt for the Yorkshire Ripper. London: HarperCollins.

Bindman, G. (1989) 'Spycatcher: judging the judges' New Law Journal, 139: 94.

Bingham, T. (1996) 'Should there be a law to protect rights of personal privacy?', European Human Rights Law Review, 5: 455–462.

Blackstone, Sir William (1776) *Commentaries, Book IV*. London: University of Cambridge.

Blackstone, Sir William (1825) *Commentaries on the Laws of England* (16th edn). London: University of Cambridge.

Böll, H. (1974) 'Die verlorene Ehre der Katharina Blum'. *Wie Gewalt entstehen und wohin sie führen kann.* München: Deutscher Taschenbuch Verlag (DTV).

Bonnington, A.J. and McInnes, R. (2010) *Scots Law for Journalists* (8th edn). Edinburgh: W. Green/Sweet & Maxwell Ltd.

Bower, T. (2006) *Conrad and Lady Black: Dancing on the edge.* London: HarperCollins.

Brecht, B. (2005) *Leben des Galilei. Schauspiel.* Neuauflage. Berlin: Suhrkamp.

Brems, E. (1996) 'The margin of appreciation in the case law of the European Court of Human Rights', *Zeitschrift für ausländisches öffentliches Recht und Völkerrecht* (Heidelberg Journal of International Law), 56: 240–314.

Brisby, P. (2006) 'The regulation of telecommunications networks and services in the United Kingdom', *Computer and Telecommunications Law Review*, 12(4): 114–139.

Britton, D. (1989) *Lord Horror.* London: Savoy Books.

Broadway, J. (2008) 'Aberrant accounts: William Dugdale's handling of two Tudor murders in the antiquities of Warwickshire', *Midland History*, 33(1): 2–20 (Spring).

Brooke, H. (2010) *The Silent State. Secrets, surveillance and the myth of British democracy.* London: William Heinemann.

Burchill, R., White, N.D. and Morris, J. (eds) (2005) *International Conflict and Security Law: Essays in memory of Hilaire McCoubrey.* Cambridge: Cambridge University Press.

Burke, E. (1790) *Reflections on the Revolution in France and on the Proceedings in Certain Societies in London Relevant to the Event in a Letter Intended to have been Sent to a Gentleman in Paris* (10th edn). London: Printed for J. Dodsley in Pall Mall.

Burns Coleman, E. and White, K. (2006) *Negotiating the Sacred in Multicultural Societies: Blasphemy and sacrilege in a multicultural society.* Canberra: University of Australia National University Press.

Capp, B. (2004) 'The Potter Almanacs', *Electronic British Library Journal (eBLJ)* 2004: 1–2: <http://www.bl.uk/eblj/2004articles/pdf/article4.pdf>, accessed 26 November 2010.

Carey Miller, D.L. and Irvine, D. (2005) *Corporeal Moveables in Scots Law* (2nd rev. edn). Edinburgh: W. Green Publishers.

Carney, D. (2008) 'Self regulation of unlawful newsgathering techniques', *Communications Law*, 13(3): 76–81.

Carter-Ruck, P.F. (1990) *Memoirs of a Libel Lawyer.* London: Weidenfeld & Nicolson.

Carter-Silk, A. and Cartwright-Hignett, C. (2009) 'A child's right to privacy: Out of a parent's hands', *Entertainment Law Review*, 20(6): 212–217.

Christie, A. and Gare, S. (2008) *Blackstone's Statutes on Intellectual Property* (9th edn). Oxford: Oxford University Press.

Clark, A. (1993) *Diaries.* London: Weidenfeld & Nicolson.

Clark, B. (2009) 'Princess Caroline: German Federal Supreme Court again considers the lawfulness of the publication of a celebrity photograph'. *Entertainment Law Review*, 20(3): 107–111.

Clayton, R. and Tomlinson, H. (2009) *The Law of Human Rights* (2nd edn). Oxford: Oxford University Press.

Clegg, C.S. (2001) *Censorship in Jacobean England.* Cambridge: Cambridge University Press.

Clutterbuck, R. (1981) *The Media and Political Violence.* London: Macmillan.

Coad, J. (2005) 'The Press Complaints Commission: Are we safe in its hands?', *Entertainment Law Review*, 16(7): 167–73.

Cobbett, W. (1806) *Cobbett's Parliamentary History of England*, Vol. 6, col. 1063. London: House of Commons. Oxford University Digital Library.

Colligan, C. (2003) 'Race of born pederasts: Homosexuality, and the Arabs', Nineteenth Century Contexts, 25(1): 1–20 (March).

Colston, C. and Galloway, J. (2010) Modern Intellectual Property Law (3rd edn). London: Routledge.

Cook, T. (2010) EU Intellectual Property Law. Oxford: Oxford University Press.

Cornish, W. (2009) 'Conserving culture and copyright: A partial history', Edinburgh Law Review, 13(1): 8–26.

Cornish, W. (2010) Intellectual Property: Patents, copyrights, trademarks and allied rights (7th edn). London: Sweet & Maxwell.

Council of Europe (1996) 'The European Convention on Human Rights in the New Architecture of Europe'. General Report presented by Lord Lester of Herne Hill, QC, in Proceedings of the 8th International Colloquy on the European Convention on Human Rights, pp. 227–240.

Council of Europe (2009) International Justice for Children. Brussels: Council of Europe Publication.

Council of Europe (2010) 'Blasphemy, insult and hatred: Finding answers in a democratic society', Science and Technique of Democracy 47. Brussels: Council of Europe Publication.

Craig, R. (2009) 'Non-jury courts in Northern Ireland', Criminal Law and Justice Weekly, 6 June: <http://www.criminallawandjustice.co.uk/index.php?/Analysis/non-jury-courts-in-northern-ireland.html>, accessed 26 November 2010.

Crossan, S.J. and Wylie, A.B. (2010) Introduction to Scots Law: Theory and practice (2nd edn). London: Hodder Gibson.

Crossman, R.H.S. (1976) The Diaries of a Cabinet Minister, 1964–1966. Volume I. New York: Holt, Rinehart & Winston.

Crossman, R.H.S. (1976) The Diaries of a Cabinet Minister: Lord President of the Council, 1966–68. Volume II. London: Hamish Hamilton Ltd.

Crossman, R.H.S. (1977) The Diaries of a Cabinet Minister: Secretary of State for Social Services, 1968–70. Volume III London: Penguin.

Cumberbatch, G. (2004) 'Villain or victim? A review of the research evidence concerning media violence and its effects in the real world with additional reference to video games.' A report prepared for The Video Standards Council.

Darnton, R. (1990) What was Revolutionary about the French Revolution? Waco, TX: Baylor University Press.

Davies, M. (2010) 'The demise of professional self-regulation? Evidence from the "ideal type" professions of medicine and law', Professional Negligence, 26(1): 3–38.

Deazley. R. (2008) Rethinking Copyright: History, theory, language. Northampton, MA: Edward Elgar Publishing Ltd.

Dehin, V. (2010) 'The future of legal online music services in the European Union: A review of the EU Commission's recent initiatives in cross-border copyright management', European Intellectual Property Review, 32(5): 220–237.

Denning, Lord (1949) 'Freedom under the Law'. The Hamlyn Lectures, First Series. London.

Deringer, K.F. (2003) 'Privacy and the Press: The convergence of British and French Law in accordance with the European Convention of Human Rights'. Penn State International Law Review, 22 (Summer). Carlisle, PA: Dickinson School of Law.

Devlin, Sir Patrick (1956 reprint 1966) Trial by Jury. London: Methuen.

Doley, C., Starte, H., Addy, C., Helme, I., Griffiths, J., Scott, A. and Mullis, A. (eds) (2009) Carter-Ruck on Libel and Slander. London: Butterworths.

Duncan, A.G.M., Gordon, W.M., Gamble, A.J. and Reid, K.G.C. (1996) The Law of Property in Scotland. Edinburgh: Butterworths.

Dunlop, R. (2006) 'Article 10, the Reynolds test and the rule in the Duke of Brunswick's case – the decision in Times Newspapers Ltd v United Kingdom', European Human Rights Law Review, 3: 327–339.

Dupré, C. (2000) 'The protection of private life against freedom of expression in French law', *European Human Rights Law Review*, 6: 627–649.

Edwards, L. (2009) 'Pornography, censorship and the Internet'. A paper for the Social Science Research Network (SSRN), 16 July 2009, available at <http://papers.ssrn.com/sol3/papers.cfm?abstract_id=1435093>, accessed 26 November 2010.

Edwards, L. and Waelde, C. (2009) *Law and the Internet* (3rd edn). London: Hart Publishing.

Edwards, S.M. (1997) 'A safe haven for hardest core', *Entertainment Law Review*, 8(4): 137–42.

Edwards, S.M. (2000) 'The failure of British obscenity law in the regulation of pornography', *Journal of Sexual Aggression: An international, interdisciplinary forum for research, theory and practice*, 6(1): 111–127.

Elliott, D.W. (1993) 'Blasphemy and other expressions of offensive opinion', *Ecclesiastical Law Journal*, 3(13): 70–85.

Epworth, J. (2005) 'Protecting your private life: The future of OFCOM privacy complaints', *Communications Law*, 10(6): 191–196.

Ericson, E.E. and Mahoney, D.J. (eds) (2009) *The Solzhenitsyn Reader: New and essential writings, 1947–2005*. Wilmington, NC: ISI Books (Intercollegiate Studies Institute).

European Commission (2007) *Green Paper on Copyright in the Knowledge Economy*. COM (2007) 724 final, Brussels, 20 November 2007.

European Commission (2010) *A Digital Agenda for Europe*. COM (2010) 245 final, Brussels, 19 May 2010.

Falkheimer, J. (2002) 'The Swedish Press Ethics in a Changing Media Landscape', in J. Falkheimer and S. Leijonhufvud, *Pressetiken – i vems tjänst? Report 1*. Stockholm: Institutet för Mediestudier (Institute for Media Studies).

Fenwick, H. and Phillipson, G. (2006) *Media Freedom under the Human Rights Act*. Oxford: Oxford University Press.

Ficsor, M. (2003) 'Collective management of copyright and related rights at a triple crossroads: Should it remain voluntary or may it be "extended" or made mandatory?' *Copyright Bulletin 3*. United Nations, Educational, Scientific and Cultural Organization (online publication): <http://portal.unesco.org/culture/en/ev.php-URL_ID=14935&URL_DO=DO_TOPIC&URL_SECTION=201.html>, accessed 26 November 2010.

Fox, Sir John C. (1927) *The History of Contempt of Court. The form of trial and the mode of punishment*. Oxford: The Clarendon Press.

Foxon, D. (1965) *Libertine Literature in England 1660–1745*. New York: New Hyde Park Publishing, pp. 19–30.

Freud, S. (1976) *Interpretation of Dreams*. London: Penguin Books. (1900, 1st edition, *Über den Traum*. Wiesbaden: Verlag J F Bergmann).

Fritscher, J. (2002) 'What happened when? Censorship, gay history and Robert Mapplethorpe', in D. Jones (ed.) *Censorship: A world encyclopedia*. New York: Fitzroy Dearborn Publishers, pp. 67–98.

Frost, C. (2007) *Journalism, Ethics and Regulation* (2nd edn). Harlow: Pearson Longman.

Gaber, I. (2009) 'Three cheers for subjectivity: Or the crumbling of the seven pillars of traditional journalistic wisdom', *Communications Law*, 14(5): 150–156.

Garzaniti, L. (2009) *Telecommunications, Broadcasting and the Internet: EU competition law and regulation* (3rd edn). London: Sweet & Maxwell.

Gibbons, T. (1996) 'Defamation reconsidered', *Oxford Journal of Legal Studies*, 16(4): 587–615.

Giles, P. (2000) 'Virtual Eden: Lolita, pornography, and the perversions of American studies', *Cambridge Journal of American Studies*, 34(1):41–66.

Gillieron, P. (2006) 'Performing Rights Societies and the Digital Environment', Stanford Law School: <http://www.law.stanford.edu/publications/dissertations_theses/diss/GilliieronPhilippe-tft2006.pdf>, accessed 26 November 2010.

Gilvarry, E. (1990) 'Mapplethorpe retrospective sparks pornography debate', Law Society Gazette, 87(33): 10–11.

Goldberg, D. (2009) 'Freedom of information in the 21st century: bringing clarity to transparency', Communications, 14(2): 50–56.

Goodhart, A.L. (1935) 'Newspapers and contempt of court in English Law', Harvard Law Review, 48(6): 885–910 (April).

Gordon, S. (2008) The Future of the Music Business. How to succeed with the new digital technologies. A Guide for Artists and Entrepreneurs (2nd edn). San Francisco, CA: Backbeat Books (Hal Leonard Corporation).

Gravells, N.P. (2007) 'Authorship and originality: The persistent influence of Walter v Lane', Intellectual Property Quarterly, 3: 267–293.

Griffiths, J. (2010) 'Rhetoric and the "Three-Step Test": Copyright reform in the United Kingdom', European Intellectual Property Review, 32(7): 309–312.

Groll, L. (1980) Freedom and Self Discipline of the Swedish Press. Swedish Institute.

Habermas, J. (1962 translation 1989) The Structural Transformation of the Public Sphere: An inquiry into a category of Bourgeois society (original in German Strukturwandel der Öffentlichkeit. Untersuchungen zu einer Kategorie der bürgerlichen Gesellschaft). Cambridge: Polity Press.

Habermas, J. (1994) 'Three normative models of democracy', Constellations: An International Journal of Critical and Democratic Theory, 1(1): 10 (December).

Habermas, J. (1992 translation 1996) Between Facts and Norms: Contributions to a discourse theory of law and democracy (original in German Faktizität und Geltung). Cambridge: Polity Press.

Hampel, S. (1992) 'Note: Are Samplers Getting a Bum Rap? Copyright infringement of technological creativity?', University of Illinois Law Review, 559.

Harris, D., O'Boyle, M., Warbrick, C., Bates, E. and Buckley, C. (2009) Law of the European Convention on Human Rights (2nd edn). Oxford: Oxford University Press.

Harrison, A. (2008) Music: The Business. The essential guide to the law and the deals (4th edn). London: Virgin Books.

Hauch, J.M (1994) 'Protecting private facts in France: The Warren and Brandeis tort is alive and well and flourishing in Paris', 68 Tul. L. Rev.: 1219.

Hedley, S. and Aplin, T. (2008) Blackstone's Statutes on IT and e-Commerce (4th edn). Oxford: Oxford University Press.

Henderson, G. (2009) 'A new form of libel tourist? Ewing v Times Newspapers Ltd'. Case Comment, Scots Law Times, 20: 116–118.

HM Department for Culture, Media and Sports (DCMS) and Department for Innovation, Business and Skills (BIS) (2009) Digital Britain. Presented to Parliament by The Secretary of State for Culture, Media and Sport and the Minister for Communications, Technology and Broadcasting. June 2009. London: The Stationery Office, Cm 7650.

HM Treasury (2006) Gowers Review of Intellectual Property. London: HMSO.

HM Treasury (2009) Taking Forward the Gowers Review of Intellectual Property: Second stage consultation on copyright. London: HMSO.

Hewitt, S. (2010) Snitch! A history of the modern intelligence informer. London: Continuum Publishing Corporation.

Heylin, C. (1994) The Great White Wonders: A history of rock bootlegs. London: Viking.

Hildebrand, L. (2009) Inherent Vice: Bootleg histories of videotape and copyright. Durham, NC: Duke University Press.

Hixson, R. (1987) Privacy in a Public Society: Human rights in conflict. Oxford: Oxford University Press.

Hoffmann, Lord (2009) 'The universality of human rights', *Law Quarterly Review*, 125: 416–432 (July).

Holdsworth, W., Sir (1920) 'Press control and copyright in the 16th and 17th Centuries', 29 *Yale Law Journal*, 841.

Holdsworth, W., Sir (1942) *A History of English Law* (5th edn). London: Methuen & Co.

Hollingsworth, M. and Fielding, N. (1999) *Defending the Realm: MI5 and the David Shayler affair*. London: Andre Deutsch Ltd.

Home Office (1987) *The Byford Report. Home Office papers 1981–86*. London: HMSO.

Home Office (1997) *No More Excuses: A new approach to tackling youth crime in England and Wales*. A White Paper presented to Parliament by the Secretary of State for the Home Department, Mr Jack Straw MP. November 1997. CM 3809.

Home Office (2002) *The Criminal Justice Bill: Justice for All*. Cm 5563, July 2002. London: Stationery Office.

House of Commons (1973) 'Privacy: Younger Committee's report'. HC Debate 6 June 1973. *Hansard*, Vol. 343: cc 104–178.

House of Commons (1974) *Report of the Committee on Contempt of Court*. Cmnd 5794. London: HMSO.

House of Commons (1980) *Contempt of Court. A discussion paper*. Cmnd. 7145. London: HMSO.

House of Commons (1981) *Report of the Committee on Contempt of Court*. Cmnd. 5794. London: HMSO.

House of Commons (1990) 'Calcutt Report'. HC Debate 21 June 1990. *Hansard*, Vol. 174: cc 1125–1134.

House of Commons (1994) *First Report of the Committee on Standards in Public Life: The Nolan Report*. Volume 1: Report, Cm 2850–I; Volume 2: Transcripts of Oral Evidence, Cm 2850–II. London: HMSO.

House of Commons (1995) 'Privacy and media intrusion'. HC Debate 17 July 1995, *Hansard*, Vol. 263: cc 132–139.

House of Commons (2005) *Home Affairs Committee Annual Report of the Session 2004–05*. 22 March 2005. London: The Stationery Office.

House of Commons (2009) *Intelligence and Security Committee Report: 'Could 7/7 have been prevented? Review of the intelligence on the London terrorist attacks on 7 July 2005*. Cm 7617. London: The Stationery Office.

House of Commons (2010a) *Culture, Media and Sport Committee. Second Report 'Press standards, privacy and libel'* of 9 February 2010: <http://www.publications.parliament.uk/pa/cm200910/cmselect/cmcumeds/362/36202.htm>, accessed 26 November 2010.

House of Commons (2010b) *The Government's Response to the Culture, Media and Sport Select Committee on Press Standards, Privacy and Libel. April 2010*. Cm 7851: <http://www.culture.gov.uk/images/publications/Cm7851GovResponse_PressPrivacyLibel.pdf>, accessed 26 November 2010.

House of Commons – Department of Culture, Media and Sport (2003) *Privacy and Media Intrusion. Select Committee Report. Session 2003–03*. 16 June 2003. HC 458-I. London: The Stationery Office.

House of Commons – Department of Culture, Media and Sport (2007) *Report by the Select Committee on 'Self – Regulation of the Press', 7th Report, 3 July 2007. Session 2006–07*, HC 375. London: The Stationery Office.

House of Lords (1983) 'Press Council Report. House of Lords Debate', *Hansard: HL Deb 20 July 1983*, Vol. 443: cc 1159–1170 (see also: Press Council Report 1983).

House of Lords and House of Commons (2010) *Human Rights Joint Committee. Counter-Terrorism Policy and Human Rights. 16th Report. Annual Renewal of Control Orders Legislation 2010*. Internet publication: <http://www.publications.parliament.uk/pa/jt200910/jtselect/jtrights/64/6402.htm>, accessed 26 November 2010.

Information Commissioner's Office (ICO) (2006a) *What Price Privacy? The unlawful trade in confidential personal information*, presented by the Information Commissioner to Parliament pursuant to Section 52(2) of the Data Protection Act 1998. 10 May 2006. HC 1056. London: The Stationery Office.

Information Commissioner's Office (ICO) (2006b) *A Report on the Surveillance Society*, for the Information Commissioner by the Surveillance Studies Network. September 2006. Online report: <http://www.ico.gov.uk/upload/documents/library/ data_protection/practical_application/surveillance_society_full_report_2006.pdf>, accessed 26 November 2010.

Jackson's Machinery of Justice: see Spencer, J.R. (1989).

Jackson, R.M. (1937) 'Common law misdemeanours', *Cambridge Law Journal*, 6: 193–201.

Jaconelli, J. (2007) 'Defences to speech crimes', *European Human Rights Law Review*, 1: 27–46.

James, J. and Ghandi, S. (1998) 'The English law of blasphemy and the European Convention on Human Rights', *European Human Rights Law Review*, 4: 430–451.

Jerrold, C. (1913) *The Married Life of Queen Victoria*. London: G. Bell & Sons Ltd.

Johnson, H. (2006) 'Family justice: Open justice', *Communications Law*, 11(5): 171–174.

Johnson, H. (2008a) 'Freedom of information – confidence and journalism exemptions from Disclosure', *Communications Law*, 13(5): 174–176.

Johnson, H. (2008b) 'Defamation: The media on the defensive?', *Communications Law*, 13(4): 126–131.

Judge, Lord LCJ (2008) 'Time of change: The criminal justice system in England and Wales'. Speech to the University of Hertfordshire, 4 November 2008. Ministry of Justice; Judges' Speeches website, available at <http://www.judiciary.gov.uk/media/speeches/2008/ speech-lord-judge-03112008>, accessed 30 November 2010.

Kearns, P. (2000) 'Obscene and blasphemous libel: Misunderstanding art', *Criminal Law Review*, Aug: 652–660.

Kearns, P. (2007) 'The ineluctable decline of obscene libel: Exculpation and abolition', *Criminal Law Review*, Sep: 667–676.

Keeling, D.T., Llewelyn, D. and Mellor, J. (2010) *Kerly's Law of Trade Marks and Trade Names* (15th edn). London: Sweet & Maxwell.

Kendrick, W. (1997) *The Secret Museum: Pornography in modern culture*. Ewing, NJ: University of California Press.

Kennedy, J. (2010) *Music How, When, Where You Want It – But not without addressing piracy*. London: International Federation of the Phonographic Industry (IFPI).

Kilbrandon, Lord (1964) *Report of the Committee on Children and Young Persons, Scotland* ('The Kilbrandon Report')·Cmnd 2306, HMSO.

Kilbrandon, Lord (1971) 'The Law of Privacy in Scotland', 2 *Cambrian Law Review*, 35: 128.

Klang, M. and Murray, A. (2004) *Human Rights in the Digital Age*. Oxford: Routledge-Cavendish.

Koempel, F. (2005) 'Data protection and intellectual property', *Computer and Telecommunications Law Review*, 11(6): 185–187.

Koempel, F. (2007) 'If the kids are united', *Journal of Intellectual Property Law & Practice*, 2(6): 371–376.

Koempel, F. (2010) 'The Digital Economy Bill', *Computer and Telecommunications Law Review*, 16(2): 39–43.

Kreile, R. and Becker, J. (2001) 'Rechtedurchsetzung und Rechteverwaltung durch Verwertungsgesellschaften in der Informationsgesellschaft' ('Rights Enforcement and Management by Collecting Societies in the Information Society'), *GEMA Yearbook 2000/2001*, pp. 85, 89

Law Commission (1982) *Working Paper No. 84. Criminal Libel*. London: HMSO.

Law Commission (2002) *Defamation and the Internet: A preliminary investigation*, Scoping Study No 2, December 2002. London: HMSO.

Lawrence, D.H. (1928; first UK publication 1960) *Lady Chatterley's Lover*. London: Penguin Classics.

Lee, S. (1987) 'Spycatcher', *The Law Quarterly Review* 103: 506.

Leigh, I. (1992) 'Spycatcher in Strasbourg', *Public Law*, 200.

Leiner, B.M., Cerf, V.G., Clark, D.D., Kahn, R.E., Kleinrock, L., Lynch, D.C., Postel, J., Roberts, L.G. and Wolff, S. (2003) *A Brief History of the Internet*. The Internet Society. <http://www.isoc.org/internet/history/brief.shtml>, accessed 17 November 2010.

Lester, Lord of Herne Hill (1993) 'Freedom of expression', in Macdonald, R. J., Matscher, F. and Petzold, H. (eds) *The European System for the Protection of Human Rights*. Dordrecht: Martinus Nijhoff, pp. 465–81.

Lester; Lord Lester of Herne Hill, Panick, Lord David and Herberg, Javan (eds) (2009) *Human Rights Law and Practice* (3rd rev. edn). London: LexisNexis.

Lichtenberg, J. (1995) 'Foundations and limits of freedom of the press', in Lichtenberg, J. (ed.) *Democracy and the Mass Media*. Cambridge: Cambridge University Press.

Lindon, M. (1998) *Le Procès de Jean-Marie Le Pen*. Paris: POL.

Lipstadt, D E. (1994) *Denying the Holocaust: The growing assault on truth and memory*. London: Penguin.

Lipstadt, D.E. (2006) *History on Trial: My day in court with David Irving*. New York: Harper Collins.

Lloyd-Bostock, S. (2007) 'The Jubilee Line jurors: Does their experience strengthen the argument for judge-only trial in long and complex fraud cases?', *Criminal Law Review*, Apr: 255–273.

Loveland, I. (1998) 'The constitutionalisation of political libels in English Common Law?', *Public Law*, 633.

Loveland, I. (2000) *Political Libels: A Comparative Study*. Oxford: Hart Publishing.

Lovelace, L. (Linda Susan Boreman) (1976) *Inside Linda Lovelace*. London: Pinnacle Books.

Lowe, N. and Douglas, G. (2006) *Bromley's Family Law* (10th edn). Oxford: Oxford University Press.

Macmillan, K. (2009) 'Internet publication rule survives', *Communications Law*, 14(3): 80–82.

MacQueen, H. (2006) *Studying Scots Law* (3rd edn). Edinburgh: Tottel Publishing.

Mahoney, P. (1997) 'Universality versus subsidiarity in the Strasbourg case law on free speech: Explaining some recent judgments', *European Human Rights Law Review*, 4: 364–379.

Manchester, C. (1988) 'Lord Campbell's Act: England's first obscenity statute', *Journal of Legal History*, 9(2): 223–241.

Markesinis, B.S. and Unberath, H. (2002) *The German Law of Torts: A comparative treatise*. London: Hart Publishing.

Matthews, R., Hancock, L. and Briggs, D. (2004) *Jurors' Perceptions, Understanding, Confidence and Satisfaction in the Jury System: A study in six courts*. Research Development and Statistics Directorate. Home Office Report No. 05/04/2004.

McGonagle, M. and Barrett, N. (2007) 'Reforming media law in Ireland: Broadcasting', *Communications Law*, 12(1): 11–17.

McInnes, R. (2009a) 'Footballers' faces: Photographs, identification and publication contempt', *Scots Law Times*, 21: 123–126.

McInnes, R. (2009b) 'The ones which got away? Reporting of criminal trials', *Scots Law Times*, 25: 149–152.

McKittrick, D. and McVea, D. (2001) *Making Sense of the Troubles*. London: Penguin.

McLagan, G (2004) *Bent Coppers: The inside story of Scotland Yard's battle against police corruption*. London: Orion.

McLeod, K. (2004) 'How Copyright Law Changed Hip Hop', *Stay Free Magazine*, Issue 20, 23 June 2004: <http://www.stayfreemagazine.org/archives/20/public_enemy.html>, accessed 26 November 2010.

Mill, J.S. (1859) *On Liberty* (4th edn). London: Longmans, Green, Reader and Dyer.

Miller, F.P., Vandome, A.F and McBrewster, J. (eds) (2009) *Intellectual Property: Government-granted monopoly, exclusive right, copyright, trademark, patent, industrial design right, trade secret, history of patent law, history of copyright law*. Beau Bassin, Mauritius: Alphascript Publishing/VDM Publishing House Ltd.

Milmo, P., Rogers, W.V.H., Parkes, R., Walker, C. and Busuttil, G. (eds) (2010) *Gatley on Libel and Slander* (11th edn: 1st supplement). London: Sweet & Maxwell.

Milo, D. (2008) *Defamation and Freedom of Speech*. Oxford: Oxford University Press.

Milton, J. (1644) *Areopagitica: A speech of Mr. John Milton for the liberty of unlicensed printing to the Parliament of England, London printed in the Yeare, 1644*. Reprinted edition: Milton, J. (1915) *Areopagitica*. London: MacMillan and Co. Limited.

Ministry of Justice (Home Office) (1965) *Report of the Departmental Committee on Jury Service* ('The Morris Report'), Cmnd 2627. London: HMSO.

Ministry of Justice (2001) *A Review of the Criminal Courts of England and Wales by The Right Honourable Lord Justice Auld* ('the Auld Review'). London: HMSO.

Ministry of Justice (2007) *Diversity and Fairness in the Jury System*, Research Analysis by Thomas, C. and Balmer, N., Ministry of Justice Research Series 2/07 June 2007. London: HMSO.

Ministry of Justice (2009a) *Sensitive Reporting in Coroners' Courts – Response to Comments 2006–2008*, Coroners and Burials Division, January 2009: <http://www.justice.gov.uk/publications/docs/sensitive-reporting-coroners-courts.pdf>, accessed 26 November 2010.

Ministry of Justice (2009b) *Defamation and the Internet: The Multiple Publication Rule*, Consultation Paper, CP20/09, 16 September 2009: <http://www.justice.gov.uk/consultations/docs/defamation-consultation-paper.pdf>, accessed 26 November 2010.

Ministry of Justice (2009c) *Defamation and the Internet: The Multiple Publication Rule*, Response to Consultation, CP(R) 20/09, 23 March 2010: <http://www.justice.gov.uk/consultations/docs/defamation-internet-response-web.pdf >, accessed 26 November 2010.

Ministry of Justice (2010a) *Are juries fair?* Research conducted by Professor Cheryl Thomas of the Centre for Empirical Legal Studies, University College London. Ministry of Justice Bulletin Number 39, March 2010.

Ministry of Justice (2010b) 'A study of the impact of changes to court rules governing media attendance in family proceedings. Summary of responses to stakeholder feedback'. January 2010: <http://www.justice.gov.uk/publications/docs/media-family-proceedings.pdf>, accessed 26 November 2010.

Mitchell, P. (1999) 'Malice in qualified privilege', *Public Law*, Summer: 328–340.

Mitchell, P. (2005) *The Making of the Modern Law of Defamation*. Oxford/Oregon, OR: Hart Publishing.

Mitchell Waldrop, M. (2002) *The Dream Machine: J.C.R. Licklider and the revolution that made computing personal*. London: Penguin.

Mommsen, T. (1954) *The History of Rome, Volumes I–V.* (orig. Römische Geschichte 1854–1856). New York: Appleton & Co.

Moore, Barrington (1984) *Privacy: Studies in Social and Cultural History*. Armonk, NY: M.E. Sharpe Publishing.

Moreham, N. A. (2001) 'Douglas and Others v. Hello! Ltd: The protection of privacy in English private law', *The Modern Law Review*, 767.

Moreham, N. A. (2008) 'The right to respect for private life in the European Convention on Human Rights: A re-examination', *European Human Rights Law Review*, 1: 44–79.

Morgan P. (2005) *The Insider: The private diaries of a scandalous decade*. London: Ebury Press.

Mullins, A. and Scott, A (2009) 'Something rotten in the state of English Libel Law? A rejoinder to the clamour for reform of defamation', *Communications Law*, 14(6): 173–183.

Music Managers Forum (2003) *The Music Management Bible* (2nd edn). London: Sanctuary Publishing Ltd.

Nabokov, V.V. (1958; 1955 – first published in French, Paris, Olympia Press; 1959 – first British edition, published by Weidenfeld and Nicolson, London) *Lolita*. New York: Berkley Publishing Group.

Nagle, E. (2009) 'Keeping its own counsel: The Irish Press Council, self-regulation and media freedom', *Entertainment Law Review*, 20(3): 93–99.

National Audit Office (2009) *The Procurement of Criminal Legal Aid in England and Wales by the Legal Services Commission*. Report by the Comptroller and Auditor General. Session 2009–10. HC 29. London: HMSO.

National Council for Public Morals (1917) 'The Cinema: Its present position and future possibilities', *Report of Chief Evidence*. London: Williams and Norgate.

Neethling, J., Potgieter, J.M and Visser, P.J. (1996) *Neethling's Law of Personality (1996)*. Cape Town: Juta Legal and Academic Publishers.

Neethling, J., Potgieter, J.M. and Scott, T.J. (1995) *Casebook on the Law of Delict /Vonnisbundel oor die Deliktereg* (2nd edn). Cape Town: Juta Legal and Academic Publishers.

New York Times (2001) *Political Censorship. 20th Century Review*. Chicago, IL: Fitzroy Dearbourn Publishers.

Nokes, G.D. (1928) *A History of the Crime of Blasphemy*. London: Sweet & Maxwell.

Normand, the Right Hon Lord (1938) 'The Law of Defamation in Scotland', *The Cambridge Law Journal*, 6: 327–338.

Oats, L. and Sadler, P. (2002) '"This great crisis in the republick of letters" – the introduction in 1712 of stamp duties on newspapers and pamphlets', *British Tax Review*, 4: 353–366.

Ormerod, D. (1995) 'Publicity and Children Cases', *Family Law*, 25: 686.

Ormerod, D. and Williams, D.H. (2007) *Smith's The Law of Theft* (9th end). Oxford: Oxford University Press.

Orwell, G. (1941) '*The Art of Donald McGill*', *Critical Essays*. London: Horizon (also in *Critical Essays* (1946). London: Secker and Warburg).

Oswald, J.F. (2009) *Contempt of Court, Committal, and Attachment and Arrest Upon Civil Process*. London: BiblioBazaar.

Owen, L. (ed.) (2007) *Clark's Publishing Agreements: A Book of Precedents* (7th edn). Haywards Heath: Tottel Publishing

Oxford Economics (2009) *Respect for Film: Economic impact of legislative reform to reduce audio-visual piracy*. March 2009, Final Report. Oxford: Oxford Economics.

Page. W. (2007) 'Economics: It's time to face the music'. *The Report*, 178: 7–8 (18 October).

Palmer, H. (1997) 'Queen Victoria's not so "Victorian" writings: About pregnancy, children, marriage and men', *Victoriana Magazine*. Online publication: <http://www.victoriana.com/doors/queenvictoria.htm>, accessed 26 November 2010.

Palmer, T. (1971) *Trials of Oz*. London: Blond & Briggs.

Passman, D. S. (2008) *All You Need to Know about the Music Business* (6th edn). London/New York: Penguin.

Pedley, P. (2008) *Copyright Compliance: Practical steps to stay within the law*. London: Facet Publishing.

Pfeifer, K-N. (2008) 'The return of the commons: Copyright history as a helpful source?', *International Review of Intellectual Property and Competition Law*, 39(6): 679–688.

Phillips, J. (2009) *Copyright in the UK and the European Community*. London: Butterworths.

Pike, L.O. (1894) *A Constitutional History of the House of Lords*. London: Macmillan.

Pila, J. (2010) 'Copyright and its categories of original works', *Oxford Journal of Legal Studies*, 30(2): 229–254.

Pimlot, N. (2007) 'ICSTIS – 20 years on', *Entertainment Law Review*, 18(4): 135–137.

Poole, T. and Shah, S. (2009) 'The impact of the Human Rights Act on the House of Lords', *Public Law*, (April): 347–371.

Press Council (1983) 'Fair trial and the presumption of innocence', *Report on Media Events Surrounding the Peter Sutcliffe Trial*. London: The Press Council (as reported in House of Lords Debates, *Hansard* – see above).

Press Complaints Commission (2009) *The Editor's Code Book* (2nd edn). London: Press Complaints Commission.

Pullman, P. (2007) *His Dark Materials Trilogy: Northern Lights, The Subtle Knife, The Amber Spyglass*. New York: Alfred A. Knopf Publishing.

Pullman, P. (2010) *The Good Man Jesus and the Scoundrel Christ*. Edinburgh: Canongate.

Rachels, J. (1975) 'Why privacy is important'. 4 *Philosophy and Public Affairs*, 323.

Raento, M (2006) 'The data subject's right of access and to be informed in Finland: An experimental study', *International Journal of Law & Information Technology*, 408ff.

Rampal, K. R. (1981) 'The concept of the Press Council', *International Communication Gazette*, 28: 91–103.

Rana, I.S. (1990). *Law of Obscenity in India, USA and UK*. London: Mittal Publications.

Rawls, J. (1971; 1999 reprinted edn) *A Theory of Justice*. Oxford: Oxford University Press.

Raymond, J. (1998) 'The newspaper, public opinion, and the public sphere in the seventeenth century', *Prose Studies*. 21(2): 109 –136 (August).

Reid, K.G.C. (1993) *The Laws of Scotland, Stair Memorial Encyclopaedia,Vol 18*. Edinburgh: Butterworths.

Reid, K.G.C. and Zimmermann, R. (2000) *A History of Private Law in Scotland*. Oxford: Oxford University Press.

Rimington, S. (2002) *Open Secret:The autobiography of the former Director-General of MI5*. London: Arrow Books Ltd.

Robertson, G. and Nicol, A. (2007) *Media Law* (5th edn). London: Penguin.

Rogers, W.V.H. and Parkes, R. (eds) (2010) *Gatley on Libel and Slander* (11th edn). London: Sweet & Maxwell.

Rogerson, P. (2010) 'Conflict of laws – foreign copyright jurisdiction', *Cambridge Law Journal*, 69(2): 245–247.

Routledge, G. (1989) 'The Report of the Archbishop of Canterbury's Working Paper on Offences against Religion and Public Worship', *Ecclesiastical Law Review*, 1 Ecc LJ (4): 27, 31.

Royal Commission (1993) *Report of the Royal Commission on Criminal Justice* ('The Runciman Commission'). London: Stationery Office Books

Rushdie, S. (1989; new edition 1998) *The SatanicVerses*. Minneapolis, MI/ London: Consortium Press.

Samuels, A. (2009) 'Obscenity and pornography', *Criminal Law and JusticeWeekly*, 173(12): 187–189.

Samuels, E. (2001) *The Illustrated Story of Copyright*. New York: Palgrave Macmillan.

Sanders, K. (2003) *Ethics and Journalism*. London: Sage.

Sanjek, D. (1992) '"Don't have to DJ no more": Sampling and the "autonomous" creator', *Cardozo Arts and Entertainment Law Journal*, 10(2): 612–615.

Schilling, K. (1991) 'Privacy and the press: Breach of confidence – the nemesis of the tabloids?', *Entertainment Law Review*, 2(6): 169–176.

Schudson, M (2003) 'The sociology of news media', in Alexander, G.C. (ed.), *Contemporary Societies*. New York: W.W. Norton & Co.

Schwartz, E. and Childs, B. (1992) 'Introduction to Bela Bartok: The influence of peasant music on modern music', Contemporary composers on contemporary music. *University of Illinois Law Review*, 559.

Senftleben, M. (2004) *Copyright, Limitations and The Three-Step Test: An analysis of the Three-Step Test In International and EC Copyright Law*. The Hague: Kluwer Law International.

Sentencing Guidelines Council (2009) *Overarching Principles: Sentencing youths*. London: Sentencing Guidelines Council (November).

Sereny, G. (1998) *Cries Unheard:The story of Mary Bell*. London: Macmillan.

Shannon, R. (2001) *A Press Free and Responsible: Self regulation and the press complaints commission, 1991–2001*. London: John Murray Publications.

Simpson, A.W.B. (2004) *Human Rights and the End of Empire. Britain and the genesis of the European Convention*. Oxford: Oxford University Press.

Singh, S. and Ernst, E. (2009) *Trick or Treatment: Alternative medicine on trial*. London: Transworld Publishing.

Smartt, U. (1999) 'Constitutionalism in the British Overseas Territories', *European Journal of Crime, Criminal Law and Criminal Justice*, 3: 300–314 (June).

Smartt, U. (2004) 'Stay out of jail: Performance, multimedia and copyright laws', in L. Hill and H. Paris, *Guerrilla Performance and Multimedia* (2nd edn). London/New York: Continuum Press.

Smartt, U. (2006) *Media Law for Journalists*. London: Sage Publications.

Smartt, U. (2007) 'Who still observes the law of contempt?', *Justice of the Peace Journal*, 171: 76–83 (3 February).

Smartt, U. (2008) 'Crime and punishment in the Turks and Caicos Islands', *Justice of the Peace Journal*, 172: 200–203 (April).

Smartt U. (2009) *Law for Criminologists*. London: Sage Publications.

Smartt, U. (2010b) 'Crime and punishment in the Turks and Caicos Islands', in J.P. Stamatel and H.-E. Sung (vol eds); G.R. Newman (ed.) *Crime and Punishment Around the World. The Americas,Vol. 2*, pp. 322–8. Santa Barbara, CA/Denver, CO/Oxford, UK: ABC-CLIO, LLC-Greenwood Press.

Smith, T.B. (1964) 'Civil jury trial: A Scottish assessment', *Virginia Law Review*, Vol L.

Smith's *The Law of Theft*; see Ormerod, D. and Williams, D.H. (2007).

Solzhenitsyn, A. (1962) *One Day in the Life of Ivan Denisovich*. London: Penguin. (reprinted in 1996. London: Bantam Press).

Spencer, J. R. (1977) 'Criminal Libel: A skeleton in the cupboard', *Criminal Law Review*, 383.

Spencer, J. R. (1981) 'Blasphemy: The Law Commission's Working Paper'. , *Criminal Law Review*, 810.

Spencer, J. R. (1989) *Jackson's Machinery of Justice* (8th edn). Cambridge: Cambridge University Press.

Spencer, J.R. (2000) 'Naming and shaming young offenders', *Cambridge Law Journal*, 59(3): 466–468.

Stahl, J.M (1997) 'CDA is DOA: Zoning the information superhighway to exclude adult motels and community service organisations', *Entertainment Law Review*, 8(5): 166–175.

Stair, Viscount (The Stair Society, 1981) *The Tercentenary of the First Publication of Viscount Stair's Institutions of the Laws of Scotland. Papers delivered at a Conference held in the University of Glasgow. The Stair Society.* Edinburgh: W. Green & Son.

Stein, E. (2000) *Thoughts from a Bridge. A retrospective of writings on new Europe and American federalism.* Michigan, MI: University of Michigan Press.

Stephen, J.F. (1883) *A History of the Criminal Law of England*. London: Macmillan and Co.

Sterling, A.L. (2008) *World Copyright Law* (3rd edn). London: Sweet & Maxwell.

Strachan, James Frederick Strachan, Lord (1959) 'Civil jury trial in Scotland', The Scotland Committee on Civil Jury Trial. Edinburgh: HMSO.

Strachan, J. and Singh, R. (2002) 'The right to privacy in English law', *European Human Rights Law Review*, 2: 129–161.

Tomkinson, M. and Gillard, M. (1980) *Nothing to Declare: Political corruptions of John Poulson*. Richmond, Surrey: Calder Publications.

Traub, F. (2009) 'Bob Dylan's Albums Protected in Germany', *Entertainment Law Review*, 20(4): 144–146.

Travers, P. and Reiff, S. (1974) *The Story Behind 'The Exorcist'*. New York: Signet Books.

Van Vechten., V. (1903) 'The History and Theory of the Law of Defamation I', 3 *Colum. L. Rev.*, 546.

Van Vechten, V. (1904) 'The History and Theory of the Law of Defamation II, 4 *Colum. L. Rev.*, 33.

Wallis, R., Baden-Fuller, C. Kretschmer, M. and Klimis, G.M (1999) 'Contested collective administration of Intellectual Property Rights in music: The challenge to the principles of reciprocity and solidarity', *European Journal of Communication*, 14(1): 5–35.

Warren, S. and Brandeis, L. (1890) 'The right to privacy', *Harvard Law Review*, 4: 193–220.

Weber, R.H. (in collaboration with M. Grosz and R. Weber (2010) *Shaping Internet Governance: Regulatory challenges*. Zürich: Springer.

Whitty, N.R. (2005) 'Rights of personality, property rights and the human body in Scots law'. *Edinburgh Law Review*, 9(2): 194–237.

Williams, D.G.T. (1972) 'Oz and obscenity', *Cambridge Law Journal*, 30(1).

Winfield, P. H. (1937) *A Textbook of the Law of Tort*. London: Sweet & Maxwell.

Wooler, S. (2006) *Review of the Investigation and Criminal Proceedings Relating to the Jubilee Line Case*. HM Crown Prosecution Service Inspectorate (HMCPSI), June 2006. (*Hansard*, HC Vol. 455, col. 1594>)

Wright, P. (1987) *Spycatcher: The candid autobiography of a secret intelligence officer*. Australia: William Heinemann Publ. and Viking Press.

Young, J. (1981) 'The Contempt of Court Act 1981', *British Journal of Law & Society*, 8(2): 243ff.

Zimmermann, R. (1996) *The Law of Obligations: Roman foundations of the civilian tradition*. Oxford: Clarendon Press.

Zweigert, K. and Kötz, H. (1998) *An Introduction to Comparative Law* (3rd edn). Oxford: Clarendon Press.

Internet Sources and Useful Websites

Access Info Europe: www.access-info.org
Advertising Standards Authority (ASA): www.asa.org.uk
Association of American Publishers: www.publishers.org
Association of Independent Music (AIM): www.musicindie.com
Associated Press (AP) (Global News Network): www.ap.org
Association for Journalism Education (AJE): www.ajeuk.org
Association for Television on Demand (ATVOD): http://atvod.co.uk
Attorney General's Office (England & Wales): www.attorneygeneral.gov.uk
Authors Guild: www.authorsguild.org
Authors' Licensing and Collecting Society (ALCS): www.alcs.co.uk
BBC News Online: www.bbc.co.uk/news
BBC Northern Ireland Service online: www.bbc.co.uk/northernireland
BBC World Service: www.bbc.co.uk/worldservice
BMI – Broadcast Music, Inc: www.bmi.com
British Board of Film Classification (BBFC): www.bbfc.co.uk
British Phonographic Industry (BPI): www.bpi.co.uk
CISAC (Confédération Internationale des Sociétés d'Auteurs et Compositeurs – the International Confederation of Societies of Authors and Composers: www.cisac.org
CNN International: http://edition.cnn.com
Department for Business, Innovation and Skills: www.bis.gov.uk
Department for Culture, Media and Sport: www.culture.gov.uk
Deutsche Presseagentur (German News Agency): www.dpa.de/en/unternehmenswelt/index.html
English PEN: www.englishpen.org
European Advertising Standards Alliance (EASA): www.easa-alliance.org
European Commission: http://ec.europa.eu
European Court of Human Rights: www.echr.coe.int/echr
European Court of Justice (ECJ): www.curia.eu.int
European Parliament: www.europarl.eu.int
European Patent Office: www.european-patent-office.org
Featured Artists Coalition (FAC): www.featuredartistscoalition.com
Federation Against Copyright Theft (FACT): www.fact-uk.org.uk
Freedom of Information Advocates: www.freedominfo.org
GEMA (Gesellschaft für musikalische Aufführungs- und mechanische Vervielfältigungsrechte – Musical copyright association): www.gema.de
Hansard: www.parliament.the-stationery-office.co.uk/pa/cm/cmhansrd.htm
Index on Censorship: www.indexoncensorship.org
Intellectual Property Office UK: www.ipo.gov.uk
International Federation of Journalists: www.ifj.org/en
International Federation of the Phonographic Industry (IFPI): www.ifpi.org
Information Commissioner's Office (ICO): www.ico.gov.uk

International Confederation of Societies of Authors and Composers (Confèdèration Internationale des Sociétés d'Auteurs et Compositeurs): www.cisac.org

International Press Institute (IPI): www.freemedia.at

Internet Corporation for Assigned Names and Numbers (ICANN): www.icann.org

Internet Watch Foundation (IWF): www.iwf.org.uk

Irish Department of Justice and Law Reform: www.justice.ie

Irish Parliament for the Dáil – Houses of the Oireachtas: www.oireachtas.ie

Irish Patent Office: www.patentsoffice.ie

Mechanical Copyright Protection Society (MCPS) – see: PRS

Music Managers Forum (MMF): www.musicmanagersforum.co.uk

Music Publishers Association (for sheet/printed music): www.mpaonline.org.uk

Musicians Union (MU): www.musiciansunion.org.uk

National Archives: www.nationalarchives.gov.uk

National Union of Journalists (NUJ): www.nuj.org.uk

Northern Ireland Assembly: www.niassembly.gov.uk

Northern Ireland Courts and Tribunal Service: www.courtsni.gov.uk

Ofcom (Office of Communications): www.ofcom.org.uk

Office for Harmonization in the Internal Market (OHIM) (EU Trademark Office): http://oami.europa.eu

Office of Fair Trading (OFT): www.oft.gov.uk

Office of National Statistics (UK): www.statistics.gov.uk/glance

Office of Public Sector Information: www.opsi.gov.uk

Parliament, UK: www.parliament.uk

Performing Rights Society (PRS): www.prsformusic.com

Phonographic Performance Ltd (PPL): www.ppluk.com

PhonepayPlus (regulates phone-paid services in the UK): www.phonepayplus.org.uk

Press Association: www.pressassociation.com

Press Complaints Commission (PCC): www.pcc.org.uk

Scots Law Online: www.scottishlaw.org.uk

Scottish Arts Council: www.scottisharts.org.uk

Scottish Court Service: www.scotcourts.gov.uk

Scottish Information Commissioner: www.itspublicknowledge.info/home/ScottishInformationCommissioner.asp

Scottish Law Commission: www.scotlawcom.gov.uk

Scottish Parliament: www.scottish.parliament.uk

Society of Authors: www.societyofauthors.net

Society of Editors: www.societyofeditors.co.uk

Trading Standards Institute (TSI): www.tradingstandards.gov.uk

UK Copyright Service: www.copyrightservice.co.uk

Universal Music Publishing Group for Artists & Writers: www.umusicpub.com/artistswriters_newsignings.aspx

US Patent Office (Patents & Trademarks): www.uspto.gov

Video Standards Council (VSC): www.videostandards.org.uk

Welsh Music Foundation: www.welshmusicfoundation.com

WIPO Phonogram Treaties: www.wipo.int/treaties/en/ip/phonograms

World Intellectual Property Organization (WIPO): www.wipo.int

World Summit on the Information Society (WSIS): www.itu.int/wsis

World Trade Organization (WTO): www.wto.org See Chapter 2

Index